Independent Traveler's

USA 2000

Forthcoming titles in this series include:

Independent Traveler's Europe 2000
The Budget Travel Guide

Independent Traveler's Australia 2000
The Budget Travel Guide

Independent Traveler's New Zealand 2000
The Budget Travel Guide

Independent Traveler's

USA 2000

THE BUDGET TRAVEL GUIDE

Edited by Caroline Ball
Consultant Editor: Barbara Rogers

The Globe Pequot Press
Guilford, Connecticut

Thomas Cook Publishing

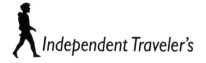

Published by Thomas Cook Publishing
The Thomas Cook Group Ltd
PO Box 227
Thorpe Wood
Peterborough PE3 6PU
United Kingdom

The Globe Pequot Press
PO Box 480
Guilford, Connecticut USA
06437

ISBN: 0-7627-0673-2

Library of Congress Cataloging-in-Publication Data is available

Publisher: Stephen York
Commissioning Editor: Deborah Parker
Map Editor: Bernard Horton
Text Design: Tina West

Layout: Leyla Davies, Tina West
Cover Design by Pumpkin House
Copy editor: Katy Carter
Proofreader: Linda Bass
Route maps: Polly Senior Cartography

Text typeset in Book Antiqua and Gill Sans using QuarkXPress
Picture research: Image Select International
Imagesetting: Z2 Reprographics, Thetford
Printed in Spain by GraphyCems, Navarra

HELP IMPROVE THIS GUIDE

This guide is updated each year. However, the information given may change and we would welcome reports and comments from our readers. Similarly we want to make this guide as practical and useful as possible and are grateful for any comments, criticisms and suggestions for improving future editions.

A free copy of this guide will be sent to all readers whose information or ideas are incorporated in the next edition. Please send all contributions to the Editor, Independent Traveller's USA, Thomas Cook Publishing at the address/email address given at the top of this page.

Written and researched by:
Tom Bross
Ann Carroll Burgess
Tony Kelly
Tim Nollen
Lura Rogers
Kirk Schneider
Roberta Sotonoff
Wendy Wood

Transport Information:
Peter Bass, Assistant Editor,
Thomas Cook Overseas Timetable

Consultant Editor:
Barbara Radcliffe Rogers

Book Editor:
Caroline Ball

The Authors

Caroline Ball is a freelance editor and writer (well, ghost-writer), who covers subjects from gardening to petcare as well as travel, food and wine. After a peripatetic childhood, she worked in foreign-language publicity and advertising and has now settled with her husband in the Surrey hills.

Barbara Radcliffe Rogers is the author or co-author of more than a dozen travel guides and other books about places from New England to South Africa.

Tom Bross is a Boston-based freelance travel writer with 20 years' experience covering New England destinations and attractions for US and Canadian magazines and newspapers.

Ann Carroll Burgess, travel writer, editor and broadcaster based in Atlanta, Georgia, has travelled North America and Europe extensively. She never misses an opportunity to tour the Southwest and Southeast United States for her weekly radio program *Postcards.*

Tony Kelly took up travel writing after teaching English in Sudan and China. Among his recent books are guides to Mallorca, Catalonia and New York City.

Tim Nollen hails from Washington, DC, though he has frequently fled the US for extended stays in Europe. His many guidebooks and travel articles include destinations from Prague to Philadelphia.

Lura Rogers is the author of books about Switzerland and Dominican Republic, and wrote about New England in Frommer's *America on Wheels.*

Kirk D. Schneider is a travel writer based in Northern California. He has travelled extensively throughout the USA and Canada. Schneider is editor and publisher of *California By Train, Bus & Ferry* and contributed to *Thomas Cook's International Air Travel Handbook.*

Roberta Sotonoff is a confessed travel junkie whose favourite mode of transportation is a 747. To support her habit, she became a Chicago-based travel writer.

Wendy Wood, intrepid adventurer, studied at Oxford and now frequently enjoys global tip-toeing. She has a great love of America, particularly Arizona, and has written and researched for several Thomas Cook publications.

The authors and Thomas Cook Publishing would like to thank the following for their help during the production of this book:

Connecticut River Valley & Shoreline Visitors Council; Robert A. Gregory; Greater Providence Convention & Visitors Bureau; Newport County Convention & Visitors Bureau; Zion National Park Visitor Centre; Ralph Walden; Charlie Pepe; Glen Faria of DestINNations New England; Lucy Arnold at Mobile CVB; the helpful staff at CVBs in New Orleans, Philadelphia, St Louis and Washington; Paul Haught and Emily, Josh Nickerson, Andrew Maraniss, Nicky Short and Tim Nollen's Mom; Ellie Shelton; Matthew Dolling.

The following are thanked for supplying the photographs (and who hold the copyright):
Colour section p. 32/33 all Ethel Davies except (ii) Niagara Falls, Spectrum Colour Library
p. 160/161 all Spectrum Colour Library except (i) Bar Harbor, Ethel Davies; (ii) Portland Indoor Market, Ethel Davies; (iv) Charleston, Image Select
p. 288/289 all Spectrum Colour Library except (iv) Buffalo, Yellowstone; Old Faithful, Yellowstone, Image Select
p. 416/417 all Maxine Cass except (i) Grand Canyon; Natural Bridge, Bryce Canyon NP; (iv) Amtrak loco, Spectrum Colour Library

Cover photo of New York taxi by Ethel Davies.

Contents

General Information

Routes & Cities

Routes are shown in one direction only but can, of course, be travelled in the opposite direction. See pp.10–11 for a diagrammatical presentation of the routes.

REFERENCE SECTION

CONTENTS

INTRODUCTION

The United States is a huge, dynamic, exciting, varied and often puzzling place to visit. Just as you think you know it, you can travel to another region and find an entirely different atmosphere, culture, climate, topography and even a different way of speaking the English language.

Forget about trying to understand what makes America and its inhabitants tick. Americans are as varied as the peoples of the world, partly because they *are* people from all over the world. No other country on earth contains so many people whose national ancestry is so short. Apart from the relatively few Native Americans (the correct term for those who used to be called Indians), Americans are all sons and daughters of immigrants. Descendants of the first families – those whose ancestors arrived on the *Mayflower* and other early ships – are still immigrant in origin.

People from every corner of the earth have settled here, bringing some of their ways and discarding others, blending with neighbours from other places into the rich soup that is the uniquely American heritage. The soup is far from bland, and it contains hearty chunks of cultures that have been preserved intact, or mostly intact. Americans have come to value their ethnic roots, and are fond of celebrating the customs and traditions of homelands, even ones they never knew, in holidays and festivals throughout the year.

Americans are proud of their rebellious history, and cling to a stubborn independence, especially in rural areas and small towns.

History is everywhere, especially along the coasts, where the first settlers built cities and the pivotal events of America's early history took place. To explore America's past and find the most significant sites of its early history, see the Timeline on p. 51. But whatever your quest in America, take time to enjoy its variety, to lose yourself in the zest of its lively cities, to explore its quiet rural corners and to see some of the monumental natural attractions that decorate and shape its land. Don't expect to understand it, but do expect to have fun trying.

Barbara Rogers

PRICES

The price indications given below have been used througout this book. Please bear in mind that prices do fluctuate – these symbols have been given for guidance. Occasionally we do mention accommodation, food and highlights that are very expensive (shown $$$$+) but these are included in this budget guide if the attraction is an unmissable one or in case you want to splash out on a special treat.

Accommodation

$	=	under $30
$$	=	$30–75
$$$	=	$75–100
$$$$	=	over $100

Based on standard double room, no meals but including all taxes.

Food

$	=	under $7
$$	=	$7–12
$$$	=	$12–20
$$$$	=	over $20

Based on the price of a mid-range main course.

Highlights

If an admission charge is made:

$	=	under $6
$$	=	$6–$12
$$$	=	over $12

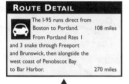

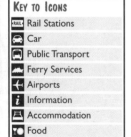

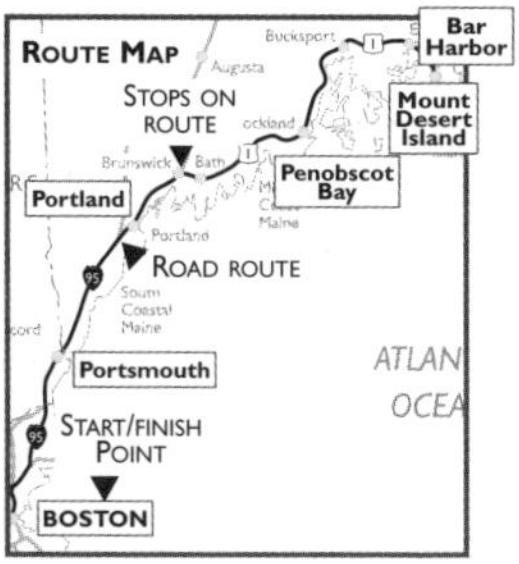

BOSTON SOUTH–PORTSMOUTH
OTT TABLE 315/517

TRANSPORT	FREQUENCY	JOURNEY TIME
Bus	20 Daily	1hr10mins

Note: Most trips go via Logan Airport.

PUBLIC TRANSPORT DETAILS

Mode of travel, journey time, frequency of service and *OTT* table numbers are given.

ROUTE DETAIL

The I-95 runs direct from Boston to Portland. 108 miles
From Portland Rtes 1 and 3 snake through Freeport and Brunswick, then alongside the west coast of Penobscot Bay to Bar Harbor. 270 miles

ROAD DETAILS
Route details and approximate cumulative mileages given.

KEY TO ICONS

- Rail Stations
- Car
- Public Transport
- Ferry Services
- Airports
- Information
- Accommodation
- Food

ABOUT THIS BOOK

Independent Traveller's USA provides you with expert advice and details on over 60 different routes, cities and regions, each in its own chapter. Reflecting the tremendous variety of the United States, as well as its almost daunting size, these chapters vary in their approach, each featuring the best way to see and enjoy that part of the country. Some routes take advantage of the rail routes that connect major cities across the land. Others use cross-country bus, local bus and train lines, or even boats, to show you the best of a smaller region. In other areas the routes are best explored by hired car, and these detail the exact driving routes, town by town. In each case, stopovers and the most important attractions are described, with their price ranges, opening hours and other details. The remaining chapters feature cities or attractions which are worth longer stops, each including detailed information on how to get there, get around by local transport and make the most of your time there. All chapters give suggestions for budget-friendly accommodation and places to eat, as well as how to find the best of local entertainment.

The order of these routes and cities moves from the north-east to the south-east, across the mid-west to the south-west and north through California to the north-west.

Each chapter is accompanied by a map, showing the route or city or its environs and the stops described in the text. Each also has a route description or a summary of ways to get there: either a table showing bus and train times or a list of driving approaches, and sometimes both. Throughout the book you will see notes and tips in the margins. These provide added information, suggest places to stop en route or day trips from the main destination, tell you about interesting boat trips or walking tours, and suggest an onward route connecting this with other chapters.

Think of the USA as a banquet, and this book as the menu from which you can select each delectable course.

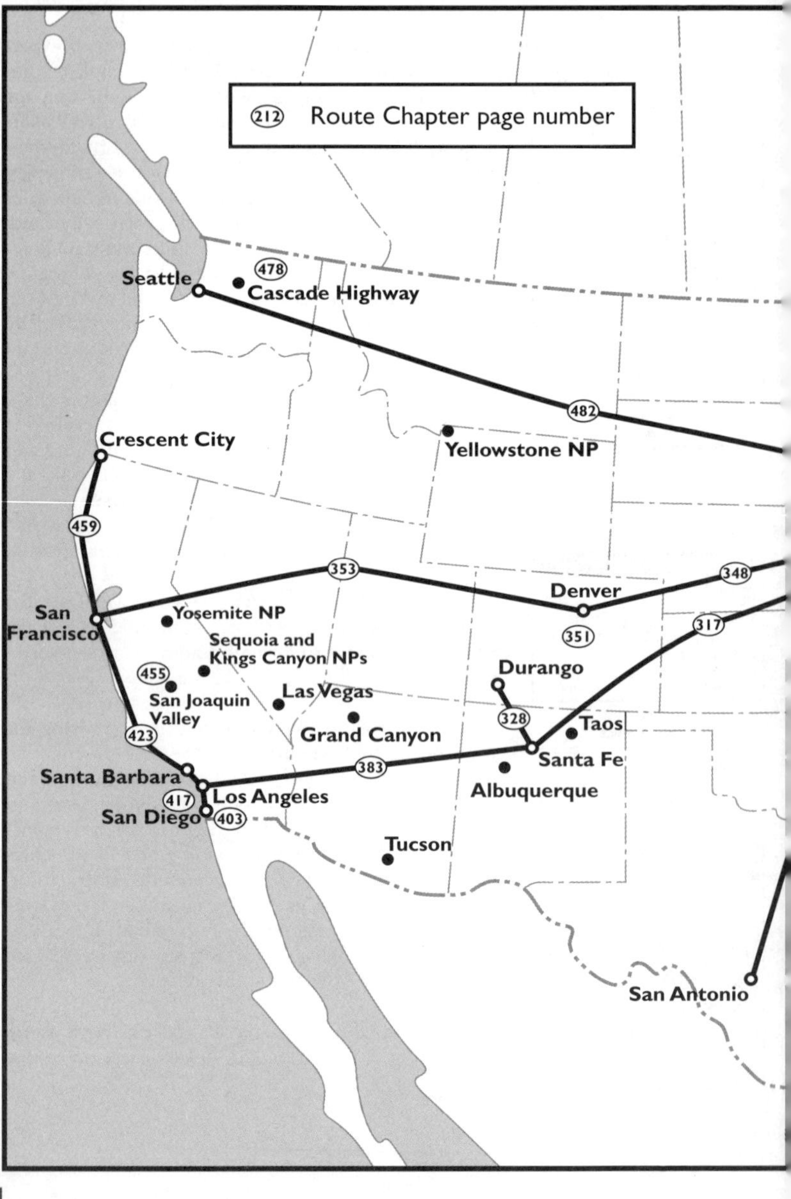
212 Route Chapter page number
Seattle
478
Cascade Highway
482
Yellowstone NP
Crescent City
459
353
348
Denver
351
317
San Francisco
Yosemite NP
Sequoia and Kings Canyon NPs
455
San Joaquin Valley
Las Vegas
Grand Canyon
Durango
328
Taos
Santa Fe
423
Santa Barbara
383
Albuquerque
417
Los Angeles
San Diego
403
Tucson
San Antonio

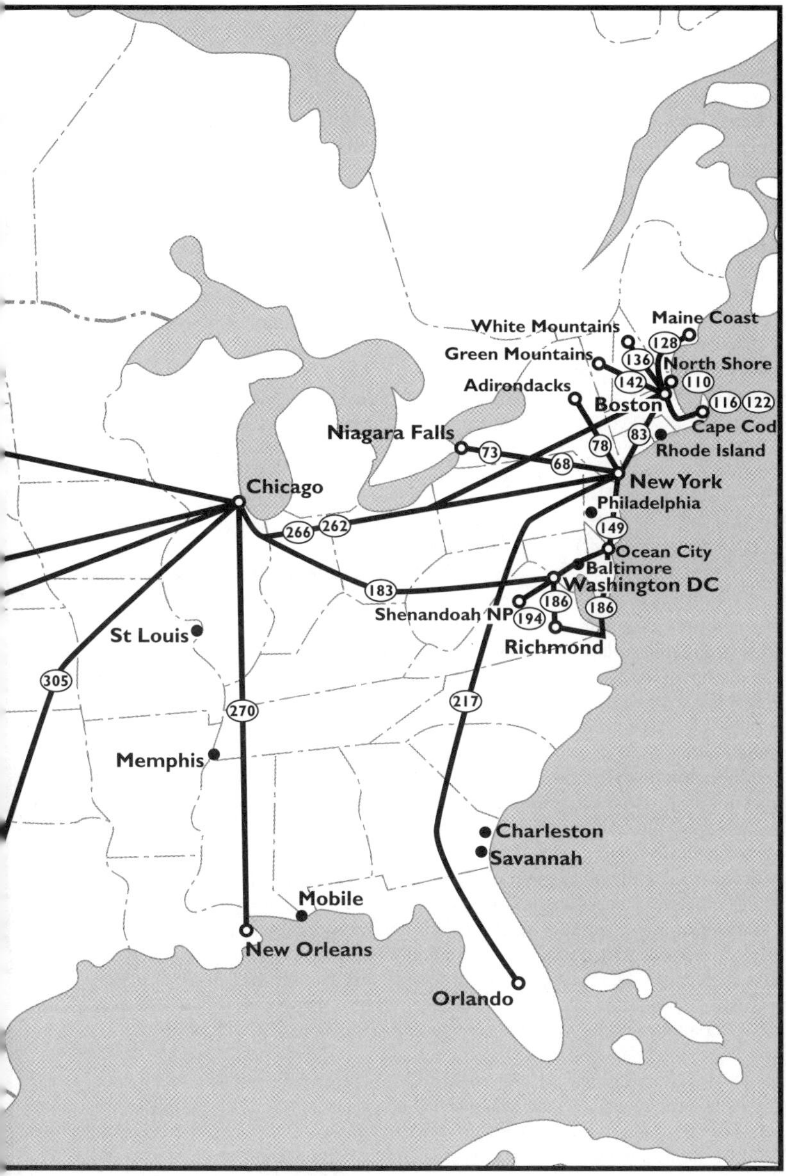

Maine Coast
White Mountains
128
Green Mountains
136
North Shore
Adirondacks
142
110
Boston
116
122
Cape Cod
Niagara Falls
78
83
Rhode Island
73
68
New York
Chicago
Philadelphia
266
262
149
Ocean City
Baltimore
183
Washington DC
186
186
Shenandoah NP
194
St Louis
Richmond
305
270
217
Memphis
Charleston
Savannah
Mobile
New Orleans
Orlando

Reaching the United States

Most international travellers from Europe arrive at Boston's Logan International Airport, New York's John F. Kennedy International Airport, Newark International Airport in New Jersey, Baltimore-Washington International Airport in Baltimore or Atlanta International Airport. Those from Australia or New Zealand usually arrive in Los Angeles, San Francisco, Seattle or Vancouver, British Columbia. For entry formalities, see Travel Directory, p. 489.

> Check with a travel agent, look at the travel pages of newspapers or airline internet sites to find the cheapest flights to the USA. Apex, Pex, Superpex and Standby tickets are cheaper than Economy fares, but what you save in money you lose in flexibility. In general, the cheaper the ticket, the more restrictions placed upon your air travel.

After clearing Customs and Immigration, onward-bound passengers re-check baggage and transfer to flights to smaller or inland airports. There are car hire facilities at any airport (always reserve in advance) and public transport of some type (train, bus, limousine, taxi) into the nearest city.

Travelers' Aid desks provide tourist information; airport information booths and kiosks cover airport facilities, airport-to-city transport and accommodation. For flight information and bookings, contact individual airlines, not the airport. All major airports have foreign exchange and banking services as well as car hire facilities. Secondary airports have cash machines (ATMs) and car hire desks, but seldom currency exchange facilities. Public transport from secondary airports to the nearest city is sometimes available, but seldom practical in terms of routes or time. Luggage trolleys are generally free for international arrivals; elsewhere, there is a charge of a dollar or so. Be prepared for long walks through terminals on arrival – moving walkways are few and far between.

Unless you have a reason to be in New York, arrival and departure are generally easier at Boston or Baltimore. They are much smaller, and easier and cheaper to get in and out of. If you do fly into New York, keep in mind that Newark Airport is smaller, less crowded and slightly closer to Manhattan than JFK. It is always a good idea to book your first night's room in advance, but in Boston and New York it is absolutely essential because rooms can be hard to find.

Consider going without a car if you will begin your stay in a city – after all, public transport into and within cities is quick and simple, while parking places are scarce and expensive. If you must pick up your hire car on arrival at a major airport, arrange parking in advance with your city hotel. However, if you stay outside the city proper, a car is usually a necessity and parking might well be free.

Don't let airlineflight schedules mislead you into a full first day of touring. Jet lag intensifies the effects of long-distance air travel. Expect to arrive fatigued, disoriented, short-tempered and *not* ready to drive or engage in complicated travel activities. Night-time flights seem to offer an extra day of sightseeing upon arrival. Resist the temptation. Most travellers do better by timing their flights to arrive in the late afternoon or early evening, then getting a good night's sleep before tackling the sights. Since many airport-area hotels and motels offer a free shuttle service to and from the airport, you can take a shuttle to the hotel, recover from the flight and pick up the rental car the next morning at no additional cost.

Many fly-drive programmes offer what looks like an easy first-day drive, e.g. Los Angeles International Airport to the Disneyland area in Anaheim. Although this should be a 45-min jaunt, it can stretch to hours in heavy commuter traffic. Better to spend the first night in an airport-area hotel and hit the road refreshed in the morning – especially if youu're not accustomed to urban traffic or driving on the right-hand side of the road.

The reverse is equally true. Don't plan a tight schedule that gets you into a city and on to the airport just the requisite two hours before an international departure. Unexpected volumes of traffic can leave you stranded on a highway as your plane takes off overhead. Airlines won't hold an entire flight for a carload of passengers flying on non-refundable bargain fares, but they will happily allow you the privilege of paying full fare for single tickets home on the next available flight. Allow a safety margin by spending your last night near the departure airport, or at least in the same city.

TRAVEL ARRANGEMENTS It is a great temptation for independently minded travellers to make all their arrangements separately, instead of locking into a packaged plan. However, the many types of air ticket and the range of temporary deals available on busy routes make it advisable to talk to your travel agent before booking to get the best bargain.

In fact, taking a fly-drive package such as one of Thomas Cook's own, or one of the many others offered by airlines and tour operators, can be more economical than making all your own arrangements. All include the air ticket and car hire element; some also follow set itineraries which enables them to offer guaranteed and pre-paid *en route* accommodation at selected hotels. Programmes such as Thomas Cook's America for the Independent Traveller allow the flexibility of booking the airline ticket at an advantageous rate and then choosing from a 'menu' of other items, often at a discounted price, such as car hire, hotel coupons (which pre-pay accommodation but do not guarantee availability of rooms) and other extras such as excursions.

INSURANCE

Experienced travellers carry insurance that covers their belongings and holiday investment as well as their bodies. Travel insurance should include provision for cancelled or delayed flights and weather problems, as well as immediate evacuation home in the case of medical emergency. Thomas Cook and other travel agencies offer comprehensive policies. Medical cover should be high – at least $1 million.

REACHING THE UNITED STATES

Travelling around the USA

The most difficult thing for travellers planning trips to the USA is to remember just how big it is. Once you leave the smaller states of New England and the north-east, it can take an entire day's driving to cross just one state. And since your purpose is to see something while you are there, you won't want to spend all your time moving from point to point. However you decide to travel, beware of planning to cover too great a distance. It is better to see one area of the country, enjoy it and get to know it a little, than to flit from place to place without time to see any of them.

If you arrive in the eastern USA and plan to visit the west coast, flying is the most practicable way to get there unless you have plenty of time for overland travel. Transcontinental train and motor coach travel is slow, cramped and unpredictable, although Amtrak operates popular north–south coastal services. Air travel is even more cramped, but travel time is counted in hours rather than days and timetables are almost always accurate.

TRAVELLING BY AIR

The US domestic air service is extensive and cheaper than within Europe. There are shuttle flights into Boston and other eastern cities every hour from New York's LaGuardia Airport and from Baltimore, plus regularly scheduled flights from cities all over the USA and Canada. Currently, Southwest Airlines (tel: 210 617 1221) is revolutionising domestic air fares with its 'no frills' flights at prices that rival bus and train fares. Other airlines are being forced into competitive pricing.

Cover major cross-county routes by air – at least one way – and you can save days for sightseeing at your destination. Many overseas carriers include options for additional flights within the USA at reduced rates; and local airlines, as noted above, often have special fares. These are arrangements you should make well in advance, however, since special fares often apply only to a certain number of seats on each flight. In general, the closer you are to flight time, the

Bumped off

Being 'bumped' from your flight can throw your travel plans into chaos – or it can be profitable. If you are flying on a busy route, and could just as easily take a somewhat later flight, you could find yourself with a coupon toward a future ticket. To best position yourself for voluntary bumping, check in early, then go to the gate and sit close to the desk. If the flight over-fills, you can be the first one at the desk when the call for volunteers comes. The initial offer is usually a $200 certificate toward another flight and a guarantee of a seat on the next flight to your destination. Wise travellers usually accept this offer, even though a larger reward may be offered later. The coupon is issued immediately, so you can use it whenever you like.

AIR PASSES

A number of major airlines offer VUSA (Visit USA) air passes which can be purchased by those travelling from outside the US when booking a flight to the US. These passes, which offer good value if you are going to stick to an itinerary, pre-pay your air travel within the USA. Conditions and restrictions vary depending on the carrier – you usually have to pre-book all your flights before you reach the US, and may not be allowed to alter these arrangements. Check with the airline or enquire at your travel agent before booking your transatlantic flight.

rarer bargain seats become. Within the last seven days, rates are rarely reduced. Amtrak has arrangements with United Airlines to combine cross-country train travel with a return by air, under their Air Rail scheme.

In making air arrangements, keep in mind that return air fares are cheaper than single tickets. If you are only travelling one way by air, always give a return date, and as far in the future as possible, to take advantage of the lowest rate. Do not tell the ticketing agent that you do not plan to use the return portion, however; agents are not allowed to sell you a return ticket if they know it won't be used.

TRAVELLING BY TRAIN

Amtrak is the official passenger train transport company in the United States: tel: (800) 872-7245. Main routes along the west coast run from California to Portland, Seattle and Vancouver. Along the east coast, principle routes run from Boston to Miami, through New York, Philadelphia, Baltimore, Washington and Atlanta. Four major routes travel east–west across the USA: one just south of the Canadian border, one along the Gulf coast and Mexican border, and two across the centre: north–south is Chicago–New Orleans. **VIA Rail** handles passenger traffic in Canada; tel: (888) 842-7245. Trains do not stop at each town en route, so check if there is a stop at your destination.

USEFUL ADDRESSES AND TELEPHONE NUMBERS

Greyhound Bus Lines, Customer Service, 901 Main St, Dallas TX 75202; tel: (800) 231-2222;

For telephone numbers of other regional bus lines and local commuter, bus and ferry systems, consult the appropriate table in the bi-monthly *Thomas Cook Overseas Timetable* which contains timetables and much more additional travel information

Train times for many Amtrak, VIA Rail and local services are published in the *Thomas Cook Overseas Timetable* (see p. 50). Amtrak sell a Far West Rail Pass, which gives 15 or 30 days of unlimited train travel on its system in the west. Similar plans cover the entire west (from Chicago), the north-east (from Virginia to Montreal), all points east of Chicago, and the east coast routes. A National Rail Pass, covering the entire USA and nearby Canadian cities, ranges from $285 to $425 for 15 days and $375–$535 for 30 days. These are available in the UK through Rail Pass Direct, tel: 01733 50280.

TRAVELLING AROUND THE USA

AMTRAK PASSES

Amtrak passes pay for unlimited train travel for 15 or 30 days, valid for peak season (1 June–6 Sept) or off peak (all other times). Passes pay for travel (supplements are payable for sleeping accommodation and on Metroliner services), but reservations must be made on most routes.

Route	15/30-day	Peak 1999/2000	Off-peak 1999/2000
National	15-day	$425/$440	$285/$295
Rail Pass	30-day	$535/$550	$375/$385
Far West	15-day	$240/$245	$185/$190
Pass	30-day	$310/$320	$240/$250
West Pass	15-day	$315/$325	$195/$200
	30-day	$395/$405	$260/$270
Northeast	15-day	$200/$205	$180/$185
Pass	30-day	$235/$240	$220/$225
plus a 3-day pass ($130) and 5-day option ($150)			
East Pass	15-day	$250/$260	$205/$210
	30-day	$310/$320	$255/$265
Coastal Pass	30-day	$275/$285	$225/$235

For prices in sterling, contact (in the UK) Rail Pass Direct; tel: 01733 503596

Amtrak Explore America Passes allow travel within 1, 2, 3 or 4 regions over 45 days and permit three stops on the way. The regions covered are: Florida; east from the Atlantic to Cincinnatti and Atlanta; from Atlanta/Cincinnatti/Detroit to Wolf Point/Denver Albuquerque/El Paso; from Wolf Point/Denver Albuquerque/El Paso to the Pacific. Peak season is 18 June–22 Aug and 17 Dec–2 Jan.

Remember, however, that these passes are only economical if you will be spending many days within that period on the train. If you plan to spend several days sightseeing at each of several destinations, you may well do better to buy single tickets. All long distance and several of the New York – Boston trains require advance reservations even if you have a pass. Other discounts, including 15% reductions for students and travellers over 62, and half fare for children aged 2–15, can bring individual ticket rates lower than passes for those who qualify. Current offers are shown on the Amtrak website: www.amtrak.com.

In deciding whether these schemes will save you money, keep in mind that return fares (called round-trips in the USA) usually cost very little more than one-way fares and that advance reservations make fares even cheaper. Consider this, too, when deciding between bus and train. Return bus fares are usually simply double the one-way rate. Since most comparison charts use one-way as a base, these charts are not entirely reliable. Always ask for both single and return fares.

EXPLORE AMERICA PASSES

(1999 Prices quoted)	Peak	Off Peak
Florida	$99	$79
1 region	$239	$209
2 adjoining regions	$339	$279
3/4 adjoining regions	$399	$339

Train travel is somewhat less useful as a way of connecting closer destinations, except along the well-used coastal routes.

Amtrak offers dining and snackbar service on long-distance trains and on some shorter runs, but prices tend to be high. You can save substantially by taking a picnic meal on board. Most larger stations have facilities for leaving luggage while you tour; a complete list of station facilities is shown in Amtrak's National Timetable. In many places, Amtrak carries passengers from central railheads to nearby destinations by special shuttles or Thruway coach service.

TRAVELLING BY BUS

Bus (coach) lines serve many more destinations than do the railways. Bus lines also cover the same long-distance routes as trains, often in the same time. The Boston–New York bus trip, for example, is comparable to the train in both duration and price.

Greyhound Bus Lines (www.greyhound.com; (tel: 01342) 317317 in the UK) provide long-distance bus services between cities (and stops en route) nationwide. Trailways, an association of independent operators, provides a complete connected bus network in many areas, and in some parts of the US are the major operator.

GREYHOUND PASSES

Passes have to be presented to the station/ terminal ticket agent for validation before travel.

Ameripasses
(bought outside US)

4 days	$119
5 days	$139
7 days	$179
10 days	$229
15 days	$269
30 days	$369
45 days	$399
60 days	$539

Greyhound offer discounts for seniors (over 55), disabled travellers and their helpers and children (under 12) riding with a full-fare paying adult. The International Ameripass offers special discounts for adult travellers not resident in North America.

Greyhound's (International) AmeriPass (see left), like rail passes, may not necessarily be a lower price than individual tickets, especially if you reserve and buy individual tickets at least 3 days in advance. Because these are not 'flexi-passes' they are not good for those who are only travelling for a short time and visiting a few destinations. But for long-distance travel, they are a very good buy. The Greyhound pass is valid on most other operations including Trailways. Seats are not guaranteed on Greyhound buses. It's best to turn up 45 mins before departure, but if a bus is full another bus will usually be laid on to take the overflow.

If you're buying tickets locally enquire about the **Ameripass**, which, depending on distance travelled, may be more economical (but slightly more expensive if bought within the US). Local transport companies listed in the telephone directory under individual cities and towns provide a local service, or consult the *Thomas Cook Overseas Timetable*.

Greyhound also offer a number of regional passes including: Northeast pass (10-day $199, 21-day $299); Northeast/Central pass ($329 for 30 days); West Coast pass (21 days for $299); and the Southern pass (10-day $199, 21-day $299). The Floripass is $99 for 7 days, but options are available that allow entrance to theme parks ($269 for 3 parks, $299 for 4 parks, reduced rates for children.

TRAVELLING BY BOAT

The USA has very little regularly scheduled boat travel, except on short ferry connections. Long-distance boat trips, such as steamboat trips on the Mississippi and coastal travel, are by cruise packages of several days to a week. These tend to be luxury holidays, too pricey for budget travellers.

TRAVELLING BY CAR

Possibly one of the most difficult things for non-Americans to understand about the United States is how important a car is for getting to places. Public transport is quite good between cities of any size, passable between many smaller cities, but generally inadequate for smaller towns and rural areas. It serves the needs of commuting workers, but not of travellers. Because so many of the 'sights' of the USA are away from cities, often (especially in the west) remote from settled areas, getting to them without a car can be quite challenging, even impossible. In the east, many of the best places to go are lovely scenic rural areas, such as New England's small towns and villages or the great plantation houses of the south. Other attractions, such as museums and living history villages, may be miles from anywhere. Being without 'wheels' puts you at the mercy of erratic local buses or expensive and crowded rush-through tours.

Being without a car also leaves you little option in accommodation. In the USA, most budget accommodation (other than fleabag boarding houses and by-the-hour hotels) is outside city centres, along the Interstate highway or other approaches to a city. Here you will find rows of budget chain motor inns offering plain but clean and comfortable rooms at a tiny fraction of their in-town counterparts in the same range. The saving in hotel rooms alone can pay for car hire.

If you plan to spend days sightseeing in the city, it is often easiest to stay in hotels on the outskirts and drive to a nearby free commuter car park at a railway or bus station. You will usually be travelling during 'commuter hours', when buses and metro systems run frequently and in the right direction. For example, the area around Concord and Acton, Massachusetts, has several nice budget hotels, and is served by commuter rail that takes you right to Porter Square in Cambridge or into North Station, both stops on the city's subway system.

Many budget travellers plan to spend their days in the city, returning to the outskirts at night to find dining in the budget restaurants that often surround 'motel row' or in small suburban village centres where more upmarket restaurants congregate. A car gives you this flexibility.

Some US Driving Terms

Big Rig – A large lorry, usually a tractor pulling one or more trailers.

Boulevard stop – Slowing at a stop sign, but not stopping.

CNG – Liquified petroleum gas used as fuel

Connector – A minor road connecting two freeways

Crosswalk – Pedestrian crossing

Curve – Bend

Divided Highway– Dual carriageway

DUI – Driving Under the Influence of alcohol or drugs, aka Drunk Driving. Drink-driving laws are very strictly enforced.

Expressway – Motorway

Fender – Bumper

Garage/Parking Garage – Car Park

Gas(olene) – Petrol

Grade – Gradient, hill

Highway – Trunk road

Hood – Bonnet

Metering lights – Traffic signals controlling access to bridges, freeways etc.

Motor home – Motor caravan

Pavement – road surface. A UK pavement is a Sidewalk

Ramp – Slip road

Rent – Hire

Rubberneck(er) – Slowing down to peer while driving past the scene of an accident or some unusual event

RV (Recreational Vehicle) – Motor caravan

Shoulder – Verge

Sidewalk – Pavement

Sig-alert – An official warning or unusually heavy traffic, usually broadcast over local radio stations

Shift(stick) – Gear lever

Switchback – Serpentine road

Tailgate – Driving too close to the vehicle immediately in front

Tow Truck – Breakdown lorry

Traffic cop – Traffic Warden

Trailer – Caravan

Truck – Lorry

Trunk – Boot

Unpaved Road – Rough gravel or dirt road – check car hire restrictions on driving

Windshield – Windscreen

Yield – Give way

GETTING FROM HITHER TO YON The extensive US Interstate highway system brings car traffic smoothly into and around cities, travelling across and up and down the entire country. The best of US roads, these are dual carriageway, limited-access highways carrying two, three, four or more lanes of traffic in each direction. Most major cities have circular 'beltway' highways, also part of the Interstate system.

Although they don't all run north–south or east–west, you can generally tell the principal direction of an Interstate highway by its number. Odd two-digit numbers run north–south, even two–digit numbers east-west, and three digit numbers are either connectors or beltways around cities. Washington DC, for example, is linked to New York and the south by I-95, while I-66 leads west. I-495 circles the city and I-295 and I-395 are short connector routes.tes.

Some Interstate highways are toll roads, others are free. Some have toll segments and free segments. Interstates are the quickest, most direct routes but offer little to see. Petrol stations, restaurants and motels generally cluster at exits, off the highway; rest stops between some exits offer parking and often toilet facilities. Rest stops along other, non-Interstate toll roads offer petrol and food as well.

Most major bridges charge tolls, as do scattered small private bridges, but the latter are becoming more rare. These tolls usually range from less than $1 to $4; most expensive is the bridge-tunnel across the mouth of the Chesapeake Bay, about $10. Some toll highways use a card system, giving you a card as you enter and tallying the correct toll as you exit, based on how far you have travelled. Some (the bane of through-motorists) stop you every so many miles to collect a small fee. Some of the pay points (called toll plazas) are manned, others use a collecting machine that signals with a green light when the money is received.

It is wise to carry a small change purse filled with 25-cent pieces (quarters) and smaller change, as well as $1 bills, enabling you to choose the exact change lane at toll plazas. A common failing of these is not advising motorists of the exact toll until changing lanes becomes more difficult; this cache of small change assures that whatever it is, you will have it handy.

CAR HIRE One of most important decisions that must be made well in advance is whether to rent a car, and if so, where, what kind and from whom. In general, it is cheaper to include car hire as part of your flight package, although this might require that you pick the car up at your destination city, which might not be the best choice. If, for example, you plan to arrive in New York, see the sights, and move on to see Providence, Newport and Boston before touring northern New England, you might prefer to pick up your car as you leave Boston, using public transport where it serves the best.

Car categories vary, but most hire companies offer sub-compact, compact, economy, mid-sized, full-sized, luxury and sport utility (SUV) vehicles. The larger the car, the faster it accelerates and consumes petrol. Standard features usually include automatic transmission, air conditioning and unlimited mileage.

Recreational Vehicles, or RVs (camper vans and caravans), are an increasingly popular way to travel, with the higher cost of hiring and operating an RV offset (in theory) by savings on accommodation and meals and the convenience of not packing and unpacking at every stop. Make sure that you are given operating manuals and a full demonstration for all systems before leaving the hire company. In planning your itinerary, allow extra time for shopping, cooking and cleaning. For more details on RVs as an accommodation alternative, and for useful contact addresses, see Accommodation, p. 31.

It is usually cheaper to pick up a vehicle at an airport than in the city centre (and it's also easier to leave town from one). A surcharge, or drop fee, may be levied for dropping the vehicle off somewhere other than the place of hire. If considering an RV, ask about one-way rates if you aren't planning to arrive and leave from the same place. Most car hire companies require a credit card deposit, even if the hire has been prepaid. Before accepting the car, be sure you have all necessary registration and insurance documents and that you know how to operate the vehicle. To minimise safety problems, try to spend the first night in a hotel near the airport rather than jump from an exhausting international flight into a strange car.

Many states require third-party liability insurance cover of at least $15,000 for death or injury to one person, $30,000 for death or injury to more than one person and $5000 for property damage. US and Canadian drivers may be covered by their own insurance, but other drivers are strongly advised to take out their own cover or buy the collision damage waiver (CDW), sometimes called loss damage waiver (LDW), offered by hire companies. Without the waiver, hirers are personally liable for the full value of the vehicle. CDW is often required as part of fly-drive packages.

Your home country driving licence is valid in the USA, but you must have the licence in your possession while driving. The minimum driving age is 16, but most car hire companies require that all drivers be at least 25. Be sure to have the vehicle registration and proof of liability insurance handy at all times.

PICKING UP YOUR HIRE CAR A few car hire companies have desks near luggage claim areas of major airports, but for most you have to take a coach to an off-airport facility to pick up your hire car. Follow terminal signs for Rental Cars to the proper coach or van loading area.

Once there, have your booking number, passport, credit card and driving licence ready. Everyone who might drive the vehicle must show his or her driving licence and be listed on the rental contract. If an unlisted driver has an accident, you will probably have to pay for repairs yourself.

If hiring an RV, ask the hire company about airport pick-up and drop-off when making your booking. Most hire companies provide free or low-cost transport to and from their offices, which are usually located some distance from the airport.

DRIVING Before you leave the car park, take a 'tour' of your car: test the gear lever (although most US hire cars have automatic transmissions), and find the headlight and other light switches – it doesnn't help to reach for the wrong lever in an emergency! Be sure you know how to operate windscreen cleaning systems to avoid being suddenly blinded by a splash.

The most immediate problem will be for those from right-hand drive countries, such as the UK and South Africa. The operating equipment will be on the other side from where you expect it. When you are in normal traffic, driving will begin to seem natural as you follow other drivers, but at roundabouts (called rotaries or traffic circles in the USA) or on dual-lane highways, it becomes more difficult, because your natural instincts give you the wrong signals. Be especially alert and continue to remind yourself of this danger.

The most difficult time for some is in starting out in the morning on a road without other traffic. You can sometimes drive for some distance without realising that you are on the wrong side of the road. To solve this, attach a card to your keys, with the words 'Drive Right!' printed in large letters. Whenever you leave the car, and need to pocket your keys, this will be in your way. Remove it and tape it to your steering wheel. That reminds you as soon as you enter your car, at which time you return the card to your keys. A roll of tape is a small price to pay for avoiding a head-on collision.

RVs drive more like lorries than cars and are treated as lorries by traffic laws. In most places, the RV highway speed limit is 55 mph, as opposed to 65 mph for cars. Be cautious while driving. RVs are blown about by the wind more than cars and are more subject to rollover. They are also taller and wider than cars, which can create hazards at petrol stations, toll booths, car parks and low-hanging trees or signs.

It's wise, but not obligatory, to leave headlights on at all times for safety. Headlights must be used from dusk to dawn, or whenever conditions such as rain, fog or snow require. In some states, including California, it is illegal to drive with only parking lights illuminated.

In many states the driver and all passengers must wear seat belts. Nearly everywhere, children under the age of four or weighing less than 40 lb must ride in approved child safety seats. Safety seats can be hired with a car, or bought for under $100 at a discount store. In an RV, passengers riding behind the driver's seat need not wear belts, but should be safely seated.

By now you will have noticed that no single set of rules governs driving in the USA.

Travelling around the USA

Each state makes its own laws, which may vary in detail. As you cross a state line, be sure to slow down to read any signs by the roadside. These often inform you of ways in which laws differ. For example, many states require that you come to a complete stop whenever a school bus (indicated by a sign or its bright yellow colour) is loading children. While its flashing red lights are illuminated, all traffic, in both directions, must stop. Bus drivers can report violators, who will be charged.

Fuel Petrol (called gasoline) and diesel are sold at petrol stations in US gallons (there are about 4 litres to the gallon). Most vehicles take unleaded petrol, which comes in regular, premium and super grades. Buy regular unless the car hire company specifies otherwise. Most stations are self-service, although some offer a higher priced full-serve alternative. Pump prices include all taxes. Petrol stations generally accept credit cards and some take $20 travellers' cheques but will not take $50 or $100 bills in case they are counterfeit.

Parking Parking garages and parking lots (car parks) are usually, but not always, indicated by a white P on a blue background. Prices are posted at the entrance. Some city centre garages charge $20 or more per hour, especially for short-term stays.

Kerbside parking time is usually limited, either by posted signs or by coin-operated parking meters. Costs range from nothing to several dollars per hour. Kerbs in some places may be colour-coded. In California, for example, *red* means no stopping or parking at any time; *white* is for passenger loading/unloading only; *green* means limited time parking (usually 10 mins); *yellow* is a commercial loading zone; *blue* is handicapped parking. The general rule is that if the kerb is painted, don't park there. In most places, parking is not allowed within 15 ft of a fire hydrant, within 3 ft of a disabled kerb ramp, at bus stops, zebra crossings (crosswalks), on the pavement or on freeways. Fines vary from a few dollars to several hundred, depending on the infraction and jurisdiction. Fines levied against hired cars are charged against the hirer's credit card.

Driving Conditions The United States has almost every difficult driving condition imaginable, sometimes just an hour or two away from each other. Here is a survey of those you may encounter.

Desert travel For desert travel, be sure that air conditioner and heater are both in good order. Carry extra water, food, warm clothing and a torch in case of trouble. If the car breaks down on a highway, one person should walk to the next phone box and call for help, then return to the car to wait. On secondary roads, raise the bonnet. Either way, *always stay with your vehicle*. It's the only shade in sight and the breakdown lorry will be looking for a stranded car, not someone on foot. Sandstorms can reduce visibility to zero. If visibility drops, pull off the road on to a spot higher than the surrounding terrain and wait it out.

Winter driving Blowing snow can reduce visibility to zero in minutes, not only on mountain roads, but on Interstate highways. Many passes over the Sierra Nevada mountains are closed late Nov–June, and even in northern New England some mountain roads close Nov–Apr. In the mountains of the west, highways that remain open frequently require the use of chains or other traction devices. If youou're planning mountain driving in winter, ask the car hire company to include chains or buy your own (under $50). When chains are required, petrol station attendants and roadside workers will install them for about $20.

For any long-distance winter driving, carry warm clothing and food in case of traffic delays and always keep the petrol tank at least half full. Useful items include an ice scraper and a small shovel.

Avoid driving in snow or on icy roads; listen to weather predictions and plan your route or activities around the weather in winter. Be especially cautious when temperatures hover just around freezing and it is raining. The road may be wet one minute and icy the next.

Other hazards In California, fog and blowing dust are frequent hazards, causing massive chain-reaction collisions in the Central Valley each year. When visibility drops, *slow down* and turn your headlights on low beam. High beams blind oncoming drivers and reflect back to reduce your own vision. Fog can be a problem in any coastal area, more so at night.

Driving across the long, flat, straight roads of America's midlands, the greatest hazard may be falling asleep. Be sure to have someone else awake in the car, keep the radio on and carry small boiled sweets or fresh fruit to eat. Stop often and, if necessary, get out and jog on the spot beside the car.

Most state highway maps have a number to call for information on conditions, including road closures, and roadside signs often give call numbers of dedicated radio reports for motorists. Local radio stations also broadcast weather and driving information. In urban areas, most stations have regular traffic reports during morning and evening rush hours, which is why you may sometimes see a helicopter hovering overhead as you sit in a traffic jam.

Speed Limits The speed limit on Interstate highways is 65 mph for cars (55 mph for trucks and RVs) unless posted otherwise. Some rural freeways have a limit of 70 mph. In town, the speed limit is usually 25 or 30 mph unless otherwise indicated. If driving conditions are poor, drivers are required to keep to a safe speed, no matter how slow. Police use radar, lasers and planes to track, stop and ticket speeders, but highway traffic normally flows at least 10 mph above the limit.

Police signal drivers with flashing red and blue lights, sirens and loudhailers. Pull off the roadway as quickly as possible, turn off the engine and roll down the driver's side window a few inches. Stay inside the vehicle unless asked to step out. Have your driving licence and vehicle registration ready for inspection. Officers occasionally let drivers off with a verbal warning. If they issue a ticket – a citation – arguing will only make a bad situation worse.

It is sad but true that some localities support their police departments with 'speed traps', places where signs are misleading or confusing, or where speed limits are deliberately lower than conditions require. Often these are just as you leave or enter a town, often when a low speed limit continues far outside a congested area. Drivers resume normal speed, believing that they have simply failed to see the sign indicating higher limits. In these cases, there is little you can do but pay the fine as soon as possible and leave town. Arguing will usually lead to a court appearance several days or weeks hence. Although speed traps are becoming less frequent on major roads, you may encounter them in the south, and in small communities anywhere. The best rule is to watch speed limit signs carefully and obey them, however odd they may seem.

IN CASE OF TROUBLE If your car breaks down, pull as far off the road as possible, turn on the flashing hazard lights, and if it is safe to get out, raise the bonnet and return to the vehicle. Do not split passengers up. Change tyres only when out of traffic. Emergency phone boxes are placed every half-mile on some highways; otherwise, dial 911 from any telephone for police or medical assistance, but not for a tow truck (breakdown lorry). Lights on emergency vehicles are red or red and blue, so do not stop for flashing white lights or flashing headlights. Ask directions only from police, at a well-lit business area, or at a service station.

AAA or other auto club membership is especially valuable in case of breakdown. Membership usually includes free towing service to the nearest garage for repairs. Most hire car companies either pay for repairs directly or reimburse the cost shown on repair receipts. If a hire car will be out of service for more than a few hours, ask the hire company for a replacement vehicle.

If you are involved in a collision, stop. Call the highway patrol or local police if there are injuries or more than minor scratch damage to either vehicle. Show police your driving licence, vehicle registration, proof of insurance and contact information, and exchange the same information with the other driver. Get the names and addresses of any witnesses. Accidents must also be reported to your car hire company.

In most states (and the responding officer can tell you) collisions resulting in death, injury or property damage over $500 must be reported to the state's Department of Motor Vehicles (DMV) within ten days. DMV offices are listed in the telephone book white pages. In some states, such as Nevada, property damage amounting to only $350 or more must be reported to police.

Driving under the influence of alcohol, or any other drug, is illegal. The blood alcohol limit is 0.01% in most states and strictly enforced. Drivers suspected of drunk driving have the choice of a breath, blood or urine test; refusing the test is an admission of guilt. Police establish random checkpoints and frequent roads near wine-tasting rooms and popular roadside restaurants.

ROAD SIGNS European-style road signs are widely used, but not universal. *Red* signs indicate stop, do not enter, or wrong way. *Yellow* signs are warnings or direction indicators. *Orange* means road repairs or detours. *White* shows speed limits and distances, almost always in miles. *Brown* indicates parks, camping and other recreation opportunities. *Blue* gives non-driving information such as services in a nearby town.

VEHICLE SECURITY AND SAFETY Try not to accept a vehicle with a hire company decal or logo visible–itt's an advertisement for theft. You probably can't hide the hire company advert on an RV, but the rolling homes are obvious targets already. Whether you have an RV or a car, lock your vehicle when you're in it as well as when you leave it. Check for intruders before getting in, especially at night and in RVs at any time. Never leave the engine running when the driver isn't behind the wheel and always park in well-lit areas.

Ask car hire counter personnel to recommend a safe, direct route on a clear map before you leave with the vehicle. Take all valuables with you if possible; if not, lock all valuables and luggage in the boot or glove box so that nothing is visible to passers-by or other drivers. Don't leave maps, brochures, or guidebooks in evidence – why advertise that you're a stranger in town?

Always keep car doors and windows locked. Do not venture into unlit areas, neighbourhoods that look seedy, or off paved roads. Do not stop if told by a passing motorist or pedestrian that something is wrong with your car, or if someone signals for help with a broken-down car. If you need to stop, do so only in well-lit or populated areas, even if your car is bumped from behind by another vehicle. At night, have keys ready to unlock car doors before entering a car park. Check the surrounding area and inside the vehicle before entering. Never pick up hitchhikers.

In general, you and your car will be far safer in rural areas (except possibly in the south) than in and around cities. Hundreds of thousands of people travel in the USA each year without incident or danger, but not knowing the territory does put you at risk anywhere. You can minimize that risk by being well informed, aware, cautious and alert.

TRAVELLING ON FOOT

While walking remains the best way to see most cities, and is practical in parks, nature reserves and other wilderness areas, it is not generally a good way to tour in the USA. Long-distance walking paths are rare, and routes often involve long stretches of roadside. But within local areas, especially those with considerable parkland, such as the White and Green Mountains of New England, walking and hiking are the only ways to see many of the natural wonders such as waterfalls and mountain views.

Hitchhiking

In an earlier, more trustful era, hitchhiking was the preferred mode of travel for budget travellers. Today, hitchhiking or picking up hitchhikers is asking for violent trouble, from theft to physical assault and murder. Don't do it.

The same cautions that apply anywhere else are good in the USA, particularly in mountain and wilderness areas. Know the route; carry a map, compass and basic safety gear; carry food and water. Stay on marked trails. Wandering off the trail, easy to do in the forest, adds to erosion damage and increases the danger of getting lost.

For maps, and information on health hazards for hikers, see the Travel Directory at the back of this book.

TRAVELLING BY BICYCLE

Cycling is popular for countryside day touring – less so for overnight trips, due to geography. Bikes can be hired by the hour or the day in most country and urban areas as well as in major parks.

For serious bikers (as cyclists are called in the USA), biking tours are available at all levels, from easy day trips to arduous pulls over the Cascades or Rockies. On-your-own bike tours are also possible, but beware of unexpected distances and make plans based on topographical maps that show mountains between towns.

Time

Continental USA is divided into four time zones:

Eastern Time:	GMT -5 hrs
Central Time:	GMT -6 hrs
Mountain Time:	GMT -7 hrs
Pacific Time:	GMT -8 hrs.

If you are crossing into Canada, there is Atlantic Canada Time (GMT -3 hrs) and Newfoundland (GMT -3.5 hrs) to bear in mind. Daylight saving, when all clocks are advanced one hour, runs from the first Sun in April until the last Sun in Oct – something not to forget if you are travelling at these times of the year and have a train or a plane to catch.

Many highways have narrow or non-existent verges, which can make cycling a nerve-racking experience as well as dangerous in heavy traffic. Local law in many places requires cyclists to wear protective helmets while riding. Sensible cyclists always wear them, whatever the law says.

Remember how big the USA is before planning to see it from coast to coast. If you have only a week, don't even think about it. If you have two, you will spend most of it in a bus, train or car unless you fly the cross-country routes. But if your schedule is longer, you might want to travel one or both ways by land, just to get a fuller sense of the great expanses that lie between the two oceans.

By Train To plan a cross-country return train trip, consider making a giant loop, going through the northern cities westbound, and southern destinations eastbound, or vice versa. In the chapters that follow, several train routes are detailed, describing the attractions of the route and the cities it passes through. By connecting those that appeal to you most, and filling in the spaces between them with through-train travel, you can create a custom-tailored itinerary. Be sure to do it with a copy of the *Thomas Cook Overseas Timetable* at hand, to ensure that you arrive in stopover cities at an appropriate time of day and travel the most scenic stretches by daylight.

Chicago, at the base of the Great Lakes, is the central point through which all but one east–west rail route passes, so unless you plan to see the Deep South, your routes can begin and end there. If you plan to travel both ways by train (or bus) you could choose different routes on each side of it, forming a huge figure 8.

For example, your northern east–west route from New York or Boston to Seattle via Amtrak might stop at Niagara Falls, Chicago, Milwaukee and Glacier Park. Possible side trips, using VIA Rail and Amtrak Thruway bus connection respectively, could take you to Toronto and Vancouver. You can get to Chicago from New York or Boston on the *Lake Shore Limited*, following the shores of three Great Lakes and the Erie Canal, whose locks you can see from a seat on the right. This is also the side to be on for the route along the Hudson River if you begin in New York. If you begin in Boston you'll pass through the Berkshire Mountains in western Massachusetts. Or you could travel the portion of the trip from New York to Niagara on the *Maple Leaf*, for more stops along the way. This train continues on to Toronto, just across the border in Canada.

You can continue to Seattle from Chicago via the northern route on the *Empire Builder*. This route goes through seldom-visited Milwaukee and the twin cities of Minneapolis and St Paul. Milwaukee is a German city, with breweries, good museums, parks and festivals. (Both the Amtrak station and the Greyhound terminal are in unsafe neighbourhoods, so take taxis to the city centres.)

The *Empire Builder* continues through the wide open spaces of Montana and Glacier National Park, over the Rockies, and follows the Columbia River Gorge to the Cascade Range before dropping dramatically to Puget Sound.

The southern route, from Chicago to Los Angeles, goes through the heart of the Wild West. Dodge City, the Santa Fe Trail, Grand Canyon – some of the most famous names of the west are along this one route. Stop in Lamy, New Mexico, to visit Santa Fe, and at Flagstaff, Arizona, to see the Grand Canyon. Leaving Chicago on the *Southwest Chief*, the boring parts of the corn belt are mostly travelled through at night, so there is daylight to see parts of the original Santa Fe Trail.

The *Sunset Limited* runs 3 times a week along the southern edge of the US. The 3000-mile trip, from Orlando to LA, crosses 8 states.

A middle option goes from Chicago to San Francisco. One of the most scenic rail routes in the west is followed by the *California Zephyr*, through Omaha, Denver, Salt Lake City and Reno, Nevada. The best of the scenery is west of Denver, and climaxes as the train follows the Colorado River along a succession of canyons, crossing and recrossing it. Before arriving, the train has to cross over the Sierra Nevada mountain range, along a canyon and through Gold Rush country. Or you can choose a route through the south-west, from Chicago to San Antonio. *Amtrak's Texas Eagle* takes you deep into the heart of Texas, passing St Louis about midnight, but with a great view of the huge arch. The ranchlands and flower-filled fields of Texas are seen by daylight.

The *Coast Starlight*, Amtrak's most popular train, connects the west coast cities of Seattle, Portland, San Francisco and Los Angeles, offering some stunning views from the northern forests and Cascade mountains, California's fertile valleys to the shoreline of the Pacific.

On your return, perhaps Amtrak's most scenic long route in the eastern USA is the trip from Chicago to New York on the *Cardinal*, which leaves Chicago in the evening, saving daylight hours for the trip through mountainous West Virginia. You can see the New River Gorge, and its bridge hundreds of feet above the river.

BY BUS Cross-country bus travel can follow much the same routes, although bus travellers have more flexibility in varying the stopover cities and can add destinations not accessible by train. Plan for a slightly longer trip crossing the country by bus, but for a greater choice in schedules.

BY AIR Unless you have a lot of time to spend travelling both ways by train, you may wish to opt for a compromise – travelling one way by land, the other by air. Southwest Airlines – and often others, spurred by Southwest's competitive rates – offers fares so low that they often beat train or bus travel. This is ideal for anyone who tires quickly of flatlands, cornfields and amber waves of grain, and wants to see both coasts. In a few hours, instead of a few days, you can move from Baltimore/Washington International Airport (a major east coast hub) to Santa Fe, New Mexico – or any of several other western destinations. If you decide to opt for this, look into Amtrak's return flight agreement with United Airlines, which discounts tickets for passengers who don't wish to take the train both ways.

This chapter contains useful information for planning your travels across the USA. As travellers may consider crossing the northern border – Amtrak's North America Rail Pass allows travel on the VIA rail network in Canada and the Greyhound Ameripass includes services to Vancouver, Montreal and Toronto – information useful for visitors to Canada has been included.

ACCOMMODATION

The United States offers accommodation of every style and price level imaginable, from five-star hotels and posh resorts to youth hostels and campsites. Local tourist offices can provide accommodation lists and telephone numbers, but many cannot make bookings.

HOTELS AND MOTELS

At chain hotels and motels, even with budget prices, expect a clean, comfortable, relatively spacious room with either one or two double- or queen-sized beds and a private bathroom. Some independent hotels and motels provide a lower standard, but others have good quality facilities plus charm and character.

> Hotel and motel rates, unless otherwise noted, are quoted for single or double occupancy; children usually stay cheaply or for free with parents. Advance bookings generally require a voucher or credit card number to guarantee the booking. When checking in, always ask if there's a cheaper room rate than the one you pre-booked. It's often cost effective to find accommodation day by day, especially in off-peak seasons (see Seasonal pricing, p. 35). Also ask about any discounts (see p. 35–36).

Motels are often the best bet, especially if you travel by car. Literally 'motor hotels', motels are one- to three-storey buildings with a modest version of a hotel's accommodation and facilities. Most belong to nationwide chains which enforce service and safety standards. Motels fill up fast during high season, but last-minute rooms are usually available in the off-season, especially during the week.

Motels often line major roads and advertise availability with 'vacancy' signs, as well as signs advertising special rates or offers. Most chains have toll-free reservation telephone numbers that can be reached from anywhere in North America (see Travel Directory, p. 504).

Budget hotels are sometimes acceptable, but those in cities, especially close to railway or bus stations, tend to be dim, dirty and dangerous. Look for a motel or youth hostel instead.

Bed-and-breakfasts (B&Bs) can be a homelier alternative, but they are seldom such a bargain as their English cousins, especially in cities or in highly visited areas, such as New England or California wine country. The accent is more often on luxury than on value. The typical urban bed-and-breakfast is a refurbished room in a Victorian mansion, complete with chintz curtains, down quilts, fireplace, bric-à-brac atop antique furniture, and private facilities. If 'Victorians' are in short supply, any ordinary mansion will do, even a converted garage or barn, so long as it's suitably luxurious.

Bed-and-breakfast accommodation in smaller towns and rural areas is much closer to the original concept, a tidy room with antique furnishings and homespun quilts in a restored 19th-century home or a comfortable bedroom in a farmhouse. Bathroom facilities may be private or shared. Usually the owner lives in the house, but some B&B owners live in an adjacent house. By their very nature, each is as different as its owners and the home they share; some join guests for a glass of wine in the evening, others keep a discreet distance.

Breakfasts vary, but the standard includes fruit juice, coffee or tea, an egg dish, home-made bread and a dessert. Some, however, serve these only at weekends, serving a continental breakfast of fruit or juice and home-baked breads on weekdays.

Country inns are a very fine line away from B&Bs, but most offer charm and personal attention. A small inn might have the look and feel of a B&B, but with more rooms and breakfast choices. Bigger inns typically include a full restaurant with hearthside dining, a wide porch with rocking chairs for relaxing, and higher prices.

CAMPING Camping means a tent or a recreational vehicle (RV) in a rural campsite. Those in state or national parks and forests are the quietest and most primitive, with firewood available but facilities limited to pit toilets and cold showers. Private sites usually offer more facilities but may be crowded with RVs, with pitches crowded close together.

Kampgrounds of America (KOA) is a private chain of RV parks that accepts tents (address p. 35). Many other campsites are public; most are operated by federal, state or provincial authorities. Overnight fees range from $7 to more than $20, depending on location and season. Standard facilities include a fireplace for barbecues, food storage locker (where bears are a problem), tent site, nearby showers/toilets, and, during high season, daytime guided hikes and evening educational programmes around a large campfire.

The latest introductions in camping are the yurt – a permanent fixture modelled on traditional Mongolian nomad tents – teepees, and covered wagons. All three are available at selected parks in

Colour Section

(i) New York (pp. 53–67); inset: The Statue of Liberty

(ii) Niagara Falls (p. 75); New England fall colour;

(iii) Boston (pp. 88–102); the Old State House; inset: Quincy Market

(iv) Cape Cod (pp. 122–127); Falmouth Lighthouse; Woods Hole

MetLife

Booking ahead

Although you may not want to lock into an itinerary by making advance reservations for every night, it is comforting to know that you have a bed waiting for you at the end of each day's travel. Thomas Cook or any other good travel agent can handle room bookings when you purchase air tickets, as well as car or other local transportation. All-inclusive fly-drive arrangements, and 'do-it-yourself packages' such as Thomas Cook's America for the Independent Traveller programme, can provide hotel coupons, exchangeable at a range of hotel chains, which guarantee a prepaid rate at participating chains, although they do not guarantee rooms – it's up to you to phone ahead as you go, or take a chance on availability. It is particularly important to pre-book the first and last night's stay to avoid problems when connecting with international air flights.

It is also important to confirm pre-booked rooms by telephone if you will arrive after 1800. Many hotels and motels automatically cancel bookings at 1800, especially during high season, even if rooms have been guaranteed with a credit card. The best time to make the reconfirmation is 1600–1800 on the day of the late arrival.

If you do not want to book so far ahead, it is still well worth while to carry the toll-free numbers for hotel and motel chains with you. This way you can stop at midday, when you have an idea of how far you are likely to travel that day, and call to secure a room at your destination. Several tips may make that easier:

If you don't know what is available in the area you need, call the toll-free number of major chains to locate the nearest ones (see Travel Directory).

Begin with the chain nearest to your ideal budget and work upwards.

Take a map to the telephone with you, since operators in a central reservations office rarely know what other towns may be nearby.

If you belong to an automobile club with AAA affiliation, a call to AAA's central reservations office can often turn up a room even when they are scarce – and with a member discount..

If the central reservations office tells you that a hotel is full, ask for the local number of the hotel. If you fail to find a room from any other chain, it is worth calling the individual properties, since they often keep a room or two for 'regulars' and may also put your name on a waiting list in case of 'no-shows' or cancelled reservations.

Have your credit card handy when you call, so you can immediately reserve a room.

If all else fails, go to the hotel anyway and ask to see the manager. A good manager will often try to find a room by calling managers of other establishments or local B&Bs you might never have found.

If you are truly desperate, ask permission to sleep in your car in the hotel parking lot. This often procures a room when nothing else does.

When staying in a chain hotel, always ask for a copy of the chain's directory of properties to take with you. A collection of these will be helpful as you travel and you can discard them before flying home.

Local tourist offices also provide accommodation lists and telephone numbers, but generally cannot make bookings. Where available, local services are noted in each chapter.

the north-west through Reservations Northwest, tel: (800) 452-5684 or (503) 731-3411. As a guide, expect to pay around $25 per yurt per night for up to five people, including beds, mattresses, table and lights.

At many state and provincial park campsites, a place can be reserved in advance. Nearly all private campsites accept reservations.

CAMPERS AND RVs The freedom of the open road, housekeeping on wheels, a tinker's delight: an RV, caravan or motor home provides a kitchen, sleeping and bathroom facilities, all integrated atop a lorry chassis.

Fly-drive holiday packages usually offer the option of hiring an RV. The additional cost of hiring an RV can be offset by the economies of assured accommodation for several people, space for meal preparation and eating, plus the convenience of comfort items and souvenirs stored nearby. However, RVs are cramped, designed to stuff you and your belongings into limited space. The economics work only if advance planning assures that the pricey spur-of-the-moment allure of a hotel shower or unplanned restaurant meal doesn't overcome you too often. You should also add in the cost of petrol – an RV guzzles three to four times more than a medium-sized car. And remember that you will travel more slowly than a car on long hauls, especially over mountain roads. After all, you are hauling your house around; remember the turtle.

Systems may be interdependent, or more complex than anticipated. If you decide to carry your home with you, consider the following:

Be prepared to pre-plan menus and allow additional time each morning and afternoon/evening to level the RV (perfect levelling is essential for correct operation of refrigerators), and to hook up or disconnect electricity, water and sewage hoses and cable television plugs – many RVers carry a pair of overalls.

Without hook-ups, water and electricity are limited to what you carry with you from the last fill-up or battery charge. If you camp in a park without hook-ups, locate the nearest toilets and washing facilities before dark. Using showers and toilets in RV parks or public campsites will save time cleaning up the RV shower space and emptying the toilet holding tank.

Buy a pair of sturdy rubber washing gloves to handle daily sewage chores. Pack old clothes to wear while crawling beneath the vehicle to hook up and disconnect at each stop.

As at home, some basic housework must be done; also allow time for laundry at RV parks.

When on the road, expect anything that's not secured to go flying, or to shake, rattle and roll.

Quickly get into a routine of allotted tasks and assign a handy spot for maps, snacks, cameras and valuables.

RV travel information for planning your trip can be obtained from:

Recreation Vehicle Industry Association (RVIA), Dept RK, PO Box 2999, Reston VA 22090-0999; tel: (703) 620-6003. To plan RV camping, request *Go Camping America* from Camping Vacation Planner, PO Box 2669, Reston VA 22090; tel: (800) 477-8669, covering the USA and Canada.

Camping clubs offer RV information for members: some, including the Good Sam Club, PO Box 6060, Camarillo CA 93011; tel: (805) 389-0300, offer roadside assistance for breakdowns and tyre changing. Many camping clubs publish magazines or newsletters with tips on operating and driving an RV. For a hilarious insight into RV travel, find a copy of *Out West*, 9792 Edmonds Way, Suite 265, Edmonds WA 98020; tel: (206) 776-1228; fax: (206) 776-3398; email: outwestcw@aol.com, a periodic tabloid with bizarre pictures of signs and stories about Western characters. The publisher packs his family and computer into an RV for several weeks at a time, and they deliver a flavourful picture of the best and the worst of home-on-wheels travel.

Campsite directories and state/provincial tourist office guides list private RV park locations, with directions and details of facilities. Directories cover parks in the USA and Canada. Popular directories include: *Trailer Life Campground & RV Services Directory*, TL Enterprises, 2575 Vista del Mar Dr., Ventura CA 93001; tel: (805) 667-4100 ($19.95); *Woodall's Campground Directory* (Western Edition), 13975 W. Polo Trail Dr., Lake Forest IL 60045; tel: (800) 823-9076 ($13.70); *Wheelers RV Resort & Campground Guide*, 1310 Jarvis Ave, Elk Grove Village, IL 60007; tel: (708) 981-0100 ($15.50); and *Kampgrounds of America (KOA) Directory*, PO Box 30558, Billings MT 59114-0558; tel: (406) 248-7444 ($3 or free at KOA campsites).

YOUTH HOSTELS **Hostelling International** (HI) was created for tight budgets. Youth hostels are much less common in the USA than in Europe; many cities have none. Most US hostels provide a dormitory-style room and shared bath for $8–$16 per night. Some have family rooms; all offer discounts to local attractions. However, when two or more people are travelling together and can share a room, budget motels may be even cheaper than hostels. In accommodation listings for each location in this book, prices given for hostels are based on beds for two people, to allow comparison with double room charges in the other listings. For a complete description of all Hostelling International hostels in the USA and Canada, contact Hostelling International in the UK; tel: (01727) 845047, or in the US, American Youth Hostels, 733 15th St N.W., Washington DC 20005; tel: (202) 783-6161.

SEASONAL PRICING Accommodation may be hard to find in major tourist destinations during high season – Memorial Day (end of May) to Labor Day (early Sept). In Vermont, New Hampshire and western Massachusetts, the hardest time to find a room is foliage season (mid-Sept–mid-Oct); many inns and hotels are completely booked a full year in advance by return clients. At ski resorts, high season prices arrive with the first good snowfall.

Expect to pay as much as 60% over low season rates during the high season, and even more at beach resorts. It is sometimes possible to avoid the higher tariffs by travelling during the 'shoulder' season, one or two weeks before or after high season, when crowds are smaller and rates lower. It is also possible to travel out of season, but many attractions, especially in smaller towns, close when high season ends.

DISCOUNTS Like everything else, accommodation has its deals. Senior and disabled persons should ask if discounts apply. Members of automobile clubs may find discounts through affiliated clubs in the USA. Military personnel (even foreign) on holiday may get special rates, as they do at Super 8 Motels. Other chains, such as Holiday Inn, give children free meals in their restaurants.

If you are visiting more than four or five national parks, monuments or historical sites for which entrance fees are charged, purchase a Golden Eagle Passport for $50, which covers the holder and one other person. Blind and disabled travellers can request a free-of-charge Golden Access Passport upon arrival. These passes usually include discounted prices at campsites.

Canada has a similar scheme for its national parks, Canada's Great Western Annual Pass, costing $35 per person or $70 per family from individual parks or Parks Canada Service Centre, Rm 220 Canada Place, 9700 Jasper Ave, Edmonton, Alberta T5J 4C3; tel: (800) 748-7275.

Another programme to consider is Entertainment Guides: this provides books of coupons and discounts purchased annually (about $40–$65) that allow half-price rates at hundreds of hotels. While the 50% discounts are usually at higher priced hotels and are based on the 'rack' rate, not any special seasonal or promotional rates, they still bring prices down noticeably. Budget chains, such as Day's Inn, Comfort Inn and Econo Lodge take 20% off their regular rates for Entertainment members. Reservations for all rooms must be made in advance. To learn more about these, contact Entertainment Publications, Book Order Dept, 2125 Butterfield Rd, Troy MI 48084; tel: (248) 637-3999; www.AskUs@epi.cendant.com.

FOOD AND DRINK

American meal portions tend to be large, beginning at breakfast, which may include thinly sliced bacon, eggs cooked to order, fried potatoes, toast and endless refills of coffee. Or it may be a plate heaped with pancakes or French toast (bread slices dipped in egg and fried). Crumpets (confusingly called English muffins), waffles, bagels, fresh fruit, yogurt, porridge and cereal are other possibilities. A 'continental breakfast' is juice, coffee or tea, and bread or pastry.

For most Americans, midday lunch includes light dishes, such as soups, salads and sandwiches, although most restaurants also offer dinner-type main courses (known as entrées), usually at prices lower than in the evening. Evening dinner menus offer appetisers, salads, soups, pastas, entrées, and desserts. While pasta is listed as a separate course, most Americans (especially those not of Italian descent) order it in place of a meat entrée.

Sunday brunch (usually 1100–1400) is typically a self-service buffet piled high with hot and cold dishes, which can be good value for teenagers and other hearty eaters, or can be the day's main meal, with only a light supper to follow.

You will be surprised not only at the number and variety of places to eat nearly everywhere, but at the wide span of price ranges. Small-town family-style restaurants, diners and self-service cafés are usually at the lower end of the scale, while resort dining rooms and trendy city watering holes can become quite pricey.

For hearty eating, try a steak house where salad, baked potato and beans accompany a thick steak, be it beef or salmon. Italian restaurants serve pizza, pasta, seafood and steaks, with heavy doses of tomato and garlic. Mexican cooks use thin wheat or corn tortillas as the base for beans, rice, cheese, tomatoes, spicy sauce and other ingredients. The Chinese cuisine offered in most restaurants is Cantonese with bean sprout chow mein and fried rice. More authentic Chinese dishes can be found with regional variations, from spicy Hunan to rich, meaty Mandarin. Bite-size dim sum (filled dumplings) or any variety of won ton soup makes a filling lunch. Japanese, Vietnamese and Thai food are other easy-to-find Asian cuisines.

The melting pot of cuisines in major cities includes Basque, French, German, Spanish, Cuban, Ethiopian, Salvadoran, Indian and a hundred others. 'Fusion' is the key word these days, describing the cuisine of the 'New American' restaurants, where talented chefs blend ingredients and techniques from the entire world. At these restaurants, your sandwich of Maine lobster may be seasoned with Japanese pickled ginger. The brightest and best chefs are not confined to big city culinary capitals; look for them in country inns and in small cities, too.

America made fast food an international, if dubious, dining experience. Fast meals on the road can be found at the abundant chains with drive-up windows where food is ordered, paid for, and picked up from a service counter, all within a few minutes. Some fast-food outlets have drive-through service, where the driver pulls up to a window, orders from a displayed menu, pays, and gets the meal, all without leaving the vehicle. Hamburgers, hot dogs, tacos, fried chicken and barbecue beef are common offerings. McDonald's golden arches and KFC's grinning chubby colonel are easy to spot. Other fast food chains include A & W, Arby's Roast Beef, Burger King, Carl's Jr, Del Taco, Domino's Pizza, Jack-in-the-Box, Little Caesars Pizza, Pizza Hut, Subway and Taco Bell.

Chain restaurants are ubiquitous, with pre-measured portions and the same menu in Miami as in Seattle. Chains include Friendly's (ice cream, sandwiches and simple meals), Bertucci's (Italian), Boston Market (roasted chicken) and International

House of Pancakes (IHoP), which serves all-day breakfast plus safe, unexciting lunch and dinner choices. They are hardly the best America has to show of its culinary talents, and they are not necessarily a bargain. Far better to sample what each region has to offer at a locally owned eatery where the chef is also the owner.

> **RESTAURANT TIPPING**
>
> Service charges are not added to bills and tipping is expected and part of the waiter's pay, which is proportionately lower to allow for it. Expect to add about 15% of the tab, and up to 20% for exceptional attention. In luxury restaurants, also be prepared to tip the *maître d'* and sommelier a few dollars, up to 10% of the bill. If the service is terrible, leave only small change as a lesson, instead of no tip at all, which might be interpreted as an oversight. In bars and pubs (you do not serve yourself at the bar here) tips should be about 10% when drinks are all that's served at a table, or $0.50 to the bartender.

Expect to pay $5–$8 per person for breakfast (much more at hotels), $5–$12 for lunch, and $10–$25 for dinner (plus drinks).

You can keep to your budget by having breakfast at local diners or family restaurants (instead of hotel dining rooms), and lunch at carry-outs (takeaways) and little cafés, or as picnics. If you stay in B&Bs or inns with giant-sized breakfasts, you may decide to skip lunch and take advantage of the 'early-bird specials' that many restaurants offer between 5 and 6 pm.

Another way to save money if you plan to be in one area or city for a time, is to purchase an Entertainment Guide, which are full of dining as well as accommodation discounts (see p. 35). These are available by region and include everything from fast food discounts to coupons offering a free entrée at better restaurants.

Each region of the USA has its own traditional foods, based on its climate and growing season, its proximity to the sea, its ethnic mix and a dozen other factors. Although some dishes are unique to certain regions, many regional dishes have become favourites far beyond their home town. With the advent of refrigerated air cargo, it is almost as easy to get fresh Maine lobster in San Diego as it is in Wiscasset.

Lobster is considered by many Americans to be the festive 'big occasion' food of choice. On a menu it will probably be labelled as 'Maine Lobster'; this is the stamp of quality and authenticity. Lobster is the main event at clambakes and shore dinners along New England's coast, and you can eat it in fine dining rooms or from picnic tables on the wharves where the lobsters first saw land.

Another of New England's favourite treats now enjoyed everywhere is fried clams. These are dipped in a crumb coating (sometimes a batter, to the despair of purists) and deep fried. Delicious and virtually indigestible.

If you want to start a fight in the north-east, get residents of different states talking about chowder. The real thing, whether it's clam, fish or corn chowder, besides the main ingredient, will have chunks of potato and onion suspended in a savoury cream base seasoned with salt and pepper. 'Manhattan style' has tomatoes, not cream, and to New Englanders it's not chowder at all, but a poor excuse for fish-flavoured vegetable soup.

Americans still enjoy the first foods the Pilgrims met – turkey, pumpkin (or similar winter squashes), cranberries, seafood and maize (called corn). So close are these to the hearts of most Americans, these are essential to the dinner menu for the national feast of Thanksgiving Day.

Americans have puddings such as bread pudding or Indian pudding (milled maize with molasses), but the sweet course is always called dessert.

Americans are fond of food festivals, usually celebrating a local crop. In rural areas at various seasons you may find strawberry festivals, apple festivals, or those celebrating blueberries, mushrooms (in Pennsylvania) and even garlic (in California). These are filled with fun and food, and a good place to meet people in a relaxed and friendly local setting.

ALCOHOL Some small restaurants without liquor licences allow you to bring your own wine – the term for this is BYOB – but most are licensed. Beware that occasionally you will encounter a 'dry' town where restaurants are not allowed to serve wine or beer and you must bring your own from a neighbouring town. Buying alcoholic drinks by the bottle varies by state; wine and/or beer may be available in grocery or convenience stores. In some places, alcohol cannot be sold on Sunday. Not only do these laws vary by state, but by municipality as well, so if in doubt, ask whether a restaurant is licensed when you make dinner reservations.

DRINKING AND THE LAW

You must be 21 (and able to prove it, so keep your passport handy) to drink – anywhere, at any time. In most states you cannot carry an open container of any alcohol – even wine or beer – in the car. In many towns you cannot drink in public places, such as parks or beaches, so be careful about picnics with a loaf of bread and a bottle of wine.

BEVERAGES Coffee has become something closer to a religious experience than a hot drink in some cities, especially in the Pacific north-west. *Espresso* carts are a way of life where: they purvey breakfast, lunch and tea on city pavements. Motorists stuck in traffic jams jump out for a quick shot of espresso to speed the drive home, while petrol stations sell *cappuccino* and *latte* alongside the motor oil and tyre chains. Drive-through *espresso* stands have become common in some urban areas.

Urban residents are fiercely loyal to their chosen brand. Expect descriptions such as 'strong', 'nutty', 'smooth', ' delicate' etc. *Espresso* is the basic brew, black and thick. *Latte* is similar to *cappuccino*, without the foam or the spice dusting. And if basic coffee is too strong for your taste buds, most coffee bars offer more than a dozen flavours, from vanilla and hazelnut to banana and coconut. The latest fashion is iced coffee drinks, often whipped. Apart from the coffee bars, the majority of places still serve 'American coffee', a tad weak for most European tastes.

Two centuries after the Boston Tea Party, Yankees are again drinking the beverage they once boycotted; in some places they've re-adopted the proper way of preparing it, forgoing the teabag-in-a-cup-of-warm-water travesty for the real stuff, and even enjoying fine blends in place of the once ubiquitous orange pekoe. But don't expect good tea most places: you still have to look hard. American tea drinkers usually carry their own premium-brand of teabags with them when they travel, and you might wish to follow their example.

Don't be surprised if your classy B&B or inn offers you afternoon tea with all the accompaniments. Two cautionary notes, however. 'Tea Room' does not necessarily mean that afternoon tea is served. More often, it is simply a restaurant retaining an old-fashioned name for a spot where respectable ladies would feel comfortable dining. It may be a centre for psychic readings, as in tea leaves. Remember also that Americans often drink their tea without milk, so before you pour, be sure to check and make sure you have not been given a jug of cream, a distinction non-tea drinkers sometimes fail to make.

Bottled water is popular, but rarely necessary for health reasons. However, water from streams and ponds in natural areas should be avoided (see below). Soft drinks (called soda or tonic) and fruit juices are available in stunning variety.

DISABLED TRAVELLERS

Access is the key word. 'Physically challenged' is synonymous with disabled. Physical disabilities should present less of a barrier in the USA than in much of the world. Federal and state laws, particularly the Americans with Disabilities Act (ADA), generally require that all businesses, buildings and services used by the public be accessible to handicapped persons, including those using wheelchairs. Every hotel, restaurant, office, shop, cinema, museum, post office and other public building must have access ramps and toilets designed for wheelchairs. Most cities and towns have ramps built into street crossings and most city buses have some provision for wheelchair passengers. Even many parks have installed paved pathways so disabled visitors can get a sense of the natural world.

The bad news is that disabled facilities aren't always what they're meant to be. Many older facilities do not yet comply with the standards. Museums, public buildings, restaurants and accommodation facilities are usually accessible, but historic homes and properties often are not. Special controls for disabled drivers are seldom an option on hired vehicles.

Airlines are particularly hard on disabled passengers. Carriers can prevent anyone who is not strong enough to open an emergency exit (which weighs about 45 lb or 20 kg) or has vision/hearing problems from sitting in that row of seats – even if it means not allowing them to fly. Commuter airlines sometimes deny boarding to passengers with mobility problems on the grounds that they may block the narrow aisle during an emergency.

Some public telephones have special access services for the deaf and disabled. Broadcast television may be closed-captioned for the hearing impaired, indicated by a rectangle around a double cc in a corner of the screen.

Two helpful organisations are:

SATH (Society for the Advancement of Travel for the Handicapped), 347 5th Ave, Suite 610, New York NY 10016; tel: (212) 447-7284.

RADAR, 12 City Forum, 250 City Rd, London EC1V 8AF; tel: (0171) 250 3222..

MONEY

Try to arrive with a few dollars in US currency and coins. Luggage trolleys are sometimes free in the international arrivals area but must sometimes be paid for. Some trolley stands accept credit cards, usually Visa or Access/Mastercard, but others require cash – and currency exchange facilities are located outside the arrivals area.

SMOKING

Be careful about lighting up. More often than not, smoking is forbidden in public buildings and on public transport; in several states it is prohibited by law in all public places. All plane flights in North America are non-smoking, and some hire cars are designated as non-smoking. Most hotels/motels set aside non-smoking rooms or floors; bed-and-breakfast establishments are almost all non-smoking. Restaurant dining regulations vary by locality: some forbid all smoking; others permit it in the bar or lounge only; some have a percentage of the eatery devoted to smokers. Smoking is prohibited in most stores and shops. Always ask before lighting a cigarette, cigar or pipe. When in doubt, go outside to smoke.

International airports have currency exchange facilities in the international terminal which are usually open at times when overseas flights are arriving. Domestic terminals and smaller airports have no exchange facilities at all. But nearly all will have automatic cash dispensers or ATMs.

ATMs offer the best currency exchange rates and never close. Star and Cirrus are the most common international ATM networks, but check with your card issuer before leaving home to ensure that you have the proper four-digit PIN (personal identification number) for US outlets. Expect to pay transaction fees to both the bank which owns the ATM and your own bank for each transaction, but also expect to get the best rate of exchange for that day, since electronic transfers use the commercial exchange rate.

For security reasons, avoid carrying large amounts of cash. The safest forms of money are travellers' cheques and credit or debit cards. Both can be used almost everywhere.

US dollar travellers' cheques from Thomas Cook and other major issuers are accepted almost everywhere, but travellers' cheques in other currencies must be cashed at a bank, and not just any bank, either. Except in large commercial and city banks, expect, at the very best, delays as staff telephone the main office in search of exchange rates and procedures. In smaller cities and towns you may not be able to cash travellers' cheques in foreign currencies at all. Eurocheques and personal cheques drawn on banks outside the United States are generally not accepted. Don't even bother trying to exchange coins: it costs banks in both countries more to collect and process them than they're worth.

A number of Thomas Cook locations offer MoneyGram, a quick international money transfer service. To contact Thomas Cook offices while in the USA, tel: 1-800-CURRENCY (toll-free).

If possible, bring at least one, preferably two, major credit cards such as Access (MasterCard), American Express or Visa. Nearly all US shops accept both MasterCard and Visa. Plastic is the only acceptable proof of fiscal responsibility. Car hire companies require either a credit card imprint or a substantial cash deposit before releasing a vehicle, even if the hire has been fully prepaid. Hotels and motels also require either a credit card imprint or a cash deposit, even if the bill is to be settled in cash. But you cannot travel entirely on plastic: some shops, cheaper motels, hostels, small local restaurants, and low-cost petrol stations require cash.

FINANCIAL EMERGENCIES

If you lose your Thomas Cook travellers' cheques, tel: (800) 223-7373 (toll-free 24 hr service). In the event of loss or theft of a MasterCard, or for assistance with other card-related emergencies, call MasterCard Global Service at 1 (800) 307-7309 (toll-free 24 hr service). Thomas Cook locations also offer replacement and other emergency services if you lose a MasterCard.

MoneyGram provides money transfer by telegraph, with locations all over the USA and around the world. If you need to have funds sent to you in an emergency, call (800) 926-9400 (toll-free) .

CURRENCY US dollars are the only currency accepted in the USA; Canadian dollars are used in Canada, but shops in border towns will usually accept American dollars, sometimes at a favourable exchange rate.

US banknote denominations are $1, $2 (very rare), $5, $10, $20, $50 and $100. All banknotes are the same colour – green and white – and the same size, so take great care not to mix them up. The only differences, apart from the denominations marked on them, are the US presidents pictured on the front and the designs on the back. Very confusing at present are the new bills which have been issued to foil counterfeiters. Their new design is unfamiliar to many people, who hesitate to accept them in denominations over $20.

There are 100 cents to the dollar: coins include the copper 1¢ piece, 5¢ nickel, 10¢ dime, 25¢ quarter, 50¢ half-dollar (rare), and a seldom-seen Susan B. Anthony dollar which is almost identical to the quarter.

Canadian banknotes come in $1, $2, $5, $10, $20 and $100 denominations, all the same size but each a different colour. $1 and $2 bills are being replaced by coins. $1 coins are popularly called 'loonies' after the image of the loon, a native bird, on the original issue. $2 coins, a small silvery disk surrounded by a golden disk, are popularly called 'toonies'. There are 100 cents to the dollar: coins include the copper 1¢ piece, 5¢ nickel, 10¢ dime and 25¢ quarter. Size and weights of US and Canadian coins are slightly different and seldom work in the other country's vending machines or coin-operated telephones.

TIPPING Acknowledgement for good service should not be extorted. That said, tipping is a fact of life, to receive, to repeat, or to thank someone for service.

Hotel porters generally receive $1 per bag; a bellperson who shows you to the room expects several dollars; in luxury properties, tip more. Room service delivery staff should be tipped 10–15% of the tariff before taxes, unless there's a service charge indicated on the bill. Expect to hand out dollars for most services that involve room delivery. Pay $1–$5 for valet parking each time your car is delivered. Some hotels have a chambermaid name card placed in the room: it's a hint for a tip of a few dollars upon your departure, but is never obligatory. The pricier the hotel and the more services it offers, the more you will be expected to tip.

In an emergency, phone 911. See also Emergencies in the Travel Directory, p. 496.

TAXES

There is no value added tax in the USA, but many other kinds of sales taxes can raise the cost of your holiday. Sales taxes vary with the state; a few do not have them at all. Cities can also add sales taxes to each purchase, although various items are usually exempt, including food in most jurisdictions. Nearly all states add taxes on accommodation and on restaurant meals. There may also be special taxes or fees on rental cars. None of these is refundable on departure.

SAFETY AND SECURITY

Despite well-publicised incidents of street violence, millions of people travel (and live) in perfect safety in the USA. So can you if you follow commonsense precautions. Throwing caution to the winds is foolhardy at any time, and even more so on holiday.

The best way to avoid becoming a victim of theft or bodily injury in the USA, as in any other part of the world, is to walk with assurance, and try to give the impression that you know where you are going and are not worth robbing. Sightsee with a known companion, or in a group. Solo travel, in urban areas or in the countryside, is not recommended.

Never publicly discuss travel plans, or money or valuables you are carrying; keep to well-lit areas; do not wear or carry expensive jewellery or flash rolls of banknotes. Use a hidden money-belt for your valuables, travel documents and spare cash. Carrying a wallet in a back pocket or leaving a handbag open is an invitation to every pickpocket in the vicinity. In all public places, take precautions with anything that is obviously worth stealing: use a handbag with a crossed shoulder strap and a zip, and in restaurants wind the strap of your camera case around your chair or place your handbag firmly between your feet under the table.

Never leave luggage unattended or with strangers, no matter how pleasant and trustworthy they appear. At airports, security officials may confiscate unattended luggage as a possible bomb. In public toilets, handbags and small luggage have been snatched from hooks, or from under stalls. Airports and bus and train stations usually have lockers. Most work with keys; take care to guard the key and memorise the locker number. Hotel bell staff may keep luggage for one or more days on request, sometimes for a fee – be sure to ask for receipts for left luggage before surrendering it.

Concealing a weapon is against the law. Some defensive products resembling tear gas are legal only for persons certified in their proper use. Mugging, by individuals or gangs, is more of a problem in larger cities than in smaller ones and rural areas. If you are attacked, it is safer to let go of your bag or hand over the small amount of obvious money, as you are more likely to be attacked physically if the thief meets with resistance. Never resist. If you do encounter trouble, dial 911 on any telephone for free emergency assistance from police, fire and medical authorities. Report incidents immediately to local police, even if it is only to take a copy of their report for your insurance company or to show authorities should your passport be included in the stolen property.

SLEEPING SAFELY

When sleeping rough, in any sort of dormitory, train, or open campsite, the safest place for your small valuables is at the bottom of your sleeping bag. In train sleeping carriages, padlock your luggage to the seat, and ask the attendant to show you how to lock a compartment door at night. If in doubt, it's best to take luggage with you.

In hotels, motels and all other accommodation, lock all doors from the inside. Check that all windows are locked, including sliding glass doors. Ground-floor rooms, while convenient, mean easier access by anyone intent on breaking in. Never leave the room at night without leaving a light on. Lights deter prowlers, and when you return, any disturbance to room contents will be visible.

Use a door viewer to check before admitting anyone to your room. If someone claims to be on the hotel staff or a repair person, do not let the person in before phoning the office or front desk to verify the person's name and job. Money, cheques, credit cards, passports and keys should be with you, or secured in your hotel's safe deposit box. When checking in, find the most direct route from your room to fire escapes, lifts, stairwells and the nearest telephone.

For safety on the road, see p. 25.

Ushers in legitimate theatres, arenas and stadiums are not tipped; cinemas seldom have ushers, nor are tips expected. You are not expected to tip petrol station attendants. It *is* expected, however, that you tip taxi drivers; in New York if you do not, you risk injury or at least verbal abuse. For tipping in restaurants, see p. 38.

SHOPPING

Airports do not have duty-free shopping for incoming travellers, but it's no great loss. Prices for alcohol and other duty-free items are almost always lower in supermarkets and discount stores than in duty-free shops. (For duty-free allowances, see Travel Directory, p. 494.)

The same goes for other goods. Airport prices are generally higher than in similar shops nearby and the selection is smaller. Airport fast food outlets are comparable to chain outlets anywhere, but airport restaurants are generally higher in price than in quality.

DISCOUNTS

Reductions and concessions on entrance fees and public transport (including most Amtrak services)for senior citizens, children, students and military personnel are common. Some proof of eligibility is usually required. For age, a passport or driving licence is sufficient. Military personnel should carry an official identification card. Students will have better luck with an International Student Identity Card (ISIC) from their local student union, than with a college ID.

The most common discount is for automobile club members. Touring guides from AAA (Automobile Association of America) and CAA (Canadian Automobile Association) affiliates list hundreds of member discounts throughout the country. Always ask about 'Triple A discounts' and 'CAA discounts' at attractions, hotels, motels and car hire counters. Most recognise reciprocal membership benefits. Some cities will send high-season discount booklets on request, which may cover shops, restaurants or accommodation.

WHAT TO PACK

What you will need travelling in the USA depends largely on what you plan to do, where you plan to go, and when you will be travelling. It's an old rule, but still a good one, to bring half as much clothing as you think you will need, and twice as much money. Of the two, money is the lighter to carry. Less is more where luggage is concerned. Porters don't exist outside the most expensive hotels and luggage trolleys (baggage carts) are rare outside airports. Luggage has to be light enough to carry. The normal luggage allowance is two pieces, each of 70 lb (32 kg) maximum, per person, but you will find that too much to carry around as you travel.

Luggage must also fit into the car or other form of transport. North Americans buy the same cars as Europeans, Australians and the rest of the world, not the enormous 'boats' of the 1960s. If it won't fit in the boot at home, don't expect to cram it into a hire car.

Absolutely everything you could ever need, except your own personal teddy bear, is available, so don't worry if you've left anything behind. In fact, most North American prices will seem low: competition and over-supply keeps them that way. Pharmacies (also called drug stores but never chemists) carry a range of products, from medicine to cosmetics to beach balls. Prepare a small first-aid kit before you leave home with tried and tested insect repellent, sunscreen cream, and soothing moisturising lotion. Carry all medicines, glasses, and contraceptives with you, and keep duplicate prescriptions or a letter from your doctor to verify your need for a particular medication, as well as the note of its generic name – brand names will vary.

Other useful items to bring or buy immediately upon arrival are a water bottle, sunglasses, sunhat or visor with a broad brim, umbrella and light rain gear, Swiss Army pocket knife, torch (flashlight), padlock for anchoring luggage, money belt, travel adaptor plug, string for a washing line, alarm clock and camera. Those planning to rough it should take a sleeping bag, sheet liner and inflatable pillow. Allow a little extra space in your luggage for souvenirs.

A small daypack that is easy to carry can be handy for picnic lunches, guidebooks and daily use items, and can double as a spare bag for souvenirs on the trip home. On the way over, it can be folded flat in your suitcase.

Because the USA is such a big place, where you go will govern what clothes you will need. In general, if you plan to spend most of your time in cities, you will want dressier clothes, especially if you plan to attend the theatre and concerts. But if you plan to hike or ski during your trip, space will quickly be filled with sturdy boots and heavier clothing. The biggest problem comes in packing for multi-activity trips that include a little of everything or a number of different climates.

In any season, take plenty of layers, from shorts for the beach and interior valleys to jumpers and jackets for the mountains. Cotton and wool, worn in layers, are the traveller's favourite fibres. One layer is cool, several layers are warm. Adding and removing layers makes it easier to stay comfortable no matter how many times the weather changes in a single day. Umbrellas and lightweight rain gear are indispensable along the coast.

Informality is the norm throughout the USA, with the exception of a handful of elegant city restaurants which require jackets and ties for men. Trainers (sneakers), sandals and hiking boots are far more common than wingtips and high heels, even in fancy hotels. When in doubt, leave it at home. US clothing prices are cheaper than almost anywhere outside the Third World, so if you suddenly realise you need something you left at home, you can quickly replace it. But do take good, broken-in walking shoes.

CLIMATE

Climate is what you expect; weather is what you get. Being so big, the USA can harbour several major weather systems all at once, which you can see moving about weather maps on TV evening news programmes, or by tuning to special weather channels. To find these from your hotel room, consult the directory that usually accompanies the television set, or call the reception desk. In looking at a weather map, remember that most storm systems and high and low pressure areas move west to east, with others moving northwards up the Atlantic (east) coast. New England occasionally suffers from storms moving down the coast from Canada.

While the climate is variable nearly anywhere in the USA, some trends prevail for each region. Mountains and the sea are the primary geographical features that affect weather, as are the Great Lakes. Although no one weather pattern governs the entire country, nearly all areas share a tendency toward great variations within short periods of time. Especially in the north-east and in the Great Plains (between the Appalachian and Rocky Mountains), conflicting air masses may bring changes of as much as 50° within a few hours.

New England's weather is known more for changeability than for extremes. In general, expect cold and snow from December to March, and warm days and cool nights from June to September. Depending on locale, daytime temperatures in summer are in the 70s or 80s (°F); July and August usually bring short spells of uncomfortably humid weather with temperatures above 90°F. Winter snows are heaviest in the mountains of Maine, New Hampshire and Vermont. Snowfall is generally light in southern New England, except for occasional big storms, with temperatures in the 20s or 30s. September and October can be the most pleasant months, with daytime temperatures from the 50s to 70s, and leaves turning colour dramatically.

The middle Atlantic region, around Chesapeake Bay, has hot, sunny summers, a balmy spring and autumn, and fairly mild but crisp winters with little if any snow. Intermittent storm systems that bring snow to the north-east here bring rain, and occasional freezing rain around the Chesapeake. The closer you are to water, the less likely it is to snow. Average coastal temperatures in July and August rarely exceed the low 90s, but it can become much hotter in Washington DC, where city pavements and buildings absorb and store the heat. All along the east coast, September is hurricane month. In severe storms coastal regions are evacuated, but these do not strike without warning, and travellers can easily learn if one is brewing further south and heading their way. A good sign of an approaching hurricane, if you haven't tuned to the weather forecast, is when you see locals hammering large sheets of wood over their windows.

The climate warms noticeably in the southern Atlantic states, becoming almost tropical in Florida. Summers don't get much warmer than in the Washington DC area, but they last much longer. Florida, surrounded by water, has a more moderate climate, warmer in the winter and cooler in the summer than neighbouring southern states. Snow is rare in the south, but summer thunderstorms are frequent. Florida is the sunniest state, particularly in the winter.

Mid-west winters are cold and summers quite warm, with frequent droughts and heatwaves. Snow can be heavy, especially in the north, where blizzards sweep down from the Arctic without mountains to divert them. Generally the eastern part of this region is rainier than the west, but throughout, the area tends to be sunny much of the time. Average daily temperatures hover around the freezing mark in Chicago, where summer averages range from the mid 70s to the low 90s. To the south, the Gulf states (Alabama to Texas) have similar weather without the winter snows, and with longer (but not significantly hotter) summers.

In the north-west, you can expect grey skies west of the Cascade Range and blue skies to the east, but weather can change abruptly on either side of the mountains. Rain and snow are more likely between October and April, but don't be surprised by a downpour in August. Fog is common along the coast all year. Portland, Seattle and Vancouver are known for cloudy skies and rain all year round, but the sun shows itself for at least a few minutes on most days from May to September. Sunshine is a treasured experience on the western side of the Olympic Peninsula, where tall mountains wring rain from prevailing winds off the Pacific Ocean. The San Juan Islands, sheltered by those same mountains, are much drier and sunnier.

The Pacific Ocean moderates temperatures west of the Cascades. Expect greater extremes east of the range, colder in winter and hotter in summer. Summer is also fire season. Forest fires may be allowed to burn unchecked unless human lives or major property damage are threatened. Regular burning is a natural renewal mechanism and necessary for the regeneration of many forest species. If a patch of forest has not burned in several years, deliberate fires, called controlled burns, are set during wet weather to burn out accumulated dead growth and prevent later conflagrations. Smoke-jumpers – airborne fire-fighters who parachute into remote areas to fight fires – and water bombers are at their busiest in late summer.

In the south-west, expect sunshine in southern California, fog along the coast, and heat inland. However, uneven terrain creates a patchwork of weather patterns with no apparent rhyme or reason. Summer fog can hang heavily or burn away to reveal deep blue skies and a blistering sun. Winter temperatures generally drop with altitude and distance north, with snow above 6000 ft. In summer, expect increasing heat inland and to the south.

TRAVELLING WITH CHILDREN

Whether at home or abroad, this is rarely easy, but nearly always rewarding. Preparation helps. Children become bored and cranky on long drives. Pack favourite games and books, and pick up a book of travel games. A traditional favourite is to count foreign, i.e. non-local, licence plates. The winner – always a child – gets a special treat later in the day.

If the children are old enough, suggest that they keep a detailed travel diary. It will help them focus on where they are instead of what they might be missing back home. A diary also helps them to remember details later to impress friends and teachers. So does collecting anything from postcards to admission tickets, dropped into the child's own backpack and pasted into a diary each evening. Even children too young to maintain a diary can enjoy this visual record of the places they have visited.

Instead of focusing your travel on made-for-children attractions, such as theme parks and amusement parks which are much the same everywhere, aim for places that are unique to the area or to the USA, but with plenty of activities aimed at the young. Living history museums and restoration villages nearly always have special events, hands-on experiences, tours, and even activity-filled guidebooks for children. Look for aspects of a place that will delight your children, and find themes for them to follow wherever they go, such as how many different kinds of transport they can ride on. Older children may gain more from a trip if they read books set in some of the places they will visit; a librarian can help you discover these. From museums to transport, check for children's rates, often segmented by age. A student card must be shown to use student rates.

Most hotels and motels can arrange for babysitters, though the price may be steep. Many motel chains allow children under 12, 14, and sometimes up to 18, to stay free in their parents' room. A rollaway child's bed, usually called a cot, should come free or at low cost. At mealtimes, picnics offer flexibility, as does a small cooler filled with cold drinks and snacks. Most towns have roadside restaurants with long hours, cheap children's menus and familiar names. If your children like fast food at home, they'll like it in California or Maryland.

USEFUL READING

Referred to throughout this guide as the **OTT**, the *Thomas Cook Overseas Timetable* is published every two months, price £8.99 per issue. Indispensable for independent travellers using public transport in the USA, it contains timetables for all the main rail and bus services in North America, plus details of local and suburban services. It is available from UK branches of Thomas Cook or by mail order, phoning (01733) 503571/2 in the UK. In North America, contact Forsyth Travel Library Inc., 226 Westchester Ave, White Plains, New York 10604; tel: (800) 367 7984 (toll-free). A special edition of the *Overseas Timetable* is available from bookshops and from the outlets given above – the *Thomas Cook World Timetable Independent Traveller's Edition* include bus, rail and ferry timetables, plus additional information useful for travellers.

Please note that the OTT table numbers very occasionally change – but services may easily be located by checking the index at the front of the *Overseas Timetable.*

If you are considering spending more than a couple of days in a city or region of the USA, then it may be worth obtaining a localised guidebook. Most guidebook series include separate volumes covering the major cities and regions of the USA, and may issue titles that cover more remote areas that are beyond the scope of this guide.

For further accommodation recommendations, the *AAA Tourbook* series gives comprehensive listings. Titles cover groupings of states or guides to the major cities, and can usually be obtained from specialist travel bookshops outside the USA.

Before 1500 Native Americans inhabit most of North America, some as nomadic hunter-gatherers, others in agricultural villages.

1492–1535	Early European explorers make first contact with native populations.
1539–42	Spanish explorers De Soto and Coronado claim Pacific coast for Spain.
1565	Spanish establish first permanent European settlement in St Augustine, Florida (see p. 243).
1603	Samuel de Champlain begins exploration and colonisation of what is now eastern Canada for France.
1607	First British colony established at Jamestown, Virginia (see p. 192).
1609	Henry Hudson explores Hudson River, leading to Dutch trading colony of New Amsterdam, later New York. Santa Fe (see p. 321) founded by Spanish.
1620	Pilgrims land at Provincetown, then settle at Plymouth, Massachusetts (see pp. 122 and 117).
1675–6	King Philipp's War between native tribes and New England colonists.
1692	Witch trials begin in Puritan colony of Salem, Massachusetts (see p. 113), bringing European practice of witch-burning to New World.
1700–90	Population of the 13 original colonies increases from 260,000 to 3,900,000
1754–9	French and Indian War, ending with the fall of Quebec to the British and the end of French control in North America.
1763	Britain gains Florida and all lands east of the Mississippi by treaty, ending all Dutch and Spanish control in eastern North America.
1765	Stamp Act Congress of the 13 colonies meets to protest against taxation without representation and British trade restrictions. Sons of Liberty and other 'subversive' groups form. Rebellion brews.
1773	Protesters attack taxation and trade restrictions at 'Boston Tea Party' and similar incident in Annapolis, Maryland.
1775	First shots of Revolution fired at Lexington and Concord, Massachusetts, followed by Battle of Bunker Hill in Boston (see p. 101).
1776	British evacuate Boston; American independence is declared in Philadelphia.
1777	Burgoyne defeated at Saratoga, New York.
1881	Cornwallis surrenders at Yorktown, Virginia, ending Revolutionary War (see p. 192).
1787	Constitution is signed in Philadelphia.
1789	George Washington inaugurated as first president.
1790	Industrial Revolution begins in Pawtucket, Rhode Island and elsewhere; inventors' rights protected by copyright law.
1803	President Jefferson buys most of central continent from Napoleon.
1804–6	Lewis and Clark explore the north-west.
1812	War with Britain to establish American shipping rights.
1831	Northern Abolitionists begin serious crusade to end slavery.

TIMELINE OF AMERICAN HISTORY

Timeline of American History

1836	Texas wins independence from Mexico, becoming a state ten years later (see p. XXX).
1845–8	Through treaty and war with Mexico, USA acquires lands to Pacific, creating borders almost as they stand today.
1848	Gold discovered in Sacramento Valley, beginning California Gold Rush of 1849 (see p. XXX).
1850s	Immigration soars to 400,000 a year, with 40% from Ireland; the Cotton Kingdom reaches its height in the south.
1860	Lincoln elected president; southern states secede from Union, precipitating Civil War in 1861.
1865	Civil War ends at Appomattox, Virginia, after Confederate capital of Richmond falls to Grant's army.
1869	Railroad spans the nation from ocean to ocean, meeting at Ogden, Utah.
1870s–1900	Industrialisation of both north and south heals divisions of Civil War. Telegraph, radio, and electric power spur continued growth and westward expansion.
1898	Battleship *Maine* sunk in Havana, Cuba, beginning Spanish American War. USA acquires Philippines, Guam, Hawaii and Samoa in Pacific and becomes power in the Caribbean.
1903	Wright Brothers succeed in first aeroplane flight at Kitty Hawk, North Carolina. Automobile manufacture begins in earnest.
1917	USA joins European allies and enters World War I.
1918–29	Post-war economy booms through the Roaring Twenties. Prohibition of liquor passed by Constitutional Amendment.
1929	Stock market crashes, beginning the Great Depression. The economy grinds to a halt.
1933	President Roosevelt begins New Deal to provide relief and begin economic recovery.
1941	Japanese attack Pearl Harbour, Hawaii, bringing USA into World War II, two years after it began in Europe.
1945	Atomic bomb dropped on Hiroshima, Japan, ending World War II.
1947	Marshall Plan aids European postwar recovery.
1950s	Interstate highway system begins under President Eisenhower.
1954	Racial discrimination banned in all US schools.
1961	Alan Sheppard, first man in space, launched from Cape Canaveral, Florida (see p. XXX).
1963	President John F. Kennedy assassinated in Dallas, Texas.
1963	Civil rights movement, with massive rallies in Washington DC and elsewhere.
1964	73 US intervention in Vietnam escalates; massive protests against Vietnam War follow; US involvement ends.
1969	Apollo 11 puts first man on the moon.
1972	President Nixon opens relations with Communist China.
1974	President Nixon resigns in Watergate scandal.
1980	Mount St Helens (p. 484) explodes in a violent volcanic eruption, 500 times more powerful than the atomic blast at Hiroshima.
1999	Impeachment proceedings against President Bill Clinton fail a majority vote in Senate.

New York

New York can claim, with some justification, to be the capital of the world. Not only is it the home of the United Nations, but of immigrants from every corner of the globe. Ever since Dutch settlers established their first trading post on the southern tip of *Manhattan*, buying the island from local Indians for a few dollars' worth of trinkets, New York has been the mecca of everyone wanting to share in the great American dream.

The sheer energy of the Big Apple is exhilarating. It is seen in the manic pace of the city's street life, the creativity of its artists and designers, the skyscrapers which rise ever higher only to be demolished as soon as they are built. At first, New York is exhausting and the tension impossible to escape; after a while you get used to it and everywhere else seems dull by comparison.

New York City consists of five boroughs – Manhattan, Brooklyn, the Bronx, Queens and Staten Island – but to most outsiders New York simply means Manhattan. Wall Street and Broadway may be household names across the world, but Manhattan is really just a collection of neighbourhoods, each with its own personality. Harlem and Chinatown are as different from Greenwich Village as New York is from the rest of America.

GETTING THERE

Air International flights arrive at John F. Kennedy (JFK) Airport in Queens or at Newark in New Jersey. There's a flat fare from JFK into Manhattan (plus bridge and tunnel tolls and a tip). Uniformed dispatchers will guide you towards the licensed taxi stand; avoid the 'gypsy cabs' which tout for custom at the airport. About half the price of a cab, private minibus services operated by Carey Buses and Gray Line depart regularly for various points in Midtown Manhattan, including Grand Central Terminal for connections to the subway. The cheapest way of all is to take the free shuttle bus to Howard Beach subway station, where a single subway token will get you anywhere in the city. This will take at least an hour and could be awkward with heavy luggage.

Taxis from Newark start at around $40, or you can take the transit bus to Port Authority Bus Terminal or Grand Central Terminal.

Most US domestic flights arrive at La Guardia in Queens, the closest airport to

Manhattan. Again, a minibus into Manhattan (about $10) is about half the cost of a taxi, but the cheapest way into town is on the M60 bus, with links to the various subway lines along 125th St.

RAIL/BUS Amtrak long-distance train services from the USA and Canada arrive at Penn Station, close to Midtown Manhattan and with connections to the subway network. Greyhound buses arrive at the Port Authority Bus Terminal on West 40th St, a short walk from Times Square – though a taxi would be advisable if you are arriving late at night.

ROAD I-95 runs up through New Jersey and crosses briefly into Manhattan on its way to New England. Of several exits to New York, take the I-78 at Jersey City to enter Lower Manhattan through the Holland Tunnel; the I-495 at Union City for Midtown Manhattan via the Lincoln Tunnel; or cross the George Washington Bridge into Manhattan and take the Henry Hudson Parkway down the west side of the island. Once you are settled in Manhattan, park your car securely in a garage and get around by public transport. Driving in New York is a nightmare and it is simply not worth the hassle.

GETTING AROUND

New York is a great city for walking, and Manhattan's grid system makes it easy to get about. The only real exception to Manhattan's grid system is Broadway, an ancient Indian trail. Allow one to two minutes per block if heading up or downtown, five minutes across town between avenues, and you won't go far wrong.

For longer distances, the quickest way of getting about is by **subway**. The subway system runs 24 hrs a day and is both easy and safe to use once you have mastered the map (see inside back cover). Remember that 'express' trains only stop at certain stations and if you want one of the stations in between you need to catch a 'local'. A better bet than single-ride tokens is to buy a magnetic Metrocard which can be 'loaded' in advance with multiple rides; if you plan to use the subway a lot, a seven-day unlimited Metrocard, also valid on buses, is even better value.

Buses tend to be slow but they can be a good way of seeing the city. A single flat fare takes you anywhere in Manhattan, so if you need to change buses ask your driver for a 'transfer'.

ORIENTATING YOURSELF

New York is relatively simple to navigate once you know a few basic facts and the lingo that goes with them.

From 14th St to Central Park, the **streets** run east–west and the **avenues** north–south.

Fifth Ave divides Manhattan into **East Side** and **West Side**.

Uptown is an area – from the 60s up – as well as a direction, of ascending street numbers.

Downtown is the lower (southern) part of Manhattan, and also the direction of descending street numbers.

Midtown is the middle part of Manhattan (between 14th and 59th Sts).

Two of the most scenic and enjoyable bus routes are the M5 from Greenwich Village, skirting Central Park on its way to Riverside Drive, and the M4 from Penn Station and the Empire State Building, which crawls along Museum Mile and then up Broadway on its way through Washington Heights to the Cloisters, a museum of medieval architecture in the far north of Manhattan. Change between these two routes where they meet up on Broadway and you have an enjoyable bus tour of Manhattan for a fraction of the cost of an organised tour.

Open-top bus tours are operated by a number of companies, including **New York Apple Tours**, tel: (800) 876-9868. A single ticket is valid for two days, allowing you to hop on and off as you choose. The standard 4-hr city tour ($$$$+) includes all the main sights. A Harlem gospel tour ($$$$+) includes a visit to a Sunday gospel service as well as two days unlimited travel on the Uptown tour route. Tickets are available from the visitor centre at 8th Ave and 53rd St or on the bus.

Taxis are fine if you are in a hurry, but an unnecessarily expensive way of getting about. Always use a licensed yellow cab – you can hail them on the street – and make sure that the driver switches on the meter.

INFORMATION

The **New York Convention and Visitors Bureau**, 810 7th Ave; tel: (212) 397-8200; open Mon–Fri 0900–1700, is the official tourist office and offers maps, brochures and advice. Another useful source of information is the **Times Square Visitors Center**, 1560 Broadway; open 0800–2000 daily, which also has a theatre booking service and free Internet access. Kiosks outside Grand Central Terminal and the World Trade Center have a wide range of leaflets; there are also tourist information desks in the major department stores. For up-to-date information on events, pick up a copy of *Time Out New York*, Sunday's *New York Times* or *Where New York*, a free monthly magazine available from tourist offices and hotels.

SAFETY

New York is a lot safer than it was – the 'zero tolerance' policing campaign of Mayor Rudolph Giuliani has led to a dramatic drop in crime rates – but as in any large American city it still pays to take care. The most important thing is to be aware of your surroundings and not to look too much like a tourist. Avoid the parks and poorly lit streets at night, and if a situation is starting to feel tense, just walk away.

Specific areas to avoid after dark are: Central Park; the Port Authority Bus Terminal; Midtown west of Times Square; Alphabet City, east of Avenue A in the East Village; and Harlem north of 125th St. The Financial District, though safe by day, can be deserted and therefore dangerous at night. Brooklyn and the Bronx both have no-go areas and are best avoided at night unless you know where you are going.

It is safe to use the subway after dark so long as you use common sense. At stations, stay in the

'Off Hour Waiting Area' by the ticket window until your train arrives or head for the section on the platform marked 'During off hours train stops here': this will ensure that you can be seen and also that you get on near the centre of the train, where the conductor's carriage is situated. If you still don't feel safe, take a cab.

MONEY Thomas Cook has several foreign exchange offices which are open outside normal banking hours. The office at 1590 Broadway, tel: (212) 265-6063, is open 0900–1900 Mon–Sat, 0900–1700 Sun. Others are at 29 Broadway, 1271 Broadway, 317 Madison Ave, 511 Madison Ave, 157 W. 57th St and JFK Airport. For details, tel: (212) 883-0401.

POST AND PHONES The General Post Office at 421 8th Ave is open 24 hours a day. Poste Restante letters addressed to Name, Poste Restante, c/o General Delivery, General Post Office, New York, NY 10001 will be kept at the General Delivery counter for between 10 and 30 days. Another useful post office, in the Financial District, is based in the old Cunard building at 25 Broadway; open Mon–Fri 0800–1800, Sat 0800–1300.

New York has two telephone area codes, 212 for Manhattan and 718 for the outer boroughs. For calls within Manhattan, omit the area code and simply dial the final seven digits of the number. When using a public phone, you should deposit 25¢ for a local call and have a stack of further quarters ready.

ACCOMMODATION

Hotels in New York are notoriously expensive – even 'budget' hotels charge over $100 for a double room – and to make matters worse, the rates quoted usually exclude taxes. You can sometimes get the cost down by asking for the 'corporate rate' or negotiating a discount at weekends, but the fact remains that accommodation is going to eat up a sizeable chunk of your budget in New York. If you are flexible about where you stay, you could try calling one of the discount agencies who book up rooms in advance and can usually offer a discount of 20% or more. Two of the biggest are **Take Time to Travel**, tel: (212) 840 8686; fax: (212) 221 8686; and **Hotel Reservations Network**, tel: (214) 361 7311; fax: (214) 361 7299.

If you don't mind sleeping in a dorm and sharing a communal shower, it will work out a lot cheaper to stay in one of the city's hostels. Another option is bed and breakfast in a private apartment, usually shared with the host. For a completely different experience, **Homestay New York** offers accommodation with Brooklyn families from about $90 for a double room including dinner, breakfast and a Metrocard. Tel/fax: (718) 434-2071.

DOWNTOWN (BELOW 14TH ST)

Larchmont $$$–$$$$ 27 W. 11th St; tel: (212) 989-9933; fax: (212) 989-9496. Small, arty boutique hotel on a tree-lined street in Greenwich Village.

Off SoHo Suites $$$–$$$$ 11 Rivington St; tel: (212) 979-

9808; fax: (212) 979-9801. Smart new apartment suites with kitchen and bathroom for two to four people. The Lower East Side location is good for bars and clubbing, but can get a little dodgy at night.

Washington Square Hotel $$$$ 103 Waverley Pl.; tel: (212) 777-9515; fax: (212) 979-8373. The location is everything at this old-fashioned hotel, where both Bob Dylan and Joan Baez stayed while busking in Washington Square. A bonus is the free continental breakfast.

MIDTOWN (14TH ST TO CENTRAL PARK)

Carlton Arms $$$ 160 E. 25th St; tel: (212) 684-8337. Tenement dive with funky murals in every room, popular with students, artists and backpackers. A place for atmosphere rather than creature comforts.

Gershwin $$$–$$$$ 7 E. 27th St; tel: (212) 545-8000; fax: (212) 684-5546. Bohemian hotel with Pop Art on the walls and some private rooms with baths. The rooftop terrace is good for parties.

Herald Square Hotel $$$–$$$$ 19 W. 31st St; tel: (212) 279-4017; fax: (212) 643-9208. Clean, basic, budget hotel in the original *Life* magazine building.

Hotel 17 $$$–$$$$ 225 E. 17th St; tel: (212) 475-2845; fax: (212) 677-8178. Super-hip and slightly seedy establishment where Madonna posed in her knickers for *Details* magazine. Great for fashion-conscious clubbers.

Hotel 31 $$$–$$$$ 120 E. 31st St; tel: (212) 685-3060; fax: (212) 532-1232. The sister establishment of Hotel 17.

Wolcott $$$–$$$$ 4 W. 31st St; tel: (212) 268-2900; fax: (212) 563-0096. Popular budget hotel close to the Empire State.

Best Western Manhattan $$$$ 17 W. 32nd St; tel: (212) 736-1600; fax: (212) 563-4007. Chain hotel, slightly off the beaten track in Little Korea, with a marble lobby and rooms themed by New York's neighbourhoods.

Chelsea Hotel $$$$ 222 W. 23rd St; tel/fax: (212) 243-3700. With its faded elegance and seedy Edwardian glamour, the hangout of Dylan Thomas, Andy Warhol and Sid Vicious continues to attract creative types and denizens of low life.

Comfort Inn Murray Hill $$$$ 42 W. 35th St; tel: (212) 947-0200; fax: (212) 594-3047. Small, family-oriented hotel close to Macy's and the Empire State. The free continental breakfast adds to the value.

Gramercy Park Hotel $$$$ 2 Lexington Ave; tel: (212) 475-4320; fax: (212) 505-0535. Old-fashioned European style in a quiet area of Manhattan. Guests receive a key to the private park in the square.

Pickwick Arms $$$$ 230 E. 51st St; tel: (212) 355-0300; fax: (212) 755-5029. Clean and comfortable Eastside hotel with good views from the rooftop garden.

UPTOWN (ABOVE 59TH ST)

Beacon $$$$ 2130 Broadway; tel: (212) 787-1100; fax: (212) 724-0839. Friendly hotel in a lively Upper West Side district, close to Central Park and Zabar's deli.

Broadway American $$$$ 2178 Broadway; tel: (212) 753-8841; fax: (212) 787-9521. Clean, comfortable art deco hotel with a 24-hour café.

Excelsior $$$$ 45 W. 81st St; tel: (212) 362-9200; fax: (212) 721-2994. The suites are good value for families at this cosy Upper West Side hotel, where the rooms are decorated in art deco style.

HOSTELS

Chelsea Center $$–$$$ 313 W. 29th St; tel: (212) 643-0214; fax: (212) 473-3945. Small, friendly hostel with dorm beds and a garden courtyard. Breakfast included.

Chelsea International Hostel $$–$$$ 251 W. 20th St; tel: (212) 647-0010; fax: (212) 727-7289. This good-value hostel has a few smaller rooms with private baths.

Hostelling International New York $$–$$$ 891 Amsterdam Ave; tel: (212) 932-2300; fax: (212) 932-2574. The most popular place for budget travellers, with 500 beds in dormitories. Way uptown near Harlem.

YMCA Vanderbilt $$$–$$$$ 224 E. 47th St; tel: (212) 756-9600; fax: (212) 752-0210. Somewhere between a hostel and a hotel, the Y has single and double rooms, some with bath, as well as a swimming pool.

YMCA Westside $$$–$$$$ 5 W. 63rd St; tel: (212) 787-4400; fax: (212) 875-1334. The larger of the two Ys is situated close to Central Park.

BED & BREAKFAST AGENCIES

The following offer rooms in both hosted and unhosted apartments, in the **$$$–$$$$** price range.

Bed & Breakfast (& Books): tel/fax: (212) 865 8740 during office hours.

Bed & Breakfast in Manhattan: tel: (212) 472 2528; fax: (212) 988 9818.

City Lights Bed & Breakfast: tel: (212) 737 7049; fax: (212) 535 2755.

New World Bed & Breakfast: tel: (212) 675 5600; fax: (212) 675 6366.

Urban Ventures: tel: (212) 594-5650; fax: (212) 947 9320.

FOOD

Generations of foreign immigrants have brought their cuisines to New York and it is easy to try a different style of cooking each day. Chinese, Italian and Moroccan are all popular and good value; the more adventurous can seek out Brazilian, Russian and Colombian cuisine. If you're looking for something authentically New York, the best bet is one of the delis which serve essentially Jewish food, such as doorstep-sized pastrami sandwiches with pickles on the side. Another deli option, and a symbol of New York, is a toasted bagel spread with cream cheese and lox (smoked salmon). Other Jewish classics are bialys (onion rolls from Poland) and knishes (pastries filled with buckwheat, potato or cheese).

Some of New York's restaurants may leave a severe dent in your credit card limit, but it is perfectly possible to eat both cheaply and well. Pushcarts on every street corner sell bagels, pretzels and the ubiquitous hot dogs. Look out, too, for diners, serving huge portions of pea soup, burgers and fries in unpretentious surroundings; fill up on a diner breakfast and you won't need to eat again all day. Chinatown is full of cheap Asian eateries where a bowl of rice noodles will set you back less than $5. Other good hunting grounds for inexpensive food include Little India (centred on E. 6th St between 1st and 2nd Aves), Harlem and Greenwich Village.

For picnic food, pick up a sandwich to go and a ready-made salad from one of Manhattan's high-class delicatessens. The best of these, like Balducci's in Greenwich Village (424 6th Ave) and Zabar's on the Upper West Side (2245 Broadway), have mouthwatering displays of breads, cheeses, fresh pasta and ready-to-eat dishes. New Yorkers use them when they are giving a dinner party at home; it's worth wandering in just to look around, but remember that even snack food in these places does not come cheap.

FINANCIAL DISTRICT	**Deli Maven Café** $ 26 Beaver St. A typical deli just two blocks from Wall St.
	McDonald's $$ 160 Broadway. This McDonald's has doormen, waiter service, a Wall St trading bulletin and a piano.
	Fraunces Tavern $$$$ 54 Pearl St; tel: (212) 269-0144. Colonial atmosphere and American cuisine in the tavern where Washington used to meet his troops during the War of Independence.
	Windows on the World $$$$ World Trade Center 1; tel: (212) 524-7000. The view from the 107th floor is hard to beat. If you can't afford dinner, come for a cocktail or Sunday brunch. Dress smartly.
GREENWICH VILLAGE	**Moustache** $$ 90 Bedford St. Funky Middle Eastern specials like Lebanese salads and pitta-based 'pitzas'.
	Pink Teacup $$ 42 Grove St. A long-time Village favourite, serving Southern soul food and a huge weekend brunch.

Tea and Sympathy $$ 108 Greenwich Ave. Quaint Cockney café serving comfort food like sherry trifle and scones to a mixture of gay villagers and homesick Brits.

Casa $$$ 72 Bedford St; tel: (212) 366-9410. Home-style Brazilian cuisine – the house special is *feijoada*, a casserole of chorizo, bacon, black beans and salted beef.

CHINATOWN AND LOWER EAST SIDE

Bo Ky $ 80 Bayard St. One of several restaurants in Chinatown offering filling rice and noodle dishes. Always packed out at lunchtime.

Katz's Deli $$ 205 E. Houston St. Presidents and film stars have visited this legendary deli, where Meg Ryan faked an orgasm in *When Harry Met Sally*.

Lombardi's $$ 32 Spring St. The birthplace of New York pizza, cooked in a coal oven. This is on the edge of an area known as Little Italy, with several good Italian restaurants, especially on Mulberry St.

McSorley's Old Ale House $$ 15 E. 7th St. New York's oldest pub, serves snacks and home-brewed beer.

MIDTOWN

Empire Diner $$–$$$ 210 10th Ave. The classic 24-hour diner, all gleaming chrome and steel and a popular late-night haunt of clubbers and drag queens.

Pete's Tavern $$–$$$ 129 E. 18th St. Pub grub and home-brewed beer in a 19th-century inn.

Carnegie Deli $$$ 854 7th Ave. The queues are legendary and so are the skyscraper-sized sandwiches at this famous deli near Central Park.

Coffee Shop $$$ 29 Union Sq. West. Fashion models hang out at this smoky Fifties diner offering Brazilian and American cuisine.

Grand Central Oyster Bar $$$ Grand Central Terminal, 42nd St. Seafood and oysters beneath the railway station, with a cheap lunchtime counter as well as more formal dining.

Hard Rock Café $$$ 221 W. 57th St. One of several theme restaurants which have opened on this stretch in recent years – others include Planet Hollywood, Motown Café and Harley-Davidson Café.

UPTOWN

Tom's $ 2880 Broadway. Greasy-spoon diner popular with Columbia students and known through its starring role in the *Seinfeld* TV series.

Drip $$ 489 Amsterdam Ave. This coffee bar with a dating agency attached has become one of the hottest venues in the lively West Side singles scene.

Londel's $$$ 2620 Frederick Douglass Blvd; tel: (212) 234-6114. Trendy Harlem restaurant and jazz club serving a modern version of soul food.

Sylvia's **$$$** 328 Lenox Ave; tel: (212) 996-0660. The original Harlem soul food restaurant, popular with locals and tourists, offers up giant portions of fried chicken and sweet potato pie.

Café Pierre **$$$$** Pierre Hotel, 2 E. 61st St; tel: (212) 940-8195. *The* place to take afternoon tea, in an art deco rotunda with painted murals. Not cheap, but worth doing once.

Tavern on the Green **$$$$** Central Park West at 67th St; tel: (212) 873-3200. Over-the-top decor and a Central Park setting make this a favourite with anyone out to impress a date. Amazingly, it serves more meals than any other restaurant in the USA.

BROOKLYN

Grimaldi's **$$–$$$** 19 Old Fulton St. If you've trekked over the Brooklyn Bridge, it's worth queuing for some of the best pizza in New York at this waterfront hideaway beneath the bridge.

HIGHLIGHTS

When Frank Sinatra sang 'New York, New York', he was not just getting carried away with the name – New York, New York is the official name for Manhattan. To most people, New York *is* Manhattan and this is where you will inevitably spend most of your time, though a day in one of the outer boroughs – Brooklyn, the Bronx, Queens or Staten Island – will show you a very different side to the city. In fact, there is no better place to start than by leaving Manhattan to walk over **Brooklyn Bridge**. This was the world's longest suspension bridge when it opened in 1883 and it continues to provide one of the most iconic images of New York. John Travolta danced over it, Hart Crane immortalised it in poetry and numerous New Yorkers have leapt from it to their deaths. The views back to Manhattan, through a tangle of cables and a neo-Gothic archway, are spectacular.

For more views, stroll to **Brooklyn Heights Promenade**, from where Manhattan appears as a forest of steel and glass, vividly reflected in the East River. These are the skyscrapers of the downtown Financial District, dominated by the hideous twin towers of the **World Trade Center**. It may not look much from the outside, but the views from the 107th-floor observation deck are memorable, especially at night; $$ open 0930–2130 daily (0930–2330 June–Aug).

BOAT TOURS

A Circle Line boat tour around Manhattan is a great way to get your bearings and see the skyline from every angle. Full island cruises, lasting 3 hrs, depart Mar–Oct from Pier 83 at the Hudson River end of 42nd St; $$$$. A 2-hr cruise ($$$) around the southern half of Manhattan operates year round; there are also sunset cruises in summer. For bookings and timetable, tel: (212) 563-3200; www.circleline.com. If you don't want to fork out for a cruise, take the free Staten Island Ferry instead.

The Manhattan skyline

The Swiss architect Le Corbusier called it 'a beautiful catastrophe' and it is easy to see what he meant. On such a small island (13 miles long and 2 miles wide), the only way to build is up and that is what Manhattan has been doing throughout the 20th century. The Chrysler Building, Empire State and World Trade Center were all at one stage the tallest building in the world, and the desire to build bigger and better shows no sign of diminishing.

At the heart of the Financial District, the **New York Stock Exchange** on Wall St is where half of the world's stocks and shares are traded. You can watch the frenzied activity from a viewing gallery above the trading floor; entrance on Broad St; open Mon–Fri 0915–1600.

Downtown **Battery Park**, at the southern tip of Manhattan, is the departure point for the **Staten Island Ferry** as well as boat trips to Ellis Island and the Statue of Liberty. **Ellis Island** was New York's immigration centre from 1892 to 1924, when more than 12 million immigrants passed through its doors. It is now a museum of immigration, telling the moving story of some of those who arrived – the names included Bob Hope, Irving Berlin and Golda Meir – and those who were turned away. Sailing through New York Harbor, all of them would have seen the massive female figure of the **Statue of Liberty**, with a shining torch in her hand and broken shackles at her feet. More than a century later, the statue remains a powerful and slightly kitschy symbol of 'the land of the free'. If you arrive early enough you can climb up to her crown, but most people content themselves with a close-up look from the boat. Admission to Ellis Island and the Statue of Liberty is included in the cost of the boat trip ($$).

North of the Financial District, the skyscrapers gradually disappear and give way to a succession of small neighbourhoods. **SoHo** (the name means South of Houston St) is the centre of the New York art scene, where vacant loft spaces and cast-iron factory buildings have been turned into trendy avant-garde exhibition spaces. Saturday morning is the best time for gallery hopping here. Nearby **Greenwich Village**, with its ivy-covered mews cottages and tree-lined streets, has long been popular with writers, bohemians and the gay community. **Washington Square**, on the edge of the Village, is a great place for people-watching, with buskers, rollerbladers, dope dealers and open-air chess.

Across town, the USA's largest **Chinatown** is slowly taking over the **Lower East Side**, traditionally the first port of call for European immigrants. This area has a strong Jewish flavour, with kosher bakeries and shops selling religious items, but these days many of the immigrants are Hispanic and the area is becoming known as Loisaida. North of here, the **East Village** is grungy and ultra-hip, with funky clothes shops, alternative theatres and an edginess rarely seen elsewhere.

MIDTOWN Above 14th St, the grid pattern takes over as you move into **Midtown**, the quintessential Manhattan of crowded sidewalks, speeding taxis and long, straight avenues hemmed in by skyscrapers. This is where the noise never seems to stop and the sheer energy of Manhattan hits you in the face. At the centre of all this activity is **Times Square**, the neon-lit crossroads at the heart of the Broadway theatre district. Once a seedy haunt of pushers and pickpockets, Times Square has been cleaned up in recent years as a model of the new, tourist-friendly image which the city is trying to promote. The theme stores have moved in, the hookers have moved away and many people complain that Times Square is losing its soul.

CITY PASS

If you're planning to visit most of the major sights, get hold of a City Pass which can save you 50% on admission as well as cut down on queuing times. The pass is valid for nine days and gives entry to the Empire State Building, World Trade Center, Metropolitan Museum, Museum of Modern Art, American Museum of Natural History and Intrepid Sea Air Space Museum. You can buy it at any of these sights.

The Midtown skyline is dominated by two buildings which were both at one stage the tallest in the world – the gleaming art deco spire of the **Chrysler Building** and the elegant **Empire State Building**, whose observation deck ($$) is open 0930–2400. To either side of the Chrysler Building are two more structures which in their different ways represent aspects of New York. **Grand Central Terminal** was once the gateway to the nation, the romantic railway station from which passengers would board the 'Twentieth Century' to Chicago each evening. After falling into disrepair, it has been thoroughly restored and now conjures up the glory days of the 1930s once again. Nearby, beside the East River, is the complex of buildings which make up the headquarters of the **United Nations**. A tour here is strictly for those with an interest in global politics and diplomacy. $$ 0915–1645 daily; under 5s not admitted.

Fifth Avenue is the pulse of Midtown and the most famous shopping street in Manhattan. Starting at 49th St and continuing to Central Park, it is ten blocks of consumer paradise where upmarket department stores mix with designer boutiques, jewellers and theme stores devoted to basketball and Coca-Cola. Don't miss Trump Tower, a spectacularly over-the-top shopping mall built by the property tycoon Donald Trump on the corner of 57th St – the street where many of New York's most exclusive designers have their shops. Also on Fifth Ave, facing **St Patrick's Cathedral**, is the **Rockefeller Center**, a 'city within a city' built by the financier John D. Rockefeller Jr in the 1930s.

Pick up a free leaflet in the lobby of the GE Building (570 Lexington Ave) for a self-guided tour through some of New York's best art deco art and architecture.

Around the corner, at 11 W. 53rd St, is the **Museum of Modern Art**. MoMA has one of the best collections of 20th-century paintings anywhere, with works by Picasso, Matisse, Dalí, Monet and Warhol as well as a delightful sculpture garden where concerts are held on

WALKING TOURS

Look in the *Weekend* section of Friday's *New York Times* for details of weekend walks. Between May and Oct, **Heritage Trails**, tel: (212) 269-1500, run regular 2-hr walking tours of the downtown Financial District. The **Municipal Arts Society**, tel: (212) 935-3960, has a number of interesting tours with an emphasis on the architecture of different neighbourhoods. Walking tours of various ethnic districts are organised by **Harlem Spirituals**, tel: (212) 391-0900, **Braggin' About Brooklyn**, tel: (718) 297-5107, **Brooklyn Attitude**, tel: (718) 398-0939, and **Hassidic Tours**, tel: (800) 838-8687. Ask at the Belvedere Castle visitor centre in Central Park about guided nature walks in the park. See also For Free, (p. 65).

summer evenings. Open Thur–Tues 1030–1800 (Fri to 2030); $$, children free; free entry Fri after 1630).

There are more museums along Museum Mile, the stretch of Fifth Ave which borders Central Park. Must-sees include the **Frick Collection** ($$ 1 E. 70th St; open Tues–Sat 1000–1800, Sun 1300–1800; under 10s not admitted), a collection of European Old Masters in the mansion of a 19th-century industrialist; and the **Guggenheim Museum** (open Sun–Wed 1000–1800, Fri–Sat 1000–2000; $$, children free and free entry after 1800 Fri), where modern art is displayed inside a spiral white building by Frank Lloyd Wright which critics have described as 'an inverted oatmeal dish'. The single most important museum, however, is the **Metropolitan Museum of Art**. The collections include everything from an ancient Egyptian temple to a Chinese scholar's garden and a series of American period rooms, plus 30 galleries of Old Masters and another 20 devoted to 19th-century European art – you could easily spend two days here and still not have seen it all. Open Tues–Thur and Sun 0930–1715, Fri–Sat 0930–2045; $$, children free.

UPTOWN

Central Park is Manhattan's green lung, where New Yorkers come to let off steam, walk, jog, rollerskate, picnic, row boats, take carriage rides and fall in love. Parts of it, like the wooded area known as the Ramble (popular with both birdwatchers and gays), are still virtual wilderness, but on a summer Sunday other parts can be as crowded as Times Square. Children take rides on a vintage carousel, storytelling takes place beside Conservatory Water, and there is even a small zoo with snow monkeys and polar bears. Look out for free events in summer, which include performances by the Metropolitan Opera and Shakespeare in the Park.

If you don't mind breaking the bank, you can take a horse-drawn carriage ride around the park. The starting point is from outside the Plaza Hotel on 59th St and the rate should be negotiated with the driver in advance – but don't expect change from $50. It's a little schmaltzy, but still a magical experience, especially at night.

Across the park, the **American Museum of Natural History** has a world-class collection of dinosaur skeletons as well as dioramas featuring African, Asian and American mammals in their natural habitats. The giant-screen IMAX® theatre shows wildlife films, and

AERIAL EXPERIENCE

The ultimate New York experience has to be a helicopter ride over the skyscrapers. Flights with **Liberty Tours** ($$$$+) leave from the Hudson River heliport 0900–2100 daily; tel: (212) 465-8905. If this is beyond your budget, you could always try the simulated helicopter flights inside the Empire State Building and the World Trade Center instead. For a much cheaper thrill, take the cable car across the East River from E. 60th St to Roosevelt Island.

a new Earth and Space Center, including a planetarium, is scheduled to open in 2000. $$ Open Tues–Thur and Sun 1000–1745, Fri–Sat 1000–2045. The museum is situated in the **Upper West Side**, a fashionable area with an arty, alternative feel, lots of bookshops and cafés and streets which seem designed for strolling. **Riverside Park**, overlooking the Hudson River, is quieter than Central Park and leads into Morningside Heights, where you find **Columbia University**, the oldest and most prestigious in New York, as well as the unfinished **Cathedral of St John the Divine**, which should one day be the largest in the world. The cathedral hosts regular concerts and art exhibitions and is also an outspoken supporter of radical causes – as witnessed by the chapel for Aids victims on the south side of the nave.

From here it is a short walk to **Harlem**, an area described by Nelson Mandela as 'the capital of the black world'. Despite its recent history of poverty and race riots, Harlem does not deserve its fearsome reputation and during the day it makes a pleasant place to stroll, with handsome brownstone houses in elegant tree-lined streets. The streets of Harlem echo with the sounds of black American culture, and nowhere do you feel this more than at the **Apollo Theater** (253 W. 125th St), whose Amateur Nights have been the making of performers from Ella Fitzgerald to Michael Jackson and are still the best place to catch the hip-hop and jazz stars of tomorrow.

Take a ride on the **Staten Island Ferry**, one of the most romantic experiences in New York. The ferry runs 24

FOR FREE

Stroll through the quiet streets of Greenwich Village, beside the Hudson River and up to Central Park, where numerous free events are held throughout the summer. Get there before 1300 to queue for free tickets for **Shakespeare in the Park**, a summer festival which often attracts big-name actors. Look out too for free concerts in the plaza of the Lincoln Center (Broadway and 64th St), New York's premier performance venue.

Take advantage of 'pay-what-you-wish' evenings at several of New York's museums, including the Museum of Modern Art and the Guggenheim Museum (both Fri) and the Whitney Museum of American Art (945 Madison Ave; free Thur after 1800). One interesting museum which is always free is the **National Museum of the American Indian**, at 1 Bowling Green in downtown Manhattan; open 1000–1700 daily (Thur until 2000). This is just a short walk from the New York Stock Exchange, where entry to the viewing gallery is also free (see p. 62).

Kids and techno-freaks will enjoy **Sony Wonder Technology Lab**, a free interactive museum of

For Free cont.

technology where you can surf the Net, edit a rock video and create your own multimedia soundtrack. Madison Ave and 56th St; open Tues–Sat 1000–1800 (Thur until 2000), Sun 1200–1800.

Free **walking tours** leave from the Fifth Ave entrance of the Empire State Building (Thur at 1230; 1½ hours) and from the Whitney Museum at Philip Morris, 42nd St at Park Ave (Fri at 1230; 1½ hours).

The best bargain in New York is a walk around one of

hrs a day and is probably best at night with the lights of Manhattan twinkling in the distance.

SHOPPING

People travel halfway around the world just to do their Christmas shopping in New York. The fashion boutiques and posh department stores are spread out along Madison and Fifth Aves, but it can be just as much fun to seek out the wacky, alternative shops in areas like Greenwich Village, the East Village and the Upper West Side. Also worth exploring are Manhattan's flea markets, such as the one that takes place in SoHo on the corner of

TOY STORY

At 85 Mercer St, **Enchanted Forest** is a SoHo store with old-fashioned wooden toys displayed in a fairytale setting. And your kids will adore you if you take them to the best-known toy shop in America: **FAO Schwarz**, 767 Fifth Ave.

THE BIG ONES

Century 21, 22 Cortlandt St. Discount designer store in the Financial District with a huge range of jeans, clothing and shoes.

Macy's, Herald Sq. (Broadway and 34th St). Billed as 'the world's largest store', with ten floors of clothing and household goods.

Virgin Megastore, Times Sq. The world's biggest music store is open late into the night and features a cinema as well as live performances.

Greenmarkets were started in 1976 as a way of bringing city dwellers into contact with farmers, and they are now a great source of organic food, including bread, cakes and snacks as well as fresh produce. They are held weekly at more than 20 sites across the city, but the biggest is at Union Sq. It takes place four times a week (Mon, Wed, Fri, Sat), beginning at around 0800.

New York has some great bookshops. **Barnes and Noble**'s superstores, like the one on Union Sq., stay open late into the evening, with live music, author readings and trendy cafés which have established a reputation as sophisticated pick-up joints. The **Gotham Book Mart**, 41 W. 47th St, is a wonderful old-style bookshop founded in 1920, with new and second-hand books and a heavy literary atmosphere. **Strand**, at 828 Broadway, has 8 miles of new and second-hand books including lots of books about New York. The store sells half-price review copies and has discounts on most new books.

Broadway and Grand St every Saturday and Sunday – a good place to pick up vintage Americana and second-hand clothes. For listings of other markets and street fairs, look in Friday's *New York Times*.

For Free cont.

the city's neighbourhoods with a volunteer 'greeter' specially chosen to match your interests. The service is free and tips are not accepted. Call **Big Apple Greeter**, tel: (212) 669 2896, about a week before your visit to fix things up.

NIGHTLIFE

For comprehensive listings of theatres, cinemas, music and clubs, the best sources are the weekly *Time Out New York* and the radical free newspaper *Village Voice*.

To see a Broadway show, go to the TKTS discount ticket booth in Times Sq. (Mon–Sat 1500–2000, Sun 1100–1900, Wed and Sat 1000-1400 for matinées), which offers reductions of up to 50% on the day of the performance. No credit cards. There is a second TKTS booth downtown on the mezzanine floor of World Trade Center 2 (Mon–Fri 1100–1730, Sat 1100–1530). If you don't mind paying full price plus a booking fee, the ticket desk inside the visitor centre in Times Sq. is helpful. Alternatively, some theatres sell cheap standby tickets immediately before the performance.

Manhattan's club scene is constantly on the move and the best way to find out what's hot is to pick up a copy of the monthly style magazine *Paper*. Currently hip areas include the East Village, Lower East Side and the meatpacking district around W. 14th St. Chelsea and Greenwich Village are good for gay clubs and bars. Some clubs, like **Mother**, 432 W. 14th St; tel: (212) 366-5680, have theme nights ranging from cyber-fetish on Saturdays to the lesbian Clit Club on Fridays. Cover charges vary from nothing to around $25.

Some of the biggest names in jazz play the **Blue Note**, 131 W. 3rd St; tel: (212) 475-8592, and **Village Vanguard**, 178 7th Ave; tel: (212) 255-4037, both in Greenwich Village, while **SOBs**, 204 Varick St; tel: (212) 243-4940 highlights Brazilian and Afro-Cuban bands. The covers at these places might be steep, but there are smaller bars and clubs all over Greenwich Village where you can hear live jazz and blues for free. Jerry Rose of **ET Tours**, tel: (212) 875-7019 offers evening tours ($$) of some of the lesser-known jazz clubs. Alternatively, head up to Harlem on a Wednesday, when Amateur Night at the **Apollo Theater**, 253 W. 125th St; tel: (212) 222-0992 provides some of the best entertainment in town for around $20.

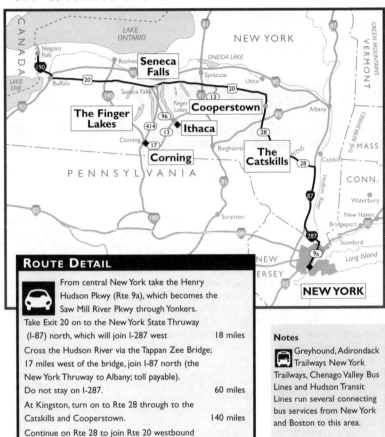

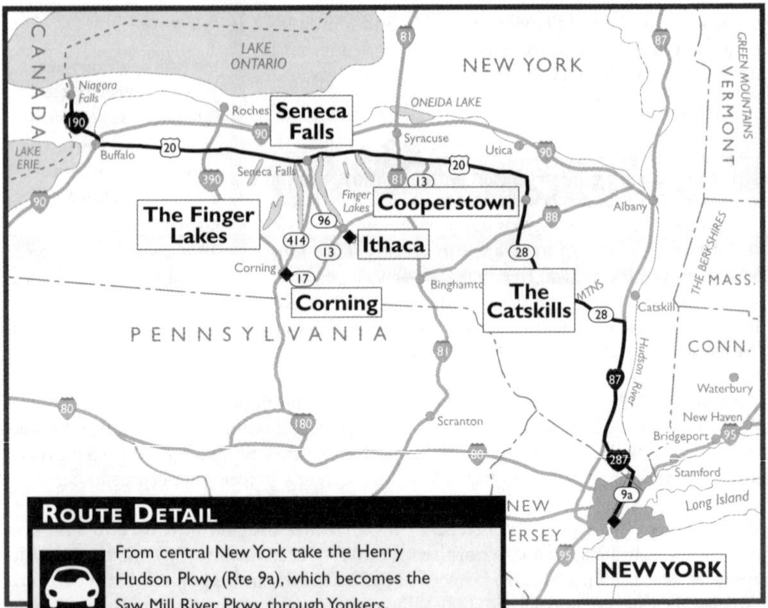

ROUTE DETAIL

From central New York take the Henry Hudson Pkwy (Rte 9a), which becomes the Saw Mill River Pkwy through Yonkers.

Take Exit 20 on to the New York State Thruway (I-87) north, which will join I-287 west	18 miles
Cross the Hudson River via the Tappan Zee Bridge; 17 miles west of the bridge, join I-87 north (the New York Thruway to Albany; toll payable). Do not stay on I-287.	60 miles
At Kingston, turn on to Rte 28 through to the Catskills and Cooperstown.	140 miles
Continue on Rte 28 to join Rte 20 westbound to Seneca Falls.	240 miles
Rte 20 continues through Finger Lake country to Buffalo and Niagara.	370 miles

Notes

Greyhound, Adirondack Trailways New York Trailways, Chenago Valley Bus Lines and Hudson Transit Lines run several connecting bus services from New York and Boston to this area.

The Catskills and Upper New York State

By car or by bus, you can wander right through rural New York state, from New York to Niagara Falls via the Catskill region, an area of charming small towns, farms, resorts, streams and hiking trails north and west of the Hudson Valley. Around the Finger Lakes is scenic wine country, together with Cooperstown and its Baseball Hall of Fame. On the Northern Tier of the Great Lakes, Seneca Falls stands out for its place in history as the birthplace of the organised women's movement in the USA.

THE CATSKILLS

The Catskill Mountains region, west of the Hudson River, is a popular holiday destination because of its natural beauty, and offers a variety of accommodation, from campsites to elegant mountain resorts.

The town of **Catskill** was where the fictional Rip Van Winkle had his lengthy sleep. It was also home to the painter Thomas Cole, who taught the artist Frederick Edwin Church, and the early training ground of world heavyweight champion boxer Mike Tyson.

In the winter ski season, nearby **Hunter Mountain** offers a 2-mile downhill ski run, the longest you'll find in these parts; tel: (518) 263-4223 for information. Out of season walk one of 33 trails to the bottom of the 1600 ft mountain at Ski Windham, CD Lane Rd, Windham; tel: (518) 734-4300 or (800) 729-7549.

The region includes a 287,989-acre forest preserve, the **Catskill Game Farm** (12 miles off I-87, exit 21) and legendary rock music haven **Woodstock**. Access to Woodstock is from I-87, exits 19–21; from Rhinebeck via Rte 9 to 199 to 28; or via Rtes 23 to 23A.

i **The Ulster County Information Office**, tel: (800) 344-5826, has information on Woodstock and the surrounding area.

North-South Lake Campground $ County Rte 18, Haines Falls; tel: (518) 589-5058.
Redcoat's Return $$ Dale Lane, Elka Park; tel: (518) 589-9858 or 589-6379. Owned by Tom Wright, who was a chef on the *Queen Mary*. Closed Apr–May.
Mohonk Mountain House $$$ 1000 Mountain Rest Rd, New Paltz; tel: (914) 255-1000. A landmark resort, built above Lake Mohonk in 1869.

In Woodstock, Tinker St, the main street, has an abundance of good restaurants, cafés and bakeries
Tinker Street Cafe $$, 59 Tinker St, tel: 914 679 2487, set

right in the heart of town; live jazz music often accompanies your meal.
Blue Mountain Bistro $$$, just outside Woodstock, tel: (914) 679-8519, junction of Rts 212 and 375. Luxurious eating.
Catskill Rose, $$, on Rte 212 outside Woodstock, tel: (914) 688-7100. Good home cooking.
New World Home Cooking Company $, 424 Zea Rd, tel: 914 679 2600, for very cheap Caribbean and Creole cuisine.
Rasher's $ 13 Tinker St, Woodstock, for a cheap drink and simple snack.

COOPERSTOWN

Tiny Cooperstown has a surprising tourist pull, largely thanks to the presence of its three museums: the Farmers' Museum, Fenimore House and the National Baseball Hall of Fame. The town gets its name from one William Cooper, landowner and also father of James Fenimore. **Fenimore House** $$ (which was also the home of Edward Clark, of the Singer Sewing Machine Co.) houses memorabilia of James Fenimore Cooper, and has seen its popularity much increased since the film of his best-known novel, *The Last of the Mohicans*.

Baseball connections from another resident, General Abner Doubleday, who was falsely credited with inventing baseball here in 1839. The connection has stuck and Cooperstown is home to the most popular sports museum in the USA. The **National Baseball Hall of Fame and Museum** is baseball's national shrine. It is home to all the important artefacts: signed hats, uniforms and balls; plaques honouring the players and photos of memorable moments. The museum has its own cinema and library. $$ Main St; tel: (607) 547 7200; open 0900–1700 (until 2100 May–Sept).

Cooperstown Chamber of Commerce, Higgins Cottage, 31 Chestnut St; tel: (607) 547 9983.

The closest campsite is the **Cooperstown Beaver Valley Campground** on Rte 28; tel: (800) 726 7314.
Bourdon Guest House $ 60 Susquehanna Ave; tel: (607) 547 9387.
Ellsworth House $$ 52 Chestnut St; tel: (607) 547 8367.
Otesaga Hotel $$$ on Otesaga Lake; tel: (607) 547 9931.

Try Main St where the restaurants between Chestnut and Fair Sts serve family-sized portions at a cheap price.
Clinton's Dam Sandwich $ Hoffman Lane; tel: (607) 547 9044.
Otesaga Hotel $$$ (as above). The elegant interior frames the view of the lake.

THE FINGER LAKES

One of New York state's most scenic and rural destinations, the Finger Lakes region is divided into Northern and Southern 'tiers'. Stretching between the two are the long, thin lakes that give the region its name, interspersed with hills dotted with vineyards.

Most of the vineyards around the Finger Lakes region are open throughout the year and offer an excellent way of taking in the hillside scenery and learning some of the history of the region, while enjoying some of its most famous produce. After California, New York is the second largest wine-producing state in the USA, with annual sales topping $300 million. Here the topology of the region, created in the Ice Age when glaciers carved out the lakes and hills, very much lends itself to the production of grapes. The result is a superb collection of wineries, linked by 'wine trails': look for giveaway signs of bunches of grapes by the roadside to point you to your stop.

The **New York Grape and Wine Foundation** is an excellent source of information on all the Finger Lakes wineries and on promotional events throughout the summer, which include jazz festivals and route picnics. 350 Elm St, Penn Yan (Northern Tier); tel: (315) 536-7442.

ITHACA AND CORNING

An easy loop detour from Rte 20 can be made to visit the Southern Tier towns of Ithaca and Corning. Rte 13 leads to Ithaca, Rtes 13 and 17 to Corning and Rte 414 returns to Rte 20 at Seneca Falls.

The university town of Ithaca is at the southern end of Lake Cayuga, surrounded by countryside that provides ample offerings at the town's farmers' market. Further south, on the Chemung River, is the town of Corning. It is known as the home of the Corning Glass Works, although the company moved to Brooklyn after the Civil War. The pretty market street area has been carefully restored to look as it did in the 19th century. The **glass museum**, tel: (607) 974 8271, is just west of Rte 17 on Cedar Street, and houses glass objects from as early as 1400 BC to the present day.

i Ithaca/Tompkins County Convention and Visitors Bureau, 904 E. Shore Dr., Ithaca; tel: (607) 272-1313; has information about the town and region.

Hill 'N' Hollow Campsites; tel: (607) 569 2711, has 40 shaded, grassy sites. Open mid-May–mid-Oct. From Rte 17, take Exit 38, go 2 miles north on Rte 54 then 6 miles east on County Rd 113.

Lando's Hotel $ William and Bridge Sts, Corning; tel: (607) 936-3612. A convenient base for the town and glass museum.
Hanshaw House Inn $$ 15 Sapsucker Woods Rd, Ithaca; tel: (607) 257 1437.
La Tourelle Country Inn $$$ 1150 Danby Rd, Ithaca; tel: 607 273 2734.

Medleys $ 61 E. Market St, Corning, tel: (607) 936 1685.
The Upstate Tuna Co. $$ 73 E. Market St, Corning; tel: (607) 936 8862. Provides chicken teriyaki or fish kebabs and lets customers cook for themselves.
John Thomas Steakhouse $$$ 1152 Danby Rd, Ithaca; tel: (607) 273 3464. One of the town's best.

SENECA FALLS

Seneca Falls is situated on Rte 20 a few miles west of Cayuga Lake, and was the home of Elizabeth Cady Stanton, who in 1848 put together the proposal for a 'Declaration of Sentiments', calling for all men and women to be created equal. Her home, **Stanton House**, 32 Washington St, has been restored and includes some original furniture; free.

Visitors Centre, 136 Fall St; tel: (315) 568 2991; sited in a complex housing Stanton House and the remains of the Wesleyan Chapel, home of the first Women's Rights Convention.

Cayuga Lake State Park $ tel: (315) 568 5163. Seven miles outside town, and offers cheap camping May–Nov.

Venice Pizzeria $ Fall St. Wholesome pizzas by the slice.

WHERE NEXT?

Rte 20 provides many interesting detours. Rte 490 can take you to Rochester, a town built on the Genesee River and housing the Kodak International Centre of Photography, and bordering Lake Ontario. Continuing westwards will take you to Buffalo on the eastern tip of Lake Erie, a short distance from Niagara Falls *(see p. 75)**.*

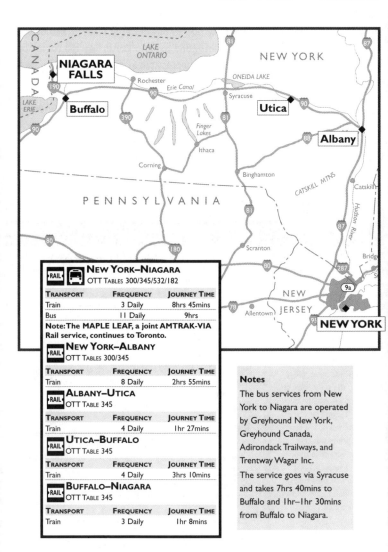

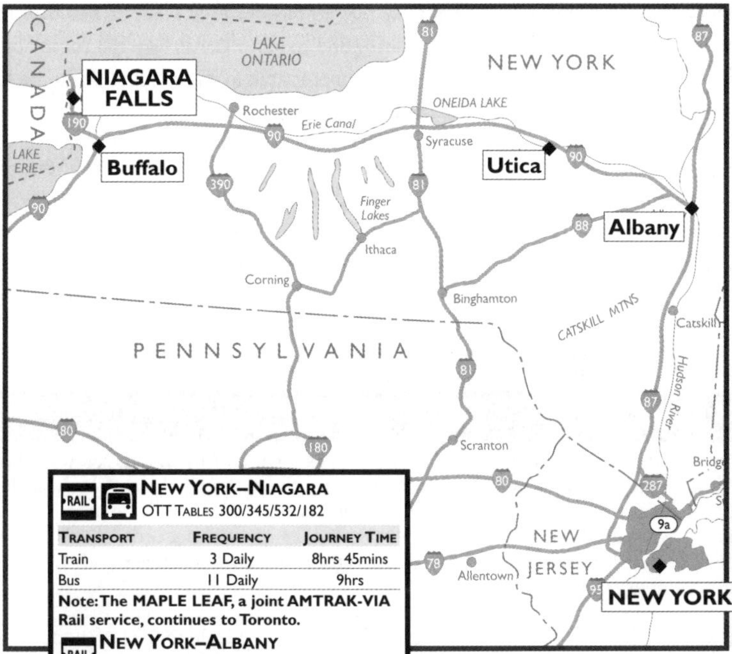

NEW YORK–NIAGARA

RAIL / BUS — OTT TABLES 300/345/532/182

TRANSPORT	FREQUENCY	JOURNEY TIME
Train	3 Daily	8hrs 45mins
Bus	11 Daily	9hrs

Note: The MAPLE LEAF, a joint AMTRAK-VIA Rail service, continues to Toronto.

NEW YORK–ALBANY

RAIL — OTT TABLES 300/345

TRANSPORT	FREQUENCY	JOURNEY TIME
Train	8 Daily	2hrs 55mins

ALBANY–UTICA

RAIL — OTT TABLE 345

TRANSPORT	FREQUENCY	JOURNEY TIME
Train	4 Daily	1hr 27mins

UTICA–BUFFALO

RAIL — OTT TABLE 345

TRANSPORT	FREQUENCY	JOURNEY TIME
Train	4 Daily	3hrs 10mins

BUFFALO–NIAGARA

RAIL — OTT TABLE 345

TRANSPORT	FREQUENCY	JOURNEY TIME
Train	3 Daily	1hr 8mins

Notes

The bus services from New York to Niagara are operated by Greyhound New York, Greyhound Canada, Adirondack Trailways, and Trentway Wagar Inc.

The service goes via Syracuse and takes 7hrs 40mins to Buffalo and 1hr–1hr 30mins from Buffalo to Niagara.

New York – Niagara

On the 'Empire'

The Amtrak 'Empire' service from New York to Niagara Falls winds across New York state via the Lower Hudson Valley, Albany and the Erie Canal. Take the route northbound, where the stunning scenery can be appreciated in daylight; and sit on the left-hand side of the train for superior views of the Hudson Valley.

Past a bevy of elegant mansions and the military academy of West Point, the train chunters to a halt in Albany, the state capital. Moving on through the Mohawk Valley, the train eventually arrives at its destination, the international boundary between the USA and Canada and the magnificent Niagara Falls. These can be viewed from almost any angle and means, including boat, platforms or aerial tramway; the brave can even venture behind the falls for an inside-out perspective.

ALBANY

New York state's capital city, Albany, began as a Dutch fur trading centre and fort on the Hudson River in 1609. It boomed with the opening of the Albany–Buffalo Erie Canal in 1825, but more recently author William Kennedy's novels, including *Ironweed*, have shown its grittier side. The main sights cluster around the massive, 96-acre **Empire State Plaza**, built by Governor Nelson Rockefeller and derided as 'Rockefeller's Edifice Complex'.

En Route

Pageantry is rich at the US Military Academy at **West Point**, on the west bank of the Hudson River, just outside Newburgh. There are great river views, and fine weather brings out the cadets on parade in the spring and autumn. West Point Tours, $, gives tours of the academy daily, and a visitor centre, at Thayer Gate is open daily 0900–1645; tel: (914) 938-2638.

Free attractions in the city include the late-19th-century **New York State Capitol**, between Washington Ave and State St; tel: (518) 474-2418, where the state legislature meets; it has tours Mon–Fri 0900–1600. **New York State Museum**, on the plaza, features the original sets for *Sesame Street*. Open daily 1000–1700; tel: (518) 474-5877.

Albany County Convention and Visitors Bureau, 52 S. Pearl St; tel: (518) 434-1217 or (800) 258-3582. Visitor centres are at Broadway and Clinton Ave; tel: (518) 434-6311.

The Amtrak station is located in Rensellear, a short walk across the Hudson on Rtes 9 and 20 from Albany.

Jack's Motel and Chinese Restaurant $ 1881 Central Ave; tel: (518) 456 5588.
Pine Haven B&B $$ 531 Western Ave; tel: (518) 482 1574.
Omni Albany $$$ State/Lodge Sts; tel: (518) 462 6611. For comfort and luxury.

ERIE CANAL

Farmers, axemen, ex-slaves, Irish labourers fresh off the boat – about 3500 'canawlers' – cleared land and dug the Erie Canal for a period of seven years. Climbing and descending 688 vertical feet over a distance of 363 miles, it linked the Great Lakes to the Hudson River and, thus, the American frontier to the port of New York City. After it opened in 1825, thousands more men, women, boys (known as 'hoggees') and mules helped move the freight barges up and down the canal. Today, waterways along the route of the original Erie Canal have been reborn for leisure, not work. Marinas, restaurants, inns and historic sites dot the banks, and nature preserves, parks and campsites have replaced mills and factories. The historic corridor, an engineering milestone that opened a path to the settlement of the West, is now a playground. For information on recreation, cruises and boat rentals, contact the New York State Canal Corp., tel: (800) 422-6254.

Restaurants to suit a range of tastes can be found at the intersection of Western Ave and Quail St.

The Ginger Man $$ 234 Western Ave; tel: (518) 427-5963. Named after J. P. Donleavy's novel, features sketches and quotations from British authors on the walls.

NIAGARA FALLS

From the USA you will first see on your right the **American Falls**, then the smaller **Bridal Veil Falls** and ahead, to the left, the larger and more famous **Canadian Horseshoe Falls**. This is the most visited scenic attraction in North America and one of the world's great natural wonders, formed when the waters of Lake Erie chiselled out an exit channel towards Lake Ontario at the end of the last Ice Age. Daredevils, sightseers and honeymooners (a trend started by Napoleon's brother) have all been drawn to see the awesome power of the foaming water as it thunders 170 ft into the Niagara River.

Amtrak stops at Lockport Rd and 27th St, just north of the centre of town. In town, connect on to the highly publicised 'people mover', a system of green air-conditioned motorcoaches travelling an 18-mile circular route from just above the Falls (Rapids View parking lot) to Queenston Heights. They operate approximately every 20 mins, with stops at all major sites. One ticket gives you a day's unlimited travel. $ Open late Apr–mid-Oct; tel: (905) 357-9340.

Most of the area near the river and around the American Falls is part of the **Niagara Reservation State Park** – take an immediate right turn from the Rainbow Bridge; tel: (716) 278-1770. From **Prospect Point Observation Tower**, you can see the view from above the Gorge and for less than a dollar take an elevator down to the base of the American Falls.

For more than 150 years visitors have cruised to the foot of the Falls on the ***Maid of the Mist*** excursion boat, 5920 River Rd; tel: (905) 358-5781. Rain gear is provided, as it is for the **Journey Behind the Falls**, in which elevators descend 125 ft from Table Rock Complex for a self-guided tour behind Horseshoe Falls. $ Open from 0900 year round. Alternatively, venture to view the Falls from high on the observation decks located at the **Skylon Tower**, 5200 Robinson St, $, and at the **Minolta Tower**, 6732 Oakes Dr., $.

The Falls are illuminated nightly, by garish multicoloured lights on the American side and by a soft rose glow on the Canadian side. On Fridays in summer there are free fireworks displays at 2200.

Niagara has some more unusual attractions away from the Falls. **Oakes Garden Theatre** is an outdoor amphitheatre at the foot of Clifton Hill, with free live entertainment 1900–2100 (mid-June–Sept). **Oh Canada, Eh?**, Pyramid Pl., 5400 Robinson St; tel: (905) 374-1995, $$$, is a fun dinner-theatre musical celebration of Canada, with a log cabin décor. There are more quirky entertainments on Clifton Hill, including **Ripley's Believe It or Not Museum** and the **Guinness Museum of World Records**. At Pyramid Pl., the **IMAX® Theatre and Daredevil Museum**, 5400 Robinson St; tel: (905) 374-4629, $, presents the history of the Falls from Native legends to modern-day daredevils on a six-storey high screen.

NIAGARA AND THE DAREDEVILS

Fame and fortune have lured many to the Falls: some lost their lives, but almost all went away empty-handed. One of the first recorded to risk life and limb in an attempt to gain celebrity status was a schoolteacher, Mrs Annie Taylor, who in the early 1900s decided to travel over the Falls in a padded barrel. She jarred and bounced the whole way down, eventually losing consciousness. Seventeen minutes later, her barrel was retrieved and the bleeding and bruised Mrs Taylor was removed, alive enough to be triumphant about her success. Sadly her fame was short-lived and she died destitute 20 years later.

The quieter nature lover can try **Niagara Parks Greenhouses**, Niagara Parkway, south of Horseshoe Falls; tel: (905) 356-2241, open from 0930; free. Nightlife, on the other hand, is not forgotten, and **Casino Niagara**, 5705 Falls Ave (temporary home); tel: (905) 374-3598 or (888) WINDFALL (946-3255), features 3000 slot machines, 123 gaming tables, snack and restaurant facilities.

i On the US side, the **Niagara Falls Convention and Visitors Bureau**, 310 4th St; tel: (800) 338-7890, will provide you with a free guide. Alternatively try **Orin Leham Visitor Center**, Niagara Reservation State Park; tel: (716) 278-1796; open daily 0800–2215.

On the Canadian side, the **Niagara Visitor and Convention**

Bureau, 5115 Stanley Ave; tel: (905) 356-6061 or (800) 56-FALLS, is open daily 0800–2000 (mid-May–mid-Oct) and Mon–Fri 0800–1800 (mid-Oct–mid-May).

Inevitably, the weight of tourist traffic generates considerable commercial nastiness, particularly around the American town of Niagara Falls. If you do want to stay the night, the NFCVB can supply a list of bed and breakfasts. There is a budget hostel:

Hostelling International $ 1100 Ferry Ave; tel: (716) 282-3700. A Victorian house several miles from the Falls; closed 0930–1600.

On the Canadian side try the Niagara Parkway, lined with B&Bs as you enter the city. Rates drop as you move away from the river. The closest **campsite** to the Falls is Glen-View, 3950 Victoria Ave; tel: (905) 358-8689. It's on the People Mover system and has a large swimming pool, but during the day helicopters land across the street.

Niagara Falls Guest House $ 4487 John St, L2E 1A4; tel: (905) 356-9037.

Butterfly Manor $$–$$$ 4917 River Rd, L2E 3G5; tel/fax: (905) 358-8988.

Skyline Foxhead Hotel $$$ 5875 Falls Ave, L2E 6W7; tel: (905) 374-4444.

Mist Fast Food Restaurant $ Maid of the Mist Plaza. Budget fast food with a view.

Capri Restaurant & Lounge $$ 5438 Ferry St; tel: (905) 354-7519. Local award winner, representing Niagara's large Italian population.

Skylon Tower $$–$$$ 5200 Robinson St; tel: (905) 356-2651. The dining room revolves once an hour 760 ft above the Falls.

WHERE NEXT?

Crossing the Rainbow Bridge takes you into Canada, either to Buffalo and Fort Erie to the west or Toronto to the east. See page 489 for visa requirements.

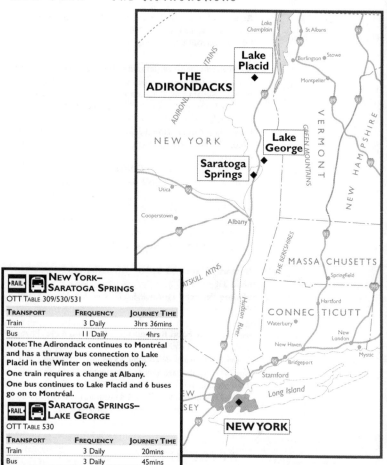

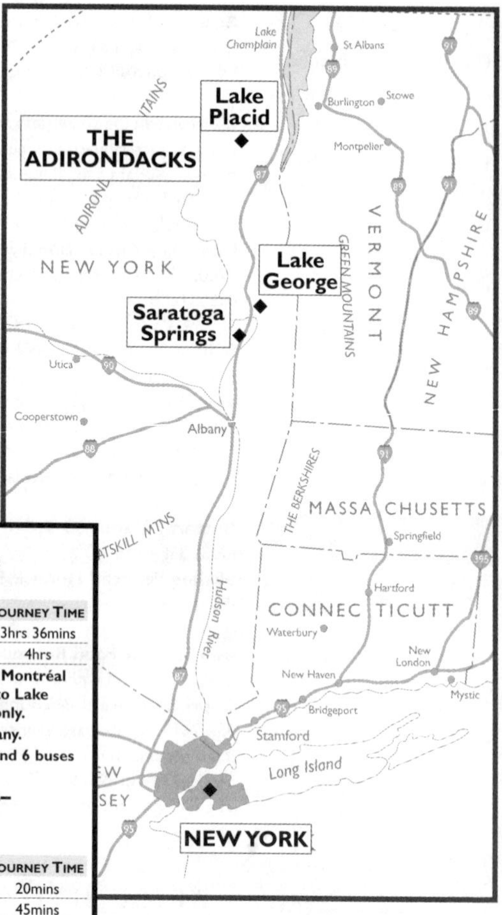

NEW YORK–SARATOGA SPRINGS

RAIL

OTT TABLE 309/530/531

TRANSPORT	FREQUENCY	JOURNEY TIME
Train	3 Daily	3hrs 36mins
Bus	11 Daily	4hrs

Note: The Adirondack continues to Montréal and has a thruway bus connection to Lake Placid in the Winter on weekends only.

One train requires a change at Albany.

One bus continues to Lake Placid and 6 buses go on to Montréal.

SARATOGA SPRINGS–LAKE GEORGE

RAIL

OTT TABLE 530

TRANSPORT	FREQUENCY	JOURNEY TIME
Train	3 Daily	20mins
Bus	3 Daily	45mins

Note: The nearest stop to Lake George is at Fort Edward.

LAKE GEORGE–LAKE PLACID

OTT TABLE 530

TRANSPORT	FREQUENCY	JOURNEY TIME
Bus	Daily	1hr 15mins

Notes

There are several extra Amtrak services to Albany and New London.

ON THE 'ADIRONDACK'

The Adirondack Mountains may not be pure wilderness, but the region does contain vast numbers of trees, peaks, lakes and streams among its 6 million acres. Adirondack history encompasses old trains, wooden boats, rustic furniture and forest estates in addition to logging, hunting and fishing. The train initially follows the Hudson Valley to Albany (see p. 74). Stop by Saratoga Springs to see the famous racetrack and splendid Victorian mansions, and to visit the mineral springs that give the town its name. In winter, a bus connects to Lake Placid, site of two Winter Olympics. The rail route parallels Lake Champlain into Canada and terminating in Montreal. Both directions of the route are travelled during daylight hours, except on Sunday, when the southbound journey is timetabled much later in the day, when much of it is after dark.

Adirondack Trailways covers much of the same route by bus, and is an alternative way of seeing this beautiful corner of the States.

SARATOGA SPRINGS

Saratoga's history and society sprang from the presence of mineral waters bubbling up from the ground. It is also renowned for its racecourses and polo ground, which attract many visitors each year. It is an elegant town of Victorian architecture, neatly clipped gardens and a famous timetable of concerts and dance performances.

The Drink Hall exhibits lend perspective to the past when you visit the Roosevelt or Lincoln bathhouses, in **Saratoga Spa State Park**, S. Broadway, where you can soak in a tub of the mineral spring water. After your bath, an attendant wraps you in warm sheets and leaves you for quiet reflection. $$ Call for appointments; tel: (518) 584-2011 or 583-2880.

Saratoga Race Course presents thoroughbred horse-racing mid July–Aug and may be the most civilised course in the USA: dresses, jackets and ties are 'appreciated' in the clubhouse. Breakfast is served at a trackside café 0700–0930. First race is 1300; closed Tues. For information, tel: (718) 641-4700 off season, (518) 584-6200 in season.

Saratoga Raceway, Crescent Ave; tel: (518) 584-2110, offers a much longer season of harness racing, mid Jan–late Nov, except for a break in Apr.

The **Saratoga Performing Arts Center**, in the park, is the summer home of the New York City Ballet, New York City Opera and the Philadelphia Orchestra. Popular music concerts are also staged here. Open June–Sept; tel: (518) 587-3330 (summer) or (518) 584-9330 (off-season).

Saratoga's other claim to fame is for a decisive battle of the American Revolution: Major-General John Burgoyne's campaign south from Canada was finally stopped when he surrendered on the heights here on 17 Oct 1777. The **Saratoga Battlefield** ($) is on Rtes 32 and 4, Stillwater; tel: (518) 664-9821.

Saratoga Springs Urban Cultural Park Visitor Center, Drink Hall, 297 Broadway at Congress, Saratoga Springs; tel: (518) 587-3241. Gives a museum-quality overview of the city's history and society. Open daily 0900–1600; closed Sun Nov–Mar. The Amtrak station is located at West Ave/ Station Lane.

Many chain hotels can be found on Rtes 50 and 9 (see p. 504). Room rates tend to jump during racing season.
Cold Brook Campsites $$ 10 miles north of Saratoga in Gansevoort. Open May–early Oct.
Kimberly Guest House $ 158 S. Broadway; tel: (518) 584 9006.
Brunswick House $$ 143 Union Ave; tel: (518) 584 6751.
Willow Walk $$$ 120 High Rock Ave; tel: (518) 584 4549.

Hattie's $ 45 Philadelphia St; tel: (518) 584-4790. New Orleans and Southern fare; home-made desserts.
9 Maple Avenue; tel: (518) 583-2582. Intimate bar that can get crowded Fri, Sat nights when live jazz can be heard.
Professor Moriarty's Dining and Drinking Saloon $$ 430 Broadway; tel: (518) 587-5981. The walls are hung with photos of his nemesis, Basil Rathbone, and other pretenders to the Sherlock Holmes throne.
Batcheller Mansion Inn $$$ 20 Circular St; tel: (518) 584-7012 or (800) 616-7012. A Victorian refuge, recently restored.

WHERE NEXT?

The Amtrak Ethan Allen *service runs from Saratoga Springs and Glen Falls. It runs to Fair Haven in Vermont, where thruway bus services take you to Rutland and Killington.*

LAKE GEORGE

You'll know you've reached Lake George when your children spot the rollercoaster of **Great Escape Fun Park**. East of the park, the town centre is a honky-tonk strip of shops, takeaway restaurants and fast-food stops. Further north along the lake you'll find more hotels and motels than homes.

The life of the region is captured best at the **Adirondack Museum**, Blue Mountain Lake; tel: (518) 352-7311, open daily 0930–1730 (late May–mid Oct).

Cannons still boom – just for show – and fife and drums are played at **Fort Ticonderoga**, strategically placed on the northern tip of Lake George and the shores of Lake Champlain. It was the site of several battles before and during the American Revolution. Built by the French in 1755 under the name of Fort Carillon, it was destroyed by the British in 1777, after its occupation by Ethan Allen and his Green Mountain Boys in May 1775. Following its restoration to original condition, it has been converted into a military museum, a must for all history buffs. Historical cruises on the lake are also on offer. $$ Open daily 0900–1700 (mid May–mid Oct); tel: (518) 585-2821.

The **Hyde Collection**, 161 Warren St, Glens Falls; tel: (518) 792-1761, is a gem – a must for art lovers – housed in a small mansion in the Italian Renaissance style. Among its attractions are small works by Van Dyck, Tintoretto and Botticelli.

Lake George Regional Chamber of Commerce, PO Box 272, Lake George; tel: (518) 668-5755. Operates a summer booth at Shepard Park, downtown on the waterfront, open daily 0900–1700 (July and Aug).

Adirondack Mountain Club, RR 3, Box 3055, Lake George, NY 12845; tel: (518) 668-4447, provides information on hiking, camping, canoeing and more in the region. It operates information booths at its Lake George headquarters on Rte 9 (south of I-87 exit 21); open Mon–Sat 0830–1700 (May–mid Oct); Mon–Fri 0830–1630 (rest of year).

High Peaks Lodge $ Adirondack Loj Rd, PO Box 867, Lake Placid, NY 12946; tel: (518) 523-3441.

Corner Birches Guest House $$ 86 Montcalm St; tel: (518) 668 2837.

Lincoln Log Colony $$$ Rte 9/Canada St; tel: (518) 668 5326.

The food in Lake George village is limited. Try:

Prospect Mountain Diner $ Canada St; tel: (518) 668 4381.

Rosie's Diner $$ Rte 9/9N junction; tel: (518) 668 2499.

LAKE PLACID

Lake Placid was the site of the 1932 and 1980 Winter Olympics. With New York state's highest mountain, Mount Marcy, looming in the background, Lake Placid draws visitors all year. US ski jumpers practise in summer on the 90 m Intervale Ski Jumps (Rte 73; tel: (518) 532-1655). The **Olympic Center ice rink**, Main St; tel: (518) 523-1655, is open in summer for public ice-skating Mon–Fri 1945–2115. Continue the Olympic theme by riding a bobsleigh, horse, or mountain bike, or go cross-country skiing at the **Olympic Sports Complex**, Mount Van Hoevenberg, Rte 73; tel: (518) 523-4436.

Ausable Chasm is a 1½ mile river gorge cut through sandstone, which you can explore on steps, steel bridges or in boats. $$ Open daily 0900–1600 (late May–mid Oct); tel: (518) 834-7454 or (800) 537-1211.

Tourist Information, The Olympic Center, 216 Main St, Lake Placid, tel: (518) 523-2445.

Lake Placid is a premier resort area, and the prices for accommodation are among the highest in the Adirondacks, rising sharply in season.

Whispering Pines Campground $ 6 miles south of the lake on Rte 73; tel: (518) 523 9322.

High Peaks Lodge $, Adirondack Lodge Rd, tel: (518) 523-3441 is a gold mine of information leaflets and provides lodging and breakfast at budget prices.

Irv-Inn $ 67 Parkside Ave; tel: (518) 523 4359. Simple but clean, and you can eat heartily at low prices.

Placid Bay Motor Inn $$ 140 Main St; tel: (518) 523 2001.

Mirror Lake Inn **$$$-$$,** 5 Mirror Lake Drive, Mirror Lake; tel: (518) 523 2544 is a palatial establishment with 120 rooms, a pool, health club and a good restaurant.

MONTRÉAL

Although it is the second largest French-speaking city in the world, Montréal is as decisively North American as it is francophone. Its early fortunes were made in furs and shipping as the furthest navigable port inland on the St Lawrence River, but today Montréal is a banking, manufacturing, software and world trade centre, and a polyglot city of great ethnic diversity. Perhaps no industry has so benefited from this immigration as the food service – it is hard to find a better place to eat in all of North America.

Vieux Montréal has most of the historic buildings and colourful, narrow streets dating from the 17th and 18th centuries. Remnants of the 1642 town lie beneath the Point-à-Callière museum. **Vieux Port**, the waterfront area of Vieux Montréal, has been recently redeveloped to create a 2-mile promenade and entertainments on the old piers. Former warehouses and chandleries on the surrounding streets are blossoming as art galleries, restaurants and boutiques. Montréal is also a sociable city, and Montréalers consider entertainment to be incomplete without the addition of good conversation and drink – either alcohol or strong coffee – so you will never be short of a good bar or restaurant. Interest in jazz has blossomed in recent years, and there are good clubs to be found too: try the downtown area, near McGill and Concordia Universities, where shows featuring jazz and blues can be found most nights.

Infotouriste Centre, 1001 rue du square-Dorchester (Métro: Peel); tel: (514) 873-2015, is open daily 0830–1930 (June–early Sept), 0900–1800 (rest of year).

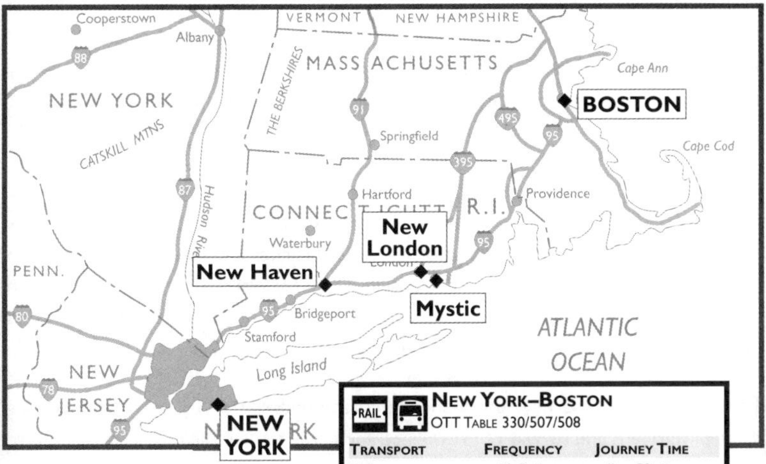

Notes

Amtrak intends to introduce the new *Acela* service on the Northeast corridor. As well as introducing new trains on this service and improving the catering facilities, the main benefit will be a reduction of the journey time between New York and Boston to three hours.

RAIL BUS New York–Boston
OTT Table 330/507/508

Transport	Frequency	Journey Time
Train	10 Daily	4hrs 50mins
Bus	45 Daily	5hrs 20mins

The New York–Boston bus service runs via Springfield

RAIL New York–New Haven
OTT Table 335

Transport	Frequency	Journey Time
Train	16 Daily	1hr 45mins

RAIL New Haven–New London
OTT Table 330

Transport	Frequency	Journey Time
Train	14 Daily	1hr

RAIL New London–Mystic
OTT Table 330

Transport	Frequency	Journey Time
Train	5 Daily	13mins

RAIL Mystic–Boston
OTT Table 330

Transport	Frequency	Journey Time
Train	4 Daily	2hrs 37mins

New York – Boston

The short distances between station stops and the good supporting infrastructure – commuter-rail lines and intercity buses link numerous towns not on Amtrak's network – make train travel along this route a viable alternative to that ultimate symbol of American mobility: the car. The Connecticut–Rhode Island–Massachusetts segment of Amtrak's NortheastDirect service is the railway's busiest route – understandably so, for this is a densely populated area, and New York and Boston are major 'anchor' destinations.

Much of this part of Amtrak's line follows the original course of the Boston Post Road, mile-posted in 1672 for mail delivery between New York City and Boston. Present-day contrasts are striking – a mixed bag of seascapes, beaches and boat harbours; pristine marshlands and nature sanctuaries; village greens; backyard-barbecue suburbia and New England academia; factories and power plants; woeful patches of urban blight; and the USA's per capita wealthiest county (Fairfield in Connecticut).

The total 205-mile journey runs along the coastal underbelly of Connecticut, curving through Rhode Island by way of Providence and finally zipping through a south-eastern stretch of Massachusetts to reach Boston. Coach passengers have access to no-frills food and beverage buffet service (smart travellers bring their own, more edible supplies on board). If you're carrying ponderous amounts of luggage, porterage is available at the larger stations. Be forewarned, however: New Haven is the only station on the Connecticut route with left-luggage facilities.

En Route

Barnum Museum, Bridgeport. The sole reason for a Bridgeport stopover is just a block away from the sizeable Amtrak station: the bizarre, neo-Byzantine-Romanesque museum recalling the career of the flamboyant circus impresario P.T. Barnum. $ 820 Main St; tel: (203) 331-9881. Open Tues–Sat 1000–1630, Sun 1200–1630; also Mon 1100–1630 (July–Aug).

NEW HAVEN

The heart and soul of this mid-size city is **Yale**. This élite university in the eastern USA's so-called Ivy League has been a hugely prestigious and influential presence here since 1717, an influence most evident in the city's cultural institutions.

New Haven's Union Station is about a mile south from downtown, but walking is not recommended because of its location in a less-than-idyllic area. Take a taxi or use the Connecticut Transit bus service.

New Haven Green, bounded by Chapel, Church, College and Elm Sts, and divided by Temple St, is a textbook example of a New England town common, laid out in 1638. It is the site of three churches exemplifying Federal, Georgian and English Gothic design. In Chapel St are two notable art galleries. The **Yale Center for British Art**, 1080 Chapel St; tel: (203) 432-2800, has the biggest and broadest-ranging collection of British art outside the UK, a bequest from billionaire Yale alumnus Paul Mellon. Open Tues–Sat 1000–1700, Sun 1200–1700. At 1111 Chapel St is America's oldest academic art museum, **Yale University Art Gallery**, tel: (203) 432-0600. It was founded in 1832 and holds paintings, sculptures and decorative arts from ancient Egypt to French and American Impressionist periods. Open Tues–Sat 1000–1700, Sun 1300–1800 (Sept–July). The collection at another Yale institution, the **Beinecke Rare Book and Manuscript Gallery Library**, 121 Wall St; tel: (203) 432-2977, includes a Gutenberg Bible, Charles Dickens manuscripts and rare Audubon *Birds of America* prints; it also has a sunken sculpture garden. Open Mon–Fri 0830–1700, Sat 1000–1700.

The **Peabody Museum of Natural History** $ at 170 Whitney Ave, tel: (203) 432-5050, was founded in 1866 and ranks among the world's best, with global 'finds' by university archaeologists. Open Mon–Sat 1000–1700, Sun 1200–1700.

SAFETY

Confine your sightseeing to Yale's immediate surroundings and areas adjoining the city-centre New Haven Green. This precaution becomes doubly applicable after nightfall.

Greater New Haven Convention and Visitors Bureau, 59 Elm St, New Haven, CT 06510; tel: (800) 322-7829 or (203) 777-8550; www.newhavencvb.org.

Yale Visitor Information Center, 149 Elm St; tel: (203) 432-2300.

The best places to stay tend to be heavily booked during spring graduation time at Yale, and also in autumn when the football team does battle against a traditional Ivy League foe on the Yale Bowl gridiron. So plan accordingly.

Hotel Duncan $$ 1151 Chapel St; tel: (203) 787-1273. A long-time favourite of touring theatrical personalities; far from ritzy, just the basics – but clean, respectable, and centrally situated.

The Colony $$$ 1157 Chapel St; tel: (800) 458-8810 or (203) 776-1234; fax: (203) 772-3929. Handsome, low-rise downtown hotel with a restaurant and lounge.

New Haven Hotel $$$ 229 George St; tel: (800) 644-6085 or (203) 498-3100; fax: (203) 098-0922. Within the city's major hospital complex, a few blocks from Yale's campus; features an indoor pool.

Streets west and south of New Haven Green have plentiful choices of moderately priced and inexpensive restaurants.

Atticus Bookstore Café $ 1082 Chapel St. Professors and students linger over breakfast and lunch in this thoroughly collegiate bookstore.

Louis' Lunch $ 261 Crown St. A little cubbyhole where, in 1895, Louis Lassen made gastronomic history by cooking the first-ever American hamburgers.
Claire's Corner Copia $–$$ 1000 Chapel St. Mingle with the 'Yalies' in this non-smoking, vegetarian establishment serving soups, pastries and creative sandwich specials.

NEW LONDON

Wrapped around its deep-water harbour, New London prospered as a 19th- century whaling port. That nautical tradition endures with America's Coast Guard Academy and – across the Thames (rhymes with James) River in neighbouring Groton – evocative submarine lore.

The main nautical attractions are along the waterfront. At the **US Navy Submarine Base** you can clamber through the world's first nuclear-powered submarine, launched in 1954. There is also a museum, definitive as regards undersea warfare. 1 Crystal Rd; tel: (800) 343-0079 or (860) 449-31741. Open Wed–Mon 0900–1700, Tues 1300–1700 (mid-Apr–mid-Oct), Wed–Mon 0900–1600 (mid-Oct–mid-Apr).

The **Lyman Allyn Art Museum** is strong on Colonial furniture, accessories and paintings – plus an outstanding collection of dolls, dolls' houses and antique toys. $ 625 Williams St; tel: (860) 443-2545. Open Tues–Sat 1000–1700, Sun 1300–1700. Eugene O'Neill grew up in **Monte Cristo Cottage**, which inspired his *Long Day's Journey Into Night* and *Ah! Wilderness*. $ 325 Pequot Ave; tel: (860) 443-0051. Open Tues–Sat 1000-1700, Sun 1300–1700 (May–early Sept).

Southeastern Connecticut Tourism District, 470 Bank St, New London, CT 06320; tel: (800) 863-6569 or (860) 444-2206; www.mysticmore.com. Information for Groton and Mystic as well as New London.

Red Roof Inn $$$ 707 Colman St; tel: (800) 843-7663 or (860) 444-0001; fax: (860) 443-71541. A short taxi ride north from downtown gets you to this basic but satisfactory motel.
Queen Anne Inn B&B $$$$ 265 Williams St; tel: (800) 347-8818 or (860) 447-2600; fax: (860) 443-0857. If you wish to splurge. A Victorian 'painted lady'; full breakfast and afternoon tea included.

Captain's $–$$ Stone and Bank Sts. Directly across from Union Station: pasta, pizzas, chicken, seafood, high-calorie desserts.
Dutch Tavern $$ 23 Green St. The oldest pub in town; have

New London's railway station itself is small but significant, designed in rusticated neo-Romanesque style by celebrity architect H. H. Richardson in 1887. It's right downtown and well served by SEAT (Southeast Area Transit) buses taking passengers to outlying attractions.

a burger and a beer where Eugene O'Neill allegedly quaffed a few.

The Lorelei $$$ 158 State St. Primarily for seafood. Pressed-tin ceilings and a convivial bar.

MYSTIC

Mystic Seaport is 19th-century maritime America recreated. Attractively (and profitably) situated at the mouth of the Mystic River, the seaport boasts the last surviving wooden whaling ship, a square-rigger and Gloucester fishing schooner, a coal-fired steamer (which takes passengers on river cruises), interactive demonstrations and craftspeople at work. It also has galleries of model ships, figureheads, seafaring paintings and the largest nautical bookstore anywhere in the world. $$$ 75 Germanville Ave; tel: (860) 572-5315. Open daily, hours variable depending upon time of year.

Mystic Seaport's stature as Connecticut's foremost tourism attraction seeps into the town in obvious ways: plenty of places to eat, sleep and shop. That could imply an overdose of touristy tackiness, but somehow Mystic retains its genuine old-time charm. See Beluga whales, sharks, penguins and bottle-nose dolphins among the 3500 aquatic creatures at the **Mystic Marinelife Aquarium** $$, 55 Coogan Blvd; tel: (860) 572-5955. Open daily 0900–1700, 0900–1900 in summer.

While in town, consider a half-day or sunset cruise aboard the *Argia* schooner, or Long Island Sound day-tripping on a Mystic Whaler cruise.

Mystic's tiny wooden train station is about a mile from downtown, considerably more from Mystic Seaport. Catch a cab or hop aboard the low-cost Mystic Trolley, a sightseeing jitney making the rounds daily during tourism's mid-year high season.

Mystic Chamber of Commerce, 16 Cottrell St, Mystic, CT 06355; tel: (860) 572-9578.

Whaler's Inn $$–$$$ 20 E. Main St; tel: (800) 243-2588 or (860) 536-1506; fax: (860) 572-1250. A grouping of four 19th-century buildings in the bustling downtown district.

Old Mystic Motor Lodge $$$ 251 Germanville Ave; tel: (860) 536-9666; fax: (860) 536-2044. Advantageously close to Mystic Seaport; outdoor pool.

Two Sisters Deli $ 4 Pearl St. Ideal for light lunch or coffee break; save room for the choice of home-baked desserts. Downtown location.

Seamen's Inne $$–$$$ 105 Germanville Ave; tel: (860) 536-9649. Restaurant and pub, a few steps from Mystic Seaport's entrance.

Boston

New England's largest city by far is widely known as The Hub – a name bestowed by Oliver Wendell Holmes, who wrote about chauvinistic turn-of-the-century Bostonians who considered their city 'the Hub of the Universe'. The oldest major US city, founded in 1630, Boston was once a class-conscious Brahmin town:

the home of the bean and the cod,
where the Lowells speak only to the Cabots,
and the Cabots speak only to God.

There's still a blue-blooded Yankee establishment, but it's matched by a feisty Irish one, and ethnic diversity is prevalent.

The city centre's compact size surprises visitors expecting Americanised urban sprawl, and then discovering that they can get nearly everywhere on foot. Walking the Freedom Trail (see p. 94) is a good introduction to historic Boston, and a trip out to Lexington and Concord (p. 100) provides a vivid lesson in what sparked the American Revolution.

Learning and culture rank high in this 'Athens of America' (another often-used, lofty title), where the nation's first public elementary school was established in 1636. Today the metro area is energised by its student population, some 25,000 strong, attending the couple of dozen colleges and universities. Harvard and almost-as-famous Massachusetts Institute of Technology (MIT) are across the Charles River in Cambridge, part of Boston and yet separate, the city's 'Left Bank'.

Getting There

Logan International Airport covers landfill in East Boston, directly across the Inner Harbor from downtown, 20–30 mins by public transport. A free shuttle connects the international terminal (E) to domestic terminals (A–D), and the Blue Line subway station. By bus or cab, downtown is 3 miles away via a toll tunnel. Hotel courtesy shuttles are available; for suburban express buses, tel: (617) 235-6426.

Also available from Logan to Boston is the harbour-crossing Water Shuttle, which docks at Rowes Wharf downtown. For schedule and fares, tel: (617) 330-8680.

THE BIG DIG

Travellers entering the city from Logan Airport and South Station can't but wonder at the blue-and-yellow barriers, cranes and monstrous pieces of earth-moving equipment that greet them. The Big Dig, officially the Central Artery Project, is the largest public-works endeavour in US history, costing billions of dollars of federal and state funds. This 7½-mile construction corridor through the heart of Boston will ultimately become a vehicle tunnel and allow for the dismantling of a traffic-clogged elevated motorway erected in the 1950s. Its removal, scheduled to commence in 2003, will reconnect the North End to downtown and Government Center, and also allow for a beautified swathe of landscaping.

Amtrak operates NortheastDirect rail service to and from South Station, Summer St at Atlantic Ave; tel: (800) 872-7245 or (617) 482-3660; www.amtrak.com.

Near South Station, the bus terminal accommodates Greyhound, tel: (800) 231-2222, Peter Pan Trailways, tel: (800) 343-9999, and other intercity motorcoach services.

GETTING AROUND

Public transport is essential in squeezed-together, traffic-congested Boston. The Massachusetts Bay Transportation Authority (MBTA or simply 'the T') operates streetcars, buses and subways in town, in across-the-river Cambridge and nearby suburbs. In addition, the T provides commuter ferryboat service between downtown landings and the Charlestown Navy Yard.

NAVIGATING THE SUBWAY

(See colour map section, inside back cover)

Stops on the **Green Line** include Government Center (close to Faneuil Hall/Quincy Marketplace), Park St (Boston Common and main shopping district), Arlington (Boston Public Garden and Newbury St), Copley (Copley Sq., Copley Pl., Boston Public Library, Back Bay) and Kenmore (Boston University, Fenway Park baseball stadium). Passengers using the Green Line's E branch reach the Museum of Fine Arts, Symphony Hall, Prudential Center and the Christian Science Center.

Take the **Red Line** northbound to Harvard and MIT, southbound to the John F. Kennedy Library and Museum and historic sites in suburban Quincy. Also on the Red Line are the Old State House and South Station.

The **Blue Line** is the one to take for the New England Aquarium and Logan Airport, while the **Orange Line** (not recommended at night) has a Chinatown stop and goes to Arnold Arboretum. **Purple** designates MBTA commuter-rail service (see p. 90).

Subway tokens are sold at all T stations; bus drivers and streetcar conductors take tokens or exact change. MBTA Information Line: tel: (800) 392-6100 or (617) 222-3200; www.mbta.com.

MONEY SAVERS

Visitor passes are available for one, three or seven consecutive days' unlimited travel on the 'T'.

Boston CityPass ticket books entitle users to half-price admittance at the Museum of Science, Museum of Fine Arts, New England Aquarium, JFK Library and Museum, John Hancock Observatory and Isabella Stewart Gardner Museum.

Both passes available at visitor information centres.

INFORMATION

CITY AND TRANSPORT MAP – inside back cover

Greater Boston Convention and Visitors Bureau (GBCVB), 2 Copley Pl. (Suite 105), Boston, MA 02116-6510; tel: (800) 888-392-6100 or (617) 536-4100; www.bostonusa.com. The bureau operates visitor information centres on the Tremont St side of Boston Common and inside the Prudential Center.

Along the Freedom Trail (see p. 94), you'll find a **National Parks Service Visitors Center**, 15 State St; tel: (617) 242-5642; www.nps.gov.

OLDEST SUBWAY

One of numerous Bostonian 'firsts in America' is the underground's short initial stretch linking Park Street Station with Boylston Station, at opposite edges of Boston Common, inaugurated in 1897.

SAFETY Inner-city Boston is well lit at night, full of people and therefore generally safe. Avoid 'fringe areas' after dark – especially the so-called, fast-shrinking Combat Zone – also edgy sections of the South End, as well as Esplanade walkways along the Charles River.

MONEY Thomas Cook has a currency exchange facility at 399 Boylston St, Copley Sq.; tel: (800) 223-9392 or (617) 267-5367. Open 0900–1700 Mon–Fri. At Logan Airport's Terminal E, you'll find a BankBoston currency exchange kiosk.

POST AND PHONES Boston's main post office, open 24 hrs daily, is behind South Station; tel: (617) 654-5326. In more central Faneuil Hall, a branch opens daily 0930–1700; tel: (617) 723-1791.

ACCOMMODATION

The city and vicinity's popularity as a vacation, convention, business and academic destination translates into heavily booked rooms all year round, so reserve well in advance. Rates are generally high (the overall average is in the very pricey $175 range). National chains are omnipresent, but exceptions do exist.

Contact **A Bed & Breakfast Agency** for moderate-price rooms in local residences (including waterfront lofts) and self-catering apartments: 47 Commercial Wharf; tel: (800) 248-9262 or (617) 720-3540; fax: (617) 523-5761; phone direct from UK: 0-800-89-51-28. **Citywide Reservation Service** books rooms in hotels, inns, guesthouses and B&Bs. 25 Huntington Ave; tel: (800) 468-3593 or (617) 267-7424; fax: (617) 267-9408.

Boston's few recommendable budget–moderate choices include:

Boston International AYH $ 12 Hemenway St; tel: (617) 536-9455; fax: (617) 424-6588. Part of the American Youth Hostel organisation. Super-inexpensive; in the Fenway neighbourhood near the Museum of Fine Arts.

463 Beacon Guest House $$–$$$ 463 Beacon St; tel: (617) 536-1302; fax: (617) 247-8876. West end of Back Bay, near Charles River Esplanade.

Boston Hotel Buckminster $$–$$$ 645 Beacon St; tel: (800) 727-2825 or (617) 236-7050; fax: (617) 262-0068. Old but respectable; overlooks Kenmore Square in the vicinity of Boston University.

A Friendly Inn at Harvard Square B&B $$$ 1673 Cambridge St, Cambridge; tel/fax: (617) 547-7851. Unusually inexpensive accommodation, close to all university attractions.

Newbury Guest House B&B $$$ 261 Newbury St; tel: (617) 437-7666; fax: (617) 262-4243. Favourably situated on Back Bay's hip Newbury St; includes continental buffet breakfast.

FOOD

Boston remains best known for fresh seafood. There's also no shortage of traditional Italian and Irish cooking, and such Yankee fare as pot roast, baked beans and Indian pudding. Added to that is a whole wider world of ethnic cuisine. Browse through the North End to take your pick of Italian eateries; do the same in Chinatown for big helpings of affordable Chinese and Vietnamese fare.

Beacon Hill and Downtown

Faneuil Hall Marketplace has restaurants and food stalls cooking everything from pizza and hot dogs, soups and sandwiches to full-course lunches and dinners. The colonnaded middle building of this bustling complex contains the largest conglomeration of cheap eateries, with communal seating beneath the dome.

	Black Rose $$–$$$ 160 State St. Irish pubs are plentiful in this most Irish of US cities. Food, drink, live Celtic entertainment, central location.
	Durgin-Park $$–$$$ 340 Faneuil Hall Marketplace; tel: (617) 227-2038. A no-nonsense taste of old Boston, with hearty New England fare.
	Union Oyster House $$$ 41 Union St. The US's oldest restaurant, in continuous existence since 1826. Enjoy oysters galore at the ancient mahogany raw bar.
WATERFRONT	**The Wharf** $$–$$$ 80 Atlantic Ave. Small, casual, chatty. On a dock poking into Boston harbour.
BACK BAY	**Bon Marché** $$–$$$ Prudential Center, Belvedere Arcade. Euro-style marketplace buzz, with quantities of serve-yourself stations. There is a huge food court elsewhere in the 'Pru'.
	Atlantic Fish Company $$$ 793 Boylston St. Boston's culinary essence: fresh-caught seafood.
	Legal Sea Foods $$ 35 Columbus Ave. Casual, noisy local chain with outlets in Copley Place, the Prudential Center and at Logan Airport.
	Vinny Testa's Bar Ristorante $$ 867 Boylston St. Serves huge portions of Italian food.
CAMBRIDGE	**John Harvard's Brewhouse** $$ 33 Dunster St. Inexpensive pub food attracts collegiate clientele.

HIGHLIGHTS

BEACON HILL AND DOWNTOWN

Boston's earliest citizens lived on a tiny fist-shaped peninsula crowned with three prominent hills; atop the tallest during Colonial times stood a blazing signal beacon. Two hills were cut down and used as landfill, but this most Bostonian of old neighbourhoods remains 'the Hill', a British-looking warren of crooked streets and red-brick terraces. Among its photogenic highlights is **Louisburg Sq.**, a fenced-in, London-type crescent and a posh address. Beacon Hill is bordered by Boston Common and antiques shop-lined Charles St. The neighbourhood's lower, 'flat' section borders Storrow Dr., with footbridges connected to the Charles River Esplanade.

'New' State House, in Beacon St, is Beacon Hill's oldest building (completed in 1798) and the seat of Massachusetts' state government. Its dome is gilded with 23-carat gold leaf and yellow Sienese marble adorns the Hall of Flags; a statue of John F. Kennedy stands alongside the main entrance. Free tours Mon–Fri 1000–1530; tel: (617) 727-3676. .

Now dwarfed by financial district high-rises, the **'Old' State House**, 206

Washington St, was the seat of British government from 1713 to 1776 (the building's eastern end still bears the royal lion and unicorn), and later that of the Massachusetts legislature. Inside is Boston's history museum ($; open daily 0900–1700), and outside is a cobblestone circle marking the site of the Boston Massacre.

THE BOSTON MASSACRE

The attempt by an impoverished British government to raise revenue by increased taxes and tighter trade regulations angered American Colonists, who had no representation in the parliament that was imposing the levies. Protests culminated on 5 Mar 1770 in the so-called Boston Massacre, in which five Colonists where shot by English soldiers facing a taunting mob. Many taxes (but not on tea) were repealed and a period of calm followed, to be broken by the Boston Tea Party (see p. 96).

Faneuil Hall, the 1742 meeting-house-atop-a-marketplace in Dock Sq., was where such firebrand orators as Samuel Adams aired the ideas that led to the American Revolution, hence its 'Cradle of Liberty' title. Still an open-forum meeting hall upstairs, it now has a cluster of shops downstairs. Its grasshopper weathervane was inspired by the one above London's Royal Exchange. Open daily 0930–1630..

Between Congress and Union Sts stands the **New England Holocaust Memorial Carmen Park**. The six luminous glass towers etched with 6,000,000 numbers, commemorating those who perished, make a haunting metaphor.

To the west of Beacon Hill, bordered by Tremont, Boylston, Charles, Beacon and Park Sts, is America's first public park, **Boston Common**. The 48-acre common was laid out in 1634 as a pasture for Colonists' cattle, and was also where that era's criminals were publicly hanged. Meandering walkways cross the open land and link monuments, memorials, fountains and the Frog Pond, frozen in winter for ice-skating.

LAID TO REST

Three of Boston's cemeteries are historically significant. **Granary Burying Ground** (1660), Tremont St, is the last resting place of such notables as Paul Revere, John Hancock, Samuel Adams and Boston-born Benjamin Franklin's mom and dad. **King's Chapel Burying Ground**, Tremont St, is the city's oldest graveyard, predating 'Old Granary' by three decades. Interred here is John Winthrop, the Massachusetts colony's first governor. Slate headstones on the crest of **Copp's Hill**, Charter St, mark the graves of 17th-century Puritan settlers.

Boston Public Garden abuts the common to the west. The nation's first botanical garden (1837), it is very Victorian in concept, with flower beds, weeping willows and a lagoon upon which the city's famous Swan Boats have taken passengers on lazy rides since 1877. (They operate Apr–mid-Sept.) Bronze ducks on the Beacon St side recall the Boston-based children's book, *Make Way for Ducklings*.

THE FREEDOM TRAIL

In the most walkable of major US cities, it makes good sense to indulge in some self-guided sightseeing on foot – best accomplished by following this 2½-mile route connecting sites associated with the city's early history. The trail begins at the visitor centre near the Park St T station on Boston Common and, designated by a red line, slithers through downtown, the North End and over the water to Charlestown. You can pick up a map at the start-point, or halfway along at the National Park Service facility, where a better free map is available. (If you prefer knowledgeable guidance, Park Service Rangers lead 90-min tours, Mon–Fri 1100 and 1400, Sat–Sun 1000, 1300 and 1400).

BACK BAY Originally a foul-smelling mudflat, this prestigious neighbourhood was created by an epic landfill project in the late 19th century. It is criss-crossed by a Boston rarity: streets laid in an orderly grid. A parallel row of them is alphabetically named (Arlington to Hereford) after English dukes. Commonwealth Ave is split down the middle by a graceful, wide promenade, tree-shaded and lined with statues. Many of Back Bay's town houses are occupied by schools, consulates and pricey condominiums.

For a panorama of the city, ride up to the **John Hancock Observatory**, atop New England's tallest skyscraper; there are spectacular views from this 60th-floor, 740-ft vantage point, plus historical exhibits. $ Copley Sq.; open daily 0900–2200 (Apr–Oct), Mon–Sat 0900–2200, Sun 0900–1700 (Nov–Mar).

The neo-Romanesque bulk of **Trinity Episcopal Church** is dramatically reflected in the John Hancock Tower's mirror-glass facade. Consecrated in 1877, it is considered by many to be H. H. Richardson's architectural masterpiece; the interiors were designed by John LaFarge. Open daily 0800–1800; free guided tours Sun 1215; organ concerts Fri 1215 (Sept–June).

Close by, in Dartmouth St, is **Boston Public Library**. Completed in 1895, it's regarded as one of the first outstanding examples of the Beaux Arts style in the US. The bronze doors were created by Daniel Chester French and a walk up the marble stairway is worthwhile to see murals by Puvis de Chavannes, Edwin Abbey and John Singer Sargent on second- and third-storey walls. You can also admire the courtyard garden and barrel-vaulted Bates Reading Room. Open Mon–Thur 0900–2100, Fri–Sat 0900–1700 all year; also Sun 1300–1700 (Oct–May).

TOURS

Old Town Trolley Tours $$$; tel: (617) 260-7010. Hop aboard a trolley at any of 16 stops for a narrated ride. You can disembark and reboard as you please; the next trolley comes along every 15 mins. Full tour takes 100 mins. It's the same procedure for separate, shorter-length Cambridge touring; tel: (617) 269-7150.

The **Institute of Contemporary Art** is housed in a former Back Bay police station, with changing exhibitions of avant-garde paintings, sculptures and photographs. It's a venue, too, for concerts, lectures, films, videos and performance arts programmes. 995 Boyston St; open Wed–Sun 1200–1700; $ (free admittance Thur 1700–2100).

Taking up a whole block of Huntington Ave, the plaza and buildings of the **Christian Science Center** are dominated by the Mother Church of the Christian Science faith, founded locally by Mary Baker Eddy. Free tours Tues–Sat 1000–1600, Sun 1130.

Sightsee by day the multi-ethnic enclave of **South End** (not to be confused with South Boston) that spreads south of Back Bay, between Columbus Ave and Washington St. It encompasses the USA's largest concentration of Victorian terrace houses, some surrounding a pair of London lookalikes – Rutland Sq. and Union Park. There are innovative restaurants and chic cafés on the main thoroughfare, Tremont St. Its broad, pleasantly landscaped Southwest Corridor takes the place of a planned-for motorway extension, defeated by civic activists.

CHARLES RIVER ESPLANADE AND THE FENWAY

A lengthy green belt, the **Charles River Esplanade**, runs along Boston's side of the river. In summertime, the Hatch Shell hosts outdoor cinemas and concert series, including Boston Pops performances. Pedestrians, joggers and bicyclists can cross bridges to more parkway along Memorial Dr. on the Cambridge side.

The **Museum of Science** at the Science Park, downriver from the Esplanade, has more than 500 exhibits, and many hands-on activities covering all things scientific from anthropology to space exploration. Combination tickets or separate admittances ($$) to the **Hayden Planetarium** and **Mugar Omnimax Theater**. Museum open daily 0900–1700 (July–Sept), also Fri 1700–2100 rest of year.

Dropping south of the Esplanade is Boston's 'Emerald Necklace' of interconnected parklands, conceived a century ago by landscape maestro Frederick Law Olmsted. **Arnold Arboretum** (125 Arborway, Jamaica Plain) is part of the necklace, a 265-acre site with thousands of trees, shrubs and flowers, including 250 varieties of lilac. Open daily dawn–dusk.

A 1901 building (plus a modernistic wing) at 465 Huntington Ave houses the **Museum of Fine Arts** (MFA). The USA's second-largest public art collection spans all periods, but is particularly strong on Asian and Egyptian art, French Impressionism (43 Claude Monet paintings) and Early American works. $$ tel: (617) 267-9300; open Mon–Tues 1000–1645, Wed 1000–2145, Thur–Fri 1000–1700, Sat–Sun 1000–1745. West Wing stays open Thur–Fri 1645–2145. Free admittance Wed after 1600.

Works by Rembrandt, Botticelli, Titian and other old masters, along with tapestry and Greco-Roman statuary, form the eclectic collection of a 19th-century socialite. The **Isabella Stewart Gardner Museum** at 280 The Fenway is in her replicated 15th-century Italian *palazzo*, complete with lush, flowering courtyard; tel: (617) 566-1401. Open Tues–Sun 1100–1700.

NORTH END AND THE WATERFRONT Cut off from the rest of Boston by the I-93, North End, Boston's 'Little Italy', overlooks the harbour and nearby downtown skyline. Its narrow thoroughfares, especially Hanover and Salem Sts, are chock full of trattorias and cappuccino cafés, and on summer weekends the streets are alive with religious festivals.

Christ Church ('Old North'), built in 1723, is another stop on the history trail. In its steeple were hung the lanterns that signalled British troop movements ('one if by land, two if by sea'), and which in April 1775 started Paul Revere on his horseback ride through the night to warn patriot leaders at Lexington and Concord of the enemy's impending arrival (see p. 101). 193 Salem St; open daily 0900–1700. **Paul Revere House** is where the silversmith-turned-patriot lived for 30 years from 1770. It contains period furnishings and Revere memorabilia. $ 19 North Sq.; open daily 0930–1715 (Apr–mid-Oct), 0930–1515 (Nov–Dec).

Further along the waterfront, on Central Wharf, is the **New England Aquarium**, which has sealion shows, a penguin rookery and exhibits of exotic ocean life. The main feature is a four-storey tubular glass tank in which aquatic creatures – including turtles, sharks, moray eels and tropical fish – swim in and out of a coral reef. Café and gift shop in the silvery new West Wing. $$ Open Mon–Tues and Fri 0900–1800, Wed–Thur 1800–2000, Sat–Sun 0900–1900 (July–Sept); Mon–Fri 0900–1700, Sat–Sun 0900–1800 (Sept–June).

At Museum Wharf there are three floors of hands-on exhibits, play areas and a kids' theatre at the **Children Museum** $$; open daily 1000–1700 (also Fri 1700–2100). The **Computer Museum** $$ explores the information revolution and its impact, via 170 interactive exhibits and vintage hardware from computerisation's early years. Open daily 1000–1800 (mid June–Sept), Tues–Sun 1000–1700 rest of year.

THE BOSTON TEA PARTY

The arrival in Boston harbour in November 1773 of three British ships bearing cheap tea threatened to undermine the boycott on the taxed leaves. An angry mob, dressed as Mohawk Indians, swarmed aboard the ships and dumped the precious cargo into the harbour. An exhibition and re-enactments can be seen at Old South Meeting House ($ 310 Washington St; open daily 0930–1700), where angry citizens gathered to curse the Brits on the evening of the Tea Party; and the Boston Tea Party Ship and Museum at Museum Wharf has a replica of one of three vessels, *Beaver II*; $$ open daily 0900–1700 (Mar–Dec).

CHARLESTOWN From downtown, take the commuter boat or cross the bridge to reach this blue-collar (but increasingly gentrified) section of Boston. Permanently docked at Pier One of Charlestown Navy Yard is **USS *Constitution*** ('Old Ironsides'), launched in 1797 and still part of the US Navy. The 52-gun frigate, the world's oldest commissioned warship, gained its nickname when its solid oak hull proved resistant to the enemy fleet's cannonballs during the war of 1812 with Britain. Open daily for free guided tours, 0930–1550. A museum telling the saga of 'Old Ironsides', with interactive exhibits, is open daily 1000–1700..

After the opening shots of the American Revolution had been fired at Lexington and Concord in 1775 (see p. 101), British redcoats tried to lift a rebel siege of Boston. The misnamed Battle of Bunker Hill (it actually took place on nearby Breed's Hill) on 17 June was a victory for Britain, though a costly one, for King George's troops evacuated Boston the following March. A 221-ft hilltop obelisk, the **Bunker Hill Monument**, marks the battleground; there are dioramas and exhibits in a building at the base, and you can climb the stairs to the top for panoramic views. Open daily 0900–1630.

Free student-led Harvard Yard tours courtesy of the Harvard Information Center Holyoke Center, 1350 Massachusetts Ave; tel: (617) 495-1573. Tours Mon–Fri 1000 and 1400, Sat 1400 (Sept–May); Mon–Sat 1000, 1115, 1400 and 1515, Sun 1330 and 1500 (June–Aug).

CAMBRIDGE Though tightly woven into the cultural and intellectual fabric of Boston, Cambridge is a separate, staunchly free-thinking, across-the-river municipality, home to Harvard University and the Massachusetts Institute of Technology.

i **Cambridge Office for Tourism**, 18 Brattle St; tel: (800) 862-5678 or (617) 441-2884; www.cambridge-usa.org.

Harvard Yard, the university's inner sanctum and the ultimate New England campus quadrangle, is surrounded by brick walls and reached through tall wrought-iron gates. The seated bronze figure memorialises the young English cleric John

MODERN ARCHITECTURE IN CAMBRIDGE

Le Corbusier's only US building (24 Quincy St) is used by the **Carpenter Center for the Visual Arts** for contemporary art exhibitions and nightly Harvard Film Archive cinemas. $ Open Mon–Sat 0900–2300, Sun 1200–2200.

MIT's **List Visual Arts Center**, 20 Ames St, is a gridlike structure designed by I M Pei, with three galleries displaying contemporary art. Open Tues–Sun 1200–1800 (Fri until 2000). On MIT's **West Campus** there is more Cantabrigian architectural bravado, this one a cylindrical brick edifice desiged by Finland's Eero Saarinen, which is both a religious and concert venue. Open dawn–dusk.

BOSTON FROM THE WATER

Boston Duck Tours $$$ tel: (617) 723-3825, provides 90-min narrated sightseeing jaunts aboard World War II amphibious vehicles, including splashdown in the Charles River for on-the-water views of Boston and Cambridge.

Boston Harbor Cruises $$$ One Long Wharf; tel: (617) 227-4321, operates a daily variety of narrated excursions with the city skyline as a backdrop, including whale-watching cruises and stopover at George's Park (one of the Boston harbour islands), site of picnic grounds and a Civil War fort.

Spirit of Boston $$$ tel: (617) 457-1450, offers a pricier way to cruise the harbour while enjoying lunch or dinner. Lunch cruise, 1130–1400; three-hour dinner cruises depart 1600, 1900, 2030 depending upon time of year.

Harvard, who left half his money and all his books to the fledgling college when he died in 1638, two years after it was founded. Buildings in and around the yard span the history of US architecture.

The **Fogg Art Museum**, 32 Quincy St, features European and North American art from the Middle Ages to contemporary times. In Otto Werner Hall on the second floor the Busch-Reisinger Museum specialises in 19th–20th-century art of Germanic-speaking countries, notably Vienna Secessionist and German Expressionist periods. $ (Sat free); open Mon–Sat 1000–1700, Sun 1300–1700.

A joint ticket gives admittance to the Fogg and the nearby **Arthur M. Sackler Museum**. This striking post-modern building, designed by Britain's James Stirling, houses Harvard's collections of classical, Asian, Islamic and late Indian art. $ 485 Broadway; open Mon–Sat 1000–1700, Sun 1300–1700.

OUT OF TOWN

The John F. Kennedy Library and Museum recalls the 'Camelot' era of the Boston-born 35th US president, in a stunning white harbourfront building out at Columbia Point (Morrissey Blvd, Dorchester), reached by free shuttle from the Red Line's JFK/UMass T Station. $$; tel: (617) 929-4500; open daily 0900–1700.

On an upper-class street north of Harvard Sq. once known as 'Tory Row' is the home of poet **Henry Wadsworth Longfellow** (1837–1882), he who gave us *Hiawatha* and, a century after the event, immortalised (and romanticised) Paul Revere's midnight ride. Owned by the National Park Service, the 18th-century Georgian-style house depicts the Longfellow family's comfortable lifestyle. Earlier in history (1775–6), this was George Washington's headquarters. $ 105 Brattle St; guided tours Wed–Sun 1000–1630 (May–Oct).

Longfellow lies buried in **Mount Auburn Cemetery**, America's first 'garden cemetery', alongside such eminent personalities as the founder of Christian Science, Mary Baker Eddy (see p. 95), the writer Oliver Wendell Holmes and the social reformer and writer Julia Ward Howe, who wrote 'The Battle Hymn of the Republic'. 580 Mt Auburn St; open daily 0800–1700 (till 1900 in summer).

SHOPPING

Boston's main shopping district is Downtown Crossing, a crowded car-free zone centred on Washington and Winter Sts, where both the big department stores (Filene's and Macy's) and a myriad of other stores are located. Bargain hunters delve into the frenzy of Filene's Basement, well known for 'automatic markdown' savings.

Back Bay's Newbury St is a people-watchers' paradise amid galleries, bookstores, indoor/outdoor cafés and boutiques ranging from stylish to offbeat. Across Boylston St from that trendiest of Boston thoroughfares is the Prudential Center's mall, an extensive galleria complex with eateries and 70 shops in various price ranges. That bazaar connects via covered walkway to Copley Pl. and its 100 stores with mostly higher price tags.

Near the harbourfront, wildly popular Faneuil Hall/Quincy Marketplace, packed with tourists and Bostonians day and night, consists of three renovated 1825 market buildings, supplemented by newer add-ons, that house 125 shops, restaurants, pubs and food stalls.

Over in Cambridge, Harvard Sq. and surroundings provide an additional splurge of shopping opportunities. The university-affiliated Harvard Coop is a sizeable department store, and this compact area boasts more bookshops per square foot than anywhere else on earth.

NIGHTLIFE

The Calendar section in each Thursday's *Boston Globe*, Scene in Friday's *Boston Herald* and listings in the weekly *Boston Phoenix* and *Improper Bostonian* tabloids contain updates of what's happening.

The theatre district around Tremont and Boylston Sts draws audiences to musicals and dramas at the cavernous Wang Center, the classy Colonial, the more intimate Wilbur and Emerson Majestic and the tiny Charles Playhouse. There's also a thriving small-theatre scene, and classical and contemporary drama are performed at the Lyric Stage (140 Clarendon St) and Boston University's Huntington Theater Company (264 Huntington Ave). More such doings in Cambridge, where Loeb Drama Center, 64 Brattle St, is home of the American Repertory Theatre (ART). Boston area colleges and universities present reputable theatrical offerings, too. Half-price, same-day-performance tickets go on sale (cash only) at Bostix booths located alongside Faneuil Hall, and at Copley Sq. and Harvard Sq.

The classical music scene is dominated by the Boston Symphony Orchestra (also the lighter-weight Boston Pops) at acoustically pitch-perfect Symphony Hall, 301 Massachusetts Ave: tel: (617) 266-1492 (information) or 266-1200 (tickets). For an ongoing school-year programme of (mostly) free concerts, Jordan Hall is at the nearby New England Conservatory, 290 Huntington Ave; tel: (617) 585-1122. Harvard-Radcliffe, Boston University, MIT, Tufts, Berklee School of Music, Boston Conservatory and the Longy School also schedule high-calibre student performances. The Schubert Theatre, 265 Tremont St; tel: (617) 542-6772, is home of the Boston Lyric Opera. For Boston Ballet performances, tel: (617) 695-6950.

The area has a hyperactive pop, rock, jazz, blues, folk, country and cabaret scene at Kenmore Sq. and on nearby Lansdowne St, in the Faneuil Hall Marketplace vicinity, the student-populated Allston neighbourhood, in various parts of Cambridge and elsewhere. Abundant, too, are comedy clubs, among them Nick's Comedy Stop, 100 Warrenton St; tel: (617) 482-0930.

DAY TRIPS

There is much to see outside the central city area. MBTA's rapid-transit lines (the Purple Line) fan out from Boston's South and North Stations to such North Shore locales as Salem and Gloucester (covered on pp. 110–115), westbound to Concord and vicinity, and south to Plymouth.

PLYMOUTH P&B (Plymouth & Brockton) intercity buses connect Boston with Plymouth, where the Pilgrims aboard the *Mayflower* first settled (see p. 117). The Purple Line from South Station will take you to Plymouth's Cordage Park, a 19th-century rope mill transformed into a marketplace.

LEXINGTON AND CONCORD Just outside the city (Lexington is only 11 miles from Boston, and Concord a further 7), these were the villages that saw the very beginning of the American War of Independence (see box, right).

Concord was also the scene of an extraordinary blossoming of American letters in the mid-19th century, when writers seized on the philosophy of Ralph Waldo Emerson ('the Sage of Concord') by creating a self-consciously national literature. The **Emerson House** has been maintained largely as he left it, with books, furniture and personal belongings. Here, too is **Orchard House**, which Louisa May Alcott described in loving detail in *Little Women*. Both writers are among the Concord literati resting in peace on **'Author's Ridge'** in Sleepy Hollow Cemetery, along with Henry David Thoreau and Nathaniel Hawthorne. Thoreau's beloved Walden Pond, just south of Concord, is now popular for swimming and boating, and park rangers can provide directions to the site of his humble cabin, still marked by its crumbled chimney hearth.

Points of interest are widespread and rambling, so a car is the easiest option (beware of heavy traffic – this is a popular tourist trail). Alternatively, Concord Depot, half a mile from the town centre, is on the MBTA commuter-rail line from Boston's South

THE FIRST SHOTS OF REVOLUTION

On 19 Apr 1775 British forces marched from Boston towards Concord for what they thought would be an easy task: to confiscate caches of arms owned by the increasingly restless Colonists. Instead they met with armed resistance from local militia – the Colonists had been forewarned of their imminent arrival by Paul Revere, riding through the night to warn the patriot leaders: 'The British are coming!' (see p. 96).

Unfair taxes (see the Boston Tea Party, p. 96) and a growing resistance to British rule meant it had been only a matter of time before a bid was made for independence, and the ensuing battles were the start of the American Revolution.

The **Minuteman National Historical Park** commemorates the events of the day the British redcoats were driven back towards their Boston encampments. Most of the park follows Rte 2A along that retreat path, now called Battle Road. **Lexington Green**, site of the initial dawn skirmish, is surrounded by white-spired churches and the yellow clapboard Buckman Tavern, where the Colonial militiamen (called minutemen, for they could be ready in a minute) assembled the night before. The next major battle site was at **North Bridge** in Concord, and costumed re-enactments of both firefights are held in the early hours each April on the fateful date.

The **Museum of Our National Heritage** in Lexington, **Battle Road Visitors Center** (open mid-Apr–Oct only) and **North Bridge Visitor Center** in Concord all commemorate these historic times – the Battle Road Center presents an excellent video and a diorama tracing the first four miles of the British retreat.

Driven back to Boston, the British tried to lift a rebel siege, but despite their victory at the Battle of Bunker Hill were forced to withdraw from Boston the following March.

Station; you could tour the outlying sites by taxicab – Colonial Livery, tel: (978) 369-3433, is a Concord-based company. Getting from Boston to Lexington is somewhat more complex. Take the Red Line T to Alewife Station; from there, take no. 62 or 76 MBTA bus to Lexington centre.

LINCOLN If you are interested in art and architecture, take a trip out to Lincoln, where you can visit **Gropius House**, the family home and first US building (1937) by architect Walter Gropius, founder of Germany's Bauhaus school of design. $ 68 Baker Bridge Rd; tel: (781) 259-8098. Open Fri–Sun 1200–1700 (June–mid-Oct).

For contemporary art and large-scale radical sculptures, try Lincoln's **DeCordova Museum and Sculpture Park**, housed in a turreted brick building set in 35 acres. $ 51 Sandy Pond Rd; tel: (781) 259-8355. Open Tues–Fri 1000–1700, Sat–Sun 1200–1700.700.

OLD STURBRIDGE VILLAGE Families, schoolchildren and history buffs enjoy this experience of what daily life was like in New England in 1830.

This makes a very long one-day trip, and as tickets to the village are valid for two consecutive days, you may like to stay over. Apart from the omnipresent chain operations (see p. 504) there are a number of distinctive inns and B&Bs. Offering good value are **Colonel Ebenezer Crafts Inn**, a Federalist famhouse on the common; **Old Sturbridge Village Lodges and Oliver Wight House** on Rte 20 W; and the **Sturbridge Country Inn** and **Sturbridge Host Hotel**, both on Main St.

Spread over 200 acres, it comprises some 40 structures including a blacksmith's, water-powered saw mill, one-room school, general store, bank and printing office. 'Villagers' in authentic period garb demonstrate workaday activities and join in community celebrations. Farming is a constant occupation, but village goings-on change with the seasons; special demonstrations include weaving and basket- and broom-making. The Village's **Bullard Tavern** does lunches and snacks, or its restaurant offers a seasonal menu of New England fare.

Sturbridge Tourist Information Center, 380 Main St, Sturbridge; tel: (508) 347-2761. $$$ Village open daily 0900–1700 (Apr–end Oct); Tues–Sun 1000–1600 (Nov–Dec and Feb–Mar); www.osv.org.

Sturbridge is 60 miles west of Boston, 50 miles north of Providence; Peter Pan/Greyhound buses from South Station normally take 95 mins (buses continue to New York City via Hartford and New Haven).

WHERE NEXT?

Boston is as much The Hub for modern-day visitors as it was for Old Bostonians. You can strike out north along the Massachusetts shore (see p. 110), perhaps travelling right up the coast of Maine (see p. 128); or head west via Concord along Rte 2 (the 'Mohawk Trail') into the Berkshire Hills, where Tanglewood is the esteemed Boston Symphony Orchestra's summer home (see p. 143). North of Concord lies Lake Winnipesaukee and the rugged scenery of the White Mountains (see pp. 136–141).

Southwards, there are Cape Cod and its islands to explore (see pp. 116 and 122). You can take the train down to New York via the old coastal towns of Connecticut (see p. 83); or detour to Providence and Newport in 'Little Rhody' (see p. 103). Amtrak also runs fast trains to New York and, via Albany, across to Chicago (see pp. 262 and 266).

RHODE ISLAND

Despite its name, the USA's smallest state is not actually an island, although numerous small islands, waterways, inlets and coves break up its scant 1214 square miles (about the same area as Cheshire or Nottinghamshire). Its capital, Providence, offers plentiful attractions and visitor amenities, but is outshone by smaller Newport.

Rhode Island's 'founding father' was Roger Williams. Upon being kicked out of the Massachusetts Bay Colony by the Puritans for his 'new and dangerous opinions', he trekked south in 1636 to establish a plantation settlement dedicated to religious freedom. This little patch of New England is still officially named the State of Rhode Island and Providence Plantation.

Newport's exclusivity as an oceanfront resort began early in Colonial times, when southern plantation owners travelled north to escape oppressive humidity in favour of cool sea breezes. By the 1850s, wealthy New Yorkers were cruising to Newport via the Fall River Steamship Line. Thus began a seasonal influx of privileged families personifying America's Gilded Age. They commissioned 'summer cottages' of palatial scope and grandeur, and this small town on the southernmost tip of Aquidneck Island became high society's 'in' place to spend millions of dollars in a binge of conspicuous consumption. The town also became a summer colony for literary notables, including Henry Wadsworth Longfellow, Julia Ward Howe and Henry James.

GETTING THERE AND GETTING AROUND

Flights from, for instance, Boston and Cape Cod, fly into T. F. Green Airport, 7 miles south of central Providence; tel: (401) 737-4000.

Providence is 45 miles south of Boston via Amtrak's Northeast Corridor rail service. From Boston travellers can also get to Providence by commuter rail and, from Boston's South Station Transportation Center, via Bonanza bus, tel: (401) 751-8800. The railway station in Providence is centrally located and has left-luggage facilities.

From central Kennedy Plaza, Providence RIPTA (Rhode Island Public Transit Authority) buses fan out for service throughout metropolitan Providence, and also to the airport, Newport, Bristol and smaller communities. For RIPTA fares and schedules, tel: (401) 781-9400.

PROVIDENCE

Providence's capital-city stature is augmented by the energising influence of upper-crust Brown University, plus a world-class school of design. Moreover, 'Little Rhody's' mini- metropolis is a top-notch restaurant town, partly because the design school has a culinary curriculum and Johnson & Wales University educates future chefs.

FOR FREE

There are free tours of the **Rhode Island State House**, an 1891–1904 hill-top whopper in white marble, crowned by one of the world's biggest self-supporting domes. Enter at 82 Smith St; tel: (401) 277-2357. Tours Mon–Fri 0830–1630.

Riverwalk and pedestrian bridges connect the handsome 4-acre **Waterplace Park** with city-centre attractions. It features an amphitheatre overlooking a lagoon and a Venetian-type gondola takes passengers on waterway rides.

The third Thursday of each month is **Galley Night**, when free ArTrolleys shuttle between galleries, museums, antiques shops, and art and performance events.

i **Providence Warwick Convention and Visitors Bureau**, 1 Exchange St, Providence, RI 02903; tel: (800) 233-1636 or (401) 274-1636; www.providencecvb.com. A **Visitor Information Center** is located in Waterplace Park's pavilion; tel: (401) 751-1177.

POST The main post office is at 24 Corliss St; tel: (401) 276 6812.

Several of the US chain hotels are in town (see page 504). Among more intimate alternatives are:

Old Court B&B $$$ 144 Benefit St; tel: (401) 751-2002; fax: (401) 272-4830. An Italianate-style Victorian mansion ideally situated for sightseeing the 'Mile of History'.

State House Inn B&B $$$ 43 Jewett St; tel: (401) 785-1235; fax: (401) 351-4261. Century-old house with ten guest rooms in a West Side neighbourhood, close to the state capitol building.

There's no lack of elegant, pricey restaurants in Providence, and Italian trattorias pack the West Side's Federal Hill neighbourhood. Other options include:

Trinity Brewhouse $–$$ 186 Fountain St. Delectable barbecued sandwiches; house brands of ale and lager.

Boathouse Restaurant $$ Waterplace Park. View the park's fountain and the city skyline over a casual meal.

Meeting Street Café $$ 220 Meeting St. On College Hill, light fare including vegetarian offerings.

Barnsider's Mile and a Quarter $$$ 375 S. Main St; tel: (401) 351-7300. Steak and seafood restaurant with popular salad bar.

Café Nuovo $$ 1 Citizens Plaza. Enjoy indoor or outdoor seating overlooking the Riverwalk while dining on Caribbean, Asian or US Southwest cuisine.

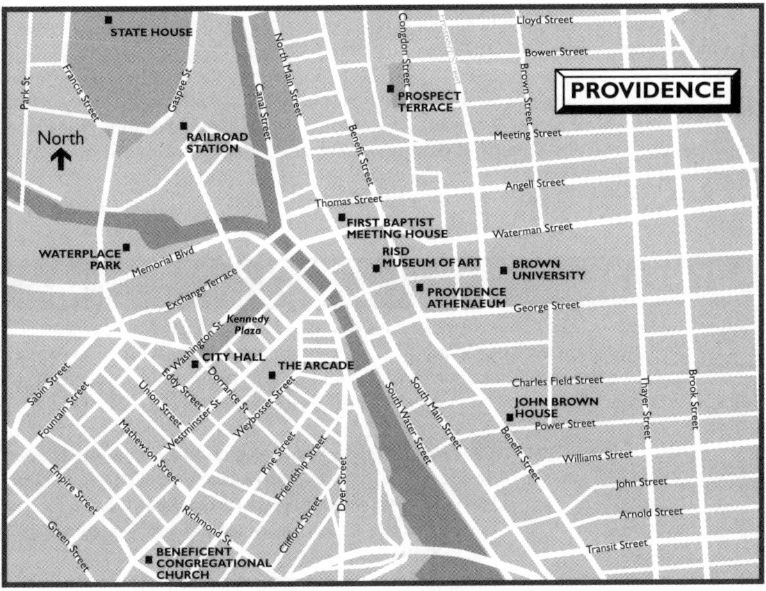

HIGHLIGHTS Providence is compact and walkable. The Seekonk River, which meets up with the Providence River before emptying into Narragansett Bay, flows through the middle of the city, dividing the city into two.

Streets on the east side of town rise steeply to **College Hill**, where there's much in the way of fascinating history plus an artsy, academic atmosphere. For a great panorama of the city, climb up to the statue of Roger Williams that stands on Prospect Terrace, Congdon St.

Benefit Street, the east side's brick-paved 'Mile of History', encompasses the USA's most impressive concentration of domestic architecture from the Colonial through Victorian periods. The **RISD Museum of Art** is the Rhode Island School of Design's cultural treasure, with collections ranging from French Impressionist paintings and 18th-century US furniture to ancient Greek bronzes and Roman mosaics. $ 224 Benefit St; tel: (401) 454-6500. Open Tues–Wed, Fri–Sat 1030–1700, Thur 1200–2000, Sun 1300–1600 (mid-Sept–late June); Wed–Sat 1200–1700 (summer).

> Take a bus from Kennedy Plaza out to the excellent Roger Williams Park and Zoo. $ Open daily 0900–1600 (Nov–Mar), Mon–Fri 0900–1700 (Apr–Oct).

Across the river, **The Arcade** connecting Weybosset

and Westminster Sts is a skylit Greek Revival enclosure that qualifies as America's first indoor mall, completed in 1828.

NIGHTLIFE Consult the daily *Providence Journal* and weekly tabloids for categorised listings. **Trinity Repertory Company** is an award-winning theatrical organisation. **Veterans Memorial Auditorium** stages ballet, opera and Rhode Island Philharmonic performances. Providence packs a steady musical barrage of jazz, folk, blues, country and rock into its relatively small size.

NEWPORT

Flanked on three sides by waterfront as it juts out into Narragansett Bay, Newport still exudes the boat-racing aura of its America's Cup heyday. It is an easy town to explore on foot; to get further afield, various bus lines and taxicab companies converge at the transportation terminal alongside Gateway Visitors Center in America's Cup Ave.

i Newport County Convention and Visitors Bureau, 23 America's Cup Ave, Newport, RI 02840; tel: (800) 976-5122 or (401) 849-8048; www.GoNewport.com. Same location for the Gateway Visitors Center, where services include accommodation bookings.

MONEY For foreign currency exchange, go to Citizens Bank, 8 Washington Sq.

POST AND PHONES Newport's main post office is at 320 Thames St; tel: (401) 847-2328.

Be mindful that room rates zoom steeply upwards during the summer. For a selection of B&Bs in various price ranges, there's no charge for bookings arranged by Taylor-Made Reservations, tel: (800) 848-8848 or (401) 848-0300; fax: (401) 849-8566; www.CityBytheSea.com.

Admiral Benbow Inn B&B **$$$** 93 Pelham St; tel: (800) 343-2863 or (401) 848-8000; fax: (401) 848-8006. Former home of a mid-19th-century sea captain.

Admiral Fitzroy Inn B&B **$$$–$$$$** 398 Thames St; tel: (800) 343-2863 or (401) 848-8000; fax: (401) 848-8006. Seventeen nicely decorated guest rooms in the Historic Hill neighbourhood.

Hotel Viking **$$$–$$$$** 1 Bellevue Ave; tel: (800) 556-7126 or (401) 847-3300; fax: (401) 849-8566. A vintage (1926) hotel in a quiet residential location three blocks from downtown.

Cycle rentals available at Ten Speed Spokes, 18 Elm St; tel: (401) 847-5609.

Ocean Coffee Roasters $–$$ 22 Washington Sq. Brews espresso, cappuccino and café au lait and purveys an inexpensive array of sandwiches, scones, soups and chilli.

Gary's Handy Lunch $$ 462 Thames St. This hangout replicates a 1950s diner and – in that vein – dishes out soups, burgers, fries, meat loaf, American chop suey and blue plate specials.

Brick Alley Pub and Restaurant $$–$$$ 140 Thames St; tel: (401) 849-6334. Very popular, therefore very busy in all seasons. Steaks, ribs, chicken, pasta and a massive salad bar. Loaded with funky antiques.

Christie's $$$ Christie's Wharf; tel: (401) 847-5400. Can't be beaten for harbour views. Ocean-fresh specialities include lobster, baked halibut and terrific Nantucket Bay scallops.

The Rhumbline $$$ 62 Bridge St; tel: (401) 849-6950. In a wooden Colonial-era house in Newport's bayfront Point district. Eclectic international menu ranges from Austrian Wiener schnitzel to Thai dishes.

Tours

Request a map detailing the self-guided **Banner Trail**, marked by colour-coded flags at points of interest. In addition to State House, city centre and Benefit St vicinities, the route covers classy Brown University's campus and surroundings on College Hill and the hip Wickenden St historic district.

Take the RIPTA bus 4 miles north from downtown to tour the riverside **Slater Mill Historic Site**, 67 Roosevelt Ave; tel: (401) 725-8638. In 1793, Samuel Slater built the USA's first reliably operative textile plant, thereby launching the nation's industrial revolution.

Shopping

Speciality stores cram Bannister's Wharf and Bowen's Wharf; the nearby Brick Market Place encompasses shops, galleries and clothing boutiques. Stores of all sorts line Thames St. Historic Hill's Spring St has a small-scale mercantile flavour with shops displaying antiques, pottery and ship models. The 1894 Armory, 365 Thames St, is occupied by antiques and fine-art dealers.

Highlights

Historic Hill, one of New England's finest early American neighbourhoods, is reached by brick pavements sloping up from the harbour. Across town, facing Narragansett Bay, **the Point** neighbourhood is another showpiece of 18th- and 19th-century houses. The **Museum of Newport History**, housed in Brick Market Building (dating from 1762), has insightful displays and artefacts that focus on colourful local history. $ 120 Thames St; tel: (401) 841-8770. Open Mon and Wed–Sat 1000–1700, Sun 1300–1700. **Trinity Episcopal Church** in Queen Anne Sq. was modelled on English churches designed by Christopher Wren and has been in use since 1776 – look out for pew no. 81, where George Washington sat. Open Mon–Fri 1000–1300; Sun services 0800 and 1030.

Newport has several 'firsts' among its historic buildings, including the nation's oldest public library, in existence since 1747: **Redwood Library**, 50 Bellevue Ave; tel: (401) 847-0292, open Mon–Sat 0930–1730. It also has North America's oldest Jewish house of worship (dedicated 1763), **Touro Synagogue**, 85 Touro St; tel: (401) 847-4794 (Fri services 1800 winter, 1900 summer; Sat services 0900).

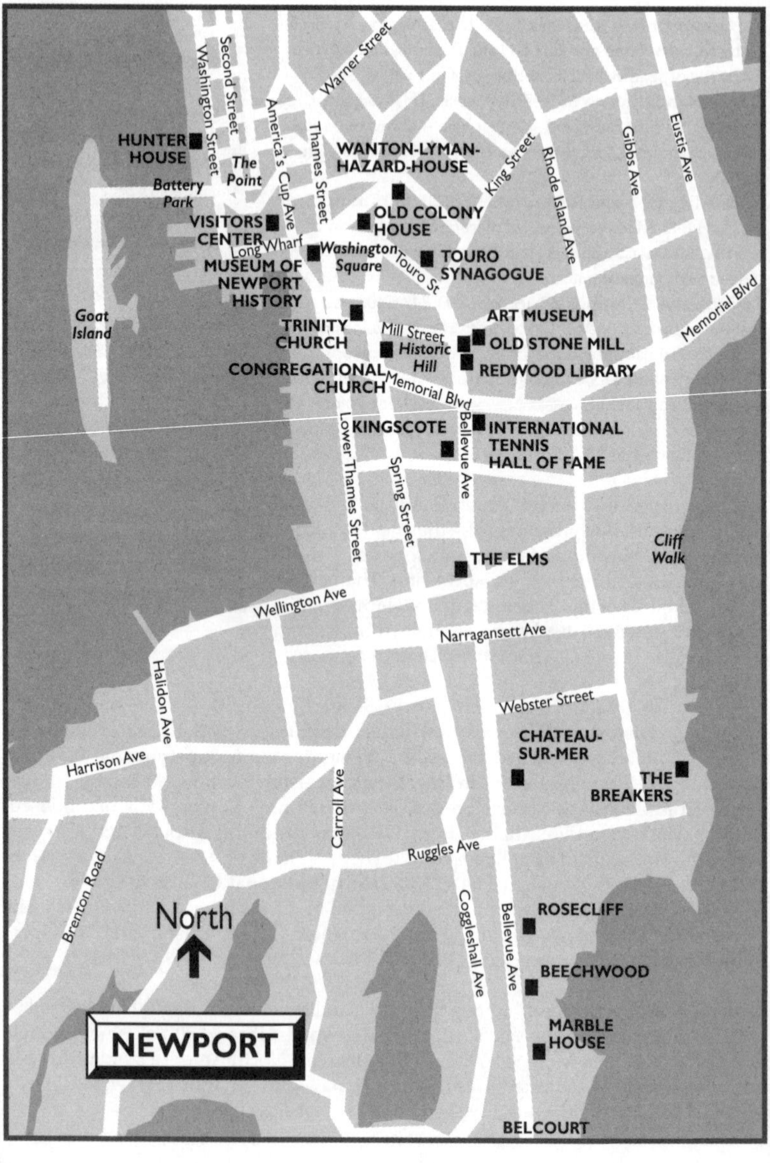
NEWPORT
North
Warner Street
Second Street
Washington Street
America's Cup Ave
Thames Street
HUNTER HOUSE
The Point
Battery Park
WANTON-LYMAN-HAZARD-HOUSE
King Street
Rhode Island Ave
Gibbs Ave
Eustis Ave
VISITORS CENTER
OLD COLONY HOUSE
Long Wharf
Washington Square
Touro St
TOURO SYNAGOGUE
MUSEUM OF NEWPORT HISTORY
Goat Island
TRINITY CHURCH
ART MUSEUM
Memorial Blvd
Mill Street
Historic Hill
OLD STONE MILL
REDWOOD LIBRARY
CONGREGATIONAL CHURCH
Memorial Blvd
KINGSCOTE
INTERNATIONAL TENNIS HALL OF FAME
Lower Thames Street
Spring Street
Bellevue Ave
Cliff Walk
THE ELMS
Wellington Ave
Narragansett Ave
Halidon Ave
Webster Street
CHATEAU-SUR-MER
Harrison Ave
Carroll Ave
THE BREAKERS
Ruggles Ave
Brenton Road
ROSECLIFF
Coggleshall Ave
Bellevue Ave
BEECHWOOD
MARBLE HOUSE
BELCOURT

Covering history of a very different sort, the **International Tennis Hall of Fame** is the sport's Valhalla. Players still use the original 13 grass courts. $$ 194 Bellevue Ave; tel: (401) 849-3990. Open daily 1000–1700.

Collectively, Newport's star attractions are its **mansions**: eleven 'summer cottages' built for the rich and famous of America's Gilded Age are now open to the public. Most of them are on or near posh Bellevue Ave, south of the centre, and outstanding among them are Cornelius Vanderbilt's The Breakers, emulating a 16th-century Italian palazzo, and 22-bedroom Rosecliff, inspired by Versailles's Grand Trianon. Ask at the Gateway Visitors Center for days, times and individual or combination admittance prices.

For an even greater choice of mansions to ogle, the looping 7-mile route of **Ocean Drive** passes some of America's costliest real estate, and is great for bicycling. Along the way look out for Brenton Point State Park, Fort Adams and **Hammersmith Farm**. This 50-acre bayfront estate of the Auchincloss family was where Jackie and John F. Kennedy had their 1953 wedding reception. $$ tel: (401) 846-0420. Open daily 1000–1700 (Apr–mid-Nov), 1000–1900 (summer).

NIGHTLIFE To sample Newport's resounding jazz and blues scene, head for the **Red Parrot**, 348 Thames St. Disco-dance at **The Daisy**, Bannister's Wharf. For what's-going-on updates, dial the 24-hr Newport Activity Line: tel: (401) 848-2000.

WHERE NEXT?

For highlights of the Connecticut coastline east of Rhode Island, see p. 83; westwards you can explore the beautiful but hugely popular Cape Cod and the offshore islands of Nantucket and Martha's Vineyard (p. 116). Beyond Boston (p. 110) the coast becomes increasingly rugged as you forge towards Maine and the Canadian border (see p. 128).

FOR FREE

For views of mansion terraces and lawns – and great sea views – take the **Cliff Walk**, a pathway high above the ocean surf that extends from Memorial Blvd 3.5 miles south to Bellevue Ave.

TOURS

Viking Tours, tel: (401) 847-6921, offers a variety of narrated sightseeing excursions. Several other organisations operate boat cruises on Narragansett Bay; enquire at the visitor centre.

DAY TRIPS

Bristol, 10 miles north of Newport, is an appealing waterfront town.

Blithewold Mansion and Gardens, the former summer estate of a coal baron, sprawls alongside Narragansett Bay. In Colt State Park, **Coggleshell Farm Museum** is a working farmstead relying solely on 18th-century agricultural methods. Pleasant restaurants and shops are on Hope St.

Information: **Bristol County Chamber of Commerce**, 654 Metacom Ave, Warren, RI 02885; tel: (888) 278-9948 or (401) 245-0750; www.bristolcountychamber.org.

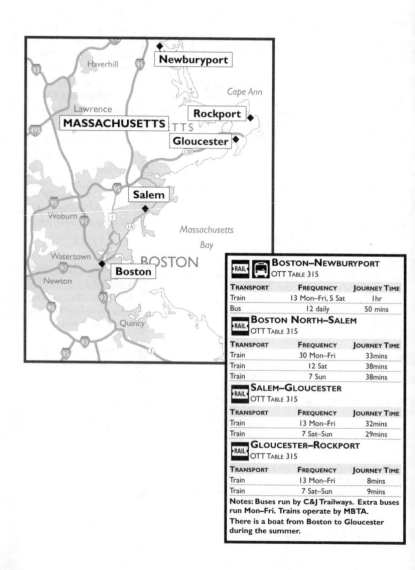

BOSTON–NEWBURYPORT
OTT TABLE 315

TRANSPORT	FREQUENCY	JOURNEY TIME
Train	13 Mon–Fri, 5 Sat	1hr
Bus	12 daily	50 mins

BOSTON NORTH–SALEM
OTT TABLE 315

TRANSPORT	FREQUENCY	JOURNEY TIME
Train	30 Mon–Fri	33mins
Train	12 Sat	38mins
Train	7 Sun	38mins

SALEM–GLOUCESTER
OTT TABLE 315

TRANSPORT	FREQUENCY	JOURNEY TIME
Train	13 Mon–Fri	32mins
Train	7 Sat–Sun	29mins

GLOUCESTER–ROCKPORT
OTT TABLE 315

TRANSPORT	FREQUENCY	JOURNEY TIME
Train	13 Mon–Fri	8mins
Train	7 Sat–Sun	9mins

Notes: Buses run by C&J Trailways. Extra buses run Mon–Fri. Trains operate by MBTA.
There is a boat from Boston to Gloucester during the summer.

The shore north of Boston distils coastal New England's chief appeals into a heady essence: ocean beaches, dramatic scenery, fresh-caught local seafood and seafaring history. Towns may share the sea as a common bond, but their styles range from the stately captains' homes of Salem and the boutiques, galleries and artfully arranged waterfront of Rockport to the lusty, gutsy reality of Gloucester's wharves.

These communities once dominated the world's cod fisheries and trade with the Far East. Today, yachts and pleasure craft far outnumber fishing boats, but the glories of the China Trade are still evident in Newburyport's fine architecture, and in antiques shops and museums.

Although you need a car to explore Cape Ann's more out-of-the-way corners, you can easily enjoy the highlights of the North Shore by public transport. MBTA commuter trains leave Boston's North Station for historic Salem (whose rich history is not confined to the notorious witchcraft trials) and for Gloucester and Rockport. Frequent buses leave Boston's South Station for Newburyport.

GLOUCESTER

Fishermen have gone to sea from the wharves here since 1623 and maritime painters have made the port their base for more than 150 years. The interplay of painting and fishing is captured at the **Cape Ann Historical Museum**, where exhibitions trace the fishing and boatbuilding heritage (Gloucester shipwrights invented the three-masted schooner). This is set against the magnificent paintings by native son Fitz Hugh Lane, America's premier maritime painter. $ 27 Pleasant St; open Tues–Sat 1000–1700; closed Feb. Lane's granite house and studio stand on a stone outcrop with a commanding view of the harbour.

Rocky Neck Art Colony, the oldest working artists' colony in the USA, sits directly across the harbour on a knob of land with a near 360-degree view of sky and water. The Neck retains a bohemian quality, and painters working on their decks or along narrow streets encourage curious visitors.

Gloucester's dramatic seascape also attracted millionaires. Inspired by European journeys, inventor John

BOAT TOURS

From Gloucester's busy fishing pier you can take a $1 Harbour Water Shuttle to Rocky Neck or to island beaches, or just enjoy the ride, 1100–1700 (June–Sept). Whale Watch Cruises $$$ carry naturalists on board and sometimes gather research data during cruises, Apr–Oct (reservations suggested). Yankee Fleet Whale Watch, 75 Essex St; tel: (978) 283-0313. Cape Ann Whale Watch, Rose's Wharf (near Rte 128); tel: (978) 283-5110. Captain Bill's Whale Watch, Harbor Loop (off Rogers St); tel: (978) 283-6995.

FESTIVALS AND PAGEANTRY

The Gloucester Stage Company presents plays with local colour; 267 E. Main St; tel: (978) 281-4099. Saint Peter's Fiesta takes place over four days in late June to honour the patron saint of fishermen: tel: (978) 283-1601. The Schooner Festival is a three-day regatta in early Sept: tel: (978) 283-1601.

Hays Hammond Jr built **Hammond Castle**, a medieval-style estate to house his collection of early Roman, medieval and Renaissance artefacts; $ 80 Hesperus Ave; open 1000–1700 (June–Oct). **Beauport**, also known as the Sleeper-McCann Mansion, is another fantasy house, where a theme from literature or history defines the decor in each of the 26 rooms. $ 75 Eastern Pt Blvd; open Mon–Fri 1000–1600 (mid May–mid Oct).

Because Gloucester lies just 15 miles from important whale feeding grounds, it is one of New England's best places for whale-watching cruises. Most operators guarantee whale sightings, usually of humpbacks and finbacks, but occasionally of northern right whales, of which only 300 remain.

TIC Cape Ann Chamber of Commerce Information Center, 33 Commercial St; tel: (800) 321-0133 or (978) 283-1601; cape-ann.com/cacc offers regional information and has menus from area restaurants.

TIC Gloucester Visitors Welcoming Center, Stage Fort Park, Hough Ave; tel: (978) 281-8865.

Cape Ann Motor Inn $$ 33 Rockport Rd; tel: (978) 281-2900. Well-run motel with some self-catering units.

The Rudder $–$$ Rocky Neck; tel: (978) 283-7967. A little rowdy in high season, with good traditional seafood dishes.

McT's Lobster House and Tavern $$ 25 Rogers St; tel: (978) 282-0950. Set amid the fish docks, serves simple preparations of exceedingly fresh catch.

ROCKPORT

Every artist in town (and there are plenty of them) seems to have painted at least one canvas of the fishing shack on Bradley Wharf, aptly named Motif No. 1. The main activity in town is browsing in the galleries, boutiques and souvenir shops crammed onto Bearskin Neck, a rocky peninsula enclosing Rockport harbour. For the best, however, climb to the Rockport Art Association, 12 Main St, open Mon–Sat 1000–1700, Sun 1200–1700, and the surrounding Main St galleries.

Rockport once supplied building granite for the entire Atlantic seaboard, and the quarries create a scenic foreground to sea views at **Halibut Point State Park**, a 54-acre reserve at the northern tip of Cape Ann. Picnic and walk trails border the ocean, one exploring a quarry: $ open dawn–2000 (Apr–Oct).

TIC Rockport Chamber of Commerce, Upper Main St; tel: (978) 546-6575.

Bearskin Neck Motor Lodge $$–$$$ 74 South Rd; tel: (978) 546-6677. Modest eight-room motel near shops and restaurants with fine ocean views.
Inn on Cove Hill $$–$$$, 37 Mt Pleasant St; tel: (978) 546-2701. A 1791 house close to beach and Bearskin Neck.

Rockport is a 'dry' town, so bring beer or wine (available in Gloucester) when you dine out.
Peg Leg Restaurant $–$$ Beach St; tel: (978) 546-3038. Old favourite dishes with a creative touch; don't miss the chowders.
Harbor Grille $$ 8 Old Harbor Rd; tel: (978) 546-3030, Bearskin Neck seawall. Try a bucket of peel-and-eat shrimps followed by seafood stew or lobster roll.

SALEM

The witchcraft trials of the 1690s can easily overshadow Salem's real claim to immortality: its 1790–1830 period as the New World's capital of the China Trade. Guided tours by rangers of the Salem National Historic Site bring to life the era when the riches of the Orient spilled onto Salem's wharves.

The astonishing collections of the **Peabody Essex Museum** vividly capture life at sea and the lands the seafarers explored. Curios from their trips formed the basis of the Peabodys' 100,000-object collection, including the world's most extensive in Asian export art. The Essex Institute branch complements this global view in galleries brimming with Salem's fine 17th- and 18th-century cabinetry. Three house museums in the grounds reflect Salem's expanding domestic wealth between 1684 and 1805. If you see nothing else in Salem, see this museum complex. $$ East India Sq., 132 and 162 Essex St; tel: (978) 745-9500. Open Mon–Sat 1000–1700, Sun 1200–1700 (Nov–late May closed Mon).

Stroll north to the 9-acre **Salem Common**, with bandstand, 19th-century cast-iron fence and leafy arcade. The houses at 74, 82 and 92 Washington St E. are associated with Samuel McIntire, Salem's self-taught master architect of the early 19th century. Chestnut St is lined with merchants' and sea captains' mansions designed or inspired by McIntire.

At the harbour stands the **House of Seven Gables**, inspiration for Nathaniel Hawthorne's second novel. The grounds include striking seaside gardens and the author's modest birthplace. $$ 54 Turner St; open daily 0930–1800 (July–Oct); 1000–1630 (Nov–June).

Haunted Happenings, tel: (800) 777-6848, celebrates Hallowe'en throughout October with candlelight tours, haunted houses and psychic fairs.

The witch trials, however shameful, are still a lucrative draw, 'inspiring' many made-for-tourist sites. The **Salem Witch Museum** features histrionic narration in darkness punctuated by suddenly lit dioramas: $ Washington Sq.; open daily 1000–1900 (July–Aug), 1000–1700 (Sept–June). The **Witch Dungeon Museum** dramatises transcripts from a trial and has recreated a dungeon: $ 16 Lynde St; open daily 1000–1700 (Apr–Nov). By contrast, the tasteful and reflective **Salem Witch Trial Memorial** stands on New Liberty St next to the old cemetery.

TIC Salem National Historic Site Visitors Center, 193 Derby St; tel: (978) 740-1660; open daily 0900-1700. Guided tours $.

The Hawthorne Hotel $$–$$$ Salem Common; tel: (800) SAY-STAY or (978) 744-4080. Member of Historic Hotels of America, well located for touring.
Inn at Seven Winter Street $$$ 7 Winter St; tel: (978) 745-9520. An 1870s Empire-style B&B decorated with period furnishings.

Derby Fish and Lobster $–$$ 215 Derby St; tel: (978) 745-2064. Fresh fish, at the counter or with table service.
Grapevine Restaurant $$ 26 Congress St; tel: (978) 745-9335. Stylish trattoria specialising in seafood.
Lyceum Bar and Grill $$ 43 Church St; tel: (978) 745-7665. Casual bar and more formal restaurant, both in dark wood and white linens; stylish updates to classic dishes.

NEWBURYPORT

The three-storey mansions crowned with cupolas in the **High St** attest to the wealth of Newburyport's 18th-century ship owners. Elegant cornices, doorways and windows carved by ships' carpenters place this district among the nation's finest examples of Federal architecture. Downtown Newburyport was built of red brick that came as ballast in ships from Asia. Cargo from later European trade was registered at the granite Custom House, now the **Maritime Museum**, where exhibitions evoke the town's overseas trade days. $ 25 Water St; open Mon–Sat 1000–1600 (closed Wed pm Nov–May), Sun. 1300–1600.

BOAT TRIPS

Yankee Clipper Harbor Tours $$, Waterfront Park; tel: (888) 975-1842; 45-min tours 1100–1830 (May–Oct), sunset cruises 1830.

Capt. Lew Deepsea Fishing $$$, 54 Merrimac St; tel: (888) 234-3530 or (978) 465-3530; all-day trips Apr–Oct.

Newburyport Whale Watch $$$, 54 Merrimac St; tel: (978) 465-7165 or (800) 848-1111; daily 0830 and 1330 (July–Aug), Mon–Fri 1000 Sat–Sun 0830 and 1330 (June and Sept), shorter schedule May and Oct.

On Merrimac, Water and State Sts are boutiques and antiques shops and nearby Waterfront Park has summer concerts and fireworks. A boardwalk provides a vantage point to watch boats on the river; and you can also board a cruise here.

TIC Greater Newburyport Chamber of Commerce, 29 State St; tel: (978) 462-6680.

Beginning on the last Saturday in July is the Yankee Homecoming, nine days of parade, concerts, fireworks, craft exhibitions and food; tel: (978) 462-6680.

Newburyport is the gateway to **Plum Island's Parker River National Wildlife Refuge**, 4662 acres of sand beach and dunes, bogs and tidal marshes, among North America's top ten bird-watching sanctuaries: $ Plum Island Turnpike; open daily sunrise–sunset.

Places to stay are scarce here, especially in budget range.
Clark Currier Inn $$$ 45 Green St; tel: (978) 465-8363. Antiques-filled rooms in a shipwright-built 1803 home.
The Windsor House $$$ 38 Federal St; tel: (888) TRELAWNY or (978) 462-3778. An 18th-century brick Federal mansion, with a British innkeeper.

The Bayou $–$$ 50 State St; tel: (978) 499-0428. Spicy Creole and southern cooking, local seafoods.
Glenn's Restaurant $$ 44 Merrimac St; tel: (978) 465-3811. Bistro with fresh fish and lively bar.

WHERE NEXT?

Buses from Newburyport continue north to Portsmouth, New Hampshire, another fine Colonial seaport and gateway to the rugged Maine coast *(see p. 128)**.*

Boston – Cape Cod by Car

Route Detail

From Boston go south on Rte 3, sidetracking into Plymouth. Continue on to the Sagamore Bridge — 50 miles

At the roundabout across the bridge, look for Rte 6A to Sandwich, 1 mile east, and continue through to Dennis and Brewster — 74 miles

Drive on to Orleans, where you join Rte 6, passing entrances to Cape Cod National Seashore Park on the way to Provincetown — 113 miles

Backtrack on Rte 6 to Orleans and follow Rte 28 south to Chatham — 157 miles

Keep going east to Hyannis — 180 miles

a southward turn on any major street will bring you to views of Nantucket Sound. Continue on Rte 28 to Falmouth, going to the town's southernmost point in Woods Hole — 205 miles

Return to Rte 28, bearing left on to Rte 28A, and later rejoin Rte 28 to Bourne — 221 miles

Cross Bourne Bridge, making an immediate right on the other side to follow Rte 6 north along the canal and rejoin Rte 3 to Boston — 276 miles

Notes

This area is well served by public transport. The Plymouth and Brockton Street Railway Co. (508) 746 0378, Bonanza Bus Lines (401) 331 7500 both operate regular bus services to the major towns and cities. The Massachusetts Bay Transportation Authority run trains to Plymouth.

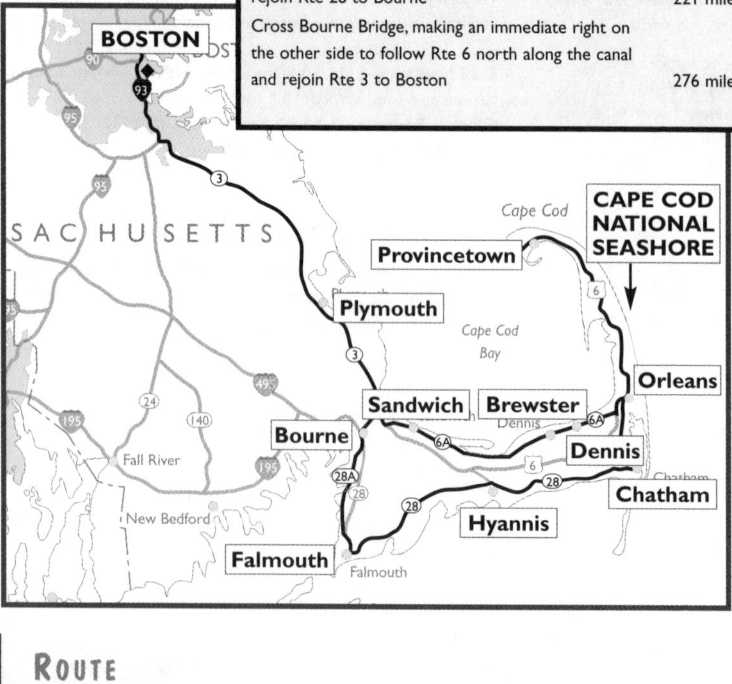

The Cape's beaches – the finest in the north-east – attract millions of summer visitors, getting far more attention than the many quiet towns, fine museums and inland natural areas. Much of the long arm of the Cape remains almost unvisited, a landscape of windswept dunes and relentless surf, or of tranquil farmland dotted with windmills. The Cape Cod National Seashore protects miles and miles of deserted shore and duneland, worlds away from the non-stop partying, dining and shopping of the holiday centres.

Driving is easy, with no mountain roads, but traffic snarls can be tedious, bordering on maddening, on Friday evenings and Sunday afternoons in summer. The two bridges over the Cape Cod Canal, at Sagamore (Rte 6) on the east and Bourne (Rte 28) on the west, are unavoidable bottlenecks.

For information on Provincetown and the islands of Nantucket and Martha's Vineyard, see pp. 122–127.

PLYMOUTH

In the American pantheon, the Pilgrims are right up there with George Washington. This grim lot of fervent religious dissidents crossed the Atlantic aboard the crowded *Mayflower* and established Plymouth – the first permanent English settlement between Newfoundland and Virginia.

Sites recalling Pilgrim endurance are close together in this handsome town. On Water St, a portico shelters **Plymouth Rock**, the supposed stepping stone where the newcomers clambered ashore. More accurate is *Mayflower II*, a faithful replica of the original three-masted barque, which actually followed its transatlantic course in 1954; State Pier, off Water St; tel: (508) 746-1622; open daily 0900–1900 (July–Aug); Thur–Sat 1000–1530 (June and Sept–mid Oct). Pilgrim Hall Museum houses Pilgrim portraits, furniture, maps, humble clothing and personal goods; $ 75 Court St; tel: (508) 746-1620; open daily 0930–1630 Feb–Dec.

The Plymouth Rock Trolley Company runs narrated tours ($) that include south-of-town **Plimouth Plantation**; tel: (508) 747-3419. This is a recreated 1627 village where 'Pilgrims' cook, harvest, tend livestock, make candles and speak with visitors in Elizabethan dialect. A Wampanoag campsite demonstrates Native American life at the time. $$$ Rte 3A; tel: (508) 746-1622; open daily 0900–1700 Apr–Nov.

i **Plymouth Visitor Information**, 130 Water St; tel: (800) 872-1620 or (508) 747-7525.

Cape Cod Chamber of Commerce and Visitor Bureau,
junction of Rtes 6 and 132, Hyannis; tel: (888) 332-2732 or (508) 362-3225. Offers information for the entire Cape.

Governor Bradford Motor Inn $$$ 98 Water St; tel: (800) 332-1620 or (508) 246-6200; fax: (508) 747-3032. Overlooks Plymouth harbour, close to *Mayflower II*.
John Carver Inn $$$ 25 Summer St; tel: (800) 274-1620 or (508) 746-7100; fax: (508) 746-8299. Central, with an indoor pool.

For seafood, choose among these waterfront eateries:
Seafood Market & Restaurant $$ Town Pier.
Weathervane $$–$$$ 6 Town Wharf; tel: (508) 746-4195.
Isaac's $$$ 114 Water St; tel: (508) 830-0001.

SANDWICH

The first in a row of placid communities strung along the Old King's Highway, Rte 6A, Sandwich overlooks Cape Cod Bay. History lines its streets in the form of 18th- and early 19th-century houses (many converted to B&Bs) and antiques shops. **The Sandwich Glass Museum** chronicles the pressed glass industry that flourished here 1828–88; $ 129 Main St; open daily 0900–1700 (Apr–Oct); Wed–Sun 0930–1600 (Nov, Dec, Feb, Mar). The charming **Thornton Burgess Museum** features a collection of the author's children's books and original illustrations; $ 4 Water St; open Mon–Sat 1000–1600, Sun 1300–1600.

For Free

Cranberry World explains growing and harvesting the area's cash crop. 225 Water St; tel: (508) 747-2350; open daily 0930–1700 May–Nov.

Shady Nook Inn and Motel $$–$$$ 14 Old Kings Hwy (Rte 6A); tel: (508) 888-0409. Set in terraced rock gardens; heated pool, free movies.
Belfry Inne $$$ 8 Jarves St; tel: (508) 888-8550. A Victorian 'painted lady' with balconies, fireplaces, and a lot of character.
Wingscorton Farm Inn $$$ 11 Wing Blvd, E Sandwich; tel: (508) 888-0534. An unusual opportunity to stay in the 1758 farmhouse of a working farm.

Beehive Tavern $ 406 Rte 6A; tel: (508) 833-1184. Friendly, fun and frugal, possibly the best food value on the Cape. Lobster pie is a speciality, as is their ice cream.
Genesis $$ 8 Jarves St; tel: (508) 888-8550. Intimate, with an eclectic menu.

Baseball

Aficionados cite the semi-professional Cape Cod League as the purest surviving example of the all-American game. The schedule is posted in the *Cape Cod Times*; admission free.

DENNIS AND BREWSTER

Along with sea captains' homes, Dennis has the **Cape Museum of Fine Arts**, showing works by local artists; $ Main St ; open Tues–Sat 1000–1700, Sun 1300–1700.

Cape Cod Playhouse, in Main St, is the last of the summer stock venues; tel: (508) 385-3911.

Almost at the geographic centre of Cape Cod, Brewster makes good use of its sedate landscape with the **Cape Cod Museum of Natural History**. Activities target children, but the 82-acre site contains three self-guided nature trails. $ Rte 6A; open Mon–Sat 0930–1630, Sun 1230–1630. For more wide-ranging roaming, the 2000 acres of **Nickerson State Park** are dotted with glacial ponds and covered with trails.

Nickerson State Park has the Cape's most popular tent and caravan (RV) pitches; tel: (508) 896-3491; camping reservations: tel: (508) 896-4615.
Michael's Cottages $$–$$$ 618 Main St, Brewster; tel: (508) 896-4025. Rooms and self-catering cottages.
Isaiah Hall B&B $$$ 152 Whig St, West Dennis; tel: (508) 385-9928 or (800) 736-0160. Relaxed 11-room inn with congenial common areas.

Cobie's $ 3260 Main St, Brewster; tel: (508) 896-7021. Fried clams, lobster and crab rolls, ice cream at picnic tables or to take away, 1100–2100 daily, May–Aug.
Gina's $–$$ 134 Taunton Ave, Dennis; tel: (508) 385-3213. Casual and family-friendly place for Italian and seafood.
Marina's Eatery $–$$$ 67 Thad Ellis Rd, Brewster; tel: (508) 896-4457. Hearty Greek food, open for three meals daily in summer, dinner for the rest of the year.

CAPE COD NATIONAL SEASHORE

Almost 45,000 acres of fragile dunes, fertile marshes, woodlands, pine barrens, cranberry bogs and long sandy beaches stretch between Chatham and Provincetown. Ranger-led programmes explore varied ecosystems, but no explanation is required to enjoy the beaches, which include Coast Guard Beach (excellent surfing), Nauset Light Beach (good surfing and surf-casting), Head of the Meadow Beach (views of dunelands), Race Point Beach (spectacular dunes and fine swimming) and Herring Cove Beach, which has the calmest waters and faces west into the sunset. Lifeguards are posted late June–early Sept. Watch for heavy surf and rip tides. Admission is free; beach parking lots $$.

Cape Cod National Seashore Salt Pond Visitor Center, Rte 6, Eastham; tel: (508) 255-3421; open dawn to dusk, mid Mar–Dec. **Provincelands Visitor Center**, Rte 6, Provincetown; tel: (508) 487-1256; open dawn–dusk, late May–early Sept.

Linnell Landing Beach, across Rte 6A from the park, is one of Brewster's best beaches, and has access for people with disabilities.

Hostelling International – Mid Capee $ 75 Goody Hallet Dr., Eastham; tel: (508) 255-2785; open mid May–mid Sept. Close to National Seashore Visitor Center and Cape Cod cycle path.

Hostelling International – Truro $ North Pamet Rd, Truro; tel: (508) 349-3889, open late June–early Sept. Within the National Seashore, close to Plymouth and Brocton bus stop at Truro.

CHATHAM

Retaining its quiet small-town air, Chatham blends old-money gentility with a working fishing industry. Art galleries and boutiques dominate the village, and its shell fishermen harvest some of the world's finest clams, oysters and mussels, which you can buy at the docks. The **Old Atwood House Museum** details local history and displays provocative murals by Alice Stallknect depicting Christ as a modern fisherman; $ 347 Stage Harbor Rd; open Tues–Fri 1300–1600 (mid June–Sept).

Sheltered Oyster Pond Beach, a block off Main St, is superb for small children, and the long strand of **Chatham Light Beach** is reached from the lighthouse parking lot. For birdwatchers, Massachusetts Audubon Society, tel: (508) 349-2615, and the Cape Cod Museum of Natural History, tel: (508) 896-3867, operate tours of **South Monomoy Island**, a barrier island bird sanctuary ($$$).

The best way to explore the marsh near Nauset Beach is by canoe or kayak; both can be hired from Goose Hummock Shop $$$ 15 Rte 6A, Orleans; tel: (508) 255-0455.

Chatham Chamber of Commerce Info Booth, 533 Main St; tel: (800) 715-5567 and (508) 945-5199.

Chatham Wayside Inn $$$ 512 Main St; tel: (800) 391-5734 or (508) 945-5550. Convenient for restaurants and shops in the village centre.

Port Fortune Inn $$$ 201 Main St; tel: (800) 850-0792 or (508) 945-0792. A recently renovated B&B near Chatham Light.

Budget lodging is hard to find in Chatham, so try along the southern shore too.

Campers Haven $ 184 Old Wharf Rd, Dennisport; tel: (508) 398-2811. A 265-pitch campsite with private beach on Nantucket Sound.

Town and Country Motor Lodge $$ 452 Main St, Rte 28, W. Yarmouth; tel: (800) 992-2340 or (508) 771-0212. About 5 miles from the beach, with pools, sauna and putting green.

Edgewater Beach Resort $$–$$$ 95 Chase Ave, Dennisport, tel: (508) 398-6922. Motel complex on private beach with indoor and outdoor pools, fitness centre and family-sized rooms with kitchens.

Sea in the Rough $–$$ Rte 28; tel: (508) 945-1700. Casual spot to sample Chatham shellfish.
Impudent Oyster $$ 15 Chatham Bars Ave; tel: (508) 945-3545. Fresh fish and cold draught beer.

FOR FREE

During July and Aug, Fri evening band concerts are held in Kate Gould Park, tel: (508) 945-5199 – best enjoyed with chocolate-covered cranberries from Chatham Candies on Main St.

FALMOUTH

Falmouth is a busy harbour, with a village green ringed by fine homes. Julia Wood House, built in 1790, is filled with Federal furniture and sailor art, with a barn of old farm implements. $ open Wed–Sun 1400–1700 (mid June–mid Sept). The boxwood-bordered garden, free, is best in May for azaleas and June for roses.

Falmouth's history is tied to the sea. The Historical Museum in picturesque Woods Hole has a small-boat museum; Woods Hole Rd; open Tues–Sat 1000–1600 (mid June–mid Sept), and conducts walking tours of the village on Tues at 1600, free. The Oceanographic Institute at Woods Hole focuses on underwater research; $ 15 Market St; open Tues–Sat 1000–1630, Sun 1200–1630 (Apr–Oct), while the National Marine Fisheries Service Aquarium eschews high tech in favour of educational exhibits of local fish. Albatross St; open Mon–Fri 1000–1600 (daily mid June–mid Sept). You can watch seals in a pool even when the aquarium is closed.

Falmouth Chamber of Commerce, 20 Academy Lane; tel: (800) 526-8532 or (508) 548-8500. Provides an excellent brochure, *A Walk Through Falmouth History*.

Admiralty Inn $$–$$$ 51 Teaticket Hwy (Rte 28); tel: (508) 548-4240 or (800) 341-5700. Motel-style, close to town centre rather than the beach.
Park Beach Ocean Front Motel $$–$$$ 241 Grand Ave S.; tel: (800) 341-5700 or (508) 548-1010. Two-storey motel at Falmouth Heights beach.
Palmer House Inn $$$ 81 Palmer Ave; tel: (800) 472-2632 or (508) 548-1230. Filled with Victorian frills in village centre.

The Quarterdeck $–$$, 164 Main St; tel: (508) 548-9900. Friendly, lively place with outstanding lunch and dinner menu.
Fishmonger Café $$ 56 Water St, Woods Hole; tel: (508) 548-9148. Creative, mostly seafood meals three times daily except Mon.

SAILING ON NANTUCKET SOUND

Cruises and fishing trips leave from Falmouth's busy harbour, the most interesting of them the sailing schooner *Liberte*; tel: (508) 548-2626 or (in Massachusetts) (800) 734-0088.

WHERE NEXT?

From Woods Hole you can take a ferry to Martha's Vineyard and thence to Nantucket (see p. 125); from the Bourne Bridge you can head south along the shore to Providence and Newport, Rhode Island (see p. 103).

Cape Cod and the Islands

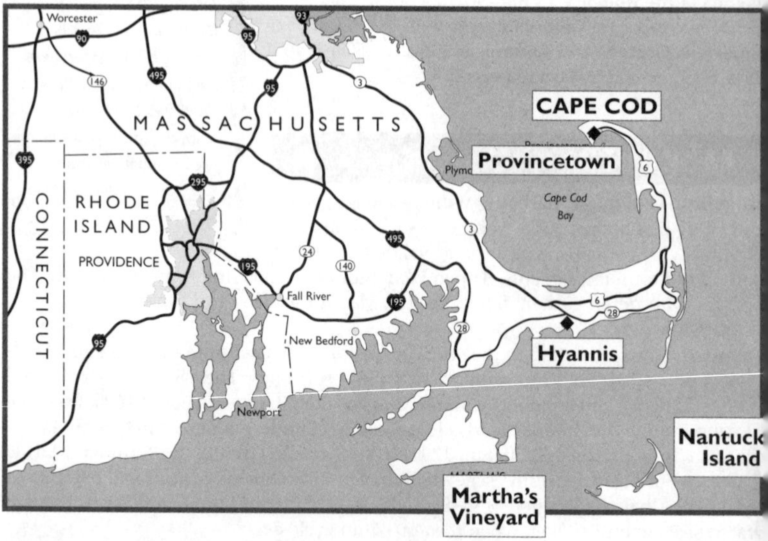

BOSTON–WOODS HOLE
OTT TABLE 522A

TRANSPORT	FREQUENCY	JOURNEY TIME
Bus	8 Daily	1hr 35mins

Note: Most buses start and finish at Logan Airport and there are extra buses Monday to Friday.

NEW YORK–HYANNIS
OTT TABLE 522

TRANSPORT	FREQUENCY	JOURNEY TIME
Bus	6 Daily	5 hr 50mins

Note: New York buses connect with Woods Hole service at Bourne.

BOSTON–PROVINCETOWN
OTT TABLE 455

TRANSPORT	FREQUENCY	JOURNEY TIME
Boat	Daily	3 hrs

BOSTON–HYANNIS
OTT TABLE 315

TRANSPORT	FREQUENCY	JOURNEY TIME
Bus	15 Daily	1hr 35 mins

Note: Most services go via Logan airport. Additional services Monday to Friday.

HYANNIS–PROVINCETOWN
OTT TABLE 315

TRANSPORT	FREQUENCY	JOURNEY TIME
Bus	2 Daily	1hr 30mins

WOODS HOLE–MARTHA'S VINEYARD
OTT TABLE 451

TRANSPORT	FREQUENCY	JOURNEY TIME
Boat	12–28 Daily	45mins

HYANNIS–NANTUCKET
OTT TABLE 451

TRANSPORT	FREQUENCY	JOURNEY TIME
Boat	20	1hr

Note: Some services take up to 2hrs. Fewer sailings in the winter.

While public transport doesn't allow travellers to wander into remote areas of the Cape, it does an exceptionally good job connecting major centres and getting visitors from Boston to Provincetown and the islands. Take your choice of plane, ferry or bus, and pay according to the speed.

Provincetown is the most swinging town on otherwise sedate Cape Cod; it is also one of America's acknowledged gay capitals. Ringed with beaches for daytime sunning, 'P'town' comes to life at night, as bronzed bodies make their way between bars, clubs and performance venues in one of New England's hottest music scenes.

Nantucket and Martha's Vineyard, by contrast, exude the aura of old money, with a healthy overlay of shiny new yuppy wealth. Don't expect bargains in either place, but do expect a pleasant, genteel atmosphere where open space is prized and protected, and where a bicycle travels at just the right speed.

PROVINCETOWN

Isolated on a narrow spit of sand at the tip of Cape Cod, Provincetown is the cape's most dynamic town. Mingling an art colony, a Portuguese fishing village and a gay and lesbian resort may seem impossible, but it works here. The town is compact, easy to get around and easy-going, although packed with people in midsummer. Everyone walks or rides a bicycle. If New Orleans is 'The Big Easy', P'town is certainly 'The Little Easy'.

No matter how you arrive, getting to your lodgings will be easy: you can walk or take a shuttle bus. If you arrive after the bus season (July–Aug), a taxi, tel: (508) 487-2222 will take you the short distance.

PEDAL OR PADDLE

Provincetown Bikes at 42 Bradford St and 306 Commercial St; tel: (508) 487-8294, rents good broad-tyred bikes that work well in sand. Arnold's, 329 Commercial St; tel: (508) 487-0844, also rents bikes.

Flyer's Boat Rental, 131-A Commercial St; tel: (508) 487-0898 or (800) 750-0898, near the Coast Guard wharf, has watercraft for hire, including Sunfish, powered skiffs and plastic sea kayaks, perfect along the harbour, beaches and for exploring the shore.

Beaches are what bring most people to P'town. **Race Point Beach** is the favourite, but within walking distance of town is more crowded **Herring Cove Beach**. Beachcombers and bird-watchers catch a water shuttle from Flyer's Boat Rental to Long Point Lighthouse or walk, following Commercial St and the stone breakwater. Nearby **Wellfleet Bay Wildlife Sanctuary** also draws birdwatchers; tel: (508) 349-2615; trails $ open daily 0800–dusk; visitor centre open Tues– Sun 0830–1700. Self-guiding nature trails wind through Cape Cod National Seashore (see p. 120).

In late June, the Annual Portuguese Festival includes food, music, dancing and the Blessing of the Fleet; tel: (508) 487-3424.

The other draw is art galleries, which line Commercial St, along with music in bars and clubs. Top performers and artists gravitate here, and **Provincetown Art Association** has an outstanding collection of work by some of America's leading artists, including Edward Hopper, who painted the outer Cape; $ 460 Commercial St; tel: (508) 487-1750; open daily 1200–1700 and 2000–2200 (June–mid Sept); Sat–Sun 1200–1600 (Nov–Apr). **Provincetown Heritage Museum** covers everything from fine furniture makers to Grand Banks schooners; $ 356 Commercial St; open daily 1000–1800.

Several companies run tours with a difference. **Willy's Air Tour** combines a dramatic perspective with a rare chance to fly in a 1930 Stinson Detroiter. $$$ Provincetown Municipal Airport; reservations tel: (508) 487-0240. **Art's Dune Tours** $$, Standish and Commercial Sts; tel: (508) 487-1950, are the best way to tour the fragile dunes; book sunset tours early. **Dolphin Fleet of Provincetown** $$$, tel: (508) 349-1900, operates whale-watching boats staffed by naturalists.

Wellfleet Drive-In Flea Market, Rte 6A; tel: (508) 349-2520, is Cape Cod's largest flea market. Open Sat–Sun (mid Apr–Sept); also Wed–Thur (July–Aug).

Provincetown Chamber of Commerce, 307 Commercial St; tel: (508) 487-3424; fax: (508) 487-8966; www.ptownchamber.com; e-mail: info@ptownchamber.com.

Outermost Hostel $$ Monument Hill; tel: (508) 487-4378. A cottage colony with common kitchen, open May–Oct.
The Commons $$–$$$ 386 Commercial St; tel: (508)487-7800 or (800) 487-0784. Individually decorated rooms surrounding a garden.
Surfside Inn $$–$$$$ 543 Commercial St; tel: (508) 487-1726. Motor inn with private beach, outside town centre.
Beaconlight Guesthouse $$$ 12 Winthrop St; tel: (800) 696-9603 or (508) 487-9603. Country-house atmosphere created by transplanted Brits.

The Boatslip $$–$$$ 161 Commercial St; tel: (508) 487-2509. Three meals daily July–Aug, dinner Sept–June; inspired by cuisines from Moroccan to Yankee.
Commons Bistro $$–$$$ 386 Commercial St; tel: (508) 487-7800. Creative New American menu with chicken, meats, seafood, pizzas and vegetarian dishes.

Dancing Lobster $$–$$$ 463 Commercial St; tel: (508) 487-0900. One of the best for fish.
The Moors $$–$$$ Bradford St Ext; tel: (508) 487-0840. Portuguese flavours influence the seafood here.

HYANNIS

This sprawling commercial centre is haunted by memories of President Kennedy. Exhibits at the modest **John F. Kennedy Hyannis Museum** include photographs taken at the nearby Kennedy compound. $ 397 Main St; open Mon–Sat 1000–1600, Sun 1300–1600 (mid Apr–midOct); shorter hours off-season. **Hyannisport Harbor Cruises**, Ocean St Dock; tel: (508) 778-2600, makes narrated hour-long tours ($$) past the Kennedy compound. The Visitor Bureau in Hyannis (see p. 118) has information on the whole Cape.

DeCota Family Inn $–$$ Rte 132; tel: (508) 362-3957. The lakefront beach makes this motel good for families.

Sam Diego's $–$$ Rte 132; tel: (508) 771-8816. Informal Tex-Mex and burger place.

NANTUCKET ISLAND

Nantucket keeps its 30-mile distance from the Cape's hubbub, and the spartan influences of Quaker whalers who made Nantucket's fortunes are still felt. The island is small enough to explore by bicycle, but dense with natural and historic sites, most in Nantucket Town. The former fishing village of Sconset is now an exclusive preserve on the east end of the island.

In Bloom

The Daffodil Festival celebrates the bloom of more than 3 million daffodils in late April; tel: (508) 228-1700.

The island layout is best appreciated from the belfry of the **First Congregational Church**, 62 Centre St; $ tower open Mon–Sat 1000–1600 (mid June–mid Oct); also Wed 1800–2000 (July–Aug). After getting your bearings, spend at least a day wandering the streets of fine old homes and rose-entwined cottages. The **Nantucket Whaling Museum** explains the enterprise that made Nantucket rich; $ Broad St; tel: (508) 228-1894; open

Getting Around

The village clusters close to the ferry wharf, with most lodgings an easy walk. Nantucket Regional Transit Authority, tel: (508) 228-7025, operates buses between villages and a seasonal beach shuttle. At Steamship Wharf, Nantucket Bike Shop, tel: (508) 228-1999, and Young's Bicycle Shop, tel: (508) 228-1151 rent bicycles.

daily 1000–1700. Enquire at the museum for admission to the many historic houses the oldest of which is **Jethro Coffin House** $, Sunset Hill, built in 1686. **Hichman House** is a museum of local flora and fauna, with a busy programme of nature walks; $ 7 Milk St; tel: (508) 228-0898.

Great Point Natural History Tours $$$, tel: (508) 228-6799, traverse the dunes and barrier beach at the north-east tip of the island in four-wheel drive vehicles.

GETTING AROUND

Yellow Line Public Bus Service, tel: (508) 693-1589, connects Vineyard Haven, Edgartown and Oak Bluffs. Martha's Bike Rentals, 4 Lagoon Point Rd, Vineyard Haven; tel: (508) 693-6593, is next to the steamship docks.

Nantucket Chamber of Commerce, 48 Main St; tel: (508) 228-1700.

All the following are in Nantucket Town. Camping is prohibited on the island.

Hostelling International $ 31 Western Ave; tel: (508) 228-0433. In a historic lifesaving station on a paved bike path opposite the beach. Open mid Apr–mid Oct, reservations essential.
Sherburne Inn $$–$$$$ 10 Gay St; tel: (508) 228-4425. In the historic district, close to ferry landing; continental breakfast included.
Quaker House Inn $$$ 5 Chestnut St; tel: (508) 228-9156. Small, simply furnished but comfortable rooms.

Café at Le Languedoc $$ 24 Broad St; tel: (508) 228-2552. Cheery bargain sibling of one of Nantucket's best French restaurants.
Straight Wharf Fish Store $$ Harbor Sq.; tel: (508) 228-1095. Outstanding takeaway lobster rolls, seafood gumbo and swordfish sandwiches.
Kendrick's $$$ 5 Chestnut St; tel: (508) 228-9156. Gives Nantucket shellfish their imaginative due.

NIGHTLIFE

Hot Tin Roof at Martha's Vineyard Airport is known for its live music.

MARTHA'S VINEYARD

Smaller than Nantucket, Martha's Vineyard has more day trippers who often don't get beyond the shops and ice cream parlours of Vineyard Haven, where the ferries dock. But the 100-square-mile island is worth exploring.
Methodists used to hold summer camps at **Oak Bluffs**, across the harbour, and more than 300 of the gingerbread-pretty cottages that superseded their original tents

are lovely to stroll among. The Flying Horses Carousel $ is one of America's oldest, and still working.

The majestic white-clapboard whaling captains' homes in **Edgartown** add historic charm to the town with the best beach access. Martha's Vineyard Preservation Society offers tours of two houses and the 1843 Old Whaling Church daily in summer, less frequently in other seasons; $ 99 Main St; tel: (508) 627-8619.

Three-mile **Katama Beach** has good surfing and many shore birds; a ferry at Dock St crosses to **Chappaquiddick Island** (of Ted Kennedy fame), where the Cape Pogue Wildlife Refuge has 2 miles of stunning beach.

At the other end of the island, **Menemsha** is the Vineyard's last working fishing village and the brightly coloured Gay Head cliffs (owned by the Aquinnah Wampanoag tribe) capture 100 million years of geological history in layers of sand, gravel and clay.

Martha's Vineyard Chamber of Commerce, Beach Rd, Vineyard Haven; tel: (508) 693-0085.

Like Nantucket, Martha's Vineyard has scarcely any budget places to stay. There is camping at Webb's Camping Area $ Barnes Rd; tel: (508) 693-0233, a wooded site 3 miles from either Vineyard Haven or Oak Bluffs.
Hostelling International $ West Tisbury; tel: (508) 693-2665; fax: (508) 693-2699.
Wesley Hotel $$ 70 Lake Ave, Oak Bluffs; tel: (508) 693-6611. Victorian resort hotel with modern annexe.
Colonial Inn $$$–$$$$ 38 N. Water St, Edgartown; tel: (508) 627-4711. Central to shopping and waterfront.
Lothrop Merry House $$$–$$$$ Owen Park, Vineyard Haven; tel: (508) 693-1646. Historic B&B with tiny private beach and boats for guests' use.

Scottish Bakehouse $ 7 State Rd, Vineyard Haven. For breakfast, lunch and tea: scones, shortbread, meat pies and breads. Closed Wed.
Larsen's Fish Market $$ Menemsha Harbor. Steamers, lobsters and mussels to order and always has chowder and crab cakes.
Nancy's $$ Oak Bluffs. Excellent fish and chips, lobster rolls and stuffed clams at picnic tables overlooking the harbour.
Seafood Shanty $$$ 31 Dock St, Edgartown; tel: (508) 627-8622. Overlooks harbour and specialises in local shellfish.

WHERE NEXT

Instead of returning to Boston, take a ferry from Martha's Vineyard to New Bedford, where a bus continues to Newport or Providence, both in Rhode Island (see p. 103).

Maine Coast

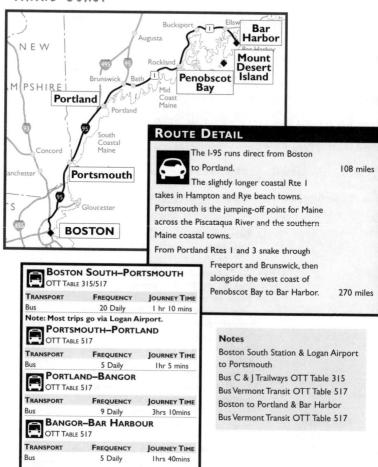

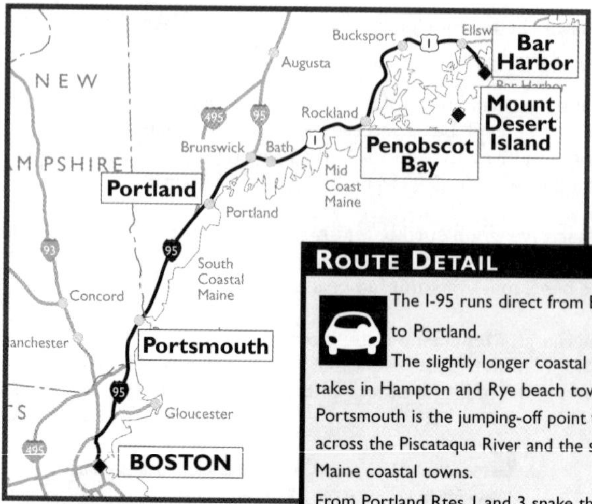

Route Detail

The I-95 runs direct from Boston to Portland. 108 miles

The slightly longer coastal Rte 1 takes in Hampton and Rye beach towns. Portsmouth is the jumping-off point for Maine across the Piscataqua River and the southern Maine coastal towns.

From Portland Rtes 1 and 3 snake through Freeport and Brunswick, then alongside the west coast of Penobscot Bay to Bar Harbor. 270 miles

Boston South–Portsmouth
OTT Table 315/517

Transport	Frequency	Journey Time
Bus	20 Daily	1 hr 10 mins

Note: Most trips go via Logan Airport.

Portsmouth–Portland
OTT Table 517

Transport	Frequency	Journey Time
Bus	5 Daily	1hr 5 mins

Portland–Bangor
OTT Table 517

Transport	Frequency	Journey Time
Bus	9 Daily	3hrs 10mins

Bangor–Bar Harbour
OTT Table 517

Transport	Frequency	Journey Time
Bus	5 Daily	1hrs 40mins

Notes

Boston South Station & Logan Airport to Portsmouth

Bus C & J Trailways OTT Table 315

Bus Vermont Transit OTT Table 517

Boston to Portland & Bar Harbor

Bus Vermont Transit OTT Table 517

This coastline is an unforgettable American composite: rocky shores with a lighthouse in the background, lobster traps stacked on a weatherbeaten dock in the foreground. To that tableau, add taciturn 'Mainers', acclimatised to whimsical weather, living in villages scarcely invaded by chainstore commercialism. Despite its splendours of ocean-side nature and pockets of architectural opulence, this is the poorest New England state, offset by admirable endurance and unspoiled simplicity.

Maine's coast measures 228 miles in linear distance, but tracing the myriad coves, inlets and bays adds up to 3478 miles of spectacular jagged shoreline. Towards the Canadian border, much of Mount Desert Island falls within Acadia National Park, with its hiking and wildlife trails, strange geological formations and dramatic scenery.

All along the Maine coast are signs pointing the way along rustic side roads that offer a dizzying choice of lobster-boat hamlets, historic seaports and artists' colonies. Out of season Maine may seem wild and remote, but in summer little seaside towns such as Ogunquit and Kennebunkport are overrun by New Yorkers, Bostonians and yachting society.

Only a car will get you to the more remote places, but buses run from Boston to Portsmouth, on the New Hampshire–Maine border, and up to Portland; in summer, they continue on to Bar Harbor on Mount Desert Island.

PORTSMOUTH

Portsmouth's long history began with original settlement in 1623 and its fervour for preservation has saved its historic architecture. Craft shops, boutiques and restaurants enliven the old harbour, and a self-guided Harbour Trail (maps available at the information kiosk on Market Sq.) points out 18th-century houses from Portsmouth's merchant and seafaring past. **Strawbery Banke**, on Puddle Dock, is where Portsmouth began, and the 10-acre site recalls 300 years of domestic life in 40 buildings $$ Marcy St; tel: (603) 433-1100. Open daily 1000–1700 (mid Apr–Oct).

i TIC Greater Portsmouth Chamber of Commerce, 500 Market St, Portsmouth, NH 03802; tel: (603) 436-1118; fax: (603) 436-5118; www.portcity.org.com. The bus drop-off point is in Market Sq.

Bow Street Inn $$$ 121 Bow St; tel: (603) 431-7760; fax: (603) 433-1680. Nine pleasant rooms in an ex-brewery overlooking the working harbour.
Inn at Strawbery Banke B&B $$$ 314 Court St; tel: (800) 428-3933 or (603) 436-7242. Spacious 19th-century inn with wraparound porch.

Seventy-five eateries are crammed into little Portsmouth.
Café Brioche $–$$ 14 Market Sq. Soups, sandwiches, French pastries, deli specials.
Portsmouth Brewery $$ 56 Market St. Varied daytime and

evening menu; serves micro-lagers and ales with offbeat names like Black Cat Stout and Weizenheimer.

SOUTH COASTAL MAINE

Old seafaring ports, ticky-tacky beach towns and upmarket summer resorts are interwoven along this stretch of 'Downeast' Maine, where rocky outcrops dip into marshlands at the ocean's edge. The Yorks and the Kennebunks are photogenically historic; Ogunquit has a lively arts scene. Stay calm: summer traffic can be slow and heavy.

York was Maine's first permanent English settlement (1624). The Old York Historical Society preserves six 17th- and 18th-century buildings as a combined museum. $$ 207 York St; tel: (207) 373-0794; open Tues–Sat 1000–1700, Sun 1300–1700 (mid June–Sept).

NUBBLE LIGHT

Seeing (and photographing) this classic beacon atop the granite bulk of Cape Neddick is worth the slight detour off Rte 1 from York Village/York Beach.

Ogunquit, Maine's most gay-tolerant resort, has clusters of galleries and boutiques downtown and at Perkins Cove. Marginal Way, a 1.2-mile clifftop footpath bordered by rose bushes, connects the cove with north-of-town beaches. The local art colony's eminence since 1900 is well represented at Ogunquit's Museum of Art $, Shore Rd; tel: (207) 646-4909. Open Mon–Sat 1030–1700, Sun 1400–1700 (July–Sept). The Oqunquit Playhouse $$$ stages summer productions; Rte 1; tel: (207) 646-2402.

Kennebunk and its oceanfront adjunct grew wealthy from 19th-century shipbuilding, hence their showpiece Colonial, Federal, Greek Revival and Victorian homes. Kennebunk's Brick Store Museum $ 117 Main St; tel: (207) 985-4802, focuses on maritime history and decorative arts. Open Tues–Sat 1000–1630 (Apr–mid Dec).

THE WEDDING CAKE HOUSE

Along Summer St (Rte 35) connecting Kennebunk and Kennebunkport, watch for a yellow and white confection, built by a sea captain whose 1826 wedding was interrupted by a call to sea duty. For his bride, the house took the place of a wedding cake.

From Kennebunk, follow the signs along very coastal Rte 9 for less commercialised **Kennebunkport** and **Old Orchard Beach**. Shops and eateries pack Kennebunkport's Dock Square area in the 'Port'. Beyond the yacht club ex-President George Bush lives the good life on Walker's Point; continue north to Cape Porpoise and Goose Rock Beach.

i TIC Kennebunk-Kennebunkport Chamber of Commerce, 17 Western Ave; tel: (207) 967-0857.

Beachmere Inn $$–$$$ 12 Beachmere Pl., Ogunquit; tel: (800) 336-3983 or (207) 646-2021; fax: (207) 646-2231. Victorian manse and modern motel with grand views; gate opens onto Marginal Way.
Fontenay Terrace Motel $$$ 128 Ocean Ave, Kennebunkport; tel: (207) 967-3556. Small motor hotel attractively situated on a tidal inlet.
York Commons Inn $$$ Rte 1, York; tel: (207) 363-8903; fax: (207) 363-1130. Ninety rooms, roadway approach to the Yorks.

Port Lobster $$ Ocean Ave, Kennebunkport. Seafood market sells takeaway lobster rolls.
Village Café $$ 226 York St, York Village. Friendly, always casual local hangout; elemental American fare.
Barnacle Billy's $$–$$$ Perkins Cove, Ogunquit. Quintessential Maine: cracking boiled lobster while seated on a deck overlooking a boat-filled cove.

EN ROUTE

Rachel Carson National Wildlife Refuge.
This haven for migratory birds totals 4800 marshy acres overlooking barrier beaches, with a mile-long interpretive trail. It was created in memory of author Rachel Carson, whose 1962 *Silent Spring* made a strong case for ecological awareness. Tel: (207) 646-9226. Open dawn–dusk.

PORTLAND

Being north-coast New England's cultural and commercial hub, this city of merely 65,000 citizens boasts more visitor amenities than many places three times its size. Far-sighted urban planning salvaged the architectural shell of Portland's Victorian-era heyday, and an influx of young professionals has reinvigorated the city centre and seaport districts. The **Old Port**, bounded by Commercial, Franklin, Congress and Union Sts, is an area of red-brick façades and cobblestone streets, rejuvenated as a shopping, dining and drinking district.

The Greyhound teminal is half a mile east of centre, at 950 Congress St.

The **Portland Museum of Art** $ 7 Congress St; tel: (207) 775-6148, has an outstanding collection of works by celebrated artists who lived in Maine, including Andrew and N. C. Wyeth, Winslow Homer, Edward Hopper and Rockwell Kent. Open Tues–Sat 1000–1700 (Thur until 2100), Sun 1200–1700. **Victoria Mansion** is over-the-top Victoriana in an 1858 Italianate villa; $ 109 Danforth St; tel: (207) 772-4841. Open Tues–Sat 1000–1600, Sun 1300–1700 (May–Oct). Danforth St leads to **Western Promenade**, a landscaped public walkway along the edge of a 175-ft high cliff in Portland's classiest neighbourhood.

South of the city (take Rte 77 across the harbour), on Cape Elizabeth rocky promontories, are Portland's much-pictured lighthouses: the 19th-century examples at **Two Lights State Park** inspired Edward Hopper paintings, and the **Portland Head Light** at Fort Williams State Park was commissioned by George Washington in 1791. There is a lighthouse museum $ in the former keeper's quarters.

Scattered over Casco Bay are the **Calendar Islands**; some are residential, others offer swimming and picnicking. Reach them from Casco Bay Lines' terminal, Commercial and Franklin St; tel: (207) 774-4871.

TIC Convention and Visitors Bureau of Greater Portland, 305 Commercial St, Portland, ME 04101; tel: (207) 772-4994; fax: (207) 874-9043; www.visitportland.com.

Portland Summer Hostel $ 645 Congress St; tel: (207) 874-3281. Super-budget accommodation (June–Aug) at University of Southern Maine's Portland Hall.
Inn at St John B&B $$$ 939 Congress St; tel: (800) 636-9127 or (207) 773-6481; fax: (207) 756-7629. Within walking distance of downtown, near the Western Promenade.
Pomegranate Inn B&B $$–$$$ 49 Neal St; tel: (800) 356-0408 or (207) 772-1006; fax: (207) 773-4426. This 1884 Italianate home and carriage house has eight guest rooms.

Portland Public Market $–$$ Preble St. A timber-ceilinged complex encloses takeaway food stands and sit-down restaurants.
Becky's Place $$ 390 Commercial St. Diner-style informality for lunch and dinner.
Dry Dock $$ 84 Commercial St. Restaurant and tavern in the popular Old Port district.
Gilbert's Chowder House $$ 92 Commercial St. This casual spot near the docks is a good bet for chowder and baked fish.
Gritty's $$ 396 Fore St. Portland's first brew pub serves English-inspired pub food.
Two Lights Lobster Shack $$ Two Lights Rd, Cape Elizabeth. Lobster, clams, shrimp, burgers; eat 'em at ocean-view picnic tables.
DiMillo's $$$ 25 Long Wharf; tel: (207) 772-2216. Harbour views from every table in a huge floating restaurant.

MID-COAST MAINE

This oceanic expanse fragments into hundreds of skinny peninsulas (Pemaquid is especially scenic) fringed by villages where lobstering, clam-digging and scallop-dragging remain primary livelihoods. At **Bath** is the Maine Maritime Museum $$,

243 Washington St; tel: (207) 443-1316, open daily 0930–1700. **Freeport** has 110 factory-outlet stores, but also L. L. Bean, the legendary outdoors outfitter, open non-stop. **Boothbay Harbor** has a small-town, seafaring charm that inspired Rodgers and Hammerstein's musical *Carousel*. Very typical, too, are **Wiscasset** and **Damariscotta**, and also **Popham**, which is the site of New England's first English colony (1606) and has a beachfront state park. Larger **Brunswick** is energised by Bowdoin College, alma mater of Nathaniel Hawthorne and Portland-born Henry Wadsworth Longfellow.

For free in Brunswick

Bowdoin's Museum of Art, Walker Art Bldg; tel: (207) 725-3275, has an international spectrum of major works; and the Peary-MacMillan Arctic Museum commemorates two Bowdoin College graduates who became North Pole explorers. Hubbard Hall; tel: (207) 725-3000. Both free-admittance museums open Tues–Sat 1000–1700, Sun 1400–1700.

Scenic side-tracking

Explore some of the slender peninsulas along this stretch of coast: the Harpswells (13 miles from Brunswick; Rte 123), Popham Beach (15 miles from Bath; Rte 209) and Boothbay Harbor (11 miles from Wiscasset; Rte 27).

TIC Bath-Brunswick Region Chamber of Commerce, 59 Pleasant St, Brunswick; tel: (207) 725-8797. **Boothbay Harbor Region Chamber of Commerce**, Boothbay Harbor; tel: (800) 266-8422 or (207) 633-2353.

Maineline Motel $$ 133 Pleasant St, Brunswick; tel: (207) 725-8761; fax: (207) 725-8300. An economical 51-room choice; town centre, close to Bowdoin College.
Admiral's Quarters Inn B&B $$$ 71 Commercial St, Boothbay Harbor; tel: (207) 633-2474; fax: (207) 633-5904. Guests staying in this renovated sea captain's house (1830) enjoy harbour-view decks.

Le Garage $$–$$$ Water St, Wiscasset; tel: (207) 882-5409. Dining room and glassed-in deck overlook the Sheepscot River.
Miss Brunswick Diner $$ 101 Pleasant St, Brunswick. For 'basic' meals plus rather surprising Tex-Mex specials.

PENOBSCOT BAY

Halfway along its length the Maine coast is split by the deep cleft of Penobscot Bay. It features some of Maine's most typical scenery. **Camden Hill State Park** has 30 miles of hiking trails, and windjammers sailing from pretty **Camden** allow you to experience the drama of the Maine coast from the sea.

Working-class **Rockland** features the Farnsworth Art Museum and Wyeth Center, with works by the Wyeths, Fitz Hugh Lane, Winslow Homer, Edward Hopper,

MAINE LOBSTER FESTIVAL

Rockland's annual bash, four days in early August, is a New England classic, with a parade, boat rides, lobster 'shore dinners' and the crowning of the Lobster Queen.

Childe Hassam and Louise Nevelson. $ 352 Main St; tel: (207) 596-6457. Open daily 0900–1700 (late May–mid Oct), Tues–Sat 1000–1700, Sun 1300–1700 rest of year. Drive or hike up Mount Battie for a stunning panorama of the town and its bowl-shaped harbour. You'll view it exactly as Edna St Vincent Millay did in 1912.

A century ago, sea captains built their Federal and Greek Revival mansions in **Belfast**, at the head of the bay. On the eastern shore rural roads pass blueberry barrens and lead to yachting and lobstering harbours. **Castine**, established in the 17th century as a fur-trading centre, has many memorials to its chequered history. The **Blue Hill peninsula** is noted for its pottery and Stonington, on Deer Isle, is the departure point for ferries to **Ile au Haut**, inhabited by shore birds and harbour seals. Isle au Haut Boat Company, Seabreeze Ave; tel: (207) 367-5193.

from *Renascence* by Edna St Vincent Millay

All I could see from where
I stood
was three long mountains
and a wood;
I turned and looked
another way
and saw three small islands
in a bay.

A ROUTE AROUND PENOBSCOT'S EAST SHORE

Two miles beyond Bucksport, take Rte 175 which meets Rte 166 and leads to Castine. Leave Castine on Rte 166 northbound, turn right onto Rte 199, then right again on Rte 175 south. After 8 miles, Rte 15 crosses the Eggemoggin Reach to Deer Isle. Back-tracking to the mainland, meet Rte 175 again for a 25-mile drive to Blue Hill.

TIC Camden-Rockport-Linconville Chamber of Commerce, Public Landing, Camden; tel: (800) 223-5459 or (207) 236-4404; fax: (207) 236-4315.

Rockland-Thomaston Area Chamber of Commerce, Harbor Park, Rockland; tel: (800) 562-2529 or (207) 596-0376.

Castine Inn $$$ Maine St, Castine; tel: (207) 326-4365; fax: (207) 326-4570. Choicest rooms in this old inn feature harbour views.

Old Granite Inn $$$ 546 Main St, Rockland; tel: (800) 386-9036 or (207) 594-9036. Non-smoking lodgings with 11 guest rooms at dockside.

Mama and Leenie's $ 27 Elm St, Camden. Bakery-café serves soups, salads, and great cookies.

Cappy's Chowder House $$ 1 Main St, Camden. The New Englandy name says it all; moosehead on the wall.

Young's Lobster Pound $$ Mitchell Ave, Belfast. Lobster fresh off the boat, then cooked to order for takeaway.

Jonathan's $$–$$$ Main St, Blue Hill; tel: (207) 374-5226. A meat and seafood restaurant among the village's antiques shops.

MOUNT DESERT ISLAND

Pronounced 'dessert' by Mainers, Mount Desert's landscape consists of deep glacial valleys and granite mountains rising straight up from the Atlantic. A road bridge crosses to the island at Ellsworth. **Bar Harbor** is the principal town to shop, stay and dine in, humanity's bustle a counterpoint to the park's serenity. Enquire about whale-watch cruises. Southwest Harbor and Bass Harbor, boat towns on the opposite shore, are less inundated with 'summer people'.

Acadia National Park $ (day use) covers nearly half the island. It has more than 120 miles of hiking trails that ascend every summit and traverse every valley. The 27-mile Park Loop Rd passes all of Acadia's better-known highlights; from it, a 3.5-mile road twists to Cadillac Mountain's 1530-ft summit for sweeping views. At Thunder Hole, tidal wave motion creates thunderclaps inside hollow rocks. An astonishing variety of life forms thrive in Otter Point's tide pools, with peregrine falcons soaring overhead.

Offshore from Southwest Harbor are a scattering of pristine islands, the Cranberries. Cranberry Cove Boating operates ferries to three of them; $$ Town Dock; tel: (207) 244-5882.

TIC Acadia National Park Visitor Center, Park Loop Rd, Hull's Cove; tel: (207) 288-3338.
Bar Harbor Chamber of Commerce, 93 Cottage St; tel: (207) 288-5103.

Bar Harbor is stuffed with some four dozen lodgings in every price niche: resorts, hotels, motels, inns, cottages, bed & breakfasts. Summertime reservations are essential. The park has two tent-pitch campsites $, Blackwoods and Sewall. Reservations required at Blackwoods; tel: (800) 365-2267.

Island Chowder House $$–$$$ 38 Cottage St. Informal, centrally located.
Jordan Pond House $$–$$$ Park Loop Rd. In the park: lunch, afternoon tea and dinner.
Maggie's Classic Scales $$–$$$ 6 Summer St. Fresh seafood; sun porch dining.
West Street Café $$$ West St. Old-fashioned restaurant offering the traditional Downeast meal of fish chowder, steamed lobster and blueberry pie.

WHERE NEXT?

The famously rocky coast continues north through Washington County's blueberry barrens, past the lighthouse at West Quoddy Head to land's end at Eastport – the easternmost US town. You can cross the Canadian border into New Brunswick province. Car ferries connect Bar Harbor with Yarmouth, Nova Scotia; Bay Ferries; tel: (888) 249-7245.

Boston – White Mountains

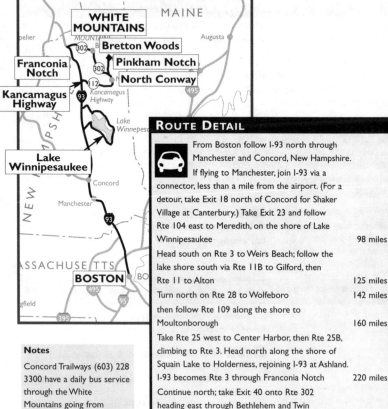

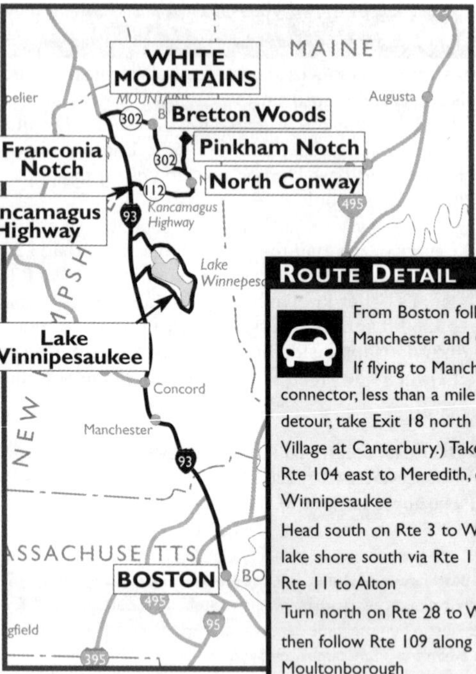

Route Detail

From Boston follow I-93 north through Manchester and Concord, New Hampshire. If flying to Manchester, join I-93 via a connector, less than a mile from the airport. (For a detour, take Exit 18 north of Concord for Shaker Village at Canterbury.) Take Exit 23 and follow Rte 104 east to Meredith, on the shore of Lake Winnipesaukee — 98 miles

Head south on Rte 3 to Weirs Beach; follow the lake shore south via Rte 11B to Gilford, then Rte 11 to Alton — 125 miles

Turn north on Rte 28 to Wolfeboro — 142 miles

then follow Rte 109 along the shore to Moultonborough — 160 miles

Take Rte 25 west to Center Harbor, then Rte 25B, climbing to Rte 3. Head north along the shore of Squain Lake to Holderness, rejoining I-93 at Ashland. I-93 becomes Rte 3 through Franconia Notch — 220 miles

Continue north; take Exit 40 onto Rte 302 heading east through Bethlehem and Twin Mountain to Bretton Woods, then south through Crawford Notch — 240 miles

(For a scenic loop from Glen, take Rte 16 north to Jackson, via a short loop on Rte 168, and Pinkham Notch. Return south through Notch, rejoining Rte 302 in Glen). Take Rte 16, which blends with Rte 302, south through North Conway, continuing through to Conway — 286 miles

Take Kancamagus Highway, Rte 112 west, returning to I-93 in North Woodstock — 324 miles

Notes

Concord Trailways (603) 228 3300 have a daily bus service through the White Mountains going from Boston to Pinkham Notch. They also have a frequent service from Boston to Concord via Manchester.

The White Mountains are the quintessence of the rugged Appalachians, reaching their highest northern elevation at Mount Washington. Grand hotels once refreshed the wealthy from the cities' summer heat, and a rare few still cater for holiday-makers, who view the mountains from their wide verandahs. On the way north, stop at a Shaker village and make a scenic detour around Lake Winnipesaukee before continuing into the heart of the White Mountains.

Take a break from driving by taking a cog railway, aerial tramway or gondola to a mountaintop for even grander views. Stop also to enjoy the outdoor pleasures of streams to fish in, rivers and lakes to canoe, waterfalls, and miles of hiking trails.

Views spread before you as you drive: row upon row of mountains, with tiny villages clustered around a white church. Expect some steep winding roads, and heavy traffic at summer weekends, especially around the shopping mecca of North Conway. Travelling in the evening or night, be wary of moose – huge creatures which have no fear of cars. In a head-on confrontation, the moose will win, so drive slowly and scan the roadsides.

LAKE WINNIPESAUKEE

Meredith borders a dock-lined lakefront with hotels, shops and eateries. At its centre, Mills Falls Marketplace, tel: (603) 279-7006, is a multi-storey complex of 18 shops, selling everything from local books to ice cream and fashionwear.

BOAT TOURS

Board the 65-foot MV *Judge Sewall*, tel: (603) 569-3016, at the Town Dock, for a narrated cruise past a loon refuge, old boatyards and several islands. MV *Sophie C* sails among Winnipesaukee's 365 islands and into secluded coves, all in a day's work for a genuine working mailboat. Day or sunset cruises are 2–3 hours; $ tel: (603) 366-5531; operates Sat–Sun (May–early June); (Sept–mid-Oct); daily (mid-June–Aug). The larger, pricier MS *Mount Washington* departs Weirs Beach for Wolfeboro, Center Harbor and Alton Bay. Evening cruises include dinner and dancing to live music; $$ tel: (603) 366-BOAT; daily, 1000 and 1230 (May–Oct); 1500 (July–Aug). Board either tour at Lakeside Ave, Weirs Beach.

Just south is **Weirs Beach**, a touristy town popular with families who flock to the water slides, wave tanks, miniature golf, bowling, kiddy rides and game arcades that seem to fill its every inch. It is port for several boat tours of the lake, for many its only redeeming feature.

Wolfeboro, on the lake's 'quiet side', is a pleasant place to stroll, with a quaint museum complex (free) of vintage buildings open on a limited schedule, and the Libby Museum, focusing on the area's natural history (native birds and animals) and a collection of local Indian artefacts; $ Main St; open Tues–Sun 1000–1600 (June–Sept).

Instead of driving around the lake, you can see its port towns and surrounding mountain scenery during a narrated boat ride.

Information Center, Dockside, Meredith; tel: (603) 279-6121; open daily May–Oct.
Wolfeboro Chamber of Commerce, 32 Central Ave; tel: (603) 569-2200 or (800) 516-5324.

Lakehurst Housekeeping Cottages $$ Rte 11-D, Alton Bay; tel: (603) 875-2492; May–June nightly, July–Sept weekly only. Well-kept lakefront cottages.
Lin-Joy Cabins $$ Robert's Cove Rd, Alton; tel: (603) 569-4973. Rustic self-catering cabins with a swimming pool.
Tuc-Me-Inn B&B $$ 118 North Main St, Wolfeboro; tel: (603) 569-5702. Comfortable, unpretentious, and downtown.

PJ's Dockside $–$$ Main St, Wolfeboro; tel: (603) 569-6747. Sandwiches, salads, lobster rolls and seafood dinners on the dock.

EN ROUTE
CANTERBURY SHAKER VILLAGE

From Canterbury Center (at Exit 18), follow brown signs east to a perfectly preserved set of 24 housing, farm and workshop buildings, now a museum perpetuating the art and ideals of the 19th-century religious sect, the Shakers. Tours not only show the buildings, but explain Shaker philosophy and daily life. $$ tel: (603) 783-9511. Open 1000–1700 daily (May–Oct); Fri–Sun (Apr, Nov–Dec). The Creamery Restaurant recreates authentic Shaker meals ($$–$$$); open daily for lunch (May–Oct); Fri–Sun (Apr, Nov–Dec); Fri–Sat 1845. Candlelight dinner $$$ by reservation only. The Summer Kitchen ($) sells snacks.

FRANCONIA NOTCH

Between the towns of North Woodstock and Franconia I-93 and Rte 3 join to become the Franconia Notch Parkway, a dual carriageway through one of the White Mountains' scenic notches. The first exit leads to the **Flume**, a natural chasm with vertical walls. A boardwalk runs through it close to river level; $$ open daily 0900–1700 (mid-May–late Oct).

The Basin is a 20-foot natural pothole at the base of a small waterfall, where melting glaciers wore away the granite with their swirling force. A short walk beyond are the sloping ledges of Kinsman Falls, a lovely series of cascades.

Notches are glacially carved passes through the mountain ranges. Low points over which roads can pass, they are characterised by their bowl-like shape, a result of the circular glacial scouring that formed them.

High above Profile Lake is New Hampshire's symbol, the 40-ft group of granite ledges forming the **Old Man of the Mountain**. A lay-by alongside the northbound lane offers clear views, or you can park at the base of the Aerial Tramway and walk down to the lake, stopping at the Old Man of the Mountain Museum, which explains the geology of the profile and its preservation; tel: (603) 823-5563; open daily 1000–1730 (June–mid-Oct).

The Aerial Tramway, one of New Hampshire's several summit lifts, begins here, carrying passengers to the 4200-ft summit of Cannon Mountain. Views extend to Canada on clear days, and trails circle the summit. $$ tel: (603) 823-5563; open daily mid-May–Oct.

White Mountain Attractions Association, Rte 112 at Exit 32 off I-93, North Woodstock; tel: (603) 645-9889 or (800) 346-3687.

Apart from camping, accommodation can be found only at either end of the State Reservation, in Thornton and North Woodstock (south) or Franconia and Sugar Hill (north).

Lafayette Campground $ Rte 3; tel: (603) 823-9513. Well-spaced tent pitches and a campers' store.

Bungay Jar $$–$$$ Easton Valley Road, Franconia 03580; (603) 823-7775. Gardens, sauna, balconies, fireplaces.

Hilltop Inn $$–$$$ Main St, Sugar Hill; tel: (603) 823-5695. B&B with well decorated, very comfortable rooms and lively hosts.

Like lodgings, dining is available outside the state reservation. Basic picnic supplies are available at Lafayette Campground.

Frannie's $–$$ Rte 3 (just south of Exit 30, I-93), Thornton; tel: (603) 745-3868. Plain decor, friendly atmosphere, very good food.

Polly's Pancake Parlor $$ Rte 117, Sugar Hill; tel: (603) 823-5575; open Mon–Fri 0700–1500, Sat–Sun 1700–1900. Serves fresh-made pancakes with real maple syrup.

Woodstock Station and Brewpub $$ 80 Main St, North Woodstock; tel: (603) 745-3951. Three meals daily, good ales.

BRETTON WOODS

The imposing **Mount Washington Hotel** is the centrepiece of this mountain valley, a last reminder of an opulent era, gleaming in meticulous restoration. Free daily tours show its historic interior, often also a water-powered print shop and Stickney Chapel, with Tiffany windows.

The **Mount Washington Cog Railway** has puffed its way up the steep mountainside to the summit since the 1860s. The very pricey 3-hr return trip allows time to explore New England's highest peak; $$$ tel: (603) 846-5406 or (800) 922-8825; operates Sat–Sun (May, daily June–late Oct); reservations suggested.

On a clear day the views from the summit of Mount Washington seem endless. The Mount Washington Observatory at the summit has clocked winds to 231 miles per hour, so hold on to your hat. To climb the mountain, wait for good weather, begin early, and take layers of warm clothing. The **Ammonoosuc Ravine Trail** begins at the Cog Railway's base station, passing a waterfall and Lake of the Clouds en route. A shorter, easier climb with a view is nearby Mount Willard, overlooking Crawford Notch's steep walls.

The Bretton Arms $$$–$$$$ Rte 302; tel: (603) 278-1000 or (800) 258-0330. In the grounds of the Mount Washington Hotel.

Top o' Quad Restaurant $$ Bretton Woods Ski Area; tel: (603) 278-5000 or (800) 232-2972. Take the chairlift or their van to dine overlooking the valley.

PINKHAM NOTCH

Rte 16 climbs from the picturesque village of Jackson, with fine views of Mount Washington, which forms its western slopes. Take the short walk to Glen Ellis Fall, dropping 65 ft through a granite cleft.

The **Pinkham Notch Visitors Center** is the headquarters of the Appalachian Mountain Club, with books, maps and information about trails, wildlife and nature, and a giant relief map of Mount Washington. Year-round programmes include nature hikes, botany, photography and travelogues, some free.

The **Mount Washington Auto Road** ($$$) is an 8-mile 12 per cent climb with breathtaking views. Drive or ride in a van. At the base are Glen House Carriage Barns (free), with vehicles that have carried passengers up the mountain since the first horse-drawn coach.

White Mountain National Forest charges $5 per vehicle for a one-week pass, currently available only in Lincoln, Conway or Pinkham Notch; tel: (603) 528-8721.

The notch is within the National Forest, without commercial ventures, so look for places to stay in Jackson (south) or Gorham (north).

Dolly Copp Campground Rte 16, Gorham; tel: (603) 466-2713.

Appalachian Mountain Club $ Rte 16, Gorham; tel: (603) 466-2727. Rustic lodging and three daily meals.

Carter Notch Inn $–$$ Carter Notch Rd, Jackson; tel: (603) 383-9630 or (800) 794-9434. B&B with great breakfasts.

Town and Country Motor Inn $$ Route 2, Gorham; (603) 466-3315. Well-kept motel with swimming pool.

Gorham House B&B $$ 55 Main St; tel: (603) 466-2271. Victorian inside and out.

Yokohama Restaurant $–$$ 288 Main St, Gorham; tel: (603) 466-2501. Asian menu, with emphasis on Japanese.
Wilfred's Turkey Dinners $$ Main St, Gorham; tel: (603) 466-2380. Turkey and other country foods.

EN ROUTE

Explore New England history at **Heritage New Hampshire**, beginning on the realistic pitching ship that brought the first settlers. Although it is designed for children, adults will enjoy the engineering of interactive displays detailing 'King's Pines', royal grants and Native Americans. $$ Rte 16, Glen; tel: (603) 383-4186; open daily 0900–1700 (mid-May–mid-Oct).

NORTH CONWAY

Shoppers' heaven, this historic resort town is also a drivers' hell on summer weekends when traffic nearly stops on Rte 16. The largest concentration of cut-price retail outlets in the north-east sells 'blems' (seconds) and overstocks, often at drastically reduced prices, even better since New Hampshire has no sales tax.

But there's more to North Conway than retail outlets and traffic. **Cathedral Ledge** rises from Echo Lake State Park, and a road leads to the top for views of the valley. The lake has a fine – although often crowded – swimming beach ($) and picnic area. **Conway Scenic Railway** $$, tel: (603) 356-5251, travels along the wide valley from the Victorian Railway Station, a free museum of vintage trains.

Mount Washington Valley Chamber of Commerce, Rte 16; tel: (603) 356-3171 or (800) 367-3364.

Fox Ridge $$ Rte 16; tel: (603) 356-3151 or (800) 343-1804. Well-decorated motel with balconies and sports facilities.
Green Granite Resort $$–$$$ Rte 16; tel: (603) 356-6901 or (800) 468-3666. Family-friendly modern hotel with pools, sauna.

WHERE NEXT?

To explore the Maine Coast (see pp. 128–135), remain on Rte 302 south of North Conway, following it eastward along Maine's Sebago Lake to Portland.

KANCAMAGUS HIGHWAY

Stretching 35 miles through National Forest from Conway to Lincoln, the road is sometimes steep and winding, but a number of lay-bys offer vistas not seen from the road. At the Conway end, Rocky Gorge and Lower Falls are popular for swimming and picnics. Shortly after a covered bridge is the trail to Sabbaday Falls, a gorge with 40-ft walls and glacial potholes.

ROUTE DETAIL

From Boston travel west on I-90, past Springfield, to Exit 2 in Lee.	107 miles
Take Rte 102 west to Stockbridge, turning north on Rte 7 to Lenox	118 miles
From Lenox, follow Rte 7, detouring to visit the Shaker Village in Hancock.	
Just north of Williamstown, cross into Vermont, continuing on Rte 7 through Bennington, and Rte 7A to Manchester	175 miles
From here take Rte 30 to Middlebury and then rejoin Rte 7 to Burlington	260 miles
From Burlington, Rte 15 leads to Jeffersonville, where Rte 108 climbs south over Smugglers Notch to Stowe	310 miles
Take Rte 100, the Skiers' Highway, south through Waterbury to Weston	395 miles
From Wilmington (43), Rte 9 leads over Hogback Mountain to Brattleboro	453 miles
From here the I-91 returns you to Springfield	500 miles
and the I-90 runs back to Boston	580 miles

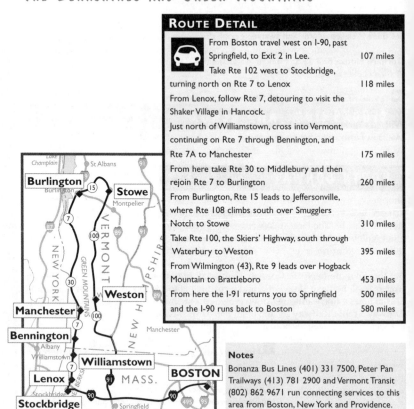

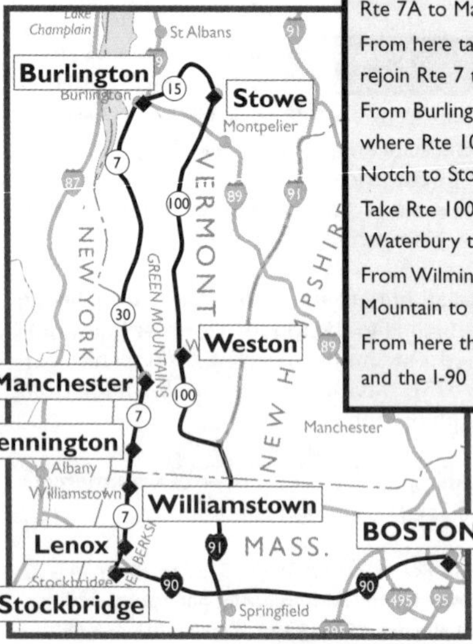

Notes

Bonanza Bus Lines (401) 331 7500, Peter Pan Trailways (413) 781 2900 and Vermont Transit (802) 862 9671 run connecting services to this area from Boston, New York and Providence.

From the manicured, gentrified Berkshires Hills in western Massachusetts to the more rustic and higher Green Mountains of Vermont, this route covers much of western New England. Wealthy New Yorkers and Bostonians 'found' the Berkshires at the end of the 19th century, building lavish summer retreats and bringing music events that still thrive a century later.

Some of Vermont's most idyllic towns lie nestled in the rolling Green Mountains, where stylish Manchester was once the darling of New York socialites. Despite these citified incursions, the Green Mountains are still filled with the elements that personify Vermont: green-clad mountains, skiing, white churches, country stores and craft studios.

Caught between the Green Mountains and huge Lake Champlain, Burlington rises from its marina to a lively downtown. Expect a steep, winding road over Smugglers Notch, but otherwise gentle gradients as you explore these hills and mountains, for which you should allow at least 4 days.

STOCKBRIDGE AND LENOX

A far cry from its Puritan origins, Stockbridge reeks of old money, its impressive Main Street homes only a hint of the sumptuous 'cottages' on its fringes. The illustrator Norman Rockwell set many of his small-town American scenes here; many are in the **Norman Rockwell Museum** $$, Rte 183; open daily 1000–1700 (May–Oct), Mon–Fri 1100–1600 (Nov–Apr).

Chesterwood was the summer estate of sculptor Daniel Chester French, best known for his Lincoln Memorial in Washington. Tours feature his house, gardens and studio, filled with drawings, casts and bronze models. $$ Williamsville Rd; open daily 1000–1700 (May–Oct).

To see how the rich summered here, visit **Naumkeag**, residence of America's ambassador to Great Britain from 1899 to 1905; it has 26 rooms filled with antiques and Chinese decorative arts. $$ Prospect Hill Rd; open daily 1000–1700 (late May–mid Oct).

Lenox is the real centre of Berkshires society, which revolves around music, theatre and dance. You'll find boutiques, restaurants and upmarket lodgings, along with more 'cottages'. Most interesting is **The Mount**, completed in 1902 for novelist Edith Wharton, who designed this estate after a Lincolnshire manor house, adding French and Italian accents. $ Plunkett St and Rte 7; tel: (413) 637-1800; open daily 0900–1500, last tour 1400 (late May–Oct).

SUMMER THEATRE AND MUSIC

The Mount's bosky grounds are the stage for Shakespeare & Company, enjoyed while picnicking on the lawn; tel: (413) 637-3353 for performance details.

Tanglewood is summer home to the Boston Symphony Orchestra, chamber music and jazz. Priciest tickets are for 'the Shed', a roofed open auditorium, but lawn tickets are more fun; bring a picnic. Tel: (413) 637-5165; performances late June–early Sept.

Berkshire Theater Festival, on Main St in Lenox, tel: (413) 298-5536, is set in a Gilded Age playhouse.

i **Stockbridge Information**, Main St, where they would as soon look straight through you as answer your question. The

EN ROUTE

Hancock Shaker Village.

A short detour off Rte 7 south of Williamstown leads to the 'City of Peace', inhabited 1790–1959 by the communal Shakers. Twenty artefact-filled buildings illustrate their ways. In the five-storey 1830 Brick Dwelling, pegs for hanging clothes, tools, chairs and brooms speak of the Shaker penchant for order. The highlight is the 1826 Round Stone Barn. $$$ Rtes 20 and 41; tel: (413) 443-0188. Open daily 0930–1700 (late May–Oct), 1000–1500 (Apr–May and Nov).

TIC Lenox Chamber of Commerce, 75 Main St; tel: (800) 255-3669 or (413) 637-3646, is much more hospitable.

Monument Mountain Motel $$ 249 Stockbridge Rd (US Rte 7), Great Barrington; tel: (413) 528-3272. Not fancy, but the in-room movies are free.
Hidden Acres $$–$$$ 35 Tremont Dr., Alford; tel: (413) 528-1028. Hidden, indeed, in the countryside near Great Barrington.
Red Lion Inn $$$–$$$$ 30 Main St; tel: (413) 298-5545. A local landmark since the 18th century. Semi-formal dining room serves traditional fare.

Cactus Café $ 54 Main St, Lee; tel: (413) 243-4300. Mexican decor and food, informal in atmosphere and service.
Theresa's Stockbridge Café $$ Main St; tel: (413) 298-5465. Refreshingly un-snooty oasis, with many vegetarian choices.
La Bruschetta $$$ 1 Harris St, West Stockbridge; tel: (413) 232-7141. Stylish and pricey, but brilliant use of local produce, cheeses and meats.

WILLIAMSTOWN

The **Sterling and Francine Clark Art Institute** puts this tidy college town on the art map with impressive collections of Renoir, Monet, Turner and Winslow Homer. $ 225 South St; tel: (413) 458-2303, open Tues–Sun 1000–1700 (Sept–June), daily 1000–1700 (July and Aug). On Main St, the **Williams College Museum of Art** complements it with modern, contemporary and non-Western art; tel: (413) 597-2429, open Tues–Sat 1000–1700, Sun 1300–1700. The annual **Theater Festival**, June–Aug, includes classics, premières and cabaret; 1000 Main St; tel: (413) 597-2429.

In the 12,500-acre **Mount Greylock State Reservation**, off Notch Rd, the mountain is laced with 45 miles of marked trails. Loops near the summit can be traversed in under an hour to see rare alpine flora and birds.

Williamstown Tourist Board, Rtes 2 and 7; tel: (413) 458-4922 or (800) 214-3799.

Bascom Lodge $–$$ Mount Greylock summit; tel: (413) 443-0011. Rustic lodge has mixed-sex bunkrooms and four private rooms.
Northside Motel $–$$ 45 North St; tel: (413) 458-8107. Convenient downtown location.

Field Farm Guest House $$–$$$ 554 Sloan Rd; tel: (413) 458-3135. Modern lodging with wild flowers and 4 miles of hiking trails.

Wild Amber Grill $$ 101 North St; tel: (413) 458-4000. Contemporary food, plus cabaret by the performers at Williamstown Theater Festival.
The Orchards $ (tea), Rte 2; tel: (413) 458-9611 or (800) 225-1517. Serves afternoon tea daily. The dining room is pricey, but superb; actor Paul Newman is often a guest here in the summer.

BENNINGTON

The 306-ft **Bennington Battle Monument** marks the turning point of the American Revolution, where General Burgoyne rethought his northward thrust. A lift to the top yields views of three states. Old Bennington is worth seeing for its fine colonial-era homes and for the **Bennington Museum**, with early American glass, pottery, quilts and primitive paintings. $ Rte 9; tel: (802) 447-1571; open daily 0900–1700 (Mar–Nov).

In North Bennington, **Park-McCullough House** is among America's earliest Second Empire homes, with a carriage barn, flower gardens and a playhouse. $ off Rte 67A, North Bennington; (802) 442-5441; open Thur–Mon (June–Oct).

Bennington Chamber of Commerce, Rte 7A; tel: (802) 447-3311.

Greenwood Lodge $ Rte 9; (802) 442-2547; open mid May–mid Oct. Mountainside hostel close to hiking trails.
Molly Stark Inn $ 1067 East Main St; tel: (802) 442-9631. Victorian inn with a homey country feel and handmade quilts.

Alldays and Onions $ 519 East Main St; open 0800–2100 Mon–Sat. Serves healthy whole-grain sandwiches and delectable pastries.
Blue Benn Diner $ Rte 7. Old-fashioned diner atmosphere, but with a modern twist to the menu.

MANCHESTER

Manchester Village's genteel gathering of impeccable large homes surround the pillared façade of the Equinox, a vintage grand hotel. Wealthy New Yorkers once summered in the mansions, including Robert Todd Lincoln's **Hildene** $, built in 1902 by Abraham Lincoln's son. Restored gardens are at their height in June and July; tel: (802) 362-1788; open daily (mid May–Oct).

The **Vermont State Craft Center**, opposite the Equinox, features works by top craftsmen in all media, from pottery and wood to weaving and art glass. Behind the hotel rises Mount Equinox, reached via the 5-mile **Mount Equinox Skyline Drive**. $$ tel: (802) 362-1113; open May–Oct.

Just north is **Manchester Center**, a succession of factory outlet malls selling cut-price brand-name clothing and home decorations.

Manchester and the Mountains Chamber of Commerce, 2 Main St, Manchester Center; tel: (802) 362-2100; www.manchestervermont.com.

Barnstead Instead $$ Rte 7A, Manchester Center; tel: (802) 362-1619, fax: (802) 362-1619. In a converted barn, a short walk from shops and restaurants.

The Inn at Ormsby Hill $$$–$$$$ Rte 7A, 1842 Main St. Manchester tel: (802) 362-1163; www.ormsbyhill.com. Antique-furnished mansion, now a classy inn with working fireplaces and full-course breakfast in a magnificent dining room.

Garlic John's $–$$ Rtes 11 and 30, Manchester Center; tel: (802) 362-9843. Casual setting where families are welcome.

BURLINGTON

Lake Champlain is part of downtown Burlington, bordered by parks, cycling/foot paths, beaches and playgrounds. **Church Street Marketplace** is alive with activity, especially in good weather, filled with sidewalk cafés, vendors and music. A free shuttle trolley connects the two.

Ten miles south, **Shelburne Museum** features folk arts: early New England quilts, roundabout horses, horse-drawn sleighs, carriages, covered bridge, and the SS *Ticonderoga* are among the 80,000 artefacts. $$ Rte 7; tel: (802) 985-3346; open daily late May–mid Oct 1000–1700, shorter winter hours.

Shelburne Farms is a 1400-acre working 'gentleman's farm' with wagon tours of gardens, historic barns, a children's farmyard where you can try milking a cow, and a dairy where cheese is made. $ Harbor Rd; tel: (802) 985-8686; tours daily 0930–1330 (June–mid Oct).

BOAT TOURS

The wooden schooner *Northern Spy* takes passengers for 2-hr sails $$, tel: (802) 343-3645; and the *Spirit of Ethan Allen II* does narrated dinner and sunset cruises $, tel: (802) 862-8300.

Lake Champlain Regional Chamber of Commerce, 60 Main St; tel: (802) 863-3489.

Look for 'Motel Row' on Rte 7 south of the city.
Mrs Farrell's Home Hostel $ (directions with reservation); tel: (802) 865-3730. Curfew 2200.
Anchorage Inn $$ 108 South Dorset St, South Burlington; tel: (802) 863-7000 or (800) 336-1869; fax: (802) 658-3351. Modern hotel with pool, sauna, breakfast included.
Burlington Redstone B&B $$ 497 So Willard St (Rte 7); tel: (802) 862-0508. Historic home within easy walking distance of downtown.

Five Spice Café $–$$ 175 Church St; tel: (802) 864-4045. Asian eclectic with New England touches.
Trattoria Delia $–$$ 152 St Paul St (City Hall Park); tel: (802) 864-5253. Unforgettable Mediterranean dining with wild game specialities.

STOWE AND SMUGGLERS NOTCH

The road over Smugglers Notch, Rte 108, is so narrow that caravans are unable to manoeuvre the sharp turns between giant boulders that line its sides. Park between them and climb a short distance for a panoramic view of Vermont, New York State and Canada. When the road closes for the winter, you can ski over the top, Alpine-style, from Smugglers Notch Ski Resort; tel: (802) 644-8851 or (800) 451-8752; www.smuggs.com.

TO THE TOP

The Gondola Skyride $, tel: (802) 253-3000, scales Mount Mansfield for sweeping views and access to hiking trails, or a 4.5-mile Auto Road $$ leads to the summit.

On the Stowe side, a short trail leads to **Bingham Falls**, one of the state's most beautiful, with potholes carved by swirling waters.

Stowe is popular year-round for shopping, restaurants and lodgings. Crafts and hand-made goods shops predominate in upmarket Main Street, where you can rent bicycles at Stowe Hardware Store, tel: (802) 253-7205, to cycle the paved 5.3-mile Stowe Recreation Path.

Stowe Area Association, Main St; tel: (800) 24-STOWE; www.stoweinfo.com.

The Gables $$–$$$ 1457 Mountain Rd; tel: (802) 253-7730 or (800) GABLES-1; www.Stoweinfo.com/saa/ gables. Warm and family-owned inn with fireplaces, whirlpool tubs and

STOWE EVENTS

At the Trapp Family Lodge the hills *are* alive with the sound of music, all summer long, when the von Trapps host Meadow Concerts (bring a picnic and watch the sunset to music). $$; performances late June–Aug. The Vermont Mozart Festival $$ takes place in late July. Tel: (800) 24-STOWE.

The Smugglers Notch Area Winter Carnival, in early February, has Nordic races, snow sculptures, food, snowshoe hikes and social events; tel: (802) 644-8851.

EN ROUTE

Vermont's favourite ice creams are made at **Ben and Jerry's Ice Cream Factory**, where you can sample this stuff everyone raves about and see it made. Tours include samples. $ Rte 100; tel: (802) 244-5641; open daily year round.

mega-breakfasts.

Green Mountain Inn $$–$$$ Main St; tel: (802) 253-7301 or (800) 253-7302; fax: (802) 253-5096; www.genghis.com. Canopy beds, whirlpool baths, afternoon cider and fresh-baked biscuits.

The restaurants at The Gables and Green Mountain Inn are both open to the public ($–$$).

Gracie's $ Main St; tel: (802) 253-8741. Big burgers, sandwiches and generous dinners until 2400 daily.

WESTON

Clustered around its village green and bandstand, Weston is home to the **Vermont Country Store**, a real original, complete with high button shoes, pot-bellied stove, and rows of penny candy jars. More than a museum, it's an emporium of carefully chosen country clothing, housewares and foods; open Mon–Sat 0900–1700. The **Weston Bowl Mill** has made wooden wares since 1902; open Mon–Sat 0900–1500, Sun 1000–1500. **Weston Playhouse** presents Broadway musicals late June–early Sept, with pre-theatre dinner and cabaret; tel: (802) 824-5288.

Colonial House Inn and Motel $ Rte 100; tel: (802) 824-6286. A homey B&B-cum-motel, with home-cooked meals and a bakery famed for peach pie.

Village Sandwich Shop $; open daily 1000–1730. Sandwiches, light meals and pastries.

WHERE NEXT?

From Brattleboro you can follow Rte 9 east, which becomes Rte 101 in Keene, NH, continuing to Manchester for the start of the White Mountains Route (see p. 136). Or you can continue on Rte 101 to the coast to join the Maine Coast Route (p. 128). Lake Champlain straddles the border with Canada and from Burlington it is just under 100 miles on to Montreal.

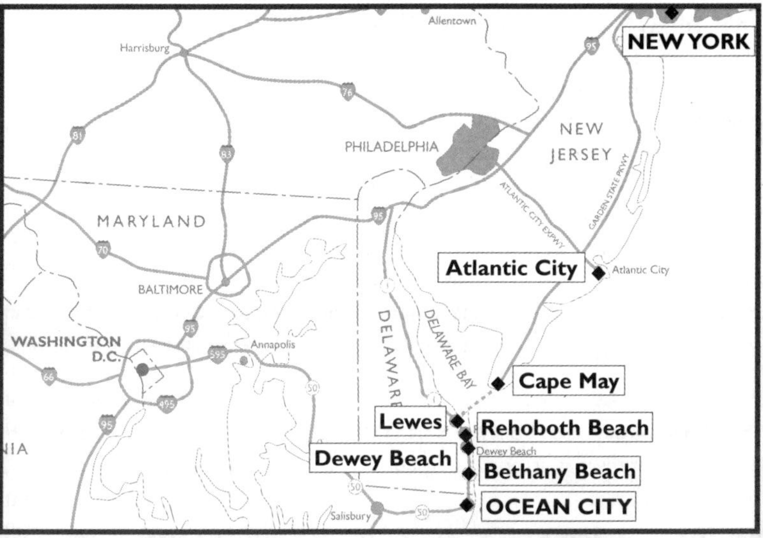

NEW YORK–PHILADELPHIA
OTT TABLE 340

TRANSPORT	FREQUENCY	JOURNEY TIME
Train	10 Daily	54mins
Bus	42 Daily	2 hrs

Note: There are an extra 26 trains that run on Monday to Friday, 16 on Saturday and 10 on Sunday.

NEW YORK–ATLANTIC CITY
OTT TABLE 355 AND 550

TRANSPORT	FREQUENCY	JOURNEY TIME
Bus	17 Daily	3hrs

ATLANTIC CITY–CAPE MAY
OTT TABLE 550

TRANSPORT	FREQUENCY	JOURNEY TIME
Bus	3 Daily	1hr 56mins

PHILADELPHIA–ATLANTIC CITY
OTT TABLE 366

TRANSPORT	FREQUENCY	JOURNEY TIME
Train	13 Daily	1hr 30mins
Bus	41 Daily	1hr 30mins

PHILADELPHIA–CAPE MAY
OTT TABLE 366

TRANSPORT	FREQUENCY	JOURNEY TIME
Bus	6 Daily	3hr 15mins

CAPE MAY–LEWES
OTT TABLE 472

TRANSPORT	FREQUENCY	JOURNEY TIME
Ferry	6 Daily	1 hr 15mins

Note: At least 13 extra sailings daily between late June and Mid September.

REHOBOTH BEACH–BETHANY BEACH
OTT TABLE 718

TRANSPORT	FREQUENCY	JOURNEY TIME
Bus	2 Daily	20mins

BETHANY BEACH–OCEAN CITY
OTT TABLE 718

TRANSPORT	FREQUENCY	JOURNEY TIME
Bus	1 Daily	25mins

WASHINGTON–OCEAN CITY(MD)
OTT TABLES 718/720

TRANSPORT	FREQUENCY	JOURNEY TIME
Bus	1 Daily	4hrs

Note: Also 2 buses daily changing buses at Baltimore.

New York – Ocean City

The Shores of New Jersey and Maryland

The eastern seaboard may not be as well known as the California coast, but the Jersey shore is summer holiday home to untold numbers of New Yorkers and Philadelphians. There are lots of good beaches, and the attractions range from the outlandish gambling haven of Atlantic City to the Victorian-era refinement of Cape May. A ferry ride across the Delaware Bay takes you to Lewes, from which a string of beaches and offshore islands runs south through Delaware and Maryland. Lewes and the adjacent Cape Henlopen State Park are quiet and peaceful places, while nearby Rehoboth Beach is much more vigorous. On southward, and Dewey and Bethany beaches are again more reserved, but summer sun-and-fun reaches its zenith in raucous Ocean City. At the end of this road is Assateague Island, a wildlife preserve and a wonderful space to unwind.

Public transport will get you to Atlantic City and Cape May from Philadelphia and New York. Trailways buses run from Washington DC to Rehoboth Beach and to Ocean City once a day, but there is no public transport along the Delaware–Maryland coast.

ATLANTIC CITY

Atlantic City today is an East Coast version of Las Vegas, with 24-hr casino action and glittery shows featuring big-name entertainers. This identity only dates back to 1976, though, when the run-down, has-been resort introduced the casinos as a means of financial rescue. Absecon Island, on which Atlantic City sits, has been a seaside resort since the 1850s, when a newly built railway helped the masses to escape the steamy summers of Philadelphia and New York City. Atlantic City has had a hand in creating much of America's pop culture: in 1870 its famous Boardwalk appeared, and in 1921 it launched the Miss America Beauty Pageant. The city's street names (such as Baltic Ave and Park Place) have been immortalised in the American version of 'Monopoly'.

Arrival Points

The **bus terminal** is downtown at Arctic and Arkansas Aves; the train station is a few blocks over at the end of the Atlantic City Expressway. If you're driving, the Atlantic City Expressway runs you right into town.

The 4.5-mile **Boardwalk** is the place for strolling, bicycling and people-watching – or let an attendant push you in a three-wheeled, wicker 'rolling chair' (price depending on distance). The usual fun-fair entertainment – mini-rides and games – is available at the Central Pier, and the sandy beaches offer good swimming and boating.

Gamblers can try their luck at any time of day or night at the casinos. You must be 21 to enter, and you're expected to be presentably dressed – don't just wander in from the beach. The 'oldest' casino is **Sands**, at the Boardwalk and Indiana Ave, a boisterous place which also features occasional boxing matches. **Caesars**, at the Boardwalk and Arkansas Ave, is loaded down with bogus statues and images from the ancient Mediterranean, while the **Taj Mahal**, at the Boardwalk and Virginia Ave, is an outrageous mega-palace of eastern delights.

SAFETY

Beyond all the pseudo-glitz and crowds of the Boardwalk, the back streets can be dangerous.

The Atlantic City Convention and Visitors Authority, 2314 Pacific Ave; tel: (1-800) BOARDWK or (888) AC-VISIT; www.atlanticcitynj.com, is open 0900–1630. They have a helpful information booth in the new Convention Hall at Boardwalk and Mississippi Ave.

Many hotels offer package rates (especially midweek) that include casino coins and free or discounted show tickets, meals and parking; ask at the visitor centre. The casinos on the Boardwalk all have pricey rooms, but cheaper chain motels line the streets behind the Boardwalk. Campsites are available nearby in Pleasantville and Mays Landing.

Ascot Motor Inn $$$ Iowa and Pacific Aves; tel: (609) 344-5163 or (1-800) 225-1476. Good enough location and decent rooms.

Mid town Bala Motor Inn $$$–$$$$ Indiana and Illinois Aves; tel: (609) 348-3031 or (1-800) 932-0534. Another lower-end place that's good, but still quite expensive.

Trump's Taj Mahal Casino and Resort $$$$ Boardwalk and Virginia Ave; tel: (1-800) 677-7378. Since you're here, you might as well go all the way.

Gamblers often don't bother to leave the casino at meal-time, relying instead on casino-hotel restaurants. There's no shortage of fast-food joints along the Boardwalk for your beach snacks.

White House Sub Shop $$ 2301 Arctic Ave. Great submarine sandwiches: the photo-covered walls advertise 75 years' worth of famous patrons.

Dock's Oyster House $$$ 2405 Atlantic Ave. Good local seafood.

CAPE MAY

Cape May, 50 miles away at the southernmost tip of New Jersey, is a far cry from

Atlantic City's crassness, offering a glimpse of the architecture and ambience of America's Victorian era. It was founded in 1620 and became a resort in the mid-19th century, when exuberant, colourful homes were put up by wealthy Philadelphians and Southerners. Many of these are today on the register of national historic buildings, and although the resort has spread in all directions, it maintains its serenity. The beaches are excellent, and among the highlights in warm weather is the opportunity to go whale-watching.

The Victorian homes on and around Jackson St are great fun to gawk at; most are now B&Bs. The beach itself is, of course, Cape May's *raison d'être*, and the waves here can be particularly exhilarating. To use the beaches, though, you must purchase a pass ($). A few miles south of the central beach area, **Cape May Point State Park** is a preserved wetland. Its lighthouse is visible for miles around, and a boardwalk leads through the marshes. The beach here is less crowded than in Cape May.

Information on whale- and dolphin-watching cruises and on bike rental is available at the information centres, or pick up any of the free visitor guides available from shops and restaurants.

The Welcome Center, 405 Lafayette St; tel: (609) 884-9562; open daily 0900–1600 (Apr–Oct), can help with accommodation. **The Mid-Atlantic Center for the Arts**, 1048 Washington St, gives guided tours of the town. A good website to peruse is www.beachcomber.com/Capemay.

New Jersey Transit buses use a tiny station just west of centre on Lafayette St.

B&Bs abound in the city's Victorian homes, but they don't come cheap and you'll have to book well in advance. Weekday rates can be significantly lower than weekends. There are several campsites around the town, though, and a cluster of lesser-priced motels at the southern end of the beach – though these too are more expensive than usual.

Surf Motel & Apartments $$–$$$ 211 Beach Dr.; tel: (609) 884-4132. Quiet location near the southern end of the beach.

The Chalfonte $$$–$$$$ 301 Howard St; tel: (609) 884-8409. Victorian-looking hotel, pleasant and a tad less pricey than others.

Windward House $$$$ 24 Jackson St; tel: (609) 884-3368. Cosy antique-laden rooms right in the Victorian centre.

The seafood is excellent here, but at a price. Cheap sandwiches are available on the waterfront, and a number of good cafés and pubs line the pedestrian Washington St mall.

Ugly Mug $$–$$$ Washington Mall at Decatur St. Good local pub with relatively inexpensive sandwiches and seafood platters.

Ebbitt Room $$$$ 25 Jackson St. Fine place for dinner right on Cape May's most Victorian street.

LEWES AND CAPE HENLOPEN STATE PARK

Delaware's oldest settlement dates from 1631, when a Dutch colony was established here. The **Zwaanendael Museum**, at Savannah Rd and Kings Hwy, has artefacts relating to the original settlement and other aspects of the town's history. Open Tues–Sat 1000–1630, Sun 1330–1630; donations accepted. Many old buildings in town date from as far back as 1730, and form the **Lewes Historical Complex** on and around Shipcarpenter Sq. and Front St. Most of these were actually moved here from neighbouring villages; they include an early 18th-century farmhouse, a turn-of-the-century doctor's office and country store, and a log cabin of unknown origin. Open Tues-Fri 1000–1500, Sat 1000–1230 (mid June–early Sept). Also along here, the Lewes–Rehoboth Canal sports the Lightship *Overfalls*, a sea-going lightship that patrolled the entrance to Delaware Bay from 1892 to 1961.

One mile east of Lewes, **Cape Henlopen State Park** is a beautiful area of shady trees and sandy beaches, including the highest dunes in the mid-Atlantic. It also has a nice campsite.

The **Visitor Centre**, 120 Kings Hwy, Lewes; tel (302) 645-8073, is a useful source of information on sites and accommodation in the region.

This should not be the problem that it is in Cape May or Rehoboth Beach.

Cape Henlopen Motel $$$ Savannah and Anglers Rds; tel: (302) 645-2828 or (1-800) 447-3158. Centrally located and convenient for Delaware Bay and the historic district.

Wild Swan Inn $$$ 525 Kings Hwy, Lewes; tel: (302) 645-8550. A B&B in a Queen Anne-style house.

Lewes Crab House $$–$$$ corner of Bay and Henlopen Sts. Serves up piles of steamed crabs.

Gilligan's Harborside Restaurant and Bar $$$ Front and Market Sts. Waterfront dining and a canalside bar.

REHOBOTH BEACH

Of the beach communities along the 24 miles of Delaware coast, Rehoboth Beach has the most video games, mini-carnival rides and nightlife. The name sounds biblical – and it is: Rehoboth appropriately means 'room enough'. Permanent residents number fewer than 1300, but people swarm in from Washington DC at the first sign of spring and throughout the hot weather, giving the resort its 'Nation's Summer Capital' tag. The thing to do is just laze on the beach and stroll the boardwalk, chew salt-water taffy and dine in one of the many seafood restaurants.

Rehoboth Beach/Dewey Beach Chamber of Commerce, 501 Rehoboth Ave; tel: (302) 227-2233 or (1-800) 441-1329. Ask here too about local outdoor activities like crabbing or para-sailing.

Rooms are heavily booked in July and Aug.
The Sandcastle Motel $$–$$$ 123 2nd St; tel: (302) 227-0400 or (1-800) 372-2112. Just off the Boardwalk.
Delaware Inn $$$–$$$$ 55 Delaware Ave; tel: (302) 227-6031 or (1-800) 246-5244. A very pleasant B&B, one of several that line Delaware and Baltimore Aves.

The usual beach junk food is available on the boardwalk, with **Grotto Pizza** a local favourite. Try the seafood, though. **Jakes Seafood House Restaurant**, 1st St and Baltimore Ave, is good, as is **Dogfish Head Brewings and Eats**, 320 Rehoboth Ave (both $$$).

DEWEY BEACH AND BETHANY BEACH

If the crowds are a bit much in Rehoboth, there's less hoopla in Dewey Beach, connected to its southern edge, and Bethany Beach, some 10 miles down the shore. The long and narrow **Delaware Seashore State Park** has a campsite and beach.

Journey's End $$ Atlantic Ave, Bethany; tel: (302) 539-9502. Gracious, simple and central.

ASSATEAGUE ISLAND

A greater contrast to Ocean City could not be imagined. Assateague Island National Seashore, just a few miles south of the stampede, is an utterly tranquil stretch of pine forest and empty beaches. It is maintained as a wildlife preserve, and wild horses roam free from here all the way down to Chincoteague, 30 miles south (see p. 195). Several campsites dot the island: tel: (410) 641-2120 for information, and there are three nature trails taking in this special ecosystem.

OCEAN CITY

The last of this string of beaches is Ocean City, Maryland, and it's the gaudiest of them all. Drunken college students, redneck bars and a general sense of sun-blinded fun prevail on this long strip of land just off the coast. If this is your scene, then find a place to stay and jump right in.

Don't expect seclusion, especially when summer sun warms its 10-mile beach – four million visitors annually tread Ocean City's 3-mile boardwalk, alive with shops, restaurants, music and entertainment. The beach and sundry seaside amusements are the draw, although **Ocean City Life-Saving Museum** takes an enlightening look at everything from wrecks and storms to marine life and mermaids. $ Boardwalk at the Inlet; open daily 1100–2200 (June–Sept); 1100–1600 (May and Oct); winter weekends 1200–1600.

Stop at **Trimper's Rides**, opened in 1890, to ride the 1902 Herschel Spellman carousel with hand-carved and painted animals; $ Boardwalk; open 1300–2400.

Chamber of Commerce, 40th St and Hwy 1; tel: (410) 289-8181 or (1-800) 62-OCEAN. They can also assist with rooms.
Ocean City Visitors and Convention Bureau, PO Box 116, 4001 Coastal Hwy, Ocean City; tel: (410) 289-8181; or 40th St, Ocean City; tel: (800) OC-OCEAN.

Along with 9500 rooms Ocean City has 25,000 condominium units, apartments and beach houses, and several B&Bs, so beds aren't scarce. But expect a room that costs $55 in the winter to approach $200 in summer.
Commander Hotel $$–$$$ 1404 Baltimore Ave; tel: (410) 289-6166 or (888) 289-6166. Newly restored with spacious rooms overlooking the beach..
Ocean City Weekly Rentals, 7th St, 54th St and 87th St, Oceanside; tel: (410) 524-7486. Apartments sleeping 4–10, with fully equipped kitchens, from $500 a week in season.
Sun 'n' Fun Motel $$–$$$ 29th St and Baltimore Ave; tel: (410) 289-6060. Rooms with refrigerator and microwave.
There's a cheap hostel called **Summer Place** $ at 104 Dorchester St (no reservations accepted), plus zillions of hotels and motels along Hwy 1, though these fill up fast in summer.

Eateries line the streets and boardwalk; seek local advice to navigate this changing scene.
Cadillac Jack's Bar and Grill $–$$ 106 S. Boardwalk. Serves burgers, pizzas and overstuffed sandwiches, with dancing to golden oldies.
Brass Rail Restaurant $$ 4801 Coastal Hwy. Tex-Mex all-you-can-eat buffet Mar–Oct.

Ocean City Princess runs deep-sea fishing and nature cruises with an expert on hand to interpret the dolphins, whales, sea turtles and marine life which you see. Cruises run May–Sept; tel: (410) 213-0926.

WHERE NEXT?

Hwy 50 heads inland across the Peninsula to Washington (see p. 168), 145 miles away. Many of the small towns along the way are worth a stop for a taste of Chesapeake Bay backwater life; Annapolis is also en route (see p. 206). Or continue south to the Chesapeake Bay Bridge-Tunnel and the heart of American Revolution country (pp. 187–197 in reverse)

Philadelphia

Anyone returning to Philadelphia after a gap of several years will be gratified to find the city has done much to turn around its bad reputation, which was only partly deserved. Its selling points – a rich colonial history, excellent museums, and good dining and nightlife – are worth the trip.

Philadelphia is the birthplace of the nation. William Penn founded the City of Brotherly Love in 1682, and it quickly became the centre of Colonial America. The Declaration of Independence was signed here, the US constitution written here, and the city served as the nation's first capital from 1791 to 1800. But as Washington and New York became major political and commercial centres, Philadelphia was elbowed out and went into a long, slow period of urban decline. In the early 20th century it was an industrial powerhouse and one of the largest cities in the world, but heavy industry bottomed out by the 1950s, and comments such as local resident W.C. Fields' 'On the whole, I'd rather be in Philadelphia', took a lot of living down. In the 1990s, though, the city pulled itself up by the bootlaces, invested in its future and put itself back on the tourist map.

The Independence National Historical Park and the Philadelphia Museum of Art, one of the finest in the world, are complemented by a whole host of other museums and galleries. Don't visit the city without exploring one of its many intriguing neighbourhoods: Philadelphia's working-class soul opens its heart in the gritty, exuberant Italian Market, while other areas worth exploring include Society Hill, and arty, historic Manayunk.

GETTING THERE AND GETTING AROUND

Air Philadelphia airport was recently voted best airport in America in terms of convenience, appearance and safety. It is in fact very handy – easy and cheap by public transport to the Center, clean, manageable (not too big), but with lots of flights, including a growing number to Europe.

Train/Bus The reasonably priced Airport Rail Line operates between Philadelphia International Airport and Center City daily every half hour 0530–2325.

PARKING
Parking is not easy downtown on the street, but there is no shortage of parking lots in the centre. Try around Penn's Landing (for Old City, Society Hill and South Street) or Locust or Walnut Sts downtown.

Trains and buses connect New York and Washington via Philadelphia almost every hour. The suburban sprawl between New York and Washington, in effect one megalopolis, has precious little appeal, but the fast track can be fast indeed: Amtrak's Metroliner trains reach Philadelphia from New York in just 1¼ hrs, while Northeast Direct trains take a few more minutes. Amtrak trains from New York, Washington, Chicago and Lancaster use the beautiful 30th St Station, just across the Schuylkill River from Center City at 30th and Market Sts (take the subway into the centre).

For bus travel between New York and Philadelphia, Peter Pan is preferred, and between Philadelphia and Washington, use Greyhound. Both lines compete for service from two adjacent stations at 11th and Filbert Sts downtown.

CAR Signs to the I-95 spur via either I-195 or I-295 will take you into Philadelphia from the New York–Washington I-95. If you want more scenery from Washington, Hwy 301 traverses rural eastern Maryland before crossing the dramatic Chesapeake Bay Bridge; it joins I-95 just south of Wilmington.

SEPTA (Southeastern Pennsylvania Transportation Authority) runs a subway system, buses and an extensive commuter rail network. Buy tokens in advance from a station if you plan to take more than one trip – packs of two or more tokens work out cheaper.

INFORMATION

The Philadelphia Visitors Center is at 16th St and John F. Kennedy Blvd; tel: (215) 636-1666; open daily 0900–1700 (1800 in summer); www.libertynet.org. A separate visitor centre handles the monuments of Independent National Historical Park at 3rd and Chestnut Sts; tel: (215) 597-8974; open daily 0900–1700.

SAFETY Philadelphia is not the safest city in America, but the central area, particularly the tourist parts, is fine during the day. At night, the main, well-lit streets are generally safe – just don't stray away from these after hours. South St develops a hard edge at night, and the subway can be a little intimidating as well.

MONEY Thomas Cook Currency Services is central at 1800 John F. Kennedy Blvd; open Mon–Fri 0900–1700. Banks all over town have automatic cash dispensers.

POST AND PHONES The main post office at 30th and Market Sts is open 24 hrs (use zip code PA 19104 for poste restante), but more convenient post offices are located at 3rd and Market Sts and at Sansom and S. Broad Sts.

PHILADELPHIA
North
PHILADELPHIA MUSEUM OF ART
Eakins Oval
Fairmount Park
The Benjamin Franklin Parkway
Pennsylvania Av
RODIN MUSEUM
FREE LIBRARY OF PHILADELPHIA
Logan Circle
FRANKLIN INSTITUTE SCIENCE MUSEUM
GOLDIE PALEY GALLERY AT MOORE COLLEGE OF ART
ACADEMY OF NATURAL SCIENCES MUSEUM
CATHEDRAL OF SAINTS PETER & PAUL
30th ST STATION
SCHUYLKILL
MUSEUM OF AMERICAN ART OF THE PENNSYLVANIA ACADEMY OF THE FINE ARTS
QUAKER INFORMATION CENTRE
PENNSYLVANIA CONVENTION CENTRE
READING TERMINAL MARKET
CITY HALL
STOCK EXCHANGE
ACADEMY OF VOCAL ARTS
ROSENBACH MUSEUM & LIBRARY
CIVIL WAR LIBRARY & MUSEUM
Rittenhouse Square
CURTIS INST. OF MUSIC
PLAYS & PLAYERS THEATRE
TEMPLE CENTRE CITY
ACADEMY OF MUSIC
MERRIAM THEATRE
UNIVERSITY OF THE ARTS
PHILADELPHIA ARTS BANK
FORREST THEATRE
HENRY GEORGE HOUSE
TOMB OF THE UNKNOWN SOLDIER
SOCIETY HILL PLAYHOUSE
Washington Square
GREYHOUND BUS TERMINAL
CHINESE CULTURAL CENTRE
AFRO-AMERICAN HIST. & CULT. MUSEUM
WHYY/FORUM THEATRE
Franklin Square
U.S. MINT
U.S. FEDERAL BUILDING
GRAFF HOUSE
LIBERTY BELL
NORMAN ROCKWELL MUSEUM
Independence National Historical Park
INDEPENDENCE, CONGRESS, OLD CITY & PHILOSOPHICAL HALLS
NAT. MUS. OF AMERICAN JEWISH HISTORY
FRANKLIN'S GRAVE
ARDEN THEATRE
NEW HALL
ARMY-NAVY MUSEUM
TODD HOUSE
BISHOP WHITE HOUSE
POWEL HOUSE
PHYSICK KEITH HOUSE
KOSCIUSZKO NATIONAL MEMORIAL
MUSEUM & INDEPENDENCE SEAPORT
PENN'S LANDING
COLUMBUS MEMORIAL
VIETNAM WAR MEMORIAL
DELAWARE
EDGAR ALLEN POE NATIONAL HIST. SITE
Christopher Columbus Blvd
Ben Franklin Bridge
JFK Blvd
Market St
Chestnut St
Walnut St
Locust St
Spruce St
Pine St
Lombard St
South St
Bainbridge St
Fitzwater St
Delancey St
Sansom St
Ludlow St
Arch St
Race St
Cherry St
Vine St
Callowhill St
Hamilton St
Spring Garden St
Green St
Mt Vernon St
Winter St
Noble St
Filbert St
Franklin St
Dock St
Front St
26th St
25th St
24th St
23rd St
22nd St
21st St
20th St
19th St
18th St
17th St
16th St
15th St
14th St
13th St
12th St
11th St
10th St
9th St
8th St
7th St
6th St
5th St
4th St
3rd St
2nd St
0
500 m
500 yds

ACCOMMODATION

Philadelphia's primary role as a business centre means there is no shortage of chain hotels, and some have good weekend rates. The central area is also blessed with several good value B&Bs, though you'll have to book in advance. **Bed and Breakfast of Philadelphia**, tel: (215) 735-1917 or (1-800) 448-3619; fax: (610) 995-9524; www.bnbphiladelphia.com, can set you up in fun neighbourhoods such as Society Hill, Rittenhouse Sq., the Art Museum area or University City for $50–150.

Bank Street Hostel $ 32 S. Bank St; tel: (215) 922-0222. HI hostel in perfectly central, atmospheric location.

HI – Chamounix Mansion $ Chamounix Dr., West Fairmount Park; tel: (215) 878-3676. An alternative if Bank Street is full, situated in a lovely mansion in sprawling Fairmount Park, but a little awkward to get to. Take bus 38 from Market St downtown to the corner of Ford and Cranston Sts, then walk along Ford St to Chamounix Dr.

Antique Row B&B $$ 341 S. 12th St; tel: (215) 592-7802; fax: (215) 592-9692. Good value and a full breakfast in 180-year-old townhouse.

International House $$ 3701 Chestnut St; tel: (215) 387-5125. Part of a dormitory complex of the University of Pennsylvania; call ahead for availability.

The Gables Bed & Breakfast $$$ 4520 Chester Ave; tel: (215) 662-1918. Lovely Victorian home with period furnishings in West Philadelphia, just beyond the University of Pennsylvania campus. Take subway-surface trolley 13 (the Green Line) from Market St downtown to 46th and Chester.

La Reserve $$$ 1804 Pine St; tel: (215) 735-1137. A well-preserved townhouse on a pretty street near Rittenhouse Sq.

Best Western Center City Hotel $$$–$$$$ 501 N. 22nd St; tel: (215) 568-8300 or (1-800) 528-1234; fax: (215) 557-9448. In the heart of the museum district, just off the Benjamin Franklin Pkwy.

Shippen Way Inn $$$–$$$$ 416–18 Bainbridge St; tel: (215) 627-7266. Family-run inn dating from the 1750s, in an interesting and pretty little part of town just south of South St.

Thomas Bond House $$$–$$$$ 129 S. 2nd St; tel: (215) 923-8523 or (1-800) 845-BOND; fax: (215)

> The city's asinine liquor laws mean many restaurants don't serve alcohol, but are happy to pour wine or beer that you bring yourself (BYOB means 'bring your own booze').

923-8504. Restored guesthouse, circa 1769, in Independence National Historical Park; owned by the National Parks Service. Price includes breakfast.

FOOD

Visitors to Philadelphia are utterly spoilt for choice, with a whole atlas of cuisines offered by hundreds of restaurants. The local favourite, though, is something far more mundane: cheesesteaks are a thoroughly messy sliced-beefsteak submarine sandwich, topped with onions, peppers and gooey cheese. These can be had just about anywhere, though a couple of shops at the corner of 9th St and Passyunk Ave in South Philly are hailed by locals as the original and best. Good areas to look for restaurants are South St between Front and 8th Sts for anything from cheesesteaks to fine Italian dining, Chinatown for a variety of Asian places, and Walnut St between about 10th and 20th Sts for anything from Indian to Irish. Main St in suburban Manayunk has some great cafés and bistros as well.

Judy's Café $$ 3rd and Bainbridge Sts; tel: (215) 928-1968. The type of place where locals queue outside the door; famous especially for its meatloaf and its luscious desserts. Just off South St; BYOB.

Manayunk Brewing Co. $$ 4120 Main St. Large brewpub in hip suburban Manayunk serving the usual American burgers, nachos and salads; some outdoor tables overlook the Schuylkill River.

Audrey Claire $$–$$$ 276 S. 20th St; tel: (215) 731-1222. Tiny bistro with Mediterranean specialities like grilled tuna and roast chicken. BYOB; no credit cards.

Jow's Garden $$–$$$ 319 S. 47th St. Quite possibly the best Thai food anywhere; worth the trip out to West Philly (take bus 42 from Walnut St downtown to 47th and Spruce Sts). Open for dinner only from 1700; closed Mon.

Vietnam $$–$$$ 221 N. 11th St. Good, reasonably priced Vietnamese cuisine in Chinatown.

Brigid's $$$ 726 N.

Colour Section

(i) Maine (pp.128–135): Bar Harbor; Portland indoor market

(ii) Washington (pp. 168–182): Cherry blossom time; National Air and Space Museum

(iii) Baltimore's Inner harbour (pp. 206–216); on parade in Williamsburg; (p. 190)

(iv) Chicago skyline at night (pp. 246–261); inset: antebellum house in Charleston (pp. 219–225)

SHERMAN'S
SHERMAN'S BOOK STORE

A.J. KENNEDY'S
Fruit & Vegetables

NASA
66670
U.S. AIR FORCE
FUEL VENT

24th St. The menu includes duck chambord, bouillabaise ostendaise and a splendid collection of Belgian beers.

Philadelphia Fish & Co. $$$ 207 Chestnut St. Excellent grilled fish, plus nightly specials and good beer. Try to get an outdoor table.

Buddakan $$$–$$$$ 325 Chestnut St. Ultra-hip pan-Asian establishment.

Ristorante Primavera $$$–$$$$ 146 South St; tel: (215) 925-7832. In a city loaded with Italian restaurants, this is one of the best, and not too dear.

Happy Rooster $$$$ 118 S. 16th St at Sansom St. Eccentric little place offering American, continental and Russian fare, and claiming the best-stocked bar in town.

TOURS

Philadelphia is compact enough for most of it to be covered on foot. A quick way from A to B is to use the little purple Phlash buses, which whisk tourists around the central area in a loop for a modest fare. The service runs daily 1000–1800. Old Town Trolley Tours move in a loop covering 15 major tourist stops with narration, and passengers may board and alight at will.

HIGHLIGHTS

OLD CITY AND SOCIETY HILL

Independence National Historic Park (INHP) covers the area between Market St and Walnut St, from 2nd St to 6th St, and encompasses some of the most hallowed historical shrines in the USA. Buildings within the park are open daily 0900–1700 year round and admission is free. The real highlight of the park is **Independence Hall**, the 'birthplace of the nation'. This solemn, pretty, Georgian hall and tower was host to the signing of the Declaration of Independence on 4 July 1776, and the writing of the US constitution in 1787. It is connected to **Carpenters' Hall**, where the First Continental Congress met in 1774, and **Congress Hall**, where the US Senate and the House of Representatives met in the early days of the young nation. These are all somewhat overshadowed by neighbouring office buildings. Equally renowned in American lore is the **Liberty Bell**, the bell with the famous crack, which used to hang from Independence Hall's tower. It now sits low down in an unseemly modern pavilion opposite, the better to gaze upon it.

Outside Independence Hall you'll see horse-drawn carriages lined; you can trot off in one of these for a narrated tour of INHP and Society Hill.

Resounding in colonial glory just off 2nd and Market Sts, the red-brick and creamy-white **Christ Church** dates from 1727, and is where the American Episcopal Church was created in 1789. The interior is a testament to Georgian-era values of solemnity, simplicity and grace.

The streets around here, particularly 2nd and 3rd Sts north of Market St, are packed with galleries and bars. On the first Friday of each month, all open their doors to the eclectic crowds who descend on the area, creating a sort of open block party. **Elfreth's Alley**, off 2nd St between Arch and Race Sts, is a quaint cobblestoned passage of homes continuously inhabited since 1727, said to be America's oldest street.

Abutting the southern edge of the INHP, **Society Hill** – really no more than a swell – is one of Philadelphia's most exclusive districts, though the name comes from the Free Society of Traders, a colonial merchants' social organisation. Strolling the brick and cobblestone streets here is a joy more for the colonial atmosphere than any particular sites. While wandering, take note of Head House Sq., Philadelphia's original covered market, which has been preserved as a graceful public space. Wander down Pine St to 3rd St and St Peter's Episcopal Church and Cemetery, where George Washington worshipped. The building and grounds are almost bucolic. Further on down Pine St at 8th St, the Pennsylvania Hospital was America's first, founded by Benjamin Franklin. The gorgeous domed edifice includes an authentic surgery theatre, open to the public.

SOUTH PHILADELPHIA A quick dip south from here takes you to lively South St. Push on a few more blocks to the marvellous **Italian Market**, a real Philadelphia institution and the heart and soul of working-class South Philly. This festive, open-air street market stretches several blocks down 9th St, concentrated particularly between Christian St and Washington Ave. This is the place to come for fresh fruit and vegetables, fresh-cut pasta, meats, cheeses and spices and, most of all, the atmosphere itself. On Fri and Sat mornings especially, the market is frenetic with activity, and it's impossible not to get caught up in the energy. Connoisseurs of the bizarre will get a kick out of butchers' shops selling ostrich and rattlesnake meat, and spice shops selling things you may never have seen before.

LITTLE ITALY

A world unto itself, South Philadelphia was populated in the late 19th century by Italian immigrant labourers, who settled into block after block of low terraces, and whose descendants manage to keep the old world alive today in a unique east coast urban setting. Along with the Italian Market, Passyunk Ave is its unofficial main street – a fun place simply to wander and enjoy a pocket of a different America; you'll probably even hear Italian spoken.

CENTER CITY Philadelphia's so-called Center City is its financial and commercial focus. Parts of it are fairly run-down, but it's coming back with flashy new skyscrapers and some good shops and restaurants.

The locus is **City Hall**. Some love it; most hate it. This colossus was the largest municipal building in the USA when it was built in 1901. Its only noteworthy feature today is its tower's observation deck, which offers fine, if quite unflattering, views of the city.

A few streets north and east of here the elaborate Chinese Arch at 10th and Arch Sts announces the presence of lively, bustling **Chinatown**, one of America's largest such neighbourhoods. Streets on all sides are lined with restaurants, herb and spice shops, and busy electronics shops. **Reading Terminal Market**, nearby at 12th and Arch Sts, is in the former main railway station. This is a favourite lunchtime rendezvous, with plenty of ethnic eateries, speciality food and craft stalls.

For a piece of urban calm after the rush of Center City, make for **Rittenhouse Square**, at 18th and Walnut Sts. One of the original four squares planned for William Penn's 'green countrie towne', this is a fine place to bring a picnic or catch a free summer evening concert. One of the city's more bizarre attractions is nearby at 22nd and Chestnut Sts. The **Mutter Museum** in the College of Physicians is crammed with medical oddities, such as the preserved bodies of Siamese twins, the 'Elephant Man' and the 'Soap Woman'. $ Open Tues–Sat 1000–1600.

Admission to the Museum of Art is free Sun before 1300, and on Wed nights it stays open until 2100 for talks, films and special dinners all focused around a theme.

MUSEUM ROW Philadelphia's greatest cultural treasures are clustered in the north-west corner of centre, along the broad, green, flag-decked Benjamin Franklin Parkway.

Though not quite as large as New York's Met or Paris's Louvre, the **Philadelphia Museum of Art** is often mentioned in the same breath. Its top-flight collection of art spans virtually all eras in European, American and Asian history. The gallery's particular strengths include sections on Impressionism and 20th-century art – with an entire room full of Marcel Duchamp. Other enticements include glorious reconstructions of a Gothic cloister, a Buddhist temple and a Japanese tea garden, and a lively collection of Shaker furniture. $$ Open Tues–Sun 1000–1700.

The elegant **Rodin Museum** contains the largest collection of Rodin statues outside Paris, including several casts of The Thinker as well as The Gates of Hell. Open Tues–Sun 1000–1700; donation requested.

Up 22nd St a few blocks, the **Eastern State Penitentiary** is one of Philadelphia's more enticing offbeat attractions. This enormous crumbling structure looks like a medieval fortress, and functioned as a prison until 1971. It was originally inspired by Quaker ideals of rehabilitation, which meant solitary confinement in vaulted cells supposed to resemble mini-chapels, with a Bible as the only decoration. $$ Open Sat–Sun 1000–1800 (May and Sept–Nov); Wed–Sun 1000–1800 (June–Aug).

FOR FREE

All of the INHP sites are free, and much of Old City and Society Hill's charm is the streets themselves. Similarly, the Italian Market and South Philly are all about strolling – and the Museum of Art is free on Sun mornings.

Fairmount Park, starting behind the Art Museum, is acclaimed as the world's largest landscaped city park – 8900 acres of meadows, woodland, creeks and trails on both sides of the Schuylkill River, and several intriguing early American mansions. Kelly Dr., behind the Art Museum, contains a series of pretty boathouses, and you can rent bicycles and in-line skates here to explore the park.

The historical suburb of Manayunk has spruced itself up to become a super-hip shopping and dining centre. To reach it, take SEPTA's commuter rail R6 line from 30th St Station, Suburban Station (15th and Market Sts) or Market East Station (11th and Market Sts).

WEST PHILADELPHIA Across the Schuylkill River, the university campus dominates the scene. The **University of Pennsylvania Museum of Anthropology and Archaeology** at 33rd and Spruce Sts is a marvellous collection of antiquities and artefacts from cultures as diverse as the Canadian Inuits, Ancient Egyptians and Javanese monks. Much of the material comes from the university's own work around the world, and highlights include some scarily preserved mummies. $ Open Tues–Sat 1000–1630, Sun 1300–1700. Across campus at 36th and Sansom Sts, the **Institute of Contemporary Art** is a hotbed of current trends in the art world: Andy Warhol and Roy Liechtenstein had early-career exhibitions here. $ Open Thur–Sun 1000–1700 (Wed until 1900); (free Sun am).

SHOPPING

Philadelphia's many neighbourhoods make it a good city to window-shop. South St is trendy with New Age bookshops, antique shops and random off-beat places appealing to anyone with an eye for the unusual. Nearby Pine St, between about 8th and 13th Sts, has been designated Antique Row for its series of small antique shops. Some of the city's finest upmarket shops are located near Rittenhouse Sq.

NIGHTLIFE

Philadelphia is something of an unheralded mecca for the fine and performing arts. The Philadelphia Orchestra has long been regarded as one of the best in the world, and it performs most Tues, Thur, Fri and Sat nights in the glorious **Academy of Music** at Broad and Locust Sts, an opera house modelled after Milan's La Scala. Best of all, you can get super-cheap upper-gallery tickets at the door for most shows. The Opera Company of Philadelphia and the Pennsylvania Ballet also perform here.

Theatres include the **Walnut Street Theatre**, 9th and Walnut Sts (which claims to be the longest continually running theatre in the English-speaking world); the **Forrest Theatre**, 1114 Walnut St; the **Merriam Theatre**, 250 S. Broad St; and the **Wilma**

Theatre across the street. All of these feature Broadway-type shows, and the Wilma also does modern dance and avant-garde film.

The city's hottest club spot of the moment is the **Delaware River Waterfront**, along Delaware Ave heading north from the Benjamin Franklin Bridge. South St between Front and 8th Sts continues to be one of the city's liveliest areas after dark, and a string of bars and clubs has popped up recently around the corner of 2nd and Chestnut Sts.

Pick up the free weekly *Philadelphia City Paper* or the *Philadelphia Weekly* at just about any street corner or bar for information on entertainment and nightlife.

Monk's Café, 264 S. 16th St. Fabulous place for Belgian beers – close to 100 different kinds. Excellent dinner menu too, with steamed mussels.

Dickens Inn, 421 S. 2nd St. Atmospheric English-style pub, renowned for its array of whiskies.

Khyber Pass, 56 S. 2nd St. One of Philly's most established bars, with a long beer list and good local bands.

Warmdaddy's, Front and Market Sts, is the city's top jazz club, drawing big names and charging a high cover.

Egypt, N. Delaware Ave. Raunchy dance club with a different theme on each of its three floors.

Katmandu, N. Delaware Ave. Pumps out world music until all hours.

Trocadero, 10th and Arch Sts. Converted art deco theatre, with good live rock and alternative bands most nights.

Woody's, 202 S. 13th St. Popular gay bar and nightclub, friendly to all.

North Star Bar, 2639 W. Poplar St. Excellent bar food, good drinks selection, and lively rock-'n'-blues bands most nights.

WHERE NEXT?

As well as New York (see p. 53) and Washington (see p. 168), Philadelphia is well connected with Atlantic City (see p. 150). Or experience the other side of Pennsylvania in the rural communities of the Pennsylvania Dutch (see p. 166).

Pennsylvania Dutch Country

A side track west from Philadelphia takes you into beautiful Lancaster County, also known as Pennsylvania Dutch country, where you get a chance to explore a totally unique culture, that of the fundamentalist but friendly Amish and Mennonites.

The countryside here is rolling, pretty and utterly pastoral, particularly with the unusual absence of electrical and telephone wires, and the presence of so many horse-and-buggies on the roads. Lancaster County is home to some 80,000 Amish and Mennonite farmers, who continue to thrive without electricity, telecommunications or cars. The town of Lancaster is the focus, but you may find yourself in or around Strasburg (7 miles south-east) or in numerous villages dotted about – many of which have great names like Intercourse, Paradise and Bird in Hand.

GETTING THERE AND GETTING AROUND

Amtrak runs from Philadelphia to Lancaster nine times daily (1½ hours), but you really need a car or bicycle to get out into the countryside. By car from central Philadelphia, take I-76 west to King of Prussia (20 miles), then Hwy 202 approximately 12 miles to the Hwy 30 interchange. Hwy 30 goes all the way to Lancaster, some 40 miles further on.

Most of the things to see are not really 'sights' themselves, but simply the countryside and the people, so forget the tourist brochures and explore the back roads. Cycling is by far the best way to get out and see things, and bikes can be rented at the Strasburg Historic Railroad, on Rte 741 just east of Strasburg. And remember: you are likely to see more horses than cars on the road, so drive carefully.

The Amish and Mennonites

The term Pennsylvania Dutch is a misnomer, 'Dutch' deriving from the 'Deutsch' or German that the Amish and Mennonites spoke (and on occasion still do speak). They came from Switzerland at the invitation of William Penn in the early 18th century, and are descendants of strict Anabaptists. The Amish adhere rigorously to the Bible, which they believe forbids them from using machinery that may link them with the outside world. Their dress is strictly conservative: men wear black trousers, braces, a straw hat and beard, and women wear simple dresses just above the ankle, and lace bonnets. They also consider photography in the same light as phones and cars, so no matter how tempting it may be, don't point a camera at them – buy postcards instead. The Mennonites, similar in appearance and belief, are more integrated into the modern world.

INFORMATION

In Lancaster, the **Pennsylvania Dutch Convention and Visitors Bureau**, 501 Greenfield Rd, off Hwy 30; tel: (717) 299-8901, is open daily 0830–1700. The **Mennonite Information Center**, 2209 Millstream Rd; tel: (717) 299-0954, is mainly about the Mennonite Church, but also has information on inns and Mennonite guest houses. Open Mon–Sat 0800–1700.

ACCOMMODATION AND FOOD

There are many motels and campsites just outside Lancaster around Hwy 30 E. Food is central European with a dose of Americana, meaning meat-and-potato dishes in huge portions. A local dessert is shoo-fly pie, made chiefly from eggs and molasses. Many restaurants are alcohol-free, but Lancaster has several downtown pubs.

Garden Spot Motel $$ 2291 Hwy 30 E.; tel: (717) 394-4736. Decent motel 3 miles east of Lancaster.

Hotel Brunswick $$–$$$ Chestnut and Queen Sts; tel: (717) 397-4801 or (1-800) 233-0182. Comfortable, central accommodation in Lancaster.

Historic Strasburg Inn $$$ Rte 896, Strasburg (8 miles south-east of Lancaster, off Hwy 30); tel: (717) 687-7691 or (1-800) 872-0201. Colonial-style inn overlooking Amish country.

Good'n'Plenty $$–$$$ Eastbrook Rd (Rte 896), a few miles north of Strasburg. Amish food place where you don't even order, they just serve piles of different meats and vegetables.

Family Style Restaurant $$–$$$ 2323 E. Lincoln Hwy (Hwy 30), 3 miles east of Lancaster. Buffet breakfast and lunch and an all-you-can-eat dinner. Beer and wine available.

HIGHLIGHTS

Some of the most interesting independent touring can be done on either side of Hwy 30, just east of Lancaster city. For a taste of unchanging Amish life, visit the **Amish Village**, Rte 896, 2 miles north of Strasburg: there are guided tours of an Amish house, blacksmith's shop, one-room schoolhouse, operating smokehouse and water-wheel. $$ Open daily 0900–1700 (spring and autumn); 0900–1800 (summer). A few miles north, in **Intercourse**, the People's Place interprets the beliefs and lifestyle of the local Mennonites and Amish. $ Open Mon–Sat 0930–1700 (until 2130 end May–early Sept). Lancaster, a pleasant college town, has examples of local crafts in the **Heritage Center Museum**, Penn Sq.; open Tues–Sat 1000–1600; donation requested. A few miles south, off Hwy 222, the **Hans Herr House** is considered the finest example of medieval-style German architecture in North America, dating from 1719. $ Open Mon–Sat 0900–1600 (Apr–Nov).

Washington DC

The nation's capital happens to be one of its most unusual and appealing cities. Power is, of course, Washington's defining feature, but many visitors are surprised both by its seemingly small size and by its wealth of cultural attractions. The city feels different from most other American cities, mainly because it has no skyscrapers (no commercial building in the city may stand taller than the Capitol). And when the skies are clear, the marble of its classical architecture is dazzling. The downside to this is that Washington has a certain sterility: the glamour of so many impressive – and similar – monuments can wear off, and given the city's high residency turnover rate (due to the frequent change in governments) it's difficult to pin down the city's actual character.

Until recently DC was a sleepy, slightly Southern town where little happened beyond daily politics. The 1960s changed all that: demonstrations for civil rights and against the Vietnam War brought it into the world's headlines and culminated in a series of riots in 1968. Racial tensions are still not fully resolved, although Washington is one of the country's most ethnically diverse cities.

District of Columbia

To its residents Washington DC is just DC. Uniquely, it is a federal district ('Columbia' is a reference to Christopher Columbus), not a state – and not to be confused with Washington State, on the west coast. The city was founded in 1791 specifically to be the nation's seat of government, and the location was chosen for its nearness to the Mason–Dixon line dividing North and South; common perception holds that its unbearable summer heat and humidity would ensure the city would maintain its role as centre of government and little else.

Most of what you'll see is in the centre of town, although this is quite spread out. The main monuments are located on or near the National Mall, and one of Washington's greatest features is that admission to virtually all buildings, museums and galleries is free. For dining and nightlife, however, you'll want to get just out of the centre to the Georgetown and Adams-Morgan districts.

Getting There

Air DC is served by three airports: Washington Dulles International, Reagan National and Baltimore/Washington International (BWI). Dulles, the largest, is about 26 miles west of downtown; Washington Flyer buses run every half hour to several central locations (free for children under six), and to the West Falls Church metro station. Taxis to the centre cost about $40–50.

BWI, often used by international carriers, is on the southern fringes of Baltimore, a 45-min drive from DC. Buses and vans run every hour (0700–2200) to central Washington and BWI also has its own railway station (catch a shuttle bus from the arrivals terminal) with regular MARC rail and Amtrak connections to Baltimore and to Washington's Union Station.

The newly renamed Reagan National Airport is almost in the centre of town, and handles shorter domestic routes. Taxis charge $12–15, and Washington Flyer buses also run into the centre, but the easiest and cheapest trip is from the airport's own metro station.

RAIL/BUS Amtrak's Union Station has been gloriously reconstructed, and serves routes north to New York and Boston, south to Miami, and to various points west. It is located at 1st St and Massachusetts Ave N.E., just a few blocks from the Capitol, and is connected to the city by metro. Greyhound and Peter Pan buses run from adjacent lots a few blocks north, at 1st and L Sts N.E.

CAR Arriving in DC by car is pretty confounding to those unfamiliar with the city's grid system, which is complicated by large avenues criss-crossing in all directions. I-495, the Beltway, skirts the city, and various roads lead from it into the centre. Follow signs for Downtown Washington.

GETTING AROUND

The city's sites are somewhat spread out, which is why the nearest metro stations are given alongside accommodation, restaurant and sightseeing details in this chapter. The Metrorail system – one of the cleanest and safest you'll see anywhere – covers the DC area (including suburban Maryland and Virginia) pretty comprehensively and makes getting from place to place easy. There's a metro map in the colour section inside the back cover. Fares vary according to distance travelled and time of day; you'll need to check the fare to your destination station from the well-lit signs at farecard machines. Buy your farecard in the machine, and be sure to hold on to it as you'll need it to exit the system. Up to two children under five travel free with a fare-paying adult. A Metrorail One Day Pass costing $5 gives unlimited travel from 0930 to closing time (around midnight) on weekdays, and all day otherwise; pick it up at Metro Center station.

Buses fill in where the subway does not, and there is a quite cheap flat rate for journeys within the city. The only route you're likely to use is the 30 line (any of buses 30, 32, 34, 35 or 36), which runs from the Mall along Pennsylvania Ave to Foggy Bottom–GWU metro, on through Georgetown and north to the National Cathedral.

INFORMATION

CITY AND TRANSPORT MAP – inside back cover

Tourist Offices The **Washington DC Convention and Visitors Association**, 1212 New York Ave N.W., tel: (202) 347-2873, is open Mon–Fri 0900–1700. Accommodation information is available, but there is no reservations service. More handy is the **White House Visitor Center**, at 1450 Pennsylvania Ave N.W.; tel: (202) 789-7000.

Safety Washington has a bad reputation when it comes to crime. It consistently led the nation in homicides per capita in the late 1980s and early 1990s, but the serious crime rate has since dropped considerably. None of this should dissuade you in any way, however, as nearly all the violent crime is the result of drug or gang conflicts, and is confined to particular areas in which you're unlikely to find yourself. Visitors on the general tourist trail (including all the sites mentioned below) are no more at risk here than in any other American city – which simply means don't stray from well-lit streets at night.

At night, exercise caution in the downtown, Georgetown, Dupont Circle and Adams Morgan. Stay on the main streets and keep to yourself. The area around 14th and U Sts has revitalised in the past few years, but again be careful here – there's lots of fun to be had but consider taking a cab at night.

Money A central Thomas Cook exchange office is at 1800 K St N.W.; tel: (1-800) CURRENCY or (202) 872-1427 (metro: Farragut North or Farragut West). Open Mon–Fri 0900–1700. There are also offices at all airports and one at Union Station, tel: (202) 371-9219, which is open late and at weekends.

Post and Phones The main post office is next to Union Station at 2 Massachusetts Ave N.E. A handy post office near the Mall is in the Post Office Pavilion at 11th St and Pennsylvania Ave N.W.

ACCOMMODATION

Central hotels are expensive during the week, but rates drop at weekends and in July and Aug, when Congress is in recess and business and convention travel slows down. In addition, many hotels extend their lower weekend rates to cover a seven-day stay, and similar low-priced packages are available during holiday periods. Always call ahead for reservations, as the city is a hugely popular tourist destination.

No district of the city is favoured with either expensive or cheap accommodation, but as downtown feels quite empty at night, you may wish to look for rooms in the more lively areas of Dupont Circle, Adams-Morgan, and Georgetown. Budget travellers with cars should try the motels in Arlington, particularly along Glebe Rd and Jefferson Davis Hwy.

Reservations services include **Capitol Reservations**, tel: (1-800) VISIT-DC or (202) 452-1270; **Washington DC Accommodation**, tel: (1-800) 554-2220 or (202) 289-2220; and **Bed and Breakfast Accommodations**, tel: (202) 328-3510.

DOWNTOWN

HI – Washington International Hostel $ 1009 11th St N.W.; tel: (202) 737-2333 (metro: Metro Center). Huge hostel with kitchen, laundry, information desk and tours. Very central, though nondescript area.

Allen Lee Hotel $$ 2224 F St N.W.; tel: (1-800) 462-0186 or (202) 331-1224 (metro: Farragut West). Quaint budget place close to the monuments.

Harrington Hotel $$$–$$$$ 1100 E St N.W.; tel: (202) 628-8140 or (1-800) 424-8532 (metro: Metro Center). Decent old hotel near the White House and the Mall.

Best Western Downtown Capitol Hill $$$–$$$$ 724 3rd St N.W.; tel: (1-800) 242-4831 or (202) 842-4466 (metro: Judiciary Sq.). Chain hotel handy for the US Capitol and Union Station.

DUPONT CIRCLE/ ADAMS-MORGAN

Simpkins' B&B $$ 1601 19th St N.W.; tel: (202) 387-1328 (metro: Dupont Circle). No-frills guesthouse near Dupont Circle. Show a passport (US or foreign) for half-price rates.

Adams Inn $$–$$$ 1744 Lanier Pl. N.W.; tel: (202) 745-3600 (metro: Woodley Park–Zoo). Small budget establishment in the Adams-Morgan neighbourhood.

Kalorama Guest House $$–$$$ 1854 Mintwood Place N.W.; tel: (202) 667-6369; and 2700 Cathedral Ave N.W., tel: (202) 328-0860 (metro: Woodley Park–Zoo). Long-time favourite B&B in several fine town houses in Adams-Morgan and Woodley Park.

Windsor Inn $$$–$$$$ 1842 16th St N.W.; tel: (202) 667-0300 (metro: Dupont Circle). B&B-style hotel in the active Dupont Circle area.

FURTHER OUT

Americana Hotel $$ 1400 Jefferson Davis Hwy, Arlington; tel: (703) 979-3772 (metro: Crystal City). Cheap, convenient enough place near the metro and Reagan National Airport, but in a lifeless neighbourhood.

Latham Hotel $$$$ 3000 M St N.W.; tel: (202) 726-5000 (metro: Foggy Bottom). Esteemed hotel in Georgetown, with shopping, dining and entertainment on the doorstep.

FOOD

As might be expected of the world's most powerful capital city, Washington offers a culinary choice that sweeps across the international spectrum. Adams-Morgan (around 18th St and Columbia Rd N.W.) is the ethnic hotspot in town, with a rich selection of Ethiopian, Mexican and French restaurants, and lots of great bars and clubs. The nearby area surrounding U St N.W., between 13th and 16th Sts, is becoming a happening restaurant and nightlife centre. Georgetown (around Wisconsin Ave and M St N.W.) is a long-established part of social life in DC, with everything from cheap diners and Irish pubs to fine Italian restaurants, and lively nightlife. Old Town Alexandria in suburban Virginia (along King St) is another historical and spirited part of town, with several good seafood places. Most of the Smithsonian museums have café/restaurants, which are good for a cheap lunch or snack.

DOWNTOWN/14TH AND U STS	**Old Post Office Pavilion** $–$$ 11th St and Pennsylvania Ave N.W. (metro: Federal Triangle). Great lunchtime food court in an impressive hall; a variety of cheap eats from burgers to Greek and Indian.
	Polly's Café $$–$$$ 1342 U St (metro: U Street–Cardoza). Pleasant pub in this up-and-coming urban neighbourhood.
	Red Sage $$–$$$ 605 14th St N.W. (metro: Metro Center). South-western cuisine in the budget-priced chilli bar, or the more pricey formal dining room.
DUPONT CIRCLE/ ADAMS-MORGAN	**Kramerbooks and Afterwords Café** $$ 1517 Connecticut Ave N.W. (metro: Dupont Circle). Satisfy mind and body in this bookstore and café, which serves salads, sandwiches, vegetarian dishes and weekend brunch.
	Meskerem $$–$$$ 2434 18th St N.W. (metro: Woodley Park–Zoo or Dupont Circle). The best of many Ethiopian restaurants in Adams-Morgan; don't miss the honey wine.
	Lebanese Taverna $$$ 2641 Connecticut Ave N.W. (metro: Woodley Park–Zoo). Fine Middle Eastern cuisine.
GEORGETOWN	**Clyde's** $$–$$$ 3236 M St (metro: Foggy Bottom–GWU). Great Georgetown place serving 'American saloon food' – burgers, seafood, fajitas, soups and salads, plus excellent home-brewed lager.
	Bistro Français $$$–$$$$ 3128 M St (metro: Foggy Bottom–GWU). Excellent and reasonably priced French cuisine in a romantic setting.
FURTHER OUT	**Yosaku** $$$ 4712 Wisconsin Ave N.W. (metro: Tenleytown). Excellent, unpretentious Japanese food with full sushi bar in upper north-west DC.
	Monocle $$$–$$$$ 103 D St N.E. (metro: Union Station). Capitol Hill gathering place for politicos, lobbyists and journalists, dishing up crabcakes and prime beef.

HIGHLIGHTS

THE MALL AND AROUND

The **National Mall** is the city's centrepiece, a long rectangular swathe of open green, book-ended by the US Capitol and the Washington Monument, and lined by several grandiose and spectacular museums of the Smithsonian. The Mall is often the scene of national marches and demonstrations; beyond the Washington Monument the Reflecting Pool stretches to the Lincoln Memorial, from where Martin Luther King Jr delivered his electrifying 'I Have A Dream' speech in 1963.

FOR FREE

Almost everything in DC is free; in fact only a very few of the sites mentioned here charge admission. But where you save on admission fees, you'll spend the money saved on the restaurants and hotels.

The **Smithsonian Institution** is one of the finest museum complexes in the world, with 18 separate institutes plus the National Zoo – all begun with a bequest from an English chemist who had never been to the USA. All are open daily 1000–1730, except the Air and Space Museum and the National Museum of American History, which stay open a bit later in summer. All are free, and you could easily spend a solid week in the museums on the Mall alone. For general information, tel: (202) 357-1300. All sites on the Mall are served by the Smithsonian metro station.

By far the most popular Smithsonian museum is the fantastic **National Air and Space Museum**, at the south-eastern corner of the Mall near the Capitol. A big hit with kids, it can't fail to impress visitors of all ages with its incredible array of real air- and space-craft. Notable exhibits include the first plane ever flown (by the Wright Brothers), Charles Lindbergh's *Spirit of St Louis*, in which he made the solo transatlantic flight, and the first glider plane to fly around the world non-stop. You can also see here an original Saturn V rocket and several (decommissioned) American and Soviet nuclear warheads. The museum shows spectacular IMAX® films, for which you must buy tickets up to several hours in advance.

The **Hirshhorn Museum** next door is a weird cylindrical structure holding some excellent 19th- and 20th-century works of art, including masterpieces by Picasso, Matisse, Jackson Pollock and Francis Bacon. The grounds of the museum, as well as a sunken garden across the street, are an open-air sculpture garden full of surprisingly intriguing modern works.

Further down the Mall, the **Freer Gallery** is a smaller collection of works donated by the 1920s industrialist James Freer: his personal favourites were James McNeill Whistler, as well as pieces from ancient China and Byzantium. Beneath the Freer, two new museums are connected in a three-level underground gallery. The **Sackler Gallery** features precious manuscripts and objects from ancient China and the Middle East, and the **National Museum of African Art** covers a broad range of sculptures, paintings, and crafts from the African continent, including several beautiful ivory carvings.

TOURS

Tourmobile Sightseeing, tel: (202) 554-5100, offers a narrated shuttlebus service ($$), with unlimited reboarding at 18 major sites all day. The service runs daily every 15 mins 0930–1630. **Old Town Trolley Tours**, tel: (202) 872-1765 runs 2-hr narrated tours ($$$) every half hour, daily 0900–1600; free reboarding at 17 sites. **DC Foot Tour**, tel: (703) 461-7364, does walking tours of major historical sites. (See also p. 178 for some suggested independent walking tours.)

Along the north side of the Mall, the first building west of the Capitol is the **National Gallery of Art**. Not actually a Smithsonian museum, this marvellous collection exists thanks to the generosity of industrialist Andrew Mellon. There are in fact two galleries, the original, gold-domed West Wing, and the super-modern (even now, a quarter century later) East Wing; the two are connected by an underground walkway. The original gallery houses an excellent collection of art, featuring the likes of Rembrandt, Rubens, Botticelli, Monet, Gauguin and Van Gogh. The East Wing focuses on contemporary art, and has a steady stream of visiting exhibitions. Its permanent collection includes works by Picasso, Liechtenstein and Warhol, and the building itself is something to marvel at.

The **National Museum of Natural History** next door is a wonderful collection of the planet's physical being. Highlights include reconstructed skeletons of dinosaurs such as a brontosaurus and a pterodactyl; an elaborate collection of precious gems, including the notorious Hope Diamond (the largest in the world); displays on the lives of native American peoples such as Eskimos and Plains Indians; and a creepy crawly insect zoo, with live tarantulas, scorpions, and lots more.

One of the finest of the Smithsonian's museums is the **National Museum of American History**, with constantly changing exhibits of important events in America's eventful and troubled history. Its greatest strength is that it doesn't try to glamorise: exhibits include rich displays on, for example, the so-called Great Migration of African Americans northwards after the Civil War, and the altered lives of Navajo and Zuni Indians in New Mexico today. Other sections are pure fun, such as turn-of-the-century locomotives and the banquet gowns of recent First Ladies.

The **Washington Monument**, on the Mall at 15th St N.W., is one of the city's most recognisable symbols. The 555 ft obelisk is undergoing a thorough facelift, due to be completed by 2001. Views from the top on clear days spread all the way to the Blue Ridge Mountains. Beyond the Monument, the long, narrow Reflecting Pool stretches nearly 600 yd to the **Lincoln Memorial** (metro: Foggy Bottom– GWU). A statue of a seated Abraham Lincoln lurks inside this Grecian-style memorial temple.

Near the Washington Monument, on the Tidal Basin, you can rent paddle-boats in warm weather. This is particularly appealing in early April, when the famous cherry blossom trees are out (see p. 180).

THE MIGHTY DOLLAR

At the **Bureau of Engraving and Printing** you can be mesmerised at the sight of dollar bills being printed at the rate of 7000 sheets an hour, totalling millions of dollars a day. This is such a popular place to visit that from May to Aug a same-day timed ticket system is in operation: for free tickets tel: (202) 874-3019 early in the day, and return at the time assigned to you. The Bureau is opposite the Holocaust Museum (entrance at 14th and C Sts S.W.); open Mon–Fri 0900–1400.

Lincoln's gaze falls kindly on the **Vietnam Veterans' Memorial**, just north of the Reflecting Pool. More than 58,000 names of those who died or remain missing in the Vietnam War are inscribed on the black granite V-shaped memorial, and the site is particularly moving as it's well visited by relatives of the dead. Across the pool, the **Korean War Veterans' Memorial** is composed of stainless steel sculptures of 19 ground troops.

More tragedy is on hand in the **US Holocaust Memorial Museum**, on 15th St just south of the Washington Monument (metro: Smithsonian). The harrowing story of the Nazi genocide is told here through photographs, artefacts, film, videotaped histories and other exhibits. Particularly moving is the Tower of Faces, an actual barrack building from Auschwitz. Open daily 1000–1730; free, but timed tickets are required, and you may well have to arrive early to get tickets for later in the day.

THE WHITE HOUSE **The White House**, 1600 Pennsylvania Ave N.W. (metro: Metro Center or McPherson Sq.), is high on most visitors' lists. Parts of the ground floor can be visited, but because of its nature as the official residence of the US president, security is tight, tours may be subject to change or cancellation, and you don't get to see the most important parts. The White House Visitor Center at 1450 Pennsylvania Ave is worth seeing in its own right, with historical exhibits and displays of photographs showing life and special functions at the White House down the years. This is where you come to pick up free tickets, which disappear fast: arrive as early as possible, as tickets may be gone by 0830. Tours run only Tues–Sat 1000–1200; the visitor centre is open daily 0700–1900 (summer) and 0800–1700 (rest of the year); tel: (202) 456-7041.

Leafy **Lafayette Sq**. opposite the mansion is a gathering point for low-key protestors of all ilks. Security, as you would imagine, is tight here (Pennsylvania Ave was closed to vehicular traffic in 1995 after numerous terrorist threats) but peaceniks, pro- and anti-abortion demonstrators and homeless advocates are usually camped out in the park. **St John's Episcopal Church**, on the northern edge of the park at 1525 H St N.W., is the church of the presidents – every one of them since James Madison has worshipped here in pew 54. The pretty landmark dates from 1816.

CAPITOL HILL The US Capitol building is the prominent focus of this section at the eastern edge of the Mall. Capitol South metro station is convenient to all sites in this area. The buildings lining Constitution Ave to the north house Senate offices, and those lining Independence Ave to the south are used by members of the House of Representatives.

The **US Capitol**, the seat of the US government, is the nerve centre of all that is Washington. All four city districts converge on this point, and the building has obvious appeal for its physical beauty (its white dome is particularly striking at night) as well as the fact that you can witness Congress in session. The Capitol building is open Mon–Fri and some weekends 0900–1630, and a 20-min guided tour starts daily from the Rotunda 0900–1545. Because of the magnificent art works and historic associations, you may well want to spend time in the galleries and look around on your own.

Behind the Capitol are a number of other buildings important to America. The **Library of Congress**, at 1st St and Independence Ave S.E., is a research library created in 1800 to serve Congress, and now holds close to 100 million books and documents. A room in the James Madison building (there are three library buildings in the complex) contains the Gutenberg Bible and Martin Luther King's 'I Have a Dream' speech. Open Mon–Fri 0830–2130, Sat 0830–1800.

The **US Supreme Court** building, a block up at 1st St and Maryland Ave N.E., has displays and a film outlining procedures in the nation's highest court. Lectures are given every hour on the half-hour Mon–Fri 0930–1530 when not in session. Court hearings may be watched on a first-come, first-served basis, but public seating is limited. For a brief look, join the 3-min queue; to attend an entire case, join the regular queue. The court sits weekdays 0900–1630.

THE GOVERNMENT AT WORK

To get a Congressional pass and watch the proceedings, Americans apply to their senator or representative, but foreign visitors may obtain House passes at the gallery check-in desk on the third floor and Senate passes at the Senate appointment desk on the first floor, all subject to availability. *The Washington Post* records when Senators and Representatives are sitting.

Also in the area is the surprisingly good **Folger Shakespeare Library**, 201 E. Capitol St S.E., a recreation of Shakespeare's original Elizabethan theatre and one of the world's greatest collections of Shakespearean and Renaissance material. Open Mon–Sat 1000–1600.

DOWNTOWN The central business district itself is no great joy, lacking the verve of many American cities, but there are several more museums and historical sites here. Near the Mall, the **National Archives** at 8th St and Pennsylvania Ave N.W. (metro: Archives–Navy Memorial) has a permanent display of the original US constitution, Declaration of Independence and Bill of Rights. Open daily 1000–2100 Apr–early Sept (until 1730 rest of year).

The **FBI Headquarters**, 9th St and Pennsylvania Ave N.W., runs free tours revealing the latest crime-fighting techniques. A favourite is the collection of firearms heisted from criminals, and demonstrations of weapons that FBI agents currently use. Open Mon–Fri 0845–1615.

A block up, at 511 10th St N.W., the pretty restored **Ford's Theatre** is the place where Abraham Lincoln was shot on 14 Apr 1865. The president's box, above the stage, was a fairly easy target for his assassin, John Wilkes Booth. Lincoln died several hours later in Petersen House across the street, which is also open to the public. A museum underneath Ford's Theatre has more information on the assassination. Open daily 0900–1700.

There are several more art galleries of note downtown as well. The **National Museum of Women in the Arts**, 1250 New York Ave N.W. (metro: Metro Center), contains more than 1500 works by 400 women from 28 countries. Open Mon–Sat 1000–1700, Sun 1200–1700; donation requested. Near the White House, the **Corcoran Gallery of Art** at 17th St and New York Ave N.W. (metro: Farragut West) is a fine collection of romantic and contemporary American art, with some Dutch and Flemish masterpieces. Open Mon, Wed, Sun 1100–1700, Thur 1000–2100; donation suggested. Fanning out a little to the north, the **Phillips Collection**, 1600 21st St N.W. (metro: Dupont Circle) is an excellent private collection of 19th- and 20th-century paintings, including works by Renoir, Georgia O'Keeffe, Paul Klee and Jacob Lawrence. $$ Open Tues–Sat 1000–1700 (Thur till 2030), Sun 1200–1900.

For something a little different, the **National Geographic Society** headquarters at 1600 M St N.W. (metro: Farragut North) has exhibits covering early humans, the earth, its geography, and the fragile balance between its inhabitants. Open Mon–Sat 0900–1700, Sun 1000–1700.

Beyond Central Washington

Georgetown is a wonderful place just to wander around, window-shop and stop for a meal. This was the city's first suburb, a port just west of centre on the Potomac River (the intersection of Wisconsin Ave and M St is its centre) and today its mostly 19th-century buildings, including several private mansions, are gorgeous to stroll by. The Chesapeake and Ohio Canal, built for trade between the Georgetown docks and rural Maryland in the mid-19th century (see Great Falls Park, p. 182), runs parallel to M St and the river, and is a pleasing little stretch to walk along.

> The National Zoo is carved into a slope in part of the park (same hours as Smithsonian museums, and also free). Orang utans live here, as do Komodo dragons.

A few miles up Wisconsin Ave at Massachusetts Ave, the **Washington National Cathedral** bears stunning similarity to many of Europe's finest cathedrals. Craftsmen used 14th- and 15th-century skills to build and adorn this gothic house of worship for the Episcopal Church. It was completed in 1990 and is the world's sixth largest cathedral. The gardens make a soothing respite from the summer heat. Take Metrobus nos. 30, 32, 34, 35 or 36 from Foggy Bottom-GWU or Tenleytown metro stations, or walk the 1½ miles from Tenleytown. Open daily 1000–1630. Guided tours Mon–Sat 1000–1515, Sun 1230–1445; donations appreciated.

Rock Creek Park is a quite remarkable phenomenon, a forest right in the city, extending from the river right out into suburban Maryland. From Woodley Park–Zoo metro follow through to the bottom of the zoo, and from here you can walk in either direction along the creek. If you follow the creek northwards, you reach the 18th-century Pierce Mill after a mile or so, and from here, Tilden St runs back up to Connecticut Ave and Van Ness–UDC metro.

Arlington National Cemetery, across the river from the Lincoln Memorial (metro: Arlington Cemetery), is the final resting place of hundreds of thousands of US servicemen and women, and of President John F. Kennedy. One of its most serene sites is the Tomb of the Unknown Soldier. Open daily 0800–1900 (summer); 0800–1700 (winter).

EXPLORING ON SHANKS'S PONY

DC is a good city for walking, with lots of green space and broad streets. Here are a few suggested walks, all with approximate times for fit walkers, assuming no stops; allow much longer to stroll and take it all in.

Potomac River: Georgetown to the Mall. This is a pleasant way to see the river and several interesting buildings along the way. From K St in Georgetown walk through Washington Harbor (an office, apartment and restaurant complex) along the banks of the Potomac past the **Watergate** and **Kennedy Center**. Cross the street at the Lincoln Memorial and continue on to the Mall. Total walking time: 45 mins to the Lincoln Memorial; another 45 mins across the Mall to the Capitol.

Embassy Row: Massachusetts Ave north-west of Dupont Circle has the highest concentration of embassies in the city, hence its nickname. Many of these are in fine mansions. Along the way you will also see the beautiful **Islamic Mosque and Cultural Center** (2551 Massachusetts Ave), which is open daily 1000–1700 – women must be modestly clothed and everyone must remove their shoes; and the **Vice President's Mansion**, 34th St and Massachusetts Ave (not open to the public). Total walking time: 45 mins, all uphill.

Old Town Alexandria: the town of Alexandria, a few miles south of central DC, was established in 1749 by Scottish tobacco merchants, and its prominent citizens included George Washington and Robert E. Lee. Many historical structures have been preserved. King St metro is an easy access point to Old Town, and King St itself is the main street leading straight toward the river. Stop off at **Christ Church** (118 N. Washington St), **Carlyle House** (121 N. Fairfax St) and **Ramsey House** (221 King St), all dating from the early to mid-18th century. Total walking time: 20–30 mins from King St metro to the river.

Not far away is one of the city's more bizarre sites, the **Pentagon** (metro: Pentagon). This is the largest office building in the world, a Cold War-era construction that captures the grandeur and bureaucracy of its time. Its size lies in its extraordinary five-sided girth rather than height, and it draws many tourists just for its name. Free guided tours are given Mon–Fri 0900– 1530, but in fact the building is rather drab and unappealing.

One site off the beaten track but worth the trip into south-east Washington is the **Frederick Douglass home**, 1411 W St S.E. (metro: Anacostia, then bus B2). Douglass, a self-educated African-American who was one of the great figures in the emancipation of slavery, became a successful businessman, and his home has been restored to its mid-19th-century appearance. Open daily 0900–1700 (spring–summer); 0900–1600 (autumn–winter). This area can be dangerous, so travel in a group.

In upper north-east Washington are two religious centres worth visiting if you have time. The **National Shrine of the Immaculate Conception**, on the campus of the Catholic University of America at 4th St and Michigan Ave N.E. (metro: Brookland–CUA), is the largest Catholic church in the USA, with more than 50 chapels and a wealth of stained glass. The enormous dome is nearly 240 ft high, and the beautiful 329 ft Knights' Tower has a carillon of 56 bells. Open 0700–1800 daily (until 1900 Apr–Oct). Not far away, the **Franciscan Monastery**, 1400 Quincy St N.E. (metro: Brookland–CUA) is a retreat in the Byzantine style, with replicas of Holy Land shrines. A statue of St Francis stands in the enclosed garden. Open daily 0900–1700.

SHOPPING

The Smithsonian museums' gift shops are excellent places to pick up anything from souvenirs to fine quality art posters and books. Political memorabilia is a hot item, including quirky T-shirts proclaiming 'Nixon 2000' and the like. Washington's busiest shopping area is probably along Wisconsin Ave and M St N.W. in Georgetown, which has many good speciality boutiques.

NIGHTLIFE

Washington has a buzzing concert and theatre scene. Listings of current shows, plays and concerts are given in *Where Washington*, *Washington City Paper* and the *Washington Post*. World-class orchestral, opera and dance performances take place at the **John F. Kennedy Center for the Performing Arts**, Virginia and New Hampshire Aves N.W., tel: (202) 467-4600 (metro: Foggy Bottom–GWU). The **National Symphony Orchestra**'s season runs Sept–May.

Top theatres in town include:

National Theatre, 1321 Pennsylvania Ave N.W.; tel: (202) 628-6161 (metro: Metro Center). Broadway shows.

Warner Theatre, 1299 Pennsylvania Ave N.W.; tel: (202) 783-4000 (metro: Metro Center). Beautifully remodelled theatre.

Ford's Theatre, 511 10th St N.W.; tel: (202) 347-4833 (metro: Metro Center). See p. 176.

Folger Shakespeare Library, 201 E. Capital St S.E.; tel: (202) 544-7077 (metro: Capitol South). See p. 176.

A night out in DC is not quite the same as in Manhattan, but Georgetown (particularly Wisconsin and M Sts) and Adams-Morgan (around 18th St and Columbia Rd) are happening neighbourhoods with plenty of bars and clubs. The area around 14th and U Sts has undergone a complete renaissance in the past ten years, and now has several good restaurants and bars – though it's still rough around the edges, so exercise caution at night. DC has an unusually good collection of jazz and blues spots, and many bars and clubs take up politically inspired themes. Most clubs have a fairly nominal cover charge ($5–10), but in some it can be much more.

DUPONT CIRCLE/ ADAMS-MORGAN

Brickseller Inn, 1523 22nd St N.W.; tel: (202) 293-1885 (metro: Dupont Circle). Large but cosy pub with an amazing menu of more than 600 beers.

Ireland's Four Provinces, 3412 Connecticut Ave N.W. (metro: Cleveland Park). Guinness and Murphy's on tap, plus live rock and folk bands weekend nights.

City Blues Café, 2651 Connecticut Ave N.W. (metro: Woodley Park–Zoo). Small and popular blues/jazz bar.

Madam's Organ, 2461 18th St N.W. (metro: Woodley Park–Zoo). Playing on the name of its Adams-Morgan location, this bar/club offers a variety of music from world to bluegrass.

FESTIVAL TIME

DC puts on a number of colourful events throughout the year. Here are a few of the very best:

National Cherry Blossom Festival (usually early Apr). A week-long exultation of more than 6000 Japanese cherry trees in bloom at various monuments. The bright pink flowers are stunning, but it's hard to predict when the trees will be at full bloom, and it only lasts a few days.

Festival of American Folklife (late June/early July). Music, arts, crafts and cuisine attract more than a million people to the Mall.

Independence Day. Washington celebrates 4 July with activities on the Mall all day, a free concert by the National Symphony Orchestra on the west steps of the Capitol in the evening, and a glorious fireworks display at night.

Adams-Morgan Day (Sun following Labor Day; see p. 96). This culturally diverse district presents live music, handicrafts and the cuisine of its people in an old-fashioned street festival.

	Heaven & Hell, 2327 18th St N.W. (metro: Woodley Park–Zoo). Drink and be cool in Hell downstairs, or dance the night away upstairs in Heaven.
GEORGETOWN	**Blues Alley**, rear of 1073 Wisconsin Ave N.W. (metro: Foggy Bottom–GWU 20 mins, bus 30/32/34/35/36). Long-established, upmarket, intimate jazz club in Georgetown, presenting the top names. Shows are twice nightly Sun–Thur, thrice Fri and Sat. Hefty cover charge.
	Saloun, 3239 M St (metro: Foggy Bottom–GWU 20 mins, bus 30/32/34/35/36). Usually a fine place tocatch local jazz and blues bands, and a good beer list.
DOWNTOWN/14TH AND U STS	**The Black Cat**, 1831 14th St N.W. (metro: U Street–Cardoza). Good bar and connected hall featuring good alternative local and national bands.
	9:30 Club, 815 V St N.W. (metro: U Street–Cardoza). DC's long-time best venue for rock and pop acts.
	State of the Union, 1357 U St (metro: U Street–Cardoza). Not the 'union' you would expect: eye-catching Soviet décor in this eclectic bar/nightclub.

DAY TRIPS

MOUNT VERNON A must-see for American history fans, and an enjoyable day trip from DC, is Mount Vernon, the home of George Washington. The hilltop home is set in 500 rolling acres of riverfront Virginia countryside 16 miles south of Washington, and is the place where the great American general and first president retired. The home retains its simple, gracious appearance, and among the furnishings you can see are a key to the Bastille presented by General Lafayette, and the bed in which Washington died in 1799. The grounds include slave quarters – an irony of many founding fathers was their ownership of slaves, despite proclamations that 'all men are created equal' – and George and Martha Washington's tombs, plus an innovative 16-sided threshing barn, built using hand-made bricks and hand-forged nails. The almost circular design served as an indoor arena for a horse to trample the straw, causing the grain to sift through to the floor below.

A more exciting way to reach Mount Vernon is by boat. Spirit Cruises, 6th and Water Sts S.W., Pier 4, tel: (202) 554-8000 (metro: Waterfront) sails boats down the Potomac to Mount Vernon Apr–Oct ($$$).

Mount Vernon is open daily 0900–1700 (Mar and Sept–Oct); 0800–1700 (Apr–Aug); 0900–1600 (Nov–Feb); $$. Fairfax Connector bus 101 runs every 30 mins (rush hour) or every hour (non-rush hour and weekends) from Huntington metro station to the house. By car, take the George Washington Memorial Pkwy, which runs along the west bank of the river through Arlington and Alexandria.

GREAT FALLS PARK The fall line of the Potomac River is about 15 miles upstream from Georgetown, a dramatic, rocky narrowing through which the river shoots with extraordinary velocity – the kind of wild river scenery you would expect to find in the West.

The falls are part of the Chesapeake and Ohio Canal National Historical Park, straddling both the Maryland and Virginia sides of the river. The Virginia side has better views, but the Maryland side is by far the more interesting, as the C&O Canal passes alongside the northern bank. The canal offers a glimpse into an intriguing part of America's 19th-century industrial history – the building of an inland waterways system to transport goods from rural Maryland and Ohio to Washington, DC. Soon after construction of the canal began, however, the railway began its romp across the country, and the romantic endeavour of the canal was overwhelmed. You can gain a perspective on the canal at the Great Falls Tavern Visitor Center, and witness the mechanically ingenious lift-lock system in action as mule-drawn barges ply the conduit (Apr–Oct only).

To see the falls, cross the bridge onto Olmsted Island for superb views. You can also stroll along the canal bank for miles in either direction, and slip down to the river for a little peace and quiet: this is a popular weekend destination for Washingtonians.

Great Falls Park is open daily from dawn to dusk; $. There is no public transport – by car take Macarthur Blvd from Georgetown (an extension of M St).

WHERE NEXT?

The District of Columbia is an enclave of Maryland and Virginia, both of which have stunning scenery and many attractions: historic Jamestown, Richmond and Williamsburg and the shores of Chesapeake Bay (see pp. 187–197) lie to the south-east, and the dramatic sweep of the Blue Ridge Mountains and Shenandoah National Park to the south-west (see p. 198). Baltimore, Annapolis (see pp. 206–216) and Philadelphia (see p. 156) are just an hour or so away by road or rail.

RAIL **WASHINGTON–CHARLOTTESVILLE**
OTT TABLE 356

TRANSPORT	FREQUENCY	JOURNEY TIME
Train	Wed/Fri/Sun	2hrs 33mins

RAIL **CHARLOTTESVILLE–HINTON**
OTT TABLE 356

TRANSPORT	FREQUENCY	JOURNEY TIME
Train	Wed/Fri/Sun	4hrs 49mins

RAIL **HINTON–CINCINNATI**
OTT TABLE 356

TRANSPORT	FREQUENCY	JOURNEY TIME
Train	Wed/Fri/Sun	7hrs 12mins

RAIL **CINCINNATI–INDIANAPOLIS**
OTT TABLE 356

TRANSPORT	FREQUENCY	JOURNEY TIME
Train	Mon/Thur/Sat	2hrs 27mins

RAIL **INDIANAPOLIS–CHICAGO**
OTT TABLE 356

TRANSPORT	FREQUENCY	JOURNEY TIME
Train	Daily except Tues	5hrs 24mins

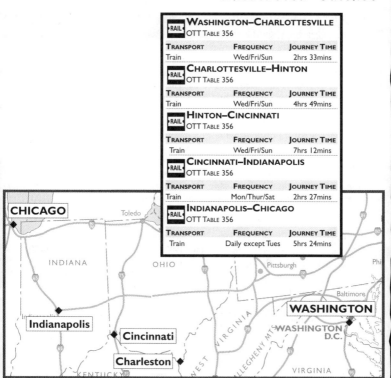

ON THE 'CARDINAL'

The 'Cardinal' certainly gives scenic value for money, perhaps to make up for its winding route. The most direct way to Chicago would be due west from DC, but the train swoops south-west through magnificent Virginia countryside and the forbidding hills of West Virginia. Stops en route include Jefferson's Charlottesville and West Virginia's capital, Charleston, but the highlight is stunning New River Gorge.

Beyond West Virginia lies serene Kentucky bluegrass country, famed for its horses and for the odd tint of blue in the grass. The 'Cardinal' crosses the Ohio at lively Cincinnati, by far the most worthwhile big city en route to explore. It then cuts diagonally across Indiana, through eminently missable Indianapolis and across fields of grain to Chicago.

CHARLESTON

Surrounded by neatly-clipped lawns, dotted with fountains and statues (spot Abraham Lincoln and Stonewall Jackson), the **Capitol Complex** at Kanawha Blvd houses the Cultural Center, the Governor's Mansion (a fine Georgian Colonial building) and the WV Veteran's Memorial Plaza. The Capitol Building itself is the largest in the country, and was designed by Cass Gilbert. Open Mon–Sat 1200–1900.

Downtown Charleston, the **Village District** stands out as a beautifully restored turn-of-the-century shopping area with a tempting array of clothing and speciality stores. For information, call Charleston Renaissance Corporation, tel: (304) 345 1738.

The curious will be enthralled by the **Sunrise Science Hall** and Art Museum Complex $, 746 Myrtle Rd, Charleston $, tel: (304) 344 8035. There are over 30 interactive exhibits and programs, as well as a Planetarium. Open Wed–Sat 1100–1700; Sun 1200–1700.

EN ROUTE

The 50 mile long canyon of New River Gorge can only be crossed by rail – or by raft on the water itself. This can be done in the picturesque town of Hinton, where the train stops before the gorge. Motel accommodation is available here.

Tourist Information at the **Capitol Complex**, The Cultural Center, 1900 Kanawha Blvd, tel: (304) 558 0220.

Charleston is not short of cheap motor inns just on the outskirts of the town: try MacCorkle Ave, lined with budget accommodations.

Embassy Suites Hotel, 300 Court St, Charleston, tel: (304) 347-8700, is a more luxurious option, primarily geared for the business traveller although they do offer some good short break deals.

Microtel Inn $$, 600 2nd Ave, Charleston, tel: (304) 744-4900, is located five minutes from the centre of Charleston, at exit 56, of Hwy 64.

Heart O'Town $–$$, 100 E Washington St, E. Charleston, tel: (304) 343-4661, is, as the name suggests, minutes from the centre and the town mall.

The Wren's Nest Restaurant, 1 mile out on Coal River Road, St Albans, tel: (304) 727-3224, is a charming log cabin roadside supper club, where you can dine, listen and dance to the best of wartime songs.

Fifth Quarter, $$, tel: (304) 345-2726, is a steakhouse located on the corner of Clendenin and Quarrier Sts, specialising in tender prime rib seafood, and with an award-winning 65-item salad bar.

Southern Kitchen, $, MacCorkle Ave and 53rd St, tel: (304) 925 3154, for nourishing home-style cooking

BLUEGRASS

The 'Cardinal' could just as well have been named the 'Bluegrass', as it cuts a line through Appalachia, the home of bluegrass music. Characterised by fast-picking banjoes, mandolins, fiddles and twangy, high-pitched vocals, bluegrass emerged from the lives of coal miners and farmers in Virginia, West Virginia, Kentucky and Tennessee. Today's distinctive style was developed by Bill Monroe and imitators in the 1940s, and deeply influenced the rise of rock 'n' roll a decade later: one of Elvis's first hits was Monroe's 'Blue Moon of Kentucky'. Often derided as hillbilly wailing, bluegrass remains popular as a uniquely American folk element.

CINCINNATI

Europeans settled here on the banks of the Ohio in the late 18th century, building on a native American trading post, and hilly Cincinnati soon became a major Midwest commercial centre. This wealth is evident today in the city's attractive buildings, and with its excellent art galleries, 'Cincy' makes a good break on the route. Its energetic centre appeals primarily for its setting, with a lively riverfront, rolling hills and gleaming skyscrapers striking a good balance. **Fountain Square** is the heart of it all, at 5th and Vine Sts, named for its massive spewing fountain. Imposing **Carew Tower** has an observation deck on its 48th floor. The riverfront has some nice open space upstream past the stadium and highway overpass. There are steamboat tours of the river from here.

A few streets in from the river, at Pike and 4th Sts, the **Taft Gallery** has beautiful glassware, china, and paintings from the likes of Rembrandt and Goya. $ Open Mon–Sat 1000–1700, Sun 1300–1700. Fine art at the **Cincinnati Art Museum**, 2 miles or so north-east, runs from the ancient Middle East to impressionist France. $$ Open Tues–Sat 1000–1700, Sun 1100–1700. Back towards Fountain Sq., the **Contemporary Arts Center** houses cutting-edge modern art; $ 115 E. 5th St; open Mon–Sat 1000–1800.

i Greater Cincinnati Convention and Visitors Bureau, 300 W Sixth St; tel: (1-800) 344-3445; www.cincyusa.com.

Amtrak's station is about a mile north-west of centre in the Union Terminal, with an easy bus link to the centre.

Chains are best for a cheap sleep (see p. 504).
Holiday Inn $$–$$$ 800 W. 8th St; tel: (1-800)HOLIDAY. Good position and fair prices, particularly at weekends.
Symphony Hotel $$$–$$$$ 210 W. 14th St; tel: (513) 721-3353. European style B&B near the Music Hall

Delis, pizzerias, bars and grills are abundant downtown.
Schlotzsky's Deli $$ 415 Vine St. Downtown hotspot for fresh-baked bread, big sandwiches and individual pizzas.
Arnold's Bar and Grill $$ 210 E. 8th St. Claims to be Cincinnati's oldest inn; solid food and live music at night.

INDIANAPOLIS

Hardly a tourist destination of the first order, Indianapolis nevertheless has a spot or two of interest, and is host to the annual Indianapolis 500 stock car race. Race fans turn up en masse – to the tune of nearly a half million people – for the Memorial Day-weekend extravaganza, traditionally the biggest event of the American car-racing season. Outside of this, Indianapolis is basically just a quiet place. Recent attempts to bring life to things are evident in the Circle Center mall, a haven of shops and restaurants downtown. One unusual thing about the city is its lack of a river: the site was chosen as state capitol merely for its centrality.

Some of the city's earliest wooden buildings survive in the **Lockerbie Sq. Historic District**, just east of downtown at East and New York Sts. On the other side of town, the **Eiteljorg Museum of American Indian and Western Art** is a grand collection of everything to do with the Wild West. Native American artefacts and an evocative group of paintings conjure up the romance and adventure. The museum is located at 500 W. Washington St, $$ open Tues–Fri 1000–1700, Sat–Sun 1200–1700; $6.

i **Indianapolis Convention & Visitors Association**, in the billowy white RCA Dome stadium at 2nd St and S. Capitol Ave; tel: (317) 639-4282 or (800) 958-INDY; icva@indianapolis.org. can help out with accommodation.

Rooms are fairly cheap, with many chains (see p. 504). **Comfort Inn City Centre** $$–$$$ 520 S. Capitol Ave; tel: (317) 631-9000 or (1-800) 228-5150. Well equipped and close to the RCA Dome.

You can settle your food and drink needs in the **Alcatraz Brewing Co.**, Circle Centre, 49 W. Maryland St. which makes its own beers and serves up pizzas, sandwiches and steaks.

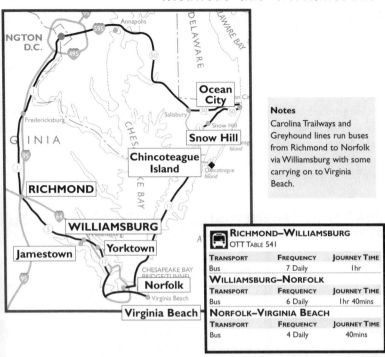

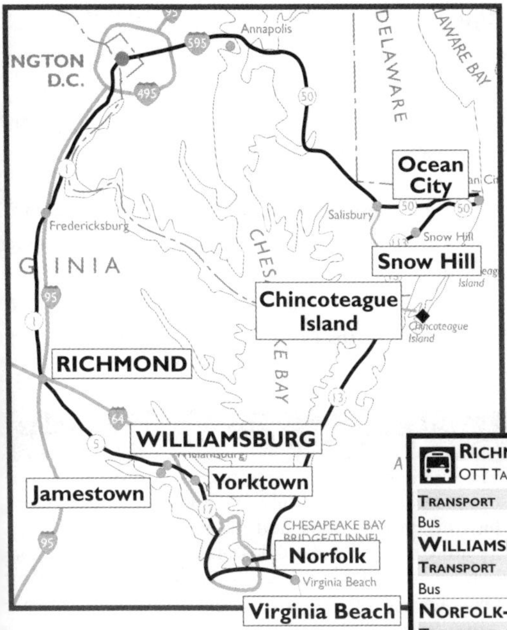

Notes

Carolina Trailways and Greyhound lines run buses from Richmond to Norfolk via Williamsburg with some carrying on to Virginia Beach.

RICHMOND–WILLIAMSBURG
OTT TABLE 541

TRANSPORT	FREQUENCY	JOURNEY TIME
Bus	7 Daily	1hr

WILLIAMSBURG–NORFOLK

TRANSPORT	FREQUENCY	JOURNEY TIME
Bus	6 Daily	1hr 40mins

NORFOLK–VIRGINIA BEACH

TRANSPORT	FREQUENCY	JOURNEY TIME
Bus	4 Daily	40mins

ROUTE DETAIL

Leave Washington on I-395, taking exit 11 to Washington St through historic Alexandria, then the Mount Vernon Memorial Hwy to Mount Vernon (16 miles). Rte 235 joins Rte 1 south to Fredericksburg and, 60 miles further on, Richmond. Beside it is the faster I-95 (124 miles). From Richmond Rte 5 meanders to Williamsburg (179 miles). Colonial Parkway leads west to Jamestown and on to Yorktown (201 miles). Go south on Rte 17 to I-64, which leads through Newport News and Norfolk. For downtown Norfolk take exit 276, heading south on Rte 460 (Granby St) (227 miles). (For Virginia Beach, 13 miles further on, continue on I-64 to exit 284 and take Rte 44 east.) Atlantic Ave heads north, becoming Rte 60; turn right on Rte 13, signposted Chesapeake Bay Bridge-Tunnel. Leaving the bridge-tunnel, Rte 13 travels north up the narrow peninsula; sidetrack onto Rte 175 to Chincoteague Island (325 miles). From Pocomoke City, follow Rte 113 north through Snow Hill to Berlin then Rte 50 east to Ocean City (362 miles). From Ocean City, head north on Rte 528 and turn left on to Rte 90 to join Rte 50 for Salisbury (395 miles). Continuing north-west, Hwy 50 passes through Cambridge, then Easton (444 miles). Join Rte 301 and cross Chesapeake Bay to Annapolis (488 miles) (exit 24 leads into town on Rte 70 south). Rte 50 returns you to Washington (total 523 miles).

Richmond and Williamsburg

Tidewater Driving Tour

Not quite in the Deep South, though filled with gracious plantations, Maryland and Virginia's tidewater country is a beautiful land all its own. From the gently rolling hills and well-groomed estates of the mainland to the flat farmlands and rough-and-ready watermen of the Eastern Shore peninsula, the region is diverse, interesting and beautiful.

Set like gems in this fine setting are such diverse places as the entire restored Colonial city of Williamsburg and the wild, barrier island of Chincoteague, where wild ponies roam. Spring comes early in a profusion of blooming trees and flowers; miles of beaches beckon in the summer; autumn paints the land in glorious colour, and winter is filled with holiday festivities and cultural events. Hospitality is the way of life all year round.

Richmond

En Route

Stop off at Mount Vernon, George and Martha Washington's beautifully maintained former home and gardens (see p. 181).

The state capital of Virginia and capital of the Confederacy between 1861 and 1865, Richmond offers historic sites, gardens, and pleasant diversions. Close by are Civil War battlefields and riverside plantation homes. Monument Ave, with its statues of Civil War generals and others, is considered one of America's most beautiful streets. The Fan, streets fanning out westward from Monroe Park, is possibly the largest intact Victorian neighbourhood in the USA.

TIC Metro Richmond Convention and Visitors Bureau, 550 E. Marshall St; tel: (804) 782-2777 or (800) 365-7272, can assist with lodging reservations, as well as provide a wide range of information.

Visitor Center, 1710 Robin Hood Rd, Richmond (Exit 78 on I-95); tel: (804) 358-5511. Open daily 0900–1700 (until 1900 June–Aug).

For reservations throughout the Richmond area, tel: (800) 444-2777. **Americamps** $ 396 Air Park Rd, Ashland (on Hwy 1); tel: (804) 798-5298, has camping about 20 miles north of the city .

Red Roof Inn $$ 4350 Commerce Rd; tel: (804) 271-7240 or (800) THE ROOF. Basic budget motor inn, south of downtown Richmond.

West-Bocock House $$–$$$ 1197 Grove Ave; tel: (804) 358-6174. An 1871 home convenient for museums, restaurants

and shopping; includes full breakfast.
Willliam Catlin House B&B $$$ 2304 E. Broad St; tel: (804) 780-3746. An 1845 home furnished with antiques.

Browse in the Fan District or Shockoe Slip, bounded by 15th, 21st, Dock and Broad Sts, where many former warehouses are now restaurants and bistros.
O'Toole's $–$$ 4800 Forest Hill Ave; tel: (804) 233-1781. Family-owned place offering barbecued dishes.
Southern Culture $–$$$ 2229 West Main, in the Fan; tel (804) 355-6939. Lively and casual, serving generous updated Southern dishes.
Strawberry Street Café $$–$$$ 421 N. Strawberry St, in the Fan; tel: (804) 353-6860. Famous for its salad bar and diverse menu.
The Frog and the Redneck $$$ 1423 E. Cary St; tel: (804) 648-3764. Continental menu uses local ingredients; popular.

HIGHLIGHTS Survey downtown from the free **Skydeck** of the City Hall at 9th and Broad Sts, open Mon–Thur 0800–2000, Fri–Sun 0800–1700. Its most visible landmark is Virginia's State Capitol, designed by Thomas Jefferson in 1785 as the first neo-classical building in the New World. Open Mon–Sun 0900–1700.
Nearby, the **White House of the Confederacy** was the Civil War home of Confederate President Jefferson Davis. The adjacent museum claims the world's largest collection of Confederate artefacts, including General Robert E. Lee's military tent. $ 1201 E. Clay St; tel: (804) 649-1861. Open Mon–Sat 1000–1700, Sun 1200–1700.

THE NATION'S OLDEST DINNER THEATRE?
Barksdale Theatre presents professional dramas, comedies and Broadway musicals year-round in a 1723 stagecoach inn, the Hanover Tavern, PO Box 7, Hanover (north of Richmond on Rte 301); tel: (804) 731-4860.

A block west is **Valentine Museum** $ 1015 E. Clay St, illustrating social history, decorative arts, costumes and architecture, and adjoining 1812 **Wickham House**, with outstanding neo-classical wall painting; tel: (804) 649-0711. Open Mon–Sat 1000–1700, Sun 1200–1700.

Valentine Riverside, on the site of an ironworks that supplied armaments for the Confederate army, has state-of-the-art living history displays, rafting trips at the falls of the James River, cycle tours and archaeological digs. $ 500 Tredegar St; tel: (804) 649-0711; open June–Aug Mon–Sat 1000–1700.

Church Hill is a historic neighbourhood, bounded by Broad, 29th, Main and 21st Sts. Here are some 70 antebellum homes, many with cast-iron ornamentation. The **Richmond National Battlefield Park Visitor Center** can supply you with a detailed

97-mile self-guided motoring tour of battlefields and sites around Richmond: 3215 E. Broad St (Rte 60); open daily 0900–1700.

The 1753 **Wilton House Museum** typifies the opulent homes of wealthy planters, with noted interior panelling and antiques: $ 215 S. Wilton Rd; tel: (804) 282-5936; open Tues–Sat 1000–1630, Sun 1330–1630. **Lewis Ginter Botanical Garden** has an extensive display of flowers, a mansion and a teahouse: $ 1800 Lakeside Ave; tel: (804) 262-9887; open Mon–Sat 0930–1600, Sun 1300–1600.

EN ROUTE

Two particularly fine plantations border the James River, on Rte 5 between Richmond and Williamsburg. **Shirley**, Virginia's oldest plantation, has a unique flying staircase and fine antiques: $$ tel: (804) 829-5377; open daily 0900–1630. Just beyond is **Berkeley** $$, open daily 0800–1700. Coach House Tavern, on the plantation, serves lunch and traditional dinners by candlelight: $$$ tel: (804) 829-6003.

WILLIAMSBURG

There is Williamsburg, and there is Colonial Williamsburg, a 173-acre museum town of houses, shops, taverns and public buildings peopled with costumed shopkeepers, craftsmen, soldiers, slaves, housewives and public officials, all vividly recalling the look and feel of Virginia's pre-Revolutionary capital. It provides a rare chance to step into another era, one very important to America's history.

To reach the Historic Area you must use the shuttle buses (included in admission) from the visitor centres (free parking) around the old town's perimeter. James City County Transit, tel: (757) 220-1621, connects the modern town of Williamsburg with the restored one for a $1 fare.

TIC Williamsburg Area Convention and Visitors Bureau, PO Box 3585, 201 Penniman Rd, Williamsburg, VA 23187; tel: (757) 229-2047, provides information on the entire area.

Colonial Williamsburg Foundation, PO Box 1776, Williamsburg, VA 23187-1776; tel: (757) 220-7645 or (800) HISTORY (447-8679), arranges accommodation and dining reservations in the Historic Area. Purchase tickets at the **Visitor Center** on Colonial Parkway at Rte 60; tel: (757) 220-7645, see an introductory film, and pick up the *Visitor's Companion* for details and to help plan your time. Open Mon–Fri 0900–1700, Sat–Sun 0830–1800.

Williamsburg's busiest periods are Apr, May and Oct; the cheapest months are Jan and Feb. **Williamsburg Hotel and Motel Association**, tel: (800) 899-9462 runs a free

reservations service. Private guest homes $–$$ are listedin the *Visitors' Guide*, which you can request in advance.
Guests in Colonial Williamsburg-owned hotels get discounted admission, free tours and preferential reservations in colonial taverns (see below). The most budget-friendly of these is:
Governor's Inn $$–$$$ 506 N. Henry St; tel: (757) 229-1000 or (800) HISTORY). A modern motel three blocks from the Historic Area.
Colonial Gardens B&B $$–$$$ 1109 Jamestown Rd; tel: (757) 220-8087 or (800) 886-9715. In woodland 5 mins by car from Colonial Williamsburg, furnished with antiques and original art.
Campsites include **Anvil Campground**, 5243 Mooretown Rd; tel: (757) 562-2300 or (800) 633-4442, which also has cabins, and **Jamestown Beach Campsites**, next to the Jamestown Settlement on Rte 31 south, 4 miles south from Colonial Williamsburg; tel: (757) 229-7609 or (800) 229-3300.

Four Colonial taverns ($–$$$) in the Historic Area serve dishes that would have been familiar to Redcoats and Patriots, in an atmosphere of minstrels and serving wenches:
Chez Trinh $–$$ 157 Monticello Ave; tel: (757) 253-1888. Vietnamese food in a casual atmosphere or to take away.
Old Chickahominy House $$ 1211 Jamestown Rd; tel: (757) 229-4689. A local favourite for plantation cooking in a non-touristy 18th-century setting; open daily 0830–1015, 1130–1415.
Chowning's Tavern, tel: (757) 229-2141, recalls an English alehouse.
Christiana Campbell's Tavern, tel: (757) 229-2141, was George Washington's favourite; open Wed–Sat 1700–2130.
The King's Arms Tavern, tel: (757) 229-2141, as posh as in Colonial times, open daily 1130–2130.
Shields Tavern, tel: (757) 229-2141, has a sampler offering tastes of several 18th-century dishes. Open Fri–Tues, 0830–1000, 1130–1500, 1700–2130.

HIGHLIGHTS Colonial Williamsburg $$$ takes more than a full day to see. Begin with an Orientation Walk (daily 1000–1500). Along with the primary sites, visit the 20 shops – apothecary, blacksmith, carpenter, foundry, gunsmith, shoe maker, silversmith, wigmaker etc – where interesting demonstrations are always in progress.

The imposing **Governor's Palace** is a reconstruction of the 1722 residence of seven royal governors, furnished in 1770s style. The **Capitol** reconstructs the seat of colonial government from 1701. It was here that a resolution declaring independence from England was unanimously adopted in May 1776, nearly two months before the Declaration of Independence was adopted in Philadelphia. **Raleigh Tavern** reconstructs the 1717 tavern where patriots plotted these events.

Bruton Parish Church, in continuous use since 1715, may be toured Mon–Sat 0900–1700, Sun 1200–1700. The **Public Gaol** is where wrongdoers – including the pirate Blackbeard – were incarcerated. **Brush-Everard House** is another original building, showing slave life in Williamsburg.

Adjoining the restored area, the **Abby Aldrich Rockefeller Folk Art Center** preserves American folk art in 18 galleries, with a collection of primitives, weathervanes, toys, needlework and other folk arts. The **DeWitt Wallace Decorative Arts Gallery** on Francis St houses an exceptional collection of English and American decorative arts to 1830, including Virginia-made furniture; tel: (757) 220-7724. Both $ open daily 1000–1800.

EVENTS DIARY

Mid Mar–Oct: weekly costumed drills in Market Square Green.

Apr–Oct: the Fife and Drum Corps performs in the Historic Area.

Early Sept: Publick Times recreates a colonial market, with craft show, auctions and military displays.

Early Dec–early Jan: Colonial Williamsburg is lit up over the Christmas period and there are firework displays and parades.

Carter's Grove, Rte 60, east of Williamsburg, is an 18th-century James River plantation, with a colonial mansion once described as America's most beautiful house, slave quarters and the Winthrop Rockefeller Archaeology Museum, interpreting the partly reconstructed site of an early English settlement here. Tel: (757) 229-1000; open Tues–Sun 0900–1800 (1000–1600 Nov–Dec). Included in Williamsburg pass.

In contrast to the tasteful historic ambience elsewhere, **Busch Gardens**, 3 miles south on Rte 60, is a theme-park version of 17th-century Europe – nine 'hamlets' filled with thrill rides, live shows, eateries and shops. $$$$+ plus parking; tel: (757) 253-3000; open Fri–Sun (mid Apr–mid May); daily (mid-May–Aug); Fri–Tues (Sept–Oct); closed winter.

JAMESTOWN AND YORKTOWN

Tree-lined Colonial Parkway connects these two major sites in American history, on either side of Williamsburg. **Jamestown** was the first permanent English settlement in North America. An extensive visitor centre has museum displays and a 15-min film. With a guide or rented audiotape, you can tour excavated ruins of early homes and of a 1608 glass furnace in the 1500-acre woodland. $ Open daily 0830–1700.

Jamestown Settlement, along Rte 31, depicts life for the first settlers in full-sized replicas of ships, a recreated fort and Powhatan Indian village; $$ tel: (757) 253-4838; open daily 0900–1700.

If you are stopping for more than a day and want to explore the area, the Discover Tidewater Passport gives unlimited access for 1–3 days on Tidewater Regional Transit (TRT))'s buses, ferries and trolleys; tel: (757) 640-6300.

Yorktown Battlefield is where the British army under Lord Cornwallis surrendered to Washington's allied French and American forces in 1781, events which are described in a film and exhibits. You can see tents used by Washington and parts of a reconstructed British frigate; pick up a brochure and audiotape for self-guided driving tours. Highlights are Moore House, where the Articles of Capitulation were drafted, and Nelson House, home of patriot Thomas Nelson, open daily 0830–1730.

Yorktown Victory Center describes the American Revolution through a timeline walkway, galleries, a film, a recreated continental camp and 18th-century farm where costumed interpreters demonstrate cooking, military and rural skills. $ tel: (757) 253-4838; open daily 0900–1700.

If you tire of national shrines, try the **Watermen's Museum** at 309 Water St, telling the story of those who sailed wooden Chesapeake wooden craft. Open Tues–Sat 1000–1600, Sun 1300–1600.

TIC: Colonial National Historic Park Visitor Center, Colonial Parkway, Yorktown; tel: (757) 898-3400.

Nick's Seafood Pavilion $–$$$ Water St (near bridge); tel: (757) 887-5269. Local favourite for seafood.
Duke of York Motor Hotel $$–$$$ 508 Water St; tel: (757) 898-3232. Has a pool and restaurant.

NORFOLK AND VIRGINIA BEACH

Side-by-side cities, one dominated by the navy, the other by beaches, guard the entrance to Chesapeake Bay. Travellers with a passion for things nautical will explore the former, while those who enjoy fun-filled beach resorts will head east to Virginia Beach, where a 2-mile boardwalk borders part of its 28-mile beach.

TIC Norfolk Convention and Visitors Bureau, Ocean View, I-64 exit 273; tel: (757) 441-1852 or (800) 368-3097, can help find accommodation. Open daily 0900–1700 (until 1900 mid June–Aug).
Virginia Beach Information Center, 2100 Parks Ave, Virginia Beach, VA 23451; tel: (757) 437-4888, (757) 437-4700,

WATER TOURS

American Rover, a three-masted schooner modelled on the 19th-century Chesapeake Bay craft, takes narrated cruises under sail Apr–Oct: $$$ tel: (757) 627-SAIL.

Dolphins swim alongside *Miss Virginia Beach* cruises: $$ 200 Winston Salem Ave; tel: (757) 422-5700.

For a nominal fare you can also ride on the *Waterside*, the charming little stern-wheeler that acts as a ferry across the Elizabeth River to Portsmouth.

EN ROUTE

Although it's flat, narrow Cape Charles is an interesting drive, especially if you wander off to the tiny watermen's harbours. Look for the picturesque village of **Wachapreague**, from which you can cruise to barrier islands; **Melfa**'s restored colonial architecture; and **Onancock**, with one of the East Coast's oldest general stores.

On the way to Chincoteague, on Rte 175, is the **NASA Visitor Center**, open Thur–Mon 1000–1600 (Mar–Nov); daily (July–Aug).

(800) 822-3224 or (800) 446-8038.

Tides Inn $$ 7950 Shore Dr., Norfolk; tel: (757) 587-8781 or (800) 284-3035. Motel with outdoor pool, close to restaurants and shops.

Old Dominion Inn $$–$$$ 4111 Hampton Blvd, Norfolk; tel: (757) 440-5100 or (800) 653-9030. Modest, with complimentary continental breakfast.

In Virginia Beach, contact **City of Virginia Beach Reservations**, tel: (800) VA-BEACH (800 822-3224), or, to rent furnished cottages, **Judy Andrassy International Realty**, 3309 Atlantic Ave; tel: (757) 428-8800.

Angie's Guest Cottage Hostel $ 302 24th St; tel: (804) 428-4690. Hostelling International member, a block from the beach and no curfew; open Apr–Sept.

Dunes Family Lodge $$ 9th St and Oceanfront; tel: (757) 428-7757. Especially welcomes children.

La Quinta Inn $$ 192 Newtown Rd; tel: (757) 497-6620. Has a pool and includes continental breakfast.

First Landings/Seashore State Park and Natural Area Campground, 2500 Shore Dr.; tel: (757) 481-2131 for information, (800) 933-7275 for reservations. Also has housekeeping cabins. Open Mar–Dec.

THE CHESAPEAKE BAY BRIDGE-TUNNEL,

which opened in 1964, is nearly 18 miles long and an extraordinary feat of engineering that serpentines above and below the water. If you want to pause before going under the waves, there is a viewing point with café on the southernmost of the four man-made islands. Keep to the right of the entrance as you go through the toll, and make sure you do a U-turn to get back to the tunnel entrance afterwards – otherwise you will have to pay the toll again.

ENTERTAINMENT

The Waterside Festival Marketplace on Waterside Dr. has live entertainment and concerts. A brick promenade leads to Towne Point Park, venue for free outdoor concerts and festivals. Through the summer Virginia Beach has band concerts on the beach and nightly entertainment on the boardwalk.

Browse around Norfolk's waterfront and in the Ghent neighbourhood's turn-of-the-century streets. Try **Elliott's $$** 1421 Colley Ave, Ghent; tel: (757) 625-0259, for down-to-earth seafood, burgers and vegetarian dishes.

Among Virginia Beach's hundreds of eateries, **Taste Unlimited $–$$** has three locations for sandwiches and picnics: 36th St and Pacific Ave, 4097 Shore Dr., and Hilltop West Shopping Center.

Duck-In and Gazebo $$–$$$ Shore Dr. at Lynnhaven Inlet; tel: (757) 481-0201. Locals' 'Best of the Beach' award choice; all-you-can-eat buffet Fri–Sat.

Famous Uncle Al's at the Beach $ 300 28th St. Sells hot dogs – satisfying and cheap.

Heritage Café $–$$ 310 Laskin Rd; tel: (757) 428-0500. Serves 'natural' foods.

HIGHLIGHTS Norfolk's **Nauticus** interprets the whole maritime world, from sciences and exploration to shipbuilding, international trade and warfare. High-tech exhibits let you navigate, chase submarines and design ships. You can also tour US Navy and foreign vessels in port. $$ 1 Waterside Dr.; tel: (757) 664-1000 or (800) 664-1080; open daily 1000–1900 (May–Sept); Tues– Sun 1000–1700 (Oct– Apr).

NORFOLK TROLLEY TOUR departs from Norfolk's Waterside Festival Marketplace for hop-on hop-off tours through historic downtown and neighbourhoods. $ Waterside Dr.; tel: (757) 640-6300; tours daily 1200–1600 (May–Sept).

Norfolk Naval Base is the world's largest naval installation. Guided bus tours ($) run daily June–Aug 1000–1330 from the Waterside or Nauticus and there are free on-board ship tours Sat–Sun 1300–1630. 9079 Hampton Blvd; tel: (757) 444-7955.

For a panorama, climb **Old Cape Henry Lighthouse** in Virginia Beach, built in 1791 to warn mariners entering Chesapeake Bay. $ Open daily 1000–1700 (mid Mar–Oct).

Birdwatchers should visit **Back Bay National Wildlife Refuge**, 7700 acres of beach, dunes, woodland and marsh filled with migratory waterfowl. Dec–Jan is best for peregrine falcons and bald eagles. The 10 miles of hiking and biking trails are open daily dawn–dusk. $ 4005 Sandpiper Rd; tel: (757) 721-2412; visitor centre open daily 0900–1600

CHINCOTEAGUE ISLAND

Chincoteague is famous for the wild ponies that roam it, frequently spotted along the roadsides. The island is also famous for oysters, shown at the **Oyster and Maritime Museum** in displays of live sea creatures. $ 7125 Maddox Blvd,

EN ROUTE

From the cheery harbour at Crisfield, summer passenger boats go to **Tangier Island**, 12 miles out in Chesapeake Bay. Its residents (fewer than 1000 of them) trace their ancestry back to 1686 and speak with an accent that even many Americans have difficulty in understanding. Tangier Island Cruises, 1001 W. Main St, Crisfield; tel: (800) 863-2338.

Chincoteague; open 1100–1700 daily (May–mid Sept); Sat–Sun (mid Sept–Nov).

Immediately to the north of Chincoteague lies the wildlife preserve of **Assateague Island**, where the ponies also run free, and the woods, dunes and marshes sustain small sika deer and 300 species of resident and migratory birds (see p. 154).

Get maps of biking and hiking trails at the **National Seashore Visitors Center**, tel: (757) 336-6577; open 0800–1800 (mid June–Aug), 0900–1600 (spring and autumn).

i TIC Eastern Shore Tourism Commission, PO Box R, Melfa, VA 23410; tel: (757) 786-2460.

Cape Charles House B&B $$ 645 Tazewell Ave; tel: (757) 331-4920. Near the beach, with bicycles available.
There are also tent pitches and caravan sites at **Kiptopeke State Park**, Cape Charles; $ tel: (757) 331-2267.
Places to stay are more plentiful at Chincoteague than further south, but also pricier.
Miss Molly's $$$–$$$$ 4141 Main St; tel: (757) 336-6686. Serves full breakfast and afternoon tea; open Mar–Dec.
Duck Haven Cottages $$$ 6582 Church St; tel: (757) 336-6290. Minutes from the beach.

WHERE NEXT?

From the tranquillity of Chincoteague, the route continues north to the contrasting non-stop summer party that is ***Ocean City****, included in the New York to Ocean City route* *(see p. 154)*.

SNOW HILL

The peninsula widens as you cross into Maryland, and the land is deeply cut by tidal estuaries lined by wildlands and cypress trees. Paddle among them from Snow Hill, renting a canoe from Pokomoke River Canoe: $$ tel: (410) 632-1700. Alternatively walk the self-guided tour of the town's 100-plus century-old homes. Nearby **Furnace Town** is a recreation of the 1840s village surrounding the enormous brick iron furnace, featuring broom and blacksmith shops, a smokehouse and a print shop. $ tel: (410) 632-2032; open daily 1100–1700 (Apr–Oct).

i Worcester County Tourism Office, PO Box 208, 105 Pearl St, Snow Hill; tel: (410) 632-3617.

River House Inn, 201 E. Market St; tel: (410) 632-2722. A gracious mansion with warm hosts.

MARYLAND'S EASTERN SHORE

Some of the loveliest villages and towns are in this part of Maryland, separated from the rest of the state by Chesapeake Bay. Close to Rte 50 are Salisbury, Cambridge, Easton, Oxford and St Michaels, each with streets lined by gracious historic homes. It would be a shame to miss any of them.

Salisbury's reconstruction following a fire in 1886 created the Newtown neigh bourhood, street after street of fine Victorian architecture. The Ward Museum of Wildfowl Art shows decoy carving as a fine art, with the world's most comprehensive collection of wildfowl carving. $ 909 Schumaker Dr.; open Mon–Sat 1000–1700, Sun 1200–1700.00.

Settled in 1682, **Easton** is an attractive community of quaint, tree-lined streets, voted one of America's top 100 small towns. **St Michaels**' postcard-perfect lighthouse is now a museum.

i TIC Wicomico County Convention and Visitors Bureau, Rte 13, Salisbury, MD 21801; tel: (410) 548-4914 or (800) 332-TOUR.
Dorchester County Tourism, 203 Sunburst Hwy, Cambridge, MD 21613; tel: (410) 228-1000.
Talbot County Conference and Visitors Bureau, PO Box 1366, Talbot Chamber Building, Tred Avon Sq., Easton, MD 21601; tel: (410) 822-4606.

The Bishop's House $$–$$$ 214 Goldsborough St, Easton; tel: (410) 820-7290 or (800) 223-7290. B&B in a restored Victorian villa furnished in period style.
Legal Spirits $$–$$$ 42 E. Dover St, Easton; tel: (410) 820-0033. Maryland crab cakes and massive salads in a former 1922 music hall decorated in Prohibition speakeasy style.

FOR FREE

Salisbury Zoo, on the banks of a stream, has some 400 mammals, birds and reptiles, including spectacled bears, spider monkeys, jaguars, bison and exotic birds in naturalistic habitats. It is open daily 0800–1630 (until 1930 in summer).

OCEAN CITY

Ocean City and Assateague Island are covered on pages 154–155.

Ocean City's municipal bus service runs round the clock and costs $1 for all day travel.

WHERE NEXT?

From Ocean City, the route described on pp. 149–155 continues up the coast all the way to New York. Annapolis (p. 212) and Baltimore (p. 206) are alternative destinations to returning to Washington DC.

ROUTE DETAIL

By car from Washington, the quickest way to Shenandoah National Park is along I-66 to Front Royal, the northern entrance to Skyline Drive (78 miles). Just over 100 miles south, this becomes the Blue Ridge Parkway, which continues to Roanoke (268 miles).

If you break the journey at Waynesboro (210 miles from Washington), Hwy 340 cuts across a few miles to Rte 11 south, which then takes you to Lexington (240 miles), and on to Natural Bridge (252 miles). From here, I-81 runs down to Roanoke (about 292 miles). From Roanoke Hwy 460 heads east to Lynchburg (347 miles) and then Appomattox (372 miles). From Appomattox to Charlottesville it's an enjoyable drive along a few back roads: take Rte 24 east to Hwy 60 east (392 miles). Turn right, and at Sprouse's Corner (399 miles), turn left onto Hwy 15 north. After 1 mile turn left onto Rte 20 north, which takes you into Charlottesville (436 miles).

Charlottesville can also be reached from the southern end of Skyline Drive via I-64 or the prettier Hwy 250, and directly from Washington by Hwy 29 off I-66 (95 miles). Charlottesville, Lynchburg and Roanoke are served by regular Greyhound buses from Washington DC, and Amtrak stops at Charlottesville, but to see more you will need your own transport.

RAIL WASHINGTON–CHARLOTTESVILLE
OTT TABLE 355/6

TRANSPORT	FREQUENCY	JOURNEY TIME
Train (Crescent)	Daily	2hrs 22mins
Train (Cardinal)	Wed/Fri/Sun	2hrs 33mins

WASHINGTON–CHARLOTTESVILLE
OTT TABLE 588

TRANSPORT	FREQUENCY	JOURNEY TIME
Bus	6 daily	2hrs 50mins

WASHINGTON–LYNCHBURG
OTT TABLE 588

TRANSPORT	FREQUENCY	JOURNEY TIME
Bus	5 daily	4hrs 5mins

WASHINGTON–ROANOKE
OTT TABLE 588

TRANSPORT	FREQUENCY	JOURNEY TIME
Bus	7 daily	4 hrs 30mins

Notes: Both trains require reservations and have a dining car.
Some buses call at Dulles Airport.
Some buses from Washington to Roanoke go via Charlottesville – journey time 5hrs 10mins.

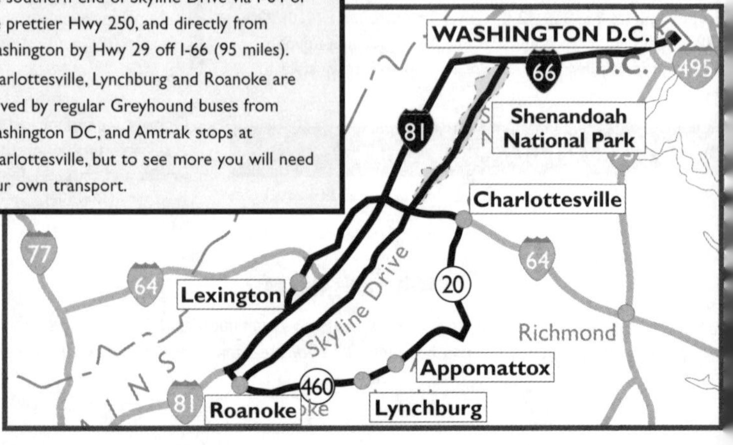

The names of two geographical features are inescapably and romantically linked to Virginia by song: the Blue Ridge Mountains and the Shenandoah River. The river flows through a broad valley between two long stretches of the Appalachian Mountains, known as the Blue Ridge here because of their rather remarkable appearance: distant peaks really do look blue most days, thanks to the presence of a particular haze that infiltrates the valley.

The Shenandoah National Park is the main draw here, and Skyline Drive rides the ridges straight through it, continuing as the Blue Ridge Parkway all the way to the Great Smoky Mountains of North Carolina. Further south in the Shenandoah Valley, the towns of Lexington and Roanoke have interesting cores and merit a brief stop.

East of the mountains lie several sites of historical importance. Appomattox is a fascinating little village and site of the signing of papers that ended the Civil War. Lynchburg and Charlottesville are attractive small cities, and the area around Charlottesville is Virginia's wine country: several dozen wineries here give free tours and tastings. Nearby is Thomas Jefferson's wonderful mansion of Monticello.

SHENANDOAH NATIONAL PARK

Straddling the eastern ridge of the Blue Ridge Mountains, Shenandoah National Park extends for about 80 miles north-east to south-west. You can traverse it along **Skyline Drive** in less than 3 hours – but only those with a soul of stone could fail to stop and take in the many stunning views, or embark on a short hike. The park is open year-round ($), though Skyline Drive may be closed at times because of bad weather conditions. There is no public transport to or through the park.

Entrances to the Park

There are four road entrances: **Front Royal** (via I-66), **Thornton Gap** (via Hwy 211), **Swift Run Gap** (via Hwy 33), and **Rockfish Gap** (via Hwy 250 and I-64).

Bird-spotting

Most commonly seen, especially from Skyline Drive, are the turkey vulture and black vulture. The turkey vulture, also known as a buzzard, has a wingspan up to 6 ft and a red head; the smaller black vulture has a pale patch on the underside of each wing. Wild turkeys, the largest of the park's bird species, are frequently seen too, especially in the northern section.

Skyline Drive affords drivers the luxury of enjoying the scenery with no physical exertion – viewpoints grace both sides of the road, so you *could* just wheel on down the road without even getting out, but this defeats the purpose of being in the mountains. There are some 300 miles of trails here, and the brochure given out at the park entrances gives some tips on hikes – everything from quick jaunts to take in a view or a waterfall, to longer circuits that can take several hours or even days. The Appalachian Trail, which extends over 2200 miles from Maine to Georgia, winds through the park, marked with a white blaze. To plan longer hikes, including overnight camping, pick up a map at any visitor centre.

WILDLIFE IN THE PARK

The mountains are home to an estimated 500 black bears. There are two species of poisonous snake: the copperhead and rattlesnake. Less fearsome creatures include Virginia white-tail deer, red and grey foxes, skunks, bobcats, raccoons, groundhogs and chipmunks. More than 1000 species of plantlife are found in the park, including 18 types of orchid (picking flowers is forbidden). Most of the park's trees are deciduous, with oaks and hickories predominating.

Skyline Drive continues south some 350 miles as the **Blue Ridge Parkway**, linking up with the Great Smoky Mountains National Park in North Carolina. While less 'developed' than Shenandoah National Park, the Parkway has much to offer. Virginia's **Explore Park**, at milepost 115, is a living history museum on 1300 acres, featuring a settlement from the 19th century, with costumed interpreters, a Native American village and bluegrass musicians. $ Open Sat–Mon, 0900–1700 (Apr–Oct).

TWO MINI-WALKS

Just north of Skyland is a 1.5-mile walk up to **Stony Man Mountain**, or take the 0.7-mile stroll down to **Dark Hollow Falls** from just south of Big Meadows.

ON THE HOOF

An exhilarating way of exploring the area is on horseback. There are stables with horses for hire at Skyland, and a guide accompanies all trips. Tel: (540) 999-2210.

All entrances to Shenandoah National Park are staffed with helpful rangers, who give out maps and information. There are regular visitor centres at Dickey Ridge (Mile 4.6) and Big Meadows (Mile 51), both open daily 0900–1700. For general park information, tel: (540) 999-3500.

Two lodges – at Skyland (Mile 41.7) and Big Meadows (Mile 51.2) – offer motel-type accommodation and rustic cabins for rent. A few cabins are also available at Lewis Mountain (Mile 57.5). The lodges are usually open early April–Nov and Lewis Mountain cabins May–late Oct; it is imperative to book well in advance: tel: (800) 999-4714. There are four campsites, at Big Meadows, Mathews Arm (Mile 22.2), Lewis Mountain and Loft Mountain (Mile 79.5). Reserve in advance for Big Meadows, and arrive early to get a spot at the others.

There are dining facilities every 20 miles or so along Skyline Drive, and you can pick up groceries at Skyland, Big Meadows and Loft Mountain (all Apr–Oct only).

LEXINGTON

Home to two universities and several historic buildings, Lexington is a pleasant place to break the journey and soak up small-town Virginia. The presence of the **Virginia Military Institute** (VMI) has much to do with the town's identity: it supplied the Confederacy with soldiers throughout the Civil War, and two of its most famous sons have museums here in their honour. Stonewall Jackson, a celebrated commander of the Confederate army, taught at VMI and owned a house in the centre of town which has recently been restored. George C. Marshall, author of the Marshall Plan to rebuild countries destroyed in World War II, graduated with the institute's class of 1901. Main St and Nelson St have some quaint boutiques and antique shops.

A visitor centre is located at 106 E. Washington St, tel: (540) 463-3777.

Of the many motels on the northern edge of town, **EconoLodge** $ tel: (540) 463-7371, is the cheapest.
Tourist Home $ 216 W. Washington St; tel: (540) 463-3075. No real name but remarkably cheap.
The Southern Inn Restaurant, 37 S. Main St. Features tasty main dishes and local wines.

EN ROUTE
NATURAL BRIDGE

The 90-ft span of this natural stone bridge is part of Rte 11, but you may scarcely be aware of it until you marvel at it from the bank of Cedar Creek 215 ft below. The setting is beautifully rural, but the lure of tourist dollars means an extravagant hotel, a silly wax museum, and an admission fee ($$) to see the archway. Despite these annoyances, the bridge is quite spectacular, and a path beneath it leads along the creek to some deep-pocket caverns.

ROANOKE

Roanoke is a surprisingly urbane city with enough attractions to keep you busy for a few hours at least. It was settled by German, Welsh and Scottish immigrants in the mid-18th century, but didn't come into its own until over a hundred years later. A slight European tinge pervades, from an ochre-coloured neo-classical church to the very German-looking Hotel Roanoke. Greyhound buses pull in to 26 Salem Ave, right in the centre.

In operation since 1882, the open-air farmers' market sets up daily at the intersection of Market St and Campbell St.

The central area has the feel of the important industrial centre it once was, and the nearby railway tracks seem to assert its continued sense of purpose. Campbell St is a trendy stretch of arty shops and international restaurants – good for a stroll.

Roanoke has made it easy for visitors to wallow in culture for hours at a time without flagging. Three independent museums and theatre are housed under one roof at the Center in the Square, 1 Market St, a restored and converted warehouse. All are open Tues–Sat 1000–1700, Sun 1300–1700. The **Science Museum of Western Virginia** ($) is a big hit with kids, while the **Art Museum of Western Virginia** (free) displays nationally important American art of the 19th and 20th centuries, as well as folk art of the region. On the top floor, the very good **Roanoke Valley History Museum** ($) gives an insight into the development of the area from the days before Colonial settlement, through the Civil War and the arrival of the railway, which brought prosperity and expansion.

The **Visitor Centre** is at 114 Market Place; tel: (540) 342-6025 or (1-800) 635-5535; open daily 0900–1700.

The nearest campsite is in neighbouring Salem, or you could head on to the Blue Ridge Parkway for the **Peaks of Otter Campground** at milepost 86.
Jefferson Lodge $$ 616 S. Jefferson St; tel: (540) 342-2951. Central and reasonably priced.
Mary Bladon House $$$ 381 Washington Ave; tel: (540) 344-5361. More atmospheric.

Stroll down Campbell St and Market St for a surprising range of restaurants that includes Vietnamese, Indian, Brazilian and Chesapeake Bay seafood.
Star City Diner $$ 118 Campbell Ave. Fun, family-oriented place, open late.
Awful Arthur's $$–$$$ 108 Campbell Ave. Extensive raw bar and fresh seafood, and live entertainment Wed and Thur evenings.
Carlos Brazilian International Cuisine $$$–$$$$ 312 Market St. Popular restaurant representing a range of cuisines.

Lynchburg

For free

The riverside **Miller-Claytor House** on Rivermont Ave dates from 1791 and is now a free-admission 'living history' museum, with demonstrations of early crafts. Open Thur–Mon 1300–1600 (May–Sept).

Settled in 1727, Lynchburg sprawls across seven steep hills above the James River. The city began as a ferry crossing and developed as a tobacco town; for more than a century tobacco was processed, auctioned and made into cigarettes and plugs for chewing. During the Civil War, the city was a major Confederate storage depot and a burial place for the war dead.

Several streets are designated historic districts. Start by walking around the central area, around Main St, Church St and Court St between 5th and 12th Sts. The

Old Court House, at 901 Court St, dates from 1855 and contains a decent museum on the city's history; $ open daily 1300–1600. On the corner of 12th and Main Sts, the **Community Market** was a favourite of Thomas Jefferson, and is still the place to come for fresh produce and home-made crafts. Across town, the **City Cemetery** at 4th and Taylor Sts contains the graves of men who fought in the Revolutionary War; most poignant is the Confederate section with the graves of 2701 soldiers from 14 states who died in the Civil War.

Lynchburg Visitors Center, 216 12th St; tel: (804) 847-1811, is very helpful, particularly with local accommodation.

The usual budget motels are located just off Rte 29 south of centre, or for more comfort in town, there are several B&Bs to choose from.

Lynchburg Mansion Inn $$$–$$$$ 405 Madison St; tel: (804) 528-5400 or (800) 352-1199. A comfortable inn in the Garland Hill historic district.

Madison Bed and Breakfast $$$–$$$$ 413 Madison St; tel: (804) 528-1503 or (800) 828-6422. Just down the street from Lynchburg Mansion and equally atmospheric and cosy.

Cattle Annie's $$$ 4009 Murray Place. For country fun – the style is Southern Americana with smoked meats, fresh salads and barbecue sandwiches, plus live country music and dancing.

APPOMATTOX

This quiet little community was the scene of one of the most significant events in the history of the USA – the ending of the Civil War. Here, on 9 April 1865, General Robert E. Lee surrendered the Confederate army of Northern Virginia to General Ulysses S. Grant, commander of the Union forces. Though skirmishes flared up in a few southern states for another two months, the agreement between Lee and Grant effectively began the long period of reconciliation.

Appomattox Court House National Historical Park $, 3 miles from the modern town (open daily 0900–1730), encompasses the original vil-

WAR'S END

The Civil War ended miserably for the 28,000 Confederate soldiers. They had made slow and rain-sodden progress westward across Virginia and on 6 April fought what proved to be their last major battle. Their dawn attack on the Union army at Appomattox three days later was short-lived – by 10 am it was clear that further fighting was useless, and General Lee signed the surrender document the same day.

lage, restored to its 1865 appearance after falling into disrepair. This was only a tiny village at the time, with a courthouse, jail, tavern, store, law office, and a few homes; many still stand or have been rebuilt, and can be visited on a self-guided tour. The courthouse contains the visitor centre and museum, but the momentous document signing actually took place in a private home, the McLean House, which has been reconstructed. Appomattox is really very small, but there is something haunting about the village and the gently rolling countryside around that makes it a must-see.

The first battle of the Civil War had been fought almost on the doorstep of the McLean family's previous home – they had moved south to Appomattox hoping to find peace.

CHARLOTTESVILLE

An elegant yet lively city dating from colonial times, Charlottesville is dominated by its beautiful university. The compact residential downtown area is worth investigating, and the countryside around is not to be missed, especially Thomas Jefferson's Monticello and the local wineries.

The **University of Virginia** campus is a stately collection of dignified red-brick buildings, smooth green lawns and carefully placed trees, and has been designated an important architectural site. Much of it was designed by Thomas Jefferson himself, who founded the university. The centrepiece is the Rotunda, from which you can join a free guided tour of many university buildings.

ARRIVING
The Amtrak and Greyhound stations are near each other on W. Main St, which links downtown Charlottesville with the university campus.

Central Charlottesville has a pedestrianised main street known as the Downtown Mall, with several buildings from the 19th century – a pleasant place to stroll and stop for ice cream. Two blocks north at 5th and Jefferson Sts, the **Albemarle County Court House** includes an 1820s chapel that was shared by Baptists, Episcopalians, Methodists and Presbyterians; worshippers included Presidents Jefferson, Monroe and Madison.

MONTICELLO Charlottesville's *pièce de résistance* is the stately, though eccentric home designed by Thomas Jefferson, the third president of the United States. Preserved as a national monument to Jefferson, Monticello is located on a hilltop just south of Charlottesville off Rte 20, and allows an insight into the mind of the squire revered as one of the founding fathers of the United States. Inside are many of the original furnishings, and the grounds – which include an orchard, vineyard and 1000-ft long kitchen garden – are well worth a visit. $$ Open daily 0800–1700 (Mar–Oct), 0900–1630 (Nov–Feb).

Charlottesville/Albemarle Convention and Visitors Bureau, tel: (804) 977-1783, shares a building with the **Monticello Visitor Center**, tel: (804) 984-9822, on Rte 20 south of town; both open daily 0900–1700.

There is a KOA campsite on Rte 1 about 10 miles south of Charlottesville. The usual cheap motels are clustered on Emmett St (Business Rte 29) west of centre.

Budget Inn $$ 140 Emmett St; tel: (804) 293-5141 or (1-800) 293-5144. Reasonable motel within walking distance of campus.

English Inn $$$ 2000 Morton Dr.; tel: (804) 971-9900 or (1-800) 986-5400. Pleasant enough place with pool, sauna and fitness centre.

200 South Street $$$$ 200 South St; tel: (804) 979-0200. Gracious Southern home right in the centre.

The **Downtown Mall** has several dining options; follow it west towards campus for more student-oriented establishments.

Hardware Store Restaurant $$–$$$ 316 E. Main St. A century ago this really was a hardware store and some of the old ironmongery and advertising signs are on display. Specialities include seafood, chicken and huge deli sandwiches.

C&O Restaurant $$–$$$$ 515 E. Water St. French-American restaurant, with formal dining upstairs or a casual setting downstairs; excellent wine list.

Wineries

Jefferson Vineyards, between Ash Lawn and Monticello on Rte 53, stands on the site where Jefferson planted the colony's first vines. Open daily 1100–1700.

Oakencroft Winery, Barracks Rd, west of Emmet St (Rte 29 north). Charlottesville's nearest vineyard is said to be one of Virginia's most picturesque. Tours and tastings offered daily 1100–1700 (Apr–Dec); 1100–1700 weekends in Mar; Jan–Feb by appointment only.

Barboursville Vineyards, Rte 777, Barboursville, 17 miles north-east of Charlottesville off Rte 20. Open Mon–Sat 1000–1700, Sun 1100–1700.

Horton Cellars, 6399 Spotswood Trail, Gordonsville, off Hwy 33 west. Tastings are held daily in a magnificent stone winery. Open daily 1100–1700 (weekends only during Mar).

Baltimore and Annapolis

Developed beside a natural harbour in Chesapeake Bay, Baltimore began as a distribution port for 18th-century grain farmers and tobacco growers. The city grew quickly, as shipwrights and merchants anxious to carry flour to distant reaches of the British Empire settled round the harbour fringes. Today, Baltimore is the thirteenth largest city in the USA and the fifth busiest port, filled with evidence of its rich Colonial and maritime history. It is a gutsy 'blue collar' city, a high-spirited place, with its busy Inner Harbor, restaurants, entertainment and activities along its hilly streets.

Annapolis, just 25 miles to the south, is one of America's most charming small cities. It rises from a boat-filled harbour to a gracious brick-clad hilltop crowned by a State House built at the time of the American Revolution. It was, briefly, the nation's capital in 1783–4. Founded in 1649, the entire city is today a National Historic Landmark, with many houses and public buildings more than 200 years old. It has more surviving Colonial buildings than anywhere else in the USA. The nautical character remains, bolstered by the US Naval Academy, whose buildings fill the eastern end of town and whose cadets are a vibrant part of the community.

Getting There

Air Baltimore/Washington International Airport (BWI); tel: (410) 859-7100, is a major gateway for passengers arriving from Europe.

A free shuttle runs between the main terminal and the airport station, and Amtrak and MARC (Maryland Area Rail Commuter), tel: (800) 325-RAIL, connect the airport and Baltimore, a 20-min journey which MARC makes only Mon–Fri. Bus no. 17, operated by MTA (Mass Transit Administration), tel: (410) 539-5000, connects the airport with the city centre and the BWI Airport Van Shuttle, tel: (800) 435-9294, serves Inner Harbor hotels.

Rail/Bus Amtrak connects Baltimore to New York and Washington, DC. The Amtrak station is nearly 2 miles from the harbour, accessed by bus nos. 3 or 11. MARC connects Baltimore and Washington, a 1-hr trip. MTA buses link Baltimore and Annapolis, also an hour apart. Greyhound/Trailways connect Annapolis to Washington, DC, 45 mins away.

ROAD Baltimore is reached by I-95, the major East Coast route, and from the north by I-83. The city is surrounded by I-695, the Baltimore Beltway, from which roads lead in to the city centre.

Rte 301/50 runs east–west across the north of Annapolis. Follow Rte 70 south to the city centre. Rte 2 leads from the south to Rte 450 W, which ends near the State House.

BALTIMORE

CITY MAP – inside back cover

You can buy tickets, often discounted, for museums, concerts, tours and cruises at the City Life Tickets kiosk, Inner Harbor Promenade, West Shore (between Harborplace and Maryland Science Center); tel: (410) 396-8342.

Baltimore Area Visitors Center, 300 W. Pratt St (in the Constellation Building on the Inner Harbor, across from Harborplace's Pratt St Pavilion); tel: (410) 837-INFO or (800) 282-6632. Well located among the major waterfront attractions but crowded during busy periods.

Maryland Office of Tourism Development, Department of Business and Economic Development, 217 E. Redwood St, Baltimore, MD 21201; tel: (410) 767-6270.

SAFETY The usual commonsense precautions apply. Don't walk around alone late at night and stick to well-lit streets.

MONEY Cash machines in Baltimore-Washington International Airport are located at the Main Terminal, Pier C; also at nearly all downtown banks.

POST AND PHONES The main post office is at 900 E. Fayette St; tel: (410) 655-9832. When using the phone you must dial the area code even for local calls.

As in most major cities, budget accommodation is scarce, but you can save by staying 3–4 miles from the Inner Harbor; and there are offers in the current issue of the *Baltimore Quick Guide* and *Baltimore Street Map and Visitor Guide*, both available at the TIC.

Reservation services include **Maryland Reservations Center**, 68 Maryland Ave, Annapolis, MD 21401; tel: (410) 269-5620; and **Amanda's Bed and Breakfast Reservations Service**, 1428 Park Ave, Baltimore, MD 21217; tel: (410) 225-0001.

Hostelling International $ 17 W. Mulberry St; tel: (410) 576-8880. Near bus and Amtrak stations, within walking distance of Inner Harbor. Check-in is 1000–1100.

Comfort Inn $$ 6700 Security Blvd, West Baltimore; tel:

BALTIMORE AND ANNAPOLIS

airport shuttle and free breakfast.

Holiday Inn Express $$$ 1401 Bloomfield Ave; tel: (410) 646-1700. Four miles from the Inner Harbor, with generous continental breakfast.

Mr Mole Bed and Breakfast $$$ 1601 Bolton St; tel: (410) 728-1179. Highly regarded non-smoking accommodation in an 1870 renovated terraced house furnished with antiques. Complimentary Dutch-style breakfast.

Days Inn Baltimore/Inner Harbor $$$$ 100 Hopkins Pl.; tel: (410) 576-1000. Children under 17 stay free and the under-12s can even *eat* free.

You could spend two weeks dining in a different Baltimore restaurant every night and still not sample all its ethnic cuisines. Some 125 restaurants are in Harborplace alone, at Pratt and Light Sts, and many more throughout the downtown area and central communities like Fells Point and Little Italy. Seafood is abundant, with crab cakes a local speciality. Buy food for picnics at Lexington Market, 400 W. Lexington St; open Mon–Sat 0800–1800.

Bertha's $ 734 S. Broadway, Fells Point; tel: (410) 327-5795. *The* place to go for mussels, chowder and afternoon tea with scones.

Sisson's Restaurant and Brewery $–$$ 36 E. Cross St; tel: (410) 539-2093. Cajun/Creole cooking.

Germano's Trattoria $$ 300 S. High St, Little Italy; tel: (410) 752-4515. Busy place specialising in good Tuscan fare.

Kawasaki $$ 413 N. Charles St; tel: (410) 659-7600. Hailed as one of the top Japanese restaurants in the USA; lunch and dinner Mon–Sat.

Wayne's Bar-B-Que $$ Harborplace Pavilion, 301 Light St; tel: (410) 539-3810. Trendy barbecue place, with country music and good beer selection.

Henninger's Tavern $$–$$$ 1812 Bank St, Fells Point; tel: (410) 342-2172; dinner Tues–Sat. American dishes served in a century-old tavern.

Lista's $$–$$$ 1637 Thames St/Brown's Wharf; tel: (410) 327-0040. Mexican food and music with live jazz Fri.

GETTING AROUND

Most major attractions are within walking distance of the Inner Harbor; sights further out are reached by tourist trolley or MTA bus and rail services. Intended to serve commuters, not tourists, buses may involve a number of transfers. None of the Metro's half-dozen downtown stations is closer than three blocks from Inner Harbor.

More fun, and cheaper, is the Water Taxi; tel: (410) 563-3901 or (800) 658-8947, a year-round service with 15 stops near sights around the Inner and Outer Harbors. Passengers are given a useful *Waterfront Guide* with maps and information on attractions and restaurants. It operates Wed–Sun Nov–Mar, daily the rest of the year. Buy an all-day pass on board.

TOURS

Baltimore Trolley Tours, tel: (410) 752-2015 or 724-0077, offers narrated tours aboard replica Victorian trolleys revealing history, culture and folklore, between 20 stops. All-day pass $$; daily half-hourly 1000–1600, less frequent Nov–Feb.

Maps for a city walking tour (free at the TIC) will lead you to Federal Hill, Little Italy, Fells Point and the Otterbein area of restored houses.

HIGHLIGHTS **Central Area**: in a convenient cluster, Baltimore City Life Museums depict the city's history: the **Exhibition Center**, **Carroll Museum**, **Center for Urban Archaeology** and the **1840 House** are at Museum Row, sharing a single entrance at 800 E Lombard St; $ tel: (410) 396-3523. Most open Tues–Sat 1000–1700, Sun 1200–1700 (closing 1600 Nov–Mar). The Carroll Museum has period furniture and decorative arts showing the style in which the city's 19th-century élite lived. 1840 House is the reconstructed home of a local wheelwright. The Center for Urban Archaeology examines the role of archaeologists, with an excavation pit, industries and shops from the past and glassware and ceramics exhibits.

The 234-ft **Shot Tower**, built in 1828 with a million wood-fired bricks and once a leading supplier of lead shot, is one of the few remaining in the USA; interactive exhibits and a sound-and-light show illustrate how gun shot was made. 801 E. Fayette St; tel: (410) 837-5424; open Wed–Sun 1000–1600.

It is worth calling in at **Baltimore City Hall** to see its 110-ft rotunda capped by a rare segmented dome; exhibits illustrate Baltimore history. 100 N. Holliday St; open Mon–Fri 1000–1630.

Continue to head north to Mount Vernon Place, to the **Washington Monument** ($). This was the first in the nation honouring George Washington, and the 228-step climb rewards you with a bird's eye view of the city.

Just to the south, the **Basilica of the National Shrine of the Assumption of the Blessed Virgin Mary**, at Cathedral and Mulberry Sts, was the first Roman Catholic cathedral in the USA. Designed by Benjamin Latrobe, architect of the White House, it is one of the world's best examples of neo-classical architecture. Tours after 1045 Sun mass or by appointment.

Just west of the monument, the **Maryland Historical Society Museum and Library** includes the Radcliffe Maritime Museum, the Darnall's Children's Gallery, Enoch Pratt House and Civil War and War of 1812 galleries. The original manuscript of 'The Star-Spangled Banner' is here, along with important collections of American silver, decorative arts and paintings. $ 201 W. Monument St; open Tues–Fri 1000–1700, Sat 0900–1700.

A block away, the **Walters Art Gallery** $$, 600 N. Charles St, represents 5000 years of art from four continents, from medieval armour and Fabergé eggs to Ancient Egyptian and art nouveau. Asian arts are at **Hackerman House**, 1 Mount Vernon Pl.; open Tues–Sun 1100–1700, free Sat 1100–1200.

Inner Harbor: the highlight of the waterfront is the USS *Constellation* ($), launched in Baltimore as a frigate in 1797 and rebuilt as a sloop of war in 1854. Her missions included blocking slave ships off Africa. The *Pride of Baltimore II* is a replica of the famous Baltimore clipper, many of which were built between the Revolutionary War and the mid-19th century. The 160-ft topsail schooner sails as Maryland's goodwill ambassador, but you can board if it's in port; tel: (410) 539-115.

Three more ships are part of **Baltimore Maritime Museum**: the coastguard cutter *Taney* is the only ship still afloat that survived the attack on Pearl Harbor; the US submarine *Torsk* sank the last Japanese combatant ship of World War II; and the *Chesapeake* is a 1930s floating lighthouse. $ tel: (410) 396-3453; open Mon–Fri 0930–1700, Sat–Sun 0930–2000; Fri–Sun 0930–1700 (Dec–Feb).

Next door is the **National Aquarium**, a world-class aquatic museum, where 7000 creatures, representing at least 500 species of fish, birds, reptiles, amphibians and marine mammals, live in recreated habitats. Highlights are a giant octopus, an Atlantic coral reef, an Open Ocean exhibit that brings visitors face to face with sharks, and a reproduced South American rain forest. Dolphins perform daily in 25-min shows. $$ Open daily 1000–1800 (Fri–Sat until 2000); opens 0900 July–Aug.

> Near the aquarium entrance at the harbour is an outdoor rock pool where you can watch – at no cost – cavorting harbour and grey seals.

Across the harbour is the **Maryland Science Center**, covering space exploration, television, energy and Chesapeake Bay through hands-on exhibits. The IMAX® theatre has a screen five storeys high, and the Davis Planetarium has excellent shows. $$ 601 Light St; open daily 1000–1800 (1000–2000 Fri–Sun in summer).

Away from the Center: the star-shaped brick fort at the end of E. Fort Ave is **Fort McHenry National Monument**, sacred to Americans. It was built in 1790, and successfully thwarted the British attack on Baltimore in 1814. (The battle inspired Francis Scott Key to compose 'The Star-Spangled Banner', the national anthem.) You'll see officers' quarters, guardrooms, and powder magazine; re-enactments of life in the garrison are presented by guardsmen in period uniform on weekend afternoons mid-June–Aug. $ open daily 0800–1700 (0800–2000 June–Aug).

HARBOUR CRUISES

Baltimore Defender and Guardian, tel: (410) 685-4288, shuttles between Inner Harbor Finger Piers and Fort McHenry (see below) and Fell's Point, May–Sept. The *Baltimore Patriot*, tel: (410) 685-4288, gives 90-min narrated harbour cruises departing from Constellation Dock. The *Minnie V* is a historic Chesapeake Bay oyster boat that gives narrated tours: **$$** tel: (410) 522-4214; or for a tour under sail, board the tall ship *Clipper City* at Harborplace: **$$–$$$** tel: (410) 539-6277.

Also a little way out of the city centre is **Mount Clare Museum House** in Carroll Park, Baltimore's only pre-revolutionary war mansion. Built in 1760, it is considered one of the finest examples of Georgian architecture in the USA. The 18th- and 19th-century furniture are original to the house. $ tel: (410) 837-3262; tours hourly Tues–Fri 1000–1500, Sat–Sun 1300, 1400, 1500.

On the way, admirers of Edgar Allan Poe can detour to 203 N. Amity St. The house where Poe lived for three years (1832–5) at the beginning of his writing career contains Poe artefacts and period furniture. $ tel: (410) 396-7932; open Wed–Sat 1200–1545.

Even closer to Carroll Park, the **B&O Railroad Museum**, at 901 W. Pratt St, is the birthplace of the oldest railway in the country, dating from 1829, and the site of the first American passenger railway station. Here are many of the nation's oldest steam and diesel locomotives, plus passenger cars and freight wagons, and a garden of model trains. $$ open daily 1000–1700. Excursion trains run at weekends; tel: (410) 752-2490.

A BASEBALL LEGEND

The new, updated home of the Baltimore Orioles, Oriole Park at Camden Yards, seats 48,000 fans. Daily tours (Mar–Dec) include the scoreboard control room and press box, and interactive computer and laser technology enable you to stand in the batter's box and slam at the ball; tel: (410) 547-6234. The birthplace of one of baseball's greats, Babe Ruth, is nearby in Pratt St and can also be visited.

NIGHTLIFE Along with top-class music and theatre, Baltimore has a busy club and pub scene, with comedy and dance clubs and live bands in bars and taverns.

The Vagabond Players, 806 S. Broadway, Fell's Point; tel: (410) 563-9135. Affordable, quality theatre year-round Fri–Sun.
Fell's Point Corner Theatre, 251 S. Ann St; tel: (410) 276-7837 or 466-8341. Premières of off-Broadway plays Fri–Sun.
Baltimore Opera Company, Lyric Opera House, 140 W.

Mount Royal Ave; tel: (410) 727-6000. Resident company for grand opera with international artists and full orchestra.
Baltimore Symphony Orchestra, Joseph Meyerhoff Symphony Hall, 12121 Cathedral St; tel: (410) 783-8000. High-profile programmes with guest performers.
Peabody Conservatory of Music, 1 E. Mount Vernon Pl.; tel: (410) 659-8124. Student and guest artist recitals, symphony and opera.
Fat Lulu's, 1818 Maryland Ave; tel: (410) 685-4665. Jazz and blues with your Cajun and Creole meal.

ANNAPOLIS

TIC Annapolis and Anne Arundel County Visitors Bureau, 26 West St, Annapolis, MD 21401; tel: (410) 280-0445. A tourist information booth is located on the City Dock.

Annapolis has 20 B&Bs in the historic district alone, with budget motels along Rte 301/50. During late May, accommodation is almost impossible to find. Reservations services include **Amanda's Bed and Breakfast**, 1428 Park Ave, Baltimore, MD 21217; tel: (410) 225-0001; **Annapolis Accommodations**, 66 Maryland Ave, Annapolis, MD 21401; tel: (410) 280-0900 or (800) 715-1000; and **B&B of Maryland**, PO Box 2277, Annapolis, MD 21204; tel: (410) 269-6232 or (800) 736-4667.
MainStay Suites $$–$$$ 120 Admiral Cochrane Dr.; tel: (800) 660-MAIN. A bargain for those with a car, offering full kitchens, pool and weekday breakfast.
Historic Inns of Annapolis $$$–$$$$ 16 Church Circle; tel: (410) 263-2641. Four inns from the 18th and early 19th centuries – the Maryland Inn, Governor Calvert House, Robert Johnson House and State House Inn – are clustered around the two circles at the heart of Annapolis.
Gibson's Lodgings $$$–$$$$ 110 Prince George St; tel: (410) 268-5555. Near the City Dock in the historic district, with courtyard parking, complimentary sherry and continental breakfast.

Downtown, the greatest concentration is along West St, Main St and around the City Dock. Eastport/Annapolis Neck south of Spa Creek, at the end of Duke of Gloucester St, has an eclectic mix.

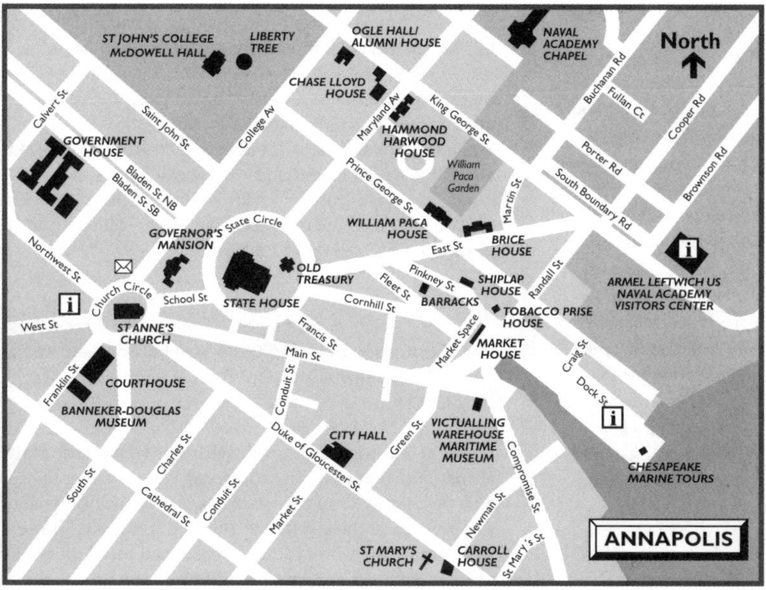

City Dock Café $ 18 Market Space. Small, casual and friendly coffee house with freshly baked confections. A good place for people-watching.

Acme Bar and Grill $–$$ 163 Main St; tel: (410) 280-6486. Serves American cuisine – chicken wings, crab cakes and pastas – in a classic saloon setting, daily 1130–0200.

Ram's Head Tavern $–$$ 33 West St; tel: (410) 268-4545. Restaurant and home of the Fordham Brewing Co., a traditional tavern featuring 26 beers on draught and lunch and dinner daily.

Carrol's Creek $$–$$$ 410 Severn Ave, Eastport; tel: (410) 269-1406. Overlooking the marina and a superb view of Annapolis, serving inspired versions of regional seafood and more.

Middleton Tavern Oyster Bar and Restaurant $$–$$$ 2 Market Space; tel: (410) 263-3323. Traditional Maryland fare served in a restored 1750 building overlooking the harbour.

GETTING AROUND Narrow streets, while lovely for strolling, leave few parking places. It's best to park all day (at a reasonable rate) at the Navy-Marine Corps Memorial Stadium, north of College Creek, and take the Annapolis Trolley

TOURS

Knowledgeable guides in Colonial costume lead 2-hr tours daily of the historic district ($$). Contact **Three Centuries Tours of Annapolis**, 48 Maryland Ave; tel: (410) 263-5401. Self-guided audio-cassette tours may be purchased at the **Historic Annapolis Foundation Museum Store**, 77 Main St, open daily; tel: (410) 268-5576. Or be guided by an architectural historian ($$) from **Annapolis Walkabout**, 223 S. Cherry Grove Ave; tel: (410) 263-8253.

Express Shuttle downtown. It stops at the visitor centre, Maryland Ave, the Naval Academy and Main St.

Most attractions are an easy walk apart in the central area. Other places – especially the restaurants along Spa and Back Creeks – are reached by Jiffy Water Taxi, Slip 20, City Dock. In summer (mid-May–early Sept) boats depart hourly: Mon–Thur 0930–2400, Fri 0930–0100, Sat 0900–0100, Sun 0900–2400; shorter hours during spring and autumn.

HIGHLIGHTS

Annapolis is a joy for budget travellers, rich in free sights. The streets themselves, and the houses that line them, are an open-air architectural museum with more than 1000 buildings of 15 different styles predating 1900.

Begin at the top of the hill, with the **Maryland State House**, on State Circle. The focal point of Annapolis and the country's oldest state house in continuous use, this was once the capitol of the USA and was the setting for George Washington's resignation as commander-in-chief and the ratification of the Treaty of Paris, which officially ended the American Revolution. Tours daily 1100 and 1500.

Government House, also on State Circle, was built during the Victorian period, to be the official residence of the Governor of Maryland. Open Tues–Thur 1000–1400 (closed Wed Jan–Mar). Tours of its collection of art and antiques are by reservation; tel: (410) 974-3531.

Church Circle adjoins State Circle via School St, and in its centre is the graceful **St Anne's Church**, rebuilt in 1859, more than 150 years after its founding. Its Tiffany window won first prize at the Chicago World's Fair in 1893; open daily 0800–1800.

Just off Church Circle, **Banneker-Douglass Museum**, at 84 Franklin St, is the state repository of African-American cultural material. Collections include artefacts and photographs of black life in Maryland, as well as African and African-American art and rare books; tel: (410) 974-2893. Open Tues–Fri 1000– 1500, Sat 1200–1600.

All in the same area, between State Circle and the Naval Academy, are three outstanding historic homes to visit. **Chase-Lloyd House** $, 22 Maryland Ave, was built in 1769 by a signatory to the Declaration of Independence. The Georgian town house, noted for fine interior detail, is open Tues–Sat 1400–1600 (Tues, Fri and Sat only, Jan–Feb); tel: (410) 263-2723.

Hammond-Harwood House, at 19 Maryland Ave, was built in 1774 for Matthias Hammond, a Revolutionary patriot. Considered one of the most beautiful examples of late Colonial architecture, the house stands in a charming garden and features late 18th- and early 19th-century Maryland furniture and paintings. $ tel: (410) 269-1714; open Mon–Sat 1000–1600, Sun 1200–1600.

William Paca House and Garden, 186 Prince George St, home of another signatory, was built between 1763 and 1765 in a 2-acre garden featuring five terraces of formal parterres. $ tel: (410) 263-5553; open Mon–Sat 1000–1600, Sun 1200–1600 (Fri–Sun only Jan–Feb).

THE NAVAL ACADEMY

Annapolis is synonymous with the US Navy, and the Naval Academy has several interesting sights, all of which are free. The Visitor Center, inside Gate 1, off King George St, is the starting point for guided tours; $ tel: (410) 263-6933; open daily 0900–1700 (until 1600 Dec–Feb).

Bancroft Hall is home to the entire brigade of midshipmen, with 1873 rooms along 5 miles of corridors; you can visit a sample midshipman's quarters.

The Chapel, often called the Cathedral of the Navy, contains Tiffany windows and the Crypt of John Paul Jones, naval hero of the American Revolution, whose remains were returned in 1905 after more than a century of obscurity in a Paris cemetery. Class of 1951 Gallery of Ships is an exhibition of model ships dating from the 17th century, made of bone, gold and wood. The Naval Academy Museum contains 50,000 items, including arms, model ships and aircraft, paintings and prints; open Mon–Sat 0900–1700, Sun 1100–1700.

South of the Circle, towards the bridge to Eastport, is **Charles Carroll House**, 107 Duke of Gloucester St. The restored birthplace of Charles Carroll, one of the wealthiest men in Colonial America and the only Catholic to sign the Declaration of Independence, has terraced gardens. $ tel: (410) 269-1737; open Fri and Sun 1200–1600, Sat 1000– 1400.

In Eastport itself, the **Barge House Museum**, on Bay Shore Dr. (end of Second St), features boat building, historic and maritime artefacts, maps and photographs, Sat 1100–1600 and by appointment; tel: (410) 268-1802.

SHOPPING In spite of its popularity with visitors, Annapolis manages to maintain a small-town ambience, where shopkeepers welcome browsers along Main and West Sts and around the City Dock.

Watch potters work at Annapolis Pottery, 40 State Circle, and visit Historic Annapolis Foundation Museum Store, 77 Main St for souvenirs that reflect the heritage of Annapolis, including reproductions of 18th-century artefacts and books. Save the Bay Shop, 188 Main St, sells books, clothing and gifts to support the Chesapeake Bay environment.

Baltimore and Annapolis

Nightlife Annapolis is a lively, busy place, with around a dozen organisations involved in the performing arts. Major performances are staged at the **Maryland Hall for the Creative Arts**, 801 Chase St; tel: (410) 263-5544. Calendars for all events are published in *The Capital* daily, and *The Publick Enterprise*.

Annapolis Opera, tel: (410) 263-2710 or 267-8135. Performs opera, operettas and musicals year-round.

Annapolis Chorale, tel: (410) 263-1906. 150-voice chorus and chamber orchestra.

Annapolis Summer Garden Theatre, 143 Compromise St; tel: (410) 268-9212. Presents Broadway musicals nightly late May–early Sept.

Annapolis Symphony Orchestra, tel: (410) 269-1132. Performs a classical repertoire.

Ballet Theatre of Annapolis, tel: (410) 263-8289. Classical and modern ballet.

Colonial Players, 108 East St; tel: (410) 268-7373. Presents plays in a 180-seat theatre-in-the-round.

NEW YORK – ORLANDO

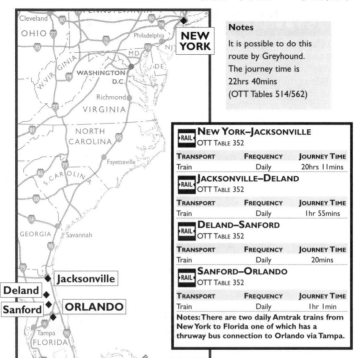

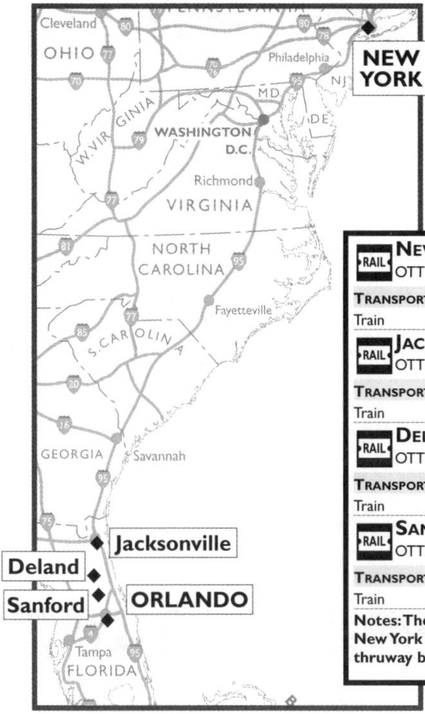

Notes

It is possible to do this route by Greyhound. The journey time is 22hrs 40mins (OTT Tables 514/562)

RAIL NEW YORK–JACKSONVILLE
OTT TABLE 352

TRANSPORT	FREQUENCY	JOURNEY TIME
Train	Daily	20hrs 11mins

RAIL JACKSONVILLE–DELAND
OTT TABLE 352

TRANSPORT	FREQUENCY	JOURNEY TIME
Train	Daily	1hr 55mins

RAIL DELAND–SANFORD
OTT TABLE 352

TRANSPORT	FREQUENCY	JOURNEY TIME
Train	Daily	20mins

RAIL SANFORD–ORLANDO
OTT TABLE 352

TRANSPORT	FREQUENCY	JOURNEY TIME
Train	Daily	1hr 1min

Notes: There are two daily Amtrak trains from New York to Florida one of which has a thruway bus connection to Orlando via Tampa.

ON THE 'SILVER STAR'

Amtrak runs trains daily from New York down the Atlantic coast to Florida via the 'Silver Star,' 'Silver Palm' and 'Silver Meteor' trains. The 'Silver Star', departing in the morning, offers the more scenic opportunities during daylight hours. From New York your morning journey will transport you through the heavily industrialised 'north-east corridor' connecting New York, Philadelphia and Washington DC, with only snippets of scenery visible. Leaving Washington in late afternoon, the train continues through the gently rolling hills of Virginia. Night-time deprives you of the sight of the edges of the Appalachian mountains, but early morning offers views of the Carolina Lowcountry. From Jacksonville, your introduction to Florida, you can access the beaches of Amelia Island, quaint St Augustine and Daytona. By midday you will have left the scrubby landscape of Florida's eastern coast behind, and be headed for the tourist havens of central Florida.

JACKSONVILLE

Jacksonville, like a large gangly puppy, sprawls in many directions, and is not easy to see on foot. To see the city at its best, stroll along the **Southbank Riverwalk**, a 1¼ mile boardwalk that runs from just east of Acosta Bridge to about ½ mile east of the Main St Bridge; or take a cruise on the river. The 12-mile bus ride to the beaches can take up to an hour, but the wide and wild expanses of sand are worth the trip.

Rarely for Florida's east coast, you can horse-ride on the beach at unspoilt Fernandina Beach, **Amelia Island**, just north of Jacksonville; the Sea Horse Stables offer a 5-mile guided trek ($$$). Take time to explore the 19th-century mansions of the town and **Fort Clinch State Park** with its brick fort and nature trails.

Jacksonville and the Beaches Convention and Visitors Bureau, 3 Independent Dr.; tel: (904) 798-9111 or (800) 733-2668; www.jaxcb.com. Open Mon–Fri 0800–1700.
Amelia Island Chamber of Commerce, tel: (904) 261-3248.

Chain hotels and basic motels are plentiful (see p. 504).

The Amtrak station is 6 miles north-west of downtown and the Riverwalk, at 3570 Clifford Lane.

DELAND

Deland Academy (later renamed Stetson University) was once envisaged as an 'Athens of Florida'. **Blue Spring State Park**, 3½ miles south-west, is a haven for manatees that congregate Nov–Mar.

Deland Chamber of Commerce, tel: (904) 734-4331.

SANFORD

This historical town on the south shore of Lake Monroe traces its routes to Fort Mellon, established in 1837. The **Sanford Museum**, 520 E. 1st St, tel: (407) 330-5698, depicts Sanford's glory days as a river port in the late 1880s.

Greater Sanford Chamber of Commerce, tel: (407) 322-2212.

CHARLESTON

Enduring elegance is the hallmark of Charleston, a city that has survived and thrived in spite of three turbulent centuries of epidemics, fires, earthquakes, hurricanes and revolution. This genteel lady of a city has a spine of steel and a soul of velvet.

Charleston is at the epicentre of the Carolina Lowcountry, a sweeping landscape uninterrupted by hills and carpeted with marsh grass, rivers and tidal creeks protected by windswept barrier islands.

Charleston is not all magnolias and moonlight. One of the most charming aspects of its personality is that it has managed to escape the contemporary architectural homogenisation that has overtaken most American cities. Generations of Charlestonians have toiled tirelessly to rescue and renovate the old downtown homes and commercial buildings, and their efforts have created one of the South's best-preserved cities. Not even Hurricane Hugo, which caused extensive damage in 1989, could significantly alter the cityscape.

FLOWER TIME

Spring is the prime time to visit Charleston, when the city is ablaze with azaleas, magnolias, dogwood and flowering jasmine. But the city blooms year round – in summer you'll find day lilies, magnolias and hydrangea, while autumn blooms with crape myrtles and gerberas, and in winter camellias and pansies abound.

The Spanish were the first to arrive here in 1521, soon followed by French Huguenots fleeing religious persecution, but it was the arrival of English settlers in 1670, in pursuit of land to farm, which laid the groundwork for what exists today. In part, the British colony's economic success led to its participation in rebellion against British rule (the first significant victory of the American Revolution was fought off the coast at Charleston, at Fort Multrie on Sullivan's Island). Charleston enjoyed a brief period of prosperity following the revolution, but the Civil War once again impoverished the area, and it was not until the development of resort hotels in the 20th century that the area was able to re-establish itself.

Charleston is a city of firsts – the first regularly scheduled passenger train service; America's first golf course; site of the first successful submarine battle; and it was a local resident, Joel R. Poinsett, who in 1820 introduced the popular poinsettia plant to the country.

No group contributed more to the colony's character than the slaves from Africa and Barbados, and 'Gullah' culture is still dominant in the cuisine, crafts and lifestyle of Charleston.

GETTING THERE AND GETTING AROUND

Charleston International Airport, 12 miles west of the city centre on I-26, is served by several major carriers. The Amtrak station, at 4565 Gaynor Avenue, North Charleston, is 8 miles north of the centre in an unsavoury neighbourhood. The Greyhound terminus is also in North Charleston, at 3610 Dorchester Road. CARTA (Charleston Area Regional Transit Authority) buses run from both these arrival points to the city centre every 30 mins.

By car, Charleston is reached from north or south by I-26, a turning east off I-95. US 17, a north–south coastal route, passes through the city.

CARTA, tel: (843) 747-0922, operates bus services within the city and to North Charleston and the beaches. Fares are cheap and the service operates 0500–0100 daily.

DASH (Downtown Area Shuttles), tel: (843) 724-7240, operates an extensive network of routes through downtown and the historic district at a reasonable fare (children under six travel free). Services operate every 15 mins, Mon–Fri, from 0800 (last bus times vary). Charleston is easily walkable.

INFORMATION

Charleston Visitors Center, 375 Meeting St; tel: (843) 853-3000 or (800) 868-8118; www.charlestoncvb.com. Housed in a renovated freight depot and open daily 0830–1700; closed on Thanksgiving, Christmas and New Year's holidays.

The Post and Courier is Charleston's daily newspaper.

SAFETY Lone travellers should avoid the area around the Amtrak station at night. North Charleston is best avoided.

MONEY The Visitors Center can exchange small amounts of currency.

POST AND PHONES The central post office is at 11 Broad St; open Mon–Fri 0800–1700; Sat 0800–noon.

ACCOMMODATION

Cheaper lodgings can be found in Mt. Pleasant, 3 miles from the centre.

Maison Du Pré $$$ 317 E. Bay St; tel: (843) 723-8691 or (800) 844-4667. This B&B manages to be both elegant and cosy at the same time. Continental breakfast and afternoon tea are included.

1837 Bed and Breakfast and Tea Room $$ 126 Wentworth St; tel: (843) 723-7166. Not as fancy as the Maison Du Pré but comfortable and cosy, with canopied beds. Rate includes generous breakfast and afternoon tea.

King Charles Inn $$ 237 Meeting St; tel: (843) 723-7451 or (800) 528-1234. Clean and convenient; some rooms have balconies.

FOOD

Lowcountry food is simply sensational. Dominating the menu are shrimp, crab and oysters, combined with rice (or that creamy maize gruel of the South – grits) and an array of vegetables. Try the roasted oysters, okra gumbo and palmetto heart pickle for an authentic taste of the area.

Gaulart and Maliclet French Café $ 98 Broad St. Casual café with counter service, specialising in sandwiches, soups, quiches and omelettes.

Magnolias Uptown/Down South $ 185 E. Bay St; tel: (843) 577-7721. Popular with locals. Seafood and innovative appetisers.

Mike Calder's Deli and Pub $ 288 King St; tel: (843) 577-0123. Soups, salads, sandwiches and more than a dozen different draught beers. Closed Sun.

82 Queen $$$ 82 Queen St; tel: (843) 723-7591. Famed for its she-crab soup and other Lowcountry specialities. Reservations recommended.

HIGHLIGHTS

If you only have a short time to spend in Charleston, you'll want to concentrate on the historic district in the heart of the city, where historic sites, graceful antebellum houses and captivating cafés are footsteps apart from each other. The district is compact, a mostly residential area bounded by Calhoun St on the north and King St on the west, and the best way to see it is on foot. Less taxing, particularly in the

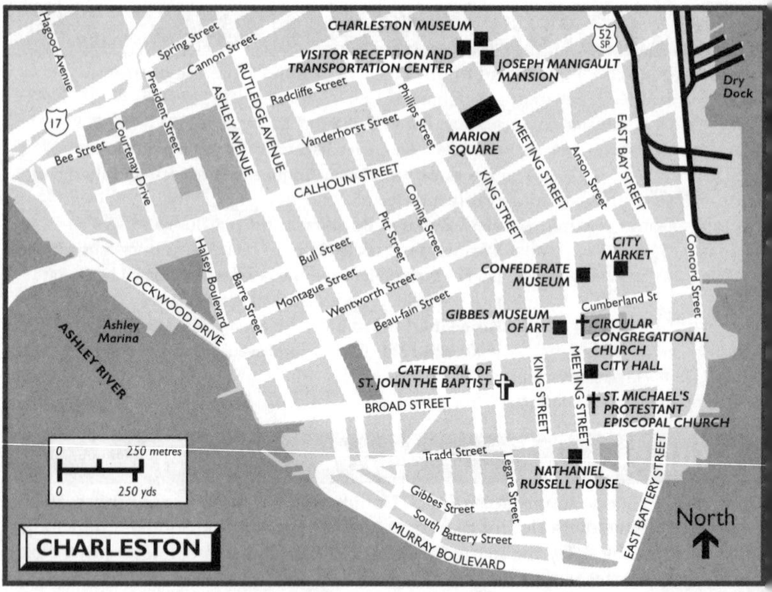

summer heat, is to take a carriage or trolley tour departing from the Market area. The visitor centre in Meeting St is a good place to start, and it's worth taking time to watch *Forever Charleston*, an excellent film that explains the city's history and orientates you to what you'll be seeing.

Across the street from the visitor centre is the **Charleston Museum**, the oldest city museum in the United States, founded in 1773. It is incomprehensible that a city that lives on its historical reputation could ever have allowed such an architecturally nondescript building, but it houses an extensive collection of South Carolina decorative arts and an eclectic range of objects focusing on aspects of Charleston and its history, ranging from silversmithing, fashion, plantation life, slavery and Native American life to the region's flora and fauna. $$ 360 Meeting St; open Mon–Sat 0900–1700, Sun 1300–1700 (combination ticket available for museum and houses – the Heritage Pass is available from the Visitors Centre, $32, or from the attractions it covers).

Many of the historic homes are open to the public, but plan carefully, as individual admissions can add up quickly. The **Joseph Manigault Mansion** is an outstanding example of neoclassical architecture; the stunning front hall boasts a beautiful curving staircase. Furnishings include rare tricolor Wedgwood pieces. A fascinating feature is the secret stairway between the second and third floors. $$ 350 Meeting St;

open Mon–Sat 1000–1700, Sun 1300–1700 (visit with combination ticket from the Charleston Museum).

To the untrained eye, many of Charleston's historic homes appear simple and unassuming when viewed head-on – the first impression is just of an unadorned façade broken by windows and a doorway to one side. But glimpse to the side and you'll find the door actually opens onto a porch or piazza that runs front to back along the side, transforming the house into a stately and elegant home.

The Holy City

The immigration of French Huguenots in the 1560s established Charleston's reputation for religious freedom. Today, Charleston boasts more than 185 churches of 25 denominations and is still referred to as the 'Holy City'.

Walk south along Meeting St to Market Hall, modelled after the Temple of Nike in Athens. Inside you'll find the **Confederate Museum** with uniforms, swords and other Civil War memorabilia. The museum was heavily damaged by Hurricane Hugo in 1989, but is scheduled to reopen in 1999. In the meantime, costumed guides are frequently seen outside and describe the museum.

Fort Sumter

On 12 April 1861, Confederate troops fired on Fort Sumter, the start of a two-day bombardment that resulted in the surrender of the fort by Union troops. The Confederacy held the fort until it was evacuated on 17 February 1865. During that time, the fort experienced one of the longest sieges in history – almost two years – during which 46,000 shells were fired at it. When the Confederate forces finally evacuated the fort it was little more than a pile of rubble.

Between Market Hall and E. Bay St you'll discover the **Old City Market**, a series of low roofed sheds that once were home to produce and fish markets. Here you'll find the 'basket ladies' carrying out their skilful craft. Unabashedly touristy, this is now one of the liveliest parts of town: the fish and produce have given way to restaurants and shops filled with all the trash and trinkets a tourist could desire. Open daily from 0900 to sunset.

Continuing south on Meeting St, the **Gibbes Museum of Art**, at no. 135, has a notable collection of more than 400 portraits of 18th- and 19th-century Carolinians. Don't miss the miniature rooms that have been decorated with fabrics and furnishings. Open Tues–Sat 1000–1700, Sun–Mon 1300–1700. Across from the Gibbes Museum is the unusual **Circular Congregational Church**, built with its corners rounded off so that 'the devil would have no place to hide', says local legend. The interior is simple but elegant, with its vaulted beamed ceiling.

At the intersection of Broad and Meeting Sts, known as the Four Corners of Law, the buildings at each corner represent the laws of nation, state, city and church. The dominant building is City Hall, but more interesting is **St Michael's Episcopal Church**, 14 St Michael's Alley. Charleston's oldest surviving church was modelled after St Martin-in-the-Fields in London, and its steeple clock and bells were imported from England. Open Mon–Fri 0900–1700, Sat 0900–noon.

Towards the southern end of Meeting St, graceful Nathaniel Russell House (no. 51) represents the epitome of the Adam style, with its daring flying staircase that rises, apparently unsupported, for three floors. $$ Open Mon–Sat 1000–1700.

ON THE WATERFRONT Not all of Charleston's treasures are indoors. **Waterfront Park**, located just off East Bay and Concord Sts, is a magnificent park on the harbour. Once a seedy neighbourhood of derelict warehouses, this stretch of riverfront along the Cooper River has been transformed with grassy areas, flower-filled planters and fountains.

Across the river, **Patriot's Point Naval and Maritime Museum** at Mount Pleasant (reached along Hwy 17) is the world's largest naval and maritime museum. It is the home of the submarine *Clamagore*, the World War II aircraft carrier *Yorktown* and the destroyer *Laffey*. The Medal of Honor Museum here features displays of vintage weapons and military aircraft. This living and working area for ships is open daily for touring, 0900–1700; tel: (843) 884-2727. $$.

From Patriot's Point you can board a ferry boat to tour the **Fort Sumter National Monument**, where the Civil War began. Located on a small man-made island at the entrance to Charleston harbour, it is accessible only by boat. Fort Sumter Tours, 205 King St; tel: (803) 722-2628, organise daily tours at 1330, more frequently during holidays. $$.

DAY TRIPS

Magnolia Plantation and Gardens, 10 miles north of the city along Hwy 61, has over 250 varieties of *Azalea indica* and 900 varieties of *Camellia japonica*. There are cycling and walking paths, a pet zoo, a canoe trail and picnic areas. $$ Open daily 0800–1730; admission to the house is extra ($).

The early years of Charleston have been brought to life at **Charles Towne Landing**.This 80-acre park is an outdoor interpretative centre of the Lowcountry's earliest European settlers. There is a 'settler village'; a 17th-century replica of a coastal trading vessel; and the Animal Forest 'wilderness', complete with wildlife. You can take a tram tour or explore on your own – bikes can be rented by the hour. The park is 6 miles from the city, along Hwy 171 between I-26 and Hwy 17, $, open daily 0900–1700.

Public beaches close to the city and easily accessed by public transport include Sullivan's Island, Isles of Palms, James Island, Folly Beach and Beachwalker Park on the west end of Kiawah Island.

The **Spoleto Festival** begins in late May and lasts for about 18 days, bringing the best of international theatre, music, art and dance to Charleston. It's a magical time to be in the city. This popular festival fills Charleston's hotels, so book early. Tel: (843) 722-2764 for information.

THE DOCK STREET THEATER

The theatre combines the early playhouse (one of the nation's first) that originally stood on this site and the preserved Planter's Hotel. Visitors can partake of a backstage tour, except on those days that technical work for a production is taking place. 135 Church St; tel: (803) 720-3968. Open Mon–Fri 1000–1600.

NIGHTLIFE

Charleston has several theatres, including the historic **Dock Street Theater**, with its intimate box seats and terrific acoustics. The **Charleston Stage Company**, 133 Church St; tel: (843) 965-4032 or (800) 454-7093, performs original works and family-oriented productions, and the **Footlight Players**, 20 Queen St; tel: (843) 722-4487, are an old-established community theatre company. Try the following for relaxed entertainment:

DANCING THE CHARLESTON

The dance craze of society flappers in the 1920s originated with black children, dancing for pennies on the city's streets.

Pusser's Landing, 17 Lockwood Blvd; tel: (843) 853-1000. Terrific view of the City Marina from the deck. Music and great food. Open Thur–Sun.

Mills House, 115 Meeting St; tel: (843) 577-2400. Good place to gather for an after-dinner drink while listening to big band tunes or jazz guitar.

Tobacco, Teas and Spirits, 364 King St; tel: (843) 577-0027. Jam sessions and bourbon bring the locals to this spot.

PORGY AND BESS

In 1925, Du Bose Heyward immortalised one of the traditional stories of the Lowcountry when he created *Porgy*, the tale of a lame Charleston street vendor and his love for Bess. Gershwin brought *Porgy and Bess* to Broadway in 1935, but it was not until 1970, when Charleston was finally desegregated, that it played in Charleston's Gaillard Auditorium.

Savannah

From its early days Savannah has been a beautiful city. So beautiful, in fact, that Northern General William Sherman could not bring himself to burn it down in his famous March to the Sea during the Civil War. The English General James Oglethorpe designed the city in the 1730s on a defensible grid pattern of 24 tree-filled squares. Savannah today, with its trees draped romantically in Spanish moss, has a pervasive spirit of fun.

A major port for the growing cotton industry, Savannah bounced back from the Civil War much faster than its neighbours and remained prominent until the collapse of the cotton market at the beginning of the 20th century. Seeing their city's fine architectural heritage in decay, a group of Savannah women established the Historic Savannah Foundation in 1955, the country's first restoration attempt.

March and early April are good times to visit, before the summer's scorching heat and while the city's many gardens are in their full glory. December is another good time, with pleasant weather and a round of Christmas activities, including festivals, parades and tours of private homes decked for the holidays. Tourism has soared in Savannah since John Berendt's bestselling *Midnight in the Garden of Good and Evil*; everyone wants to see the places mentioned in the book and shown in the film, which was shot here.

Getting There and Getting Around

Trains and buses connect Savannah to Charleston, Jacksonville and Washington DC. The Greyhound bus station is the more accessible to downtown, near the TIC at 610 E. Oglethorpe Ave; tel: (912) 232-2135. The Amtrak station is about 4 miles out of the city, a short cab ride away, at 2611 Seaboard Coastline Dr.; tel: (912) 234-2611.

If you arrive by car, follow I-95 from either direction to I-16 East, which leads directly into the city. US 17 also runs north–south through the centre of the city.

King Cotton

In 1793 on a plantation near Savannah, Eli Whitney invented the cotton gin. This machine to separate the seeds from the cotton revolutionised the industry. Soon traders were referring to the bountiful product as 'white gold', and the industry itself gained the title King Cotton.

Chatham Area Transit (CAT); tel: (912) 233-5767, running daily 0600–2400. C&H Bus, 530 Montgomery St; tel: (912) 232-7099, offers the only public transport to Tybee Beach. Buses leave from the Civic Center three times a day in the summer.

INFORMATION

Savannah Area Convention and Visitors Bureau, 222 W. Oglethorpe Ave, Savannah, GA 31401, responds to written information requests.

The Savannah Visitors Center, housed in a restored 1860s railway station at 301 Martin Luther King Jr Blvd; tel: (800) 444-2427 or (912) 944-0456, is open Mon–Sat 0900–1700, Sun 1100–1700. It has free maps and leaflets on attractions, dining, accommodation and tours. It offers four walking tour maps of the city and recorded cassette tapes for walking and driving tours, along with cassette players. An audiovisual presentation gives a general view of history and places to visit. Ample free parking and free reservations for accommodation.

SAFETY The railway station is in a seedy area that turns grimmer after dark. Even in the daytime, take a cab to the historic city centre instead of relying on public buses. Avoid low-cost hotels and boarding houses in outlying districts, sticking to the area known as the Historic District. This coincides with the downtown area, a square bordered by Martin Luther King Jr Blvd, Gwinnet St, East Broad and the river.

The midsummer heat can be oppressive and even dangerous. Stop often for non-alcoholic drinks and seek shade in the leafy squares at every opportunity.

MONEY Most banks have automated cash access from credit cards, but cashing travellers cheques in anything but dollars is unlikely here.

POST AND PHONES Savannah's main post office, 2 N. Fahm St; tel: (912) 235-4646, is open Mon–Fri 0830–1700. Use the zip code 31402 for poste restante.

ACCOMMODATION

Savannah has a wealth of major hotels and a couple of dozen historic bed-and-breakfast inns. The TIC has a complimentary reservations system for accommodation; tel: (800) 444-2427. RSVP **Bed and Breakfast Reservation Service of Savannah**, 219 W. Bryan St; tel: (800) 729-7787 or (912) 232-7787 (Mon–Tues, Thur–Fri 0930–1730), represents 32 inns and guesthouses in the city.

Hostelling International – Savannah $ 304 E. Hall St; tel: (912) 236-7744. Office hours 0700–1000 and 1700–2300; closed Feb. Close to the Riverfront Plaza and many other attractions, the hostel is in an 1884 home. No curfew.

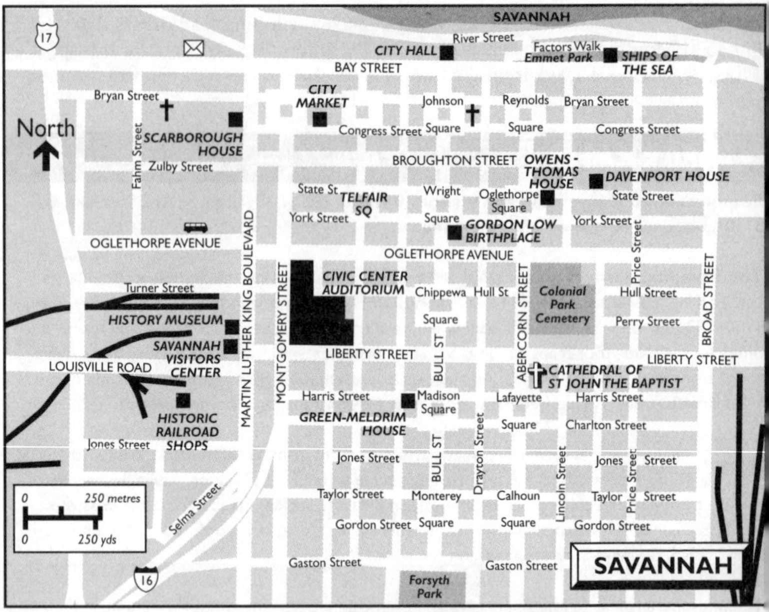

Azalea Inn $$–$$$ 217 E. Huntington St; tel: (800) 582-3823. Historic inn in 1889 home.

Best Western Savannah Historic District $$–$$$ 412 W. Bay St; tel: (912) 233-1011; fax: (912) 234-3963. Attractive locally owned hotel in good neighbourhood.

The Colophon $$–$$$ 609 Whittaker St; tel: (912) 233-2446. Historic 1880s home, now a guesthouse.

Quality Inn Heart of Savannah $$–$$$ 300 W. Bay St; tel: (912) 236-6321. Adjacent to River St, half a block from the city market. In the heart of the historic district, probably the best buy in Savannah.

Savannah's Bed and Breakfast Inn $$$ 117 W. Gordon St; tel: (912) 238-0518. 1853 house with home-cooked breakfasts.

Foley House Inn $$$$ 14 W. Hull St (Chippewa Sq.); tel: (800) 647-3708 or (912) 232-6622. One of 25 historic inns that sit around the city's squares.

Hampton Inn Historic District $$$$ 201 E. Bay St; tel: (800) 426-7866 or (912) 231-9700. Across from the river.

FOOD

The City Market area, particularly Congress St, offers a variety of cuisine and styles. Cheap eateries are not hard to find.

Mrs Wilkes' Boarding House $–$$ 107 W. Jones St; tel: (912) 232-5997. Open weekdays for breakfast and lunch, Mrs Wilkes's is an institution serving huge amounts of Southern specialities – especially buttermilk biscuits; queues are long.

The Lady & Sons $$ 311 W. Congress St; tel: (912) 233-2600. Open daily for lunch, Thur–Sat for dinner, for dishes like mouthwatering she-crab soup and mustard-fried catfish with cornbread and collards.

The Pirates' House $$–$$$ 20 Broad & E. Bay Sts (Trustees' Garden); tel: (912) 233-5757. Lunch, brunch and dinner in 16 dining rooms in a 10-acre, 18th-century garden modelled after Chelsea Physic Garden.

The Shrimp Factory $$–$$$ 313 E. River St; tel: (912) 236-4229. Seafood and pine bark stew in an 1820s cotton warehouse along the riverfront.

HIGHLIGHTS

Along the western edge of the Historic District runs Martin Luther King Jr Blvd. Opposite the TIC is the **Savannah History Museum**, where the story of Savannah's cotton industry unfolds, along with its part in the Civil War and its railway glory days; $ tel: (912) 238-1779; open daily 0900–1700.

The Historic Railroad Shops continue the story, and are acclaimed as the USA's oldest and most complete pre-Civil War railway manufacturing and repair facilities. The 13 original structures (including roundhouse and turntable) are filled with rail memorabilia, machinery and restored locomotives. $ 601 W. Harris St; tel: (912) 651-6823; open daily 1000–1600.

Ralph Mark Gilbert Civil Rights Museum covers Savannah's African-American history, too easy to neglect in the opulence of the grand antebellum homes to follow. $ 460 Martin Luther King Jr Blvd; tel: (912) 231-8900; open Mon–Sat 0900–1700, Sun 1300–1700.

Continuing north almost to the river, **Ships of the Sea Maritime Museum** has over 50 model ships, including Viking warships and the SS *Savannah*, the first steamship to cross the Atlantic, plus a ship-in-the-bottle collection. $ 41 Martin Luther King Jr Blvd (Scarborough House); tel: (912) 232-1511; open Tues–Sun 1000–1700.

TOURS

It is easy and enjoyable to get around the 2.2 sq. mile Historic District on foot. To see the highlights, begin at the City Hall, near the river, and walk south on Bull St through five of the historic squares to Forsyth Park. Walk east two blocks to Abercorn St, turning left (north) to return through four more squares and along the edge of Colonial Park Cemetery. Though there is plenty to see on the route itself, many of the other highlights described here are within a block or two.

In the heat of summer you may prefer a narrated bus or trolley tour. **Old Town Trolley Tours** $$$ 601 Cohen St; tel: (912) 233-0083, leave from the Visitor Center daily, every half hour 0900–1630 (motorists park free there for 4 hrs while sightseeing – obtain a windscreen sticker from the centre). The complete tour lasts 90 mins with reboarding at designated stops.

Carriage Tours of Savannah $$ 9 E. River St; tel: (912) 236-6756, has horse-drawn historic tours, evening Ghost Story tours (one based on Margaret Debolt's *Savannah Spectres and Other Strange Tales*) and a private Cobblestone Classic (around $60 for two).

The **historic squares** are Savannah's heart. Romantic history oozes from Savannah's pores; secret gardens hint of indiscreet liaisons; fancy grillework conjures actual or imagined murders. Historic markers, many relating to Civil War personalities, plaster the historic districts. In Thunderbolt, east of the city centre, is Bonaventure Cemetery, where many generations of old families are buried, and where Berendt heard true tales of murder and intrigue, later retold in his book. The best place to begin touring these gracious squares is at the riverfront, where the recently restored Factor's Walk, once the thriving centre of the city's shipping, runs between Bay St and the riverbank bluff. The street is cobbled with stone brought from Europe as ballast for ships returning full of cotton. Bay St marks the northern boundary of Oglethorpe's original grid, now the Historic District.

THE NEGRO HERITAGE TRAIL

Daily tours from the King-Tisdell Cottage, a museum of Afro-American history at 514 E. Huntington St, highlight the city's black heritage; $ tel: (912) 234-8000.

Two blocks west of Bull St, at Telfair Sq., is the **Telfair Mansion**, designed in 1819 by English architect William Jay. Many of the rooms are furnished with period furniture, including the fine Octagon Room. The mansion also displays several Impressionist paintings by European and American artists. $ 121 Barnard St; tel: (912) 232-1177; open Tues–Sat 1000–1700, Sun 1300–1700, Mon 1200–1700.

The **Juliette Gordon Low Birthplace**, at 142 Bull St, honours the woman who founded the Girl Guide movement in the USA in 1912. Her birthplace, a National Historic Landmark, has been restored in late 19th-century style with many of the family furnishings and a Victorian garden surrounded by the original outbuildings. $ tel: (912) 233-4501; open Mon, Tues, Thur–Sat 1000–1600, Sun 1230–1630.

The **Green-Meldrim Home**, facing Madison Sq., further south on Bull St, was General Sherman's headquarters during the occupation of Atlanta during the

Savannah Riverboat Cruises $$$ 9 E. River St; tel: (912) 232-6404 or (800) 786-6404, offers a selection from 1 hr sightseeing tours to brunch and dinner cruises. Reservations needed for all meals.

Civil War. Sherman's memory is tolerated here for the fact that he did not burn the city, although for many it still rankles that Savannah was presented to President Lincoln as a birthday gift. The house is a fine example of southern Gothic Revival architecture; open Tues and Thur–Sat 1000–1600.

Two blocks east, at Lafayette Sq., is **Andrew Low House**, built in 1848 and home of Juliette Gordon Low (see above). Its rooms, embellished with crystal chandeliers and intricate woodwork, once housed General Robert E. Lee, commander of Confederate (southern) forces in the Civil War. $ 329 Abercorn St; tel: (912) 233-6854. Tours every half hour Mon–Wed and Fri–Sat 1030–1600, Sun 1200–1600.

The **Owens-Thomas House and Museum**, designed by William Jay in 1816, and facing Oglethorpe Sq., is an interesting example of an American home modelled on an English villa, with rare antiques, a restored carriage house, slave quarters and an English parterre garden. $$ 124 Abercorn St; tel: (912) 233-9743; open Tues–Sat 1000–1700, Sun 1400–1700, Mon 1200–1700.

On Columbia Sq. stands **Davenport House**, built about 1815 and the first historic site to be saved by the Historic Savannah Foundation. Period furnishings are both English and American made and the delicate ironwork and plasterwork and an unusually elegant elliptical staircase make this one of the best houses to visit. $ 324 E. State St; tel: (912) 236-8097. Tours every 30 mins Mon–Sat 1000–1600, Sun 1300–1600.

Out of town a little, but of special interest to World War II aficionados is the mighty **Eighth Air Force Heritage Museum**, celebrating a unit formed in Savannah which served in World War II and was later moved to the UK. $$ 175 Bourne Ave (from I-95 take exit 18); tel: (912) 748-8888; open daily 0900–1800.

For Free

Forsyth Park, at the southern end of the historic district, has 75 acres of landscaped green space with playgrounds, a beautiful fountain, and fragrant gardens for the blind. The park is particularly beautiful in the early spring when filled with blooming azaleas.

The **Cathedral of St John the Baptist** is one of the largest in the south. Just wander and marvel at the extensive marble work, stained glass and impressive woodcarvings, or join a free tour (available Mon–Fri 0900–1700, Sun 0800–1700 unless a service is in progress). 222 E. Harris St; tel: (912) 233-4709.

Just out from the centre, on the banks of the Savannah River, **Old Fort Jackson** was started in the early 19th century and includes exhibits depicting the American Revolution, the War of 1812 and the Civil War, in each of which it played an active role. Entrance is free, but in spring and summer there are frequent special 'living history' exhibitions ($); tel: (912) 232-3945.

SHOPPING

The local speciality is sweetgrass baskets, woven of sweet-scented grass, which you will find at The Basket Place, 305 E. River St; tel: (912) 232-4546. The **City Market** is a renovated four-block sector of the Historic District. Among the cafés, shops, clubs and restaurants many artists work and exhibit their works for sale – fun to browse even if you're not buying. Specialist shops of the **De Soto Historic District** and the galleries and boutiques of **River St**'s nine blocks provide gifts and mementoes. River Street Gallery, 207 E. River St, has paintings and prints from the Southern states, hand-made jewellery and other crafts. River Street Zoo, 215 W. River St, specialises in childrenswear and toys. Renowned Shaver's Bookshop, 326 Bull St; tel: (912) 234-7257, has 12 rooms of books. Très-cool vintage clothing and bibelots are at Once Possessed, 141 E. Bull St (corner of York Lane).

SPECIAL EVENTS

First Saturday is a monthly festival at Riverfront Plaza, with arts, crafts, entertainment and street buskers.

River St goes unexpectedly Irish on 17 Mar with a wild **St Patrick's Parade**, and later in Mar, **Night in Old Savannah** at the Visitors Center features decorated booths displaying and selling food from the 15 different coastal cultures represented in the city, accompanied by traditional music. **Savannah's Tour of Homes and Gardens** – a tradition for more than 60 years – takes place in late Mar–early Apr. Contact Historic Savannah Foundation, 18 Abercorn St, Savannah, GA 31401; tel: (912) 234-8054. The Coastal Heritage Society; tel: (912) 651-6895, schedules historical re-enactments associated with Civil War battles.

ST PATRICK'S DAY SOUTHERN STYLE?

It's not known how or why Savannah's became the second largest St Patrick's Day celebration in the country, but it has been for more than 150 years. Beer, food and anything else you can think of is dyed green – even the 40,000 people on parade. One year locals tried to dye the river green. The parade begins at 1015, with live music at the City Market, and the festivities go on until midnight; tel: (912) 233-4804.

NIGHTLIFE

River St's cobblestones are the place for living it up in Savannah. Container ships and luxury yachts sail by on the river and lively music belts out of restaurants, taverns and shops in converted cotton warehouses. Some restaurants, especially those in City Market, offer weekend entertainment. To hear what's hot from local bands, try **Velvet Elvis**, 127 W. Congress St; tel: (912) 236-0665.

Savannah Pops concerts, tel: (912) 236-9536, are regular performances of 1920s–1940s popular music. The **International Arts Festival**, tel: (912) 236-5745, holds 40 arts events and concerts in historic downtown venues, many events free.

ORLANDO

Once upon a time Orlando was a sleepy Southern town surrounded by orange groves and pine forests. Then Walt Disney turned 43 square miles of swampland into the Magic Kingdom and life has never been the same. The orange groves have given way to a multitude of hotels and motels, shopping malls, and many non-Disney theme parks. Orlando is for tourists seeking sun, fun, shopping and more than a dash of fantasy.

Downtown Orlando itself sprawls north of the East-West Expressway (Hwy 50) but many of the attractions are spread over a wide area to the south, along International Drive (the locals call it I-Drive) and down to Kissimmee. Walt Disney World is at Lake Buena Vista, 20 miles south of Orlando. Big improvements in public transport, shuttle buses, monorails and the like mean that the attractions can be seen without a car, but no matter how you get to an attraction, there will be a fair amount of foot-slogging.

GETTING THERE AND GETTING AROUND

AIR Orlando International Airport (MCO); tel: (407) 825-2001 or (407) 825-2352, is 9 miles south of the city. The airport is served by cheap buses to both downtown and the International Dr. area. The service operates daily, but is reduced at weekends. The stop for both services is on the airport's 'A' side and the journey takes about 70 mins.

THE MARK OF THE PAW

Lynx, the regional transport authority, operates on the basis of a cheap flat fare (exact money only) – check out cheap transfers, multi-ride tickets and other discounts available from the Downtown Bus Station, 78 W. Central Blvd; tel: (407) 841-8240. Lynx bus stops carry a paw mark logo.

Lynx also operates I-Ride, the International Drive Resort Area Shuttle. These trolley buses run along the tourist strip, from Sea World at the south end to Wet 'n' Wild at the north – a great way to get to Beltz Outlet Mall and other discount emporiums. Again, there's a flat fare, and children under six travel free.

RAIL/BUS Amtrak stations are at 1400 Slight Blvd, Orlando (about 23 miles from Disney World) or 111 Dakin Ave, Kissimmee (about 15 miles from Disney World). Greyhound buses pull into 555 N. Magruder Blvd, Orlando; tel: (407) 292-3422, and 16 N. Orlando Blvd, Kissimmee tel: (407) 847-3911; van

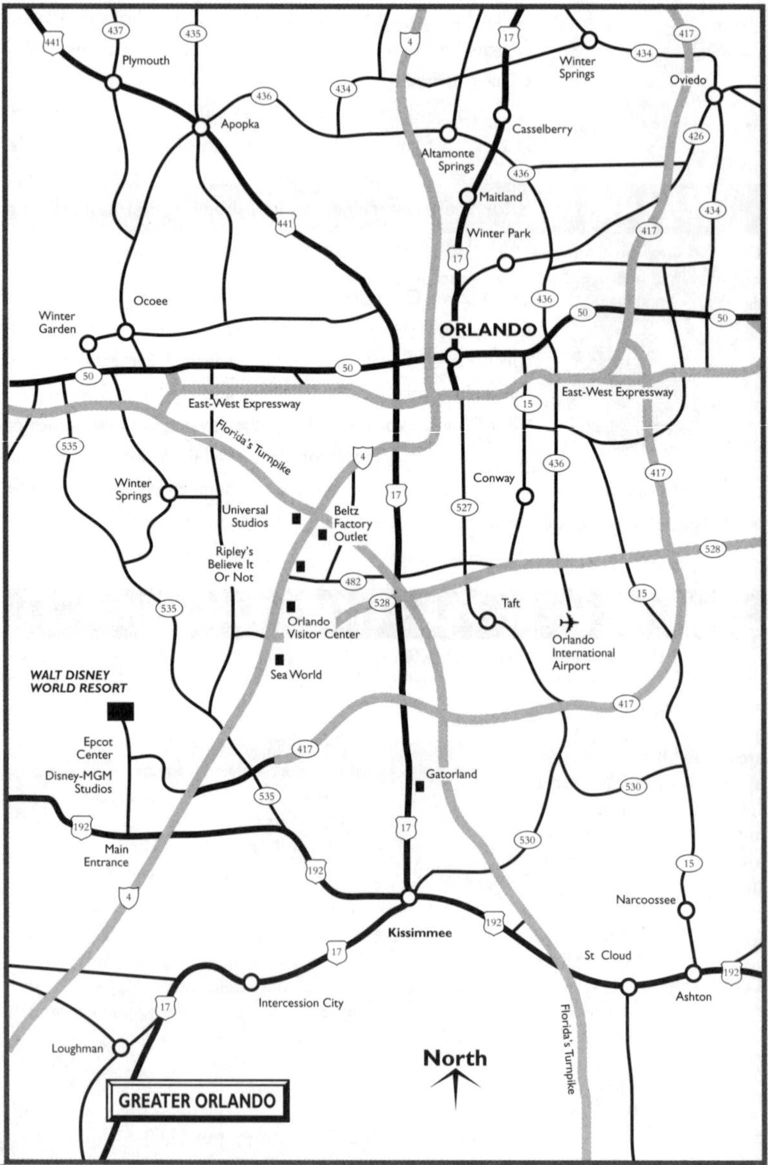
441
437
435
Plymouth
436
434
4
17
434
Winter Springs
417
Oviedo
Apopka
Casselberry
426
Altamonte Springs
436
Maitland
434
441
Winter Park
417
17
Ocoee
436
Winter Garden
50
ORLANDO
50
50
50
East-West Expressway
East-West Expressway
15
Florida's Turnpike
535
4
436
417
Winter Springs
Conway
17
527
Universal Studios
Beltz Factory Outlet
Ripley's Believe It Or Not
528
482
15
528
Taft
535
Orlando Visitor Center
Orlando International Airport
Sea World
WALT DISNEY WORLD RESORT
417
Epcot Center
417
Disney-MGM Studios
Gatorland
530
535
192
17
530
Main Entrance
192
15
4
Narcoossee
192
Kissimmee
17
St Cloud
192
Ashton
Intercession City
17
Florida's Turnpike
Loughman
North
GREATER ORLANDO

shuttle to and from the Kissimmee terminal is available from most hotels and motels.

Taxi, shuttle bus and limousine services operate between the airport, hotels and attractions – round-trip shuttle bus service is the most cost-effective.

INFORMATION

Orlando/Orange County Official Visitor Center, 8723 International Dr., Suite 101 (south-east corner of International Dr. and Austrian Ct); tel: (800) 551-0181 or (407) 363-5872. Open daily 0800–2000.

SAFETY Orlando is generally a safe destination, and most crimes are opportunistic. You should exercise caution late at night and keep belongings stowed in the boot of your car. Tourist Oriented Police Services (TOPS) provide assistance to distressed travellers in the International Drive area and around theme parks; tel: (407) 354-3924. If they are not available, dial 911.

MONEY Thomas Cook Foreign Exchange, 55 West Church St, Suite 120; tel: (407) 839-1700; open Mon–Fri 1000–2000, Sat 1200–2000. Automatic cash dispensers are available in the theme parks, mostly near the entrance area. Travellers' cheques and credit cards are widely accepted.

POST AND PHONES Branches of the US post office are to be found in most Orlando neighbour-hoods. The main office, open 24 hrs, is at 10401Post Office Blvd; tel: (407) 850-6288.

ACCOMMODATION

If the many worlds of Disney are your target it makes sense to stay within The World. You will avoid the cost of shuttle transportation (complimentary from Disney properties), get a head start with early opening hours for Disney guests, and have access to recreational facilities at other Disney hotels. Contact Walt Disney World Resort, Lake Buena Vista; tel: (407) 934-7639 to book rooms at any of the many resorts; also dining, theme parks, cruises.

DISNEY WORLD

Disney's Wilderness Campground Lodge $$. Rustic, piney and a tad removed from the rest of the park. Civilised camping with two swimming pools, white sand beach, volleyball and boat rentals.

Disney's All-Star Music Resort $$$. 1920-room hotel with giant musical instruments and a swimming pool in the shape of a guitar. Rooms are small but attractive.

Disney's Port Orleans Resort $$$. Disney's version of turn-of-the-century New Orleans. Good-sized rooms, food court, Scat Cat's bar for evening entertainment.

Outside, almost every international hotel chain has at least one property in the area (see p. 504).

OUTSIDE DISNEY WORLD

Fairfield Inn by Marriott $$ 8432 Jamaican Ct; tel: (407) 363-1944 or (800) 228-2800. In a safe and quiet location, with restaurants within walking distance (mind the traffic crossing I-Drive!), free newspapers and complimentary continental breakfast.

Perrihouse B&B Inn $$$ 10417 Centurion Ct; tel: (407) 876-4830 or (800) 780-4830; email: Birds@Perrihouse.com. Set in an orange grove 3 mins from the Disney Main Gate. Transport to the B&B can be arranged in advance.

Kissimmee Youth Hostel, Hwy 192; tel: (407) 843-8888; fax: (407) 841-8867.

Orlando/Kissimmee Resort Hostel $–$$ 4840 West Irlo Bronson Highway; tel: (407) 396-8282 or (800) 909-4776, access code 33. Motel style hostel with dormitory and private room accommodations. Set on a lake (don't swim in it), with a swimming pool, barbecue grill, and laundry facilities. Shuttle from airport and to Disney theme parks.

CAMPSITES

Kampgrounds of America (KOA), Kissimmee/Orlando KOA, 4771 W. Hwy 192, Kissimmee; tel: (407) 396-2400. Tent village, RV pitches and cabins, close to Walt Disney World (shuttle service to the attractions).

Fort Wilderness Campground and Lodge. The campground ($$) has restrooms, showers, lifeguards, canoe rentals, grocery shopping and restaurants nearby. Over 700 sites are available; for reservations tel: (407) 824-2900. The lodge ($$$) is a magnificent multi-storey log cabin, replete with totem poles and a massive stone fireplace. Complimentary transport to and from Disney theme parks.

FOOD

International Dr. has the widest choice, but the Church St area downtown and Hwy 192 out towards Kissimmee are also well served. Each of the area's major attractions has a host of restaurants, cafés and food stalls. You can bring your own snacks into the various theme parks: picnic facilities are not available, and the park operators frown if you eat your own food at restaurant tables.

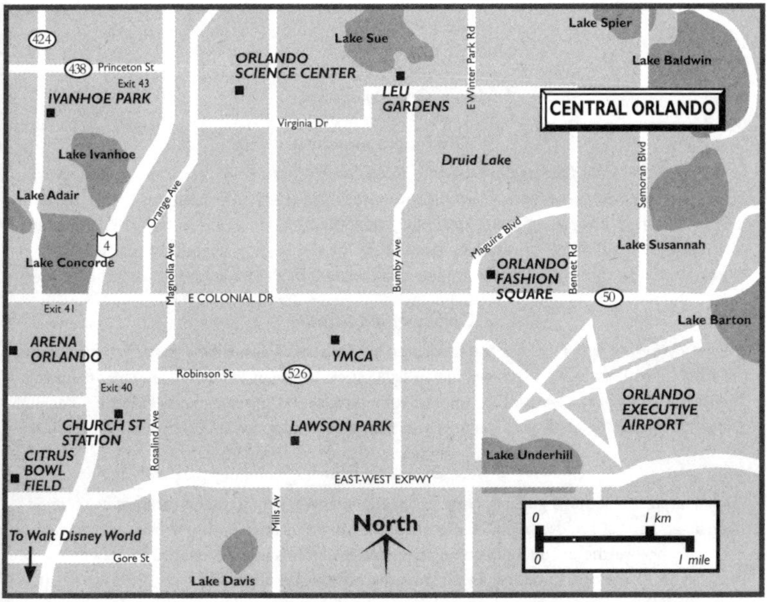

The B-Line Diner at the Peabody Hotel $ 9801 International Dr.; tel: (407) 345-4460. Serves classic burgers, steaks, seafood and home-made ice cream in the chrome and pastel décor of the 1950s.

Guitar-shaped Hard Rock Café $$ 5800 Kirkman Rd; tel: (407) 351-7625. Adjoins Universal Studios; for those who care more about rock 'n' roll than they do about food.

Ming Court $$$$ 9188 International Dr.; tel: (407) 351-9988. A favourite with Orlando business folk; pricey, but the Chinese dishes are legendary.

HIGHLIGHTS

THEME PARKS **Universal Studios Florida** is a working production studio with movie-theme attractions and daredevil stunt shows. Ride the Movies features take you right inside blockbuster films like *Jurassic Park*, *Earthquake* (feel the heat of the flames), *King Kong* (smell his banana breath), *Back to the Future* (hurtle through fog made of liquid nitrogen), *Jaws* (hang on tight as he tries to capsize your boat) and *ET* (travel through space amid hundreds of planets and thousands of

WALT DISNEY WORLD

For many, Orlando *is* Disney . . .

The Magic Kingdom

The first of the Walt Disney World theme parks features nearly 50 major shows and adventures divided into seven fantasy lands. Cinderella's Castle is its most famous landmark, and this is where Mickey and friends hang out. The dripping slime of the ExtraTERRORestrial Alien Encounter may or may not appeal, but ride the Skyway from Tomorrowland to Fantasyland as the fireworks begin and you will feel as though you are flying through the stars.

Disney-MGM Studios

This is a working film, TV, radio and animation studio as well as a theme park. Experience the Indiana Jones Epic Stunt Spectacle, the Twilight Zone Tower of Terror (its elevator drop will leave you with your heart lodged close to your tonsils) and others; go on the Studio Backlot Tour. Each evening ends with Fantasmic, a laser, fireworks and water animation spectacular.

Epcot Center

Dominated by the huge golfball shape of Spaceship Earth, Epcot is a celebration of technological and social achievements. There are whizzbang effects at Future World, a chance to see and use the products of tomorrow at Innoventions and a global tour in World Showcase's 11 national pavilions. Don't miss the nightly laser light show over the lagoon (for a good view in comfort, grab an outside table at the UK pavilion's Rose and Crown).

Animal Kingdom

This latest extravaganza opened in April 1998 with real and fabricated critters. Rescue dinosaurs from extinction, or take a photo safari. The Tree of Life dominates the park and houses a riotous 3D film, *A Bug's Life*. Go early or stay late as many animals are nocturnal and not particularly active during the heat of the day.

In addition to the four theme parks, there are three water adventure parks (**Blizzard Beach, Typhoon Lagoon** and **River Country**), **Discovery Island** zoological park, 26 resort hotels (16 owned by Disney), the **Disney Institute, Disney's Wide World of Sports** and **Downtown Disney**, an entertainment-shopping-dining complex. All the parks are open daily, including all holidays, mostly 0900–2300 (0900–2100 Sept–Jan), but times can vary. For complete information tel: (407) 824-4321, or check out the Disney website: www.disneyworld.com.

Visitors have a memorable time, but not a cheap one – a one-day admission to an individual theme park is upwards of $40, with little discounted for children. It may be worth investing in a Park Hopper Pass, which permits unlimited entry to all the parks. The passes are sold in 3, 4 and 5 day segments and do not expire, so any unused days on your present trip will remain good for a future experience.

stars). $$$$ (parking extra); opening times vary according to the season.

More than 20 major shows and displays are featured at **Sea World** (7007 Sea World Dr.). This long-established marine life park enables you to enter the underwater world of whales, dolphins, manatees and other marine mammals, and there are daily shows. $$$$ (plus parking); open daily 0900–1900 (hours vary during summer and holidays).

More than 5000 alligators and crocodiles inhabit **Gatorland**'s extensive pools. There is alligator wrestling, a marsh with an observation tower, a natural cypress swamp and lots of other animals, birds and reptiles. When hunger strikes, try alligator cooked Southern style. $$$ 14501 S. Orange Blossom Trail; open daily 0900–dusk.

Splendid China has replicas of 60 Chinese historical and cultural landmarks and sites, most – like the Great Wall of China and the Terracotta Warriors – miniaturised. $$$ 3000 Splendid China Blvd, Kissimmee; open daily 0930–1900. **Chinatown**, the dining, shopping and entertainment area, open 0930–2200, is free.

MUSEUMS The **Orlando Science Center**, downtown at 777 E. Princeton St, is likely to be crowded with children trying out the interactive exhibits *you* would like to try. $$ Open Mon–Thur 0900–1700, Fri–Sat 0900–2100, Sun 1200–1700; CineDome and parking extra.

North of the centre is the **Orlando Museum of Art**. Its

WINTER PARK

Set among the lakes just north of Orlando, this is a charming place to while away an afternoon. Stroll the smart boutiques of Park Ave, visit the **Morse Museum** for its collection of Tiffany windows, or cruise the lake on a pontoon boat. The leisurely cruise is a delightful way to observe the canals, magnificent lakeside mansions and the cypress swamps filled with dozens of marsh birds. **Scenic Boat Tour**: tel: (407) 644-4056, open daily 1000–1600.

ALMOST FREE ORLANDO

Turkey Lake Park, 3401 Hiawassee Rd; tel: (407) 299-5594. Picnic tables, bicycle and hiking trails, beaches, swimming pool, fishing pier, canoe rentals and pet zoo. $ Open daily 0930–1900.

Disney's Boardwalk Entertainment Complex, Walt Disney World; tel: (407) 824-4321. Waterfront village in the style of the 1930s Atlantic coast resorts, offers shopping, restaurants and nightlife.

Downtown Disney, Walt Disney World; tel: (407) 939-7727. Shopping in the market place, upmarket restaurants that require reservations or patience for a table, cinema complex and a bustling street life.

Farmers Markets, I-4 and Church St, Sat mornings. Fresh produce, baked goods, plants and flowers. Mingle with the locals; tel: (407) 623-3200.

Universal Studios City Walk, Universal Studios, is filled with restaurants and music venues. Admission is free, but the price for individual venues varies. You'll find the Hard Rock Café Orlando, Jimmy Buffet's Margaritaville, NASCAR Cafe, City Jazz and the Latin Quarter; tel: (407) 363-8000.

pre-Columbian gallery houses more than 250 pieces from Mexico, Guatemala, Colombia, Costa Rica, Panama and Peru dating from 1200 BC to AD 1500. Among its permanent collections is an exhibition of 20th-century American and African art. $ 2416 N. Mills Ave; open Tues–Sat 0900–1700, Sun 1200–1700. In less reverential mood, **Ripley's Believe It Or Not!** has hundreds of unbelievable exhibits in an eccentric showplace. $$ 8201 International Dr.; open daily 0900–2300. **Titanic, Ship of Dreams** is an interactive museum which features over 200 artefacts and memorabilia from the film *A Night To Remember*; White Star 'staff' welcome you aboard. $$ Mercado Mall, International Dr.; tel: (407) 248-1166; open daily 1000–2200.

The adventurous and early risers may like to take to the air. For an expensive but exciting experience, a number of companies offer hot-air balloon flights over the theme parks and lakes. Contact Aviation Services, 11475 Rocket Blvd; tel: (407) 841-8787, or Rise and Float Balloon Tours, 5767 Major Blvd; tel: (407) 352-8191.

WILDLIFE In addition to showpieces like Sea World and Gatorland (see p. 237), and Disney's Discovery Island, Orlando has a couple of animal attractions. **Jungleland Zoo** has alligators, crocodiles, birds, big cats and monkeys. $$$ 4580 W. Hwy 192; open daily 0900–1800. Out at Maitland, **Audubon of Florida** is the headquarters of the Florida Audubon Society, one of the state's oldest and largest conservation organisations. At the Audubon House visitors view live bald eagles, owls, hawks and other birds of prey. Guided tours are conducted. 1101 Audubon Way, Maitland (take I-4 east to Lee Road exit); tel: (407) 644-0190; open Tues–Sun 1000–1600; entry by donation ($5 suggested for adults, $4 for children).

SPORT AND ACTIVITIES Like the rest of Florida, Orlando is golf and tennis crazy and many facilities are available to visitors. There are five major splash parks in the Orlando area, of which Disney operates three – River Country, Typhoon Lagoon and Blizzard Beach. **Wet 'n Wild** $$$$, 6200 International Dr., has 25 acres of rides, slides and flumes, and **Water Mania** $$$$, 6073 W. Hwy 192, adds outdoor concerts for pool occupants and picnic grounds by the water rides.

NEW FOR 2000

Orlando's major theme parks are constantly adding new attractions. Continuing until 1 January 2001, **Walt Disney World** will celebrate the new millennium with fifteen months of 'New Year's Eves'. New rides include: Rock 'n' Roller Coaster featuring the music of Aerosmith, at Disney-MGM Studios; Buzz Lightyear's Space Ranger Spin, The Many Adventures of Winnie The Pooh, and the return of the Main Street Electrical Parade at the Magic Kingdom.

Universal Studios has added a new theme park 'Islands of Adventure' featuring the Marvel Super Hero Island, Jurassic Park, Toon Lagoon, The Lost Continent, and Seuss Islands.

SHOPPING

The area's largest factory outlet (over 180 stores) is **Beltz Factory Outlet World**, 5401 W. Oakridge Rd (at the north end of International Dr.); tel: (407) 352-9600; open Mon–Sat 1000–2100, Sun 1000–1800. For international travellers, thousands of tax-free items are available at **Orlando Duty Free**, 8480 Palm Parkway; tel: (407) 239-8165, which runs a free shuttle bus service to and from hotels. Open daily 1000–2200.

NIGHTLIFE

Orlando is devoted to entertainment, day and night. The daily newspaper, *Orlando Sentinel*, lists concerts, operas, recitals, ballets, plays and other entertainment and cultural activities in its calendar section published on Fri.

For theatre lovers, Orlando Broadway Series presents a late Oct–May season of national and touring productions of Broadway plays and musicals at the 2500-seat **Bob Carr Performing Arts Centre**, 201 S. Orange Ave; tel: (407) 423-9999. The professional **Orlando Opera Company** performs at 1111 N. Orange Ave; tel: (407) 426-1717.

DINNER SHOWS

Dinner shows form a major part of Orlando's night-time entertainment programme, and if you like your dinners packaged and served in a regimented, if lively, fashion, there are several to choose from. $$$$ (inclusive prices).

Arabian Nights Dinner Attraction, 6225 W. Hwy 192; tel: (407) 239-9221 or (800) 553-6116, combines virtuoso horsemanship with a four-course prime rib dinner. Italian fare accompanies speakeasy entertainment with gangsters, molls and cops at **Capone's Dinner and Show**, 4740 W. Hwy 192; tel: (407) 397-2378, while **Wild Bill's Wild West Dinner Extravaganza** at Fort Liberty, 5260 W Hwy 192; tel: (407) 363-3550 or (800) 883-8181, is a dinnertime romp with the US Cavalry, cowboys and chorus girls.

Downtown Orlando's night-time entertainment centre is **Church Street Station**, at 129 W. Church St; tel: (407) 422-2434. This complex of restaurants, shopping arcades, bars and discos is an eccentric collection of restored warehouses, hotels and shops associated with the old downtown railroad station. Open daily 1100–0100; admission free until shows begin at 1915 ($$$). At the **Cricketers' Arms**, 8445 International Dr.; tel: (407) 354-0686, there's budget eating and drinking with an English pub atmosphere and nightly entertainment. Open daily 1100–0200.

New Year's Eve is celebrated every night of the year at **Pleasure Island**, part of the Walt Disney World complex. Lots of music here: rhythm and blues, modern jazz, rock-'n'-roll, and country and western. The nightly New Year is announced with cannon fire, bells, fireworks and dancing in the streets. Open daily 1900–0200; admission for all clubs $$$.

WHERE NEXT?

When Mickey et al have exhausted you, Florida has an abundance of resorts and wildlife and, of course, the Kennedy Space Center *(see p. 245).*

Florida Beyond the Theme Parks

There is a great deal more to Florida than sunshine and hype, retirees and refugees. The beaches *are* superb – high society made Palm Beach an exclusive winter retreat long before the masses discovered Fort Lauderdale or the Gulf Coast – and the winter sun is a bonus (don't forget, winter is the *high* season here). There is a downside – parts of Miami, hurricanes, mosquitoes, overdevelopment – but there's also dramatic wildlife, some charming towns and non-theme park attractions from prehistoric caves to the launch pads of Cape Canaveral.

GETTING THERE AND GETTING AROUND

The major Florida airports are Miami International, Orlando International and Tampa International. Fort Lauderdale-Hollywood, West Palm Beach, Jacksonville and Key West all have smaller international airports. Fort Myers' Southwest Regional Airport is one of Florida's busiest.

Amtrak Silver Services run once daily between New York and Miami with a number of stops along the Florida Atlantic Coast. The Sunset Limited runs into Orlando from Los Angeles.

Greyhound buses link most of the main centres and make the run right down Hwy 1 to Key West. The nearest stop to the Everglades is Homestead, 10 miles north. The St Augustine stop is centrally located in a busy area, and the stop for Tampa is located downtown in a relatively safe area.

CITIES AND RESORTS

If Orlando is Florida's playground, then **Miami** is its night spot. This bustling city is a chaotic and curious blend of pensioners, moguls, models and movie actors. Spend your days exploring the delights of Key Biscayne and Virginia Key, with its oasis-like Bill Baggs State Park, or enjoying the art deco ambience and people-watching potential of South Beach; by night, South Beach's lively night scene will keep you club hopping. For some of Miami's best and least expensive restaurants head for Calle Ocho (S.W. 8th St) – Little Havana – where salsa rhythms blare and old men huddle over games of dominoes. Miami is not an easy city for the tourist on foot and the buses are notoriously unreliable. Be cautious: some sections of the city, such as Little Haiti, are to be avoided, especially if you are alone.

i **Greater Miami Convention and Visitors Bureau**, 701 Brickell Ave; tel: (305) 539-3063 or (800) 283-2707; www.miamiandbeaches.com.

Fort Lauderdale, north of Miami, has overcome its raucous reputation and now boasts museums, concert halls and a plethora of tourist attractions that include an IMAX® theatre, Everglades expeditions and sea sports. However, a spectacular beach remains the big draw.

i Greater Fort Lauderdale Convention and Visitors Bureau, 1800 Eller Dr., Suite 303; tel: (800) 356-1662 or (800) 22-SUNNY or (954) 765-4466; open Mon–Fri.

Charming and picturesque **St Augustine** is 40 miles south of Jacksonville (p. 218).. Its 18th-century Spanish architecture and narrow, palm-fringed streets are a pedestrian-friendly delight. This is the place to see the 'oldest' in America – St Augustine was founded in 1565, 55 years before the Pilgrims put their feet on Plymouth Rock. Sightseeing trolleys and horse-drawn carriages ply a 7-mile loop, stopping near major attractions.

The narrow strip of Florida that runs along the north coast of the Gulf of Mexico, like a finger pointing towards New Orleans, is called the Panhandle.

i St Augustine Visitor Information Center, 10 Castillo Dr.; tel: (904) 825-1000; open daily.

Tallahassee, the state capital, has the gracious atmosphere of a Southern country town quite different from the resort world of peninsular Florida. It's often overlooked, but is a useful base from which to explore the Panhandle's nature and wildlife reserves (see below). For a taste of the town itself you can't get a better deal than a free narrated tour on the Old Town Trolley, with its wooden slatted seats and shining brass fittings.

i Tallahassee Area Convention and Visitors Bureau, New Capitol Building, West Plaza Level, PO Box 1369; tel: (800) 628-2866 or (805) 413-9200; fax: (904) 487-4621; open daily.

Tampa, on the Gulf Coast, has one foot firmly planted in its Cuban heritage and the other in its ever-growing tourist industry. The biggest attraction, Busch Gardens, has thrill rides, animal habitats and all the souvenir shopping your heart could desire. It captures the spirit of turn-of-the-century Africa – ride in a gondola above a Serengeti-like plain, plunge down river rapids or dig for treasure in the sands of 'Egypt'. Ybor City, Tampa's historic Latin quarter, is famous for cigars and the largest Spanish restaurant in the world – among the art galleries, shops and nightclubs of Ybor Square you'll still find shops hand-rolling cigars. This area is well patrolled, but be cautious and do not travel solo.

i Tampa Bay Visitor Center, 3601 Busch Blvd.; tel: (813) 985-3601.

Tampa/Hillsborough Convention and Visitor Assoc. 111 Madison St; tel: (813) 223-5752 or (800) 44-TAMPA.

St Petersburg, across the bay, is Tampa's cultural *alter ego*. It has no shortage of beaches (and an excellent sunshine record), while the Pier, jutting out into Tampa Bay, is alive with shops and restaurants; but it also has more than a dozen museums and galleries, including the world-class Salvador Dalí Museum. Great Explorations, a block away from the Dalí, is the ultimate in hands-on participation ... wear loose, comfortable clothing!

i St Petersburg/Clearwater Convention and Visitors Bureau, 14450 46th St N., Suite 108, Clearwater; tel: (800) 345-6710 or (813) 464-7200; fax: (800) 89-4607; open Mon–Fri.

THE KEYS

The main fascination here is what is *under* the water (the Gulf Stream has swept away most of the beaches, although some islands have artificial stretches of sand). **Key Largo** is one of the world's most popular scuba-diving destinations, and most of the islands offer diving or snorkelling, or a trip in a glass-bottomed boat, to glimpse the fragile coral reef and old shipwrecks. Bahia Honda, on **Big Pine Key**, has the largest beach, and good swimming, fishing and diving.

US Hwy 1 links this chain of islands like a necklace, and when you reach the end of the road, throw away your watch, slip on your sandals and prepare to enter the 'Conch Republic', **Key West**. This land's-end community of bohemians, adventurers and misfits made famous by Ernest Hemingway welcomes tourists to partake in its rituals of margarita sipping and sunset watching, so join the locals at Mallory Square to watch the sun go down. Places of interest are concentrated around Duval St, and the easiest way to get around is on foot – or the Conch Tour Train and the Old Town Trolley will give you a 90-min tour of Old Town. For your safety, watch out for drunken drivers at night; street crime is rare in the historic district, but stay away from Little Bahama, west of Whitehead St and south of Petronia St.

Big Cypress is at the southern end of the Florida National Scenic Trail, a hiking trail that runs almost the entire length of the state up to Osceola Forest and the protected Panhandle shore.

i Key West Chamber of Commerce, 402 Wall St (behind the Sponge Market); tel: (800) 527-8539 or (305) 294-2587; open daily.

i The **Everglades National Park Headquarters**, 40001 State Rd 9936, Homestead; tel: (305) 242-7700; and **Big Cypress National Preserve**, HCR 61, Box 11, Ochopee; tel: (941) 695-2000, have maps and brochures and information on hiking, accommodation etc.

Other nature-watching ideas: Orphaned **manatees** are cared for at the Homosassa Springs State Wildlife Park on the Gulf Coast. Big Pine Key was set up to save the remarkably tame **Key deer** from extinction – several hundred can now be seen there. Dry Tortugas, a group of coral islands west of Key West (access by boat or seaplane only) supports a diverse bird and marine life among the coral reefs and seagrass beds.

Not all Florida's natural phenomena are marshy. Stalactites and stalagmites abound in the caves of the **Florida Caverns State Park**, and **Falling Waters** is a mysterious cascade in a park of geological formations. Both are in the Panhandle, west of Tallahassee.

Many stretches of Florida's 1800 miles of coastline are wildlife refuges. The **Canaveral National Seashore** and **Merritt Island National Wildlife Refuge** on the Atlantic coast attract giant sea turtles and an amazing number of bird species, unperturbed at sharing this undeveloped wetland with an unlikely partner: NASA.

JOURNEY INTO SPACE

To tour the **John F. Kennedy Space Center** is to take one small step into both the history and the future of space travel. The Mission Countdown, Gallery of Space Flight and the Galaxy Center with its IMAX® cinema ($) are just some of the hands-on attractions at Spaceport USA. Launch schedules permitting, there are bus tours ($$) of the working areas of the Center and out to Cape Canaveral, taking in the Saturn V rocket and a simulated Apollo 11 moon launch. Spaceport USA is an all-day experience that will bring you closer than you ever dreamt to the excitement of space exploration; amazingly, bus tours and the IMAX® cinema apart, it is all *free*.

i The **Space Cost Office of Tourism**, 2725 Judge Fran Jamieson Way, Viera; tel: (800) 872-1969, also has a visitor centre at the Space Center.

The bus tours and IMAX® cinema are understandably popular – book for these as soon as you arrive, so you don't miss out.

NATURE AND WILDLIFE

Think of Florida wildlife and you conjure up the **Everglades**: careening across the water in an airboat at 60 mph, floating silently past gators basking among the mangroves, marvelling at pink clouds of flamingoes and roseate spoonbills. A proportion of this rich wildlife habitat, a relic of the swamps and seas of reeds that once covered southern Florida, is preserved within the Everglades National Park and Big Cypress National Preserve. You'll need a vehicle for access, but there are plenty of opportunities for boat tours, canoeing and ranger-led walks. Airboats may not enter the parks themselves, but many companies offer tours outside the park boundaries – a chance to explore this watery world from an unparalleled viewpoint.

Winter is the best time to visit, when the bird population is at its height and the air mercifully free of the mosquitoes that plague the area from Apr to Nov (but beware of the hunting season mid-Nov–Dec).

Chicago

It's called the Second City, but that's a misnomer – Chicago's spectrum of sights, sounds and activities is second to none. Nestled on the shores of Lake Michigan are everything from ethnic neighbourhoods to esteemed educational institutions, from commerce to culture, from skyscrapers to stupendous shopping. Even the shadows of Chicago's notorious past – the great fire of 1871, 'hot air' politicians who gave Chicago its 'Windy City' nickname, the Capone/Dillinger gangster era of the Twenties and Thirties, and the Democratic National Convention and race riots of the Sixties – can't diminish its positives.

Chicago has been the birthplace of famous people and famous things – novelist Ernest Hemingway and poet Carl Sandburg, McDonald's, Cracker Jacks and deep-dish pizza, steel-framed skyscrapers, Walt Disney and the zip. Corporate giants like Sears, Amoco, Motorola, Sara Lee, Caterpillar and United Airlines call it home, as do famous personalities such as Oprah Winfrey and basketball's Michael Jordan. And the wheels of a global economy whirl on the trading floors of its exchanges.

Trade has been at the core of Chicago since its meagre beginnings. Jean Baptiste Point du Sable, a French-African Haitian, built a fur trading post here when he saw the potential of the site beside great Lake Michigan, with access to the Chicago River and the Des Plaines River which flowed into the Mississippi. In 1803, the US Army also appreciated its strategic value and built Fort Dearborn, the core of what is now downtown Chicago.

But history is a small part of the story. A visit to Chicago, preferably between April and November (winters are bitter), can be as varied as the city. Architecture and art, culture and cuisine, sports and sandy beaches, water and watering holes: you will find them all here.

GETTING THERE AND GETTING AROUND

Air **O'Hare International Airport** is the world's busiest. Its new Airport Transit System connects the terminals to each other and to economy parking lots. Information booths are located on the lower levels of the domestic terminals and the upper and lower levels of the International Terminal. For Travelers Aid at O'Hare, tel: (312) 686-7562.

The Chicago Transit Authority (CTA) provides cheap, rapid service (40 mins)

FOR KIDS
On the International Terminal's lower level is **Kids on the Fly**, a branch of the Chicago's Children's Museum.

between the airports and downtown (connections between other CTA trains are free). Departures are every 5–10 mins (every 30 mins 0100–0500). Continental Airport Express is a frequent shuttle service that runs to downtown hotels, the North Shore and Oak Brook suburbs (purchase tickets at counters located across from the baggage claim). A taxi to downtown Chicago will cost around $30 (there is also a flat Shared-Ride rate).

Midway Airport is located 30 mins from downtown and has the same local transport as O'Hare. CTA leaves from the east side of the airport, and Continental Airport Express leaves every 15–20 mins; taxis into the centre are around $20–25 (again, there's a Shared-Ride flat rate). An information booth is located in the main lobby.

RAIL/BUS Fifty Amtrak trains arrive and depart daily from Union Station, at 210 S. Canal St. The Greyhound main terminal is at 603 W. Harrison St.

ROAD Interstate 90 runs half a mile west of downtown Chicago – take the Eisenhower Expressway into the Loop. I90 runs from Boston, Buffalo and Cleveland and passes through Chicago on to Billings and Seattle. To reach the centre from Minneapolis and Milwaukee, take I94 which connects with I90 10 miles north of downtown. Interstates 55 (en route for St. Louis) and 57 lead into the city from the south – again joining I90/94 a few miles outside the centre.

A citywide and suburban bus and train system is provided by the CTA, PACE (which covers the suburbs) and Metra (commuter trains). Locals call the CTA train system the L (for Loop, as the downtown area is called) which is an elevated rapid rail transit system. For information tel: (312) 836-7000. A day pass ($$) on a Chicago Motor Coach Double Decker bus or on Chicago Trolley's San Francisco type streetcars will give you unlimited stops in the Loop area.

Drivers carry no change, so check on the current fare (usually a flat rate, and senior citizens and children pay less) and have the right money ready.

Guided tours ($$–$$$) are run by **Gray Line of Chicago**; tel: (312) 251-3107.

INFORMATION

Chicago Convention and Tourism Bureau; tel: (312) 567-8500.

Chicago Office of Tourism (COT), Chicago Cultural Center, 77 E. Randolph St; tel: (312) 744-2400. For the hearing impaired, tel: (312) 744-2964. Open Mon–Fri 1000–1800, Sat 1000–1700, Sun 1200–1700; closed holidays.

CHICAGO

Visitor Information Centers at Historic Water Tower (806 N. Michigan Ave) and Illinois Market Place (Navy Pier, 700 E. Grand Ave) are open daily.

For a free visitor information pack, tel: (800) 2CONNECT or visit www.ci.chi.il.us/Tourism. Free weekly publications like the *Reader*, found at restaurants and local businesses, and *Key: This Week In Chicago*, available at hotels, include lists of attractions and activities.

SAFETY As in any large city, caution is the key. Avoid areas west of downtown (beyond the south branch of the Chicago River) and walking alone in open areas such as parks or unfrequented streets after dark unless there is a special event. Exercise caution on the South Side and when travelling on the subway, especially at off-peak hours. For those times, a car or taxi is advised.

MONEY Banks are plentiful in downtown Chicago. Cash dispensers are everywhere. Thomas Cook currency offices are located at 9 S. LaSalle St; tel: (312) 807-4941; open Mon–Fri 0900–1730; and Naperville, 150 N. Naper Blvd, Suite 152, Naperville; tel: (630) 955-0536; open Mon–Fri 0900–0530, Sat 0900–1500.

POST AND PHONES The main post office is at 433 W. VanBuren St; open Mon–Fri 0700–1730, Sat 0800–1730; 24-hr self-service window.

ACCOMMODATION

Downtown hotels are expensive. Check hotels for special rates, promotions and cheaper winter rates. To make hotel reservations, contact **Illinois Reservation Service**, tel: (800) 491-1800. For B&Bs try **Bed & Breakfasts of Chicago, Inc.**, tel: (800) 444-7666. Hostels are not recommended.

DOWNTOWN

Northwestern University Dormitory Housing $ 850 N. Lake Shore Dr.; tel: (312) 503-8514. Dorm rooms available May–July, seven-night minimum stay required.

Days Inn Lincoln Park North $$$ 644 W. Diversey Parkway; tel: (773) 525-7010 or (888) LPN-DAYS. Old World charm close to the lake, zoo, and theatre and restaurant district. Special rates.

Essex Inn $$$–$$$$ 800 S. Michigan; tel: (800) 621-6909; tel: (312) 939-1605 fax. Check special promotional rates.

Ho Jo Inn $$$–$$$$ 720 N. LaSalle St; tel: (312) 664-8100; fax (312) 664-2365. Meagre but adequate hotel about five blocks west of the Magnificent Mile.

Motel 6 Chicago $$$–$$$$ 162 E. Ontario St; tel: (312) 787-3580. Charming European-style hotel one block east of Michigan Ave, near shopping, museums and Navy Pier.

Ohio House Motel $$$–$$$$ 600 N. LaSalle St; tel: (312)

943-6000. Located about six blocks west of Michigan Ave, near Planet Hollywood.

Ramada Congress $$$ (winter)–$$$$ (summer); 520 S. Michigan Ave; tel: (800) 635-1666; tel: (312) 427-7264 fax. Older hotel with small but adequate rooms. Located across from Grant Park.

NEAR NORTH

The House of Two Urns Bed & Breakfast $$$–$$$$ 1239 N. Greenview; tel: (312) 810-2466 or (800) 835-9303; www.twourns.com; email: twourns@earthlink.net. Close to downtown.

Surf Hotel $$$–$$$$ 555 W. Surf; tel: (773) 528-8400; tel: (773) 528-8483 fax. Small, attractive property near the lake in the Lakeview area.

Park Brompton Inn $$$$ 528 Brompton Place; tel: (773) 404-3499; tel: (773) 404-3495 fax. Quaint hotel located in the Lakeview area, not far from downtown.

EVANSTON

This northern suburb has some reasonable places within walking distance of downtown and about 40 mins from the city centre.

Seabury-Western Seminary $$ 2122 Sheridan Rd, Evanston; tel: (847) 328-9300. Located across from Northwestern University, near the lake and within walking distance of public transport, the school offers a limited number of rooms for guests.

Margarita Inn $$$–$$$$ 1566 Oak Ave, Evanston; tel: (847) 869-2273. Opened in 1915, its original purpose was to render 'proper lodgings for young working women'. The charming European inn is furnished with antiques and located near Northwestern University and shopping.

NILES

Leaning Tower YMCA $$ 6300 N. Touhy; tel: (847) 647-8222. About the cheapest rooms around, but located in the north-west suburb of Niles, about 90 mins from downtown by public transport.

FOOD

Chicago is most famous for hot dogs (wieners) and Chicago-style pizza. Its multicultural roots also mean a rich pool of culinary delights, from Vietnamese and South American to Polish and Irish, so in addition to the selective listing here, explore the diverse cuisines of the old Chicagoan neighbourhoods (see pp. 254–257).

Amarit $$ 1 E. Delaware. Tasty Thai food in an informal setting with good service.

Hi Ricky $$ 941 W. Randolph. Asian noodles and rice dishes. Open for lunch and dinner.

Lou Mitchell's Restaurant $$ 565 W. Jackson (by the Amtrak station). For large portions, good food and service. This place is always busy, and free ring doughnuts are served while you wait to be seated. Ladies get a free box of Milk Duds.

Pizzeria Uno $$ 29 E. Ontario and **Pizzeria Due**, 619 N. Wabash. One can't visit Chicago and not go to the places where deep-dish pizza originated.

Portillos $$ 100 W. Ontario St. For juicy hot dogs.

Stagedoor Express Deli $$ 3rd floor, Lyric Opera Building, 20 N. Wacker. NY-style, serving large portions. Open for lunch Mon–Fri.

Wishbone Restaurant $$ 1001 W. Washington. Serves large portions of Southern-style cooking. The Hoppin' John (black-eyed beans or black beans and rice) is a dish that gets rave reviews.

Heaven on Seven $$$ 111 N. Wabash, 7th floor (breakfast and lunch) and 600 N. Michigan (lunch and dinner). A favourite with the locals, who like Cajun and Creole cuisine. Each table comes with salt, pepper and 26 different hot sauces.

Russian Tea Time $$$$ 77 E. Adams; tel: (312) 360-0000. Expensive, but portions are large enough to share. Try the chicken breast roulade with oyster mushrooms à la St Petersburg. Its accompaniments, beet caviar and carrot salad, are extremely tasty. Dinner reservations advised.

HIGHLIGHTS

From 'Prairie' style to sleek skyscraper, the Chicago skyline casts a stunning silhouette against Lake Michigan. The Windy City's exterior is a tribute to the design brilliance of such notable architects as Louis Sullivan, Helmut Jahn, Frank Lloyd Wright and Ludwig Mies van der Rohe.

Those who like to see the skyline from cloud level can view the lake and the city from the 1000-ft high skywalk at the **Hancock Observatory** ($$) or go higher and see it from the **Sears Tower Skydeck** ($$).

The steel, glass and concrete towers look very different when cruising past their foundations and viewed from pylon level. **The Chicago Architectural Foundation**, tel: (312) 922-3432 and **North Pier Architectural and Historical Cruises**, tel: (312) 527-2002 give tourists that opportunity on their informative 90-min guided cruises along the Chicago River. The Architectural Foundation runs more than 50 bus, walking and river tours, affording a good prospect of the city's unique heritage. Walking tours allow a more intimate peek at the more eminent structures.

FRANK LLOYD WRIGHT

Aficionados of the distinctive work of perhaps the best known name in modern American architecture can visit the remodelled lobby of the **Rookery Building** and **Robie House**, near the University of Chicago, both fine examples of his Prairie school of architecture, as well as the **Frank Lloyd Wright Home and Studio** in Oak Park ($$–$$$), tel: (708) 848-1976.

The 100-year-old **Chicago Cultural Center** is a good place for self-guided architectural aficionados to start. The rich detail of its interior is crowned by the world's largest Tiffany glass dome. **The Museum of Broadcast Communications**, part of the facility, contains the late comedian Jack Benny's vault and the Kraft TV studio. Become an aspiring news anchor and tape a news programme ($$$).

The Cultural Center is also home to the Chicago Office of Tourism. Mid-June–mid-Oct the COT offers a free Loop history and historical tour aboard the L. Visitors can rent ($) a self-guided walking tour tape, *Audio Architecture*, which highlights the highest building in the western hemisphere, the Sears Tower, the Federal Plaza and the rooftop gargoyles of the new public library.

THE LOOP Downtown Chicago is designated by the encircling loop of the CTA, known as the L (for Loop). World-class museums and galleries abound in Chicago, and many of the best are located near downtown – the ideal place for a culture crawl.

Artefacts, photographs and exhibits at the **Chicago Historical Society** (at Clark and Dearborn) trace the city's roots from frontier days to the present. $ (Mon free); open Mon–Sat 0930–1630, Sun 1200–1700.

OUTDOOR ART

Many of downtown's architectural gems are graced by the creations of world-renowned artists. Masterpieces include the six-storey high Picasso at the Civic Center, Joan Miró's *Miró's Chicago* at the Brunswick Building Plaza, and Jean DuBuffett's *Monument With Standing Beast* at the State of Illinois Building. Marc Chagall's *The Four Seasons* can be found at Dearborn and Monroe, and Claes Oldenburg's huge baseball bat, *Batcolumn* and Alexander Calder's red *Flamingo* are at the Chicago Federal Center. All these can be discovered on a leisurely stroll around the Loop. A free booklet which gives details of all these sculptures is available from the COT.

Art lovers may already be acquainted with the **Art Institute.** The fine collection of French Impressionist paintings and drawings, as well as sculptures, textiles and art treasures that date from 3000 BC to the 1990s, reinforces its well-deserved reputation. $ (free Tues); 111 S. Michigan St; open Mon,

Wed, Thur, Fri 1000–1630; Tues 1030–2000; Sun 1200–1700. Unique hanging mobiles, paintings and sculptures created since 1945 make up the exhibits at the **Museum of Contemporary Art**. Works by Calder, Magritte and Warhol are well represented. Check out Cattlelan's *Novecento*: it is a horse hanging from the ceiling. $$ (free first Tues of each month); 220 E. Chicago Ave; open Tues–Sun 1000–1700 (Wed until 2000).

THE LAKESIDE Between Michigan Ave and the lake lies **Grant Park**, venue for dancing waters on summer evenings and a series of food and music festivals (see p. 259). Walk through the park towards the lake and a little north and you'll see **Navy Pier**, 600 E. Grand. It stretches for 50 acres out into the lake, making it easy for tour boats, dinner cruises and visiting vessels to dock there. The pier includes the unusual (fried dough, sand-bottle 'art', squeezable eyeballs) and the entertaining (an IMAX® theatre and merry-go-round), one of the world's largest McDonald's, a beer garden, shops and restaurants. The enclosed Ferris wheel moves so slowly even the worst acrophobe will feel safe, and kids love the exhibits at the **Chicago Children's Museum** such as the Art and Science of Bubbles, PlayMaze and the Stinking Truth About Garbage. $$ Open Tues–Sun 1000–1700, plus Thur 1700–2000, when it is free.

KIDS' STUFF

Chicago abounds with activities and museums that are geared towards children or those who act like them. Besides **Chicago's Children's Museum** there is the **Kohl Children's Museum**, where the young ones will come away happy and with cheeks covered with face paint. $ 165 Green Bay Rd, Wilmette; open Tues–Sat 0900–1700, Sun 1200–1700.

The **Art Institute** (see p. 251) has a children's area and a magnificent collection of miniatures, The Thorne Rooms. Budding physicists can witness a nuclear chain reaction at **ComEd's Powerhouse Museum,** 100 Shiloh Blvd, in the far north suburb of Zion; open Mon–Sat 1000–1700. Free.

Something wild is always going on at the city's **Lincoln Park Zoo**. Over 1000 animals live in this lovely setting alongside the lakefront. Cannon Dr. at Fullerton Pkwy; open 0900–1900 (until 1700 in winter). Free.

From late spring to early autumn, visitors to **Brookfield Zoo** can ride motorised safari vehicles to visit a swamp, a 5-acre savannah and many different creatures. $ 8400 31st St, Brookfield; open daily 1000–1630.

The giant chills and thrills amusement park **Six Flags Great America** is north of Chicago, at Gurnee (off I–94). Bugs Bunny and friends hang out around the park's attractions and its 130 rides, which include eight roller-coasters and a 227 ft free-fall tower. $$$ Open special weekends in May and Oct and daily June–Aug.

> **TOURS WITH A DIFFERENCE**
>
> To see the city from the water, try the popular **Windella Boat Tour**. It leaves from Wacker Dr. and Michigan and runs end Apr–Oct.
>
> Native Chicagoans look to do the unusual. Some visit the famous people who have made their eternal home at Graceland Cemetery. The 2-hr **Chicago Architectural Foundation Graceland Cemetery Tour** describes the former notables and their unique tombstones and mausoleums. $ Clark and Irving Park; daily at 1400 (Aug–Oct).

If going from the depths of the ocean to the outer limits of space, with a look at life through the ages in between, seems more appealing, visit the Museum Campus, 1200–1300 S. Lake Shore Dr. Dolphins and beluga whales perform five times a day at the **Shedd Aquarium**'s oceanarium. while over 6000 creatures lurk in the world's largest aquarium. $$ Open 0900–1800. And you can reach for the stars at the domed Sky Theater of the **Adler Planetarium:** $ (free Tues); open Mon–Thur 0900–1700; Fri 0900–2100; weekends and holidays 0900–1800. Mummies and the bones of Sue, the largest T. Rex ever discovered, are some of the former living creatures at the **Field Museum of Natural History**: $$ (free Wed); open 0900–1700.

The temptation to reach out and touch the elusive, three-dimensional pictures at the **Museum of Holography** escapes no one. Museum director Loren Billings enthusiastically explains the basic principles of this technical science which has helped to further advances in medicine, engineering and entertainment. $ 1134 W. Washington Blvd; open Wed–Sat 1230–1700.

Many Chicagoans love to walk, bike and rollerblade down the **lakeshore path** where, at every turn, there is another postcard view of the city. That's one reason it is so crowded on weekends. Though the path actually starts on 71st St, it is safer to use only the section north of Navy Pier. For those who prefer wheels to feet, rollerblades and bikes can be rented ($$) at any one of Bike Chicago's four locations, weather permitting; tel: (800) 926-BIKE.

Another favourite walk starts along the lake at Fullerton, goes to the LaSalle St overpass and then back to Fullerton through Lincoln Park Zoo. In the summer walkers also stroll along the lake north from Monroe St, to the Merchandise Mart and along the Chicago River, passing murals and sculptures along the way. They climb back up to the hustle and bustle of street level at Michigan and Wacker. These walks are not safe after dark.

SOUTH OF THE LOOP

Tucked away at 1801 S. Indiana is the **National Vietnam Veteran Art Museum**. This contains over 500 pieces of haunting artwork created by both allied and enemy Vietnam veterans. A blend of art and artefacts helps the visitor to understand the Vietnam conflict from the perspective of those who experienced it. $ Open Tues–Fri 1100–1800, Sat 1000–1700, Sun 1200–1700.

Further south is the **Museum of Science and Industry.** Its multitude of hands-on and permanent exhibits – the space capsule, vintage aeroplanes, Pioneer Zephyr train, Colleen Moore's fairy castle, coal mine, model railway, Omnimax Theatre and a U-505 submarine – leave no doubt as to why it is considered one of the 15 best museums in the world. $ (Thur free; some exhibits extra); S. Lake Shore Dr. and 57th St; open 0930–1600 (weekends and holidays until 1750).

At the south end of the museum, in Jackson Park, is the **Japanese Garden**. Lily pools, arched bridges, dwarf pines, stone lanterns and a ceremonial bamboo tea house are designed to evoke tranquillity.

Situated on the University of Chicago campus is the **Oriental Institute**, 1155 E. 58th St; tel: (773) 702-9521 for opening hours. University archaeologists gathered the fine collection of Egyptian sculpture, jewellery and statues as well as other Middle Eastern artefacts.

NORTH SHORE It is worth renting a car to visit Chicago's North Shore. Take the Outer Drive and continue down Sheridan Rd to the first suburb, Evanston. Walk along the paths of the beautiful lakeside campus of **Northwestern University**. There are only about 25,000 native Americans residing in Chicago, but the **Mitchell Indian Museum** at Central Park and Central has a fine collection of over 2000 pieces of Indian artefacts, including pottery, textiles, basketry from the Plains, Western Great Lakes, Pueblo and Navajo Indians. $ Open Tues–Sun 1000–1800.

Continue on to Wilmette's delicately sculptured **Bahai Temple**, one of seven in the world and the North Shore's foremost landmark. In the summer, its gardens are lovely.

Follow Sheridan Rd through ravines and past beautiful homes to Lake Cook Rd. Turn left to the **Chicago Botanic Gardens** (East of Edens Expressway); free, but there is a charge for parking. You can meander along its numerous promenades around the lake and through English gardens, Japanese bonsai, expanses of roses and changing landscapes.

The drive further north will take you past Ravinia Park, through Lake Forest and past many elegant mansions. In the north-west suburb of Des Plaines is the **McDonald's Museum**. Tourists addicted to Big Macs will enjoy seeing the original arches, cooking equipment, advertising and even the 'Speedee' road sign at the 1955 restaurant. 400 Lee St, Des Plaines; open Wed, Fri, Sat 1000–1600 (free).

THE NEIGHBOURHOODS If Chicago's architecture is its skin, and the Loop its brain, then the city's heart lies in its myriad cultures. Maybe poet Carl Sandburg named it 'the city of big shoulders' because of the strength it takes to support all that diversity. The flavour of the roots that have made up Chicago permeates the city – visit the neighbourhoods and see the world. Do it on your own or take one of the **Chicago Neighborhood Tours** that depart from the Chicago Cultural Center every Sat ($$$). If you plan to explore the neighbourhoods on your own, do it during daylight hours as some are not always safe after dark, especially the South Side.

NEW CHINATOWN

The red pagoda at the Argyle L stop signals New Chinatown, the Argyle/Broadway/Sheridan Rd area that has become a new hot spot for locals and visitors seeking Korean, Thai, Filipino, Vietnamese and Cambodian grocery stores, gifts shops and restaurants.

To reach **Chinatown**, take CTA Red Line south to 22nd St/Argyle. Asia is well represented here, just south of the Loop in Chinatown Sq. Messages of peace, harmony and co-operation welcome visitors at the **Chinatown Gate** (Wentworth and Cermack). Exotic aromas emanate from the Chinese herb stores, bakeries and groceries housed in the brightly coloured Asian architecture. They whet one's appetite for dim sum. Served at local restaurants between 1000 and 1400, this parade of carts brimming with tantalising oriental delicacies adds a finishing touch to an interesting afternoon. Try the **Three Happiness Restaurant** $, 2130 S. Wentworth.

Bronzeville is reached via no. 4 bus south to 56th St and Cottage Grove. For African-Americans, one of the final stops on the Underground Railroad was the **Olivet Baptist Church** (35th and King Drive) in what came to be known as Bronzeville. Life in Bronzeville between 1919 and 1948 rivalled New York's Harlem. Many of its buildings have attained National Historic Landmark status, and the once vibrant community is coming back to life.

The **DuSable Museum of African American History** details points of interest such as Martin Luther King's living quarters during his campaign for open housing and equal justice. $ 740 E. 56th Place; open 0900–1700, Sat–Sun 1200–1700. The Chicago Historical Society and other major museums often feature exhibits on African America. And rib and soul food lovers can find an abundance of ethnic restaurants throughout the city.

To travel from Africa to Europe, take the Blue Line west to Cicero/Polk. **Little Italy and Greektown** are just west of the Loop and south of the Congress St Expressway, especially around the University of Illinois–Chicago (UIC) area. Italian roots go back to the turn of the century. At first it was extortions and murders, then it was the 'booze wars' of the Twenties. The North Side Italian Community (bounded by Goose Island, North and Chicago Aves) became known as Little Hell. Later, Italian immigrants settled Little Italy around Taylor and Halsted. Though the UIC campus has taken over much of the neighbourhood, many original buildings have been preserved. The early 20th-century structures and the old country cuisine of the Taylor St restaurants make the neighbourhood appealing.

UIC also swallowed up most of the original Greektown, but a two-block segment of Halsted St west of the Loop is still devoted to bellydancers and cries of 'Opaa!' To make the area more of a tourist attraction, there are three 45 ft columns, each representing a high point in Greek culture. A spit-roasted lamb in the window of the **Parthenon Restaurant** ($$ 314 S. Halsted St) stimulates nostalgia, as do several other traditional Greek restaurants. The 1927 **St Basil's Greek Orthodox Church**, 733 Ashland, was once a Jewish synagogue. Though the church has recently been renovated, it has maintained the stained-glass windows and the seat-name plaques of the original congregation.

One of the main Jewish shopping areas during the late 1940s to the early 1960s was **Rogers Park**, between 2300 and 2900 blocks of Devon Ave. Since then, the kosher delicatessens, butcher shops and bakeries of Rogers Park have been replaced by a hodgepodge of Pakistani, Israeli, Russian, Assyrian, Thai, Korean and Indian ethnic grocery, bookshops and restaurants. This United Nations is a bargain hunter's paradise for electronics, jewellery and saris. To get there, take the Red Line north to Sheridan, then bus 155 west.

IRISH BROGUE

The main **Irish area** is found by taking the Red Line to 35th St. Anyone who knows Chicago knows that the Irish have long dominated its politics – there has been an Irish mayor for most of the last 40 years. The tree- and bungalow-bordered streets of South Side Bridgeport (Pershing/Stevenson Expressway/ Princeton and the river) were home to long-time late mayor, Richard Daley.

John Comisky built the White Sox ball park as a monument to the Bridgeport Irish. Traditional Irish pubs, gift shops and restaurants are plentiful throughout the city and suburbs. Tasty pub grub, like shepherd's pie and potato boxty, are served up with Irish music at **Fadó**, 100 W. Grand ($$–$$$).

UIC expansion halted the pushcarts and peddlers of Maxwell St, which was a staple to Jewish immigrants. Most of the urban Jewish communities have made an exodus to the suburbs, but religious artefacts, paintings, sculpture and costumes pertaining to Judaic culture are regular exhibits at **Spertus Museum of Judaica** $, 615 S. Michigan Ave; open Sun–Wed 1000–1700, Fri 1000–1500, Thur 1000–2000.

'**Polish Main Street**' is Milwaukee Ave, directly north-west of the Loop; take the Green Line to Milwaukee and Augusta. The **Polish Museum of America** features permanent exhibits of Casmir Pulaski, ethnic and military costumes and a Maritime Room; Milwaukee and Augusta; open daily 1100–1600; free. The 3000 block of Milwaukee Ave is a potpourri of authentic bakeries, gift shops, delis and restaurants where pierogi is plentiful. Enjoy tasty and authentic Polish cuisine at **Orbi Restaurant and Lounge**, 2954 N. Milwaukee, or at **Grota**, 3112 N. Central Ave. It is cheap.

Lincoln Square Mall is Chicago's **Germantown**. A huge mural depicting the German countryside colours the 4600 block of 'Sauerkraut Boulevard' (Lincoln Ave), and although 'the boulevard' does not always reverberate with oom-pa-pa, there is an abundance of ethnic restaurants, delis and shops. Take the Blue Line north to Montrose, then no. 78 bus east to Lincoln Sq.

Scandinavian settlement in the northern part of the city in **Andersonville** (Foster to Bryn Mawr near Clark St; no. 22 bus north to Clark and Foster) peaked about 1930. The **Swedish American Museum** (5211 N. Clark St; and the **Ebenezer Lutheran Church** (1650 Foster) remain. Descendants of the original immigrants still run the Clark St craft and food establishments, and a visit to Andersonville would be incomplete without sampling Ann Sather's mouthwatering cinnamon rolls at 5207 N. Clark plus five other locations.

FOR FREE

Several television shows originate in Chicago, the most popular being the *Oprah Winfrey Show*. To obtain free tickets for her show, out-of-towners must contact the ticket hotline at least a month in advance; tel: (312) 591-9222. If you can't get to see Oprah, you might try to get tickets for the outrageous *Jerry Springer Show*, tel: (312) 836-9485; or the *Jenny Jones Show*, tel: (312) 836-5365.

TRADING PLACES

Get your ups and downs at Chicago's commerce exchanges. All have videos explaining how the exchanges work and a visitors' gallery where you can watch the frenzy of trading options, foreign currency, stock or agricultural commodities. It is a good idea to call ahead. Choose from the **Chicago Board of Options Exchange**, 400 S. LaSalle St; tel: (312) 930-8249; **Mercantile Exchange**, 30 S. Wacker; tel: (312) 930-8249; and the **Chicago Stock Exchange**, 440 S. LaSalle St; tel: (312) 663-2980. All are open 0730–1530 (Mercantile closes 15 mins earlier).

The *corazón* of Mexico beats in the **Pilsen/La Villita** area (no. 60 Cermack bus west to Lawndale). A pink gateway arch at Albany and 26th welcomes visitors to La Villita. Ethnic music and the murals that decorate 25th and 26th St groceries, shops, news-stands and restaurants give Chicago's South of the Border residents a sense of the homeland. Prominent Mexican artists perform concerts, folk music, children's theatre, readings and display art at the **Museum of Mexican Fine Arts**, 1852 19th St; open Tues–Sun 1000–1700; free.

SHOPPING

Speciality boutiques, Water Tower Place (in the historic sole survivor of the great 1871 Chicago fire), and the best upmarket department stores are on N. Michigan Ave's **Magnificent Mile**. From just over the Chicago River Bridge to Oak St, it is one of the city's best places to people-watch. Stop off at FAO Schwarz, the giant toy store: the electronic keyboard on the floor plays every note you step on (like the one on which Tom Hanks danced in the film *Big)*. Turn down Oak St to check out the international designers like Ultimos, Armani and Versace.

Chicago

If you don't have the wallet for designer labels, shop in **State St**. It is Chicago's original shopping mecca, with the original Marshall Field and Carson, Pirie, Scott. There are great deals on designer merchandise at T. J. Maxx and Filene's Basement in the 1 N. State St shopping complex, but it takes time to rummage through the merchandise.

Take Me to the Ballgame

Sportsmania is part of the Chicago scene. Didn't ex-Bull basketball player Michael Jordan put Chicago on the world map? Whatever the time of year a professional team is playing. In the cooler months, it is the **Bulls** (basketball), **Bears** (football), **Chicago Blackhawks** or **Wolves** (hockey). Summer is the baseball season, and you'll find the **White Sox** at Comisky Park and the **Cubs** at Wrigley Field. It's fun just to watch the fans. Wrigley Field, one of the grand old ballparks, is where you'll find 'bleacher bums' swigging beer, yelling and predicting the plays.

Since game tickets are expensive, many fans opt instead for sports bars. You can find dancing and big screens at the **Alumni Club**, 2251 N. Lincoln. The college-aged crowd likes **Hi-Tops** by Wrigley Field (3551 N. Sheffield), where by 2300 you can expect people to be dancing on the tables. **Murphy's Bleacher Bar** on Sheffield and Waveland is *the* pre- and post-Cub game place to talk about the game, chow on brats and chug oversized cans of Old Style beer.

EVENTS AND FESTIVALS

Chicagoans love to celebrate – anything. There are ethnic festivals and parades throughout the year (the Chicago River is even dyed green for **St Patrick's Day**, 17 Mar). Check with the COT to see where the party is.

In Grant Park the sounds of great classical, jazz, country, gospel and blues ride the summer breezes on warm summer nights against a backdrop of coloured spotlights and the dancing waters of the Buckingham Fountain. Grant Park hosts three great celebrations under the stars. The **Blues Festival** (early June) and the **Jazz Festival** (early Sept) are free. Food can be costly at the week-long **Taste of Chicago** celebration, a hodgepodge of speciality and ethnic cuisines that culminates with a gala 4 July fireworks display.

In late July, Lake Michigan is aglow with boats, planes and fireworks as the city celebrates **Venetian Night** at Monroe Harbor. The Monroe Avenue Yacht Club hosts a free open house.

NIGHTLIFE

From autumn through to spring the world-class **Chicago Symphony** performs at Symphony Center, 220 S. Michigan. Solo jazz greats such as Grover Washington or Dave Brubeck and classical artists such as cellist Yo-Yo Ma or violinist Pinchas Zuckerman also play there. In the summer the musicians take their acts on the road and perform outdoors at Ravinia Park in the northern suburb of Highland Park. Reduced price 'rush' tickets for students and those aged 64 and over go on sale at the box office 2 hrs before the concert.

PLAY THE CASINOS

There is riverboat gambling outside Chicago at the Empress Casino, Joliet, the Grant Victoria Casino, Elgin, and the Hollywood Casino in Aurora. In Indiana, there is the Empress Casino in Hammond and the Majestic Star Casino in Gary.

Theatres offer everything from lavish productions to intimate pieces – many small theatres and great restaurants have sprouted up in a 2 mile section around the Lincoln/Halsted Ave area. Half-price, day-of-performance tickets are available at Hot Tix booths, tel: (312) 977–1755.

The **Second City**, 1616 N. Wells St, is the socio-political, satirical comedy club where such notables as John Belushi, Alan Arkin, Gilda Radner, Bill Murray and Dan Aykroyd started out. It is one of the great places for improvised comedy. For tickets, tel: (312) 377-3992.

Chicago has some great jazz and blues clubs. Expect to pay a cover charge in most.

Buddy Guy's Legends, 754 S. Wabash. Arrive early to get a good seat for local and top name blues performers.

Dick's Last Resort, 435 E. Illinois St. Billed as having no cover, no dress code and no class, this is the place to watch the boats float by North Pier at sunset and listen to live Dixieland music.

Green Dolphin Street, 2200 N. Ashland. Hip jazz if you can stand the cigar smoke.

Green Mill, 4802 N. Broadway. There is great jazz here, but the neighbourhood warrants caution.

House of the Blues, 329 N. Dearborn, at the base of Marina City. Features rhythm and blues music with New Orleans-style cuisine. Cover for live music and concert. At the Sunday Gospel Brunch, 0930–1430, wild designs and African-American folk art surround patrons as their ears and stomachs are filled with soul food and sacred music.

CHICAGO

If you fancy dancing the night away, try:

Hangge-Uppe, 14 W. Elm. Dance mixes played upstairs, while downstairs the 1950s-through-1970s music prompts sing-alongs. Ceilings are decorated with old 45 records. Free popcorn, but a cover charge.

Polly Esthers, 213 W. Institute. Besides dancing, there is plenty to see at this groovy local hangout – there is alighted dance floor with authentic Seventies décor and music upstairs, and Eighties paraphernalia and music downstairs. Drink concoctions are named after Seventies and Eighties movie stars and TV shows. No cover before 2100, then a fairly hefty charge.

WHERE NEXT?

The whole US transport network radiates out from Chicago like a spider's web. In addition to the transcontinental routes, Amtrak routes trace the course of the Mississippi down to New Orleans (see p. 289) or cross the vast grain fields of Kansas and Oklahoma to San Antonio (see p. 310) and Santa Fe (see p. 321). Discover more of the Great Lakes with a visit to the Erie Canal and Niagara Falls (see p. 95).

DELIVERING A CAR

Driveaway schemes can provide travellers with a low-cost way to drive across the continent, but are not exactly free car hire, as often suggested. For a deposit of $300 cash, a licensed driver at least 21 years of age can deliver a car from one coast to the other for the price of the petrol. The catch is that you must drive at least 400 miles each day. Assuming interstate highways at legal speeds with no traffic tie-ups, this is about 7 hours driving a day, leaving you little time for sightseeing. The only way it might be advantageous is to return to a gateway city after sightseeing across the country by other means.

One firm offering this service is Auto Driveaway Co., 310 S. Michigan Ave., Chicago, IL 60 604; tel: (800) 346-2277. It is important to reserve 7–10 days ahead. Most deliveries are from the west coast to the east.

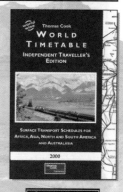

CHICAGO – NEW YORK (THREE RIVERS)

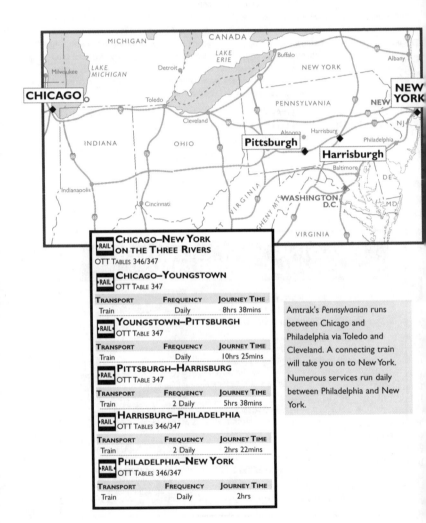

RAIL CHICAGO–NEW YORK ON THE THREE RIVERS

OTT TABLES 346/347

RAIL CHICAGO–YOUNGSTOWN

OTT TABLE 347

TRANSPORT	FREQUENCY	JOURNEY TIME
Train	Daily	8hrs 38mins

RAIL YOUNGSTOWN–PITTSBURGH

OTT TABLE 347

TRANSPORT	FREQUENCY	JOURNEY TIME
Train	Daily	10hrs 25mins

RAIL PITTSBURGH–HARRISBURG

OTT TABLE 347

TRANSPORT	FREQUENCY	JOURNEY TIME
Train	2 Daily	5hrs 38mins

RAIL HARRISBURG–PHILADELPHIA

OTT TABLES 346/347

TRANSPORT	FREQUENCY	JOURNEY TIME
Train	2 Daily	2hrs 22mins

RAIL PHILADELPHIA–NEW YORK

OTT TABLES 346/347

TRANSPORT	FREQUENCY	JOURNEY TIME
Train	Daily	2hrs

Amtrak's *Pennsylvanian* runs between Chicago and Philadelphia via Toledo and Cleveland. A connecting train will take you on to New York. Numerous services run daily between Philadelphia and New York.

ON THE 'THREE RIVERS'

The confluence of the Allegheny and Monongahela Rivers at Pittsburgh marks the start of the Ohio River's 1000-mile journey westwards, and gives this route its name.

Overnight, the train covers long stretches of agricultural land in Indiana and Ohio. Corn, beans and livestock are the main agricultural commodities throughout the Midwest, and heavy industries such as metals and chemicals are concentrated here, especially in northern Indiana. Farms and factories are very much a part of the American heartland, and you can start to gain a perspective on how truly big the country is when you realise it has taken the whole night to roll across just two states.

Although Pittsburgh has had its share of hard knocks, it has recovered from a severe slump – as well as horrid pollution – which followed its steel-and-coal glory days, to emerge as a spirited city with a good share of museums and parks. Once clear of Pittsburgh, the train whistles through the Allegheny Mountains, on its way to Harrisburg and the chocolate fantasyland of Hershey Park, then speeds through the wonderfully picturesque landscape of Lancaster County before being caught by the dense grasp of the east coast.

PITTSBURGH

Once the world's largest steel producer and a major coal centre, Pittsburgh suffered a long depression that had almost gutted the city's economy by the 1970s. Its image as a working-class town was personified at this time by its football team, the Steelers, which won four Super Bowl championships in six years. Most Americans think of Pittsburgh as merely a polluted, industrial city gone bust, but surprisingly, they are wrong. While it may never have the attractions to make it a real tourist destination, Pittsburgh has revamped in the past decade, cleaned itself up, and established itself as a pleasant, even attractive place.

The downtown financial district is a great place to feel the city's past prosperity as well as its recent rise. The newly dubbed 'Golden Triangle', wedged between the rivers, retains elements of its former industrial might in the form of restored warehouses and other turn-of-the-century buildings, while the shiny new skyline juts upwards in a profusion of steel and glass. Much of this is concentrated around the very central **Market Square**, and along Penn Ave to the north. Penn Ave continues out through what is known as the Strip District, a great place to come for busy produce and junk markets by day, and lively pubs and clubs by night.

Pittsburgh started off as a frontier post, guarded by **Fort Pitt** at the rivers' convergence. Fought over by successive waves of French and British expansionists, the fortress was destroyed several times before today's structure survived. Set in the midst of **Point State Park**, and fronted by an impressive fountain, the fort provides a good viewpoint over the city skyline. The **Fort Pitt Museum** within has displays on its frontier days. $ Open Wed–Sat 1000–1630, Sun 1200–1630. From here, it's not hard to imagine the rows of steel mills which until only recently lined the rivers.

Glancing towards the south bank of the Monongahela, you can also picture the many 19th-century coal mines of **Mount Washington** that kick-started the city's industrial drive. Cross the highway bridge and head to the right to catch the cable car up **Duquesne Incline**, on top of which is a museum demonstrating both the pluses (wealth) and minuses (appalling pollution) of Pittsburgh's industrial age.

Just north of downtown, across the Allegheny River, the new **Andy Warhol Museum** at 117 Sandusky St is a rich collection of this city's favourite son. Warhol's family emigrated to America from what is now eastern Slovakia in the 1920s. He was born in Pittsburgh in 1928, and went on to define the pop era through his paintings and films of numerous personalities and objects of the 1950s, 1960s, and 1970s. The museum is a grand-scale homage to the creator, and is helping bring tourist recognition to the city. $$ Open Wed–Sun 1100–1800, often later for events.

EN ROUTE

Between Pittsburgh and Harrisburg the train pulls in at Johnstown, renowned in American folklore for its history of tragic floods. The most devastating occurred in 1889, when the protective dam just upstream burst and raging waters drowned some 2000 unsuspecting residents in just 10 minutes. The reason is the town's precarious position at the meeting of three small rivers which flow out of the Allegheny Mountains, but poor dam construction has played its part as well. Johnstown today is pretty enough, but there is little to see other than the beguiling Johnstown Flood National Memorial.

The visitor centre is downtown at Liberty Ave near Point State Park; tel: (1-800) 366-0093; www.pittsburgh-cvb.org.

Amtrak is located at Liberty Ave and Grant St, at the north-east corner of downtown.

Central hotels are geared toward conventions, but prices are lower at weekends. Special rates can be arranged through the **Weekend Package** hotline, tel: (1-800) 927-8376.
HI Youth Hostel $ E. Warrington Ave; tel: (412) 431-1267 or (1-800) 909-4776. The cheapest option.
The Priory $$$$ 614 Pressley St; tel: (412) 231-3338; fax: (412) 231-4838. Exceptionally comfortable, a converted monastery on the north side of the Allegheny River.

Downtown Pittsburgh's revitalisation includes a surge in restaurants. The Strip District, just north-east of centre, is a lively area of markets, bars and various eateries.
Southwest Bistro $$ 129 6th St. Well-balanced combination of South-west and European cuisines.
Valhalla $$ 12th and Smallman St. Restored warehouse with home-brewed beer and an outdoor deck.

HARRISBURG

Pennsylvania's state capital, while certainly lacking the verve and grit of Philadelphia or Pittsburgh, nevertheless maintains a pretty atmosphere, with numerous old homes and interesting buildings. Predominant among these are the **State Capitol**, with a dome modelled on St Peter's in Rome. Nearby **River Park** is a lux uriant stretch of landscaped gardens.

ALTOONA

One of America's favourite thrills for railway enthusiasts is the great hairpin turn the tracks take near Altoona.

America's fascination with the big and the tacky is put on display in Hershey, 10 miles east of Harrisburg. The town was established as a planned community for workers at the Hershey chocolate factory, one of the country's largest. Chocolate is still churned out here en masse, and in addition to the pseudo-chocolate factory tour at **Hershey Chocolate World**, you can spend the day whirling on the roller-coaster rides at adjacent Hershey Park.

PENNSYLVANIA DUTCH COUNTRY

The farmland of Lancaster County has been shaped by the European religious communities that settled here. The Mennonites and Amish rejection of the technological trappings of modern life mean a pleasing lack of billboards, telephone wires and agricultural machinery, with quaint pastoral scenes from a bygone era.
See p. 166.

i Harrisburg-Hershey-Carlisle Tourism and Convention Bureau, 114 Walnut St; tel: (717) 232-1377, www.visithc.com. **Historic Harrisburg Resource Center**, 1230 North Third St; tel: (717) 233-4646, has an array of brochures and information and organises bus and walking tours.

The Harrisburg and Hershey area has plenty of accommodation options and is well represented by the familiar hotel and motel chains (see p. 504).
The nearest KOA campsite is six miles south of Hershey on Rte 743.

EN ROUTE

Philadelphia, the last major stop before New York, is a city that is at long last shaking off a bad reputation and industrial slump to enjoy its ethnic diversity and status as birthplace of the nation (see p. 156).

Chicago – New York (Lake Shore)

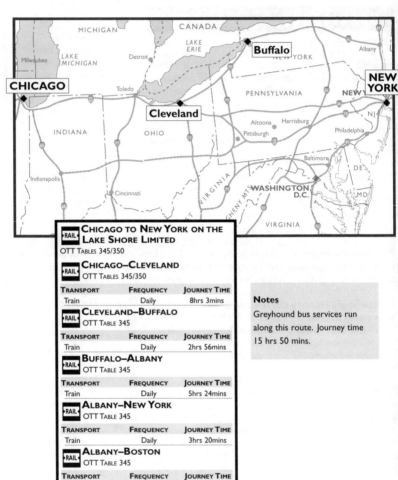

Chicago to New York on the Lake Shore Limited

OTT Tables 345/350

Chicago–Cleveland

OTT Tables 345/350

Transport	Frequency	Journey Time
Train	Daily	8hrs 3mins

Cleveland–Buffalo

OTT Table 345

Transport	Frequency	Journey Time
Train	Daily	2hrs 56mins

Buffalo–Albany

OTT Table 345

Transport	Frequency	Journey Time
Train	Daily	5hrs 24mins

Albany–New York

OTT Table 345

Transport	Frequency	Journey Time
Train	Daily	3hrs 20mins

Albany–Boston

OTT Table 345

Transport	Frequency	Journey Time
Train	Daily	5hrs

Notes

Greyhound bus services run along this route. Journey time 15 hrs 50 mins.

ON THE 'LAKE SHORE LIMITED'

Of the two Chicago–New York rail routes, the Lake Shore Limited is the more roundabout, following the shores of Lake Erie right up to Buffalo and touching the southern shore of Lake Ontario before dropping south 100 miles along the Hudson River valley to New York. The extra mileage is worth it, though, especially when the stunning autumn foliage turns the entire Hudson valley a rich golden red.

The route is interesting for its cross-sector views of American life, from smooth, easy agricultural lands to newly fashioned industrial cities and well-heeled rural serenity. Cleveland, only recently considered a place with absolutely no redeeming qualities, has suddenly come into its own with a tidied-up downtown and the great new Rock and Roll Hall of Fame. Buffalo has the massive draw of Niagara Falls, while Albany, the state capital, is the gateway to New England.

CLEVELAND

Like many cities in America's so-called Rust Belt, Cleveland has made great strides since its economic collapse of the 1960s and 1970s, to become a much more livable and enjoyable place. One of America's great industrial centres, along with the likes of Philadelphia and Pittsburgh, Cleveland hit rock bottom in the early 1970s, when the Cuyahoga River actually caught fire, so polluted was it from decades of heavy metal waste.

This event was the catalyst in the city's urban renewal drive, which by the mid-1990s reached full tilt when Cleveland opened its showpiece, the **Rock and Roll Hall of Fame**. On the spanking new North Coast Harbor, the Hall of Fame is a hugely popular testament to the musical genre. Tracing the roots of rock back to influences as diverse as blues and bluegrass, the museum has exciting interactive exhibitions on great names such as Chuck Berry, Elvis Presley, Aretha Franklin and John Lennon. The building itself is a striking piece of work by I. M. Pei, and contains wacky displays such as stage items from Rolling Stones tours. Because of the museum's popularity, it's a good idea to reserve tickets in advance. $$$ tel: (800) 493-ROLL; open Tues–Sun 1000–1730 (Wed 1000–2100).

After the novelty of Cleveland's claim to fame, take time to wander around more of the city. **Public Sq.** is a rather grand statement of its former wealth and enduring working-class pride. Meander south-west towards the notorious Cuyahoga River to drink up the gritty exuberance. The **Historic Warehouse District**, once busy with crates and forklifts, is now a lively row of shops and eateries leading towards **The Flats**, an active riverside hotchpotch of grandiose century-old mills and bridges; this is the place to come at night.

CHICAGO – NEW YORK (LAKE SHORE)

Another good way to spend a lazy afternoon or evening is at a baseball or football game. Baseball's Cleveland Indians, after decades of dormancy, are now one of the league's best, and their home is the beautiful new **Jacob's Field** stadium downtown. The Cleveland Browns, after decades as the city's – and the nation's – favourite hard-luck football team, relocated to Baltimore in 1996, but a new team formed for the 1999 season. Check with the tourist office for schedules and tickets.

The Convention and Visitors Bureau of Greater Cleveland is at the epicentre, in the Terminal Tower at 50 Public Sq.; tel: (216) 621-4110 or (1-800) 321-1001.

Amtrak lets you off on the cusp of the downtown area and the lakefront on Hwy 2.

For B&B reservations, call **Private Lodgings**, tel: (216) 321-3213. Aside from this, cheap rooms are scarce.
Comfort Inn $$–$$$ 1800 Euclid Ave; tel: (216) 861-0001. The most central budget place.

Cleveland has no particular culinary claim to fame, but its plethora of bar-and-grill joints, particularly in the Warehouse District and The Flats, along the Cuyahoga River, should keep you full of burgers and beer.
River's Edge Nite Club and Deli $$ 1198 Old River Rd. Just what the name says, and one of several bars and restaurants in The Flats.
Winking Lizard Tavern $$ 811 Huron Rd. Downtown pub with a huge beer menu.

THE GREAT LAKES

The five Great Lakes – Ontario, Erie, Huron, Michigan and Superior – together total nearly 100,000 square miles. Linked by short waterways, they practically form one enormous water system, and conceived as such they are the largest composite body of fresh water in the world. They also form one of the world's busiest shipping arteries: the Erie Canal connects Buffalo and Lake Erie to New York City and the Atlantic, and the Illinois Waterway links Chicago and Lake Michigan to the Mississippi and the Gulf of Mexico.

This extensive network was largely responsible for the USA's tremendous rise in agricultural and industrial might in the 19th century. Chicago is the world's biggest agricultural commodities market, and iron-and-steel-cities such as Cleveland have benefited from their accessibility to shipping. Likewise, Milwaukee's prominent breweries are well situated to exploit the area's rich grain fields, and Detroit became automobile capital of the world – Motown – in large part because of its ease of receiving raw materials, and of sending the finished product both nationwide and overseas.

BUFFALO

Perhaps more than any city in the region, Buffalo's fortunes have risen and fallen with the lake on which it stands. The completion of the Erie Canal (see p. 75) was a boon to the city's emerging shipping industry, as goods could now be transported between the Great Lakes cities and New York. Buffalo handled grain, iron ore, limestone, coal and oil, and although its importance has diminished in recent decades, it is still an economic force.

As a primarily commercial city, Buffalo lacks the cultural attractions of other mid-size cities. But if you're heading for **Niagara Falls** (see p. 75) Buffalo makes a good base, and its passable arts and entertainment scene will seem particularly appealing after the crass and unavoidable tourist exploitation at the famous falls.

The most noteworthy building is the tall **City Hall**, while the most interesting is the **Albright-Knox Art Gallery**, at 1285 Elmwood Ave in Delaware Park. Its rich collection from the late 19th and 20th centuries is well worth a look. $ Open Tues–Sun 1200–1700.

The **Greater Buffalo Convention and Visitors Bureau**, 617 Main St, tel: (1-800) BUFFALO, has information on the city and Niagara Falls.

Amtrak lets you off in the suburb of Depew, where you can get a connection to station downtown o Exchange St and Washington St, which is where trains to Niagara Falls depart from.

There is an **HI Youth Hostel** $ close to the Visitors Bureau, at 667 Main St; tel: (716) 852-5222; or you could head a few blocks further north to the **Red Carpet Inn** $$, a cheap chain motel at 1159 Main St; tel: (716) 882-3490.

You have to try the nationally renowned local speciality, buffalo wings: spicy chicken wings in a hot pepper sauce with blue cheese dressing, messy but scrumptious. The **Anchor Bar**, at 1047 Main St, serves them up by the dozen.

WHERE NEXT?

At Albany (see p. 74) the route divides, and instead of continuing on to New York, you have the choice of taking a separate train across Massachusetts to Boston (see p. 88).

Chicago – New Orleans

Chicago–New Orleans
OTT Tables 380/730

Transport	Frequency	Journey Time
Train	Daily	19hrs 50mins
Bus	4 Daily	20hrs 15mins

Note: There is another daily train service as far as Carbonbale. Both trains require a reservation.

Chicago–Carbondale
OTT Table 380

Transport	Frequency	Journey Time
Train	2 Daily	5hrs 35mins

Carbondale–Jackson
OTT Table 380

Transport	Frequency	Journey Time
Train	Daily	9hrs 40mins

Jackson–New Orleans
OTT Table 380

Transport	Frequency	Journey Time
Train	Daily	4hrs 21mins

ON THE 'CITY OF NEW ORLEANS'

Amtrak's 'City of New Orleans' was captured in song by Arlo Guthrie, expressing the spirit of adventure that travelling America's rails entails. And while the hobo life that the song portrays has all but disappeared, this is still one of Amtrak's most culturally appealing routes, running almost directly north–south between two of the nation's most exciting cities.

Once free of the reins of Chicago's endless suburbs, the 'City of New Orleans' flies across rolling Illinois cornfields and through the hilly westernmost corners of Kentucky and Tennessee. The major stop *en route* is Memphis (see p. 282), well worth a stopover as it's virtually an open-air museum of the blues and rock and roll. The blues were created in Memphis in the early 20th century, and dozens of rock luminaries, including Elvis Presley himself, hail from here.

The rails just nudge the Mississippi River here before levelling out across the flat, hot cotton fields of the state of Mississippi, where you gain a perspective on a very different life and culture. The state has yet to recover from its 19th-century heyday, and the poverty today is tangible. The most appealing stop is probably Jackson, the state capital, with two good museums on the state's turbulent history and culture. The train then rolls on down to New Orleans (see p. 289).

THE BLUES TRAIN

The 'City of New Orleans' links Chicago and New Orleans via Memphis – all cities that have been pivotal in the creation and development of jazz and blues. It is not coincidental that the tracks trace the path that hundreds of thousands of migrant black workers took northwards in the late 19th and early 20th centuries, bringing with them the experience and the sound that gave rise to the music.

CARBONDALE

At Carbondale, Illinois, an Amtrak Thruway Bus connects to St Louis (see p. 282), a Mississippi riverside city with plenty of exciting monuments and museums to explore.

JACKSON

The small city of Jackson, Mississippi, provides a foretaste of the grand Old South.

CHICAGO – NEW ORLEANS

THE MISSISSIPPI RIVER

The mighty Mississippi holds a special point of reverence for those who live within its powerful tug of influence. The river is a way of life for millions of people in the Midwest and South, providing major shipping opportunities and helping create the conditions for America's rich farm belt. It also effectively marks the east–west boundary of the country.

The name comes from the Algonquin Indian *Misi sipi*, meaning 'big river', and one of its many nicknames is Big Muddy, derived from its incredible breadth (over a mile at some points) and brown, earthy make-up. 'Old Man River' has its own lore, captured in literature by Mark Twain, who was raised on the waters and based his two most famous rabble-rousing characters, Tom Sawyer and Huckleberry Finn, on his own boyhood adventures. (Twain, whose real name was Samuel L. Clemens, worked as a pilot on the Mississippi and took his *nom de plume* from the boatmen's call as they plumbed the river's depth.)

The Mississippi is not, in fact, the longest river in North America – the Missouri and Mackenzie Rivers are longer – but it discharges the largest volume of water as it takes in the flow of the Missouri and Ohio Rivers along the way. The wealth that it brings to Midwestern cities such as Minneapolis/St Paul and St Louis, however, is diluted by the time the river winds south. The state of Mississippi used to be one of the nation's economic powerhouses, at the time when cotton was king and slaves were its subjects. Today, Mississippi is one of the very poorest states in the Union, along with Arkansas and Louisiana, with which it shares the river as a border. Add to this the incredible humidity that the river creates in summer and the tendency it has to flood (almost the entire length of the river is hemmed in by fortified banks), and its effect is all the more humbling.

It is, by any measure, an awesome sight. The colourful steamboats that were once a mainstay for shipping and passenger transport are still around, many converted to casinos or pleasure cruise ships. Nostalgic (not to mention pricey) tours of up to two weeks can be arranged with companies such as the **Delta Queen Steamboat Company**, tel: (1-800) 543-1949, whose boats ply the waters between all the major southern cities. If your budget doesn't allow for this, you can gain good vantage points, and take hour-long sightseeing rides, on the river in Memphis (p. 282), St Louis (p. 274) and New Orleans (p. 289).

A city of grace, Jackson also recognises the appalling conditions wrought by slavery and segregation throughout its history. Start your tour at the **Old State Capitol**, a stern structure built in the Greek Revival style. It served as the capitol building until 1903, when the current State Capitol was erected at 400 High St. The Old State Capitol was later converted into a museum, which now has a very good permanent exhibition entitled 'Native American, European, and African Cultures in Mississippi, 1500–1800'. Open Mon–Fri 0800–1700, Sat 0930–1630, Sun 1230–1630; free.

Just near the new capitol, at 528 Bloom St, is the highly informative **Smith Robertson Museum and Cultural Center**, located in the former heart of Jackson's black community. Displays portray the lives of blacks during the slave era and the equally difficult Reconstruction, when severe racism effectively kept blacks as second-class citizens. Photographs and artefacts bring the experience to life. $ Open Mon–Fri 0900–1700, Sat 0900–1200, Spun 1400–1700.

EN ROUTE

South of Jackson the route skirts the vastness of the Mississippi Delta, through the bayous and swamps of Louisiana. Look out of the left-hand side of the train for Lake Pontchartrain as the train approaches New Orleans.

i The train station and tourist office are both very central. Tourist information from **Metro Jackson Convention and Visitors Bureau**, PO Box 1450, Jackson, MS 39125-1450; tel: (601) 960-1827. www.visitjackson.com.

Accommodation is plentiful and your should have no difficulty finding somewhere to stay. Try the **Old Capitol Inn $$** 226 N. State St; tel: (601) 359-9000 or (1-888) 359-9001.

Field's Café $$ 100 W. Griffith St. Offers live music and dancing Fri and Sat nights to go with your meal.

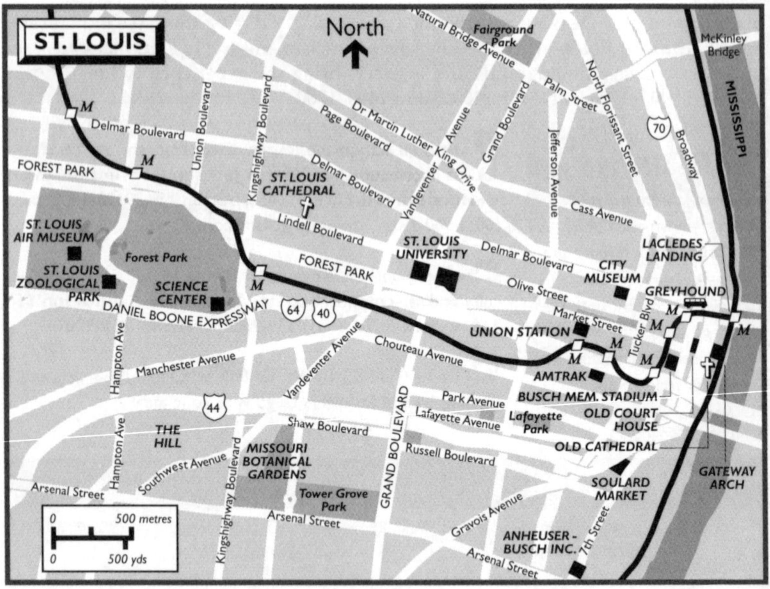

St Louis is generally known for two things: the Gateway Arch and the Anheuser-Busch brewery. While these are strong draws, St Louis offers more: it is a busy Midwestern commercial centre with a surprisingly active cultural life. Its location, just downstream from the confluence of the Mississippi and Missouri rivers, made it a profitable juncture for fur traders, westward pioneers and steamboat shippers, and drew a thoroughly mixed bag of French, German and Italian immigrants. Blacks moved in as slaves when Missouri was admitted to the union in 1821, and this mix of ethnicities, along with a new influx of Asians, thrives in the city's various pockets. Because the Mississippi commands such a presence here, summers are often unbearably hot and humid. Locals escape to Forest Park and its many museums, or kick back at a baseball game.

The sights are scattered throughout the city. The famous Arch sits on the riverfront, near the Laclede's Landing historic district – good for a wander at night, when the restaurants and clubs come to life. Forest Park, 4 miles west of the centre, contains many good museums, while the Central West End and, to the east, the University City neighbourhoods, are great to stroll around and seek out a coffee shop or deli. Working-class South St Louis has several ethnic enclaves, such as Soulard and the Hill.

GETTING THERE AND GETTING AROUND

Lambert–St Louis Airport is 12 miles north-west of centre, easily accessible by local bus or by the Metro Link light-rail system. Metro Link runs from the airport to most of the main tourist sites; rides are free 1000–1500, otherwise just $1.

Amtrak trains pull in at Union Station, at the corner of S. 16th and Market Sts. This was once the largest railway station in the world, and has been rejuvenated to a shiny version of its former grandeur, filled with shops and restaurants. The clock tower at the front is another St Louis landmark.

Buses serve the suburbs; the central bus station is at 809 N. Broadway.

INFORMATION

The city's main **visitor centre** is at 308 Washington Ave, near the Arch; tel: (1-800) 916-0092; open daily 0930-1700; www.st-louis-cvc.com (a very good website).

SAFETY St Louis is fairly safe as far as American cities go, but don't wander around Forest Park at night. East St Louis, across the river in Illinois, was once a fertile production ground for jazz and blues artists but is now a notoriously dangerous suburb.

MONEY Thomas Cook Currency Services operates out of AAA Missouri. The most convenient office is at 3917 Lindell Blvd near Forest Park; tel: (314) 523-7350.

POST AND PHONES The main post office is next to Union Station at 1720 Market St; open Mon–Fri 0700–1700, Sat 0700–1200. The zip code for poste restante is MO 63155.

ACCOMMODATION

Check with the visitor centre for special hotel rates. The Greater St Louis Reservation Service, tel: (314) 961-2252, can help with budget accommodation, including B&Bs.

St Louis RV Park, 900 N. Jefferson. Surprisingly central camping ground, geared toward RV travellers.

Huckleberry Finn Youth Hostel $ 1904–08 S. 12th St (at Tucker Blvd); tel: (314) 241-0076 or 1-800 909-4776 code 70; fax: (314) 436-0170; email: huckfinn@mindspring.com. HI hostel in three historic brick buildings in Soulard (closed 20 Dec–20 Jan). Bus no. 73 from the Arch or a 21 from Locust St and 12th St.

Days Inn at the Arch $–$$ 333 Washington Ave; tel: (314) 621-7900. Very good prices for the location.

Super Inn $ 1100 N. 3rd St; tel: (314) 421-6556. Just off Laclede's Landing, and one of the cheapest places in town.

Lister House $–$$ 4547 McPherson Ave; tel: (314) 361-5506. Reasonable B&B near Forest Park.

Best Western at the Park $$ 4630 Lindell Blvd, tel: (314) 367-7500 or (1-800) 373-7501. Simple chain hotel in the Central West End.

Lafayette House $$–$$$ 2156 Lafayette Ave; tel: (314) 772-4429 or (1-800) 641-8965. Charming Victorian home in the Lafayette Sq. area.

Napoleon's Retreat $$–$$$ 1815 Lafayette Ave; tel: (314) 772-6979 or (1-800) 700-9980. Pleasant B&B in the pretty Lafayette Sq. area.

Park Avenue Bed & Breakfast $$–$$$ 945 Park Ave; tel: (314) 241-6814 or (1-800) 430-2506. Well situated near the centre; some rooms come with jacuzzi.

FOOD

The Hill neighbourhood is great for authentic Italian food, particularly around the 5200 block of Shaw Ave. For a trendy blend of Asian, African and neo-American, there's a stretch of N. Euclid Ave in the Central West End between about the 100 and 500 blocks; also the University City, particularly around the 6200—6500 block of Delmar Blvd.

CENTRAL

Kennedy's $ 612 N. 2nd St. Laclede's Landing joint with American-style lunch and dinner menus.

Key West Café $–$$ Union Station, 18th and Market Sts. Specialising in innovative seafood sandwiches and platters.

CENTRAL WEST END

Ted Drewe's Frozen Custard $ 6726 Chippewa St. Old Route 66 hangout, famous for its 'concrete' milk shakes – so thick they're served upside down; closed Jan–Feb.

Culpepper's $ 300 N. Euclid Ave. Soups, salads, and sandwiches on a trendy street; open late.

Kopperman's $ 386 N. Euclid Ave. Grocery store and deli with excellent breakfast and lunch platters. Outdoor seating, or you can wrap it up and take it to the park for a picnic.

Sunshine Inn $ 80 S. Euclid Ave. Solid vegetarian fare, including soups, salads and burritos.

Bar Italia $–$$ 4656 Maryland. Genuine Italian cuisine, and serving up coffee and desserts on weekend evenings. Closed Mon.

Duff's $$ 392 N. Euclid Ave. Neo-French/international cuisine with no pretensions and good prices; a reliable local favourite.

Crazy Fish Fresh Grill $$–$$$ 15 N. Meramec St. Popular new place serving up – yes, fresh grilled fish, as well as pasta and vegetarian meals.

SOUTH ST LOUIS

The Bevo Mill $$ 4749 Gravois. German cuisine in a reconstructed Dutch windmill, near the Anheuser-Busch brewery.

Charlie Gitto's 'On the Hill' $$–$$$ 5226 Shaw Ave. Creative Italian dishes such as toasted ravioli and home-made tiramisù. Dinner only; closed Tues–Wed.

Giovanni's on the Hill $$–$$$ 5201 Shaw Blvd. Casual-dressy Italian restaurant in the Hill neighbourhood which has won several local awards for its pasta. Dinner only; closed Sun.

HIGHLIGHTS

St Louis's defining feature is the magnificent **Gateway Arch**, a graceful 630-ft half-loop of stainless steel that symbolises the city's role as gateway to the West during the mid-19th century. It sits on a swathe of land cleared of abandoned warehouses in the 1960s in order to create the Jefferson National Expansion Memorial, in honour of President Thomas Jefferson's Louisiana Purchase, which opened the way for westward expansion in the 19th century. The arch is particularly striking at dawn and at sunset when it catches the sun's rays. A specially designed lift takes you to the top, stopping every few moments to reposition itself in the curve of the arch. It's justifiably popular, so you may wish to purchase tickets ($) early in the day and return at your allotted time. The lift runs 0900–1715 in winter, 0800–2000 in summer. The visitor centre underneath shows films about the arch's construction and about the journey of Lewis and Clark, who set sail from St Louis up the Missouri in 1804 to explore the newly purchased western territory. The Museum of Westward Expansion further documents this extraordinary voyage, which took the party more than two years.

Just north of the arch, the **riverfront** has been cleaned up since the 1970s, when the shipping trade had ground to a halt and left the city gasping for life. Riverboats are docked along the wharf here, forming a sort of floating entertainment complex which includes fast food outlets and America's latest rediscovery: casinos.

Laclede's Landing Historic District, just beyond Eads Bridge, is a restored waterfront named after Pierre Laclede, founder of the city. It's hard to get a feel for how bustling the city was in its heyday as the area has been prettified and converted to shopping, restaurant, bar and club space, but it has its own atmosphere none the less: cobblestone streets and cast-iron lamps add authenticity. The **Basilica of St Louis** (the 'Old Cathedral' as the locals call it) at 209 Walnut St, was built in the 1840s, the first cathedral west of the Mississippi. Its presence is overshadowed – literally – by the I-70 overpass and the colossal **Busch Stadium** nearby, which devours several city blocks. There's little reason to visit unless you're intent on catching a Cardinals baseball game – not a bad idea, as the fans here are known for their exuberance. Right behind it at 8th and Walnut Sts, the **St Louis Cardinals Hall of Fame** shares premises with the **National Bowling Hall of Fame** – both of which are more interesting than they sound. Bowling, it turns out, goes back 5000 years, while the Cardinals have been around close to 100. $ Open Mon–Sat 0900–1700, Sun 1200–1700 (all until 1900 in summer).

DRED SCOTT AND THE SLAVE CASE

Dred Scott was a slave whose master took him to the northern (non-slave) states of Illinois and Wisconsin. Upon his return, Scott argued that because he had spent time in the north, he ought by law to be considered a free man. In 1847 he won his court case, and the restored courtrooms in which this pivotal trial took place can be seen at the grand **Old Courthouse** (once used for slave trading) at 11 N. 4th St; open daily 0800–1630; free.

The verdict given here, however, was overturned by the US Supreme Court, which ruled that because he was born in a slave state, he was forever the property of his owner. The decision helped bring the issue of slavery to the fore, leading to increasingly fractured governmental debate until the Civil War broke out ten years later.

St Louis Cardinals paraphernalia – baseball caps, jerseys, etc. – are worn with pride by the locals and make fun souvenirs. Cardinals' first baseman Mark McGwire captivated the nation in 1998 as he set a new single-season home-run record.

One of St Louis's newest and best attractions is the **City Museum**, 701 N. 15th St. A great place for kids, it explores art, science and history with lots of interactive displays. $ Open Wed–Fri 0900–1700, Sat–Sun 1000–1700.

WEST OF CENTRE Much of St Louis's appeal lies in its arty and ethnic neighbourhoods, so don't limit yourself to a quick trip to the Arch. About 4 miles west of the city centre, the Central West End is a hip enclave of speciality shops, outdoor cafés, art and antique galleries, and imaginative restaurants. The tree-lined streets themselves are pleasant for a stroll, and the highlight is the wonderful **Cathedral Basilica of St Louis** at 4431 Lindell Blvd, the 'New Cathedral' to the locals. The design is nouveau-Romanesque with Byzantine influence, and the interior, appropriately enough, contains one of the largest collections of mosaic art in the world.

The Central West End abuts the expansive **Forest Park**, a classic urban park designed in the late 19th century. In addition to the welcome green space, there are small lakes where you can rent boats and take gondola cruises, and the park contains a large amphitheatre for summer concerts. It is also home to many of the city's best museums.

Towards the western end, the impressive **St Louis Art Museum**, built in the *beaux-arts* style for the 1904 World Fair, houses a good collection of works from the Renaissance, pre-Columbian Mexico and the German expressionist era. Open Tues 1330–2030 and Wed–Sun 1000–1700. The **Missouri History Museum**, along the park's northern strip, tells the tale of this state, whose identity is part Midwest and part South. Among its famous sons are Charles Lindbergh, who made the first solo transatlantic flight in *Spirit of St Louis* in 1927. Other exhibits cover life on the Mississippi and the city's rich history of black music: Scott Joplin, Chuck Berry, Miles Davis and Tina Turner all were born or lived here. Open Tues 0930–2030, Wed–Sun 0930–1700. The **St Louis Science Center and Planetarium**, at the southern edge of the park, features displays on dinosaurs, space exploration and a new interactive DNA gallery. Open Mon–Thur and Sun 0930–1700, Fri–Sat 0930–2100; free except for planetarium and films. The **St Louis Zoo** is similarly child-friendly: in addition to a number of rare animals, the zoo has high-tech exhibits and a petting zoo. Open daily 0900–1700 (until 2000 on Tues in summer).

Beyond Forest Park, **University City**, also known as 'U-City' and 'the Loop', is home to thousands of students, and so is a good place to find lively bars and cafés. One of its other attractions is the **St Louis Walk of Fame**, a series of 75 plaques in the 6500 block of Delmar Ave commemorating famous St Louisans like T. S. Eliot and Arthur Ashe.

South St Louis St Louis's ethnic neighbourhoods are really on display in the working-class south side, particularly in Soulard and the Hill. **Soulard** is noted for its signature 19th-century red-brick buildings, and is a favourite local spot for live jazz, blues and casual dining. The Soulard Market, at Broadway and Lafayette, has been in existence since 1779, and from Wed to Sun teems with fresh produce and bric-à-brac.

A half mile or so west of Soulard Market, **Lafayette Park** is a nice swathe of urban green, surrounded by wonderful, colourful Victorian homes referred to as the 'painted ladies' for their effusive displays of pastel orange, yellow, purple and green. A little further west, **Tower Grove Park** has been designated a national historic landmark for its ornate bandstands. Linked to its northern edge on the 4300 block of Shaw Blvd, the **Missouri Botanical Garden** is a fantastic landscaped park, the third largest in the world, with sections including a Japanese tea garden, an English rose garden and a tropical rainforest greenhouse. $ Open daily 0900–1700 (winter); 0900–2000 (summer).

The Hill district, a few streets further west down Shaw Blvd, is St Louis's Italian

TOURS

The visitor centre has information on various **neighbourhood walking tours** and, because the city is so spread out, bus tours taking in the main sites. **Gateway Riverboat Cruises**, tel: (1-800) 878-7411, offer a 1-hr narrated tour of the Mississippi River, as well as Dixie dinner cruises with live bands. For something really substantial (and expensive) take a 2- to 12-day **steamboat tour** aboard the *Delta Queen*, the *Mississippi Queen* or the *American Queen*; tel: (1-800) 543-1949.

FOR FREE

A lot can be done with no money in St Louis, and a good place to start is Forest Park and its free museums. Other free visual entertainment abounds – just strolling down Euclid Ave in the Central West End, Delmar Blvd in University City, the Soulard Market, or Shaw Blvd in the Hill, is fun in itself, though the many shops and cafés can be tempting.

neighbourhood, distinguished by its much-vaunted red-white-and-green fire hydrants. As you might expect, this is the place to come for *gelato*, espresso, fresh baked bread and great Italian restaurants.

The German made their presence felt in St Louis as well, and the area south of Soulard still has a slightly continental flavour to it. The air is also tinged with the scent of malt emanating from the **Anheuser-Busch brewery** at Broadway and Pestalozzi St – the largest in the world. Budweiser and its many watery cousins are produced here *en masse*, and tours give the history of the family, some insight into beer-making, and free samples at the end. Tours run Mon–Sat 0900–1600.

NIGHTLIFE

St Louis has a jazzy, bluesy soul: it's been home to many esteemed musicians, and bars and clubs around town turn out some great performances. There are several places to scout out: Laclede's Landing tends toward the ritzy, but is alive at night; Soulard thumps with live blues, and Delmar Blvd in University City lives and breathes the student life. St Louis also has an excellent symphony orchestra, and concerts are given at the lovely restored **Powell Concert Hall**, 718 N. Grand.

DOWNTOWN

Laffite's Restaurant and Nightclub, 809 N. 2nd St. Schmoozy restaurant and jazz club in the Laclede's Landing entertainment district.

Mississippi Nights, 914 N. 1st St. Great place to catch biggish-name rock, reggae and heavy metal bands.

Side Door Music Club, 2005 Locust St. Live bands from the alternative scene perform here nightly.

SOULARD

BB's Jazz, Blues and Soups, 700 S. Broadway. Upmarket jazz club with St Louis cuisine.

Broadway Oyster Bar, 736 S. Broadway. Cajun cooking and St Louis blues.

1860s Hard Shell Café and Bar. Seafood

restaurant turning into an energetic dance floor at night, with live blues and rock.

Mike and Min's, 925 Geyer. Local bar with honest blues bands at night.

CENTRAL WEST END AND UNIVERSITY CITY

Club Viva, 408 N. Euclid St. World beats from Brazil, Senegal and the Mississippi delta.

Delmar Lounge, 6235 Delmar Blvd. Good place for martinis and other mixed drinks.

Blueberry Hill, 6504 Delmar Blvd. Part burger place, part dance club, and part gallery of American pop culture; live pop/rock bands most nights.

DAY TRIPS

St Charles, 25 miles south of St Louis, is a charming little riverside town, well preserved despite numerous floods. And if for you the Mississippi is synonymous with Tom Sawyer and Huckleberry Finn, make the 100-mile trek north to Hannibal, where Mark Twain's boyhood home and a museum dedicated to him are the main draws.

Memphis

While it was New Orleans which unleashed jazz on the world from the mouth of the Mississippi, Memphis, upriver, is the home of the blues and its offspring, rock-'n'-roll. Music is its heart and soul. Memphis is also known in many Americans' minds as the place where civil rights leader Martin Luther King Jr was assassinated in 1968. The city continues to endure this tragedy, while converting the site to a civil rights museum.

Memphis today draws life from its colourful past century, and a number of new constructions give the city a bold commercial appeal. Downtown is the obvious place to start, with a number of museums on and around Beale St, though this whole area is clearly tourist-oriented. Mid-town Memphis is coming into its own, with good dining options and some excellent museums. The city's top tourist draw, though, is about 10 miles south of the city centre: Elvis Presley's suburban home, Graceland, should not be missed.

GETTING THERE AND GETTING AROUND

Memphis International Airport is a major regional hub, and Northwest/KLM has daily flights to Amsterdam. Van service is your best way into town. The Amtrak station is in a scruffy part of town just south of the centre at 545 S. Main St. Greyhound buses stop at the central terminal at the corner of Union and 4th Sts.

Most of the sites are a short walk from one another; you can hop on the historic Main St Trolley to shuttle you north–south across the centre. Buses serve sites further out.

INFORMATION

The **Memphis Convention and Visitors Bureau**'s visitor centre is very convenient at 340 Beale St; tel: (901) 543-5333 or (1-800) 873-6282; open Mon–Fri 0900–1700, Sat 0900–1800, Sun 1200–1700 (weekdays until 1800 in summer). The **Tennessee Welcome Center** at the Pyramid has more regional information. Websites to peruse include the city's official www.memphistravel.com; also very good, not least for its irreverence, is www.memphisguide.com, which has a thorough rundown of the history and sites of Beale St.

Money Banks with automatic cash dispensers abound. Thomas Cook Currency Services is situated at 84 N. Evergreen, No. 4; tel: (901) 276-6060; about 2 miles east of the centre.

Post and Phones The post office is at 555 S. 3rd St, and is open Mon–Fri 0830–1730, Sat 1000–1400. For poste restante, include the zip code TN 38101.

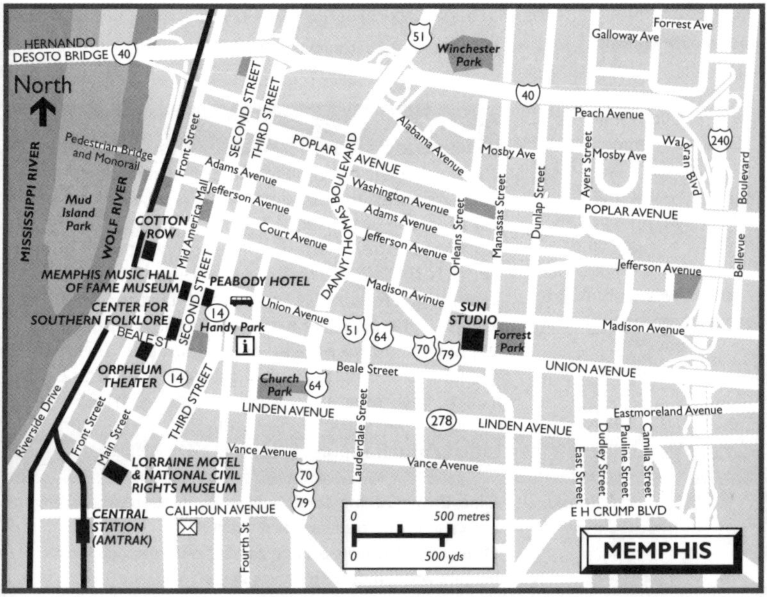

ACCOMMODATION

Your best bet for centrally placed budget rooms are the chain hotels (see p. 504). Elvis Presley Blvd, which runs south to Graceland, also has several motels and campsites to choose from. For more homely accommodation, B&B in Memphis, tel: (1-800) 206-5829, can set you up in (mostly suburban) pensions.

Days Inn $ 340 West Illinois St; tel: (901) 948-9005; fax: (901) 946-5716. Not far south of centre near the river, but a fairly drab neighbourhood.

Days Inn Downtown $–$$ 164 Union Ave; tel: (901) 527-4100 or (1-800) 325-2525; fax: (901) 525-1747. Good value for its great location.

Lowenstein-Long House $$ 1084 Poplar Ave; tel: (901) 527-7174. Not far from the centre, part hostel ($) and part B&B.

Comfort Inn Downtown $$ 100 N. Front St; tel: (901) 526-0583 or (1-800) 228-5150; fax: (901) 525-7512. On the Main St trolley line just opposite the Pyramid; try to get a room with a view of the river.

Comfort Inn East $$ 5877 Poplar Ave; tel: (901) 767-6300

The **Peabody Hotel**, 149 Union St, is distinguished not only by its costly rooms, but its marching ducks, who promenade to a Sousa march up to the hotel fountain at 1100, where they swim peacefully until roused up to return home promptly at 1700. This silly scene has drawn huge crowds since the 1930s.

or (1-800) 645-0098; fax: (901) 767-0098. Decent mid-town location, with a restaurant and pool.

FOOD

Pit barbecue is big time in Memphis, and the combination of blues and BBQ downtown is an essential ingredient in the city's social life. Beale St and Union Ave are good streets to wander when you're hungry, though the area is really quite touristy. To get away from the crowds, try the Pinch Historical District, which extends several blocks north of the Pyramid around N. Main St. Mid-town Memphis (also called the Overton Square area), 3 miles or so east of centre, is also becoming a hip place to eat and drink. Several clubs listed in the Nightlife section (p. 288) serve food as well. Pick up the *Dining out in Memphis* guide from the visitor centre for more listings.

CENTRAL

Ciao Baby Cucina $ 135 S. Main St. Italian bistro, bakery and café – good for lunch or a snack.

Huey's Restaurant $ 77 S. 2nd St. Well regarded for its burgers and a wide selection of beers.

Automatic Slim's Tonga Club $–$$ 83 S. 2nd St. A fun blend of Southwestern and Caribbean cuisine – wild lunchtime sandwiches are a speciality.

The Little Tea Shop $–$$ 71 Monroe. Extremely popular lunch-only spot since 1918 – southern cuisine.

The Rendezvous $–$$ 52 S. 2nd St. A local favourite for fantastic charbroiled ribs.

Blues City Café $$ 138 Beale St. Jumbo shrimp, huge steaks, and the like; this place makes big of its appearance in the film *The Firm*.

Elvis Presley's Memphis $$ 126 Beale St. Kitschy Elvis-themed American restaurant.

King's Palace Café $$–$$$ 166 Beale St. Cajun/Southern/BBQ place with late-night jazz and blues.

Sleep Out Louie's $$–$$$ 88 Union Ave. Great oyster bar with live music on weekends.

MID-TOWN

Bayou Bar and Grill $ 2100 Overton Sq. Lane. Cajun and BBQ.

The Cupboard $$ 1495 Union Ave, and **The Cupboard, Too**, 149 Madison Ave. Home-cooked meals, including vegetarian specials.

HIGHLIGHTS

Beale St is synonymous with Memphis blues, arguably the city's greatest contribution to world culture, and surely the heart of any visit to Memphis. The story of the street is intriguing, though today's Beale St Historic District is far cleaner and more polished than in its colourful past.

Beale St's real heyday was the 1910s and 1920s, when segregation was in full force, and Beale St became a centre of commerce for blacks, many of whom worked on the river or came into the city from outlying towns and farms for shopping and entertainment. The 1920s was also the era of Prohibition, and at night the street became a haven for rowdy pleasure-seekers and various vagabonds: liquor, prostitution and gambling were rife. By the 1940s the rage had subsided, and in the 1960s the area fell victim to a depressed economy and subsequent bulldozers, which wiped out most of the street. Shops, bars, and businesses retain, or at least imitate, the original flavour, and a number of good museums keep the culture alive – plus this is still the place to come for solid live blues, soul and rock-'n'-roll.

One building that was spared the demolition was the **Orpheum Theater**, which stands pretty at the corner of Beale and S. Main Sts. Once the home of Memphis's vaudeville theatre, it now stages plays and musicals. The **Center for Southern Folklore** has an entertaining collection of photos and films of Memphis and Southern culture in general. $ 130 Beale St; open Mon–Thur 1000–2000, Fri–Sat 1000–2400. Diagonally opposite at no. 163, **A. Schwab's Dry Goods Store** has been in operation since 1876, stocking the same articles it always has, such as supposedly indispensable voodoo potions: its motto is 'If you can't find it at Schwab's, you're better off without it'. Open Mon–Sat 0900– 1700; like all good Christian-owned shops in the Bible Belt, it's closed on Sunday.

Continuing east down Beale St, you pass **W.C. Handy Park**, a gathering spot for amateur street musicians named after the man who, in 1909, wrote what is considered the first blues tune. His house, a few steps

TOURS

A good number of tour companies are eager to lead you around town and the surrounding area. **Sample Memphis Tours**, tel: (901) 541-5215, offers three different insightful tours of downtown Memphis, with peeks into hidden places, Elvis's favourite hangouts, and tales of the ghost of Beale St. **Heritage Tours**, tel: (901) 527-3427, offers good cultural and historic group tours of all of Memphis's main sites, including many important off-the-beaten-track places such as the Alex Haley House Museum and various Civil War sites. **Blues City Tours**, 164 Union Avenue; tel: (901) 522-9229, does much the same, and is a little more geared to the showy side, with tours including casinos and riverboat show cruises.

FOR FREE

Several museums in town are free, including the Sun Studio, the Mississippi River Museum, and the Memphis Brooks Museum of Art. Beale St and the pedestrianised S. Main St are good for simple strolling, and you can pop over to one of the parks along the river with your picnic lunch.

down the street at no. 352, is a little turn-of-the-century home converted into a **museum** to the father of the blues. $ Open Mon–Sat 1000–1700, Sun 1300–1700. Across the street at no. 329, the **Beale Street Blues Museum** is a little studio filled with information and artefacts recording the spirit that created rock-'n'-roll music in Memphis. The museum is housed in the old Daisy Theater, where the legendary Bessie Smith performed in 1917. $ Open daily 1200–2000 with tours every hour. The gift shop offers a good collection of guitars, rare recordings and such-like, and you can book a karaoke-style recording session here, just to pretend you're Elvis.

THE BLUES

It's only natural that the blues should emanate from Memphis. The city grew rich in the 19th century from the cotton trade, and the blood, sweat and tears of the slaves who harvested that cotton also produced a rich, spiritual mourning music as they incorporated the sounds and styles of African music into their experience in America. The blues developed into a uniquely American form of music, gaining a hard edge in the raucous corridors of downtown Memphis, particularly Beale St. In the 1950s, the blues fused into a new style popularised initially by Elvis Presley – rock-'n'-roll – and kick-started a new generation of Memphis musicians.

For even more on the city's rich musical tradition, make for the excellent **Memphis Music Hall of Fame** at 97 S. 2nd St. The city's great blues heritage is presented here through photos, videos, rare recordings, mock-ups of the Sun Record Company's control room and the P. Wee Saloon – where Handy penned 'St Louis Blues' – and the instruments and personal effects of all the local legends. $$ Open Mon–Thur 1000–1800, Fri–Sat 1000–1700, Sun 1200–1800.

Quick tours of the real **Sun Studio**, at 706 Union Ave, are given daily, 0930–1830 (summer); 1030–1730 (winter). Sam Phillips opened a small recording studio here in 1950, and over the next 20 years helped launch the careers of Elvis Presley, Jerry Lee Lewis, B.B. King, Howlin' Wolf, Johnny Cash, Carl Perkins and Roy Orbison, to name a few. Out-of-hours it still functions as a studio.

Right around the corner from the Music Hall of Fame the pedestrianised **Main St Mall** stretches for several blocks, and you can take a ride on the restored antique Main St Trolley to bring back a taste of the old days.

Since blacks contributed so much to Memphis's riches, it is telling that Martin Luther King Jr chose to participate in a black workers march here in 1968. On the evening before the march, 4 April, King was shot by James Earl Ray while standing on the balcony outside his room at the Lorraine Motel. The site is now preserved as the **National Civil Rights Museum**, a few blocks south of Beale St at 450 Mulberry St. Highlights include a historical tracing of various black activists, a bus (from Montgomery, Alabama) commanding black riders to sit in the rear, and the balcony and room where MLK was shot. $ Open Mon–Sat 1000–1700, Sun 1300–1700 (Sept–May); Mon– Sat 1000–1800, Sun

THE UNDERGROUND RAILROAD

The antebellum **Slavehaven/Burkle Estate Museum**, several blocks north at 826 N. 2nd St, was originally a station on the 'Underground Railroad', one of many throughout the South owned by sympathetic whites who provided secret tunnels and hiding places for runaway slaves during their quest northwards. The house also contains exhibits on the slave era. Tours must be booked in advance through Heritage Tours (see p. 285).

1300–1800 (June–Aug).

Memphis today makes a point not only of preserving its unique past, but also of pushing forward into the 21st century. Some of its newer constructions really stand out, such as the unmissable **Pyramid**, on the river just below the I-40 overpass. The tourist office calls this 32-storey stainless steel model of the Great Pyramid in Egypt 'a tribute to Memphis's Egyptian heritage', though that heritage really is in the city's name and the similarity it shares in lying on a great river. Inside is a 22,000-seat arena used for concerts and sporting events.

THE MISSISSIPPI The river itself is a prime destination in town, and **Mud Island** in the middle of it has plenty of leisure and educational attractions. Getting there is fun too, on the new **Monorail and Walkway** from Adams Ave. Mud Island is part city playground – with a swimming pool, a beach, an amphitheatre, and the World War II B-17 bomber the *Memphis Belle* – and part river history lesson, with a large-scale model of the Mississippi and the entertaining **Mississippi River Museum**, documenting the great waterway's geographic features, folklore and importance in American commerce. Grounds open daily 1000–1900 (June–Aug); 1000–1600 (Apr–May and Sept–Nov).

Sightseeing cruises of the mighty Mississippi are given from April through November on **Memphis Queen Line** paddlewheelers, lasting 1½ hours. They also have dinner cruises and moonlight music cruises: tel: (901) 527-5694 or (1-800) 221-6197; www.memphisqueen.com.

MID-TOWN Overton Park is a lovely stretch of near-forest, and contains the very good **Memphis Zoo**, which has been recently revamped and houses several exotic and endangered species. $$ Open daily 0900–1700 (Mar–Oct); 0900–1630 (Nov–Feb). Also in the park, the **Memphis Brooks Museum**, at 1934 Poplar Ave, features fine and decorative arts from antiquity to the present. Open Tues–Wed and Fri 0900–1600, Thur 1100–2000, Sat–Sun 1130–1700. Bus no. 50 runs down Poplar Ave from the city centre. Another good art museum in the area is the small **Dixon Gallery and Gardens** at 4339 Park Ave, with Impressionist works by Renoir, Degas and Monet, plus some lovely gardens. $ Open Tues–Sat 1000–1700, Sun 1300–1700.

GRACELAND Billing itself as 'the most famous home in America after the White House', **Graceland**, 10 miles south of Memphis on Elvis Presley Blvd, is the beloved home of the king of rock-'n'-roll. Regardless of your level of devotion to Elvis – his fanatical followers make regular pilgrimages here – you'll probably be pleasantly surprised. There are a number of sites on the estate, and it's all nicely packaged, with personal headphones that tell the stories and play the music.

In the home itself you can visit the King's kitchen, living room, dining room, music room, TV room, and 'jungle' den – complete with floor-to-ceiling carpets. Other buildings house his own racquetball court (which didn't get much use during his later, drug-and-food-bingeing years), business office and trophy collection – including his huge collection of gold records and various articles of his elaborate stage costumes and jewellery. Elvis's many cars, including the famous 1955 pink Cadillac, and motorcycles, are stored in the Automobile Museum, while the Airplanes Tour takes in his own luxuriously equipped private planes, which shuttled him back and forth to his Las Vegas shows during his twilight years. The Sincerely Elvis museum portrays Elvis's more personal side through candid photos, personal effects and a 22-minute film tracing highlights of his career. Finally, the Meditation Garden contains the remains of Elvis and his immediate family. $$$ Ticket office open daily 0730–1800 (June–Aug); 0830–1700 (Sept–May); house and each museum require a separate ticket, and the house tour is closed on Tues Nov–Feb.

NIGHTLIFE

Beale St is still the place to head for live music, and if you've only got one night in Memphis, you shouldn't miss this.

B.B. King's Club, 139–145 Beale St. An obvious starting point, with live jamming almost every night – and occasional appearances by the man himself. Pork barbecue and fried catfish are among the house specialities.

Rum Boogie Café and Blues Hall, 174–178 Beale St. Another hot spot, decorated with memorabilia from lots of blues greats.

Silky O'Sullivan's Patio, 177–181 Beale St. Popular saloon with live pop-blues and outdoor seating.

Beale Street Barbecue and Piano Bar, 205 Beale St. A restaurant with a stage featuring blues, country, and rock-'n'-roll.

Willie Mitchell's Rhythm 'n' Blues Club, 326–328 Beale St. Formerly owned by Jerry Lee Lewis, continuing the tradition today.

Club Six-One-Six, 600 Marshall St. Alternative rock with a big dance floor, a few streets east of centre.

Colour Section

(i) St Louis arch and skyline (p. 274); New Orleans (pp. 289–300): Natchez paddle steamer; Bourbon Street musician.

(ii) San Antonio: (pp. 310–316): Mission San Jose; inset: Santa Fe trail sign; The Alamo.

(iii) Taos pueblo (p. 338); Albuquerque, old town (pp. 339–342)

(iv) Tombstone, Arizona (p. 347); inset: Yellowstone (pp. 367–374): Old Faithful geyser; buffalo.

NATCHEZ
STEAMER
NATCHEZ
NATCHEZ.

OLD SANTA FE TRAIL

INDIAN JEWELRY & LEATHER KING
201

John B
STETSON
4X 5X 10X Quality
BEAVER HATS
SINCE
SALOON

NEW ORLEANS

The Big Easy, the Crescent City, the Birthplace of Jazz – New Orleans is a city unlike any other, moving to its own sultry beat. The elegance of its colonial buildings, Spanish moss dangling from massive oak trees, the mysteries of jazz, blues and voodoo, along with the scents of spicy shrimp and roasted chicory, mingle with the ever-present swelter of the Mississippi delta to create an aura of constant excitement and expectation.

The city's unique atmosphere stems from a rich and complex heritage. At the end of the 17th century the first French colonists (dubbed 'the kids' – *las criollas* or Creoles – by rival Spanish merchants) began to penetrate the Louisiana swamps, establishing the trading post of New Orleans on a bend in the Mississippi in 1718. The site, bordered by the Mississippi River, Lake Pontchartrain and endless swamps in the hinterlands, was not a healthy one and even today the summer heat and humidity in the city can be unbearable. Traders and slaves added Spanish, Caribbean and African influences to the cultural mix, and this complex personality gives New Orleans a peculiar disjointedness: stunning architectural beauty rubs shoulders with abject poverty, while blacks and whites still maintain an uneasy coexistence.

CAJUNS

In the 1750s, dispossessed French fleeing the new British rule in Canada came here from Acadia, Nova Scotia. These 'Acadians' became 'Cajuns', and their farming and trapping communities survived in quite distinct isolation until the mid-20th century, retaining their own forms of language and music. These are remarkably intact today – turn on a radio in southern Louisiana and you're likely to find stations broadcasting in a free mix of Cajun French and English. See p. 299 for visits to Cajun country.

Inevitably, such exotic promise brings mass tourism, especially to the French Quarter, sitting pretty on the Mississippi River, with its tidy European-influenced architecture and infamous jazz clubs. A couple of miles west, the residential Garden District is green and graceful, with some good restaurants and nightlife, while beyond the city centre are two contrasting worlds: the fabulous plantation homes along the banks of the Mississippi, and the swampy bayous, with their Cajun communities and unique wildlife.

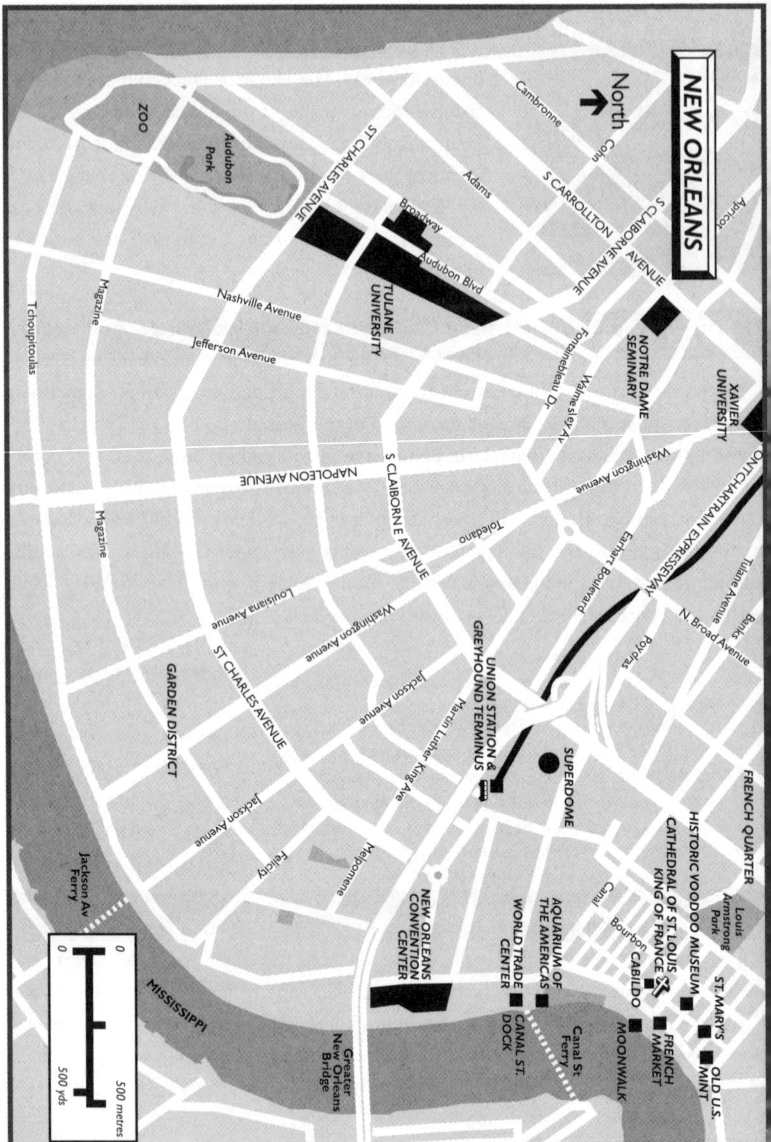
NEW ORLEANS
North
ZOO
Audubon Park
ST CHARLES AVENUE
Broadway
Audubon Blvd
TULANE UNIVERSITY
Cambronne
Adams
Cohn
S CARROLLTON AVENUE
S CLAIBORNE AVENUE
Apricot
Nashville Avenue
Jefferson Avenue
Magazine
Tchoupitoulas
NOTRE DAME SEMINARY
XAVIER UNIVERSITY
Fontainebleau Dr.
Walmesley Av
Washington Avenue
NAPOLEON AVENUE
S CLAIBORNE AVENUE
PONTCHARTRAIN EXPRESSWAY
Toledano
Earhart Boulevard
Tulane Avenue
Banks
N. Broad Avenue
Louisiana Avenue
Washington Avenue
Poydras
ST CHARLES AVENUE
GARDEN DISTRICT
Jackson Avenue
Martin Luther King Ave
UNION STATION & GREYHOUND TERMINUS
SUPERDOME
FRENCH QUARTER
Louis Armstrong Park
HISTORIC VOODOO MUSEUM
CATHEDRAL OF ST. LOUIS KING OF FRANCE
ST. MARY'S
OLD U.S. MINT
FRENCH MARKET
CABILDO
MOONWALK
Canal
Bourbon
AQUARIUM OF THE AMERICAS
WORLD TRADE CENTER
CANAL ST. DOCK
Canal St Ferry
NEW ORLEANS CONVENTION CENTER
Felicity
Melpomene
Jackson Av Ferry
MISSISSIPPI
Greater New Orleans Bridge
0
500 metres
0
500 yds

GETTING THERE

New Orleans International Airport is about 12 miles west of centre just off I-10, the interstate that cuts east–west through New Orleans. Taxis from the airport are a flat rate, or a public bus follows a circuitous route to Tulane Ave in the centre, and a van shuttle service is available from a number of competitors.

The Amtrak and Greyhound stations are next door to each other at 1001 Loyola Ave near the Superdome, a shortish walk from the French Quarter – though this is inadvisable at night.

INFORMATION

The main **Visitor Information Center** is located at 529 St Ann St, on Jackson Sq. They have a recorded message on their visitor information line, tel: (504) 566-5005, and a good, thorough website at www.neworleansonline.com. Another decent source of online information is www.thetrip.com. The Louisiana State Museum, in the Cabildo on Jackson Sq., has stacks of tour brochures.

SAFETY New Orleans has a reputation as one of the more dangerous cities in the USA, and you're best advised to drive or take a taxi just about anywhere outside the French Quarter or Uptown/Garden District areas.

MONEY There is no shortage of banks in the Central Business District, and the French Quarter and Garden District similarly have plenty of automatic cash dispensers – though they charge nearly $3 for the service. Thomas Cook is way over on the other side of the river, at 3201 General de Gaulle Dr.; tel: (504) 367-4095.

POST AND PHONES The main post office is at 701 Loyola Ave, in the Central Business District: open Mon–Fri 0800–1630, Sat 0800–1300. Poste restante is handled here (zip code LA 70140). There's also the French Quarter Postal Emporium, at 940 Royal St; open Mon–Fri 0930–1800, Sat 1000–1500.

ACCOMMODATION

Rooms don't come particularly cheap in New Orleans, and for Mardi Gras you'll pay even more and have to book several months in advance. Many visitors aim straight for the French Quarter, though some good budget possibilities – such as several B&Bs – exist Uptown within an easy ride on the St Charles Streetcar.

The visitor centre can help with budget accommodation, and many of the national chain hotels have rooms at fairly good prices outside the French Quarter. Another good source is Bed & Breakfast, Inc., 1021 Moss Street; tel: (504) 488-4640 or (1-800)

729-4640; fax: (504) 488-4639; email: bedbreak@gnofn.org, an accommodation service for just about every price range.

FRENCH QUARTER

French Quarter Guest House $$$ 623 Ursulines St; tel: (504) 529-5489; fax: (504) 524-1902. Friendly, homely place in a relatively quiet part of the Quarter.

New Orleans Guest House $$$ 1118 Ursulines St; tel: (504) 566-1177 or (1-800) 562-1177; fax: (504) 566-1179. Pleasant enough establishment with decent rates.

French Quarter Courtyard Hotel $$$–$$$$ 1101 N. Rampart Street; tel: (504) 522-7333; fax: (504) 522-3908. On the northern edge of the Quarter.

Le Richelieu $$$$ 1234 Chartres St; tel: (504) 529-2492 or (1-800) 535-9653; fax: (504) 524-8179. There are dozens of upmarket hotels in the French Quarter, but given the fine furnishings, pool and garden courtyard, this one is good value.

DOWNTOWN

International YMCA Hotel $$ 920 St Charles Ave; tel: (504) 568-9622 or (1-800) 565-9622; fax: (504) 523-7174. Not a pretty building, but clean, safe, and midway between the French Quarter and Garden District.

LaSalle Hotel $$–$$$ 1113 Canal St; tel: (504) 523-5831; fax: (504) 525-2531. Simple budget hotel near the Quarter and downtown.

Days Inn Canal $$–$$$ 1630 Canal St; tel: (504) 586-0110 or (1-800) 232-3297; fax: (504) 581-2253. Eight blocks north of the French Quarter downtown; not the most beautiful setting, but cheap enough.

UPTOWN AND THE GARDEN DISTRICT

Magnolia Garden Apartments $–$$ 2253 Carondelet St; tel: (504) 523-3014; fax: (504) 529-5933; email: HINewOrle@aol.com. HI hostel located in a grand antebellum house; some simple double rooms.

Best Western Patio Downtown Motel $$–$$$ 2820 Tulane Ave; tel: (504) 822-0200; fax: (504) 822-2328. Decent uptown location; standard chain hotel décor.

Prytania Inns $$–$$$ 1415 Prytania St; tel: (504) 566-1515; fax: (504) 566-1518. These people run several B&Bs in historic homes in the Garden District; very close to the St Charles Streetcar.

Quality Inn $$–$$$ 3900 Tulane Ave; tel: (504) 486-5541; fax: (504) 488-7440. This national chain won't win any award for atmosphere, but the location and price are fine.

St Charles Guesthouse Bed & Breakfast $$–$$$ 1748 Prytania St; tel: (504) 523-6556; fax: (504) 522-6340. Yet another Garden District B&B, with very reasonable rates.

FOOD

Cajun/Creole cuisine has its home in the Louisiana bayous, and New Orleans capitalises on this festive and flavourful food with a broad array of restaurants. The two are in fact distinct: Creole cuisine derives from the French and Spanish colonists, with African and native Choctaw Indian influence, and is quite refined; while Cajun is a spicier, more soulful, poor-folks' food. Restaurants today usually combine them into one, as the ingredients are almost identical: chicken, shrimp harvested from the Gulf of Mexico, red beans and rice, onions, garlic and lots of hot peppers. Some of the more unusual local fare includes crawfish and alligator, which is quite tough and fatty; both are culled from the inland swamps and bayous. A lot of the food is deep fried, though the perennial favourites, **gumbo** (a thick stew of shrimp, chicken, and vegetables in a tomato and okra base) and **jambalaya** (a rice dish made from any of the above) are healthy and hearty. For the sweet-toothed, chicory coffee and pralines – pecans glazed with butter and sugar – are consumed in large amounts.

Snack and lunch food is a treat: fabulous sandwiches such as **muffuletas** (Italian sandwiches with savoury meats, cheeses and garlic-olive oil dressing), and their poor cousin, the **po-boy** (a French bread sandwich stuffed with fried oysters or shrimp) are ubiquitous. A string of places along Decatur St in the French Quarter are perfect for picking up a takeaway lunch. The traditional Monday lunch is red beans and rice, and while most local restaurants serve it up, locals claim with all honesty that the best to be had are at any Popeye's Chicken fast-food chain.

Dining out can be a real experience, though the best restaurants take full advantage of the New Orleans image – you can quite easily shell out $50 for a full meal with drinks. Cheaper options are abundant, however, and a solid Cajun meal can easily be had for under $10. The French Quarter is an obvious place to start looking for food – most of which is Cajun/Creole – but shop carefully for value. There are lots of good options in the Garden District and Uptown as well – St Charles Ave around Jackson St, and Magazine St between Washington Ave and Louisiana Ave, and between Napoleon Ave and Jefferson Ave, are good hunting grounds.

FRENCH QUARTER

Café Du Monde $ 813 Decatur St. Settled comfortably into the French Market, and *de rigueur* for chicory coffee and people-watching.

Central Grocery $ 923 Decatur St. One of several good delis along here serving up massive, mouthwatering muffuletas.

Kaldi's $ 941 Decatur St. Cool, gothic coffee house to rival Café Du Monde.

Johnny's Po-Boy $ 511 St Louis St. Simple, tasty, greasy-fried, order-at-the-counter New Orleans eats.

Napoleon House Bar and Café $$ 500 Chartres St. Unique European-style café, with great po-boy sandwiches and excellent prices.

Rita's $$ 945 Chartres St. Another Southern tradition: soul food, like crawfish pie and corned beef with collard greens.

The Gumbo Shop $$–$$$ 630 St Peter's St. Lively Cajun/Creole place serving up everybody's favourite po-boys and gumbo.

Acme Oyster and Seafood House $$$–$$$$ 725 Iberville St. A New Orleans institution: start off with raw oysters on the half-shell, then move on to fried seafood platters.

Uptown and the Garden District

Dante St Deli $ 736 Dante St. A healthy array of soups, salads, and sandwiches in addition to coffees and teas. Outdoor seating available.

Semolina International Pastas $$–$$$ 3242 Magazine St. Innovative and trendy place, with variations on a number of favourites, like jambalaya pasta, pasta with pesto, and pad Thai.

Vaqueros $$–$$$ 4938 Prytania St. Just off the St Charles Streetcar line, and popular for its Mexican, Southwestern and native American cuisine, as well as its huge margaritas.

Café Atchafalaya $$$ 901 Louisiana Ave. Excellent alternative to the Quarter's much-hyped fine dining; quality New Orleans cuisine at competitive prices.

Getting Around

The French Quarter is small enough to be enjoyed on foot, but to get almost anywhere else you'll need to take advantage of the city's buses or, to head to the Garden District and Uptown, the magnificent St Charles Streetcar. This restored relic follows St Charles Ave westward in a swoop from the French Quarter to Audubon Park; rides cost $1.

Highlights

The French Quarter

The real highlight of New Orleans is the **French Quarter**, filled with 18th-century colonial buildings and hopping to the beat of jazz and blues joints on and around Bourbon St. Unless it's night-time and you're bent on drinking, the best thing to do is simply to wander and admire at random. It's a surprisingly small part of town, the heart of the old city, though you'll want to visit it at various times of day and night to catch its different colours and flavours.

The Quarter, as it's referred to by the locals (or Vieux Carré in the original French), is ethereal in the early morning, when the streets are almost unnaturally quiet and you can admire the smart homes, intricate balconies, dangling fuchsia and crape myrtle, and cobbled courtyards, unfettered by tourist hordes and the late-night partying crowd. During the day you're likely to wander through a Dixieland band

ON THE RIVER

Take a riverboat tour ($15) aboard the *Cajun Queen*, tel: (504) 524-0814, or splurge for the jazz dinner cruise ($$$); both leave from the dock at Canal St. Far cheaper, though, is the free commuter ferry from here to Algiers, on the west bank – catch it just before sunset or at night for the most exhilarating views of the city's skyline.

blowing in Jackson Square, and at night the bars and clubs spill on to the streets, doing their best to fulfil the image that visitors have of New Orleans.

JACKSON SQUARE AND THE RIVER Unassuming **Jackson Square** is the city's focal point, a pleasant, grassy park which anchors the French Quarter to the Mississippi River. It takes its name from Andrew Jackson, seventh president of the United States, who as a military general defeated the British here in 1815. A giant equestrian statue of the man sits proudly in the centre. American hero that he was, Jackson was also responsible for flushing out native American tribes throughout the South, so his legacy is somewhat tainted in modern historical interpretations.

St Louis Cathedral presides over the square and is the proud centre of one of the most Catholic parts of the country. Given its importance as the second most important cathedral in America, it's actually rather small. The interior is ornate and beautiful, and the building has a few secrets, related on free guided tours throughout the day.

The other buildings lining the square together make up the **Louisiana State Museum**: taken together they provide a good background to the history and culture of the city and region. $ Open Tues–Sun 1000–1700. Next door to the cathedral, the **Cabildo** is an impressive former city hall, built by the Spanish and then altered to look more French after the Louisiana Purchase, which was signed here in 1803. Today it houses a museum on the city's history, a fascinating look at its complicated and often turbulent cultural and physical development. It's not all pretty, either: while Africans, Caribbean islanders and native Americans are woven into New Orleans's ethnic quilt, the story of the city has often been one of oppression and war, floods and disease.

As a complement to the city's history, the **Presbytere**, on the other side of the cathedral, is filled with decorative arts and paintings. Flanking either side of the square are pretty rows of three-storey red-brick buildings with traditional laced ironwork

VOODOO

Appropriate to this often bizarre city, the **Historic Voodoo Museum** tries to teach the basic tenets of this religion. There is a creepy collection of rabbits' feet, bats' heads, herbs, oils, photos and drawings depicting voodoo ceremonies, and a live python, all crammed into the ground floor of a small apartment. $$ 724 Dumaine St; open 1000–dusk. The **Black Tourism Network** $$, tel: (504) 523-5652, which focuses on New Orleans's African-American heritage, offers, among other things, a voodoo tour which takes in haunted houses, a voodoo church and a cemetery.

JAZZ

Perhaps it's appropriate that jazz was cultivated in New Orleans around the turn of the century. Fuelled by the funky mix of ethnic influences, and because of its humble origins in rowdy bars in black neighbourhoods, it was long looked down upon by the music establishment. Jazz is based upon improvisation and a deep-down homey and exuberant attitude; its first big stars included Louis Armstrong and Joe 'King' Oliver, and its presence is integral to the city's identity. The **Old US Mint**, facing Esplanade Ave, houses a fairly good jazz museum.

balconies. The **1850 House** at 523 St Ann St is a restored Creole family mansion, displaying its flamboyant housewares.

A quick walk straight out of the square, across Decatur St and over the streetcar tracks, brings you to the mighty Mississippi. Some 2200 miles downstream from its source, the great river broadens through New Orleans before ploughing into the Gulf of Mexico, but while the romance of its name beckons, there isn't really all that much to see. The **Moon Walk** provides a leisurely strolling route with views of the odd oil tanker or souped-up steamboat. The nearby **Aquarium of the Americas** is one of the country's best, with massive glass tanks housing sharks, penguins and alligators. $$$ Open daily 0930–1900 (summer); 0930–1800 (winter).

Heading downstream from Jackson Square (away from downtown), Decatur St leads past some wonderful cafés before veering off to the **French Market**. An active market since the 1720s, this is a great place to load up on local specialities like hot pepper sauce, alligator heads and voodoo dolls. The Farmer's Market and the weekend flea market, just beyond, are great for fresh fruit and vegetables and antiques, respectively. The **Ursuline Convent**, 1114 Chartres St, is a lovely little piece of French colonial architecture dating from 1745 – one of the oldest buildings in the city.

BEYOND THE QUARTER

Just north of the French Quarter, **Louis Armstrong Park** was once the location of the city's slave market. Though the green space appears to be an enticing piece of urban green, this is one of the city's worst crime zones after dark. Nearby, the eerie **St Louis Cemetery No. 1** is New Orleans's oldest graveyard. The city is notorious for its cities of the dead; as it sits right at sea level, above-ground graves are used to prevent the grotesque occurrence of floating corpses. The dead are placed inside stone tombs, many of which crumble over time, so it is not unusual to come across the remains of a forearm or vertebra. Again, wander with a group, and only during the day.

This part of town, particularly around Basin St, was where jazz flourished in the early part of the 20th century. Known as **Storyville**, it used to seethe with bars and bordellos – the city realised it couldn't control the illicit sex and booze, so it set aside this area for it. Today the scene has moved to the Quarter, the I-10 overpass barrels through, and it's dangerous – so there's little reason to come.

The Central Business District has little to hold your interest, other than the wonderful views from the observation deck of the horrendously ugly **World Trade Center**.

UPTOWN AND THE GARDEN DISTRICT Further west, the graceful swoop of the Mississippi cradles a number of beautiful and lively neighbourhoods collectively referred to as **Uptown**. St Charles Ave is the main thoroughfare, and the lovely **St Charles Streetcar** trundles the length of the crescent-shaped avenue, a great way to see the area and worth the trip for the atmosphere itself.

The city's most intriguing area after the French Quarter is the luscious and ostentatious **Garden District**, home to New Orleans's rich and famous. Magnificent homes line the streets, their subtropical gardens designed partly for aesthetics and partly to help keep the inhabitants cool in the stifling summer months. None is open to the public, though it's fun just to wander the streets, and self-guided walking tour maps are available from the tourist office. The official borders of the Garden District are St Charles Ave to the north, Magazine St to the south, and Jackson Ave and Louisiana Ave on either end, but the elaborate Victorian style spreads throughout much of Uptown. Among the most notable mansions to look out for are the so-called Wedding Cake House, at 5809 St Charles Ave, and the 'Gone with the Wind' house, modelled after Tara from the film, a block in at 5705 St Charles Ave.

The streetcar terminates near the campuses of Tulane and Loyola Universities, at **Audubon Park**. The former are missable, but the latter is a wonderful urban green setting, condensing the unusual geographic features of southern Louisiana into one park. Magnificent overgrown oaks and weeping willows swoop down from overhead, and murky pools and walking paths lead to the excellent **Audubon Zoo**; $$ open daily 0900–1630 (until 1730 on weekends). Among the rare species on display here is a white alligator, and the zoo has gone to great lengths to recreate a local swamp.

NORTH OF CENTRE Contained amongst the shady lagoons of the New Orleans City Park is the very good **New Orleans Museum of Art**,

TOURS

Guided and self-guided walking tours of the French Quarter and Garden District are offered through the **tourist office** on Jackson Square; for more information, tel: (504) 523-3939. **Gray Line**, tel: (1-800) 535-7786, offers bus tours of just about everything, from city sweeps, including a day-long hop-on–hop-off deal, to rural plantation and swamp tours ($$$).

FOR FREE

The French Quarter, Garden District and Audubon Park are so pleasant to stroll through that the city could almost be adequately explored without even entering a museum. For free music, you can usually hear makeshift street bands in front of the cathedral and in Louis Armstrong Park (but don't go to the latter at night). For terrific views and a taste of 'Old Man River', catch the free commuter ferry across the Mississippi.

whose collection includes, appropriately, an array of French and Spanish paintings and sculptures. What is perhaps surprising is that among these are a number of works by Rodin and Picasso, and also Degas, who lived here in the 1870s.

SHOPPING

You'll surely want to poke around the jewellery and antique shops in the French Quarter and Garden District. Most visitors come away from New Orleans with pralines, chicory, alligator heads (it's OK – they're not endangered), and hot pepper sauce – you won't believe the variety available. The French Market is a good place to look, as is the shopping centre in the Jackson Brewery building, on the river in the French Quarter.

NIGHTLIFE

The French Quarter bops and grinds well into the night. Most places keep their doors open, so you can stroll about until you hear something you like, though anywhere you go, your drinks won't be cheap. One way to cut costs while roaming is to buy big plastic cups of beer from the many street stands: this is the only city in America where open containers on the street are legal, so take advantage.

The name **Bourbon St** inspires images of sweaty 1920s jazz and blues clubs and raunchy bordellos, and today it thrives on this reputation – which produces a sort of mass-market sterile sleaze. The place is actually pretty tacky, crammed with souvenir stalls and striptease joints, so scout out entertainment on the other streets as well. It is still packed to the hilt with live music venues, though much of the stuff spewing out of the guitars and drums is commercialised and tainted by a bland rock-'n'-roll influence. Given the city's tolerance of public drunkenness, it can be rowdy down here well into the wee hours. That said, Bourbon St and the other streets around are where you're likely to end up at night, not least to see what the fuss is all about, and presuming you've got money to burn.

Faubourg Marigny, a funky district just east of the Quarter, is an up-and-coming club spot, and there are lots of places spread across the Uptown area – Magazine

MARDI GRAS IN NEW ORLEANS

New Orleanians throw the biggest carnival of the year outside Rio – a genuine local outpouring of fun and passion that goes back several centuries. 'Fat Tuesday', as Mardi Gras translates from the French, is the last day to make merry before the sombre Lenten fast. Spectacular parades, masked balls and general drinking and dancing in the streets go on for a full week leading up to the day itself. While it's all in good fun, locals complain that Mardi Gras has been tainted in recent years by too many out-of-town visitors who come for the non-stop party.

St around Louisiana Ave and Napoleon Ave is always good. *The Gambit* is a good little paper with entertainment and club listings.

FRENCH QUARTER	**Preservation Hall**, 726 St Peter's St. The original and still the best for live jazz, and kept purposefully dingy to prove it. No drinks served and no seating available, but you'll still have to show up early to catch the music.
	Old Absinthe Bar, 400 Bourbon St. One of the few places along this street with good R and B in a genuine setting; but no longer serving absinthe.
	Molly's, 1107 Decatur St. Popular Irish bar with New Orleans-style pub grub.
	The Funky Butt, 714 N. Rampart St. Music true to its name.
	Donna's, 800 N. Rampart St. Simple place with occasional zydeco in addition to jazz and blues.
JUST OUTSIDE THE QUARTER	**Snug Harbor**, 626 Frenchman St. Cosy, established jazz and blues club a few streets east of the Quarter in Faubourg Marigny.
	Café Brasil, 2100 Chartres St. Off-beat coffee shop with poetry reading by day, Latin rhythms and drinks by night.
	Petroleum Lounge, 1501 St Philip St. At the north-eastern tip of Louis Armstrong Park, a simple bar with local musicians.
UPTOWN	**Tipitina's**, 501 Napoleon Ave. Biggish theatre/dance hall which occasionally draws some big names in rock and blues; good local stuff otherwise.
	Maple Leaf Bar, 8316 Oak St. Usually a good selection of live Cajun, blues, and zydeco in an appropriately dusty venue.
	Muddy Water's, 8301 Oak St. Across from the Maple Leaf, a rhythm-'n'-blues joint with decent food.

DAY TRIPS

The lazy swamps and bayous near the city have a perpetually exotic feel to them, and are well worth exploring, but you will need a car. **Cajun country** is truly a world apart: much of southern Louisiana is actually more water than land, and the Cajun people maintain their unique rustic culture in the form of *fais do-dos* – village celebrations with lots of food and Cajun and zydeco music, marked by its toe-tapping, accordion-and-fiddle beats. Traditionally they've lived off the water: fishing for crawfish and catfish in the bayous, hunting alligator and trapping lynx and nutria. Today, they find work in the many petrochemical plants around New Orleans, and tourism is becoming an important business. The back roads out towards the towns of **Houma** or **Thibodaux** wind through the swamps, and many villages have outfits offering guided boat trips for around $10.

Closer to New Orleans, **Jean Lafitte National Park** is the most accessible and one of the best swamps in the area. Boardwalks meander for several miles through thick watery groves of oak trees and Spanish moss, and if you look carefully, you're likely to spot an alligator. The park is named after the legendary Cajun rebel, who commanded a ragtag group of pirates who knew these swamps better than anyone: because of this he was enlisted by Andrew Jackson in the war against the British in 1815, which the Americans otherwise might not have won. Open daily 0900–1700; to get there, take the I-90 bridge from the Central Business District to route 45 south, and then to route 3134.

To see the most luxurious **plantation homes**, take Hwy 18 as it meanders west from New Orleans alongside the south bank of the Mississippi. Signs point out the historic homes of rich Creoles, many of which have been retained as house-museums in various states of repair. Some have been restored to mint condition, with extravagant furnishings inside and equally intriguing slave quarters scattered about the yard.

The graceful city of Mobile has a particular southern charm which makes it a fine place to relax for a day or two. Ancient oak trees form a lush canopy over central boulevards, providing much needed shade from the blistering summer heat. Mobile is sometimes referred to as the Azalea City, for more than 50 varieties bloom here. It's also known as the Port City: while profiting as a commercial and manufacturing centre thanks to its location on Mobile Bay, the rich ecology of the delta and the Gulf of Mexico means a host of outdoor attractions, including thick swamps, nature reserves and lovely beaches.

The pronunciation of the name – *Mobeel* – derives from the French, who were the first to settle here, in 1702. It was traded with the British and Spanish before being seized by the United States during the war of 1812. This combined heritage is celebrated in an extravagant Mardi Gras which precedes the more famous one in New Orleans by several decades.

Mobile has a few specific sights – highlights include Fort Condé, built by the French in 1718, a series of retired battleships and warplanes, and several antebellum homes and gardens – but really, the thing to do is stroll the shady central area, particularly around Government St, Dauphin St and the pretty Bienville Square areas.

GETTING THERE AND GETTING AROUND

Amtrak and Greyhound both have centrally located stations. Trains pull into 11 Government St, and buses use the terminal a few blocks down at 201 Government St.

The centre of the city can be covered on foot, and city buses run to outlying sites. As always in America, though, you can see much more with your own wheels.

INFORMATION

The **Mobile Convention and Visitors Corporation**, tel: 800 5-MOBILE, has a visitor centre in Fort Condé. Open daily 0800–1700; www.mobile.org.

MONEY There are plenty of banks with automatic cash dispensers in the centre. Thomas Cook services are handled by AAA Alabama, 718 Downtown Loop West; tel: (334) 342-5550, a rather long way out of town beyond I-65.

POST AND PHONES The main post office is in the centre at 250 St Joseph St; Mon–Fri 0830–1730.

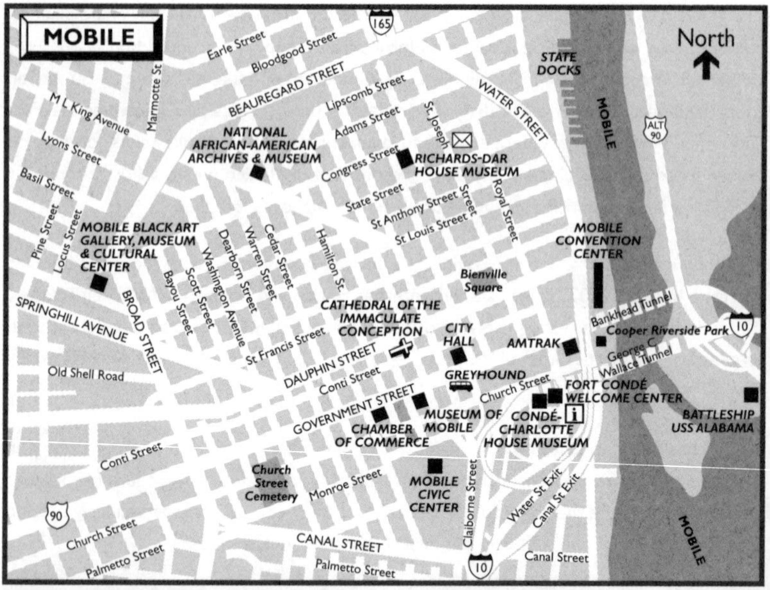

ACCOMMODATION

Check with the visitor centre for a full rundown of the budget options. Mobile's pretty streets mean a fair number of B&Bs in historic homes, with prices for most hovering around $100 per double room. Your true cheap options are the chain motels (see p. 504) on the main roads west of centre.

Olsson's Motel $–$$ 4137 Government St; tel: (334) 666-6410. Simple and friendly, and not too far from the centre.

Malaga Inn $$ 359 Church St; tel: (1-800) 235-1586. Gorgeous Southern inn with large rooms and swimming pool.

Towle House Bed & Breakfast $$–$$$ 1104 Montauk Ave; tel: (334) 432-6440 or (1-800) 938-6953; fax: (334) 433-4381. Lovely rooms and a grand breakfast spread in a beautiful neighbourhood; only three rooms, so book ahead.

FOOD

Seafood, whether steamed, fried or raw, is a real speciality this close to the Gulf of Mexico, with Gulf shrimp leading the parade. Southern cooking, in the form of steaks, pork chops and lots of fresh vegetables, is also generously served. Wash it all down with Azalea Punch, a favourite local non-alcoholic blend of fruit juices. You'll find a whole host of places on Dauphin St.

Royal Dog House $ 5 N. Royal St. Good for a quick lunch stop, eat-in or takeaway.

Wintzell's Oyster House $ 605 Dauphin St. Fried seafood and raw oysters are a favourite among locals here.

Drayton Place $–$$ 101 Dauphin St. Casual-chic image includes billiards, cigars and live jazz Wed–Sat.

Pier 4 Restaurant $$ 1420 Battleship Parkway. Fresh Gulf seafood is the speciality, and tables overlook the bay and downtown Mobile.

Spot of Tea $$ 310 Dauphin St. A beautiful Victorian-style tea parlour, serving elegant breakfast and lunch.

TOURS

Gray Line operates a 2-hr city tour trolley which departs from Fort Condé each day at 1000 and 1400 (Sun at 1400 only); tel: (334) 432-2229 or (1-800) 338-5597 for information. **Memorable Mobile Tours**, tel: (334) 344-8687 or (1-800) 441-1146, offers a full range of sightseeing and in-depth tours. **Wildland Expeditions**, tel: (334) 460-8206, runs boat tours of the estuary from Chickasaw Marina in the northern suburbs, $$$ Tues–Sat at 1000 and 1400.

HIGHLIGHTS

Fort Condé is as good a place to start as any, as it offers good views of the city from its reconstructed walls, and contains a museum with dioramas depicting the city's French, British and Spanish eras. Open daily 0800–1700.

From here it's a short walk to the pretty central area. Government St is a major thoroughfare with a number of noteworthy buildings. **City Hall**, at no. 208, dates from around 1855 and sports an architectural style drawn from the West Indies. A block down, the **Museum of Mobile** provides a good historical background to the area with relics of the past 2000 years, most interesting among which are ornate carriages and fantastical gowns from past Mardi Gras celebrations. Open Tues–Sat 1000–1700, Sun 1300–1700.

Two blocks north, the surprisingly grand and attractive **Cathedral of the Immaculate Conception** stands proudly at the corner of Dauphin St and Claiborne St. Dauphin St is another pleasant and lively stretch of pavement, and from here you can get a good taste of Mobile. The city's identity as a grand dame of the South is revealed through its many **antebellum homes**. These magnificent houses were the pleasure palaces of rich landowners who revelled in their Southern grace; all relied in large part on slave labour, and the stories of African-Americans are as fascinating as those of their masters, though for different reasons. Styles vary, but common

DAY TRIPS

Ten miles south of Mobile, off I-10, the Bellingrath Home contains a huge collection of china, crystal and silver, plus a beautiful 64-acre landscaped semi-tropical garden; it's pricey, though. $$$ Open daily 0800-dusk. At the mouth of Mobile Bay (accessible via Hwy 193), Dauphin Island is a favourite playground of Mobilians, with pretty beaches and the 164-acre Audubon Bird Sanctuary. An 'estuarium' here displays sea life in the Gulf. $$ Open Mon-Sat 0900-1700 (until 1800 in summer). At the eastern tip of the island, Fort Gaines is a neo-Renaissance construction which figured prominently in the defence of Mobile during the Civil War. $ Open daily 0900-1700. North of Mobile, you can explore the swamps and bayous of the Mobile Bay estuary, home to hundreds of species of wildlife, including alligators, black bears, bald eagles and osprey. On the opposite side of the bay, Hwy 58 is a designated scenic drive with a wetlands reserve and many pretty viewpoints. At the eastern tip of Mobile Bay (take I-10 east to Hwy 59), the tourist town of Gulf Shores is famed for its marvellous white-sand beaches.

features are two-storey columns supporting a massive front porch; the furnishings inside are always exquisite. The following are quite central and open to the public:

The **Condé-Charlotte Museum House**, right next to Fort Condé, was Mobile's first jail and is one of the city's oldest buildings; each room is furnished according to different eras in city history. $ 104 Theatre St; open Tues–Sat 1000–1600. The **Richards-DAR House Museum** is a large Italianate city home in the attractive de Tonti Square area: $ 256 N. Joachim St; open Tues–Sat 1000–1600, Sun 1300–1600. The **Oakleigh Period House Museum** was built in 1833 in the Greek Revival style: $ 350 Oakleigh Pl.; open Mon–Sat 1000–1600.

One of the city's real tourist pushes is the **Battleship Memorial Park**, towards Mobile Bay. This is the appropriate final resting place of the USS *Alabama*, the World War II battleship that led a US fleet into Tokyo Bay to accept the surrender of Japan in 1945. $$ Open daily 0800–1730 (until 2000 May–Aug).

The **National African-American Archives/Museum** documents the lives of blacks in Alabama – Mobile was a major port during the slave trade. 564 Martin Luther King Ave; open Mon–Fri 0830–1700, Sat–Sun 1200–1600.

NIGHTLIFE

Mobilians don't go in for much rollicking on Saturday nights, so you're somewhat limited to the bars around Dauphin St. Check the *Mobile Register* for theatre and concert listings.

Drayton Place (see under Food), has billiards and live jazz.

Bentley's Place, 220 Dauphin St. Pleasant for a meal or a drink, with live shows on weekend nights.

Port City Brewery, 225 Dauphin St. Microbrewery and pizzeria – try to get a balcony seat and watch the city roll by.

Chicago to San Antonio

RAIL / BUS

Train AMTRAK OTT Table 376

Bus Greyhound OTT Table 730/776

Transport	Frequency	Journey Time
Train	Tue/Thu/Fri/Sat	30 hrs
Bus	3 Daily	29hrs 20mins

Note: There are 4 more daily bus services from Chicago to San Antonio using a less direct route.

Chicago–St. Louis

RAIL

OTT Table 374/6

Transport	Frequency	Journey Time
Train	3 Daily	6hrs 4mins

St. Louis–Little Rock

RAIL

OTT Table 376

Transport	Frequency	Journey Time
Train	Tues, Thur, Fri, Sat	7hrs 28mins

Little Rock–Dallas

RAIL

OTT Table 476

Transport	Frequency	Journey Time
Train	Wed, Fri, Sat, Sun	7hrs 29mins

Dallas–Austin

RAIL

OTT Table 476

Transport	Frequency	Journey Time
Train	Wed–Fri, Sat, Sun	6hrs 13mins

Austin–San Antonio

RAIL

OTT Table 476

Transport	Frequency	Journey Time
Train	Wed–Fri, Sat, Sun	2hrs 50mins

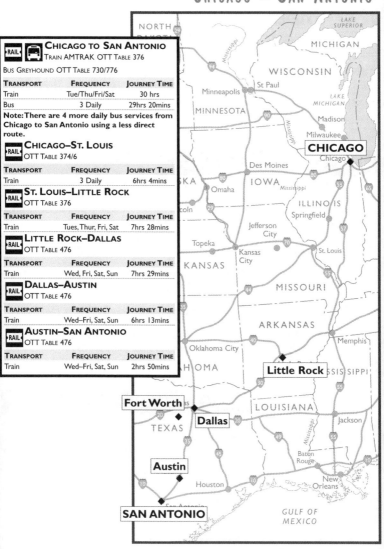

Chicago – San Antonio

On the 'Texas Eagle'

From energetic, exciting Chicago (see p. 246), the 'Texas Eagle' rolls through the flat prairieland of Illinois to quiet Little Rock. From there it cuts through tall pine forests to glitzy Dallas, where sightseers can take in the memorabilia of the Kennedy assassination, and then to the city's historical competitor, nearby Fort Worth. The university city of Austin is the next main stop before the train reaches its final destination of San Antonio (see p. 310).

LITTLE ROCK

In 1957 Little Rock shot to fame as legal, violent and brutal battles raged in the first major conflict between state and federal government over race relations. It was also the home of Bill Clinton, governor of Arkansas until he became president. Today, it is a quiet, unassuming town with little on offer apart from pretty MacArthur Park, with its **Museum of Science History** (open Mon–Sat 0900–1630, Sun 1300–1630). There is a coach connection to **Hot Springs**, a spa town 50 miles away.

Mid-morning, the train reaches Texarkana, which reputedly gets its portmanteau name from its position straddling the Arkansas–Texas state line – even the station is officially in two states.

Visitor Convention Center, Markham and Main Sts, tel: (501) 376 4781, is open Mon–Fri 0830–1700.

Distinctive station is downtown at 1400 W. Markham St.

Finding a room downtown is easy throughout the year.
Little Rock Inn $ 6th St; tel: (501) 376 8301.
Quapaw Inn $$ 1868 S. Gaines St; tel: (501) 376 4781.

DALLAS

Seated in the Metroplex region, boasting the main tourist draws of Texas, Dallas has money, glitz and glamour. Its roots are surprisingly humble: the town was not originally founded on oil as many would believe, but instead started out as a prairie trading post. A succession of investing entrepreneurs have built up its wealth in the worlds of finance and trade, and nowadays it prides itself on being the cultural capital of the region. Worldwide, it is also famous for being witness to President Kennedy's assassination in 1963, and being the host of the *Dallas* TV serial and the Cowboys football team in the 1970s.

Central Dallas is littered with skyscrapers and neon lights. Shopping is a luxurious experience: sample the **Nieben Marcus Department Store** on Main St. Walk south down St Paul St into Marila St and you will see **City Hall**, film-star famous as the police station in *Robocop*.

The **Dallas Museum of Art** is in the northern part of downtown, at 1717 N. Harwood St. European works are downstairs; upstairs are the American exhibits, including a special collection of pre-Columbian memorabilia. Open Tues, Wed, Fri 1100–2100, Sat and Sun 1100–1700; free.

Deep Ellum is the old warehouse district, made famous by its music in the 1920s. It is now the fashionable place to go with galleries, trendy clothes stores, cafés and clubs. The **Pegasus Theater**, 3916 Main St, tel: (214) 821 6005, puts on modern plays and original productions.

South of Deep Ellum is **Fair Park**, a plaza originally built to house the Texas Centennial Exposition. Inside you will find several fine museums: the **Dallas Museum of Natural History**, open Mon–Fri 1000–1300 ($, free Mon); the **Dallas Aquarium**, $ open daily 0900–1630; and a recent addition, the **Museum of African Art**.

Southfork Ranch, 25 miles out of town, at 3770 Hogge Road, Parker, is the film home of the fictional Ewing clan. It has been kitted out as a mini-theme park, with a museum where tourists can have their photograph taken in a cowboy hat at JR's desk.

A City of Conspiracy?

Dealey Plaza is quickly recognised and needs no introduction. Only a little imagination can take you to 12.30pm, 22 November 1963, when John F. Kennedy toured the streets of Dallas and was shot here by Lee Harvey Oswald.

Nearby, at 411 Elm St, you will find the **Texas Schoolbook Depository** from which Oswald fired. On the sixth floor is the aptly named Sixth Floor Museum, housing a recreation of the gunman's nest, some moving displays and the infamous film of the assassination. $ open daily 0900–1800.

It is generally accepted that Oswald acted independently (he in turn was shot in a police station by nightclub owner, Jack Ruby, to avenge the killing), but conspiracy theories still flourish. Some witnesses say they heard shots that day from the grassy knoll just to the north of Elm St. These theories and others are discussed in detail at the **Conspiracy Museum** $$, 110 S. Market St, open daily 1000–1900. Close by you will find the **Kennedy Memorial**, located in the Dallas Historical Plaza.

Dallas Visitors Center, 1303 Commerce St, tel: (214) 712 1944, is open daily 0800–1700 (Sat, Sun until 1600). **North Park Center**, 1201 Elm St, tel: (214) 746 6677, is open Mon–Sat 0830–1700.

The Amtrak service stops at Union Station, just west of downtown, at 400 S. Houston St.

Central Dallas has high prices aimed at the business traveller, but if you phone in advance you may be able to obtain

good weekend deals. There is also a B&B reservation service: **B&B Texas Style**, 4224 W. Red Bird Lane; tel: (214) 298 8586. There is camping at **Lewisville Lake Park** ($).
Adolphus Hotel $$$ 1321 Commerce St; tel: (214) 742 8200.
Stoneleigh Hotel $$ 2927 Maple Ave; tel: (214) 871 7111.

Café Brasil $ 2815 Elm St; tel: (214) 747 2730.
Blind Lemon $$ 2805 Main St; tel: (214) 939 0202.
Dinger's Catfish Café $$ 2706 Elm St; tel: (214) 741 9012.

FORT WORTH

There is strong competition between Dallas and its near neighbour. Built from fortunes in the cattle trade, Fort Worth was the home of the Sundance Kid and of Bonnie and Clyde, and in the late 19th century was the last stop on the great cattle drive to Kansas, the Chisholm Trail.

Leafy downtown is centred on **Sundance Sq.**, encircled by shops, restaurants and bars between 1st and 6th Sts. It is overlooked by two glass skyscrapers, City Center Towers, and flanked by the **Bass Performing Arts Hall**. Notice the walls covered with murals, and the theme of carvings of longhorn skulls.

If cowboy celebrations are your style, time your visit for the **Chisholm Trail Round-Up** in mid-June, or **Pioneer Days** (Labor Day weekend), western-style celebrations in the Stockyards.

Around Exchange Ave, 2 miles north, **Stockyards** is an area of restaurants, bars (some encourage you to drink first and buy later!) and shops (like the quaint M. L. Leddy's Saddle Shop) nestling together on the dusty streets to form a nostalgic cowboy heaven. **Cowtown Coliseum** holds a championship rodeo every Sat at 2000.

CVB, 415 Throckmorton St; tel: (817) 336 8791; open Mon–Fri 0830–1700.
Stockyards Visitor Center, 130 E. Exchange Ave; tel: (817) 624 4741; open Mon–Fri 0900–1800, Sat 0900–1900, Sun 1200–1800.

The historic Amtrak station is downtown at 1501 Jones St; tel: (817) 332-2931.

Sundance Sq. and the Stockyards are the most lively areas of the city. Motels can be found on the freeways both north and south of the city.

Park Central Hotel $ 1010 Houston St; tel: (817) 336 2011.
Ramada Inn Downtown $$ 1701 Commerce St; tel: (817) 335 7000.
Etta's Place B&B $$$ 200 W. 3rd St; tel: (817) 654 0267. Named after the schoolteacher girlfriend of the Sundance Kid.

Steak is the speciality at Fort Worth, and the best steakhouses can be found at Stockyards.
Flying Saucer $ 201 Commerce St; tel: (817) 877 4191.
Juanita's $$ 115 W. 2nd St; tel: (817) 654 4466.
Cattleman's Steak House $$$ 2458 N. Main St, tel: (817) 624 3945.

AUSTIN

The capital of Texas, laid-back Austin lies on the bank of the Colorado River and since the 1960s it has been favoured by artists, musicians and writers. Walk along **The Drag**, a stretch of Guadaloupe St running from Campus North, on Martin Luther King Blvd, to 24th St. Cluttered with cafés, second-hand clothes shops and bookshops, it set the scene for the 1991 Richard Linklater film, *Slacker*.

Austin is dominated by the **University of Texas**, which even has its own oil rig (Santa Rica 1, on San Jacinto Blvd), bringing in the money to make it one of the world's richest universities. Part of the campus can be visited: the Harry Ransom Centre in the south-west corner, and the art gallery (open Mon–Fri 0900–1630).

Visitor Center, 201 E. 2nd St; tel: (512) 474 5171; open Mon–Fri 0830–1700.
State Tourist Information Center, State Capitol; tel: 512 305 8400; open Tues–Fri 0900–1700.

The Amtrak station is just south-east of the centre at 250 N. Lamar Blvd; tel: (512) 476-5684.

Austin Motel $ 1220 S. Congress Ave; tel: (512) 441 1157.
HI Austin $ 2200 Lakeshore Blvd; tel: (512) 444 2294.
La Quinta Capitol $$ 300 E. 11th St; tel: (512) 476 7151.
Driskill Hotel $$$ 604 E. Brazos St at E. 6th St; tel: (512) 474 5911.

Mr Natural $ 1901 Cesar Chavez St; tel: (512) 477 5228.
Mezzaluna $$ 310 Colorado St; tel: (512) 472 6770.
Threadgills $$ 6416 N. Lamar Blvd; tel: (512) 451 5440.

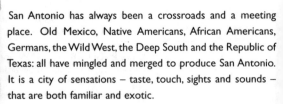

San Antonio

San Antonio has always been a crossroads and a meeting place. Old Mexico, Native Americans, African Americans, Germans, the Wild West, the Deep South and the Republic of Texas: all have mingled and merged to produce San Antonio. It is a city of sensations – taste, touch, sights and sounds – that are both familiar and exotic.

In 1836 Texas shook off the yoke of colonialism – this was the year of the Alamo (see p. 313) and Sam Houston's subsequent victory – and for ten years the territory existed as an independent republic. Surprisingly, it was the Europeans who flocked here after the revolution, and by 1850, Mexicans and Anglos were outnumbered in San Antonio by Europeans, especially Germans.

San Antonio's multi-ethnic roots are reflected in its varying architectural styles. More recently the city has returned to its Hispanic roots and new buildings flaunt red-clay roofs, Saltillo tile floors and central patios.

San Antonio is a tale of two cities. The compact, downtown area with the River Walk, Alamo and business district will keep a visitor contented for days; beyond the centre the city sprawls in several directions, laced together by an extensive freeway system.

Getting There and Getting Around

Air San Antonio International Airport is located 13 miles from the city. Transport is available by taxi or van shuttle.

Train/Bus The Amtrak station is located in St Paul Sq., 224 Hoefgen; tel: (210) 223-3226 or (800) 872-7245, on the east side of downtown, near the Alamodrome. Hop on a Via streetcar to your downtown hotel. Taxis are also available. The Greyhound terminus is downtown, at 500 N. St Marys St, two blocks from the River Walk; tel: (210) 270-5824. The station is within walking distance of many hotels, and streetcar and bus transport are nearby.

Via Metropolitan Transit Service, tel: (210) 362-2020, operates 105 routes to every major tourist attraction, including express routes from central San Antonio to Sea World and Six Flags Over Texas. It offers a bargain one-day visitor pass.

> Via San Antonio Streetcars are open-air, authentic reproductions of the rail streetcars that plied the streets of San Antonio more than 50 years ago. They now shuttle tourists and residents alike through downtown. Stops include the Alamo, La Villita, St Paul Sq. and the King William area for a flat fare.

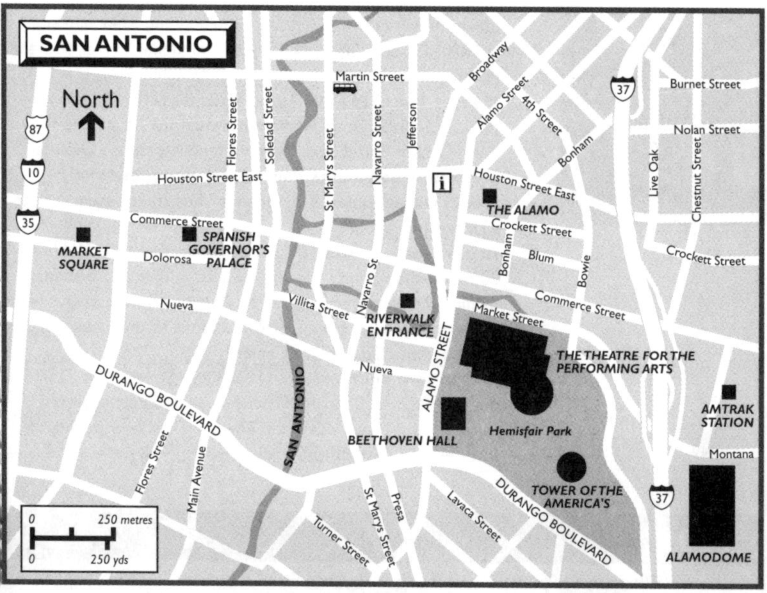

INFORMATION

Visitor Information Center, 317 Alamo Plaza; tel: (210) 270-8748 or (800) 447-3372; www.SanAntonioCVB.com. Open daily 0830–1800. Closed on Thanksgiving, Christmas and New Year.

POST AND PHONES The main post office is at 615 E. Houston St (across from the Alamo); tel: (210) 227-3399.

SAFETY The usual precautions apply, especially at night. Rangers patrol the River Walk and public parks.

ACCOMMODATION

San Antonio International Hostel $ Pierce St; tel: (210) 223-9426. Next door to the Bullis House Inn, the hostel has a reading room, small kitchen, dining areas and picnic tables. Pleasant but not particularly convenient for public transport.

Bullis House Inn $$ 621 Pierce St; tel: (210) 223-9426. Best B&B bargain in town, if you don't mind sharing a bath. Just down the street from Fort Sam Houston and filled with oak panelling, parquet floors and crystal chandeliers. Near I-35 and Hwy 281.

Menger Hotel $$$ 204 Alamo Plaza; tel: (210) 223-4361 or (800) 345-9285. Good location between the Alamo and the River Center Mall. Decor ranges from Victorian to Oriental, with a smattering of unknown periods that possess kitchenettes and balconies. If Victorian is your choice make sure to specify when booking.

Arbor House Hotel $$$ 339 South Presa; tel: (210) 472-2005. Neither quite a hotel nor a B&B (although croissants, muffins and juice are delivered to your door); 11 cottages with decor transplanted from Las Vegas. Close to the River Walk, La Villita and the Convention Center.

La Mansión del Rio $$$$ 112 College St; tel: (210) 225-2581 or (800) 292-7300. Spanish hacienda-style hotel converted from a 19th-century seminary. The balconies overlooking the River Walk are worth the price.

FOOD

Dining options run the gamut from burgers to fine French cuisine, Chinese to Cajun, and soul food to German specialities. Pure San Antonio, however, is Tex-Mex. Try the queso falmeado, chilli relleno, enchiladas, chalupas, menudo (chilli-hued stew of tripe, pig's foot and hominy, acclaimed as a hangover cure) and sopapillas. And, of course, the chilli. Note: chilli with beans is for wimps and 'con carne' (with meat) is redundant: chilli here means just that.

Mi Terra $ 218 Produce Row, Market Sq.; tel: (210) 225-1262. Open 24 hours. This is the place to go when you must have eggs and chorizo at 2 am. Fabulous bakery on site.

Carranza's Grocery and Market $$ 701 Austin St; tel: (210) 223-0903. Mesquite-smoked meats, barbecue and lots of combination plates.

Paseano's River Walk $$ 110 Crockett St; tel: (210) 22-PASTA. Because you can't eat Tex-Mex all the time! Huge portions at reasonable prices. The cheese tortellini with artichokes, spinach and cream is a delight.

Rosario's $$ 1014 S. Alamo; tel: (210) 223-1806. Great atmosphere, good food, and possibly the best margaritas in San Antonio.

Boudro's $$$ 421 E. Commerce St; tel: (210) 224-8484. Drift down the river while you feast on Tex-Mex specialities. Servers whip up fresh guacamole en route.

HIGHLIGHTS

Amid all the revolution, rebellion and reconstruction, the heart of San Antonio was, and is, the river. No other part of the city so accurately reflects its multiple personality as the **River Walk**, where European-style cafés serving Tex-Mex specialities blend smoothly with cobblestone walkways, night clubs, art galleries and gleaming high-rise hotels.

River Walk – Paseo del Rio – is the city's core, and its pride. First called 'Yanaguana' by the Papaya Indians, meaning 'place of refreshing waters', the description is no less accurate today. Lush green foliage lines the banks of this calmly flowing river. Cobbled walkways lead visitors to the river-level restaurants and shops. This is *the* place to walk, eat, cruise the river, gaze at the stars and drink in the soul of San Antonio. Its 3-mile stretch can be thronged with crowds around the restaurants or cafés, or quiet and peaceful just a short walk away. Tiny white lights in the trees create a fairytale atmosphere at night.

REMEMBER THE ALAMO

In 1718 Father Antonio Olivares founded the mission of San Antonio de Valero. Within little more than a decade the outpost had become a complex of missions, settlements and a military garrison known as the Alamo, defending itself first against hostile Indians and later from large numbers of immigrating Anglos.

The name of the Alamo became etched into American history when, in 1836, it stood against some 4000 of General Antonio Lopez de Santa Anna's Mexican troops, sent to take Texas for newly independent Mexico. The 189 defenders held out for 12 days before falling. One month later, Sam Houston spurred his troops on at the Battle of San Jacinto with the rallying cry of 'Remember the Alamo'. His victory secured independence for the new Republic of Texas.

Beyond the River Walk there is much to explore. Downtown you will find La Villita, with its shops and artisans; the King William District lined with Victorian homes, some of them now B&Bs; and, of course, the Alamo.

Located in the heart of the city (300 Alamo Plaza), the **Alamo** is a monument to the 189 men, including Davey Crockett, who sacrificed their lives during the famous battle here in 1836. Housed in the grounds of the historic mission, the museum exhibits artefacts from the battle and the period of the Republic of Texas, including manuscripts, maps and weapons. The shrine (free) is open Mon–Sat 0900–1730, Sun 1000–1730. Closed 24–25 Dec.

The **Cowboy Museum** is a real cowboy museum. Visit a replica of a Western town and see how the people of the Old West lived. $ 209 Alamo Plaza; tel: (210) 229-1257; open daily 1000–1900.

The **Spanish Governor's Palace**, 105 Plaza de Armas, has been called 'the most beautiful building in San Antonio' by the National Geographic Society. It once housed the officials of the Spanish Province of Texas. Distinguishing features include period furnishings and a cobblestone patio with fountain and foliage. Open Mon–Sat 0900–1700, Sun 1000–1700; tel: (210) 224-0601.

Step back into San Antonio's rumbustious past with a visit to **Buckhorn Saloon and Museum**. Walk into a recreation of a 120-year-old saloon and take a tour of Texan history and local entertainment. A restaurant, arcade and curio stores share space with the Hall of Horns, Fins and Feathers. Quirky, but fun. $$ 318 E. Houston; tel: (210) 247-4000. Open daily 1000–1800.

La Villita is a lovely oasis in the city centre – a unique arts and crafts community with shops, working artists, restaurants and a post office. The Old San Antonio Exhibit (located in Bolivar Hall) houses a collection of artefacts relevant to its history. Open daily 1000–1800.

The 32 shops of **El Mercado**, in Market Sq., are modelled on a Mexican market. In addition, there are over 80 speciality shops in the Farmers' Market Plaza. The square hosts many Hispanic festivals, where food and beverage booths sprout alongside the Victorian lamps and strains of mariachi music are heard. Open daily (except major holidays) 1000–2000.

The cool greenscapes and water features of **Hemisfair Park** (200 S. Alamo St) provide a refreshing retreat from the city streets. The park was the site of the 1968 HemisFair, celebrating the progress made by the confluence of civilizations in the western hemisphere. The playground is located near the Alamo St entrance and the park includes the Institute of Texan Cultures, Instituto Cultural Mexicano and the **Tower of the Americas**. This tower, 750 ft tall, was the theme structure for the fair, and you can ride up to the top for panoramic views of San Antonio and the surrounding area. There is a restaurant that serves lunch and dinner (great view, mediocre food) and after dark the lofty bar is a lovely way to drink in the sparkling array of city lights. The observation deck ($) is open daily 0800–2300; tel: (210) 207-6815.

LIFE BEYOND DOWNTOWN

Southtown, once depressed, is now teetering on the verge of trendy, and has a good mix of Hispanic shops, coffee houses and galleries. Monte Vista, north-west of the city centre, is a transitional area largely occupied by student housing for nearby Trinity University. To see how the other half lives, head for Alamo Heights, home to the city's wealthy residents and filled with expensive shops and trendy restaurants. Alamo Heights is where yuppies call home in San Antonio.

Rebellion and railways aside, San Antonio has prospered in part by a continuing military presence. The Alamo became a quartermaster depot for the US Army, and in 1876 **Fort Sam Houston** was built. The Apache war chief, Geronimo, was held prisoner here in 1886 and it was from Fort Sam that Teddy Roosevelt equipped his 'Rough Riders'. In 1910 the first military flight by an American took off from here and in subsequent years it was the location for early aviators, such as Charles Lindbergh, to sharpen their skills. By 1941, four air force bases had sprouted, making San Antonio the largest military complex in the USA, outside Washington DC. The fort is at 1212 Stanley Road, Bldg 124; tel: (210) 221-1151, north-east of the city centre, in a working-class and somewhat run-down neighbourhood. It is now home of the Army Medical Command and Headquarters, Fifth Army. The Visitor Information Centre has a leaflet giving a self-guided tour.

A highlight of visiting San Antonio is to take a gentle cruise on the river in flat-bottomed, environmentally friendly barges. Tours operate every day and last 35–40 mins. Take a tour ($), or for less than the cost of two tickets buy a shuttle pass for the day and ride as frequently as you like. A special treat is a dinner cruise. Yanaguana Cruises, 315 E. Commerce St; tel: (210) 244-5700 or (800) 417-4139 (reservations); www.sarivercruise.com.

The chain of missions established along the San Antonio River in the 18th century now collectively forms the **Missions of San Antonio National Historical Park**. Reminders of one of Spain's more successful attempts to dominate the New World, the missions were more than just churches: they served as vocational and educational centres, and bastions of trade. They formed the basis for what is San Antonio today. Within the park are the Missions Concepción, San Jose, San Juan and Espada. 2202 Roosevelt Ave; tel: (210) 534-8833; www.nps.gov/saan/. Open daily 0900–1700; free.

NIGHTLIFE

San Antonians love a fiesta and are ready to party at the drop of a sombrero. You'll find a fiesta occurring every month of the year. At the top of the list is Fiesta San Antonio, held in the third week of April. Other celebrations include: Cinco de Mayo, celebrating Mexico's independence from France in May; Oktoberfest, celebrating San Antonio's German roots; and Fiesta de las Luminarias, when the River Walk is lit by thousands of candles on the weekends before Christmas.

The rest of the year, see something of San Antonio's nightlife at:

The Landing, Hyatt Regency Hotel, River Walk; tel: (210) 737-7266. Traditional jazz from big band to Dixieland.

Blue Star Brewing Company, 1414 S. Alamo; tel: (210) 212-5506. Good beer brewed on site for a largely collegiate crowd.

Durty Nellie's Irish Pub, 715 River Walk; tel: (210) 222-1400. Quaff a lager with lime, throw your peanut shells on the floor and join the gang for a sing-along. Trite, but good fun.

DAY TRIPS

New Braunfels, north-east of San Antonio at the junction of the Comal and Guadalupe Rivers, is in the prettiest part of Texas – the Hill Country (see OTT Table 888 for details of bus services). This was the site selected in the 19th century by Prince Carl of Solms-Braunfels to bring in German settlers. The prince could not get his fiancée, Sophie, to return with him to the wilderness, but his colony prospered and by the 1850s New Braunfels was the fourth largest city in Texas.

The delights of downtown are largely historical and a walking tour with 39 points of interest will give you some insight into its heritage. The city has never lost its German flavour and today you'll find the Hummel Museum, the Sophienberg Museum (in memory of the reluctant fiancée), and a tradition of sausage making that culminates annually over two weekends in November with **Wurstfest**. What started out as a modest fair to display sausages has evolved into this yearly *Fest*, drawing over 200,000 visitors, including an excess of polka-ing, arm-linking, loud-singing, stomping, temporary 'Germans', intent on devouring 40 tons of meat and 40,000 gallons of beer. This is the place to try the 'wurst taco' you've ever had.

i New Braunfels Chamber of Commerce, 390 S. Seguin; tel: (210) 625-2385 or (800) 572-2626. Open Mon–Fri 0800–1700.

New Braunfels is an attractive town, but not as quaint as some of the other hill towns. For a more concentrated look at the past you might want to head 4 miles north-west to **Gruene** (pronounced *green*) to explore an 'almost' ghost town. Deserted during the Depression, Gruene was revived in the 1970s by businessmen seeking to create an area of speciality shops within the restored structures. Don't miss the H. P. Gruene Antique Mall for items of nostalgic Texicana.

Gruene Hall, on the corner of Gruene and Hunter Rds, tel: (210) 606-1281, is Texas's oldest and most mellow country-and-western dance hall – Lyle Lovett and Garth Brooks have played here. Learn the two-step or just listen to the music.

ROUTE DETAIL

Night travel is mostly across the expanses of the Corn Belt, the attraction of which soon palls.

The nearest Amtrak stop to Santa Fe is Lamy, from which the Lamy Shuttle Service runs into Santa Fe (included with the Amtrak USA or North America Rail Pass, otherwise a fare is payable). A working freight train also follows the route (tel: (888) 989-8600). (Note: the stop before Lamy is Las Vegas – but not *the* Las Vegas...)

RAIL CHICAGO–SANTA FE

OTT TABLE 368

TRANSPORT	FREQUENCY	JOURNEY TIME
Train	Daily	23 hrs

Notes: There is a Lamy–Santa Fe Shuttle Service which meets The South West Chief daily. Train arrives in Topeka at 0139. There is also a train from St Louis that connects with the SOUTHWEST CHIEF at Kansas City.

It is possible to travel from Chicago to Santa Fe by bus using Greyhound and TNM&O buses. If you go via Kansas City the bus will take you through Topeka, Wichita and Dodge City.

RAIL CHICAGO–KANSAS CITY

OTT TABLE 368

TRANSPORT	FREQUENCY	JOURNEY TIME
Train	Daily	6 hrs 35 mins

RAIL KANSAS CITY–DODGE CITY

OTT TABLE 368

TRANSPORT	FREQUENCY	JOURNEY TIME
Train	Daily	6 hrs 53 mins

RAIL DODGE CITY–LAMY (FOR SANTA FE)

OTT TABLE 368

TRANSPORT	FREQUENCY	JOURNEY TIME
Train	Daily	8 hrs 8 mins

CHICAGO – SANTA FE

ON THE 'SOUTHWEST CHIEF'

The changing landscape of America looms outside the windows of the 'Southwest Chief'. The train leaves the urban sprawl of Chicago in its dust as it rolls past Illinois's prairies and over two great rivers, the Missouri and the mighty Mississippi. In western Missouri, the railway begins to trace the Santa Fe Trail. Opened in 1821, the trail blazed the way for pioneers, missionaries, trappers and traders from Franklin, Missouri to Santa Fe. It crosses the spacious wheatfields of Kansas, and the legendary Old West until it ascends the towering Sangre de Cristo Mountains and the Ratón Pass into New Mexico's high country near Santa Fe.

KANSAS CITY, MISSOURI

Art deco architecture, culture, fountains, jazz and barbecues lure today's tourists to the 'Heart of America' city. In the 19th century travellers came here for supplies before embarking on the Santa Fe, Oregon or California trails. Provisions are now available amid the unique Moorish architecture of the Country Club Plaza, the nation's first outdoor shopping mall (Broadway and Ward Parkway), or within the Beaux Arts-styled Old Union Station, where there is entertainment, a city of science museum and speciality shops (opens Nov 1999).

FOR FREE

Free attractions include tours of the State Capitol (10th and Jackson Sts, Mon–Fri 0800–1600, Sat–Sun 0900–1500) and the Tiffany windows at the First Presbyterian Church, 817 S.W. Harrison St (opening hours vary). Visit a Victorian mansion at Historic Ward-Meade Park ($ 124 N.W. Filmore; open Tues–Fri 1000–1600, Sat–Sun 1300–1600), or experience the excitement of car racing at Heartland Park, 7530 S.W. Hwy 75; open May–Oct; tel: (800) 43-RACES; admission varies.

The **Hallmark Visitors Center**, Crown Center, tells you everything you ever wanted to know about greeting cards. Its inventive Kaleidoscope Workshop entices creative kids, and is free. 8450 Grand Blvd; open Mon–Fri 0900–1700, Sat 0930–1630. Former president Harry Truman lived nearby in **Independence** (take the KC Trolley, see below). His life and times are detailed at his home ($ 223 N. Main St; open daily except Mon), the Harry S. Truman Courtroom and Office ($ City Sq.; open Fri–Sat, Mar–Nov), and the Truman Library and Museum ($ Hwy 24 and Delaware; open Mon–Sat 0900–1700 (Thur until 2100), Sun 1200–1700).

Kansas City Visitors Center, 4709 Central in Country Club Plaza; tel: (800) 767-7700; info@visitkc.com has Metro bus timetables. The **KC Trolley** goes to a number of attractions and out to Independence; tel: (816) 221-3399.

The Amtrak station is located at Main and Pershing Sts.

Rodeway Inn City Center $$ 3420 Broadway.

Best Western Seville Plaza $$$ 4309 Main St.
Holiday Inn Express $$$ 801 Westport.
Contact all three by their central booking numbers – see p. 504.

Barbecue food is what Kansas cuisine is all about.
Phoenix Piano Bar and Grill $–$$ 302 W. 8th St. Features live KC Swing.
Gates Barbecue $$ 3201 Main St. Good-value, mid-town.
Winslow's City Market Barbecue $$–$$$ 20 E. 5th St. For barbecue and blues.

TOPEKA

Kansas's state capital played a large role in the prelude to the Civil War. Not only was it a stop on the Underground Railroad (the route used to smuggle runaway slaves north), but the slavery issue became so intense that the controversy here became known as 'Bleeding Kansas'. The free **Kansas Museum of History** traces the state's roots from Bleeding Kansas to Karl Menninger (founder of one of America's foremost mental treatment facilities) and from wagon trains to MacDonald's. 6425 S.W. 6th St; open Mon–Sat 0900–1630.

WHERE THE BUFFALO ROAM

Bison still live at the Finney Game Refuge in Garden City, 50 miles west of Dodge City, or the next train stop. Free tours by Friends of Finney Game Refuge: tel: (888) 445-4663, ext. 9400.

Topeka Convention and Visitors Bureau, 1275 S. Topeka Blvd; www.kansascommerce.com, has public transport timetables and other tourist information.

The Amtrak station is located on 5th and Holiday Sts.

Heritage House Bed and Breakfast $$$ 3535 S.W. 6th St; tel: (785) 233-3800. The original Menninger Clinic is now a charming B&B.
Topeka Capital Plaza $$$ 1717 S.W. Topeka Blvd; tel: (785) 431-7200. Topeka's newest hotel, near the Expo Center.

Willie C's $$ 2047 S.W. Topeka Blvd. Steaks a speciality.
Blind Tiger Brewery and Restaurant $$$ 417 S.W. 37th St. Juicy Kansas wood-grilled steak, ribs and pork chops.

DODGE CITY

Fort Dodge, established in 1865 to protect voyagers on the Santa Fe Trail, still exists 5 miles east of the modern city, on Hwy 154, and just west of the city, along Hwy 50, original wagon ruts are still visible at **Santa Fe Tracks**. Dodge City's lawlessness became legendary and so did its lawmen – Bat Masterson, Wyatt Earp and Charlie

Basset among them. Boot Hill, the cemetery where cowboys were 'buried with their boots on', is here and all this history comes alive at the **Boot Hill Museum** (3rd and Wyatt Earp Sts) and **Front Street** (Front and 5th Sts). The sites ($) can be visited aboard the Dodge City Trolley (end May–1st week Sept, $). Even Andrew Carnegie left his mark here: the **Carnegie Center for the Arts** at 701 2nd Ave features Kansas artists (open Tues–Fri 1200–1700, Sat 1100–1500; free).

JESSE JAMES

The boyhood home of cowboy outlaws Frank and Jesse James is now the **Jesse James Farm and Museum**, 25 miles north of Kansas City in Kearney, Missouri; $ open Mon–Fri 0900–1600, Sun 1200–1600.

Dodge City Convention and Visitors Bureau, 400 W. Wyatt Earp Blvd; www.dodgecity.org.

The Amtrak station is located at Central and Wyatt Earp. General public transport runs only Mon–Fri 0800–1600; tel: (316) 225-8119. The town has no taxi service, but almost everything is easily walkable. Unfortunately westbound trains arrive very early in the morning. If you are hiring a car, Hertz and Avis will arrange pick up, as will hotels.

Lodgings offer free shuttle service from the station.
Best Western Silver Spur $$ 14th and Wyatt Earp Sts.
Boot Hill B&B $$ 603 W. Spruce St; tel: (316) 225-7600; www.bbonline.com/ks/boothill. Across from Boot Hill.
Dodge House $$ 2408 Wyatt Earp St; tel: (316) 225-9900.

Mic-Leo's $ 2nd and Wyatt Earp Sts. For sandwiches.
Casey's Cowtown Club $$ 507 E. Trail. Juicy Kansas steaks.
Café Potpourri $$$ 2nd and Wyatt Earp Sts. Features continental cuisine.

THE TRAIL WESTWARDS

Time stands still at **Ratón**, one of Santa Fe Trail's original stops, and its Historic District allows a peek into the past. Sugarite Canyon and Cimarron Canyon state parks are nearby. Ratón Chamber of Commerce, tel: (800) 638-6161; www.raton.com. You can fish or explore the high country of the **Pecos Wilderness** by foot or by horse. Las Vegas/San Miguel Chamber of Commerce, tel: (800) 832-5947; www.worldplaces.com.las.vegas.new.mexico.

WHERE NEXT?

Stay in Santa Fe to explore some of the Southwest's fascinating attractions (see p. 321), or get back aboard the 'Southwest Chief', which continues westwards for almost another thousand miles, arriving in Los Angeles the following morning (see p. 383). A thruway coach links Flagstaff to the Grand Canyon (see p. 386).

Santa Fe

Santa Fe will take your breath away! This may be because of its altitude – around 7000 ft above sea level – but more likely because it is one of America's most charming and attractive cities. It feels like one giant, outdoor, interactive museum of art and history. The background of the canvas is filled with the magnificence of the Sangre de Cristo Mountains, the foreground sprinkled with adobe-lined streets that are seasonally adorned with fresh lilacs, poppies, sunflowers or a dusting of snow.

Santa Fe is proud of its rich and romantic history. By the time the Pilgrims set foot on Plymouth Rock, Santa Fe was already firmly established, and over the centuries it has been the capital for the Spanish kingdom of New Mexico, the Mexican province of Nuevo Mejico, the American territory of New Mexico and, since 1912, the state of New Mexico.

Native Indians, Spanish conquistadores, mountain men, gamblers, writers, artists and musicians have all contributed to the creative tapestry that has made Santa Fe the cultural heart of the South-west. Today you will find a city which is a multicultural wonder that seamlessly blends the varying ethnic populations.

Within a 60-mile radius of the city, forests and parks, monuments and ancient Indian ruins, Indian pueblos and the unique community of Los Alamos provide much to explore. Hiking trails, kayaking, river rafting, biking, horse-riding, tennis and golf will keep the active traveller happy.

GETTING THERE AND GETTING AROUND

Air Albuquerque International Airport (now renamed Sunport) is 65 miles south-west of Santa Fe. Shuttlejack provides a service into Santa Fe several times daily for around $20. Santa Fe Municipal Airport, tel: (505) 473-7243, is primarily used by private aircraft, but a regular scheduled service to Denver is available.

Rail/Bus Amtrak's 'Southwest Chief' stops in Lamy, 14 miles east of Santa Fe (see p. 317), from which the Lamy Shuttle, tel: (505) 982-8829, ferries passengers to local hotels and car hire agencies. Lamy also has its own entertainment (see p. 326).

Greyhound and TNM&O (Texas, New Mexico and Oklahoma) bus services and also the Shuttlejack from Sunport arrive at 858 St Michael's Dr.; tel: (505) 471-0008 or (800) 528-0447. The bus station area is quite a distance from the central plaza. The area is relatively safe during the day but exercise caution in the evening hours.

Santa Fe is the highest city in the United States at 6970 ft. Allow yourself time to adjust – the altitude can leave you breathless. Rest, drink plenty of water and limit alcohol to avoid the drowsiness, dizziness, headaches and nausea that come with altitude sickness.

INFORMATION

Santa Fe Convention and Visitors Bureau, 201 W. Marcy St, Santa Fe, 87504-0909; tel: (505) 984-6760 or (800) 777-CITY; www.santafe.org.

SAFETY Despite its benign appearance, Santa Fe on the whole is not a particularly safe city. Tourists should be particularly conscious of petty theft in hotels and bag grabbing (purses and camera bags) while on the streets.

MONEY Automatic cash dispensers abound throughout the city. You can exchange foreign currency at Nationsbank, 1234 St Michael's Dr., and First Security Bank, 121 Sandoval St.

POST AND PHONES The main post office is located at 210 S. Federal Place (two blocks north and one block west of the plaza); tel: (505) 988-6351. Open Mon–Fri 0730–1745.

ACCOMMODATION

No matter where you stay in Santa Fe you will be charged a hefty 10.25% hotel tax.

Budget Inn $$ 725 Cerillos Rd; tel: (505) 982-5592. Clean, comfortable, functional and central. Ask for a room at the back to avoid the street noise.

El Paradero $$ 220 W. Manhattan St; tel: (505) 988-1177. An eccentric, rambling old farmhouse dating from the 1880s. Rooms have skylights and fireplaces. A full breakfast is served.

Travelodge $$ 646 Cerillos Rd; tel: (505) 982-3551 or (800) 578-7878. Clean, comfortable and convenient. Rooms have mini-refrigerator and coffeemaker.

The Inn of the Animal Tracks $$–$$$ 707 Paseo de Peralta; tel: (505) 988-1546; www.santafe.org/animaltracks. A restored pueblo-style home in the centre of town, filled with hardwood floors and platform beds with feather mattresses.

Four Kachinas Inn $$$ 512 Webber St; tel: (505) 982-2550; www.southwesterninns.com/fourkachi.htm. B&B in a turn-of-the-century house. Some rooms have their own patio.

La Fonda $$$$ 100 E. San Francisco St; tel: (505) 982-5511 or (800) 523-5002. The oldest hotel in Santa Fe. Guests have included William Tecumseh Sherman, Ulysses S. Grant, Pat Garrett (who shot Billy the Kid), Errol Flynn, John F Kennedy, Robert Redford and Shirley MacLaine (just to name a few). Elegant, expensive and worthy of the splurge.

FOOD

Plaza Diner $ 54 Lincoln Ave (on the Plaza); tel: (505) 982-1644. Classic diner where New Mexican, Greek and American foods top the menu. The Kahlua flan calls for second helpings.

Downtown Subscriptions $ 376 Garcia St; tel: (505) 983-3085. Giant lattes, shady patio and the largest selection of international newspapers and magazines in town.

Celebrations $–$$ 613 Canyon Rd; tel: (505) 989-8904. Yummy huevos rancheros, eggs Benedict and home-made cinnamon rolls served all day long. Lovely place to stop and nibble between gallery stops on Canyon Rd.

Santacafé $$$ 231 Washington St; tel: (505) 984-1788. The South-west meets South-east Asia. Expensive but interesting, with an amazing twist on local cuisine. Reservations recommended.

HIGHLIGHTS

Like most cities with Hispanic origins, the city was built around a central plaza that was the focus of town life. Santa Fe's plaza, surrounded by narrow streets filled with adobe houses, has retained that role, and is the place to begin your acquaintance with the city.

In the centre of the plaza, a monument commemorates Santa Feans' valour in repelling various 19th-century invaders, such as Confederate troops and [ ] Indians (locals have eradicated the word 'savage' from the plaque, as they point out that these were not local Indians but rather Comanches who came from Texas – as, for that matter, did the Confederate soldiers).

GETTING AROUND

Santa Fe is easily explored on foot, but **Santa Fe Trails**, the public bus system, may be a welcome aid in the summer heat. It runs Mon–Fri 0630–2230; Sat 0800–2000 (no service Sun or public holidays); tel: (505) 438-1464.

Facing the plaza on the north side is the **Palace of the Governors**, housing the New Mexico Museum of History. Built in 1610 as the original capital of New Mexico, it has been in continuous public use longer than any other structure in the United States. The museum highlights the colonial and territorial eras. Permanent exhibits include photographic reproductions of Spanish colonial maps of the South-west as well as a truly beautiful full-scale reconstruction of a Penitente chapel.

The Historic Styles Act, passed in 1957, legislated that all new structures built within the downtown area must be either Spanish pueblo or territorial in appearance. Large electrical signs are prohibited and even the building height and window sizes are regulated. The result? A low-rise, earth-toned city that is easy on the eye.

Within a covered portico outside the museum you will find Indians selling jewellery and pottery. They enjoy official status as an 'exhibit' of the museum, which regulates the quality and authenticity of their goods.

One block west is the **New Mexico Fine Arts Museum** which, when it was built in 1917, sparked a resurgence in the architecture that characterizes Santa Fe today. Originally, the museum provided display space for local artists as well as a framing workshop in the basement, and monthly banquets were held upstairs. In the early days, Santa Fe's artist population was small enough to fit into one room. Today the upstairs galleries house classic paintings from early 20th-century Santa Fe and Taos. (You will need at least 2 hours to see both museums. For admission details, see box below.)

Santa Fe's latest attraction is the **Georgia O'Keeffe Museum** on Johnson Street. One of the country's leading abstract artists, O'Keeffe was drawn to New Mexico and the desert landscapes that inspired her, and was a resident of Santa Fe at the time of her death in 1986. Over 100 of her works are on permanent display at the museum

THE MUSEUM OF NEW MEXICO

Of the five individual museums that make up the **Museum of New Mexico**, three – the **Palace of Governors**, the **Museum of Fine Arts**, and the **Georgia O'Keefe Museum** – are all in the heart of Santa Fe. The **Museum of International Folk Art** and the **Museum of Indian Arts and Culture** are located just a few miles away. All are open Tues–Sat 1000–1700. You can pay separate admission to each ($) or, for the cost of two admissions, obtain a four-day pass, valid for all the museums.

Diagonally across the plaza is **La Fonda**, Santa Fe's oldest hotel. Browse through the lobby to view its unusual décor. West, up San Francisco St, is **St Francis Cathedral**, built in 1869 by Archbishop Jean Baptiste Lamy. The most notable feature is *La Conquistadora,* a blue-clad willow-wood statue of the Virgin, carried by Spanish refugees in their flight from the Pueblo Revolt of 1680. It is the oldest surviving religious carving in New Mexico. The statue is carried as the centrepiece of a thanksgiving procession that has been held annually since 1716.

Sena Plaza, just north of the plaza on E. Palace Ave, is one of the most beautiful and secluded historic sites in Santa Fe. Once the central court of a large hacienda of 33 rooms, it has been transformed into an intimate garden. Built in the 1860s and extensively remodelled in 1927, it is a classic example of how a historic building can be adapted for modern use.

Canyon Rd is the art and soul of Santa Fe. This mile-long road was once travelled by Pueblo Indians, Spanish explorers and pioneers. In recent history the path has been trodden by artists and writers from around the world. Dozens of galleries, studios, shops and restaurants are now housed within the historic buildings. Wear comfortable walking shoes: the pavement is uneven.

One block south of La Fonda, on the Old Santa Fe Trail, is the **Loretto Chapel** (chapel of Our Lady of Light) in the grounds of the Inn at Loretto. The chapel is another creation of Archbishop Lamy, patterned after the Sainte Chapelle church in Paris. It was constructed in 1873 as a chapel for the Sisters of Loretto, who had established a school for girls in 1852. The chapel's best-known feature is its 'miraculous staircase', a remarkable spiral staircase that makes two complete 360° turns with no central or other visible means of support. Many legends surround its construction, but the only element upon which all the

RIDING INTO THE SUNSET

The **Santa Fe Southern Railroad** will take you on an evening ride to Lamy (timed to connect with the 'Southwest Chief', see p. 317), where you can explore the Legal Tender Saloon. This five-car train with restored cars represents different eras of railway history. Seats covered in green velvet and walls of gleaming wood highlight the New Jersey Car of the 1920s, and the Plaza Lamy car, built in the 1950s as a lounge car, has a domed roof. The caboose was originally built in the 1940s as part of a livestock train.

stories agree is that a mysterious carpenter completed the work and vanished without waiting to be paid.

Across the river is the **Barrio de Analco**, the oldest European settlement in Santa Fe other than the plaza and the palace. Past the **San Miguel Mission** and the **Oldest House** you will arrive at the **Roundhouse**, the New Mexico State Capitol. Completed in 1966, it is the only round capitol building in the USA, and was designed to reflect the shape of a Zia Pueblo emblem. It symbolises the Circle of Life: four winds, four seasons, four directions and four sacred obligations. Surrounded by a lush garden filled with more than 100 varieties of plants and trees, with plenty of benches and sculptures by local artists, the outside is much more interesting than its functional interior.

FIESTA TIME The most famous of Santa Fe's many festivals is the **Santa Fe Fiesta**, held annually in September. This three-day celebration begins with dancing, fireworks and the burning of the 40-ft figure of Zozobra or Old Man Gloom.

SHOPPING

Santa Fe will emphasize that you are here for the art, for the history, for the culture. Yes, all that's true. But don't forget the shopping! Native American artefacts and traditional crafts, western paintings, contemporary Indian art and 'wearable art' (western fashions with an *haute* twist) will all combine to put a major dent in your budget. If you are in the market for a painting that costs more than a car, this is the city in which you will find many.

DAY TRIPS

Pecos National Park, 20 miles east of Santa Fe (head northbound on I-25), is the site of 17th-century Spanish mission and a major pueblo ruin that dates from the 13th century. The Pecos pueblo was the eastern gateway to the Rio Grande pueblo country. It was abandoned in the mid-19th century after Comanche raids decimated most of the population, and the survivors moved to the mountains north of Albuquerque and joined the Jemez pueblo. The E. E. Fogelson Visitors Center relates the history of the Pecos people with exhibits and dioramas. A 1½ mile loop trail takes you past the excavation of the Misión de Nuestra Señora de Los Angeles de Porcincula, all that remains of what was once the most magnificent church north of Mexico City. $ Open daily 0800–1700.

To visit the **Bandolier National Monument** take I-84 north approximately 16 miles to Tesuque, then head west on Rte 502. The monument, named after pioneering Swiss archaeologist Adolph Bandolier, reflects the perseverance of Bandolier's 34 years of excavation activities. Only a stone floor plan remains of what was once a three-storey, castle-like walled town. To appreciate the ruins fully climb to the Ceremonial Cave for the best view. The area is also a hiker's paradise. $$ (per car); open daily during daylight hours.

LOS ALAMOS

Further along Rte 502 is **Los Alamos,** perched atop the 7300 ft Pajarito Plateau. This odd community, best known to the world for its secret project to develop the atom bomb in World War II, was home to Pueblo tribes for well over a thousand years. Today, over 10,000 people work at the Los Alamos National Laboratory, making it the largest employer in the state.

The **Bradbury Science Museum** at the National Laboratory puts a very positive spin on nuclear production but it is a fascinating place. Make sure you see the 18-min film, *The Town That Never Was,* detailing how this community evolved in secrecy. 15th St and Central Ave; tel: (505) 667-4444; open Tues–Fri 0900–1700, Sat–Mon 1300–1700; free.

The **Los Alamos Historical Museum** is a massive vertical log building in which the history of the area, from pre-historic cave dwellers to the present, is depicted, with an excellent permanent Manhattan Project exhibit that offers a more realistic view of the devastating effects of nuclear weapons. 2132 Central Ave; tel: (505) 662-4493; open Mon–Sat 0930–1630, Sun 1100–1700 (summer); Mon–Sat 1000–1600, Sun 1300-1600 (winter); free.

BLACK HOLE

Do not take an engineer or technophile anywhere near 4015 Arkansas, Los Alamos if you have anything else planned for that day! This store/museum is filled with the remains of the nuclear age: geiger counters snuggle up to giant blenders and every other sort of technical gizmo (the owner has supplied props to many sci-fi movies). Bring a jacket or sweater as the temperature inside hovers at about 40°F.

WHERE NEXT?

The drive north from Santa Fe to Taos (see p. 334) will take you along a spectacular 80-mile route through mountains, red painted desert, villages bordered by apple and peach orchards and the foothills of the 13,000 ft peaks of the Sangre de Cristo Mountains. Equally dramatic is the Durango Driving Loop (see p. 328). Amtrak's 'Southwest Chief' will take you west to Los Angeles (see p. 383) or north all the way to Chicago (see p. 317).

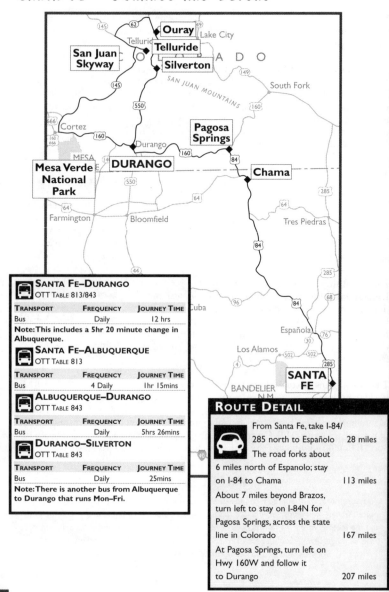

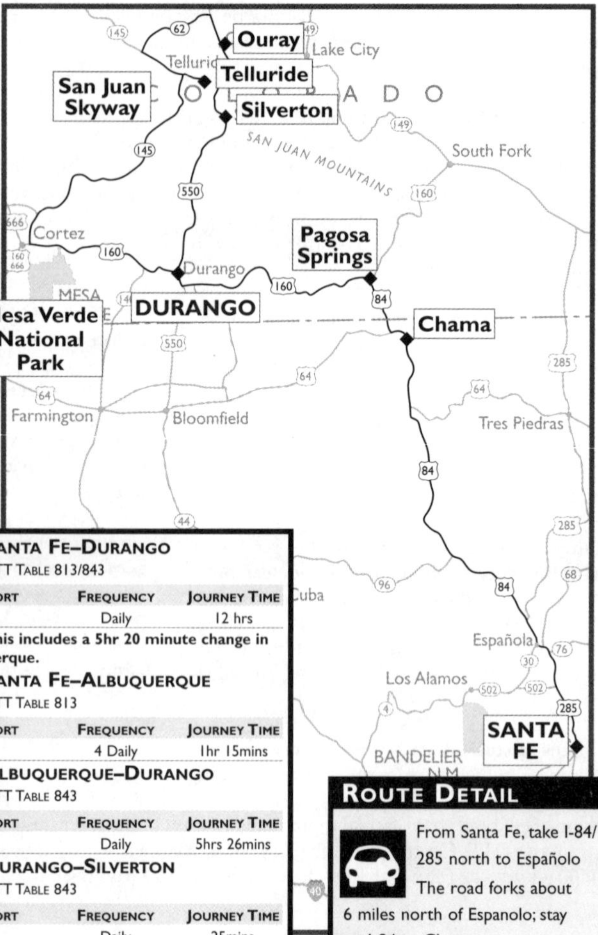

SANTA FE–DURANGO

OTT TABLE 813/843

TRANSPORT	FREQUENCY	JOURNEY TIME
Bus	Daily	12 hrs

Note: This includes a 5hr 20 minute change in Albuquerque.

SANTA FE–ALBUQUERQUE

OTT TABLE 813

TRANSPORT	FREQUENCY	JOURNEY TIME
Bus	4 Daily	1hr 15mins

ALBUQUERQUE–DURANGO

OTT TABLE 843

TRANSPORT	FREQUENCY	JOURNEY TIME
Bus	Daily	5hrs 26mins

DURANGO–SILVERTON

OTT TABLE 843

TRANSPORT	FREQUENCY	JOURNEY TIME
Bus	Daily	25mins

Note: There is another bus from Albuquerque to Durango that runs Mon–Fri.

ROUTE DETAIL

From Santa Fe, take I-84/285 north to Españolo	28 miles
The road forks about 6 miles north of Espanolo; stay on I-84 to Chama	113 miles
About 7 miles beyond Brazos, turn left to stay on I-84N for Pagosa Springs, across the state line in Colorado	167 miles
At Pagosa Springs, turn left on Hwy 160W and follow it to Durango	207 miles

Driving north from Santa Fe your journey will take you through the Santa Fe and Carson National Forests as you steadily ascend into the Rockies and the dramatic landscape that dominates south-western Colorado. En route are mineral springs and the highest narrow-gauge railway in the USA.

The one-time 'Wild West' mining town of Durango is ideal as a base camp for further exploration of the San Juan mountains, Indian settlements and Mesa Verde National Park. It also excels in outdoor sports opportunities, offering everything from horseriding and ballooning to snowmobiling, according to the season. (For travellers without a car, the Greyhound Denver–Albuquerque route stops in Durango.)

From Durango the San Juan Skyway takes a looping route for nearly 250 miles through the spectacular mountain range – an unmissable introduction to the scenic glory of the state.

The San Juan Skyway is described on p. 326.

CHAMA

Take a break and visit the **Ghost Ranch Living Museum**, a US Forest Service exhibit of regional plant and animal life. A trail through the severely eroded *arroyo* (river canyon) is an opportunity to study soil ecology and range management. A 2-mile drive from the museum is Ghost Ranch itself, a collection of adobe buildings making up an adult study centre. Georgia O'Keefe spent time at the ranch painting these canyons.

EN ROUTE

Take a dip! The **Ojo Caliente Mineral Springs**, 50 miles north-west of Santa Fe, were considered sacred by prehistoric tribes and are now a National Historic Site. No other hot spring in the world has Ojo Caliente's combination of iron, soda, lithium, sodium and arsenic. The dressing rooms are in good shape, but it could use an overall sprucing up. Open daily 0800–2000.

HIGH-LIFE DETOUR

Instead of turning left on I-84 after Brazos, stay on Hwy 17 N. to the Cumbres and Toltec scenic railway. This is the longest and highest narrow-gauge railway in North America. The journey ends in Antonito, Colorado and is a day trip of tunnels, gorges and mountains; tel: (719) 376-5483 or (505) 756-2151.

PAGOSA SPRINGS

Pagosa is an Ute Indian name given to the hot mineral springs renowned for their healing qualities. The relaxing hot mineral baths and 12 swimming pools are open all year round. After a refreshing soak – and a massage perhaps? – visit the Fred Harman Art Museum, Rocky Mountain Wildlife Park, and Chimney Rock Indian Ruins. In winter you will find great powder skiing at Wolf Creek Ski Area.

Pagosa Springs Chamber of Commerce, Box 787, Pagosa Springs, CO 81147; tel: (800) 252-2084; www.chamber@pagosa-springs.com.

DURANGO

Durango began its life as a frontier mining town. Today the romance of the Old West remains in Durango's century-old saloons, Victorian architecture and narrow-gauge railway. This lively town snuggled into the shadows of the San Juan Mountains has a wide selection of accommodation and restaurants, and activities such as river rafting, Jeep tours, relaxing hot springs and, should you feel so inclined, factory outlet shopping.

Durango Chamber of Commerce, 111 Camino del Rio, Durango; tel: (970) 247-0312. Plenty of ATMs and local banks will do currency exchanges, but you will have difficulty locating bureaux de change.

Siesta Motel $$ 3475 Main Ave; tel: (970) 247-0741. Clean and quiet, with cooking facilities and jacuzzi.
Jarvis Suites $$$ 125 W. 10th St; tel: (970) 259-6190 or (800) 824-1024. Studios and suites with kitchens, a barbecue on the patio and outdoor hot tubs.
Strater Hotel $$$$ 699 Main Ave; tel: (970) 247-4431 or (800) 247-4431. A taste of the Old West, but with hot tubs/jacuzzis, television and laundry. It also has a restaurant (see below).

Durango has even more restaurants per capita than Santa Fe but no distinctive regional cuisine. For a special treat you might dine in the Victorian atmosphere of **Henry's** in the Strater Hotel – a bit of a splurge, but you won't find another restaurant as splurge-worthy for many miles.

Highlights

Durango's premier tourist attraction is the **Durango and Silverton Narrow-Gauge Railroad**, a puffing steam train that travels a spectacular route through the Animas river valley and San Juan National Forest. The journey will transport you through an unspoilt wilderness of waterfalls, meandering creeks and dense forests. The train has been pursued by bands of 'outlaw' Hollywood extras, while its passenger cars have echoed to the footsteps of such actors as David

Niven in *Around the World in 80 Days*. Four round-trip trains operate daily between late Apr and Oct; reservations are essential. $$$$+ tel: (970) 247-2733.

UTE INDIAN RESERVATION

Ignacio, south-east of Durango on Rte 172, is the home of the Southern Ute tribe. The reservation, covering more than 680,000 acres, was established in 1886. Explore the tribe's history at the Sky Ute Event Center and Cultural Center Museum, or try your hand at limited-stakes gambling at the Sky Ute Casino or Ute Mountain Casino. In town you will find art, crafts, native pottery and jewellery in the shops and galleries that feature the work of these Native American artisans.

Durango celebrates the active life. You can take to the air with a glider ride over the scenic Animas valley (Durango Soaring Club, 3 miles north on Highway 550; or lift your spirits with a hot-air balloon trip. More earthly pursuits include horseriding, hayrides, hiking, fishing and biking. During the winter season you can try sleigh rides and snowmobiling.

THE SAN JUAN SKYWAY

This breathtaking 260 mile loop on paved highways through the San Juan mountains begins and ends at Durango. Designated an 'all-American road', the Skyway travels through alpine forests and towering mountains, some as high as 14,000 ft, and past Native American cliff dwellings. The most spectacular segment, between Ouray and Silverton, is nicknamed the Million Dollar Highway.

From Durango follow Hwy 550N to Silverton (45 miles). Continue north on Hwy 550 to Ouray (15 miles) and on to Ridgway (10 miles). At Ridgway turn west on Hwy 62 to Placerville (24 miles), then turn east on Hwy 145 south to Telluride (15 miles). Continue south on Hwy 145 past Ophir, Rico and Dolores (60 miles). Past Dolores Hwy 145 ends at the junction with Hwy 160. Turn east towards Mesa Verde National Park and Mancos, and so back to Durango – a total of 260 miles.

From Telluride the route is quite remote, and from a scenic viewpoint a little dull. It's better to turn tail at this point and head back to Durango, enjoying the scenery from the other direction.

SPECIAL DRIVING NOTE

Your journey will take you over some of the steepest mountain passes in North America. Be careful not to overheat your engine and especially careful not to 'ride the brakes': this may cause them to overheat and fail.

SILVERTON

One of Colorado's most scenic settlements lies at the end of the narrow-gauge railway from Durango. Its wide, dirt-paved streets and false-fronted Victorian-era stores along once notorious Blair Street, known for its bordellos, evoke the 'shoot 'em up' days of the Wild West when Bat Masterson was the city marshall.

Teller House Hotel $$ 1250 Greene St; tel: (970) 387-5423 or (800) 342-4338. Built above the French Bakery, it needs refurbishing, but has a quirky charm. Rooms have private or shared bath.

Wingate House B&B $$ 1045 Snowden St; tel: (970) 387-5220 or (800) 484-9547-5520. Snuggle under a satin comforter or elk hide. Non-smoking.

Romero's Cantina and Restaurant $ 1151 Green St; tel: (970) 387-9934. Enjoyable Mexican cuisine in an authentic cantina setting.

OURAY

The 24 miles between Silverton and Ouray are along the heart-stopping Million Dollar Highway. Ouray is a charmer – the entire town is listed on the National Register of Historic Districts – and also has an abundance of hiking trails and mineral hot springs.

Box Canyon Lodge $$ 45 Third Ave; tel: (970) 325-4981. Relax in mineral hot tubs on a redwood deck. Fireplace suite available, but otherwise pretty standard accommodation.

Historic Western Hotel $$ 210 Seventh Ave; tel: (970) 325-4645 or (888) 624-8403. Wooden building with an upper-storey verandah that overlooks the former stagecoach stop. It has 12 rooms with shared bath, two suites with private bath.

TELLURIDE

Tucked into a box canyon 120 miles north of Durango, Telluride's beauty is legendary. This resort town was briefly home to a young Butch Cassidy, who robbed his first bank here. Today, Telluride's reputation is based on its outstanding ski trails and Hollywood residents. The wide main street, designated a National Historic District, heads directly towards one of the most spectacular views of the Rockies.

Telluride Visitors Bureau, 700 W. Colorado Ave. Open Mon–Fri 0800–2000, Sat–Sun 1000–1600.

Ridgway/Telluride Super 8 Lodge $$, 373 Palomino

Trail, Ridgway, Colorado 81432. Tel: (800) 363-5444 or (970) 626-5444. Reasonable, quiet, clean and surrounded by breathtaking scenery. A fireplace large enough to park a Buick!

MESA VERDE NATIONAL PARK

The cliff dwellings and artefacts of the Anasazi (a Navajo word meaning 'ancient ones') were accidentally discovered in 1888 and are a must-see.The Anasazi, the ancestral Puebloans, began building communities on the plateaux of Mesa Verde as early as AD 550. After more than 600 years of living on the mesa they began to build structures in the alcoves of the sandstone cliffs. Despite decades of research and archaeological excavations, the exact reason for their departure remains unknown. Most experts speculate that a combination of overpopulation, crop failure and drought may have caused them to abandon the area.

Today's visitors will find themselves awestruck at what they accomplished. The access road to Mesa Verde is 10 miles south of Cortez on Hwy 160, 36 miles west of Durango. Entrance fee ($$) is per vehicle, and guided tours, both full day and half day, are available ($$$$). The park is extremely crowded in summer, and the best months to visit are May, Sept and Oct. Wear comfortable, non-slip shoes and make sure you take a hat and water bottle. Facilities within the park include an archaeological museum lodge, several restaurants, gift shops, petrol stations and a 425-pitch campsite.

It's a 15-mile drive from the entrance to the Far View visitor centre, and immediately beyond, the road divides to the two areas of remains: **Chapin Mesa** to the south and **Wetherill Mesa** to the west. You will not manage to do both on the same day, so Chapin Mesa is your best bet, with tours of both the Cliff Palace and Balcony House. Tours ($) run every hour during peak season. **Cliff Palace**, the largest Anasazi cliff dwelling to survive, is tucked 200 ft below an overhanging ledge of sandstone. Its 217 rooms once were home to over 200 people. Inside you will walk through empty plazas, mysterious *kivas* and gaze on fading murals. **Balcony House**, a little further on, is not for the faint of heart. Access is very difficult and involves climbing ladders and crawling through a narrow tunnel. It's not visible from above, so the only way to view Balcony House is to take the tour.

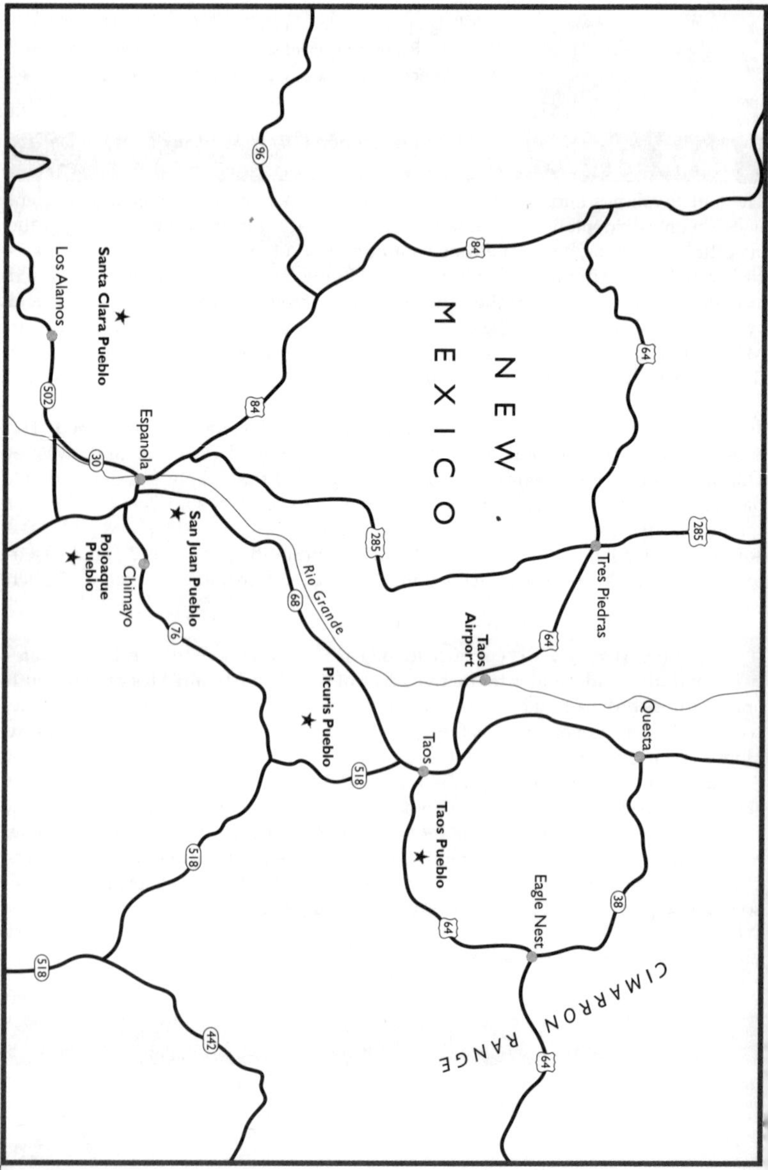
NEW MEXICO
CIMARRON RANGE
Santa Clara Pueblo
Los Alamos
Espanola
San Juan Pueblo
Pojoaque Pueblo
Chimayo
Rio Grande
Picuris Pueblo
Taos
Taos Airport
Tres Piedras
Questa
Taos Pueblo
Eagle Nest
96
84
64
502
30
285
68
76
518
38
442

TAOS

Taos began as the northernmost outpost of Spanish colonial America. Founded five years after Santa Fe, it was the third permanent Spanish settlement in what is now the United States. Bypassed by the railways in the 1880s, the economy languished until the end of the 19th century, but in 1898 two American artists, bound for Mexico on a sketching trip, made it only as far as Taos before their wagon broke down. Enchanted by the land and the exotic, vivid quality of its light, Bert Phillips and Ernest Blumenshein stayed to form the nucleus of Taos's active artist community. After World War I more artists arrived and by the end of the 1920s the area became known as 'the left bank of the American Frontier.'

A quirky little town set in the middle of a sage-covered valley, Taos is filled with narrow streets punctuated by artists' galleries and artisan shops. At first glance, the dusty streets populated with funky residents may strike the visitor as Key West moved inland. Take time to sweep the dust from your eyes and you will discover a thriving arts community with an awe-inspiring background of giant blue mountains and irrigated meadows.

GETTING THERE AND GETTING AROUND

AIR Taos has its own airport, about 8 miles north on US 64, but a more comprehensive service is to Albuquerque International Airport, about 2.5 hours away. A shuttle service is available from Pride of Taos; tel: (505) 578-8340.

BUS/TRAIN Amtrak does not run through Taos, but TNM&O (Texas, New Mexico & Oklahoma) coaches arrive at Paseo del Pueblo Sur, at the Chevron station, close to the Plaza.

Taos Transit, tel: (505) 571-2000, runs from from Kachina Lodge on Paseo del Pueblo Norte to the Ranchos Post Office on the south side of town. The flat fare is very cheap, even for an all-day or 7-day pass.

INFORMATION

Tourist Office: Taos County Chamber of Commerce, junction of US 64 and NM 68; tel: (505) 758-3873 or (800) 732-TAOS. Open daily 0900–1700; closed on major holidays.

POST AND PHONES Taos Post Office is at 318 Paseo del Pueblo Norte; tel: (505) 758-2081.

ACCOMMODATION

Most hotels and motels are located along Paseo del Pueblo Sur and Norte, with a few scattered east of the town centre. Condo accommodation (and there is lots) and most B&Bs are scattered throughout the back streets.

La Doña Luz $$ 114 Kit Carson Rd; tel: (505) 758-4874 or (800) 758-9187. You will feel part of the Taos art community in this B&B with its painted murals on the doors, wood carvings and set tile. Renovations are ongoing (1999); ask for a room in the main house.

La Posada de Taos $$$ 309 Juanita Lane; tel: (505) 758-8164 or (800) 645-4803. European antiques, New England quilts and Spanish tiles mesh very nicely within the thick walls of this adobe building. Fabulous breakfast feasts and merry hosts complement your stay.

Abominable Snowmansion Skiers Hostel $–$$ tel: (505) 776-8298. About 8 miles out of town, it offers clean beds, a common room with circular fireplace, pool table, piano, and teepees that sleep 2–4 people.

FOOD

Bent Street Deli and Café $ 120 Bent St; tel: (505) 758-5787. Homely atmosphere – dine on hearty breakfast burritos and home-made granolas or have the deli pack you a picnic to take away. Outside pavement seating area is heated.

La Luna Ristorante $–$$ 223 Paseo del Pueblo Sur; tel: (505) 751-0023. Bright and cosy, with intimate booths or outside tables in warmer months. Pastas, pizzas and very good salads.

HIGHLIGHTS

D. H. Lawrence, whose books stirred such controversy on both sides of the Atlantic, took refuge in Taos during 1924–5 to escape notoriety. However, while here, he tried his hand at painting, and the results earned him an obscenity prosecution! (and drove him from England one last time). You can view the naughty pictures in the back room of **La Fonda de Taos** in the Plaza.

The **Kit Carson Home and Museum of the West** is located a short block east of the Plaza. The 12-room adobe home was purchased by the famous mountain man, Indian agent and scout, as a wedding present for his young bride, Josefa. This was their home for 25 years until they both died within a month of each other. Furnishings, antique firearms and memorabilia are on display. The museum bookshop has a very comprehensive selection of books on New Mexico history. $ East Kit Carson Rd; tel: (505) 758-4741; open daily 0800–1800.

A block and a half south of the Plaza is an adobe house built in 1797. The **Blumenshein Home** was the home and studio of Ernest Blumenshein, a founder in 1915 of the Taos Society of Artists. Changing exhibits, European antiques and handmade Taos furniture are on display. $ 222 Ledoux Dr; tel: (505) 758-0505; open daily 0900–1700.

Martinez Hacienda is the only remaining Spanish colonial hacienda in New Mexico. Built in 1804 as a fortress-like refuge from Comanche raids, it is remarkably beautiful for a building that has thick adobe walls and no exterior windows. $ Lower Ranchitos Rd, Hwy 240; tel: (505) 758-1000; open daily 0900–1700.

Four miles north of Taos (off NM 522) is the **Millicent Rogers Museum**. Founded in 1953, the museum houses one of the most extensive private collections of Indian art in the south-west. Features are Navajo and Pueblo jewellery, textiles, Pueblo pottery and painting, and Zuni and Hopi *kachinas*, as well as some Spanish colonial folk items. $ tel: (505) 758-2462; open daily 1000–1700 (closed Mon Nov–Mar).

> You can buy a joint ticket to cover entrance to all the Kit Carson Historic Museums: the Kit Carson Home, the Blumenshein Home and the Martinez Hacienda.

Heading south about 4 miles out of Taos, at Rancho de Taos, you will find **San Francisco de Asis Church**. This adobe sculpture with no windows or doors has been the subject of many photos by Ansel Adams and paintings by Georgia O'Keefe. It contains the phenomenon of 'The Shadow of the Cross' by Henry Ault. Under ordinary light it portrays a barefoot Christ at the Sea of Galilee; in darkness, however, the portrait becomes luminescent and a shadow of the cross appears over the left shoulder of Jesus's silhouette. The artist claims this was not of his doing, and it remains a mystery why these illusions appear. Open Mon–Sat 0900–1200 and 1300–1600, or visitors may attend Mass: Sat 1800 (English), Sun 1900 and 1130 (Spanish). Donations accepted and appreciated.

THE PUEBLOS Taos Pueblo – the oldest and best known of the Rio Grande Indian pueblos – is a National Historic Landmark. It is 3 miles north-west of the town. Preserved here is the multi-storey architectural style that dates back to the 12th century.

About 1400 people live in the pueblo today. The residents still live as they did

Pueblos

Pueblos are more than just a tourist attraction. They are microcosms of Native American culture -- the past, present and future all uniquely represented in tight, family-oriented communities. They are villages that manage to welcome tourists while conducting their daily lives. The Pueblos have been thriving since the time of the Battle of Hastings. Today, you will find bread baked in the traditional horno (outdoor oven), harvest celebrations and ceremonial dances and sacred rituals perfomed.

The ceremonial dances offer the most intriguing glimpse into Pueblo culture. Each dance tells a different story and serves a different purpose. These ceremonies with the costumes brilliant with beads and headdresses, are punctuated by the insistent cadenece of the drums. Pinon smoke fills the air and the chatter of strange native dialects will transport you to another century. The sights, sounds and smells of these occassions are a feast for the senses.

New Mexico is home to nineteen Indian pueblos; Acoma, Cochiti, Isleta, Jemez, Laguna, Nambe, Picuris, Pojaque, Sandia, San Felipe, San Ildefonso, San Juan, Santa Ana, Santa Clara, Santo Domingo, Taos, Tesuque, Zia and Zuni. Most are within an hours drive of Albuquerque. And all are unique.Some pueblos have strict rules governing photography, sketching and tape recording. All visitors must abide by the laws and rules of the pueblo they visit and most pueblos have a tribal office that can answer any questions.

centuries ago, baking bread in *hornos*, drinking water that flows from the sacred Blue Lake. It is a quiet life, with an emphasis and dependence upon nature.

Ceremonies and dances held at the pueblo include the Fiesta de San Antonio in June, a corn dance in late July and the Fiesta de San Geronimo in late September. The pueblo is open to the public daily 0900–1630. Parking fees and photography fees are charged. No cameras may be used during any ceremony.

Also remember when touring the pueblos that this is their home. No peeking in windows, no wandering through open doors and at all times behave in a respectful manner – visitors have been asked to leave for acting rudely. You are expected to ask permission from individuals prior to taking photographs; some may ask for a small payment – use your discretion.

ALBUQUERQUE

Up, up and away! Albuquerque is a city that feels as free-spirited as the hot-air balloon festival it hosts each year. Even if you cannot visit the city in October when the International Balloon Festival is held, you won't go far without seeing the ubiquitous hot-air balloon motif. And on almost every weekend morning you will spot up to 50 hot-air balloons floating above the city, roaring like dragons as they sometimes bounce off suburban rooftops.

Albuquerque's heritage can be traced to early Spanish settlers, Native Americans and merchant Anglo settlers. The city never went through the lawless days of many southwestern frontier towns and by the last quarter of the 19th century, Albuquerque was already well established as a rail trade centre. Historic Route 66 weaves through the 100 square mile sprawl of modern Albuquerque, connecting the threads of its historic past.

GETTING THERE

AIR Albuquerque International Airport (now known as the Sunport), in the south central part of the city, is served by most major carriers. SunTran buses; tel: (505) 843-9200 makes airport stops, but the service is somewhat limited. Efficient taxi service and Checker Airport Express ferries passengers to and from city hotels.

RAIL/BUS Amtrak is currently at First St S.W., but a new station is being planned, so call ahead to confirm the location; tel: (505) 842-9650 or (800) 872-7245. The Greyhound terminal is close by, at 330 Second St N.W.; tel: (800) 231-2222. Sun-Tran Transit serves the city bus network. Its Sun Trolley service ($0.75 fare) operates 1000–1800 and runs every 30 mins.

INFORMATION

Albuquerque Convention and Visitors Bureau, 20 First Plaza N.W.; tel: (505) 842-9918 or (800) 284-2822; open Mon–Fri 0800–1700. An Old Town visitor centre, at 303 Romero St N.W., is open daily 0900–1700. The daily *Albuquerque Tribune* and the evening *Albuquerque Journal* are both useful sources of information.

POST AND PHONES The main post office, 1135 Broadway N.E.; tel: (505) 245-9561, is open daily 0730–1800. There are 25 branches throughout the city.

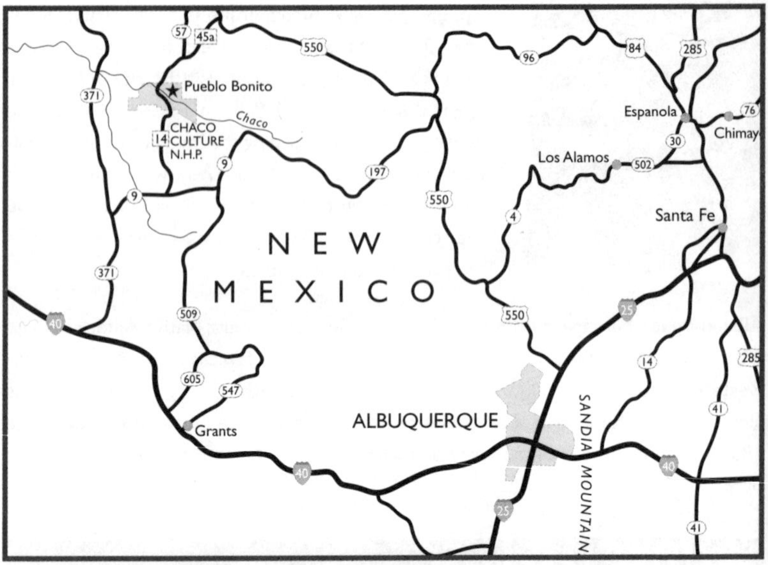

SAFETY Avoid the cluster of motels at the east edge of the town along Route 66 – this is a bad area, frequented by prostitutes and other unsavoury types.

ACCOMMODATION

Downtown or Old Town are the best places to stay. Albuquerque adds a 10.562% occupancy tax to every hotel bill.

Casas de Sueños $$–$$$ 310 Rio Grande S.W.; tel: (505) 247-6540. This compound of *casas* was all once private homes that formed a gathering place for artists and their admirers. Each room is individual, and the design and quality vary. Each accommodation has its own entrance.

Sheraton Old Town $$–$$$ 800 Rio Grande Blvd N.W.; tel: (505) 834-6300 or (800) 325-3535. No hotel is closer to Old Town. Request a southside room and you will get a balcony overlooking the Old Town and the pool.

Hyatt Regency Albuquerque $$$ 330 Tijeras Ave N.W.; tel: (505) 842-1234 or (800) 233-1234. If you are looking for luxury in the heart of downtown this is the place to be.

La Posada de Albuquerque $$$ 125 Second St N.W.; tel: (505) 242-9090 or (800) 777-5732. The first hotel built by Conrad Hilton, this place feels like Old Spain with its 19th-century hacienda-type courtyard and fountain.

William E. Mauger Estate, 701 Roma Ave N.W.; tel: (505)242-8755. B&B near Old Town. The three-storey brick Queen Anne-style mansion, built in 1896, has eight guest rooms with antique furnishings and private baths. A full breakfast is served each morning. Reservations are essential.

FOOD

66 Diner $ 1405 Central Ave N.E.; tel: (505) 247-1421. A former transmission shop has been converted into a nostalgic 1950s diner, decorated in chrome and leather with memorabilia of the glory days of Route 66. Try the fries, shakes and green chilli cheese dogs.

Duran Central Pharmacy $ 1815 Central N.W.; tel: (505) 247-4141. Yes, it does sound like an odd place to eat. Yet a plain little restaurant in the back of the pharmacy serves up authentic northern New Mexico food. Try the blue-corn enchilada plate or the huevos rancheros smothered in green chilli.

Maria Teresa $$ (for lunch) $$$ (for dinner) 618 Rio Grande Blvd; tel: (505) 242-3900. This 1840s adobe home a block north of the Plaza has been restored to hold one of Albuquerque's most appealing restaurants. You'll find beef, chicken and seafood on the menu, as well as New Mexican specialities. Reservations are recommended.

HIGHLIGHTS

The heart of Old Town, Albuquerque's original **Plaza**, dating back to 1706, has remained remarkably intact even as high-rise buildings have sprouted all around it. It is an oasis of antiquity. Browse in the art galleries and shops, bargain for handicrafts with the Pueblo Indian vendors, or pause for a quiet moment in the 18th-century San Felipe de Neri church.

The **New Mexico Museum of Natural History** contains exhibits about New Mexico's human and animal inhabitants in the last Ice Age, and a large display about the Rio Grande, including aquariums of fish that live in the river. The most unusual exhibit is a simulation of a journey into the depths of a volcano. $$ 1801 Mountain Rd N.W.; tel: (505) 841-8837; open daily 0900–1700.

Across the road, the **Albuquerque Museum** features an impressive permanent exhibit entitled 'Four Centuries: A History of Albuquerque' and contains the largest collection of Spanish colonial artefacts in the USA. 2000 Mountain Rd N.W.; tel: (505) 243-7255; open Tues–Sun 0900–1700; free.

The **Indian Pueblo Cultural Center** is owned and operated by the Native American Pueblos of New Mexico. The centre is modelled after Pueblo Bonito, a 9th-century ruin in Chaco Culture National Historic Park, and has a series of exhibit halls, screening rooms and hands-on interactive displays. The huge gift shop is filled with moderately priced items, and galleries selling Indian arts and crafts surround a central open-air dance plaza. Indian dances and craft demonstrations are held here at most weekends. $ 2401 12th N.W.; tel: (505) 843-7270 or (800) 766-4405; open daily 0900–1730. You'll also find a moderately priced restaurant specialising in Native American cuisine (a great place for a lunch stop).

Free walking tours of Old Town start from the Albuquerque Museum, Tues–Sun at 1100.

Just off the Old Town plaza, the **American International Rattlesnake Museum** has living specimens of common, uncommon and very rare rattlesnakes – more than 30 species in all. $$ 202 San Felipe N.W.; tel: (505) 242-6569; open daily 1000–1800.

A fun and exciting half-day can be spent riding the **Sandia Peak Tramway**, a journey of 2.7 miles to the top. Its base station is at 10 Tramway Loop N.E. and the tram is a jigback design: as one car approaches the top, the other is nearing the bottom and the two pass at the halfway point. The views from the peak are extraordinary, especially at night. Once at the summit you can dine in the very pricey High Finance restaurant, or picnic along one of several hiking trails (La Luz Trail is partly flat and quite easy). The schedule of operations varies from season to season and the tram can be particularly crowded during the skiing season. For operating times, tel: (505) 856-7325. $$$ (special rates apply if you have dinner at High Finance).

BALLOON FIESTA

Kodak Albuquerque International Balloon Fiesta, held every October, is the largest hot-air balloon festival in the world. Events include Mass Ascensions, a Special Shapes Rodeo and a Balloon Glow held in the evening. Mass Ascensions are held on all four weekend mornings of the fiesta. Held just after dawn, the sight of several hundred balloons taking flight with the sunrise is stunning.

If you can't resist the temptation, you'll find several balloon operators to take you up into the clear blue skies (prices average about $130 per person per hour). Contact Bradens Balloons Aloft, 3900 Second St N.W.; tel: (505) 345-6199; Rainbow Riders, 10305 Nita Pl N.E.; tel: (505) 293-0000; or World Balloon Corporation, 4800 Eubanks Blvd N.E.; tel: (505) 293-6800. Be prepared for an early morning take-off.

Tucson shines like an undiscovered gem in the Arizona desert, ringed by mountains and flanked on both east and west by the thousands of acres of Saguaro National Park.

Possessing a strong Spanish, Mexican and Native American heritage, Tucson is more than just a pretty face. It is the oldest continuously inhabited settlement in the USA – remnants of the Hohokam Indian civilisation found here date back to the 1st century AD.

Tucson is also where you find the real and 'reel' Old West. The Earps and the Clantons, Cochise and Geronimo, dance-hall girls, gunfighters and sheriffs were all part of the untamed frontier, and it's here that Hollywood created its own version of the Wild West. Countless westerns have been filmed with the saguaro-covered landscape and mountains as a backdrop.

The sun shines here 350 days a year, more than any other city in the USA. Although blessed with a more temperate climate than Phoenix because of its higher elevation, it does get a bit toasty in the summer. The clear skies, dry air and multiple mountain peaks have also made Tucson the astronomy capital of North America.

GETTING THERE AND GETTING AROUND

AIR Tucson International Airport, tel: (520) 573-8100, is 6 miles south of the city. Taxis, shuttle vans and some hotels offer transport into the city.

BUS/TRAIN The Amtrak station, 400 E. Toole Ave; tel: (520) 643-4442 or (800) 875-7245, is relatively convenient for the city centre but not safe at night; the station is as dilapidated as the neighbourhood. Although close to the Downtown Arts District and the Hotel Congress, the Greyhound terminus, at 2 S. Fourth Ave; tel: (520) 792-3475 or (800) 231-2222, is another area in which to be extremely wary.

Sun Tran, tel: (520) 792-9222, the local bus service, operates routes within the city and to the airport.

The service does not extend to such attractions as the Saguaro National Park, Old Tucson or the foothills area – better to take an organised tour or hire a car.

INFORMATION

Metropolitan Tucson Convention and Visitors Bureau, 130 S. Scott St; tel: (800) 638-8350 or (888) 2-TUCSON. The visitor centre is open Mon–Fri 0800–1700, Sat–Sun 0900–1600. Plenty of brochures and enthusiastic staff.

Safety Tucson is relatively safe for a city of around half a million people. Be careful after dark in the Downtown Arts District, except on Downtown Saturday Nights (see p. 347). To the south of downtown is a poorer area that is best avoided.

When driving be aware that many streets in Tucson are subject to flash flooding conditions. Heed warnings, find an alternative route if possible and do not attempt to cross a low-lying area that has been flooded.

Money Automatic cash dispensers are everywhere. Travellers' cheques are widely accepted; be prepared to present your driving licence for identification.

Post and Phones The main post office, at 141 S. Sixth Ave, is open Mon–Fri 0830–1700, Sat 0900–1200.

ACCOMMODATION

Hotel Congress $$ 311 E. Congress St; tel: (520) 622-8848 or (800) 722-8848. Great for the younger set, with shared hostel rooms available. The Cyber Bar, Cup Café and Library of Congress make this the coolest spot in Tucson. Convenient for the railway and bus stations.

Clarion Hotels and Suites $$$ 88 E. Broadway; tel: (520) 622-4000 or (800) CLARION. Around the corner from the Arts District, its Café Poca Cosa is a good bet for lunch.

Arizona Inn $$$$ 2200 E. Elm St; tel: (520) 325-1541 or (800) 933-1093. Old Arizona charm with all the modern conveniences. Filled with furniture made by disabled veterans of World War I. Some rooms have fireplaces. The dining room is one of the finest in the state.

FOOD

La Indita $ 622 N. Fourth Ave; tel: (520) 792-0523. Family-run restaurant with cheap and authentic Tex-Mex. Chicken mole, mushroom tacos and spinach and nut enchiladas are worth a try.

Carlos Murphy's $$ 419 E. Congress St; tel: (520) 628-1958. Mexican food with a sense of humour; fajitas and huge salads top the menu.

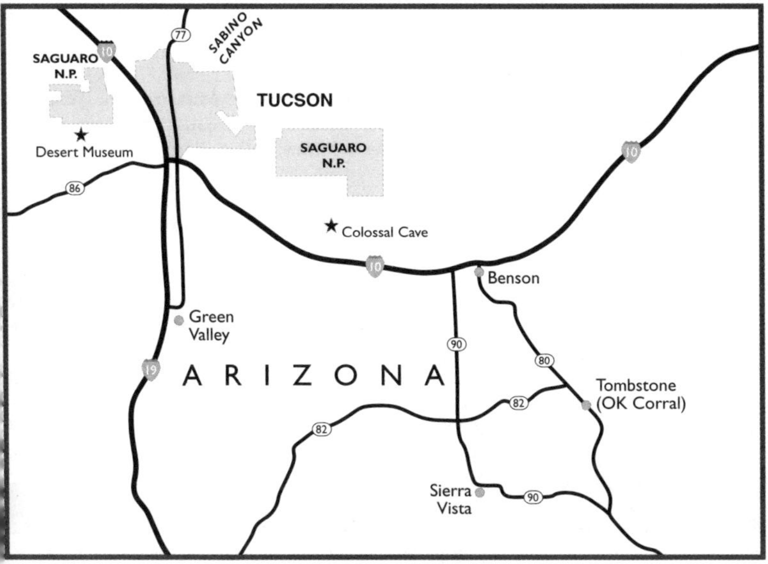

Cushing Street Bar and Grill, $$ 343 S. Meyer Ave; tel: (520) 622-7984. Housed in an old adobe building, this restaurant simply oozes old Tucson. If you like your margaritas pint size, you'll find them here.

HIGHLIGHTS

Downtown Tucson is quite compact and easily explored on foot. The narrow streets within the historical neighbourhoods are filled with reminders of life in the Old West. A walking tour of the **Museum of Art**, 140 N. Main Ave, will introduce you to five historic properties that house many of the museum's permanent collections: the Fish House, Steven's House, Corbett House, Manning House and La Casa Codova were all built in the 19th century.

Old Town Artisans, 186 N. Meyer St, is a historic 1850s adobe building, housing shops and a restaurant. Just north of here was where Tucson's élite built their homes; still fascinating to stroll by.

Between downtown and the university district you will find **Fourth Ave** and its eclectic collection of shops. More than 100 shops, galleries and restaurants are nestled into buildings from the 19th century.

The University of Arizona is home to the **Arizona State Museum**, the **Flandrau Science Center and Planetarium** and the **Center for Creative Photography**. If you've ever yearned to see an Ansel Adams or Harry Callahan original photograph, this is the place.

Beyond the City

About 25 minutes from downtown, 'Old Tucson' was built as a set for the 1939 epic western *Arizona*. Today, **Old Tucson Studios**, 201 S. Kinney Rd, is a working studio and theme-park recreation of an 1880s frontier town. Take Speedway Blvd west of I-10 over scenic Gates Pass and through Tucson Mountain Park. The road ends at Kinney Rd. Turn south, and Old Tucson is about 1/4 mile on. $$$ tel: (520) 883-0100; open daily 1000–1800.

South-east, along Old Spanish Trail, lies **Saguaro National Park**. The saguaro cactus, the 'monarch of the desert', is found only here in the Sonoran Desert, and the impressive stand of the saguaro gives a prehistoric feel to the landscape. You can picnic, photograph or hike within the park; tel: (520) 733-5100.

From 5900 N. Sabino Canyon Rd you can take a breathtaking tram ride up the 3.8 mile **Sabino Canyon**. The tram stops at nine locations, allowing time to get off and explore. If you have limited time, the Phone Line Trail is good even if you have only an hour before you must go back. $ tel: (520) 749-2861. Open daily dawn–dusk; the tram operates 0900–1600.

Stargazing

The climate and terrain around Tucson combine to provide ideal stargazing conditions. Kitt Peak Observatory, Fred Whipple Observatory on Mount Hopkins, Vatican Observatory (yes, the scientists from Rome are all practising Jesuit priests), and the University of Arizona's facilities are all nearby. Stellar research is so important to the area that Tucson even passed a city ordinance to limit light pollution.

Skywatchers Inn in the grounds of the private Vega-Bray Observatory offers not only a bed for the night but a blanket of stars. The observatory's telescopes can be rented for individual use, or you can join an astronomer-assisted programme. (With sufficient notice, Dr Vega can arrange transfer from the Amtrak station.) **$$$** (including full breakfast); 420 S. Essex Lane, Benson (between Tucson and Tombstone); tel: (520) 745-2390; www.communiverse.com/skywatcher.

Kitt Peak National Observatory, 56 miles west of Tucson on Route 86, has the greatest concentration of telescopes for stellar, solar and planetary research in the world. Guided tours are held daily, and Kitt Peak also offers an evening of stargazing beginning at sunset, including dinner, that lasts 3 hours. Reservations are required; $$$$+; tel: (520) 318-8726.

NIGHTLIFE

Do not let the preoccupation with history and astronomy lead you to think that Tucson ignores the arts! There are over 215 arts groups and organisations and over 35 galleries in the city. Add to that its own symphony, ballet, opera and theatre companies and you will understand why Tucson has been dubbed a mini-mecca for the arts.

The first and third Sat of each month Tucson throws a party – Downtown Saturday Night. It's part of the Tucson Arts District's efforts to show off downtown's many amenities. Street bands, street vendors and performance artists enhance the existing array of shops, cafés and galleries. It's free and great for people-watching.

DAY TRIP

Tombstone, 'the town too tough to die', lies 65 miles south-east of Tucson. Most famous for the Gunfight at the OK Corral, Tombstone retains all the old charm of its Wild West heritage, with frontier architecture and raised wooden sidewalks. Take a stagecoach tour of the historic district to get an overview of the OK Corral, Bird Cage Saloon and Museum of the West.

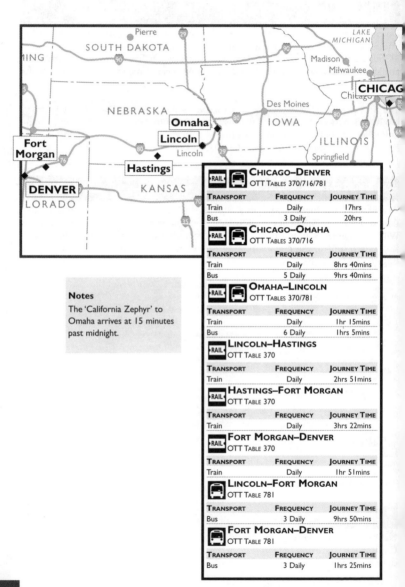

Notes

The 'California Zephyr' to Omaha arrives at 15 minutes past midnight.

CHICAGO–DENVER
OTT TABLES 370/716/781

TRANSPORT	FREQUENCY	JOURNEY TIME
Train	Daily	17hrs
Bus	3 Daily	20hrs

CHICAGO–OMAHA
OTT TABLES 370/716

TRANSPORT	FREQUENCY	JOURNEY TIME
Train	Daily	8hrs 40mins
Bus	5 Daily	9hrs 40mins

OMAHA–LINCOLN
OTT TABLES 370/781

TRANSPORT	FREQUENCY	JOURNEY TIME
Train	Daily	1hr 15mins
Bus	6 Daily	1hrs 5mins

LINCOLN–HASTINGS
OTT TABLE 370

TRANSPORT	FREQUENCY	JOURNEY TIME
Train	Daily	2hrs 51mins

HASTINGS–FORT MORGAN
OTT TABLE 370

TRANSPORT	FREQUENCY	JOURNEY TIME
Train	Daily	3hrs 22mins

FORT MORGAN–DENVER
OTT TABLE 370

TRANSPORT	FREQUENCY	JOURNEY TIME
Train	Daily	1hr 51mins

LINCOLN–FORT MORGAN
OTT TABLE 781

TRANSPORT	FREQUENCY	JOURNEY TIME
Bus	3 Daily	9hrs 50mins

FORT MORGAN–DENVER
OTT TABLE 781

TRANSPORT	FREQUENCY	JOURNEY TIME
Bus	3 Daily	1hrs 25mins

ON THE 'CALIFORNIA ZEPHYR'

A century ago pioneers used covered wagons to travel from Chicago to Denver. The 'California Zephyr' makes it much easier. As the train whirls along, the Chicago skyline melts into Illinois's prairies, America's heartland towns, Iowa and Nebraska's cornfields and through Omaha and Lincoln. Finally it climbs steadily to 'mile-high' Denver.

OMAHA

Although bustling Omaha has a diverse ethnic heritage, it is most famous for mouthwatering steaks. The city has come a long way from the sleepy, prairie outpost and transcontinental railway terminus. Trace its roots at the **Joselyn Art Museum** ($ 2200 Dodge St; open Tues–Sat 1000–1600, Sun 1200–1600) and **Mormon Trail Center** (3215 State St; open daily 0900–2100, free). The deer and the antelope still play, along with many exotic creatures, at the **Henry Doorly Zoo:** $$ open daily 0930–1700. The **Strategic Air Command Museum**: $$ 28210 West Park Hwy; open daily 0900–1700, has a collection of vintage aircraft and missiles. A turn-of-the-century atmosphere exists at the **Old Market** shops, and the beautifully landscaped grounds of **Boys Town**, founded in 1917 by Father Flanagan for troubled and homeless boys, are at 138th and Dodge Sts; open daily 0800–1630.

About a 15-minute bus ride on the No 2 Metro bus from Omaha, and the Iowa side of Missouri River, is Council Bluffs. Once a crossroads for the Lewis and Clark, Oregon, Mormon Pioneer and California Trails, crowds nowadays migrate to the gaming tables of its three casinos.

Omaha Convention and Visitors Bureau, 6800 Mercy Rd Ste 202; tel: (402) 444-4660 or (800) 332-1819; fax: (402) 444-4511; www.visitomaha.com.

The Amtrak station, at 9th and Pacific, is a mile from the downtown. Metro Area Transit schedules are available here, but as the train arrives in the middle of the night, taxis are the only means of transport from the station.

Best Western Metro Inn $$$ 3537 W. Broadway.
Hampton Inn-Central $$$ 301 S. 72nd St.
Holiday Inn $$$ 3321 S. 72nd St.

Gorats $$$ 49th and Center Sts; tel: (402) 551-3733.
Johnny's Café $$$ 4702 S. 27th St; tel: (402) 731-4774. Adjacent to this café are remnants of the old stockyards.

LINCOLN

Nebraska's capital shares much of its history with Omaha. Its crowning glory is the **Capitol** at 15th and K Sts, with its 400 ft gold dome: mosaics, marble and murals depicting Nebraska's history blanket almost every part of its interior. Entrance is free. Also free: a three-dimensional **brick train mural** on the wall at Haymarket and Iron Horse Park; **restored warehouses** with speciality shops and microbrewery (9th and P Sts), and the funky **Sheldon Museum and Sculpture Garden** (12th and R Sts).

The most interesting attractions are in Nebraska. For information, tel: (800) 228-4307 or visit the state website: www.ded.state.ne.us/tourism.html. One quirky sight en route, though, is in Iowa: Burlington's 275-foot Snake Alley is considered to be the crookedest street in the world.

Lincoln CVB; tel: (402)434-5335 or (800) 423-8212. The Amtrak station is at 7th and P Sts, and the **Visitors Center**, which has public transport timetables (StarTran) is on the other side of the building; tel: (402) 476-1234.

Cornhusker $$$$ 333 S. 13th St; tel: (800)793-7474.
Holiday Inn $$$$ 13th and M Sts; tel: (800) 405-4329. Walking distance from the station.

Valentine's Pizza $$ Local chain with four locations in town. Try the runzas, spices, ground beef, cabbage and onions baked inside homemade bread, a Nebraskan speciality.
Billy's Restaurant $$$ 1301 H St. One of Lincoln's finest, named after its native son, William Jennings Bryan.
The Green Mill $$$ at the Holiday Inn (see above). Has some of the best food in town.

HASTINGS

This little town has a great museum with an IMAX® cinema, planetarium, whooping cranes and a large exhibit on Edwin Perkins, inventor of Kool Aid. Another Hastings speciality, Eileen's Colossal Cookies, gives Mrs Field competition.

Adams County Convention and Visitors Center, tel: (800) 967-2189; www.hastingsnet.com/visitors.

FORT MORGAN

Fort Morgan Museum commemorates the life of big band leader Glen Miller, who spent his youth here. **Pawnee National Grassland**, about 50 miles north, has abundant wildlife and two huge buttes that erupt from shimmering grass-filled flatlands.

Fort Morgan Chamber of Commerce, tel: (907) 867-6702; www.fmchamber.org.

WHERE NEXT?

After Denver, the 'California Zephyr' snakes through the Rockies and across northern California to San Francisco *(see p. 358).*

The Mile High City is dwarfed by the Rocky Mountains but stands out in history as one of the main gold-rush centres of the 1860s. In fact, it was the first spot where small quantities of gold were discovered in the Colorado River. Back in those days, the town buzzed with fickle fortune-seekers. As it turned out, there was very little gold in Denver itself, and they left immediately when word came of a massive gold strike in Central City. Silver in the mountains caused the town to prosper again.

Nowadays Denver is both welcoming and enjoyable, a cosmopolitan city with a fine choice of recreational and cultural activities. Downtown Denver is formed from a regimental grid of tightly packed streets, and Lodo, or Lower Downtown, is a focus for shops, bars and cafés. To one side of the Civic Center Park, the State Capitol provides a stunning view of the Rockies, and to the other side the Denver Art Museum and the Colorado History Museum are two of the area's finest. Denver is not without its more curious attractions either: the Molly Brown House was home to 'unsinkable' Molly Brown, famous for surviving the Titanic, and Buffalo Bill's grave and museum at Lookout Mountain mark the final resting place of the famous showman William Cody.

GETTING THERE AND GETTING AROUND

Amtrak trains arrive on the north-west side of Denver, at the Old Union Station on Wynkoop St. Regular free buses run up and down 16th St pedestrian mall, one block away from the station, through the downtown area. There is also a light tram line which runs for 5 miles linking downtown and Broadway.

INFORMATION

Denver CVB, near the Capitol, 225 W. Colfax Ave; tel: (303) 892 1112; open Mon–Fri 0830–1700, Sat 0900–1700 (May–Sept); 0900–1300 (Oct–Apr). There is also an informal advice centre for travellers at the Greyhound terminal, 1055 19th St; open daily, mornings only.

SAFETY Denver is generally safe and friendly, but as with any other large city, take the usual common-sense precautions, such as not straying out of the well-lit downtown area at night. In case of emergency, the Denver Police Department is at 1331 Cherokee Street, tel: (303) 640-2011. Denver also has a large Department of Safety, with an information service, tel: (303) 640-5356

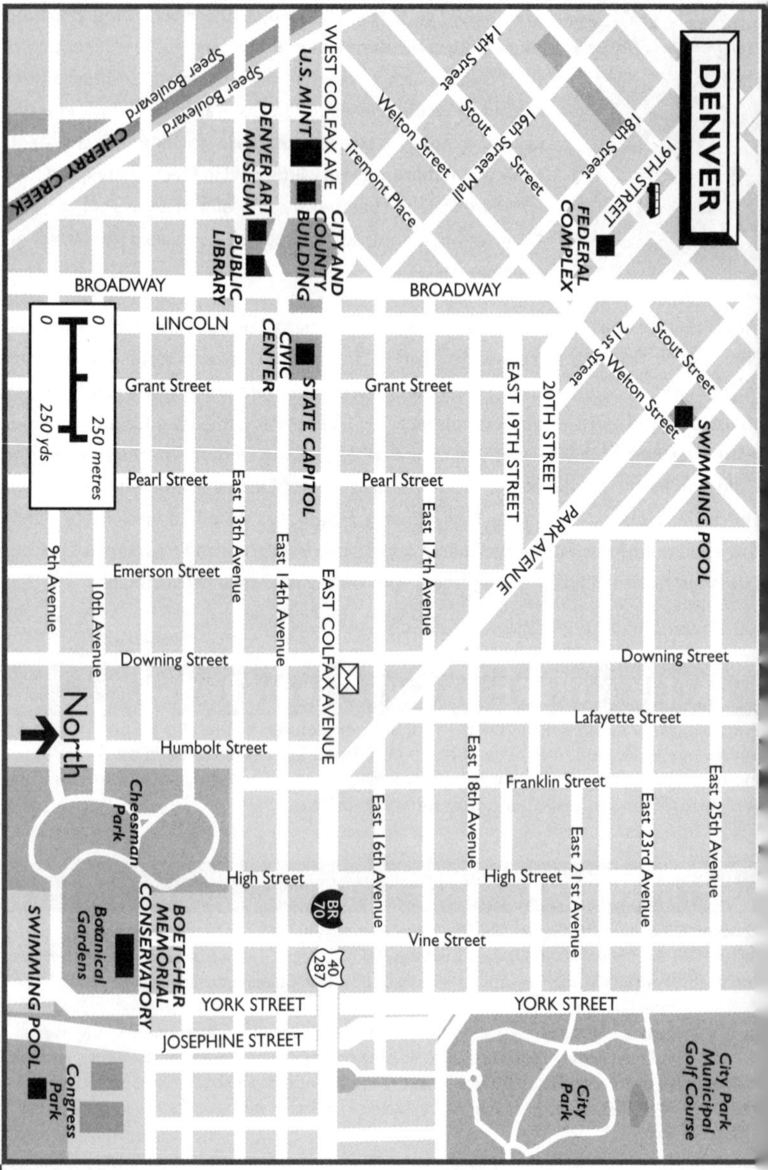
DENVER
19TH STREET
18th Street
14th Street
Stout Street
16th Street Mall
Welton Street
Tremont Place
WEST COLFAX AVE
U.S. MINT
DENVER ART MUSEUM
CITY AND COUNTY BUILDING
PUBLIC LIBRARY
FEDERAL COMPLEX
Speer Boulevard
Speer Boulevard
CHERRY CREEK
BROADWAY
BROADWAY
LINCOLN
CIVIC CENTER
STATE CAPITOL
Grant Street
Grant Street
Pearl Street
Pearl Street
Emerson Street
Downing Street
Downing Street
Humbolt Street
High Street
High Street
Vine Street
YORK STREET
YORK STREET
JOSEPHINE STREET
0 250 metres
0 250 yds
North
9th Avenue
10th Avenue
East 13th Avenue
East 14th Avenue
EAST COLFAX AVENUE
East 16th Avenue
East 17th Avenue
East 18th Avenue
EAST 19TH STREET
20TH STREET
East 21st Avenue
East 23rd Avenue
East 25th Avenue
PARK AVENUE
21st Street
Welton Street
Stout Street
SWIMMING POOL
Lafayette Street
Franklin Street
Cheesman Park
BOETCHER MEMORIAL CONSERVATORY
Botanical Gardens
SWIMMING POOL
Congress Park
BR 70
40 287
City Park
City Park Municipal Golf Course

MONEY Thomas Cook has a foreign exchange office at 299 Detroit St.

POST AND PHONES A conveniently-located post office, fairly close to the State Capitol building is 8275 E 11th Ave, tel: (303) 377-1016. Alternatively, try 1823 Stout St, or 951 20th St.

ACCOMMODATION

There is plenty of budget accommodation in Denver, ranging from hostels and B&Bs to freeway motels.

Adam's Mark Hotel $$$$ 1550 Court Place; tel: (303) 893-3333. Vast, luxurious establishment right in the centre of town.

Queen Anne Inn $$ 2147 Tremont Place; tel: (303) 296-6666. Only 14 rooms, but they are attractively themed and the inn is centrally located in pleasant park surroundings.

Franklin House B&B $ 1620 Franklin St; tel: (303) 331-9106. Simple accommodation a mile east of downtown.

The Denver International Youth Hostel $ 630 E. 16th Ave, four blocks from the centre; tel: (303) 331-9106.

FOOD

Denver has many themed Western steak and barbecue places, as well as many cosmopolitan restaurants. Try the Larimer Square area for a wide selection, or some of the city's brewpubs for good quality meals.

Josephina's $$$ 1433 Larimer St; tel: (303) 623-0166. Lively Italian restaurant with adjoining bar.

Tommy Tsunami's $$ 1432 Market St; tel: (303) 534-5050. Oriental cuisine, with trendy sushi and Thai.

St Mark's Coffeehouse $ 1416 Market St; tel: (303) 446-2925. Small but popular café good for cheap snacks and drinks.

HIGHLIGHTS

Standing proudly marking the centre of Denver is the **State Capitol** with its bright golden dome. Sited between Broadway and E. Colfax Ave, it is a copy of the one in Washington DC. For a 'mile high' view of the stunning Rocky Mountains, climb to the thirteenth step, which is exactly one mile above sea level. Inside, free tours are held Mon–Fri 0930–1530.

Mixed among the offices and shops of downtown Denver are some delightful original Victorian buildings, each with its own fascinating history. **Molly Brown House** was the home of an extraordinary survivor of the *Titanic*, who went on to become a suffragette and then ran for senator. Pictures taken in 1910 were used to restore the home with original family possessions and replicas, and ladies dressed in authentic turn-of-the-century costumes will guide visitors around. $ 1340 Pennsylvania Ave; open Tues–Sat 1000–1600, Sun 1200–1600.

THE LEGEND OF BUFFALO BILL

William F. Cody was a true character of the Wild West. Better known as Buffalo Bill for the thousands of buffalo that he killed, Cody became a national hero as a pony express rider, army scout and showman. Legend has it that early in his life he asked to be buried in Cody, but that its rich neighbour Denver 'stole' his body to bury it on Lookout Mountain. It is at this site today, above the Coors brewery, where you can find his grave and a modern museum alongside. The mountain affords some impressive views, and the museum displays buffalo rifles, clothing and Native American artwork.

The two namesakes of **Byers–Evans House**, John Evans and William Byers, were instrumental figures in the early growth of Denver. Byers was publisher of the *Rocky Mountain News* and Evans was Colorado's second territorial governor. They both worked tirelessly to ensure that the railway came to the city. The house was originally the property of Byers, but was sold to Evans' son in 1889. Today it contains most of the original elegant furnishings, and a tour of the house commences with a short film that tells all about the careers of these successful men. $ 1310 Bannock St; tel: (303) 620-4933.

The third house to see is **Pearce McAllister Cottage**. Built for mining engineer Harold Pearce, it was purchased by Henry McAllister in 1955, who was considered to be one of the most brilliant legal minds of his time. The building is a bright pumpkin yellow and is a fine example of the Colonial Revival period. $ 1880 Gaylord Dr.; tel: (303) 322-3704.

Northwest of downtown, at 320 W. Colfax Ave, is the **US Mint**, which conducts free tours Mon–Fri 0800–1435. Visitors can see millions of new coins emerging from the presses, before they are sorted, counted and bagged. Underneath the mint is the National Treasure of $100 million in solid gold bars, hidden securely in the basement behind steel framework. Don't get too many ideas, though – outside the mint machine gun turrets still guard, left over from when they were set up in the Depression.

Denver also has a wealth of museums. The **Denver Art Museum** in Civic Center Park holds examples of native American craftwork and pre-Columbian art, with many pieces by the Plains and Hopi tribes; $ (free Sat). At 1300 Broadway, the **Colorado History Museum** has several dioramas in the lower galleries depicting

THRILLS AND SPILLS

On the western edge of the city the **Elitch Gardens theme park** provides entertainment for children and adults alike, and has an extensive water park. Open daily in summer 1000–2200 (Fri–Sat until 2300). It is surprisingly close to the city, and can be reached either by a bike path along Cherry Creek or on the Cultural Connections Trolley. The park has some scary rides, the Tower of Doom, a freefall vertical drop of 70 ft, being a particular favourite of the brave – or the foolhardy.

historical scenes, including pictures of the Anasazi of Mesa Verde, and of trappers meeting with Indians at a 'Wilderness Fair'. $ Open Mon–Sat 1000–1630, Sun 1200–1630.

Two or three miles east of central Denver, between 17th and 23rd Aves and York St and Colorado Blvd, en route to the airport, is City Park. Here is undoubtedly the cream of the museums, the inventive **Denver Museum of Natural History** ($). It is internationally recognised for its travelling exhibits and scientific research programmes, and has over 90 wildlife habitat dioramas. Take a peek at the Watering Hole exhibit in the Botswana African Hall, or sample another extreme of the globe at the Alaskan exhibit. Entering the Hall of Life you will receive a 'life card', which will activate various interactive displays showing how life begins, and can provide you with a printout of information on your own vital statistics at the end of your visit. In the Dinosaur Hall, fossils draw you back to the times of the stegosaurus, tyrannosaurus rex and friends. The IMAX® theatre adds to the sense of adventure – it is equipped with a booming sound system and a 4 ft high screen and creates a breathtaking illusion of trips around the world, including stunning shots of the Grand Canyon and Stonehenge. Elsewhere in this large museum, the Planetarium shows displays of the night sky through the seasons.

A BASEBALL FRENZY

Baseball is an American institution and is one of the cheapest sports to watch (usually well under $10 for a seat). The pitcher begins play when he throws the ball upwards, at hundreds of miles an hour, towards the catcher, who crouches behind 'home plate'. A batter from the opposing team, positioned before home plate, then tries to intercept the ball and hit it into 'fair territory'. With a successful hit the batter races through the sequence of bases set at the corners of a 90-ft square diamond before the opposing team can touch the base or runner with the ball (the game has echoes of rounders and cricket). There are nine players on each side, who bat in rotation; games usually last two to three hours and are kept lively by the incessant chanting, singing and waving from the enthusiastic crowd.

Denver's own major league baseball team is the Colorado Rockies, whose home is Coors Field, 2001 Blake St. Their first game in this new stadium in 1993 served as a reminder of their popularity, attracting the highest attendance in baseball history. For ticket information, tel: (303) ROCKIES.

Also in City Park is **Denver Zoo**, well on the way to becoming a first-class natural environment park. Animals are housed in their natural habitats, rather than in traditional cages. $ tel: (303) 331-4110.

By the gates of the zoo, visitors are greeted by a simulated African savannah scene, dotted with giraffes, zebras and warthogs; there are also two okapis, a species rarely seen in North America. You cannot avoid Bear Mountain, created with the first artificial rockwork in any American zoo, which offers all the home comforts that Grizzly and Himalayan Black Bears need. The zoo also has a large selection of primates, a tantalising Tropical Discovery feature and an Australian wildlife exhibit. Check feeding times when you arrive at the park. There is a Zooliner train for non-stop guided tours of the zoo's 76 acres.

NIGHTLIFE

At night, the brewpubs in downtown Denver open up and the city centre becomes a hive of activity. At **Beckenridge Brewery**, 2220 Blake St, you can watch the beers being brewed on site as you drink. Nearby **El Chapultepec**, 20th and Market St, is a tiny, popular venue, where there is nightly live jazz and the occasional visit from a big name.

Twelve miles west of Denver is **Red Rocks Amphitheater**, which has been the setting for thousands of rock and classical concerts. Open free of charge during the day.

DAY TRIPS

Travelling around Colorado is easy: many bus services link Denver airport to the most popular resorts, including Aspen, Colorado Springs, Rocky Mountain National Park and Steamboat Springs. Book them as far in advance as possible: for information on Denver transport and links elsewhere, tel: (303) 299-000.

For a one-day ski trip catch the morning Ski Train, tel: (303) 639-1111, from the airport to **Winter Park** for a selection of slopes varying in difficulty, or to pick up the basics at the innovative Discovery/Learn-to-Ski Park.

THE BEST POWDER SNOW IN THE WORLD

Averaging 20 or 30 ft of snow and 300 days of sunshine a year, Colorado has a total of 27 ski areas and a ski season that runs from end Nov to mid-Apr. Two of the most popular resorts are Aspen and Vail: celebrities and film stars flock to enjoy the steep, lengthy runs and powder snow that have made the slopes world famous. Fashionable **Aspen** has four mountains dedicated to skiing which cater for all grades of skier, from Aerobic Avenue for the fitter enthusiasts to the beginners' favourite, Snowmass. **Vail**, king of the North American ski hills, also has a special park for snowboarders (see also p. 365).

COLORADO SPRINGS Colorado Springs was originally developed as a vacation spot in 1871 by the railway tycoon William Jackson Palmer. Nowadays it is the most popular town in south-east Colorado and provides excellent access to the gold mining country around. There are a number of cheap flights from Denver International Airport, or you can use the Greyhound Bus service, which stops downtown at 327 Weber St.

On the western edge of the city, the amazing **Garden of the Gods** is a twisted park of red sandstone rockery which has been eroded into finely balanced overhangs, pinnacles and pedestals.

Colorado Springs sits at the foot of **Pikes Peak**. Ride up to the summit, at 14,110 ft, on the cog railway (see p. 359).

CRIPPLE CREEK **Cripple Creek**, named after a calf that broke its leg trying to jump over a tumbling stream, is a gold camp which rests in a grim volcanic bowl just by Pikes Peak. In 1890, with the discovery of gold, Cripple Creek became a boom town. In its heyday it boasted two opera houses, a stock exchange, 75 saloons, eight newspapers and a large variety of brothels. Nowadays visitors still try to strike it rich at Cripple Creek's gambling casinos.

Ride the **Cripple Creek and Victor Narrow Gauge Railroad** into the heart of the gold mining district, $$ open daily 1000–1700 (June–mid-Oct); or descend 1000 ft underground into the **Molly Kathleen Mine** ($$) to learn what the rush was all about. Take your own walk into the past or join a **Ghost Walk Tour** of Cripple Creek or Mount Pisgah Cemetery Tour ($$).

WHERE NEXT?

The Colorado Driving Loop (see p. 362) explores more of the state's dramatic landscape. Denver is a major stop on the 'California Zephyr' which runs westwards to San Francisco or east to Chicago (see pp. 430 and 482).

The **Visitor Center**, 104 Cascade St, Colorado Springs; tel: (719) 635-7506, is open summer 0900–1700, and has details of hiking trails..

For tours and maps of Cripple Creek check out the **Cripple Creek Welcome Center**, 337 East Bennett Ave; tel: (877) 858-GOLD.

Old Colorado City, 4 miles west of Colorado Springs, offers the widest choice of accommodation. Try:

The Heartstone Inn B&B, 506 N. Cascade St; tel: 719 473 4413.

In Cripple Creek, cheap casino accommodation is plentiful; but for a more luxurious, traditional stay a delightful alternative is:

Imperial Hotel, 123 N. 3rd St, tel: (719) 689-2922.

There are also plenty of value places to eat.

Henri's Mexican, 2427 W. Colorado Ave, Colorado Springs; tel: 719 634 9031, is famous in the region for its fine selection of home-cooked food served up with margaritas.

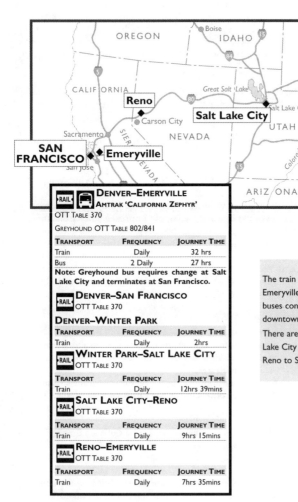

DENVER–EMERYVILLE

AMTRAK 'CALIFORNIA ZEPHYR'

OTT TABLE 370

GREYHOUND OTT TABLE 802/841

TRANSPORT	FREQUENCY	JOURNEY TIME
Train	Daily	32 hrs
Bus	2 Daily	27 hrs

Note: Greyhound bus requires change at Salt Lake City and terminates at San Francisco.

DENVER–SAN FRANCISCO

OTT TABLE 370

DENVER–WINTER PARK

TRANSPORT	FREQUENCY	JOURNEY TIME
Train	Daily	2hrs

WINTER PARK–SALT LAKE CITY

OTT TABLE 370

TRANSPORT	FREQUENCY	JOURNEY TIME
Train	Daily	12hrs 39mins

SALT LAKE CITY–RENO

OTT TABLE 370

TRANSPORT	FREQUENCY	JOURNEY TIME
Train	Daily	9hrs 15mins

RENO–EMERYVILLE

OTT TABLE 370

TRANSPORT	FREQUENCY	JOURNEY TIME
Train	Daily	7hrs 35mins

The train terminates at Emeryville and Amtrak thruway buses connect with Oakland and downtown San Francisco.

There are also 2 buses from Salt Lake City and 12 buses from Reno to San Francisco.

ON THE 'CALIFORNIA ZEPHYR'

The western half of the 'California Zephyr' route winds through the glorious mountain and desert scenery of Colorado, Utah, Nevada and California; it's pure joy just to sit and gape at the stunning panorama of the western USA. From Denver, the train wiggles uphill into the Rockies, where the first port of call is the ski centre of Winter Park. Westwards, the train follows the majestic Colorado River before crossing into Utah. Salt Lake City, the prosperous Mormon-built metropolis, is a good place to break the journey. Piling on across the salt flats, the 'Zephyr' slips into the haunting brown hills of Nevada, where the all-absorbing desert maintains a firm grasp on the eyes, all the way to the casinos of Reno. Sierra Nevada peaks loom to the west, and the train rolls through Californian Gold Rush country on its way to Oakland, on San Francisco Bay.

WINTER PARK

Excellent skiing and luxuriant summer hikes are eminently achievable by public transport in the Rockies. The train stops in Fraser, in the hills some 60 miles northwest of Denver, and shuttle buses connect to Winter Park, 5 miles south, and surrounding resorts. Contact the **Winter Park/Fraser Valley Chamber of Commerce**, tel: (800) 903-7275; www.winterpark-info.com, to help plan a visit.

SALT LAKE CITY

Utah's capital is easily the biggest city within a radius of several hundred miles. A relaxed, friendly place founded by independent-minded Mormons in 1847, it has little to detain the average visitor, but those with an interest in the Mormons' history and faith will find plenty of museums and monuments. Its position, at the base of the gorgeous Wasatch Mountains, and its pleasant climate, make it a superb base for nearby ski resorts – part of the reason it was chosen for the 2002 Winter Olympics.

The city centre is compact, with the greatest concentration of sights in Temple Sq. This landscaped park contains the city's most noteworthy building, the **Salt Lake Temple**, spiritual heart of the Mormon Church. Only Mormons can go inside, and then only at high ceremonies, but the grandiose stone spires do instil inspiration. Also on the square, the **Mormon Tabernacle** is the domed home of the Mormon Tabernacle Choir, whom you can hear singing on Sun mornings at 0930, or during evening rehearsals (Thur from 2000). For more on the Mormons, visit the **Museum of Church History and Art**, which lays out the trials and travails of these dynamic people. Open Mon–Fri 0900–2100, Sat–Sun 1000–1900; free. Salt Lake City's tallest building, appropriately enough, is the **Latter-day Saints Church Office Building** at 50 E. North Temple St, with an observation deck on the 26th floor.

THE MORMONS

The Mormon faith, or the Church of Jesus Christ of Latter-day Saints, has a fascinating history. The church was founded in 1830, when Joseph Smith claims to have discovered a set of golden tablets in upstate New York. From these, he transcribed the Book of Mormon, which the faith holds to be a restoration of the Bible in a purer form. His most important follower, Brigham Young, set up colonies in New York and further west, but was constantly hounded by more entrenched religions and the government. After a skirmish in St Louis, Young led his flock to the Salt Lake basin, where they established a semi-autonomous territory.

The Mormons are often misunderstood, largely because their services are strictly reserved for church members only, and because many people associate Mormonism with polygamy – Brigham Young had no fewer than 55 wives – though the practice was banned within the church over a century ago. Young Mormon missionaries actively travel the world, and the Mormon trademarks of clean living and a friendly, welcoming spirit endure.

Just north of Temple Sq., the **Utah State Capitol**, 400 N. State St, is a fine example of Renaissance revival architecture, and contains exhibits on Utah's history. On the edge of town, towards the hills, **Old Desert Village**, 2601 Sunnyside Ave, reconstructs early Mormon life in the area. $ Open Tues–Sat 1100–1700 (Thur until 2000).

SIDE TRIPS

The Great Salt Lake itself, north-west of the city, is the second saltiest reservoir in the world after the Dead Sea. With a car, you can visit the shores at Great Salt Lake State Park, west on I-80.

Utah sports some of the very best skiing in the world, and Salt Lake City is wonderfully close to the slopes. **Park City** and **Alta**, among others, are within easy striking distance, and the Utah Transit Authority, tel: (801) 287-4636, provides van service to various resorts in winter.

Visitor Information Center, 90 S. West Temple; tel: (801) 534-4974; open Mon–Fri 0800–1700 (until 1800 in summer), Sat 0900–1700, Sun 1000–1700. Two useful websites to inspect are www.slctravel.com and www.saltlake.org.

The Amtrak station is fairly central, at 320 S. Rio Grande St, but as both eastbound and westbound trains arrive at unsocial hours, take a taxi from the station.

Salt Lake City has a good variety of accommodation, but you should book in advance, especially in winter.
Camp VIP campsite is a longish walk from the centre: 1400 W. North Temple; tel: (801) 328-0224 or (800) 226-7752.
The Avenues Hostel $ 107 F St; tel: (801) 359-3855 or (888) 884-4752. HI hostel five blocks east of Temple Sq.; can help with bike and ski rental.
Anton Boxrud B&B $$–$$$$ 57 S. 600 E St; tel: (801) 363-8035 or (800) 524-5511. Pleasant and just east of Temple Sq.
Peery Hotel $$$ 110 W. 300 S St; tel: (801) 521-4300 or (800) 331-0073. Long-established hotel filled with antiques.

Bill and Nada's Café $–$$ 479 S. 600 E St. Well-entrenched 24-hour diner; no alcohol.

Oasis Café $$ 151 S. 500 E St. Marvellous outdoor vegetarian dining.
Red Iguana $$–$$$ 736 W. North Temple. Great authentic Mexican food, appropriate to this part of the South-west.
Old Salt City Jail Restaurant $$$–$$$$ 460 S. 1000 E St. In the former city penitentiary; steaks and salad bar a speciality.

RENO

Reno's slogan, 'The Biggest Little City in the World', blazes from a neon arch downtown casino district. Little, but growing rapidly thanks to casinos and commerce, Reno is a mini-Las Vegas. If you're not hitting the casinos, you could take a stroll down the prettily developed central riverfront, or learn more about this rather exotic state in the **Nevada Historical Society Museum**, 1650 N. Virginia St, which displays Native American artefacts, pioneer relics, antique furniture, guns and minerals.

SIDE TRIP

Lake Tahoe is one of the playgrounds of the West, sitting at the crook in the California-Nevada border. Only a few miles south-west of Reno, Tahoe's clear, cold waters are rimmed with world-class resorts, and skiing and boating opportunities abound. Reno visitor centre is really helpful in arranging visits.

The **Visitor Center** at 3rd St and Virginia Ave; tel: (888) HIT-RENO; www.playreno.com, is great for general information and advice on accommodation.

The Amtrak station is downtown, at 135 East Commericial Row; tel: (702) 329-8638.

There are plenty of central places to stay in all categories along Virginia Ave and Lake St. Casinos offer good room values midweek, but prices jump dramatically at the weekend. The leading light is **El Dorado** $$$–$$$$ 4th St and Virginia Ave; tel: (800) 648-5996.

The local speciality cuisine, oddly enough, is Basque, thanks to generations of Basque shepherds who have settled across Nevada. The best is:
Louis' Basque Corner $$–$$$ 301 4th St.

SIERRA NEVADA AND THE GOLD RUSH

Gold was first discovered in the Sierra Nevada in 1848, prompting a massive surge westwards that turned San Francisco and other cities into frenzied supply stops. Towns popped up overnight as fortune-seekers panned the rivers and bored deep into the hills in search of the precious metal, but the cost of mining rose to such a high that within twenty years most towns had gone bust and were abandoned. Many of these remain as ghost towns today – some restored, some simply faded relics, amid the dry brown Sierra Nevada hills.

Colorado Driving Loop

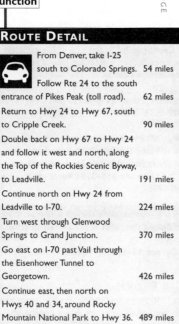

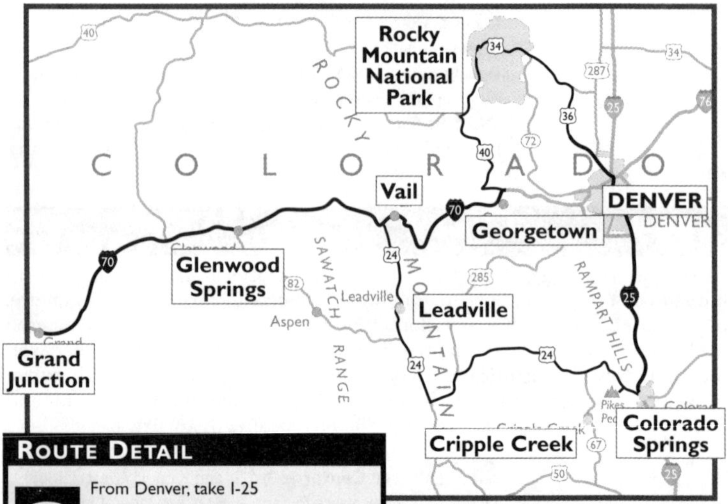

Route Detail

From Denver, take I-25 south to Colorado Springs.	54 miles
Follow Rte 24 to the south entrance of Pikes Peak (toll road).	62 miles
Return to Hwy 24 to Hwy 67, south to Cripple Creek.	90 miles
Double back on Hwy 67 to Hwy 24 and follow it west and north, along the Top of the Rockies Scenic Byway, to Leadville.	191 miles
Continue north on Hwy 24 from Leadville to I-70.	224 miles
Turn west through Glenwood Springs to Grand Junction.	370 miles
Go east on I-70 past Vail through the Eisenhower Tunnel to Georgetown.	426 miles
Continue east, then north on Hwys 40 and 34, around Rocky Mountain National Park to Hwy 36.	489 miles
Follow Hwy 36 south to Denver.	549 miles

Denver–Colorado Springs

Bus TNMO OTT Table 786/813

Denver–Colorado Springs OTT Table 786/813

Transport	Frequency	Journey Time
Bus	9 Daily	1hr 50mins

Denver–Grand Junction

Bus TNMO and Greyhound OTT Table 786/820/842

Denver–Vail

OTT Table 820

Transport	Frequency	Journey Time
Bus	4 Daily	2hrs 10mins

Vail–Glenwood Spring

OTT Table 820

Transport	Frequency	Journey Time
Bus	4 Daily	1hrs 30mins

Glenwood Springs–Grand Junction OTT Table 820

Transport	Frequency	Journey Time
Bus	4 Daily	3hrs 40mins

Denver–Grand Junction

OTT Table 786/820/842

Transport	Frequency	Journey Time
Bus	6 Daily	5hrs 50mins

On the road west, red rocks rise like sleeping giants and the pyramid-topped mountains level off to giant mesas. Bighorn sheep, elk and other abundant wildlife call its soaring heights and steep chasms home. Century-old towns, like Leadville and Cripple Creek, tell tales which parallel the rise and fall of this breathtaking topography. Smart ski resorts dot the landscape near former dinosaur domains.

BE PREPARED

Dress in layers – mountain weather systems change rapidly. Because of inclement weather, many attractions are only open end May–early Oct; check with individual visitor centres.

PIKES PEAK

Pikes Peak is a 19-mile highway to the clouds. Travelling from above the treeline, through granite fields and tundra, it passes through four climate zones to a height of 14,110 ft ($$). For the last 100 years, it has also been possible to reach the summit aboard the **Pikes Peak Cog Railway**. Reservations required; $$$ tel: (719) 685-5401.

CRIPPLE CREEK

EN ROUTE

The US Air Force Academy just off exit 156B of I-25 has free tours. Further south, take exit 146 to view the strange red rock formations at the Garden of the Gods (also free).

After Colorado Springs, possible stops along the way include the Anasazi Cliff Dwellings at Manitou Springs ($$) and the Cave of the Winds ($$).

CRIPPLE CREEK

A detour south along Hwy 67 will take you to the old gold-mining town of Cripple Creek. Casinos are now the main game in town since gambling was legalised here a decade ago (see p. 357).

LEADVILLE

Another boom town, Leadville certainly has had its ups and downs. At 10,152 ft above sea level, it is the highest incorporated town in the USA. In the 1860s, when over $5 million of gold was extracted from the nearby California Gulch, it became a town of high crime and high rollers. Gunman-gamblers like Bat Masterson, Wyatt Earp and Doc Holliday came here to ply their trade. J. J. Brown, husband of 'the unsinkable' Molly, made his fortune from the mines, and Guggenheim maintained a residence here. The downs came when the minerals ran out. Now Leadville is a working man's town with only memories of its glory days. The **National Mining Hall of Fame and Museum** $, 120 W. 9th St, showcases Leadville's mining past, and other historic buildings and recreational trails make the town worth a visit.

EN ROUTE

As it continues west, I-70 passes numerous ski areas before it becomes enveloped in the rugged red rocks of **Glenwood Canyon**. Bighorn sheep often graze alongside the road. The trail to **Hanging Lake** is steep – 1000 ft up in 1 mile – but the scenery is worth the effort.

Leadville Chamber of Commerce, tel: (888) LEADVILLE; www.leadvilleusa.com.

The Delaware $$$ 700 Harrison Ave.; tel: (800) 748-2004. Charming century-old hotel echoes Leadville's glory days – Butch Cassidy was once a guest. Breakfast included in cost.

GLENWOOD SPRINGS

The hot springs that gave this town its name are welcome after a strenuous hike. Soak away aches and pains in the **Glenwood Springs Hot Springs Pools** $$, N. River St; open daily 0730–2200 in summer; 0900–2200 in winter. If that is not enough, visit **Yampah Spa** $$ – their vapour caves were once a Ute Indian hot spot. There are also full spa services – their herbal wraps ($$$) will make you feel like a human burrito; tel: (970) 945-0667. Inside Glenwood's **Fairy Caves**, delicate crystal formations adorn limestone walls. $$ tel: (970) 945-6511; open late May–early Sept; reservations required.

Visitor Centre at 1102 Grand Ave; tel: (970) 945 6589; or try www.glenwoodguide.com.

Ramada Inn and Suites $$$–$$$$, exit 16 of I-70. Lovely rooms and friendly atmosphere, with continental breakfast.

GRAND JUNCTION

There are diverse attractions hidden in the valley of the Grand Junction area, from award-winning wineries (near Hwy 6 in Palisade) to dinosaur remains. The **Dinosaur Discovery Museum** in Fruita (Rte 6) chronicles history from 4.5 billion years ago to moon rocks. Huge creatures move and moan as hands-on exhibits familiarise kids with the extinct giants. The whimsical variety of Main Street's **Art on the Corner** sculpture in Grand Junction itself runs the gamut from bike-riding dinosaurs to a huge junk-crafted motorcycle.

The big draw of the region, however, is its natural beauty. From the Colorado River's Grand Valley, **Rim Rock Drive** (Rte 340) ascends the high country of Colorado National Monument ($). Its 23-mile journey around steep canyons and red rock sculptures is reminiscent of both the Grand Canyon (see p. 386) and Bryce national parks. Dinosaur fossils were found on Dinosaur Hill (Rte 340), so undiscovered treasure may still await any hiker or cyclist.

The **Grand Mesa Scenic and Historic Byway** (exit 46 from I-70) curves alongside imposing rock formations, then gradually ascends to the world's largest table mountain. Snow, trails and 300 lakes cover Grand Mesa's 10,839 ft summit.

The Visitor Center is found at I-70 and Horizon Dr., tel: (970) 244-1480. Open daily 0830–1700 (–2000 in summer).

Los Altos B&B $$$–$$$$ 375 Hillview Dr.; tel: (888) 774-0982; www.colorado-bnb.com/losaltos. Perched atop a high mesa, this solitary B&B offers spectacular views, great breakfasts and friendly atmosphere.

The Winery $$$ 642 Main St. Excellent food (dinner only) in an attractive atmosphere.
Crystal Café and Bake Shop $$ 314 Main St. Yummy Portobello mushroom sandwiches with pesto mayonnaise, cinnamon rolls and scones. Friendly service. Open Mon–Sat for breakfast and lunch only.
Rock Slide Brew Pub $$ 401 Main St. Tasty food and beer.

Where Next?

If you want to head west from Grand Junction instead of returning to Denver, it is 100 miles to Arches National Park (see South Utah National Parks chapter p. 390). Take I-70 for 80 miles to Crescent Junction, then head south along Hwy 191.

VAIL

Vail is not left out in the cold after the ski season: hikers, mountain bikers and white-water rafters still populate the area in summer. Within the quaint village itself is the **Ski Museum Hall of Fame**, while the **Betty Ford Alpine Gardens**, near S. Frontage Rd, has over 2000 species of native plants; both free. **Gerald Ford Amphitheater**, next to the gardens, hosts music festivals, ballets and free Tues night concerts.

Much of Vail's landscape is being lost to million-dollar homes but the sweeping beauty of the Gore Range is unsullied as it unfurls at **Eagle's Nest**. The ride up is via the Vista-Bahn Express chairlift (free; closed late April–June).

Contact Vail Valley Tourism and Convention Bureau, 100 E. Meadow Dr.; tel: (800) 525-3875; www.visitvailvalley.com for reservations, rafting companies and tourist information.

During summer and shoulder seasons, many restaurants offer half-price menus.

En Route

The Eisenhower Tunnel penetrates the mountains near the watershed of the Continental Divide. All North American waters and melting snow west of the Divide flow towards the Pacific, and those on the east side flow towards the Atlantic.

GEORGETOWN

Past and present merge in Georgetown (exit 228 from

I-70). Mining brought money and the railway from Denver brought the people. It is still the ordinary Western town it was a century ago – that is its charm. Visitors can ride into yesterday aboard the **Georgetown Loop Railroad** which climbs 600 ft on its way to Silver Plume ($$$). Antique shops, boutiques and art galleries are housed within 6th St's renovated Victorian buildings. The furnishings and exhibits in the once-smart **Hotel de Paris** $, at the street's east end, reflect century-old business life. Catch a glimpse of how Georgetown's wealthy lived at **Hamill House**, where original furniture and wallpaper still adorn the rooms; $ 3rd and Argentine Sts. The **Georgetown Energy Museum**, at the east end of 6th St, is within the plant which has powered the town since 1900 (free).

Most attractions operate only late May–early Oct. Over the first two weekends in Dec, an arts and crafts Christmas Market, carollers and holiday foods bring the town back to life.

For tourist information which has lodging and dining details tel: (800) 472-8230; www.georgetowncolorado.com.

1025 Rose Street $$$. Tasty food at reasonable prices. **Happy Cooker** $$ 6th St. Snacks and sandwiches.

ROCKY MOUNTAIN NATIONAL PARK

The park ($$ per car) is a mecca for hikers, bikers and drivers who enjoy stunning scenery. Alpine lakes, steep canyons, tundra, towering mountains, wildflowers and wildlife embellish **Trail Ridge Rd**, a byway traversing the park that has been used for about 10,000 years. Bighorn sheep graze near **Sheep Lakes**. Viewpoints on **Many Parks Curve** reveal mountain meadows vistas, and 2500 ft below Forest Canyon there is a spectacular view of a glacier-chiselled valley. Walk slowly at Rock Cut (altitude 12,110 ft) to **Toll Memorial Mountain Index**. A dazzling 360° view, strange rock formations, tundra and craggy peaks await you.

Lulu City is the site of an old mining town, while the **Moraine Park Museum** offers regional history. The 7-mile **Wild Basin Trail** takes you along the St Vrain Creek, around waterfalls and through spruce forests.

Rocky Mountain national Park, Estes Park CO 80517; tel: (970) 586-1333 or (970) 586-1200.

Yellowstone is nature's giant cauldron. It steams, spits, bubbles and burps amid an untamed landscape of deep canyons, craggy peaks, petrified forests, vast woodlands, alpine lakes and rushing waterfalls.

It took two million years and three volcanic eruptions to produce the world's oldest national park. Volcanic activity caused the central portion to collapse, and a caldera (depression) 28 miles by 47 miles was created. The same magnetic heat that caused previous eruptions continues to energise Yellowstone's hot springs, fumaroles (steam vents), spewing mud pots and geysers today.

In 1988, a great fire torched over 990,000 acres. It opened the forest canopy, and gave Yellowstone's ecosystem a new start. Vegetation has regenerated, and the Yellowstone still has the greatest variety of wildlife in the lower 48 states. Mule deer, bighorn sheep, moose, bald eagles, ospreys, trumpeter swans, elk, wolves, bison and grizzly bears reside amid a diverse landscape.

GETTING THERE AND GETTING AROUND

Tucked away in the north-west corner of Wyoming, the park has five entrances:

North Entrance, along Hwy 89 from I-90 at Livingston, Montana;
North-east Entrance, along Hwy 212 from I-90 at Billings, Montana or Hwy 296 from Cody, Wyoming;
West Entrance, from Hwy 191 from Bozeman, Montana or US Hwy 20 from Idaho Falls, Idaho;
East Entrance: US Hwy 16 from Cody, Wyoming;
South Entrance: US Hwy 89 from Jackson, Wyoming.

Entrance passes ($$–$$$ per person, per vehicle or per snowmobile) are for seven days and include Grand Teton National Parks (see p. 373).

There is no public transport available within the park, but from the end of May to mid-Sept, Amfac provides motorcoach tours from lodges, campsites, Mammoth and Gardiner, Montana ($$$). Self-guided auto audio tours can be rented for a half-day or for 24 hours ($$$). Trekking some of the 1000 miles of hiking trails, climbing aboard a stagecoach at Roosevelt Ranch ($$$), horse-riding ($$$) and cycling are alternative ways of discovering the park's wildlife and panoramas.

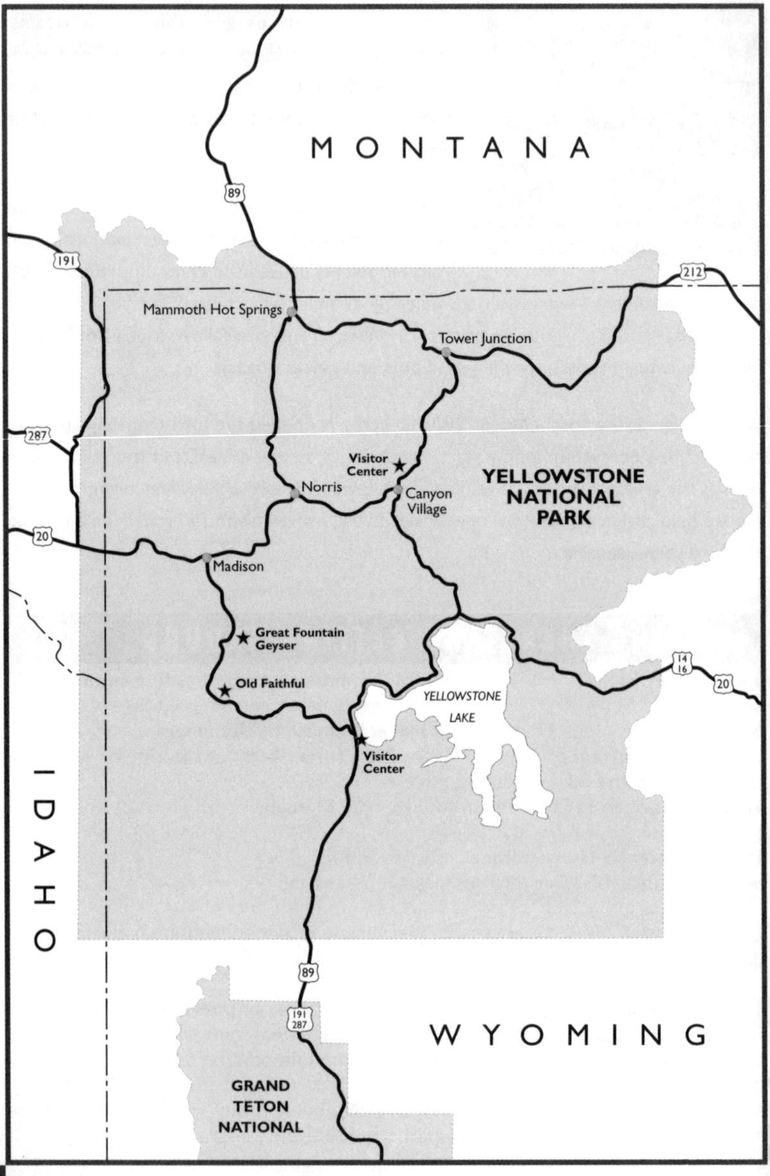
MONTANA
89
191
212
Mammoth Hot Springs
Tower Junction
287
Visitor Center
Norris
Canyon Village
YELLOWSTONE NATIONAL PARK
20
Madison
Great Fountain Geyser
Old Faithful
YELLOWSTONE LAKE
14 16
20
Visitor Center
IDAHO
89
191 287
WYOMING
GRAND TETON NATIONAL

INFORMATION

For general information before your visit contact **Wyoming Business Council Tourism Division**, tel: (800) 225-5996 or (307) 344-7381 (National Park Service Switchboard); www.nps.gov/yell/parkhigh.htm. Check with the park service for areas accessible to visitors with disabilities; tel: (307) 344-2109. TDD Access (307) 344-5395.

To promote understanding of the park's natural wonders, the **Yellowstone Institute** at Lamar Buffalo Ranch offers outdoor programmes for families and all age groups. Contact PO Box 117, Yellowstone National Park, WY 82190; tel: (307) 344-2294.

In addition to accommodation booking (see below), Amfac handles permits for fishing, boating and backpacking. Reservations should be made as early as possible; tel: (307) 344-7311.

Yellowstone has five visitor centres – **Albright** at Mammoth Hot Springs, **Old Faithful**, **Canyon**, **Grant** at the west shore of Yellowstone Lake, and **Fishing Bridge**, as well as information stations scattered throughout the developed areas of the park. Activity information is provided in English, German, French, Spanish and Japanese. Hours of operation vary.

WHEN TO GO

It is still cold, wet and snowy during May and June, but this is the time to see newborn wildlife. To see an abundance of people come between July and Aug. In Sept–Oct you will see more wildlife and fewer tourists. Snow closes most roads by Nov, except the route between the north and north-east entrances. Between mid-Dec and mid-Mar, when the park is a vision of snow, steam and ice, it is open for snowmobiling and cross-country skiing. Old Faithful Snowlodge is the only accommodation open. From 1 Mar to 1 May the park is closed for ploughing.

At whatever season, be prepared for unpredictable weather. Dress in layers and carry sunscreen, rain gear and insect repellent.

Each centre offers regional cultural and nature programmes. Ranger-led activities include hikes and nature walks. In busy parts of the park, 'Roving Rangers' are available to answer questions.

MONEY Gardiner and West Yellowstone have banks, and there are cash dispensers at Old Faithful Inn, Lake Yellowstone Hotel and Canyon Lodge. Foreign currency exchange is available at park lodges Mon–Fri 0800–1700.

SAFETY Touching thermal pools or getting too near geysers is dangerous. Lake, river and stream water is unsafe to drink without boiling. Do not try to feed the animals – view them from a distance. Stay on the trails to avoid tick bites (see p. 493).

ACCOMMODATION

Facilities open at the beginning of May. Old Faithful Inn stays open until 17 Oct, but the others, except for Old Faithful Snow Lodge, close in Sept.

Although some lodge rooms are cheap to moderate, most are expensive. Cabins range from cheap, with shared bath, to moderate. Contact **Amfac**, which handles lodging and camping; tel: (307) 344-7311 or book on the web at www.travelyellowstone.com. Outside the north-east gate are several moderately priced motels, including Comfort Inn and four Best Westerns (see p. 504).

CAMPING

Campsites ($) are located close to the lodges, but they are usually full by noon. Fishing Bridge has RV hookups, but because it is bear habitat, RVs must be hardsided. For camping information, tel: (307) 344-2114. Supplies are available at Hamilton Stores and photoshops throughout the park.

Yellowstone Canyon Village Lodge and Cabins $$$–$$$$

Lake Lodge and Cabins. The 1920s-style sunroom of this 100-year-old property has a spectacular view of Lake Yellowstone. There are cabins ($$$) or lodge rooms ($$$$).

Mammoth Hot Springs Hotel and Cabins. Choice of cabins ($$) or rooms ($$$–$$$$).

Old Faithful Inn. The huge rustic lobby has a massive fireplace. Rooms in the Old House without bath ($$), regular rooms ($$$$), or cabins ($$–$$$).

Old Faithful Snow Lodge and Cabins. The newest property has rooms ($$$$) and cabins ($$$).

Roosevelt Lodge and Cabins $$–$$$. A Western ranch atmosphere, geared to families.

FOOD

Reasonably priced fast food and snack shops are located throughout the park. Lake Lodge, Old Faithful Lodge and Canyon Lodge have cafeterias. Grant Village, Old Faithful Inn and Roosevelt have family-style restaurants – Roosevelt sports an 'Old West' atmosphere. All the hotels except Roosevelt have fine dining restaurants. Reservations are necessary; $$$$ tel: (307) 344-7901.

HIGHLIGHTS

Yellowstone has five distinct regions: the hot springs sector that stretches out from Mammoth; the geyser area reaching from Norris south past Old Faithful; the region surrounding Lake Yellowstone; canyon country with the Grand Canyon of

Yellowstone and Hayden Valley; and the north-east section, Tower-Roosevelt, with its petrified forests, falls and recapitulation of the Old West.

A 142-mile figure eight, the Grand Loop Road, traverses the park, with spur roads linking with the entrances.

MAMMOTH COUNTRY

From the north entrance the Grand Loop passes Park Headquarters in Mammoth country. Here the thermal waters undulate over the travertine **Minerva Terraces**. Primitive bacteria and algae living in the water produce the terraces' beiges, browns, greens and reddish-browns. Resident elk and bison couldn't care less about such geothermal phenomena.

On the way south to geyser country's steam and dancing waters are the black volcanic glass of **Obsidian Cliff** and snorting fumaroles at **Roaring Mountain**.

GEYSER COUNTRY

Steamboat Geyser is just past Norris. Its 300–400 ft eruptions are the world's tallest, but they are unpredictable. Nearby **Gibbons Falls**, another visitor favourite, drops 84 ft over the caldera rim. A huge amount of burping and spitting makes **Fountain Paint Pot** Yellowstone's most famous mud pot. It is near Firehole Lake Drive, where the **Great Fountain Geyser** sometimes blows 200 ft up.

At Midway Geyser Basin, you'll find the largest of the hot springs – the colourful **Grand Prismatic Spring** is 370 ft wide.

There are 150 geysers within one square mile of the Upper Geyser Basin. The most famous is **Old Faithful**. It may not be the highest or the largest, but it is certainly consistent. It spews 5000–8000 gallons of water at least 20 times a day. Ask the visitor centre for eruption times.

The trail on the backside of Old Faithful crosses Firehole River to **Geyser Hill**. The rotten egg smell of hydrogen sulphide accompanies walkers past the many geysers and boiling springs to the far end of the basin and **Morning Glory Pool**. The pool got its name from its deep blue-green colour and likeness in shape to the flower. Not far away, in **Black Sand Basin**, the clear water of **Emerald Pool** seems endless. Oranges and yellows border the deep green of the pool, the result of algae growing in the pool's depths.

YELLOWSTONE LAKE

From the Old Faithful area the Grand Loop passes the Continental Divide of the Rockies at Isa Lake, and continues to **West Thumb**. A thermal area of Yellowstone Lake, West Thumb has bubbling pots, hot springs and geysers. Fisherman used to cook their catch in the bubbling waters of the submerged **Fishing Cone Geyser**.

Yellowstone Lake is the park's fishing and boating area. Cutthroat trout are plentiful at **Fishing Bridge**, where the Yellowstone River runs into the lake. Bison, bear and bald eagles are often spotted along the 100-mile shoreline of America's largest lake above 7000 ft. Bridge Bay ponds are a favourite hangout for moose.

Park Activities

Besides hiking and camping, there is fishing, boating and horse-riding ($$$) from most of the centres, guided fishing trips ($$$), scenic cruises on Lake Yellowstone ($$) and boat rental at Bay Bridge Marina ($$–$$$).

CANYON COUNTRY Elk, deer and buffalo graze on the hillsides, meadows and sagebrush flats of **Hayden Valley**, an old lake bed from the last Ice Age. Have your binoculars handy because its upper meadows are grizzly bear land. Along the Yellowstone River, white pelicans, trumpeter swans and Canada geese hobnob with gulls and ducks.

Up the road, nature hurls football-sized mud blobs from **Mud Volcano** and **Black Dragon's Cauldron**. This is also a good place to try your hand at catch-and-release trout fishing.

From Canyon Village Visitors Center, travel to **Canyon Rim Drive**. Trek the 2½ mile one-way loop that leads to **Inspiration Point** for a spectacular view of the canyon and the Lower Falls. Cataracts tumble, foam and strike the canyon floor with great force on their 308 ft descent. The trail chiselled by the turbulent Yellowstone River reaches a depth of 1540 ft near **Artist Point**, and the vertical landscape drops 700 ft to the canyon's bottom. Bright-coloured canyon walls are the result of heat and chemical action on their rhyolite rocks. The layers of colour in the Grand Canyon of Yellowstone go from black to pink to orange to yellow – it was the bright yellow hue that gave the park its name. The path continues to **Upper Falls**, where the waters plunge 109 ft into a deep green pool.

TOWER-ROOSEVELT Subalpine fir and whitebark pine border the road from the canyon to Tower-Roosevelt as it ascends Dunraven Pass. **Mt Washburn**, at 10,243 ft, forms the northern boundary of the caldera. This is grizzly bear country.

At Tower Junction, just past the volcanic pinnacles that surround the 132 ft Tower Falls, is a one million year-old tree stump. **Specimen Ridge** contains petrified redwoods, spruce, fir and a hundred other plant species that have been preserved by multi-million year-old volcanic ash.

Towards the north-east entrance the climate is drier, and the sagebrush and grassy valleys are the winter home for many of the area's large animals. It was a favourite area of Teddy Roosevelt.

OUTSIDE THE PARK

GRAND TETON NATIONAL PARK

The Tetons lie just south of Yellowstone, and the lack of foothills dramatically underscores the range's dramatic climb from evergreen forests, alpine meadows and blue glaciers to bare granite peaks. The Snake River slithers through its valley floor. Buffalo, moose, Canada geese, sandhill cranes, trumpeter swans, beavers, elk and deer all inhabit the area's wetlands. Teton Park Road rises from the river to a sage-covered flat where it reveals the whole Teton Range. There is a first-class view of Mount Moran's massive sandstone peak at Oxbow Bend. Jackson Lake is inside a depression that was scooped out by an Ice Age glacier.

One of the park's most popular areas is **Jenny Lake**. Walkers can take a boat ($) across the lake to **Cascade Canyon Trail** for the ½-mile walk to **Hidden Falls**. The delicate cascade resembles foaming tresses. **Inspiration Point**, just up the trail, overlooks the entire lake.

Besides hiking, camping, horse-riding and biking, there are nature seminars and Snake River float trips; $$$ contact Teewinot; tel: (307) 733-3316.

Menor's Ferry and the Chapel of the Transfiguration are some of the historic settlements at **Moose Village**. There are great panoramas of the Tetons aboard the aerial tram. $$$ Jackson Hole Ski Resort; tel: (307) 733-2292.

The Old West is alive and well around the antler arches of **Jackson Hole** square. There are saddle seats and country and western music at the Million Dollar Cowboy Bar, just off the square ($$) and within it at the Jackson Hole Shoot-out (Mon–Sat 1830, free). Fine art galleries contribute to making Jackson Hole a sophisticated little ski town.

i **Jackson Hole Chamber of Commerce**, tel: (307) 733-3316; visitor information, tel: (307) 739-3600; www.nps.gov/grte. One entrance pass covers Grand Teton and Yellowstone for seven days (see p. 365–367 and above). There are cash dispensers at most lodges. The closest bank is in Jackson.

Within the park, **Flagg Ranch**, tel: (800) 443-2311; **Grand Teton Lodge**, tel: (307) 543-2811; **Signal Mountain Lodge Co.**, tel: (307) 543-2831; and **Dornan's Spur Ranch Cabins**, tel: (307) 733-2415, are expensive, but so are most facilities in Jackson Hole. Campsites are usually filled by noon.

HENRY'S LAKE STATE PARK

Wildlife and wild scenery follow Hwy 20 west out of the park to Henry's Lake State Park and Island Park

Reservoir, Idaho. This is also the place for fly fishermen to have a bout with a cutthroat trout.

Along Mesa Falls Scenic Byway (Hwy 47) the thunder of the **Upper and Lower Mesa Falls** resonates at Henry's Fork as the Snake River crams itself into a gorge that drops 65 ft. A mile south of the falls is **Harriman State Park**, a 16,000 acre wildlife reserve. Trumpeter swans make their home here, as did the Harrimans – a tour of their 1950s **Railroad Ranch** gives the impression they have only just left it. For tour reservations, tel: (208) 558-7368 ($).

i Tel: (800) VISITID (847 -4843); www.visit id.org.

BEARTOOTH Breathtaking vistas accompany the **Beartooth Highway** (Hwy 212) from the north-east entrance. A series of switchbacks climbs 11,000 ft to Beartooth Pass on its way to Red Lodge, Montana. The pass's metaphoric rocks are some of the earth's oldest.

i Tel: (800) VISITMT (800-847-4868); www.visitmt.com.

CODY, WYOMING The **Buffalo Bill Historical Center** is the home of a huge collection of Western Americana. It includes Bill Cody's personal memorabilia, the Whitney Gallery of Western Art, the Plains Indian Museum and the Cody Firearms Museum. $$ 720 Sheridan Ave, Cody (two-day admission).

As your plane approaches Los Angeles International Airport, the flat sprawl which houses 9.4 million souls within Los Angeles county is ended only by the great Pacific Ocean. Crowded? Yes – with raw opportunity. The denizens of the amorphous neighbourhoods, urban villages, slums, beach towns and creative colonies all co-exist: Angelinos are an upbeat, eternally optimistic mix. One-third are Hispanic, many from Mexico, while a good percentage are African-American or have an Asian or Pacific Island heritage. Angelinos call their home El-Lay – short, snappy, abbreviated, sassy, entertaining, like themselves: hustlers aiming to get rich enough to live the life of a star in the hills.

Most points of interest are concentrated on the trendy Westside from Beverly Hills to Santa Monica and along the coast. Most of the city's cultural attractions, shopping and nightlife are located here. Other centres of activity include Old Pasadena and the Universal CityWalk area. The strip malls and tract houses of the inland valleys are now home to immigrants from all over the world. Many Angelenos have never been downtown, although there are many interesting sights in the area, and a new metro now links the area with the rather tattered Hollywood Blvd 'Walk of Fame' in just 15 minutes. Those who do not wish to navigate the LA freeways will find downtown a good base for taking day trips by train and bus although hotels can be expensive and nighttime activity is nil. Santa Monica is another good base for seeing the sites on the Westside. In 2000, the subway will be extended to the popular Universal Studios and City Walk, making that area an excellent base.

GETTING THERE AND GETTING AROUND

AIR Los Angeles International Airport (LAX) is 17 miles west of downtown, at 1 World Way; tel: (310) 646-5252. Find all outbound transport except taxis on the Lower Level/Arrival islands outside arrival baggage carousels. There is an airport bus to downtown hotels, and a free shuttle bus to the Metro Green Line Light Rail Station; take the line to Imperial/Wilmington, then transfer to the Blue Line to 7th St/Metro Center in downtown Los Angeles. There are also free shuttles to hire car locations and airport hotels. A taxi to the downtown area will cost about three times as much as the bus – not expensive considering the distance, and well worth it if there are more than two of you.

RAIL/BUS Amtrak trains pull into cavernous, marble mosaic-lined Union Station, 800 N. Alameda St – its exterior looks like a Spanish Mission. From here Metrolink, tel: (800) 371-5465; www.metrolinktrains.com, has its Mon–Fri commuter

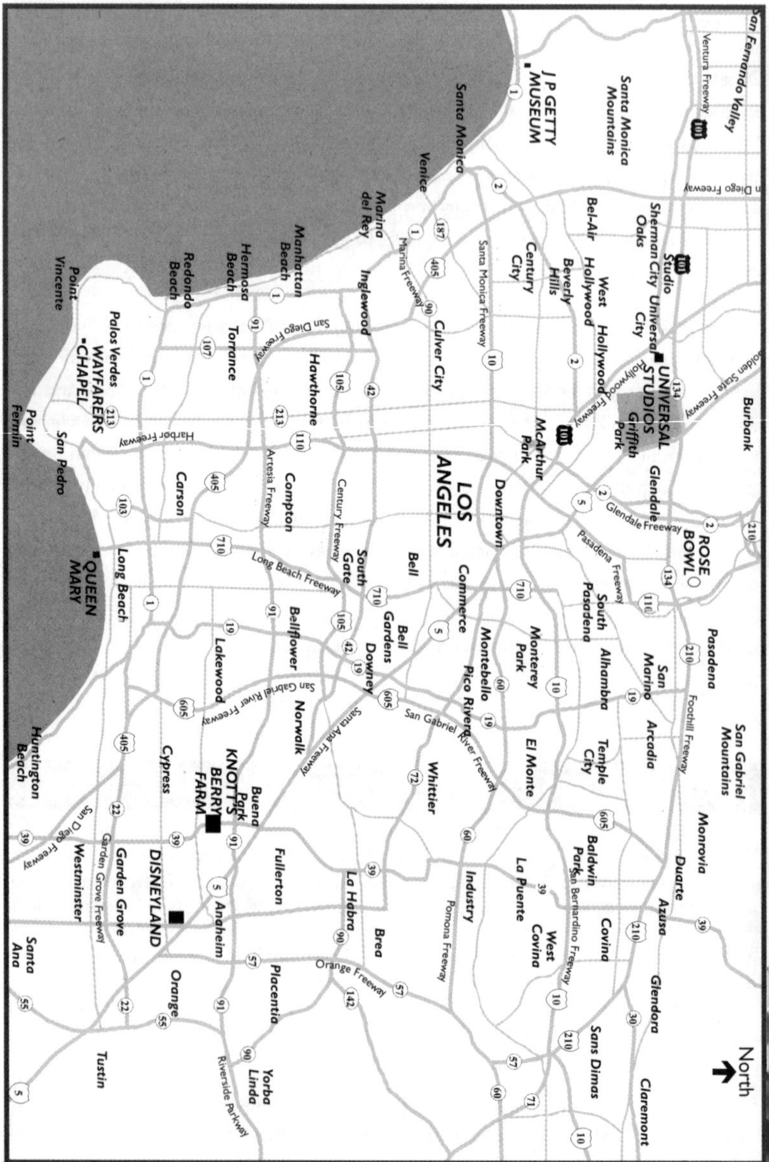
San Fernando Valley
Ventura Freeway
Santa Monica Mountains
J P GETTY MUSEUM
Santa Monica
Venice
Marina del Rey
Manhattan Beach
Hermosa Beach
Redondo Beach
Point Vincente
Palos Verdes
WAYFARERS CHAPEL
Point Fermin
San Pedro
Sherman Oaks
Studio City
Universal City
UNIVERSAL STUDIOS
Burbank
Griffith Park
Glendale
Bel-Air
Beverly Hills
West Hollywood
Hollywood
Hollywood Freeway
Century City
Santa Monica Freeway
Marina Freeway
Culver City
Inglewood
San Diego Freeway
Hawthorne
Torrance
Harbor Freeway
McArthur Park
Downtown
LOS ANGELES
Glendale Freeway
Pasadena Freeway
ROSE BOWL
Golden State Freeway
Artesia Freeway
Century Freeway
Compton
Carson
Long Beach Freeway
Long Beach
QUEEN MARY
South Gate
Bell
Commerce
South Pasadena
Pasadena
San Marino
Alhambra
Monterey Park
Montebello
Bell Gardens
Downey
Bellflower
Lakewood
San Gabriel River Freeway
Santa Ana Freeway
Norwalk
Pico Rivera
El Monte
Temple City
Arcadia
Foothill Freeway
San Gabriel Mountains
Monrovia
Duarte
Whittier
Cypress
KNOTT'S BERRY FARM
Buena Park
Huntington Beach
Westminster
Garden Grove
Garden Grove Freeway
DISNEYLAND
Anaheim
Fullerton
La Habra
Brea
Industry
Pomona Freeway
La Puente
Baldwin Park
San Bernardino Freeway
West Covina
Covina
Azusa
Glendora
Orange Freeway
Placentia
Orange
Santa Ana
Tustin
Yorba Linda
Riverside Parkway
Sans Dimas
Claremont
North

train hub for routes north-west to Oxnard, north-east to Lancaster, east to San Bernardino and Riverside and south-east to Oceanside. Lancaster and San Bernardino trains also operate Sat.

Greyhound buses arrive at a small terminal at 7th and Alameda Sts, about 1 mile east of downtown.

Much of the LA region is served by the MTA Metro rail and bus system, tel: (213) 626-4455; www.mta.net. Metro Rail connects Union Station with Hollywood (Red Line), Long Beach (Blue Line) and the airport area (Green Line) for a flat fare. Trains operate 0500–2200 daily. Metro buses operate throughout the city and suburbs, some 24 hr (same flat fare as the trains). The cheap DASH bus routes make frequent stops around the centre Mon–Sat.

INFORMATION

Los Angeles Convention and Visitors Bureau (LACVB) Downtown Visitor Information Center, 685 S. Figueroa St; 7th St/Metro Center; tel: (800) 228-2452, is open Mon–Fri 0800–1700, Sat 0830–1700. Ask for the *Destination Los Angeles* guide and small guides on shopping, dining/nightlife and entertainment.

Safety Avoid areas east of Broadway and south of 7th Street and Wilshire Blvd. Caution is advised in the Hollywood area, especially after dark. Ask at the front desk of your hotel to seek advice on travelling to areas you are uncertain of.

Money There is a Thomas Cook foreign exchange bureaux at branches of the Bank of Los Angeles at 8901 Santa Monica Blvd, West Hollywood; tel (310) 659-6093 and at 9461 Wilshire Blvd, Beverly Hills and 452 N. Bedford Dr., Beverly Hills.

Post and Phones Terminal Annex US Post Office is next to Union Station, at 760 N. Main St.

ACCOMMODATION

The LACVB lists member hotels in the *Destination Los Angeles* guide, but does not make bookings. To conserve time and energy, base yourself close to attractions you intend to see. Always ask for secure parking.

Hostelling International $1436 2nd St, Santa Monica; MTA bus 33,333 or Santa Monica bus 10; tel: (310) 393-9913; fax: (310) 393-1769. Two blocks from the beach, pier and Third Street Promenade; free airport pick-up.

IF YOU'RE DRIVING

Traffic does flow – at a few miles per hour in the rush hour – on most LA area freeways. During the rush hour, it may be as efficient to take major surface streets (arterials) in the direction desired.

Parking meters are widely available, take change, and can be a good bargain if parking for less than a couple of hours (hourly restrictions are posted on detailed signs on the kerb). Downtown and in smart areas, car parks may charge several dollars per hour, or may not. For dining in any popular area, especially at night, valet parking is de rigueur, from $5 to $15.

Hostelling International $ 3601 S. Gaffey St no. 613, San Pedro; Bus 446; tel: (310) 831-8109. In the South Bay community of San Pedro.

Kawada Hotel $$ 200 S. Hill St; Civic Center Metro; tel: (213) 621-4455. Boutique hotel located near Civic Center.

Metro Plaza Hotel $$ 711 N. Main St; Union Station Metro; tel: (213) 680-0200 or (800) 223-2223; fax: (213) 620-0200. Across from Olvera Street, ½ block from Union Station.

Omni Los Angeles Hotel and Centre $$$ 930 Wilshire Blvd at Figueroa; 7th St/Metro Center; tel: (213) 688-7777; fax: (213) 612-3989. In the downtown business district.

Hollywood Roosevelt Hotel $$$ 7000 Hollywood Blvd; tel: (323) 466-7000; fax: 462-8056; www.roosevelthotel.com. Located on Hollywood's Walk of Fame.

FOOD

Local newspapers, and the free monthly *Where Los Angeles* magazine, list restaurants and review trendy newcomers. See also Hollywood, p. 375

Phillippe the Original $ 1001 N. Alameda St; Union Station Metro. Has been serving original French dip sandwiches for over 90 years.

Original Pantry Café $$ 877 S. Figueroa St; 7th St/Metro Center. A downtown favourite serving All-American breakfasts and other hearty fare 24 hours a day, seven days a week.

Café Pinot $$$ 700 W. Fifth St; tel: (213) 239-6500. Excellent Cal-French, served inside a see-through box with the lights of downtown all around.

Water Grill $$$ 544 S. Grand Ave, between 5th and 6th Sts; Pershing Square Metro; tel: (213) 891-0900. Rated LA's top seafood restaurant. The high quality is reflected in the prices.

HIGHLIGHTS

DOWNTOWN Once shunned as dingy and crime-ridden, today's civic centre has soaring skyscrapers, a fanciful funicular, a strangely familiar City Hall and a wealth of architecture.

The **Biltmore Hotel**, built in 1923, is an LA landmark facing Pershing Sq. – stroll through its ornate Spanish Renaissance-style lobby. Three blocks away, at 9304 S. Broadway, the **Bradbury Building** features five skylit levels of intricate ironwork and an exposed lift accented by marble, tilework and rich polished wood. This fanciful $500,000 1893 masterpiece is a frequent film location; it is open to the first landing 0900–1700. Opposite is **Grand Central Market.** Since 1917, Angelinos have shopped for ingredients for their kitchens here. Look for the bronze pig heads at the Broadway entrance. Open Mon–Sat 0900–1800, Sun 1000–1730; 90 mins free parking with a $15 purchase.

> **CITY HALL**
> The shimmering white icon of City Hall, 200 N. Spring St, served as Superman's *Daily Planet* building. It is closed until 2003 for seismic repair.

Across the street from the market's Hill St entrance is the **Angels Flight Railway**, a charming funicular ride up steep Bunker Hill to California Plaza and its skyscrapers. $ operates daily 0630–2200.

Pedestrianised Olvera St at the heart of downtown is the centrepiece of the **El Pueblo de Los Angeles Historic Monument**. Among the state historic park's 27 buildings is LA's oldest building, **Avila Adobe**, dating back to 1818 and now perfectly restored and furnished as an 1850s *rancho*. A Mexican-style open-air shopping arcade has well-crafted leather goods and Mexican tourist trinkets. Restaurants serve modest, authentic Mexican food. **Sepulveda House Visitors Center** is open Mon–Sat 1000–1500.

The **Museum of Contemporary Art** (MOCA) on California Plaza presents the last 60 years of modern art with large sculpture, abstract paintings and prints. There are multimedia and video presentations in lower level galleries. $$ Open Tues–Sun 1100–1700; also Thur 1700–2000, when it is free.

Music Center, at N. Grand Ave/W. Temple St; tel: (213) 972-7200, is a performing arts complex in the heart of downtown. The Dorothy Chandler Pavilion hosts the Los Angeles Opera and the Oscars ceremony. Cutting-edge theatre is presented in the Mark Taper Forum. Broadway plays and mainstream theatre are performed at the Ahmanson Theater. A Jacques Lipchitz 'Peace' fountain in the courtyard constantly varies its water flow, creating the illusion of an erratic brook in the city centre.

> **WALKING TOURS**
> Los Angeles Conservancy Tours, 523 W. 6th St, Suite 1216; tel: (213) 623-2489, runs guided tours ($) that cover art deco, the Biltmore Hotel, Broadway movie theatres, City Hall, Little Tokyo (Japantown), Pershing Square, Union Station and architecture.

WILSHIRE BOULEVARD This long and famous street runs from the edge of downtown out to Beverly Hills – Metro buses 20, 21, 22, 302 and 322 run along it.

The **Los Angeles County Museum of Art** (LACMA) has a world-renowned Indian and South-east Asian art collection and notable textiles and costumes among its powerhouse collection. The

Japanese Pavilion is on two levels of galleries which include magnificent Japanese scrolls in a building designed in the shape of a pagoda. $$ 5905 Wilshire Blvd. Open Mon, Tues–Thurs 1200–2000, Fri 1200–2100, Sat–Sun 1100–2000.

For an introduction to LA's love affair and dependence upon the automobile, pay a visit to the **Petersen Automotive Museum**. Cars of the stars, hot rods, sport cars, roadside cafés, service stations – they're all here. $$ 6060 Wilshire Blvd; open Tues–Sun 1000–1800.

The **Armand Hammer Museum of Art** houses the late entrepreneur-philanthropist's third art collection: Old Masters, Impressionists and Post-Impressionist paintings, Dürer watercolours and satirist Daumier's lithographs. $ 10899 Wilshire Blvd; open Tues–Sat 1100–1900 (Thur until 2100, and free after 1800), Sun 1100–1700.

Tar Baby

Ice Age fossils about 40,000 years old have been found in bubbling **La Brea Tar Pits**, once mined for natural asphalt. See the discoveries at the **George C. Page Museum $$** 5801 Wilshire Blvd; open Tues–Fri 0930–1700,

Beverly Hills Beverly Hills, west of downtown and Hollywood, is a town and a state of mind. **Rodeo Drive** is three blocks of ultra-smart boutiques dripping with sophistication, where there are more tourists than shoppers. The **Museum of Television and Radio** is the best spot outside the museum's New York City venue to view television clips and listen to historic radio programmes and advertisements. $$ 495 N. Beverly Dr.; open Wed–Sun 1200–1700 (also Thur 1700–2100).

The **Museum of Tolerance**, 9786 W. Pico Blvd (take Metro bus 3) is a gripping introduction to – or reminder of – the effects of racism and intolerance. $$ Open Mon–Fri 1000–1600 (Fri until 1300), Sun 1030–1700.

Pasadena North-east of central LA, Pasadena beams into millions of homes on New Year's Day with the televised Rose Parade preceding the Rose Bowl football match. Metro buses 401, 402 and 483 will take you out there. The **Norton Simon Museum** is a marriage of a millionaire's exquisite taste with gallery display. $ 411 W. Colorado Blvd; open Thur–Sun 1200–1800. Find designer wear and casual dining at Old Pasadena's **One Colorado** complex (Colorado Blvd and Fair Oaks Ave).

An unexpected facet of LA is also out to the north-east. The **Huntington Library and Botanical Gardens** in San Marino has fine art, lovely gardens, a tearoom and medieval manuscripts. $$ 1151 Oxford Rd; Metro bus 79; open Tues–Fri 1200–1630, Sat–Sun 1030–1630.

HOLLYWOOD

The studio system has gone, the glitz may be tarnished, but Hollywood still means movieland. More than 2000 pink stars – the **Hollywood Boulevard Walk of Fame** – embedded in the pavement of Hollywood Blvd from La Brea Ave to Vine St, recall stars of film, television, radio, music and the stage. Try out the stars' autographed hand and foot imprints before the exotic pagoda facade of **Mann's Chinese Theater**, 6925 Hollywood Blvd, and take part in the interactive exhibits of the **Hollywood Entertainment Museum** $, 7021 Hollywood Blvd. Independent films feature in the newly renovated 1922 **Egyptian Theatre** $, 6712 Hollywood Blvd.

Every souvenir shop sells maps showing the location of stars' homes, but for a different take on the immortals of Hollywood, **Grave Line Tours**, tel: (213) 469-4149, run a dolorously narrated Cadillac hearse tour of death and sin sites of the famous ($$$).

A classic view of the 50 ft high letters of the landmark **Hollywood sign**, plastered across the dry hills at the top of Beachwood Canyon (near the corner of Beachwood Dr. and Franklin Ave) is from Griffith Observatory. Griffith Park is also the location of the **Autry Museum of Western Heritage**, which offers a vibrant, honestly captioned collection of Western US art, artefacts and cowboy film memorabilia. $$ 4700 Western Heritage Way; Metro bus 96; open Tues–Sun 1000–1700.

Just north of Hollywood proper, **Universal Studios Hollywood and CityWalk**, 100 Universal City Plaza, is one of the world's oldest film studios, and what Hollywood was all about. Surrounded by a cinema-themed amusement park ($$$), it offers a Backlot Tram Tour past actual set locations and sound stages with a bridge drop-out. Brace youself for an encounter with King Kong and a simulated earthquake. Dinosaurs run amok in 'Jurassic Park – The Ride'; prepare to get soaked when a humungous tyrannosaurus rex dunks the ride's car. 'Back to the Future – the Ride' is a clever motion simulator with effects of ice cliffs, lava flows and another T-rex, while 'ET Adventure' puts you on a bicycle to save the beloved Extra Terrestrial's home planet. Outside the park entrance gate is the free (with parking) Universal CityWalk, a pedestrian walking, shopping, dining, entertainment and multiplex cinema area.

Some fun, bargain places to eat in Hollywood:

Sharkey's Mexican Grill $ 1710 N. Cahuenga Blvd. Some of the best fish tacos in LA.

Chan Dara $$ 1511 N. Cahuenga Blvd, north of Sunset Blvd. Draws diners for scrumptious Thai food – especially pad Thai noodles.

Fabiolus Café $$ 6270 Sunset Blvd, east of Vine St. A pasta bowl chain that's popular with low-budget 'moguls' and struggling actors.

Hollywood Hills Coffee Shop $$ Best Western Hollywood Hotel, 6145 Franklin Ave at Vine St. American food served in what could best be described as a 'scene'.

Musso and Frank Grill $$$ 6667 Hollywood Blvd. The essence of 'old' Hollywood – martinis and chicken pot pie to die for.

INFORMATION

Hollywood Visitor Information Center, The Janes House, 6541 Hollywood Blvd; open Mon–Sat 0900–1700.

Metro Rail Red Line connects Union Station with Hollywood/Vine Station in under 25 mins. Greyhound buses stop two blocks south, at 1409 N. Vine St/Sunset Blvd; tel: (323) 466-6384.

SHOPPING

The LACVB offers a pocket-sized *Shopping in Los Angeles* guide for suggestions of where and what to purchase.

Rodeo Drive (Beverly Hills) or the Beverly Center (8500 Beverly Blvd) are starting places for smart-conservative with touches of Academy Award gown thrown in. For the raw materials, a DASH bus will take you to the Fashion District.

NIGHTLIFE

Look in the free weekly newspapers: *LA Weekly*, *New Times Los Angeles*, *Entertainment Today* and the mainstream *Los Angeles Times Sunday Calendar* for listings.

Sunset Strip, Sunset Blvd in trendy West Hollywood (Metro bus 2) still offers Whisky A Go Go, tel: (310) 652-4202; other star-making (Springsteen, Bob Marley) music venues like the **Roxy**, tel: (310) 276-2222; or American roots music at the **House of Blues**, tel: (323) 848-5100.

WHERE NEXT?

Part of the LA conurbation, but each with a separate identity, are the beach resorts of southern California – Santa Monica, Venice Beach et al (see p. 417). The Pacific Coast Highway runs down to San Diego (see p. 406) and up to San Francisco and beyond (see p. 423), or take a train up the San Joaquin Valley (see p. 455).

LOS ANGELES–SANTA FE
THE SOUTHWEST CHIEF

RAIL

OTT TABLE 368

TRANSPORT	FREQUENCY	JOURNEY TIME
Train	Daily	19hrs 20mins

LOS ANGELES–FLAGSTAFF

TRANSPORT	FREQUENCY	JOURNEY TIME
Train	Daily	10hrs 37mins

FLAGSTAFF–ALBUQUERQUE

TRANSPORT	FREQUENCY	JOURNEY TIME
Train	Daily	7hrs 38mins

ALBUQUERQUE–LAMY (FOR SANTA FE)

TRANSPORT	FREQUENCY	JOURNEY TIME
Train	Daily	1hr 5mins

GREYHOUND/TMNO

OTT TABLES 813/845/847/848

TRANSPORT	FREQUENCY	JOURNEY TIME
Bus	3 daily	20hrs 15mins

NB: You have to catch the Lamy shuttle van to Santa Fe. There is also an Amtrak thruway bus to Phoenix and the Grand Canyon from Flagstaff. The bus service takes two routes one via Phoenix and the other via Flagstaff.

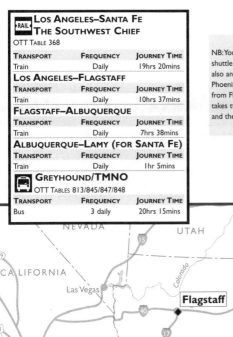

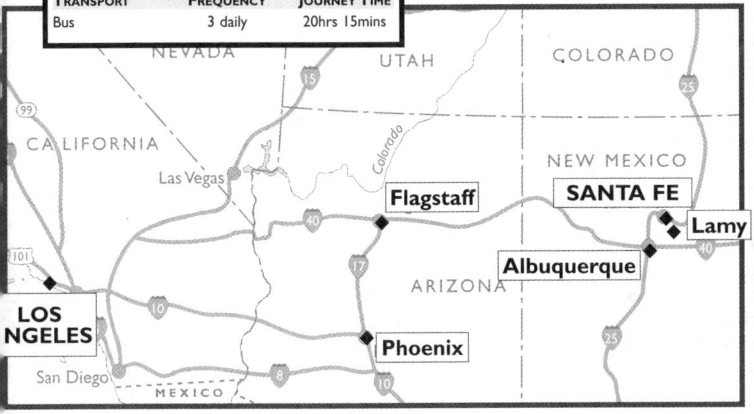

Los Angeles – Santa Fe

On the 'Southwest Chief'

There are some wonderful sights on this journey as it traverses the arid land of Arizona: pueblos hundreds of years old, lava flows, weird geological formations and extraordinary desertscapes. Breathtaking canyons are just a few feet wider than the train. The scenery is no less awesome as you continue eastwards into New Mexico and Santa Fe.

The main stop *en route* is Flagstaff, to visit the Grand Canyon. Take a detour for the day to Phoenix to see the famous America West Arena or enjoy some exclusive shopping in Scottsdale.

FLAGSTAFF

Flagstaff is a university town, a rail and trucking hub, and prosperously dependent upon the tourist trade visiting the Grand Canyon and coming to ski in winter. Historic **Route 66** still wends its way through downtown, where small cafés and bookshops foster a lively music scene at night. Flagstaff's jewel is the **Museum of Northern Arizona**, on Hwy 180. A brightly lit but cool building houses a major collection of doll-size *kachina* figures (fetishes) and an outstanding display of pottery from different archaeological eras, excavated on the Colorado Plateau. Open daily 0900–1700; tel: (520) 774-5213.

The **Riordan Mansion State Historic Park**, 1300 Riordan Ranch St, is a 40-room home covering 13,000 sq. ft, shared by two families in 1904. It is open for tours; tel: (520) 779-4395. You can also take a tour of the world-famous **Lowell Observatory**, from which Pluto was discovered in 1930; tel: (520) 774-2096.

The outstanding natural feature of the area is, of course, the Grand Canyon (see p. 386), but the landscape around Flagstaff has other wonders to offer. Snow-capped **Humphrey's Peak**, Arizona's highest point at 12,663 ft, is just north of the city, visible for a hundred miles in any direction. Unexpectedly wild scenery awaits at **Sunset Crater Volcano** and **Wupatki National Monuments**; tel: (602) 556-7042. Black lava is strewn about the one-mile circular trail near a cinder cone which last exploded in 1100 AD. Plan to arrive at the end of the day to see the sun set over the Wupatki ruins (there are several sites along the route), or the Sinagua or Anasazi villages, whose crumbling remains resemble Crusader castles. To the north, on the Navajo Nation reservation, is the **Painted Desert**.

In the **Coconino National Forest** you will see pygmy trees where high altitude and winds have stunted the conifers' growth. *En route*, as the highway descends to Valle huge statues of Fred, Barney, Wilma and the rest of the *Flintstones* TV cartoon gang lure visitors into **Bedrock City**.

Flagstaff Convention and Visitors Bureau, 211 W. Aspen, Flagstaff; tel: (520) 779-7611.
Flagstaff Visitor Center, One E. Route 66 and Beaver St (in the railway depot); tel: (800) 842-7293 or (520) 774-9541; open daily.

Be warned that because of its proximity to the Grand Canyon, Flagstaff is liable to book up several months in advance. The Grand Canyon Railway office makes bookings.
Hotel Monte Vista $$$ 100 N. San Francisco; tel: (800) 545-3068 or (520) 779-6971. Dates from around 1927, with cosy lobby and moderate rooms.

Flagstaff will always be popular, whether as a stopover for tourists traversing Rte 66, or for those visiting the Grand Canyon; so there is more than enough money to support several upmarket restaurants and some hearty steakhouses.
Black Bart's $$- $$$, 2760 E Butler Ave, tel: 520 779 4142, is a themed Western Steakhouse where the staff amuse you by singing and dancing while you eat. Try their 'Big Ribs'.
Cafe Express $$, 16 N San Francisco St, tel: 520 774 1541, serves excellent vegetarian cuisine throughout the day.
Alpine Pizza $, 7 N. Leroux St, tel: 520 779 4109, serves beer and cheap pizzas and is a student favourite.

DAY TRIP TO PHOENIX

Greyhound buses serve Phoenix from Flagstaff, or you can hire a car – the journey will take about 2 hrs on perfectly straight roads through the desert to this, the largest city in the south-west. Downtown Phoenix has little to tempt the traveller other than the **America West Arena**, the home of professional basketball and hockey teams; tours $; tel: (602) 379 2000.

A short bus journey away is **Old Town Scottsdale**, a cluster of early 20th-century buildings and some more recent buildings styled to look like those of the Old West. Scottsdale itself is pricey, but boasts the best shops and restaurants around. The **Scottsdale Centre for the Arts** has galleries, a sculpture garden and live performing artists.

WHERE NEXT?

The 'Southwest Chief' stops at Albuquerque (see p. 339) and Santa Fe (see p. 321) before making its long journey across the Midwest to Chicago (see p. 317).

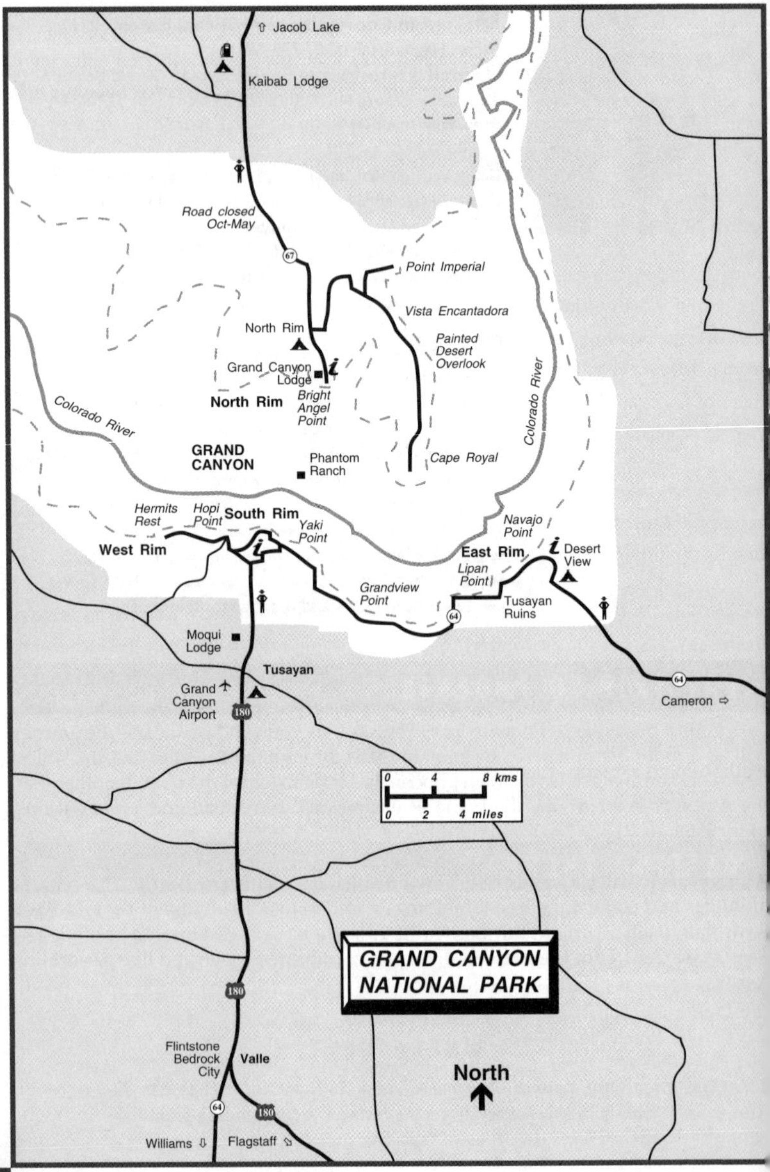

Jacob Lake
Kaibab Lodge
Road closed Oct-May
67
Point Imperial
Vista Encantadora
North Rim
Painted Desert Overlook
Grand Canyon Lodge
Bright Angel Point
North Rim
Colorado River
Colorado River
GRAND CANYON
Phantom Ranch
Cape Royal
Hermits Rest
Hopi Point
South Rim
Yaki Point
Navajo Point
West Rim
East Rim
Desert View
Lipan Point
Grandview Point
Tusayan Ruins
64
Moqui Lodge
Tusayan
Grand Canyon Airport
180
64
Cameron
0 4 8 kms
0 2 4 miles
GRAND CANYON NATIONAL PARK
180
Flintstone Bedrock City
Valle
North
64
180
Williams
Flagstaff

The Grand Canyon

'The region . . . is altogether valueless. It can be approached only from the south, and after entering it, there is nothing to do but leave. Ours has been the first, and will doubtless be the last, party . . . to visit this profitless locality.'

That 1858 US government survey estimate on the number of people who might visit the Grand Canyon was out – by more than five million visitors annually. The enormous gorge displays two billion years' worth of history, recorded in layer upon layer of red, white, buff, grey, yellow, orange, brown, pink and black rock. The first outsider to see the Grand Canyon from below was Major John Wesley Powell, who successfully navigated more than 1000 miles of Colorado River in 1869. Powell's notes from the trip, and a second in 1871–2, remain invaluable guides for modern river rafters braving the same white-water rapids.

The Grand Canyon is even larger than it appears. From the popular South Rim straight across the canyon to the less frequented North Rim measures 10 miles; go round from one to the other by road and you will cover 215 miles.

It's possible to see the Grand Canyon in a day, less if you take a flightseeing package from Las Vegas, but the ever-changing colours and the utter vastness of the canyon beg to be absorbed at leisure, far from the millions of visitors who will stop at the South Rim and Grand Canyon Village each year. At the very least, skirt the crowds by walking or cycling the South Rim Trail from Hopi Point east to Grand Canyon Village and Mather Point; a free shuttle eases the return.

Getting There

To reach the **South Rim**, take Hwy 180 north-west from Flagstaff, then continue north to the park's South Entrance; or leave Hwy 89 at Cameron and take Hwy 64 west along the East Rim of the park. To get to the **North Rim**, take Alt Hwy 89 east or west to Jacob Lake, then follow Hwy 67 south. For information on road conditions, tel: (520) 638-7888. The parking fee is $10 for private vehicles, valid for seven days on both rims.

The Grand Canyon Railway (included on some package tours) runs to the South Rim from Williams, 65 miles south of the park. The 1901 line, originally run by the Santa Fe Railway, provided the easy access that turned the Grand Canyon from geographic curiosity into an American icon. A vintage steam locomotive engine pulls the rake of restored 1920s Harriman carriages in summer, while a 1950s diesel does the duty in winter. $$ Contact 123 N San Francisco, Ste 210, Flagstaff, AZ 86001; tel: (520) 773-1976 or (800) 843-8724; fax: (520) 773-1610; www.thetrain.com. The **Railroad Express** is an alternative for visitors taking the train in one direction.

Nava-Hopi Tours, tel: (800) 892-8687, operates buses from Williams and Flagstaff Amtrak stations.

The Grand Canyon is a National Park, so there is an entrance fee ($$) however you arrive.

INFORMATION

Grand Canyon National Park, Box 129, Grand Canyon, AZ 86023; tel: (520) 638-7888; www.nps.gov/grca.

The **Main Visitor Center**, 6 miles north of the South Entrance, is open daily 0800–1700 (winter), 0800–1800 (summer). **Desert View Information Center**, **Yavapai Observation Station** and **Tusayan Museum** keep similar hours. Ask for *Grand Canyon Magazine*, free at visitor centres.

National Park Service Information Desk, Grand Canyon Lodge lobby, North Rim. Open daily 0800–1700 (mid May–Oct).

MONEY Perhaps surprisingly there is a bank (with a 24 hr cash dispenser) and post office on both the North and South Rims. Bank One will cash travellers' cheques, exchange currency, and handle wire transfers and charge card advances.

ACCOMMODATION

AmFac Parks and Resorts, tel: (303) 297-2757; fax: (303) 297-3175, operates all park accommodation and restaurants. Book as early as possible (6–12 months ahead) to ensure a place to sleep at America's most popular national park. **Grand Canyon National Park Lodges**, tel: (520) 638-2631, handles information and same-day bookings for the South Rim. South Rim is open year-round; North Rim is open May–Oct. Williams and Flagstaff, an hour south of the canyon, both offer a wide variety of accommodation.

SOUTH RIM **Tusayan**, the park's dedicated 'village' located just south of the southern entrance to the park, has an RV park and motels. **Mathe Campground**, tel: (800) 365-2267, has non-hookup pitches, and **Desert View**

Campground, on the park's east side, usually opens in April, though this depends on weather conditions.

Maswik Lodge $$ and **Yavapai Lodge** $$. Removed from the village.

Bright Angel Lodge $$$. Located near the rim.

Thunderbird Lodge $$$ and **Kachina Lodge** $$$. Offer a choice of canyon-side or park-side rooms.

El Tovar Hotel $$$. Historic lodge located near the railway station.

NORTH RIM The **National Forest Service** operates first-come, first-served campsites: the 25-pitch **DeMotte Park Campground**, 5 miles north of the boundary and the 50-pitch **Jacob Lake Campground**, 30 miles north of the park. **Jacob Lake RV Park**, tel: (520) 643-7804, has RV hookups and tent pitches, and the **North Rim Campground**, tel: (800) 365-2267, has 82-pitch, non-hookup sites; stays are limited to seven days and the campsite closes 16 Oct.

Grand Canyon Lodge $$$ tel: (435) 586-7686. Open May–Oct.

Kaibab Lodge $$ tel: (800) 525-0924 or (520) 526-0924 or (520) 638-2389. 5 miles north of the park boundary. **Kaibab National Forest** permits camping at will ¼ mile from roads and water sources.

FOOD

The Grand Canyon is ideal for picnicking – almost any spot along the rim has a scenic rock on which to dine and enjoy the vista.

SOUTH RIM

El Tovar Dining Room $$$ tel: (520) 638-2631. 'Fine' dining à la meat-and-potatoes and sweet desserts.

Arizona Steakhouse $$$ at Bright Angel Lodge. Serves dinner only.

Bright Angel Restaurant $$. Breakfast through dinner.

Bright Angel Fountain (next to the South Rim). The place for ice cream.

Hermit's Rest Snack Bar $$ end of West Rim Dr. Open mid Mar–mid Nov.

Babbitt's Delicatessen, at Babbitt's General Store. Snack bar located across the street from the Visitor's Center. There are also cafeterias at the Maswik and Yavapai lodges.

NORTH RIM

Grand Canyon Lodge Dining Room $$$, tel: (520) 638-2612, ext. 160. The main dining venue in the park, open for breakfast through dinner, for which reservations are required. There is also a tea room and a snack shop in the Lodge complex. A general store serves the North Rim Campground.

HIGHLIGHTS

SOUTH RIM From mid Apr to mid Oct, West Rim Drive, Yaki Point and the South Kaibab trailhead are accessible *only* by shuttle, tour bus, taxi or on foot. For tour information, tel: (520) 638-2631 for same-day bookings; tel: (303) 297-2757 for advance reservations.

The **Main Visitor Center Museum** has excellent explanations of early expeditions on the Colorado River, the effects of environmental pollution on air quality (242-mile visibility is occasionally reduced to 76-mile clarity), and flora and fauna on both sides of the canyon.

Bright Angel Trail began as a native American trail from the rim down to the springs at Indian Gardens. Private developers widened the trail in 1891 and began the mule rides that remain one of Grand Canyon's most popular organised activities (see p. 392).

The most popular hike along the Bright Angel Trail is rated very strenuous. The trailhead, at 6860 ft, is next to the Kolb Studios (near Bright Angel Lodge). To hike the 9.3 miles to Bright Angel Campground/Phantom Ranch is to descend to the canyon floor's 2480 ft elevation via a switchback trail, pass Indian Gardens previously tended by indigenous Havasupai, and cross the Colorado River. It is hiking in the open, aided by stops for water at Mile-and-One-Half Resthouse and Three-Mile Resthouse between May and Sept. Hiking just a portion of this trail is a challenging experience.

South Rim Trail runs 9 miles between 7120 ft Mather Point and 6640 ft Hermits Rest, with access at any point along the route. This is the path to see Yavapai Observation Point, and the lodges, restaurants and curio shops by El Tovar and Bright Angel; you can also stop at 7043 ft Hopi Point for a view of 45 miles of canyon expanse. The trail is flat and easy, skirting the edge of the canyon and offering many photo opportunities. Walk west towards Hermits Rest in the morning or east in the Mather Point direction in the afternoon for the best views with the sun behind you.

FREE SHUTTLES

The park runs a free shuttle bus system mid Mar–mid Oct through the village and the West Rim. The **Kaibab Shuttle** runs from several lodges to Yaki Point on the East Rim. The **Tusayan Shuttle** runs hourly from the village south of the park. Information from the Visitor Center, Bright Angel Lodge and Yavapai Lodge.

On the North Rim, the shuttle is non-operational until the North Kaibab Trail is reconstructed beyond Cottonwood, but the **Trans-Canyon Shuttle** operates a daily rim-to-rim round-trip service in season. Allow 4–5 hours for the transit in either direction; tel: (520) 638-2820.

GRAND CANYON VILLAGE HISTORIC DISTRICT

Ask at one of the park lodge concierge desks for a copy of the brochure, *Self-Guided Walking Tour of Grand Canyon Village Historical District.* Covering the tiny area around El Tovar and Bright Angel Lodge, the tour takes in the **1909 Santa Fe Railway Depot** (still used by the Grand Canyon Railway), as well as the log and stone **El Tovar Hotel**, the adobe South-west-style **Hopi House** and **Verkamp's Curios** (successor to a canyon floor trading post; see Shopping, p. 394), all completed in 1905.

For those wishing to stay here, the 1890 **Bucky O'Neill Cabin** near Bright Angel Lodge can still be rented. The **Red Horse Station**, once a two-storey hotel, is now a two-room guest cabin. In 1935, **Bright Angel Lodge** was opened to provide for tourists' modest accommodation near the rim. The 10 ft tall lounge fireplace is designed to show the many layers of geological strata in the canyon.

Much of the trail is not fenced or barricaded, so beware – a dozen or so people fall over the rim edge each year, drawn by the majesty of the scenery or while posing for photographs!

For more information on hikes and camping permits, consult a ranger. *The Official Guide to Hiking the Grand Canyon* by Scott Thybony (1994), Grand Canyon Natural History Association, Grand Canyon, AZ 86023, is an excellent guide to hiking trails on and between both rims.

Just inside the eastern boundary of the park, a three-storey golden rock tower hovers above the canyon. The **Watchtower** was built in 1932 to approximate prehistoric buildings in the region. Pay a few cents to walk up the tower stairs for magnificent views from windows in the wall, set between native American-style murals.

Eight centuries ago, a local band of native Americans, the Anasazi, abandoned a village along the East Rim of the canyon which they had inhabited for 1300 years. The **Tusayan Ruins** are what remain. There is a small museum and rangers lead interpretative walks on the ¼ mile of paths around the ruins.

NORTH RIM The North Rim, 1000 ft higher than the South Rim, is a different world. While the South Rim bakes in desert heat, the North Rim enjoys a cooler, mountain summer with spruce, fir and quaking aspen. And when the South Rim is dusted with snow, the North Rim is frozen beneath 25 ft of white. Although the Grand Canyon Lodge and other North Rim facilities are closed Nov–Apr, the park itself remains open to Dec, snow permitting.

A shorter season and more roundabout access mean that North Rim crowds are only about 10% the size of South Rim mobs. Hwy 67 takes you south to the promontory at **Bright Angel Point**; Grand Canyon Lodge sits close by. The Cape Royal/Point Imperial turn-off before the point is a winding road through forest which stays well away from the rim. At the T-junction, left will take you north towards the picnic area and viewpoint for **Point Imperial**; right leads south on a twisting road past rimside picnic areas at **Vista Encantadora** and the **Painted Desert Overlook**. Continue south on the Walhalla Plateau to the tip of Cape Royal.

The quickest way to enjoy the relative serenity is on foot. The canyon's north side has excellent hiking and trail rides along rim trails and routes to the canyon floor. The easiest walks are the ½ mile **Bright Angel Point Trail** and the 1½ mile **Transept Trail**. From the 0.6 mile **Cape Royal Trail** on the Walhalla Plateau, the Colorado River appears closer than from any other spot on the rims. The hardy can hike part or all of the **North Kaibab Trail** into the canyon, starting on the North Rim at 8250 ft. The multi-day return trip down to the Colorado River covers 28 miles and a 5750 ft drop. Accommodation is available at Phantom Ranch or at the Bright Angel Campground with the same reservation/permit requirements outlined for the South Rim (see p. 385).

There are several alternatives to all this foot slogging. A mule trek could take anything from an hour to several days (see below). From June to mid Oct **North Rim Mountain Bike Tours**, tel: (520) 638-2389 or (520) 526-0924, organises guided rides

MULE RIDES

Descending into the canyon on mule back has been popular for generations, and a traditional alternative to hiking on foot; aches and pains at the end of the day are comparable.

From the South Rim, one-day trips travel from the stone corral at the head of Bright Angel Trail to Tonto Platform and Plateau Point, 3200 ft below. The blue-green Colorado River twinkles another 1300 ft down. The ride takes about 7 hrs. Phantom Ranch rides stay overnight at Phantom Ranch cabins on Bright Angel Creek at the bottom of the canyon. The trip can be made in two ache-provoking days in the saddle or stretched to three days mid Nov–mid Mar.

You should book 9–12 months in advance, or get on the standby list at Bright Angel Transportation Desk the day before an intended ride. A one-day ride costs $100-plus; an overnight to Phantom Ranch with meals nearly three times as much. Contact **Mule Rides**, Grand Canyon National Park Lodges, Reservations Dept, PO Box 699, Grand Canyon, AZ 86023; tel: (520) 638-2401. One-day and overnight rides can also be arranged year-round through **AmFac Parks and Resorts**; tel: (303) 297-2757. mid Nov–mid Mar they also do three-day Phantom Ranch rides.

On the North Rim, **Grand Canyon Trail Rides**, based at Grand Canyon Lodge; tel: (520) 638-2292, offers several possibilities. A one-hour ride goes along the North Rim; a half-day ride explores the rim more fully or ventures a short way down towards the canyon floor; while the full-day ride goes into the canyon. Prices range from under $15 for an hour on mule back, to around $90 for a full day, including lunch.

Riders must be at least 4 ft 7 in tall, weigh under 200 lb (clothes and equipment included), and be fluent in English (for riding directions).

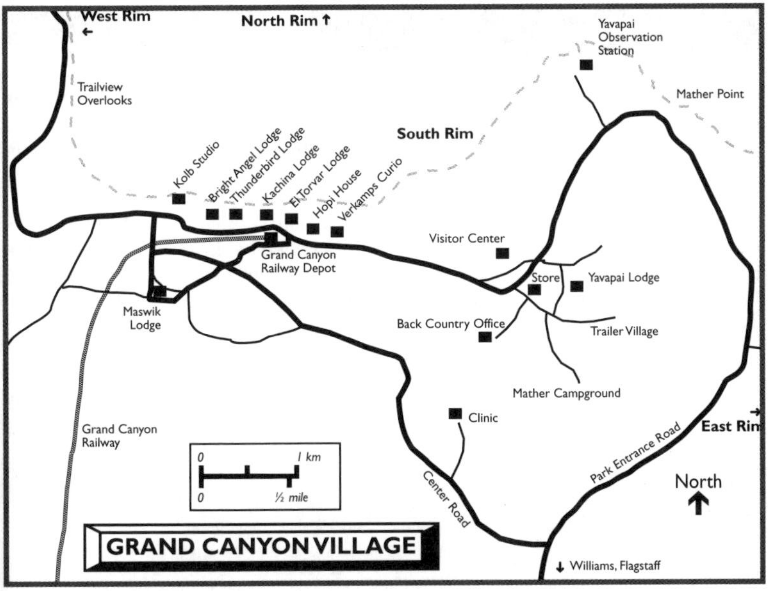

of the Kaibab Plateau and North Rim from a base at the Kaibab Lodge. For the winter, the lodge has created both tracked and marked backcountry trails for **cross-country skiing** (the area is reached using heated vans); tel: (520) 526-0924 or (800) 525-0924.

Rafting the Colorado River remains the most adventurous way to see the Grand Canyon. Allow a full day for a smooth-water float, including a picnic lunch. White-water trips last from three days to three weeks. Most departures are from Lees Ferry, upstream from the park, but a shorter trip starts at Phantom Ranch. Contact the Park, tel: (520) 638-7888, for a free trip planner that includes contact information for approved concessionaires, or check with local chambers of commerce. Summer trips get fully booked early in the season, although a few concessionaires ride the river all year. The waiting time for private river-running permits is six to eight years.

WHEELCHAIR ACCESS

Wheelchair-accessible tours can be requested in advance. The Grand Canyon National Park Accessibility Guide guides visitors who may use free wheelchairs, available from the park rangers upon request.

SHOPPING

Curio shops are everywhere on the South Rim, mostly open from 0700 or 0800 until well into the evening. Hopi House, across from El Tovar, has native American rugs, pottery, *kachina* (fetishes) and souvenir jewellery for sale; upstairs you will find museum-quality jewellery and ceramic work by contemporary native American artists.

Babbitt's General Store, across the road from the South Rim Main Visitor Center, is well stocked with provisions, and camping and hiking equipment. The visitor centres on both rims, the Kolb Studio at Bright Angel Trailhead, the Yavapai Observation Station and many of the curio shops. all stock maps and books.

Drive carefully – most accidents in Utah are due to drivers paying more attention to the scenery than to the road. In many of the national parks there are small dirt tracks that are best for 4 wheel drive vehicles only, and wide vehicles are not recommended – the National Parks advise that some of these dirt-track drives have a serious risk of vehicle damage.

You could try to do all National Parks in an exhausting seven-day tour, but it is better to choose just a couple of the parks and enjoy them at a leisurely pace.
Arches National Park is just north of Moab, off Hwy 191.
Canyonlands National Park is south-west of Moab, taking Hwy 313 off Hwy 191.
Hwy 24 leads south off I-70 and crosses Capitol Reef National Park, and from there Hwy 12 leads further south and west, crossing Bryce Canyon NP
Hwy 9 passes through Zion National Park, linked north to Hwy 12 by Hwy 89, and east to I-15 which runs north to Cedar City.

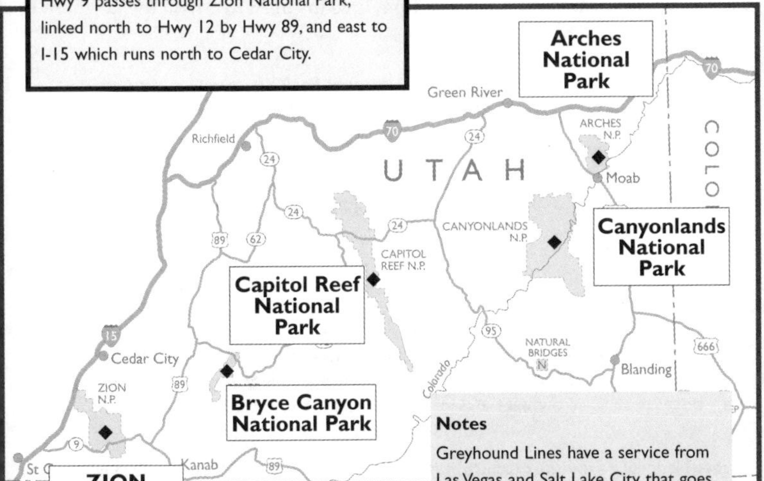

Notes

Greyhound Lines have a service from Las Vegas and Salt Lake City that goes around the perimeter of this area with stops at St. George, Cedar City and Green River. Amtrak's California Zephyr stops at Green River.

Southern Utah National Parks

Geological curiosities, gaping canyons, precipitous ravines, stone arches and needle-like towers eroded by wind and water litter the multicoloured high desert of southern Utah. The only way to see this astonishing landscape is by car, as public transport is extremely limited. Driving through the region's five outstanding national parks will take you from beside the Colorado River across the high red tableland and up into the Wasatch Mountains, through natural phenomena with evocative names like The Devil's Garden, The Maze, Rainbow Point and Weeping Rock.

ARCHES NATIONAL PARK

Travelling from Moab, you will almost immediately come to Arches National Park, where over 200 natural arches have been carved into the red stone by erosion – one of the largest concentrations of sandstone arches in the world. The park is 76,519 acres in size, and is dotted with sandstone spires, peaks and strange balanced rocks. An 18-mile road leads into Devil's Garden, where 64 closely grouped arches form a natural backdrop.

The main entrance, with visitor centre, museum and bookshop, is at the park's southern tip, near Moab; shuttles run from here to Green River, on the northern tip, which provides a handy stopping place.

Arches National Park Visitors Center, Arches National Park, Hwy 191; tel: (435) 259-8161.

There is no accommodation inside the park itself but there are places at both Green River and Moab.
Westwinds Roadway Inn $ 525 E. Main St, Green River; tel: (435) 564-3421.

SEASONALS

Peak Season is between Memorial day and Labor Day: they are hectic months and best avoided. The parks are visited throughout the year and motels and hotels are open accordingly- prices peak at midsummer and for winter weekends but are lowest in the spring after skiing season.

Arches National Park: Visitor Centre is closed only on Dec 25 ; park is open throughout the year. Canyonlands: Open throughout the year. Capitol Reef Park: Open all year. In winter, snowfall is usually light but may close some roads briefly. Zion National Park: Open all year. There is often heavy snow in winter, but the main roads are ploughed. Natural Bridges: Open all year, although some of the steeper trails are closed in winter as there is often heavy snow. Hovenweep: Open year round

RUN THE RAPIDS
Moab is gaining a reputation as a centre for white-water rafting, and from Canyonlands you can run the rapids of Cataract Canyon. Contact (435) 259-8946.

Best Western River Terrace $$ 880 E. Main St, Green River; tel: (800) 528-1234.
Castle Valley Inn $$ 424 Amber Lane, Moab; tel: (435) 259-6122.

Ben's Café $ 115 W. Main St, Green River, tel: (435) 564-3352.
West Winds Restaurant $$ 545 .E Main St, Green River, tel: (435) 564-8240.

CANYONLANDS

Seldom-visited Canyonlands is the preserve of 527 square miles of sandstone canyons, where water and gravity have carved flat layers of sedimentary rock into the landscape seen today. Between the deep-cut canyons created by the Colorado River and its tributaries is a towering mesa or tableland. The park is divided up into three land districts which are 2–6 hrs away by car: these are the Needles, named after the tall, thin rock formations that puncture the landscape, Island in the Sky and the Maze.

You can reach the park via buses from Green River, or from Grand Junction, where there is an Amtrak station.

Canyonlands National Park Information, 2282 S.West Resource Blvd, Moab; recorded information: tel: (435) 259-7164.

Inside the park there are individual campsites, which cannot be reserved in advance, at Needles Squaw Flat Campground and at Island in the Sky. Green River and Moab are alternative places to stay and eat (see above).

CAPITOL REEF NATIONAL PARK

Capitol Reef Park provides another set of geological fantasies. A 100-mile long wrinkle in the earth's crust, known to geologists as a monocline and to locals as the Waterpocket Fold, extends from nearby Thousand Lakes Mountain to the Colorado River, which here widens into Lake Powell.

Capitol Reef National Park Information Visitors Center, Hwy 24; tel: (435) 425-3791.

There are plenty of places to stay in towns near the park.

Circle D Motel $ 475 W. Main St, Escalente; tel: (435) 826-4297.

Whispering Sands Motel $$ 140 S. Highway 95, Hanksville; tel: (435) 542-3238.

Red Rock Restaurant and Campground $ 226 E. 100N, Hanksville, tel: (435) 542-3235.

BRYCE CANYON NATIONAL PARK

Bryce is a 17-mile canyon lined with hoodoos – ancient cliffs that have been eroded into parallel rows of sharp-edged pinnacles tinged with red, gold and chalk. Endless ranks of hoodoos seem to form natural stone amphitheatres, rimmed by guttered minarets, turrets, steeples and towers.

From the park entrance ($) the drive south rises 1100 ft to Rainbow Point. Sunrise is one of the most striking times of day to see the hoodoos and the easiest time of day to park. Park at **Sunrise Point** (less than a mile beyond the visitor centre) to watch the low rays of light begin to pick out the spires, then follow the **Rim Trail** down between the hoodoos to **Sunset Point**, **Inspiration Point** or **Bryce Point**. Return via the main road.

DRIVING TIPS

The road (Hwy 63) offers numerous lay-bys, but parking is extremely limited, so between spring and autumn arrive before 1000 if planning to park and explore from Sunrise, Sunset, Inspiration, Bryce or Paria viewpoints. Caravan trailers are not permitted beyond Sunset Campground, midway along the canyon drive, and RVs longer than 25 ft are prohibited from Paria View, at the end of the road, for lack of turning space.

During the day, drive directly to **Rainbow Point**, where visibility can exceed 90 miles and early visitors occasionally spot mountain lions. The one-mile **Bristlecone Loop Trail** threads through stands of rare bristlecone pines, the oldest living organisms on earth.

Sunset Point is the obvious point from which to enjoy the sunset, though parking is a problem in summer. Vistas curve east towards **Queen's Garden**, **Wall Street** and an illusory balanced rock called **Thor's Hammer**. Allow 2 hrs to walk the 1½ mile **Navajo Loop Trail** that wanders past Thor's Hammer, through the narrow clefts separating the hoodoos and through forests of pygmy Douglas fir trees. The easiest canyon trail is a 1¾ mile stroll through Queen's Garden from Sunset Point.

i **Bryce Canyon National Park**, Box 170001, Bryce Canyon; tel: (435) 834-5322; www.nps.gov/brca/. The visitor center is one mile south of the park entrance: open daily,

0800–1630 (Oct–Apr); 0800–1800 (late Apr and early Oct), 0800–2000 (May–Sept).

Bryce Canyon Lodge $$ AmFac Parks and Resorts, 14001 E. Iliff Ave, Ste 600, Aurora; tel: (303) 297-2757; fax: (303) 237-3715. Open mid Apr–Oct, the lodge is the only non-camping accommodation in the park. Advance booking required.
Best Western Ruby's Inn $$ 1 mile north of the park entrance on Hwy 63; tel: (435) 834-5341 or (800) 468-8660.

Bryce Canyon Pines, 12 miles west on Hwy 12; tel: (435) 834-5441 or (800) 892-7923.
Other accommodation is available in Tropic, east of the park on Hwy 12.

Cowboy's Smokehouse Bar-B-Q $$ 95 N. Main St, Panguitch; tel: (435) 676-8030. The best local restaurant, well worth the 6 mile drive for authentic wood-smoked meats and enormous slabs of home-made pie.
Bryce Canyon Lodge Restaurant $$. The only restaurant in the park open all year.
The General Store $$ Sunrise Point. Sells snacks and drinks mid Apr–Oct.

ZION NATIONAL PARK

The walls of Zion National Park ($) soar hundreds of feet above the river that carved them. Like the Grand Canyon, Zion has two parts: Zion Canyon (south) and Kolob Canyons (north). It's possible to combine the two in a single exhausting day, but more rewarding to allow at least a day for each.

Biblical Landscape

Zion Canyon could be a page from Mormon history, filled with names like Abraham, Isaac, Jacob and Moroni (the Mormon angel). The biblical names for the imposing formations were actually chosen by a Methodist minister, Frederick Vining Fisher, who explored the North Fork of the Virgin River.

Kolob Canyons is best known to serious hikers, but the easy 5 mile drive up Hurricane Fault to the picnic area at **Kolob Canyons Viewpoint** is not to be missed. Look for stunning views of mesa formations dropping sheer to the Lower Kolob Plateau.

The **Zion Canyon Scenic Drive** up the canyon starts from **The Watchman** (6546 ft), a mountain wedge standing sentinel near the south entrance. A short path leads from the car park to the **Court of the Patriarchs**, with Mounts Abraham, Isaac, Jacob and Moroni to the west.

OUTSIDE THE PARKS

East of the string of national parks are two remarkable national monuments in the south-east corner of the state.

Remote **Natural Bridges Monument** sits high on Cedar Mesa at 6500 ft. Intermittent streams have cut two deep canyons and sculpted three massive bridges from the white sandstone that once lined the ancient sea bed. The bridges can be viewed from overlooks or you can hike into the canyons to see them from below. Approach it from Hite, on Rte 95.

Hovenweep National Monument is 20 miles north of Aneth on a gravel road. Its incredible towers of pueblo ruins, over 1000 years old, have been compared to European castles. There are six units of towers, the largest of which is Square Tower. Hovenweep has one campsite and there is accommodation in Bluff or Blanding. More information can be obtained from Hovenweep National Monument, McElmo Rd; tel: (303) 562 4248.

The natural hanging gardens of **Weeping Rock**, ¼ mile from the car park, are watered by mists and rivulets seeping from the sandstone. Take a moment to duck beneath a well-watered overhang to see Zion's serrated peaks shimmer through the mist.

Beyond Weeping Rock, rock climbers cling like ants to cliffs that lead to the **Temple of Sinawava**, end of the road and start of a mile long **Riverside Walk** along the Virgin River to another hanging garden.

Zion National Park, Springdale, tel: (435) 772-3256; www.nps.gov/zion/. Zion Canyon Visitor Center is ½ mile north of the south entrance; tel: (435) 772-3256. Open daily.

Zion Lodge $$$ 4 miles north of the south entrance; tel: (800) 586-7686. The only indoor accommodation in the park. Reservations are essential, through AmFac Parks and Resorts, 140001 E. Iliff Ave, Ste 600, Aurora; tel: (303) 297-2757; fax: (303) 237-3715.
Other accommodation is available in Springdale, just beyond the south entrance, and the nearby towns of Hurricane or St George. The most convenient accommodation for visitors to Kolob Canyons is in Cedar City.

Zion Lodge Restaurant $$$. The only restaurant in the park. Picnic supplies can be purchased in nearby towns, a better alternative than the Lodge snack bar.

WHERE NEXT?

South from Zion, across the border in Colorado, is the Grand Canyon. Approaching from the north will bring you to the much less commercial and comparatively unvisited North Rim (see p. 391).

150 miles south of Moab (Hwys 191 and 163) is ***Monument Valley****, part of the Navajo Indian reservation, and characterised by tall, red sandstone formations. Peer closely at the rock formations: they are noteworthy as they resemble animals – look for the bear and the rabbit. It is also the scene of countless movies, Westerns in particular. Visitor Centre, off Hwy 163, tel: 801 727 3353.*

Las Vegas

The ads claim that Las Vegas never sleeps. The lure of easy money, clattering slot machines and flashing neon may slow in the hours just before dawn, but Vegas has barely paused for breath since Nevada legalised gambling in the early 1930s.

GETTING THERE AND GETTING AROUND

McCarran International Airport is 5 miles from the city centre. A taxi to the Strip averages $10; bus fares are slightly less for a return journey.

Amtrak's daily service from LA arrives at the Union Plaza Hotel Station, the world's only railway depot inside a casino.

I-15 is the main highway access from California and the Grand Canyon. Traffic along the Strip grinds to a crawl between mid-afternoon and late evening, but as a compensation, parking is plentiful, convenient and cheap. Local CAT buses operate 24 hrs a day, and trolleys run up and down the Strip until 0200.

INFORMATION

Las Vegas Convention and Visitors Authority, 3150 Paradise Rd; tel: (702) 886-0770 or (800) 332-5333, is open Mon–Sat 0700–1900, 0830–1800.

Safety Casinos are extremely security-conscious, and the Strip and 'Glitter Gulch', the casino strip on Fremont St, are safe day or night. However, avoid car parks at night (use the free valet parking every hotel offers) and don't take late night strolls away from the casino areas. Also beware the hustlers (of either sex) who work the casinos. Don't invite strangers, however alluring, to your room – too many visitors are drugged and robbed by newfound 'friends'.

Money Foreign Money Exchange, 3025 Las Vegas Blvd S. 224; tel: (702) 791-3301.

ACCOMMODATION AND FOOD

Vegas is the hotel capital of the USA, mostly concentrated along the Strip and downtown (Fremont St and nearby). New Strip hotels are most luxurious; downtown hotels less expensive. Visit midweek for the best value.

Traditionally, casino food and drink prices were kept low to lure gamblers. Prices have become more realistic, but casino buffets are still good value – the Fiesta, Rio and Station (Boulder, Palace, Sunset and Texas) score well for food as well as prices.

HIGHLIGHTS

THE RAZZMATAZZ For most visitors the **Strip** – Las Vegas Blvd S. – *is* Las Vegas. From the **Stratosphere** to the **Mandalay Bay**, its 3 miles are lined with more than 40 hotel-casinos and acres of neon. Mobster Bugsy Siegel's **Flamingo** opened here on New Year's Eve 1946 and every year seems to see a bigger, more flamboyant arrival. **Caesar's Palace** is a classic, its Forum lined with 100-plus brand name shops and restaurants – and 'living statues'. The **Luxor**'s exact replica of King Tutankhamun's tomb may prepare you for **New York, New York**'s Statue of Liberty, but what about an erupting volcano, a rain forest and white tigers at the **Mirage**? The **Imperial Palace**'s Antique and Classic Auto Collection features a 1928 Delage limousine owned by the late King of Siam and Eisenhower's parade limo.

Spectacular shows for all tastes are a major attraction. At the Mirage **Siegfried and Roy**'s tigers and explosive lighting effects transform a magic show, while **Cirque de Soleil** at Treasure Island exercise prodigious feats of balance and skill. Downtown, 2.1 *million* lights nightly create the **Fremont Street Experience**. For family-oriented entertainment, **Grand Slam Canyon** has adventure rides, Merlin fights a dragon at the **Excalibur**, and there's a free pirate battle at the **Treasure Island** (arrive early).

TIPPING

Everything in Las Vegas works better with 'green grease', or tips. Employees may be on the minimum wage or close to it, so they depend on tips, but service is generally good because of it.

GAMBLING The lure of gaming – as it's euphemistically referred to in the industry – starts with slot machines at the airport (locals say the payoff is terrible). Casinos warn against playing without knowing the rules, and they're right. If you're an innocent abroad, take a free lesson in the basics or browse in the Gambler's Bookstore (630 S. 11th St). Slot machines may seem easy to play, but they account for over half the casinos' profits. Bigger casinos generally give slightly better odds than smaller ones, and the payoff is slightly better with dollar than quarter machines.

AWAY FROM THE TABLES The **Las Vegas Natural History Museum** is a good introduction to Nevada's indigenous plants and animals. $ 900 Las Vegas Blvd N.; open 0900–1600. Be dazzled in close-up by the **Liberace Museum**: $ 1775 E. Tropicana Ave; open 1000–1700 Mon–Sat, 1300–1500 Sun.

Out in the desert, **Red Rock Canyon** (20 miles west, off Charleston Blvd) features some of the most spectacular desert scenery within easy reach of Las Vegas (visitor centre open 0830–1630). About 50 miles north-east of Las Vegas (off I-15 near Overton), the eroded red sandstone formations of rugged **Valley of Fire** seem to catch light in the sunshine; some rocks are covered with prehistoric petroglyphs. Open dawn–dusk. Man-made but hugely impressive, the mighty **Hoover Dam**, 30 miles east, on Hwy 93, is open daily 0830–1730 ($).

Route Detail

Take I-5 heading south. This takes you via Anaheim for the attractions of Disneyland. 25 miles

From Capistrano Beach, the road follows the coastline all the way into San Diego. 92 miles

For more views of the coast between Los Angeles and Capistrano Beach, you can leave LA on I-710, the Long Beach Freeway towards Long Beach, and turn left onto Rte 1, the Pacific Coast Highway.

This allows you to take in Seal Beach, Sunset Beach and Laguna Beach, before the road joins I-5 shortly before Capistrano Beach. 52 miles

Be warned – as emphasised elsewhere in this chapter, all of these roads are often very congested.

Amtrak runs frequent services between Los Angeles, Anaheim, San Juan Capistrano and San Diego – see OTT Table 405. Greyhound operate services along this route and LA to San Diego direct (OTT Table 852)

Los Angeles – San Diego

From Los Angeles south to San Diego the coast is a sunny, sandy haven for the rich and tanned. The train is a relaxing alternative to the often slow and congested highways, and the stretch between Capistrano Beach and Del Mar, in particular, affords wonderful views of the Pacific. Stops along the way include Anaheim (for Disneyland) and the old mission town of San Juan Capistrano.

ANAHEIM

All of Los Angeles has been accused of being a gigantic theme park, but even here some places are less real than others. Anaheim is the stop for Knott's Berry Farm, the USA's original theme park, and for Disney's first dreams-come-true creation, Disneyland. Amtrak trains pull into the Anaheim Stadium, about 1 mile east of Disneyland (taxis available at the station).

Just beyond Disneyland's main entrance ($$$$), **Main Street USA** is lined with Victorian-style shopfronts. Beyond, the dreamland opens up: **Adventureland, Frontierland, Critter Country, Fantasyland** (anchored by the Disney signature Sleeping Beauty's Castle), **Toontown** and the rest. **Tomorrowland** was rebuilt in 1998 to be more futuristic – 'Honey, I Shrunk the Audience' is a chance to wear 3D glasses. Evening parades and fireworks are worth waiting for, but find a vantage point early.

You may not bring food and drink into the park, but cafeterias and fast-food outlets are (of course) here in abundance, from breakfast in Main Street's **Carnation Café** to dinner in 'New Orleans' at **The Blue Bayou**. Official hotels offer children Character Dining ($$$) – they can have tea with Minnie and friends.

About 20 mins away (tel: (714) 220-5200), **Knott's Berry Farm** actually did begin life as a berry farm. The Knott family sidelined into chicken dinners to counteract the 1930s Depression, and the wagon rides they started up to entertain the ever-increasing number of visitors were the forerunners of the hair-raising amusement rides here today. The Wild West – from the partly authentic **Ghost Town** to the Bigfoot Rapids of **Wild Water Wilderness** – is a running theme. Knott's is also the home of Charlie Brown, Lucy, Linus and the rest of the Peanuts gang, with their headquarters at **Camp Snoopy**. And, yes, you can still get a Mrs Knott's Chicken Dinner here.

Disneyland Resort Hotels (tel: (714) 956-6425) include **Disneyland Hotel** ($$$) and the **Disneyland Pacific Hotel** ($$$), across from the park entrance.

SAN JUAN CAPISTRANO

Each year, on St Joseph's Day (19 Mar), legend decrees that the swallows return to Mission San Juan Capistrano. The large mission site is beautiful with fountains, lush gardens, and peaceful courtyards. The Serra Chapel (1777) is the oldest building still in regular use in California, and the ruins remain of the Great Stone Church, which collapsed during morning mass in an 1812 earthquake. $ Open daily 0830–1700.

See fine American antique jewellery, silver, glass, china, saddles, dolls, books and Orange County fruit box labels at **Old Barn Antiques Mall**, 31792 Camino Capistrano, a co-operative of antique dealers; open daily 1000–1700. The 31 structures within **Los Rios Historic District** include adobe houses, a pet farm and the 1894 Santa Fe Railroad Depot.

San Juan Capistrano Chamber of Commerce, 31931 Camino Capistrano, Ste D; tel: (949) 493-4700. For information on the month-long March swallows' return celebrations, tel: (949) 248-2049. Book accommodation in advance.

Amtrak station is in the historic town, next to the Mission.

Laguna Inn and Suites $$ 28742 Camino Capistrano; tel: (949) 347-8520.

Café Capistrano $ Camino Capistrano and Ortega Hwy. Features burgers and patty melts.
Ramos House Café $$ 31752 Los Rios St. Breakfast and lunch on an outdoor patio.

En Route

Around Oceanside is a curious mix of attractions: a surfing museum as well as real surf; tours of the Marine Corps' amphibious training base, Camp Pendleton; and, just south at Carlsbad, drag racing, motocross and the Lego Family Park.

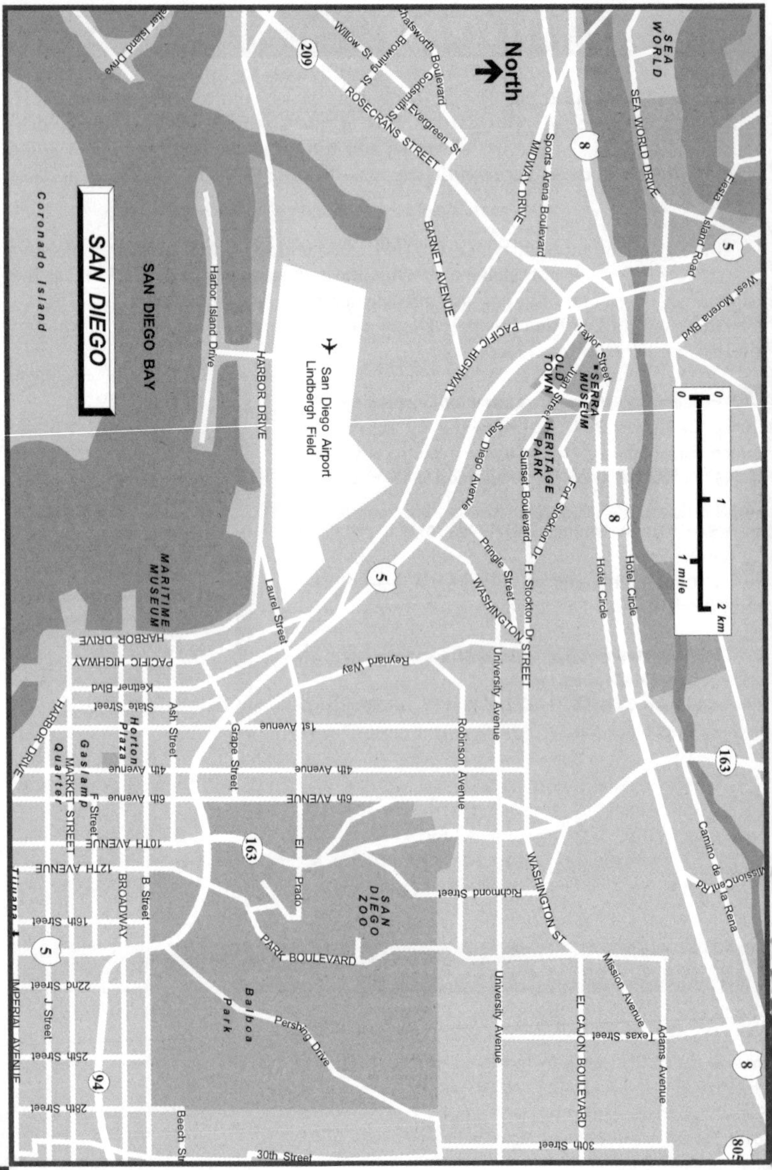
SAN DIEGO
North
SEA WORLD
SEA WORLD DRIVE
Fiesta Island Road
West Morena Blvd
Sports Arena Boulevard
MIDWAY DRIVE
ROSECRANS STREET
Chatsworth Boulevard
Browning St
Willow St
Goldsmith St
Evergreen St
BARNET AVENUE
PACIFIC HIGHWAY
Taylor Street
SERRA MUSEUM
OLD TOWN
Juan Street
HERITAGE PARK
San Diego Avenue
Sunset Boulevard
Fort Stockton Dr
Ft Stockton Dr
Pringle Street
WASHINGTON STREET
Hotel Circle
San Diego Airport
Lindbergh Field
HARBOR DRIVE
Harbor Island Drive
SAN DIEGO BAY
Coronado Island
MARITIME MUSEUM
Laurel Street
Reynard Way
University Avenue
Robinson Avenue
Kettner Blvd
State Street
Ash Street
1st Avenue
4th Avenue
6th Avenue
6th AVENUE
Grape Street
Horton Plaza
Gaslamp Quarter
F Street
MARKET STREET
10TH AVENUE
12TH AVENUE
B Street
BROADWAY
El Prado
SAN DIEGO ZOO
Richmond Street
WASHINGTON ST
16th Street
PARK BOULEVARD
Balboa Park
Pershing Drive
22nd Street
J Street
25th Street
28th Street
IMPERIAL AVENUE
Beech St
30th Street
Mission Avenue
EL CAJON BOULEVARD
Texas Street
Adams Avenue
Camino de la Rena
Mission Center Rd
0
1
1 mile
2 km
209
8
5
163
94
805

San Diego

San Diego is as tropical as California gets. Bright sun and ocean breezes combine with the influence of Mexico, 20 miles south, to concoct a casual, easy-going atmosphere in California's second largest city. Visually, San Diego is uncongested; homes and businesses do not pile above or against one another. East over the mountains is desert; north along the coast are round, eroded cliffs and beaches of golden sand. Coronado Island, in San Diego Bay, offers resort dining and shopping a few minutes from downtown, while Mission Bay has beaches, SeaWorld and marinas filled with pleasure boats. Downtown bustles with business, gracefully proportioned high-rises lining the waterfront. And just 10 inches of annual rainfall encourages alfresco dining most of the year.

Getting There

Air **San Diego International Airport, Lindbergh Field**, tel: (619) 231-7361, is 3 miles north of downtown. San Diego Transit (MTS) bus 992 will take you into the city centre, but taxis are cheap – as cheap if there are three or four of you. Hotels and other shuttles also operate from between Terminals 1 and 2.

Rail/Bus Amtrak trains connect Los Angeles and San Diego 11 times daily; the journey takes 2½ hrs. The terminus at the Santa Fe Depot has transit connections north to Oceanside on the Coaster commuter service, and via trolley to Old Town, Mission Valley, Seaport Village and the Mexican border.

Road San Diego is 120 miles south of Los Angeles via I-5; allot 3 hrs to drive from centre to centre, more in the rush hour.

Boat The Cruise Ship Terminal is across N. Harbor Dr. from the Spanish Mission-style Santa Fe Depot (1050 Kettner Blvd).

Information

San Diego Convention and Visitors Bureau, 401 B St, Suite 1400; tel: (619) 236-1212; fax: (619) 696-9371; www.sandiego.org.

International Visitors Information Center, 11 Horton Plaza (1st Ave at F St), is open Mon–Sat 0830–1700; also Sun 1100–1700 June–Aug.

San Diego Visitor Information Center, 2668 E Mission Bay Dr.; tel: (619) 276-8200; fax: (619) 276-6041; www.infosandiego.com. Open 0900–dusk.

San Diego

Safety Avoid areas east of Fifth Ave and south of Imperial.

Money Thomas Cook Foreign Exchange office at 4417 La Jolla Dr., Suite N17; tel: (619) 457 2366.

Post and Phones The main post office is at 51 Horton Plaza; tel: (619) 232-9235.

ACCOMMODATION

Coronado, Mission Bay, coastal and downtown hotels are pricey; look for large rooms, value and easy freeway access from I-8 in Mission Valley's Hotel Circle, a 15-min drive to downtown. Prices drop 15–40% Nov–Mar; what's pricey in high season may be offered at discount later. **San Diego Hotel Reservations**, tel: (800) 728-3227 or (619) 627-9300; www.savecash.com, can book accommodation area-wide.

Hostelling International Downtown San Diego $ 521 Market St; Convention Center Trolley; tel: (619) 525-1531; fax: (619) 338-0129. In the heart of the historic Gaslamp Quarter.

Hostelling International Point Loma $ 3790 Udall St; bus 35 from Old Town Trolley; tel: (619) 223-4778; fax: (619) 223-1833. Near Ocean Beach.

Heritage Park Inn $$$ 2470 Heritage Park Row; Old Town Trolley; tel: (619) 299-6832 or (800) 995-2470. Victorian cosseting two blocks from Old Town State Historic Park.

Hotel del Coronado $$$ 1500 Orange Ave, Coronado; bus 901; tel: (619) 522-8000 or (800) 468-3533. The grande dame, picture-postcard resort hotel, complete with ghosts.

Town and Country Resort Hotel $$$ 500 Hotel Circle N.; Fashion Valley Trolley; tel: (800) 772-8527. Convenient, large convention hotel with posh rooms, cheerful staff and easy freeway access.

FOOD

San Diego's proximity to Mexico makes it easy to find a variety of Mexican food, from bland to chilli-pepper spicy, especially in Old Town. San Diego is also getting a reputation for fusion cuisines, mixing California's fresh produce with delicate recipes, sauces and presentation from Asia. The Gaslamp Quarter has a good choice of restaurants, from moderate to pricey, many with live music in the evening. Seaport Village's several bayside seafood restaurants allow you to enjoy views of gleaming white boats nestled in marinas in Mission Bay.

Croce's $$ 5th Ave and F St; tel: (619) 233-4355. A choice of three venues: Top Hat Bar and Grille has nightly rhythm and blues; Croce's West has South-west cuisine; and Croce's Restaurant and Jazz Bar has all-American cuisine with live jazz.

Buffalo Joe's $$ 600 5th Ave; tel: (619) 236-1616. The place to try baby back ribs.

La Casa de Bandini $$, 2660 Calhoun St.; tel: (619) 297-8211. An adobe in Old Town serving a variety of tortillas.

Sadaf Restaurant $$ 828 5th Ave; tel: (619) 338-0008. Draws a loyal crowd for Persian dishes.

Hornblower $$$ 1066 N. Harbor Dr.; tel: (619) 686-8715. Dinner-dance and Sun Champagne brunch cruises in the Bay.

GETTING AROUND

San Diego's public transport is inexpensive, seamless and a good alternative to city driving. Different transport systems are co-ordinated by the San Diego Metropolitan Transit System (MTS), tel: (619) 233-3004; www.sandag.cog.ca.us.

The bright red **San Diego Trolley** connects the Santa Fe Depot with Mission Valley and Old Town (Blue Line), Seaport Village (Orange Line) and San Ysidro/Tijuana (Blue Line). Trolleys operate 0430–0200 daily; fares vary by distance.

San Diego Transit buses run from downtown and trolley stations to points throughout the city. Buses operate 0430–0030 daily for a flat fare.

The **Coronado Ferry** departs from Broadway Pier (across Pacific Hwy from Santa Fe Depot) on the hour 0900–2100 (2200 Fri–Sat) and returns from Coronado on the half-hour 0930–2130 (2200 Fri–Sat).

Day Tripper Passes, valid on all MTS bus and trolley routes for one, two, three and four days, are available from selected trolley ticket machines and the **Transit Store**, 102 Broadway at 1st Ave; open 0830–1730 Mon–Fri, 1200–1600 Sat–Sun.

HIGHLIGHTS

DOWNTOWN Opulent late Victorian architecture and street lamps grace downtown's 16-block **Gaslamp Quarter** (between Broadway and Harbor Dr., and 4th and 6th Aves). Alone among California's major cities, this civic and business centre has remained visually intact since its beginnings as 'New Town' in 1887, when San Francisco merchant Alonzo E. Horton bought up the waterfront and moved the action from Old Town. The 1850s **William Heath Davis House** was an early merchant-developer's residence; $ 410 Island Ave.

Through the next century, the boom town catered to lawman Wyatt Earp's three gambling halls, bordello patrons, sailors and homeless men, evolving into an infamous skid row as population and business shifted north and east. Some homeless missions remain, but the Gaslamp Quarter's 1970s restoration continues, cemented by great music clubs, fine dining and a cheerful ambience of rediscovery.

Horton Plaza, at the north edge of the Gaslamp Quarter, has 140 shops, including FAO Schwarz for toys and Nordstrom and Macy's department stores. Geometric wedges, odd angles, tilework, the eagle-topped Jessops San Diego Time Clock and 41 cheerful colours make this chic shopping mall a popular destination for San Diegans.

The **San Diego Maritime Museum** $$ on N. Harbor Dr. is dominated by the majesty of the *Star of India*'s square rigging. One of three ships open for touring, the oldest merchant vessel still afloat has been restored to the condition of her launch from the Isle of Man in 1863. The 1898 *Berkeley* ferry boat is the sister ship of the *Eureka*, displayed along the Hyde Park Pier of the National Maritime Museum in San Francisco (see p. 434). Both ferries plied San Francisco Bay. The steamer *Medea*, a Scottish-built luxury yacht, is tied up alongside.

If You're Driving

Freeways may clog abysmally in the rush hour. Hwy S21 is the much slower scenic alternative to I-5, running along the coast from Carlsbad to Mission Bay/Mission Beach.

Many city-centre streets are one-way; follow directional signs to attractions. Downtown parking meters are inexpensive: Horton Plaza offers 3 hrs' free parking with any mall purchase, a cheaper alternative to valet parking at trendy 5th St restaurants. Seaport Village has 2-hr validation.

Old Town

North-west of downtown, a larger area of motels, restaurants and shops serves visitors to the city's 19th-century settlement. In **Old Town San Diego State Historic Park** three original family adobes, **La Casa de Estudillo**, **Machado y Stewart**, and **Machado y Silvas** are beautifully restored house museums. At weekends, volunteers dressed in mid-19th-century military uniforms are inspected in front of the **Robinson-Rose House** (also the visitor centre), then drill on the green and parade around the park. A blacksmith demonstrates his skills near **Seeley Stables Museum.** Carriages and stagecoaches are on display inside, supplemented by a film on transport in California. The **First San Diego Courthouse**, the first ***San Diego Union*** (newspaper) building, a school and a dental museum offer insights into daily life while the **Wells Fargo Museum** in the reconstructed **Colorado House** explains the economics of stagecoaches and the Gold Rush in California. The park is open daily 1000–1700. For a self-guided walking tour, purchase *Old Town San Diego State Historic Park Tour Guide and Brief History* at Seeley Stables, or take a ranger-led tour. **Old Town Trolley Tours** $$; tel: (619) 298-8687, operate a hop-on hop-off tour in orange and green motorised trams. Board at Twiggs St or any of eight other stops for a 2-hr narrated circuit. Tours run 0900–1600 (last tour).

San Diegans visit Old Town to enjoy margaritas and warm tortillas at several good restaurants, such as those in the courtyard of **Bazaar del Mundo**'s hibiscus-entwined shopping arcade, complete with dancers and mariachi bands.

On the edge of Old Town, **Heritage Park** preserves six Victorian mansions and a Jewish synagogue arranged along a pedestrian walk. All the buildings are still in use, and popular with wedding parties at weekends. A turret marks the Heritage Park Bed and Breakfast Inn in the 1889 Queen Anne style **Christian House**, and there are Victorian-style souvenirs in the 1893 classical revival **Burton House**. The clean classical revival lines of the 1893 **Temple Beth Israel** appealed to Christian congregations, which also used the building before they had permanent sites for their churches.

The **Mormon Battalion Memorial** at 2510 Juan St, between Old Town and Heritage Park, celebrates the arrival in 1847 of LDS troops to support American troops in the fight against Mexico. North of Old Town, **Presidio Park** was the site of the original 1769 fort and mission. The **Junipero Serra Museum and Tower Gallery** artefacts and scale models explain San Diego's pre-American history.

BALBOA PARK *The* city park, Balboa Park is 1400 acres of greenery north-east of downtown. The collection of plants, trees, Californian-Spanish Baroque architecture, museums and the world-renowned zoo (see box) have rendered its original 1868 chaparral and cacti desertscape unrecognisable outside the sculptured **Desert Garden** (on the east side of Park Blvd). Many of the Baroque buildings were installed for the 1915 Panama-California Exposition. The park is full of interesting museums, botanical displays, artists' studios and performing arts venues. Many museums are free one Tues each month, but the seven-day, 12-museum **Passport to Balboa Park** provides bargain admission at other times. There is a visitor centre at 1549 El Prado, and a free **Balboa Park Tram** from the Inspiration Point car park makes a circuit of 11 stops.

Along El Prado, in the western segment of the park, is a varied assembly of sights and entertainments. The **Museum of Man** at no. 1350 is an eclectic, fun collection of ethnic artefacts from all over the world – don't miss the mummies; $ open 1000–1630. The **Mingei International Museum**, at no. 1439, displays worldwide folk arts; $ open Tues–Sun 1000–1600. From the formal arcaded **Alcazar Garden** behind the museum there is a picture-postcard view of California Tower's tile dome. The European art collections at the **Timken Museum of Art** (no. 1500) include magnificent Russian icons. Open Tues–Sat 1000–1630, Sun 1330–1630; closed Aug. Youth productions of ballet, theatre and dance can be enjoyed at **Casa del Prado Theater**; $$ tel: (619) 239-1311. Its elegant facade could be in Spain.

During renovation work the **Museum of Photographic Art** ($), usually housed at 1649 El Prado, has moved to the Museum of Contemporary Art downtown (across from the Santa Fe Depot). The building's lower level, however, is heaven for train buffs. The **Model Railroad Museum** has six scale-model mini-gauge train circuits, enhanced by realistic sound effects. $ Open Tues–Fri 1100–1600, Sat–Sun 1100– 1700.

Transport in all forms is well represented in the park. The combined influence of naval aviation and the aerospace industry in San Diego make the 66 aircraft on display in the doughnut-shaped Ford Building of the **San Diego Aerospace Museum** one of the best introductions to the history of flight. $$ Open 1000–1630; free fourth Tues of the month. The **San Diego Automotive Museum** rotates exhibits of southern California's *raison d'être* from a fine collection of historic vehicles. $$ 2080 Pan American Plaza; open 1000–1630 (until 1730 in summer). There are hands-on exhibits and an OMNIMAX® Space Theater at the **Reuben H. Fleet Science Center**. Open 0930–1800 Mon–Tues, 0930–2100 Wed–Sat, 0930–2000 Sun.

San Diego Zoo

This world-famous zoo was among the first to pioneer habitats for its birds and 3900 animals, freeing them from traditional caged confinement.

On several levels of jungle-type vegetation, the zoo wanders through Cat and Bear Canyons and Horn and Hoof Mesa. Queue up early for a glimpse of two pandas on research loan from China. The Polar Bear Plunge is happily incongruous in the balmy climate, but Gorilla Tropics and the South African klipspringer habitat feel like authentic exotic locations. There's also a Children's Zoo.

Guided tours in double-decker buses get round most of the zoo; Kangaroo Bus Tours provide eight drop-off points. Both depart from Flamingo Lagoon in the main area. The Skyfari Aerial Tram gives a gondola overview with a quick hop to the other side of the park. **$$$** open 0900–1700 (last entry 1600).

For art lovers, **the San Diego Museum of Art** in Plaza de Panama combines contemporary California art with Chinese, Japanese and 15th–18th-century European works, supplemented by the outdoor Sculpture Garden Café. $$ Open Tues–Sun 1000–1430. The **Spanish Village Arts and Crafts Center** has a wide, colourful courtyard full of studios where artists work, display and sell sculpture, jewellery, paintings and other arts. Open 1100–1600. The **Old Globe Theatre**, a reproduction of the London original, presents Shakespeare's plays and more on several stages.

Other curiosities and attractions in the park include **Spreckels Organ Pavilion**,where 4445 organ pipes thrill music lovers with free outdoor concerts Sun afternoons and Mon evenings June–Aug; the **Botanical Building**, whose plain name disguises the beautiful orchids and heliconia which bloom amid exotic palms (open daily except Thur 1000–1600); and **Marston House**, in the north-west corner of the park. This craftsman-style mansion has lovely landscaped English-style gardens. $ 3525 7th Ave; open Fri–Sun 1200–1630.

SEAPORT VILLAGE This nautical-theme shopping and dining area just north-west of the San Diego Convention Center lies on the bay south of the Gaslamp Quarter. A bayside boardwalk at the south end of the embarcadero gives access to year-round outdoor music, fashion shows and mimes, and shops are open late (until 2100; 2200 June–Aug). **Wyland Galleries** have the famous artist's whale paintings and marine art, and the **San Diego City Store** proffers local-name souvenirs and T-shirts. Go for a cheerful wake-up breakfast at the **Village Café** and take a spin on the 1890 Looff **Broadway Flying Horses Carousel** on the boardwalk.

CORONADO ISLAND Just a ferry ride across San Diego Bay, Coronado Island is resort, getaway, shopping opportunity, and sunset viewpoint. With the arrival of the railway in the 1880s, San Diego cried out for a resort, and the **Hotel del Coronado** met the need. The white Victorian building with bright red roof and towers still stands as a luxury landmark, a wedding-cake frippery.

The **San Diego-Coronado Bay Bridge** arcs gracefully over the bay, a lovely drive except during the rush hour. Bus no. 901 makes the journey, or catch the **Coronado Ferry** (passengers and bicycles only) from Broadway Pier to Ferry Landing Marketplace. (A fast but pricey alternative is Marriott's Coronado Island Resort's water taxi service: 6 mins to the San Diego Convention Center area.)

On the north side of the island, shops and dining are congregated around Ferry Landing Marketplace which, with four parks ½ mile west, has fine views of the afternoon sun glowing on downtown high-rises to the east. Ocean Blvd, north-west of the Hotel del Coronado, is a superb spot for sunsets. **Orange Ave**, near the hotel, is a trendy area to shop, dine, sip espresso, browse in art galleries and people-watch. The **Coronado Beach Historical Museum** displays a small collection of photographs and artefacts in an 1898 Victorian house. $ 1126 Loma Ave; open 1000–1600 Wed–Sat, 1200–1600 Sun.

MISSION BAY Mission Bay sprang from the imagination when mud dredged from San Diego Harbor created a huge waterside parkland, with beaches on the bay and Pacific Ocean. The sheltered bay offers hotels and camping, restaurants and children's playgrounds, and every sporting opportunity from swimming, jet skiing and sailing to bicycling, skating, kite-flying, fishing, tennis and golf.

The best-known attraction is **SeaWorld Adventure Park San Diego**. Its denizens of the oceans are dominated by the orca (killer whales). Special effects accompany the Shamu Adventure, with performances by Shamu, Baby Shamu and Namu. On Wild Arctic, a simulated helicopter takes off from San Diego and lands in a North Pole scenario with polar bears, beluga whales and walrus going about their business. Florida's gentle herbivores are being rehabilitated in Manatee Rescue, a 215,000-gallon freshwater tank with viewing of the sea cows from above and below. A plastic viewing tube protects visitors from the inhabitants of Shark Encounter. Bottlenose dolphins, pilot whales, sea lions, river otters and large birds perform routines, and aquariums introduce less tractable species. SeaWorld $$$ is open daily, 0900–2200/2300 mid June–Labor Day; 1000–1700/1930 rest of the year; bus no. 9 from Old Town Trolley.

POINT LOMA In 1542, three Spanish ships under Portuguese commander Juan Rodriguez Cabrillo found a 'closed and very good port' and Kumeyaay Indians. The explorers landed, claimed 'San Miguel' for their Catholic majesties, then sailed north to the Channel Islands. At the end of Point Loma peninsula sheltering San Diego Bay, the clifftop **Cabrillo National Monument** ($) is a majestic, oversized white statue of the explorer flanked by cross, crown and coat of arms of Spain. Cabrillo's head faces east, taking in the sweep of the bay channel, Coronado Island and downtown San Diego to the mountains flanking the Mexican border. Below the statue, an observation area offers stunning vistas of sailing regattas and US naval traffic.

Old Point Loma Lighthouse, a 5-min walk from the monument, sits whitely 422 ft above the Pacific. Operational from 1855 to 1891, the light tower sits in the middle of the house, furnished as it was for the last keeper's posting.

A 2-mile return **Bayside Trail** winds through prickly pear and succulents, black sage and chaparral as it descends 300 ft. A well-marked path close to the monument entrance gives on to accessible tidepools, and the **Whale Overlook** is ideal for grey whale spotting Dec–Mar. Below Point Loma, the eroded **Sunset Cliffs** are popular at sundown. Monument, visitor centre and lighthouse are open daily 0900–1715 (until 1815 4 July–Labor Day). To reach Point Loma, take Hwy 209 to Cabrillo Memorial Dr., or bus No. 26 from Old Town Trolley.

59-MILE DRIVE

The scenic San Diego 59-Mile Drive is a half-day circuit that begins at the foot of Broadway near the Santa Fe Depot, and includes La Jolla and Coronado. Follow the signs of a flying white seagull on a blue and yellow field.

SHOPPING

Perhaps because of the pleasant climate, it's easy to shop in the San Diego area, and shops are usually open until about 2100 most days. Film and TV merchandising stores in the whimsically coloured **Horton Plaza** include, for something more San Diegan than Disney or Warner, the local educational television station **KPBS Store of Knowledge**, and **Sports Fantasy** for genuine US sports team clothing and accessories. Validated parking helps the cost of window-shopping in the **Gaslamp Quarter**. Look for nautical souvenirs at **Seaport Village**, Mexican at Old Town's

Bazaar del Mundo, or search for unexpected bargains at **Kobey's Swap Meet**, 3500 Sports Arena Blvd; tel: (619) 226-0650; open Thur–Sun. **Fashion Valley Mall**, 7007 Friars Rd (Fashion Valley Trolley) in Mission Valley is filled with clothing, cosmetic and home furnishing shops, a food court and a multi-screen cinema.

NIGHTLIFE

Local newspapers and the free *San Diego Weekly Reader* list clubs, nightlife and restaurants. The **San Diego Performing Arts League** has bi-monthly listings in its free *What's Playing in San Diego Guide*. **Times Arts Tix**, south-west corner of Horton Plaza; tel: (619) 497-5000, offers on-the-day half-price tickets for theatre, dance or concert performances.

Hopping jazz, blues and rock clubs are attached to the **Gaslamp Quarter** restaurants along 5th Ave. The presence of University of California San Diego draws big-name music groups to the area.

Old Globe Theatre, Balboa Park; tel: (619) 239-2255. One of the most venerable companies in the country fills three theatres with 12 productions a year.

San Diego Lyceum Theatre, Horton Plaza; tel: (619) 235-8025. Comic and classic performances in repertory.

La Jolla Playhouse, 2910 Village Dr.; tel: (619) 550-1070.

OUT OF TOWN

California's first mission seems strangely isolated, 7 miles from the coast or downtown, but the white facade and lush front gardens of Mission San Diego de Alcalá are exactly the austere and imposing image the Spanish Church and Empire wished to project. $ 10919 San Diego Mission Rd (Mission San Diego Trolley). A small museum displays vestments and manuscripts written by California Mission's founder Fra Junipero Serra and is open daily 0900–1700.

DAY TRIPS

LA JOLLA Just north of San Diego is La Jolla (buses 30, 34), a popular resort graced with a rocky coast and fine beaches. **La Jolla Cove** affords excellent swimming, beachcombing and diving. Carved out of sandstone cliffs by centuries of wave action, **Sunny Jim Cave** is accessible via a staircase in a souvenir shop at 1325 Coast Blvd. The **Coast Walk** features international shopping and dining with ocean views. **La Jolla Tours** offer 1½–2 hr guided walking tours of historic buildings and scenic areas of the downtown coast, including Sunny Jim Cave. Reservations are required: tel: (619) 453-8219.

BASEBALL AND FOOTBALL VENUES

The San Diegans love sport. The **Padres**, tel: (619) 283-4494, play baseball Apr–Oct, and the **Chargers**, tel: (619) 280-2121, have NFL football combat Oct–Dec/Jan at **Qualcomm Park** (9949 Friars Rd through at least 1999, while a new stadium is built).

The excellent **Birch Aquarium at Scripps** is an interactive oceanographic museum with a dazzling variety of local and exotic marine life. $ 2300 Expedition Way; open daily 0900–1700. The **Museum of Contemporary Art San Diego** features a permanent collection which includes examples of minimalist, conceptual and California art. $ 700 Prospect St; open Tues–Sat 1000–1700, Wed 1000–2000.

Further along Prospect St, places to eat range from a **Hard Rock Café** ($$) to **George's at the Cove** ($$$), where contemporary California cuisine is served in a stylish dining room or with ocean views on the rooftop terrace.

WHERE NEXT?

A popular 'just to say I've been' trip is to cross the border into Mexico. Tijuana is less than a mile across the border. Have a passport and (for non-US citizens or resident aliens) a multiple entry visa or visa waiver in hand and, rather than drive, book a guided tour or take the San Diego Trolley to the border and walk across. There is an office of the Tijuana Tourism and Convention Bureau in San Diego; PO Box 43-4523, San Diego CA 92143-4523; tel: (800) 522-1516 or (629) 298-4105, which can give advice on hassle-free border crossing and visa requirements.

From San Diego the Pacific Highway follows the coast all the way up through Santa Barbara (see p. 417), San Francisco (see pp. 423 and 430) and northern California (see p. 459), eventually reaching Seattle and the Canadian border (see p. 468).

Colour Section

COME IN
ENJOY
YOURSELF
MAGIC
MOVIE
CASINO
CASINO
PARKING
75¢ BEER

Kite Flite

EL CAMINO REAL
MISSION SANTA BARBARA
MISSION SAN BUENA VENTURA 30
MISSION SANTA INEZ 48
AUTO CLUB OF SO. CAL.

362
362
Amtrak
Amtrak

SAN DIEGO – SANTA BARBARA

SAN DIEGO–SANTA BARBARA

RAIL / BUS — OTT TABLES 405/852/915

TRANSPORT	FREQUENCY	JOURNEY TIME
Train (Amtrak)	4 Daily	5 hrs 37 mins
Bus (Greyhound)	8 Daily	5 hrs 45 mins

Note: There is an additional Amtrak thruway bus connecting with the late afternoon train from San Diego. The Greyhound bus requires a change at Los Angeles.

SAN DIEGO–OCEANSIDE

RAIL — OTT TABLES 405/852/915

TRANSPORT	FREQUENCY	JOURNEY TIME
Train	11 Daily	47mins

OCEANSIDE–ANAHELM

RAIL — OTT TABLES 405/852/915

TRANSPORT	FREQUENCY	JOURNEY TIME
Train	10 Daily	1hr 5mins

ANAHELM–LOS ANGELES

RAIL — OTT TABLES 405/852/915

TRANSPORT	FREQUENCY	JOURNEY TIME
Train	10 Daily	43mins

LOS ANGELES–VENTURA

RAIL — OTT TABLES 405/852/915

TRANSPORT	FREQUENCY	JOURNEY TIME
Train	4 Daily	1hr 52mins

VENTURA–SANTA BARBARA

RAIL — OTT TABLES 405/852/915

TRANSPORT	FREQUENCY	JOURNEY TIME
Train	4 Daily	48mins

ROUTE DETAIL

Take I-5 from San Diego to Capistrano Beach	60 miles
Then follow Hwy 1 along the coast via Laguna Beach, Venice Beach and Santa Monica to Oxnard	189 miles
Continue, joining Hwy 101 to Ventura	196 miles
Follow 101 to Santa Barbara	216 miles

San Diego – Santa Barbara

By Car via Laguna Beach, Santa Monica and Venice Beach

If California has a riviera, this is it. The 30 miles of beach cities between Capistrano Beach and Long Beach are among the most affluent in the world. Million-dollar homes are on display along any street near the shore. This scenic route along the southernmost part of the Pacific Coast Highway continues north along the coast, skirting the sprawl of Los Angeles, to arrive at the attractive old mission town of Santa Barbara. Beauty notwithstanding, be warned that the beaches are jammed in summer; parking meters are de rigueur. Traffic crawls at weekends, holidays, and when schools are out (June–early Sept).

LAGUNA BEACH

Laguna Beach, started as a Plein Air School artists' colony in 1917, has continued its association with art. The **Festival of Arts and Pageant of the Masters**, in which human models enact tableaux of famous paintings, takes place each July–Aug; $$ tel: (714) 494-1145. The **Laguna Art Museum**, $ 307 Cliff Dr., is a glass-façaded building filled with changing exhibitions of modern art. From the museum, take Cliff Dr. along **Heisler Park** for outstanding views or lawn bowling. At Fairview St, walk down a beautiful path to the water and the **Laguna Beach Marine Life Refuge**. Injured sea lions are nursed back to health at **Friends of the Sea Lions Marine Mammal Center**, 20612 Laguna Canyon Rd.

En Route

The **Sherman Library and Gardens** at Corona del Mar (2647 E. Pacific Coast Hwy) is a self-described 'horticultural paradise', a botanical garden with cacti, roses and shade-plant areas supplemented by a tropical plant conservatory, all laid out among gazebos and walks. Open 1030–1600 daily.

There is no lack of activities available, all close to the highway, as an antidote to hours in the car. Play basketball, surf, bodysurf, body board or explore tidepools at **Main Beach**; scuba or snorkel at **Diver's Cove**; mountain bike or hike in **Aliso/Wood Canyon Regional Park**. You can take a bus from the bus station up to Dana Point, north of town, for an ocean vista from Top of the World Viewpoint.

Laguna Beach Visitors Bureau, 252 Broadway; tel: (800) 877-1115 or (714) 497-9229, runs a free accommodation and referral service.

Accommodation rates are moderate–pricey. Most desirable are locations near the beach.

Ruby's Autodiner $ 30622 S. Coast Hwy. One of a chain of 40s-style diners with all-American burgers, fries and milkshakes, served on an outdoor ocean-view terrace.

LONG BEACH

Economic revival has created soaring new office towers and hotels amid refurbished towers from the 1920s. The new **Long Beach Aquarium of the Pacific**, $$ 100 Aquarium Way, is a celebration of the world's largest and most diverse body of water. Planet Ocean covers the exterior of the **Long Beach Sports Arena** with the world's largest mural, life-sized paintings of whales and other local sea life. The 145-ft tall ship *Californian* docks at the harbourside shopping centre of **Shoreline Village**, at the foot of Pine St. This replica of an 1849 revenue cutter makes daily 4-hr sailing trips.

A free Runabout Shuttle connects downtown Long Beach to SS *Queen Mary*, with stops at major hotels, restaurants and attractions. Look for signposts with a seagull on top. The ***Queen Mary*** $$, permanently docked in Long Beach Harbor, is now part hotel, part museum and a stately reminder of the gracious age of the great trans-atlantic liners. Tour the bridge, engine room and first-class public areas. From the *Queen Mary* you can take a cruise (just under 2 hrs) aboard the **Catalina Express** $$$, tel: (800) 833-6685 or (310) 519-1212, out to Santa Catalina Is.

Long Beach Area Convention and Visitors Bureau, One World Trade Center, Suite 100, Long Beach CA 90831; tel: (562)-436-3645 or (800) 452-7829, open 0830–1700 Mon–Fri.

Lord Mayor's Bed and Breakfast Inn $$ 435 Cedar Ave; tel: (562) 436-0324. An historical landmark furnished with antiques.
Queen Mary $$$ 1126 Queens Hwy; tel: (562) 435-3511. A 365-state-room hotel ship.
Renaissance Long Beach Hotel $$$ 111 E. Ocean Blvd; tel: (562) 437-5900; fax: (562) 499-2512. Luxuriously furnished

555 East $$ 555 E. Ocean Blvd at Linden Ave; tel: (562) 437-0626. Classic upmarket steakhouse.
Cha Cha Cha $$ 762 Pacific Ave at 8th St; tel: (562) 436-3900. Eclectic Caribbean island cuisine.
L'Opera $$$ 101 Pine St; tel: (562) 491-0066. Italian cuisine and live opera performed Sat and Sun nights.
Simon's $$$ 340 Golden Shore Dr.; tel: (562) 435-2333. Fish house with view of harbour and the *Queen Mary*.

VENICE BEACH

Venice Beach is a seven-day circus. Oceanfront Walk is jammed with bicycles, skaters, walkers, and gawkers from late morning until dusk. The lure is sun, sand

and a constant stream of musicians, comedians, jugglers, mime artists and dancers concentrated around Windward Ave. **Muscle Beach**, just south of Windward, is the original outdoor body-building studio. Mr and Ms Universe wannabes pump iron and build bulk in public. Pick-up basketball games are popular on nearby public courts – and very physical.

Venice Chamber of Commerce, PO Box 202, Venice, CA 90294; tel: (310) 396-7016.

26 Beach Café $$ 26 Washington St. Boasts the best burgers in town.

SANTA MONICA

The pier has an antique carousel, bumper cars, roller-coaster and the three aquariums of the **UCLA Ocean Discovery Center**, plus more adult pastimes like fishing and dining. The **Third Street Promenade** is a lively indoor/outdoor pedestrian shopping and restaurant mall.

En Route

The **Santa Monica Mountains National Recreation Area** (SMMRA), tel: (818) 597-9192, stretches 18 miles north along the coast beyond Point Dume. The entire area is dotted with wide public beaches, broad parking lots and summer lifeguard stations.

Santa Monica Visitor Center, 1400 Ocean Ave, Santa Monica, CA 90401; tel: (310) 393-7593, is open daily 1000–1600.

Hostelling International $ 1436 2nd St; tel: (310) 393-9913; fax: (310) 393-1769. Two blocks from the beach, pier and 3rd St Promenade; free airport pick-up.
Santa Monica Bayside $$ 2001 Ocean Ave; tel: (800) 525-4447. Near sandy beach and bike path (free shuttle to 3rd St Promenade).

Some of LA's best restaurants line 3rd St Promenade and surrounding streets. Santa Monica Pier has budget takeaways.

VENTURA

Ventura is a mission town with broad beaches and suburbs spreading in all directions. The walkable downtown has plenty of parking on the west end of Main St near museums and **Figueroa Plaza**, a pedestrian street filled with fountains and colourful tiles.

Mission San Buenaventura, 211 E. Main St, was founded in 1782. A peaceful garden, crowded museum and gift shop are next to the church, completed in 1809. Just along the street, the **Albinger Archaeological Museum** is an archaeological dig covering a full city block. Indoor and outdoor exhibits chronicle five different cultures on the site over the past 3500 years. **Ortega Adobe**, 215 W. Main St, is the original home of the giant Ortega Chile Company. The 1857 adobe is typical of early Ventura homes. **Surfer's Point**, at the end of Figueroa St, is a great place to watch board devotees and sunsets.

Ventura Visitors and Convention Bureau, 89-C S. California St, Ventura, CA 93001; tel: (800) 333-2989 or (805) 648-2075, has a visitor centre open Mon–Fri 0830–1700, Sat 1030–1600, Sun 1000–1600.

Ventura Beach RV Resort $$ 800 W. Main St; tel: (805) 643-9137. Just north of downtown.

Shields Brewing Co., 24 E. Santa Clara St, is the best bet downtown. An alternative is **Nona's Courtyard Café**, 67 S. California St.

SANTA BARBARA

Central Santa Barbara still has the look of its mission-town origins, but the red-tiled roofs, whitewashed plaster walls and colourful wall tiles post-date the 1925 earthquake. Faced with rebuilding nearly the entire city centre, the authorities opted to create their own historic look with a strict architectural code. The result is one of the most gracious, visually pleasing cities in southern California. Built on a series of rolling hills between broad beaches and the rugged Santa Ynez Mountains, Santa Barbara happily lives up to the name Lotusland bestowed by an early opera diva who retired here.

El Paseo and State St are the centrepieces of the 1920s reconstruction. **El Paseo** is an early shopping arcade, filled with delightfully sunny niches and fountains, **El Paseo Nuevo** an updated version with the same mission motif. **State St** is Santa Barbara's high street. The 19th-century **Stearns Wharf** at the foot of State St now houses small speciality shops, restaurants and the **Sea Center**, a small museum devoted to the marine and bird life of the Channel Islands National Marine Sanctuary.

El Presidio de Santa Barbara State Historic Park is the site of the 1782 Spanish fort that first lured settlers to Santa Barbara. The restored El Cuartel is among the oldest structures in California. The padre's quarters, chapel, commandant's office and other buildings are reconstructions. 100–200 E. Canon Perdido St; open daily 1030–1630.

Most of the other highlights of Santa Barbara reflect its origins as a mission town. The beautifully preserved **Mission Santa Barbara** is dubbed the 'Queen of the

En Route

Channel Islands National Park is a calm marine sanctuary at the edge of an area of population explosion. The visitor centre is on the harbour at 1901 Spinnaker D.r, and Island Packers, next to it, is the sole concessionaire; tel: (805) 642-1393. Boat trips depart from Ventura Harbor and Oxnard's Channel Islands Harbor daily, and include half-day cruise-bys, hiking excursions, snorkelling and blue and humpbacked whale-watching trips. Ask locally for diving-boat operators.

Ten miles north of Ventura is **La Conchita**, the only commercial banana plantation in the continental United States. Many of the sunny slopes around **Carpinteria** are sown in flowers, grown for nursery stock and seed. Blooms are best in springtime. Carpinteria State Beach has one of the state's largest concentration of public beach camping facilities. The structures visible out to sea are oil platforms.

Missions' and has starred in innumerable early cinematic epics. E. Los Olivos and Laguna Sts; open daily 0900–1700. The **County Courthouse** is an extravagant take-off on the mission style, with echoing tiled corridors, heroic furnishings and a Moorish tower with fine views of city and sea. 1100 Anacapa St; open Mon–Fri 0800–1700, Sat 1000–1700.

Santa Barbara's **Museum of Natural History** specialises in local native American tribal artefacts plus regional flora and fauna. $ 2559 Puesta del Sol Rd; open daily 0900–1700 (from 1000 Sun). For more of the local flora, the **Santa Barbara Botanic Garden** along Mission Canyon Rd is devoted to native trees, cacti, shrubs and flowers. $ Open daily.

Santa Barbara Visitor Information Center, 1 Santa Barbara St, Santa Barbara, CA 93101; tel: (805) 965-3021 or (800) 927-4688, is open 0900–1800 in summer, 0900–1600 in winter.

El Encanto Hotel $$$ 1900 Lasuen Rd; tel: (805) 687-5000 or (800) 346-7039. Sweeping views and a mix of craftsman and Spanish-style cottages.

Hotel Santa Barbara $$$ 533 State St; tel: (805) 957-9300 or (888) 259-7700. A smart stop in the city centre.

Enterprise Fish Co. $$ 225 State St. The best fish house in town.

Wine Cask $$ 813 Anacapa St. One of Santa Barbara's best Central Coast wine lists. Don't miss the five-course Sun–Mon tasting menu.

Where Next?

The Pacific Coast Highway continues north to San Francisco (see following chapters), or you could strike inland (by road or the Amtrak Thruway coachlink) to take a train the length of the San Joaquin Valley (see p. 455).

RAIL BUS SANTA BARBARA–SAN FRANCISCO

OTT TABLE 377/915

TRANSPORT	FREQUENCY	JOURNEY TIME
Train	Daily	9hrs
Bus	6 Daily	7hrs 35mins

Note: Thruway bus connection to San Francisco from Emeryville.

RAIL BUS SANTA BARBARA–SAN LUIS OBISPO

OTT TABLE 377/405/915

TRANSPORT	FREQUENCY	JOURNEY TIME
Train	2 Daily	3 hrs
Bus	7 Daily	2hrs 5mins

Note: There are 3 daily Amtrak Thruway buses connecting with the trains from Los Angeles.

RAIL BUS SAN LUIS OBISPO–SALINAS

OTT TABLE 377/915

TRANSPORT	FREQUENCY	JOURNEY TIME
Train	Daily	3 hrs 4mins
Bus	6 Daily	2hrs 40mins

BUS SALINAS–MONTEREY

OTT TABLES 908/915

TRANSPORT	FREQUENCY	JOURNEY TIME
Bus (Monterey Salinas Transit & Greyhound)	13 Daily	30/50 mins

Notes: There are 18 more buses that run Monday through Saturday.

Monterey Salinas Transit operate a twice daily service from Monterey to Big Sur from late May to early September.

Amtrak have thruway bus connections to and from the Seattle – Los Angeles 'Coast Starlight' to both Monterey and Carmel

RAIL BUS SALINAS–SAN FRANCISCO (OAKLAND)

OTT TABLE 377/915

TRANSPORT	FREQUENCY	JOURNEY TIME
Train	Daily	2hrs 55mins
Bus	6 Daily	2hrs 30mins

ROUTE DETAIL

The route follows Highway 1 from Santa Barbara. Overnight stops at

San Luis Obispo	106 miles
or San Simeon	147 miles
and around Monterey Bay	242 miles

break the 367-mile journey into convenient chunks.

Driving the route in reverse, drive north–south, is even more thrilling, perhaps too thrilling for vertigo sufferers when the outer lane seems to hang over empty space.

Pacific Coast Highway South

Santa Barbara to San Francisco

The scenic coast route between southern and northern California is one of the most breathtaking and (in summer) crowded roads in the state. As far as San Luis Obispo it roughly follows the old Spanish Colonial route – El Camino Real, the King's Highway – that connected the twenty-one Catholic missions that ran in a string along the California coast from San Diego to Sonoma. Branching off on to Hwy 1 will keep you clinging to the coast, between the looming Santa Lucia Mountains and pounding surf of Big Sur. Many stretches of the coast are protected marine sanctuary (although Carmel is more associated in most people's minds with Clint Eastwood than sea otters!) and at Año Nuevo you can walk among the elephant seals.

SAN LUIS OBISPO

San Luis grew up as a mission farming community that blossomed when the railway arrived in 1894. The mission heritage remains, both in the pronunciation (Louiss, Spanish-style) and the town's common appellation, SLO, as in 'slow', the relaxed pace of life.

The walkable town centre, Higuera and Monterey Sts, contains some of the finest small-town commercial architecture in the state, from adobes to Art Deco and Frank Lloyd Wright. **Mission San Luis Obispo de Tolosa** (Chorro & Monterey Sts) pioneered the red-tiled roof that became the mission hallmark–the 1772 mission needed something more substantial than thatch to withstand fiery attacks by local Native American tribes. Open daily 0900–1700 (till 1600 Jan–May). **Mission Plaza**, fronting the Mission, is a shady park sloping down to **San Luis Creek** and the business district. Music wafts through the trees from several restaurant patios that open onto the plaza.

San Luis Obispo Chamber of Commerce, 1039 Chorro St, San Luis Obispo, CA 93401; tel: (805) 781-2777, is open daily (till 2000 Thur–Sat).

Madonna Inn $$, 100 Madonna Rd; tel: (805) 543-3000 or (800) 543-9666. A shocking pink temple of kitsch.

SLO Brewing Company $, 1119 Garden St. Enormous servings as well as beer brewed on the main floor.
SLO Perk $, 1028 Chorro St. Breakfast, lunch and coffee stop overlooking the Mission.

HEARST CASTLE, SAN SIMEON

The rolling hills of the Central Coast have long been a magnet for dreamers with money to bring their fantasies to life–none with more extravagance than millionaire newspaper magnate William Randolph Hearst. Hearst called his 165-room Renaissance-Moorish-Medieval holiday house 'The Ranch'. The official name was La Cuesta Encantada, The Enchanted Hill, but the world knew it as Hearst Castle. More estate than castle, Casa Grande, the Big House, is surrounded by guest houses and an outdoor swimming pool complex. The whole is set in lush gardens, complete with a private zoo of free-roaming zebras and other exotic creatures.

The property eventually passed to the State of California and is open by guided tour ($$). **Tour One** is an overview of the property. **Tour Two** concentrates on the unfinished upper floors of Casa Grande, including Hearst's library and bedroom suite. **Tour Three** looks at one of the guesthouses in detail. **Tour Four** (summer only) inspects the grounds and gardens. **Tour Five** (Fri–Sat evenings, spring and autumn) is a 'living history tour' with 'famous guests' and 'servants' from the 1930s.

Advance bookings are essential in summer and recommended all year – walk-in space *may* be available mid-week out of season. Contact **Hearst San Simeon State Historic Monument**, 750 Hearst Castle Rd, San Simeon, CA 93452; tel: (805) 927-2020 or (800) 444-4445.

The **Visitor Center** is worth a visit even if tours are fully booked. One wall opens on conservation laboratories and the free museum provides a good overview of the Castle and architect Julia Morgan's other and far more original work.

BIG SUR

Big Sur and its series of state parks is one of the most visited parts of California, yet manages to retain an air of isolation, mystery and mysticism. Credit the 90 rugged, craggy miles of Hwy 1 carved into trackless cliffs by convict labour in the 1930s and the scarcity of accommodation. Credit, too, the ethereal magic of the cobalt and turquoise Pacific Ocean battering soaring mountains cloaked in swirling mists and dense forests. The scenery is unendingly stunning, but the winding road demands full driving attention–drivers should wait for the frequent lay-bys.

Big Sur Valley, the centre for tourist services, stretches for six miles along Hwy 1. In the middle sits **Pfeiffer Big Sur State Park**: groves of redwoods, conifers and oaks interspersed with open meadows along the Big Sur River. There are miles of hiking trails and deep, clear river swimming holes among the boulders in summer. Pfeiffer Big Sur is headquarters for all of the Big Sur State Parks, with the best visitor and information centre. **Pfeiffer Beach** is Big Sur's best and hardest-to-find beach. (There's no sign, but take Sycamore Canyon Rd, the only paved road west off

TROPIC OF CANCER REMEMBERED

The **Henry Miller Memorial Library**, just south of Ventana, is a shrine to the infamous writer who lived in Big Sur for 18 years. The library is filled with Miller memorabilia, much of it for sale. The toilet has erotic tiles by local artist Ephraim Doner; oversized sculptures grace the lawn. Open Tues–Sun 1100–1700.

Hwy 1 between the Big Sur Post Office and Pfeiffer-Big Sur State Park.) The white strand is dominated by a rock hump that changes from brown to fiery orange as the sun sets.

Some of Big Sur's best coastline and day hikes are within **Julia Pfeiffer Burns State Park**, 12 miles south of Pfeiffer Big Sur itself. Don't miss the easy ½-mile return trail to McWay Waterfall, which drops from a bluff into the ocean. Another easy ½-mile return trail leads from Hwy 1 to Partington Point, overlooking the surging, kelp-filled waters of Partington Cove. Open daily dawn–dusk; $; tel: (831) 667-2315.

Also south of Big Sur Valley, **Nepenthe**, just beyond Ventana, is a restaurant best known for its views. The multi-storey structure, 800 feet above the crashing surf, was built in the 1940s by Orson Welles for his bride, Rita Hayworth. Café Kevah has the best views. Open daily for lunch & dinner; $$; tel: (831) 667-2345.

NEW AGE

The **Esalen Institute**, 8 miles south of Julia Pfeiffer Burns State Park, is America's original New Age retreat. The public are allowed to use some of the facilities. Open daily; $$$; reservations required (tel: (831) 667-3000).

Just beyond Big Sur Valley, the **Andrew Molera State Park** ($) is the largest and least developed of the Big Sur parks. Miles of trails wander its open beaches, meadows and hilltops. **Point Sur State Historic Park** ($), just to its north, contains the **Point Sur Lightstation**, in operation since 1889. The light is automated, but the building interiors are being restored to their turn-of-the-century appearance. The station is open for guided tours as part of a 2½-mile return hike, with moonlight tours in summer. Open Mon, Wed, Sat–Sun for guided tours.

Big Sur Multi-Agency Station, (½ mile S. of Pfeiffer-Big Sur State Park; tel: (831) 667-2315, is open daily 0800–1800 (till 1700 in winter). The most complete local guide is the *El Sur Grande* newspaper, free at ranger stations and shops.

High demand and low supply keeps prices high. Advance bookings are essential.

Big Sur Lodge $$–-$$$, Pfeiffer Big Sur State Park; tel: (831) 667-2171; fax: (831) 667-3110. Modern cabins around a swimming pool; the only non-camping accommodation in Big Sur state parks.

Deetjen's Big Sur Inn $$, tel: (831) 667-2377; fax: (831)

667-0466. A rambling, old-fashioned inn popular with long-time visitors.
Post Ranch Inn $$$, tel: (831) 667-2200 or (800) 527-2200; fax: (831) 667-2824; www.postranchinn.com. A post-modernist retreat below Hwy 1 with stunning views and rooms.
Ventana Inn $$$, tel: (831) 667-2331 or (800) 628-6500; fax: (831) 667-2419. A rougher-hewn equivalent, above Hwy 1.

At the inns above. **Deetjen's** ($$) serves good Euro-Californian cuisine with larger than average portions. **Sierra Mar** at the Post Ranch ($$$) keeps to cutting-edge California dishes, while the **Ventana** tends to supply traditional California offerings.

En Route

About 14 miles before you reach Carmel look for the solitary and much-photographed arch of **Bixby Creek Bridge** soaring high above Bixby Creek. **Garrapata State Park**, 3 miles further on, contains 4 miles of undeveloped coast, but has no car parks or other facilities. Park paths from lay-bys around **Soberanes Point** run to ocean beaches through stands of cacti and into dense redwood groves.

CARMEL

In summer and most warm-weather weekends, Carmel-bound traffic backs up on Hwy 1. The town centre, Ocean Ave and its side streets, are filled with antique, art and knicknack shops interspersed with T-shirt emporia, restaurants, ice-cream parlours and hordes of visitors. The area between 5th and 8th Sts and Junipero and the city beach is packed with quaint shingled cottages, dolls' houses loaded with gingerbread details and fake adobe homes.

California's second mission was founded in Monterey in 1770 but moved to Carmel the following year to protect Native American mission women from Presidio soldiers. The **Misión San Carlos Borromero del Rio Carmelo** is at 3080 Rio Rd; mission founder Junipero Serra is buried at the foot of the altar.

Carmel Beach City Park is an alluring crescent of sand the colour of white flour against the aquamarine of Carmel Bay, but the water is too cold and the undertow too fierce for swimming. **Carmel River State Beach**, just south of town, is less crowded, but high surf can be dangerous.

The **Tourist Information Center** is at Ocean and Junipero Sts; open Fri–Sun 1100–1600.

La Playa Hotel $$$, Camino Real and 8th Ave; tel: (800) 582-8900 or (408) 624-6476. Lush gardens and a memorable restaurant.

Hog's Breath Inn $$, San Carlos, between 5th and 6th Sts. Owned by former Carmel mayor and cinema heavyweight Clint Eastwood.

MONTEREY

Monterey was the capital of California under Spanish, Mexican and American flags. Today, it's a busy tourist capital. **Monterey State Historic Park** offers a self-guided walking tour from 20 Custom House Plaza around three dozen historic buildings dating back to 1794.

Fisherman's Wharf is home to charter fishing and whale-watching boats as well as sea lions. Sea otters also play around the pier and bay. **Cannery Row**, made famous by local writer and Nobel Prize winner John Steinbeck, has been reborn to process tourists instead of fish. The top attraction, at 86 Cannery Row, is **The Monterey Bay Aquarium**. Don't miss the three-storey kelp forest, so realistic that wild birds have taken up residence on the surface of the artificial ocean.

Monterey Peninsula Visitors & Convention Bureau, 380 Alvarado St, Monterey, CA 93942-1770; tel: (408) 649-1770, is open Mon–Fri 0830–1700.

Monterey's motel row, Munras Ave, drifts into the moderate– expensive ($$$–$$$$) range. **Room Finders**, 140 West Franklin St; tel: (831) 646-9250, makes bookings in all price categories.

Alvarado St, between Del Monte Ave and Jefferson St, is the trendy dining and shopping area.

The Poppy $, 444 Alvarado St. A budget breakfast and lunch house that was the model for the Golden Poppy Café in John Steinbeck's *Sweet Thursday*.

Rappa's $$, Fisherman's Wharf. A seafood choice with great early bird specials.

Beau Thai $$, 807 Cannery Row, is a local favourite for budget Thai food.

Supremos $$, 500 Hartnell St. A Cooper–Molera adobe dated 1840; lobster burritos feature.

SANTA CRUZ

Holidaymakers started visiting Santa Cruz during the 1890s and never really stopped. A University of California campus added an ivory tower element in the 1960s, followed by back-to-the-land refugees from San Francisco and Silicon Valley electronic wizards. The combination keeps local politics and entertainment venues in a ferment.

Don't miss the **Boardwalk**, south of the Municipal Wharf – the 1924 Giant Dipper

ELEPHANTS OF THE SEA

The **Año Nuevo State Reserve** at Pescadero is a rare mainland breeding ground for the endangered northern elephant seal. It's the only place in the world where humans can leave their cars and walk among 2–3 ton elephant seals in their natural habitat. Males arrive Nov–Dec and begin fighting for dominance. Females appear in Jan, give birth, and mate again before leaving a month or so later. A few seals remain all year. Winter access is by pre-booked guided tour only; tel: (415) 879-0595.

roller coaster is usually rated among the country's top ten. The lovingly restored 1911 Charles Looff Carousel has hand-carved horses, chariots and a 19th-century pipe organ. Open daily Memorial Day–Labor Day, weekends and holidays the rest of the year.

Santa Cruz County Conference and Visitors Council, 701 Front St, Santa Cruz, CA 95060; tel: (800) 833-3494 or (408) 425-1234; and Santa Cruz Beach Boardwalk, 400 Beach St, Santa Cruz, CA 95060; tel: (408) 423-5590.

The Bed and Breakfast Innkeepers of Santa Cruz County, PO Box 464, Santa Cruz, CA 95061; tel: (408) 425-8212, offer 12 choices.

The Boardwalk has the largest concentration of restaurants.

Gabriella Café $$, 910 Cedar St. Fanciful pottery to show off fresh northern Italian dishes.

Santa Cruz Brewing Co. and Front Street Pub $, 516 Front St, and **Seabright Brewery** $, 519 Seabright Ave, No 107, serve popular beers and food to suit tight budgets.

WHERE NEXT?

San Francisco, of course (see p. 430), from where the Pacific Coast Highway continues its journey north (p. 459). Inland across the coastal mountain range is California's capital, Sacramento, and the San Joaquin Valley (see p. 455), with access to Yosemite (see p. 446) and the Sequoia and Kings Canyon National Parks (see p. 440).

San Francisco

For those who live here, San Francisco is never 'Frisco'; it's The City, a refuge of civilisation in an otherwise Wild West. The city is an aggregation of minorities who dislike each other but still manage to live together. Precipitous hills, a sparkling bay, bridges, cable cars, 3000 restaurants and benign tolerance for almost anything short of mayhem are eternal touchstones.

Downtown is dominated by the 9 to 5 Financial District and Market St is not really the place to be after dark. The city's neighborhoods are where the action is. On Grant St, just north of the Financial District, are Chinatown and the Italian North Beach Neighborhood. Walk north along the Embarcadero to the tourist zone at Pier 39 and Fisherman's Wharf. Union St in the Marina District is popular with young heterosexuals, while Castro St and Upper Market cater to the gay population. Haight Street, near Golden Gate Park, is the area where the 'Summer of Love' took place in the 1960s.

GETTING THERE

Air **San Francisco International Airport** (SFO); tel: (650) 876-78090, is 14 miles south on Hwy 101. The cheapest way into the city is by **SamTrans** bus 7F; bus 3X goes to the Bay Area Rapid Transit (BART) station. The **SFO Airporter** to downtown hotels or door-to-door van service costs about $10–15; a taxi into town about three times as much. There are free shuttles to car hire locations and airport hotels.

Rail/Bus The Amtrak ticket office and waiting room are at the San Francisco Ferry Building (foot of Market St; the Embarcadero stop on the BART), where Amtrak buses depart for trains calling at Emeryville. Baylink (Vallejo), Golden Gate (Marin County), Oakland/Alameda and Tiburon Commute Ferries also arrive here. Greyhound buses serve the Transbay Terminal (Mission and Fremont Sts; Embarcadero BART), one block south of Market Street.

Road The scenic north–south route is Hwy 1/101. The fast north–south route, I-5, is east of San Francisco, with connections to the Oakland-San Francisco Bay Bridge via I-580 and I-680 from the north and I-580 and I-880 (with a detour on I-980) from the south. From the east, access is via I-80.

GETTING AROUND

One-way streets, steep hills and lack of parking make driving a challenge here. Coloured signs point the way to key areas: a green outline of Italy for **North Beach;**

orange crab for **Fisherman's Wharf;** blue Victorian house for **Union St**; and a white female statue for **Union Sq**. Public parking is scarce downtown – and costs $2–20 per hour. Best bets are city-operated garages: Stockton-Sutter Garage near Union Sq.; Fifth and Mission Garage between Union Sq. and Yerba Buena Gardens; Police Garage, 766 Vallejo St; Portsmouth Sq. Garage, Clay and Kearny Sts. Charges are exorbitant at Fisherman's Wharf and Pier 39. Street parking is nearly impossible in Chinatown, North Beach, Fisherman's Wharf and Union Square, and scarce elsewhere. Parking meters accept only quarters, good for 15–60 mins, depending on the neighbourhood. Try to park and explore on foot rather than driving, or use MUNI.

The San Francisco Municipal Railway, or **MUNI**, tel: (415) 673-6864, operates 24 hrs a day, all over the city. MUNI buses follow numbered routes on city streets. MUNI Metro light rail follows lettered routes underground in the city centre (sharing the Embarcadero, Montgomery, Powell and Civic Center stations with BART) and on the surface in outlying districts.

The **F-Market streetcar** operates along Market St from Castro St to the Transbay Terminal (extension to Ferry Building and Fisherman's Wharf opens late 1999). The famous **cable cars** serve Nob Hill, Fisherman's Wharf, Aquatic Park and California St. Streetcar and cable car flat fares are reasonably cheap and include up to two transfers. A **MUNI Passport**, valid on all MUNI buses, cable cars and streetcars, offers unlimited usage each day (available as a one-, 3- or 7-day pass).

FERRIES

Baylink Ferry, tel: (877) 643-3779, departs from the San Francisco Ferry Building at the foot of Market St for Vallejo (Solano County, north of San Francisco) with connecting express buses to Sacramento. A Network DayPass allows unlimited use of ferry and all connecting buses. **Blue and Gold Fleet**, tel: (415) 705-5555, departs from Pier 41 (Fisherman's Wharf) for Alcatraz, Angel Island, Marine World, Oakland/Alameda, Sausalito, Tiburon and sightseeing cruises. Oakland/Alameda and Tiburon commuter ferries serve the Ferry Building. **Golden Gate Ferry**, tel: (415) 332-6600, serves Sausalito and Tiburon from the Ferry Building.

BART, the Bay Area Rapid Transit District, tel: (415) 788-2278, operates via transbay tube from San Francisco to the **East Bay** cities of Richmond (north), Pittsburg/Bay Point (east), Pleasanton (south-east) and Fremont (south). The West Bay terminus is at Colma. Trains operate from early morning (0800 on Sun and holidays) through to midnight every day. Fares vary with distance.

In addition to MUNI and BART, various other operators run more specific services with variable fares. **Caltrain**, 4th and King Sts; tel: (650) 508-6455 or (800) 660-4287 is for commuter rail to Peninsula cities and San Jose; MUNI links with it. You can buy a weekend pass. **AC Transit**, tel: (510) 839-2931, runs buses from the Transbay

Terminal (First and Mission Sts) to East Bay cities via the San Francisco-Oakland Bay Bridge. **Golden Gate Transit** buses, tel: (415) 923-3000, run from Mission St (one block south of Market St) to Marin County, via the Golden Gate Bridge. **Samtrans** buses run from the Transbay Terminal to the airport and south to Palo Alto, with two levels of flat fare: local and express. **Bay Area Transit Information**, including fares and schedules, can be accessed on the web at www.transitinfo.org.

INFORMATION

DOWNTOWN MAP – inside back cover

San Francisco Convention and Visitor Bureau (SFCVB), Hallidie Plaza, Lower Level, Powell and Market Sts; tel: (415) 391-2000; fax: (415) 227-2668; www.sfvisitor.org, is open Mon–Fri 0900–1700, Sat–Sun 0900–1500. Tel: (415) 391-2001 for 24-hr recorded information. The *San Francisco Book* is the complete tourist reference.

SAFETY

Caution is advised south of Market St and in the Civic Center and Tenderloin areas. Golden Gate Park should be avoided after dark.

MONEY

Thomas Cook is located in the financial district, at 100 Spear St at Mission St; tel: (415) 896-1115 or (800) 287-7362; Embarcadero BART. There is also an office near Union Sq., at 75 Geary St at Market St; tel: (415) 362-3452; Montgomery BART.

POST AND PHONES

The principal US Post Offices are in the Embarcadero Center, Market and Embarcadero Sts; tel: (415) 284-0755; Embarcadero BART; and at 835 Market St; tel: (415) 543-2606; Civic Center BART.

ACCOMMODATION

San Francisco has been famous for high prices since Gold Rush days. It's one of America's most visited cities, which keeps hotels and restaurants busy all year round. Always book ahead. **Union Sq**. is the best location without a car, near the main shopping and theatre areas, most major tourist sights and public transport routes. Add $20–25 per day for parking. Motels along **Lombard St** (MUNI bus 30) and **Van Ness Ave** (Van Ness MUNI Metro) generally offer free parking; ask for a room at the back to minimise street noise. **Fisherman's Wharf** (MUNI buses 30, 32, 42 and Powell-Hyde St Cable Car) is group tour territory. **San Francisco Reservations**, 22 Second St; tel: (800) 677-1550, makes free bookings for more than 225 local hotels.

HI San Francisco Downtown $ 312 Mason St at Geary; Powell BART; tel: (415) 788-5604. A block from the excitement of Union Square, in the theatre district. Double and triple rooms; reservations essential.

HI San Francisco Fisherman's Wharf $ Fort Mason, Bldg 240; MUNI buses 30, 42; tel: (415) 771-7277. Fisherman's

Wharf, Chinatown and Ghirardelli Sq. within walking distance.

Sheraton Palace $$$ Market and New Montgomery Sts; Montgomery BART; tel: (415) 512-1111. One of the oldest, most historic hotels in San Francisco – and one of the few major buildings to survive the 1906 earthquake. Don't miss the Garden Court, a brilliant palm-filled restaurant.

Triton $$$ 342 Grant Ave; Montgomery BART; tel: (415) 394-0500. Filled with irregular shapes and wavy lines.

The Archbishop's Mansion $$$$ 1000 Fulton St; MUNI bus 5; tel: (415) 563-7872. Stately and elegant.

FOOD

San Francisco calls itself the food capital of America, a title justly contested by Los Angeles, New York and New Orleans. The weekly *San Francisco Bay Guardian* offers the best selection of current reviews. Local favourites change almost weekly.

Boudin Sourdough Bakery and Café $ 156 Jefferson; MUNI buses 30, 32, 42 and Hyde St Cable Car. The best Fisherman's Wharf sandwiches.

Pluto's $ 627 Irving St, between 7th and 8th Aves; MUNI Metro N. Large quantities of American homestyle food.

Beach Chalet $$ 1000 Gt Highway, Golden Gate Park; MUNI bus 5. Brewery, restaurant and Golden Gate Park visitor centre. Restored frescoes depict Depression-era life.

Golden Spike $$ 527 Columbus Ave; MUNI buses 15, 30, 45. Gargantuan portions of antipasto, pasta and main dishes.

McCormick and Kuleto's $$$ 900 North Point, Ghirardelli Sq.; MUNI buses 30, 32,

Seafood Restaurant 42 and Powell-Hyde St Cable Car; tel: (415) 929-1730. The food equals the views.

Aqua $$$$ 252 California St; Embarcadero BART; tel: (415) 956-9662. Possibly the best fish in town.

Boulevard $$$$ 1 Mission St; Embarcadero BART; tel: (415) 543-6084. A long-term survivor for its French-inspired dishes.

HIGHLIGHTS

FISHERMAN'S WHARF This one-time home to San Francisco's commercial fishing fleet now has more T-shirt and souvenir shops than fishing boats. Explore on foot from Pier 39 along to Aquatic Park on the edge of Golden Gate National Recreation Area.

Pier 39, the state's most popular tourist attraction, is an abandoned pier converted to retail shops, entertainment and restaurants with fine views of Alcatraz and the bay. The Pier's most famous residents are barking sealions that have taken over the north side marina. Most ferries leave from Pier 41, just west. Nearby is **The Cannery** (2801 Leavenworth). **Ghirardelli Sq**., a former bayside chocolate factory, has become a bustling retail/entertainment complex – the hot fudge sundaes at Swensonn's Ice Cream Parlor are divine.

San Francisco National Maritime Historic Park is the nation's only floating national park; $ Beach St; open daily. It includes the **Maritime Museum**, housed in a streamlined white art deco/modern building in Aquatic Park, and several historic ships docked at the **Hyde Street Pier** which are open daily for tours. The **USS** *Pampanito* submarine, also open for tours, is moored on the east side of Pier 45.

NORTH BEACH Once a northern beach on San Francisco Bay, the area has been an entertainment and nightlife district for more than a century. The topless and nude dancing dancing clubs that have spread across American began at **The Condor** (300 Columbus Ave), now a sports bar, in the 1960s. The Beatnik era survives at poet Lawrence Ferlinghetti's **City Lights Bookstore** (261 Columbus Ave) and **Vesuvio Café** (255 Columbus Ave). It's a short, if steep, walk from the coffee houses to the high point of North Beach, **Telegraph Hill**, topped by the 212 ft **Coit Tower** (1 Telegraph Hill Blvd, off Lombard St). The nozzle-shaped tower was built by Lillie Coit, an early City socialite with a notorious fondness for burly firemen. The interior features splendid Depression-era murals. Parking is limited; walk up or take MUNI bus 39.

CHINATOWN The area south of North Beach, bounded by Pine, Kearny and Powell Sts (take MUNI buses 1, 30, 45 or the cable car) began as a shanty town of miners expelled from the gold fields around 1850 and has now become the largest Chinese community outside Asia. Sun Yat Sen planned the revolution that became the Chinese Nationalist Republic from a tiny building on Spofford Alley. More recently, Chinatown's Waverly Place featured prominently in San Franciscan Amy Tan's bestselling novel *The Joy Luck Club*. **Grant Ave**, Chinatown's official high street, is a tourist trap. **Stockton St**, one block west, is crowded with fresh vegetables, live fish, smoked ducks and other necessities of life.

WALKING TOURS

City Guides, tel: (415) 557-4266. Culture, history and architecture.

Cruisin' The Castro, tel: (415) 550-8110. The City's gay subculture from 1849 to the present.

Wok Wiz Chinatown Tours, tel:(415) 981-8989. Chinatown alleys, tea and secrets.

Italians of North Beach, tel: (415) 397-8530. Italian food, history and culture.

Victorian Home Walk, tel: (415) 252-9485. Explore San Francisco's version of Victorian architecture, lifestyle and history.

Barbary Coast Trail matches San Francisco history with today's best sights. The CVB has a free self-guiding brochure.

Union Square and SOMA The heart of the shopping and theatre district, Union Sq. has many fine department stores, shops and restaurants, and is central for public transport. A couple of blocks south, Market St cuts diagonally across the city's centre. **SOMA**, the South of Market (St) Area (MUNI bus 42), once an industrial area filled with brick buildings and dark alleyways, has metamorphosed into a trendy residential and entertainment neighbourhood.

Yerba Buena Gardens, between Mission and Howard Sts, was once a SOMA slum, but has become a lively nexus with a performing arts centre, ice rink, Moscone Convention Center, cinemas, shopping, entertainment venues, hotels, restaurants and landscaped gardens. There are two museums of note here, with more planned. The **San Francisco Museum of Modern Art (SFMOMA)** is northern California's largest collection of modern art, most noted for its distinctive architectural design by Mario Botta. $$ Open 1100–1800 (Thur until 2100); closed Wed; free first Tues of each month; half-price Thur 1800–2100. The **Cartoon Art Museum**, tel: (415) 227-8666, is one of three museums in America devoted to cartoon art.

Mission District Named after **Mission Dolores**, founded in 1776, the Mission is Central and South America come north. Brilliant murals blaze messages of equality, ethnic pride and hope and there's a wide range of Mexican and other Hispanic restaurants. MUNI Metro J or mission BART, or MUNI bus 14.

Cable Cars

San Francisco's original mechanised public transport still climbs half-way to the stars up **Nob Hill** between the Bay and **Hallidie Plaza** and along California St. The **Powell-Hyde St Line** runs to Aquatic Park for easy access to Fisherman's Wharf, the historic ships at Hyde St Pier and Ghirardelli Sq.

Queue up (sometimes for hours) to board at the end of each cable car line or follow the locals who walk a couple of blocks up the street to climb aboard without waiting. To see how the system works, visit the **Cable Car Barn and Museum** (Mason and Washington Sts). Don't miss the gallery overlooking the 14 ft pulleys that haul miles of steel cable beneath city streets to power the cars at a constant 9 mph. Open daily 1000–1700.

Golden Gate Park Not to be confused with the GGNRA (see below), Golden Gate Park stretches west from Haight Ashbury to the ocean (MUNI buses 5, 6, 7, 21, 71 or Metro N to Stanyon St). This is America's second great urban park (after Central Park in New York), 1000 acres of drifting sand dunes transformed into shady forests, winding drives, lakes, open glades and museums. Don't miss jasmine tea and fortune cookies amid exquisite landscaping in the **Japanese Tea Garden**. Next to this is the **Asian Art Museum**, which houses the largest collection of Asian art and artefacts in any Western museum. It adjoins the **M. H. de Young Memorial Museum**, with its collection of 17th–20th-century American art. $$ joint entry (free first Wed of month); open Wed–Sun 0930–1700 (until 2045 first Wed of month).

Just across the Music Concourse stands the **California Academy of Sciences**, the oldest scientific institution in the western USA. Facilities include the **Steinhart Aquarium**, the **Morrison Planetarium** and the **Natural History Museum**, all included in a single admission. $ (free first Wed of month); open daily Memorial Day weekend–Labor Day 0900–1800 (1000–1700 rest of year). Don't miss the delightfully retro crocodile pit and underwater views of cavorting seals and sealions in the **Aquarium**.

GOLDEN GATE NATIONAL RECREATION AREA (GGNRA) A string of former military bases and coastal defences now forms a vast park stretching west from Aquatic Park and Fort Mason along the Bay to the **Presidio**, then south along the Pacific beyond San Francisco. It encompasses the **Marin Headlands**; **Muir Woods National Monument**; **Mount Tamalpais**, and much of **Tomales Bay** shoreline. It gives some truly splendid views of San Francisco and the Bay – especially from Crissy Field, Baker Beach, Lands End (for the best sunsets) and upper Fort Mason. Open daily.

GOLDEN GATE BRIDGE

Opened in 1938, the great bridge linked the gap above the tides churning through the Golden Gate, the narrow passage into San Francisco Bay. 'Golden' refers to the Golden Horn in Istanbul, after which adventurer-explorer John Fremont named the entrance in 1846. Park at the San Francisco end to walk or cycle across; drive to the vista point just beyond the north end of the bridge to look back toward San Francisco. There is a toll for southbound cars ($), pedestrians and cyclists free. Red-brick **Fort Point** beneath the bridge was built to defend San Francisco during the Civil War, 1861–5.

The **Exploratorium** on Marina Blvd (MUNI bus 30) is designed for children, but adults are at least as eager to try the 500 interactive exhibits. It adjoins the **Palace of Fine Arts**, built to resemble a classical ruin for the 1915 Panama-Pacific Exposition. $ joint entry; open Memorial Day–Labor Day daily 1000–1800 (Wed until 2130); rest of year Tues–Sun 1000–1700 (Wed until 2130). On the west edge of the park, beyond China Beach, is the **Palace of the Legion of Honor** (34th Ave and Clement St; MUNI bus 18). This copy of Napoleon's Hôtel de Salm in Paris displays ancient and European art from 2500 BC to the 20th century. $$ (free second Wed of month); open Tues–Sun 0930– 1700.

OUT IN THE BAY Once the main port of entry from Asia, **Angel Island** ($$), the largest island in the Bay, is a rural state park with stunning views of the Bay area. Facilities include restored immigration buildings, picnic grounds, hiking and cycling trails and a tram ride around the island. Access is by private boat and Blue and Gold Fleet ferry from Pier 41. (For cruises see p. 433).

The list of prisoners incarcerated in the infamous federal penitentiary of 'escape-proof' **Alcatraz Island** reads like a Who's Who of Hollywood celebrity criminals.

Al 'Scarface' Capone, Robert 'Bird Man of Alcatraz' Stroud and George 'Machine Gun' Kelly were among the 1554 convicts who spent an average of eight years within sight of San Francisco yet completely out of touch. The pervasive security apparently worked: only 36 prisoners tried to escape, of whom ten were killed in the attempt, 21 were captured and five were never found. The tiny island is 1½ miles off shore, accessible only by boat; Blue and Gold Fleet operates daily tours ($$). Visitors may wander freely, or take a self-guided audio tour narrated by former prison guards.

New for 2000

In the SOMA neighbourhood (see p. 435) is a new museum, **Zeum**, at the Moscone Convention Center, Fourth and Howard St. This art and technology museum is state-of-the-art, and filled with the best in multimedia learning. Also on the roof are an ice skating rink, an historic Looff roundabout and gardens overlooking the city.

Sony Metreon, also in SOMA, is a retail and entertainment complex with 15 movie theatres, restaurants, interactive games and 3-D screens with characters from Maurice Sendak's children's books. The Giants' new **stadium** (opening for the baseball season in April), Pacific Bell Park, King St, is nearby, making this the city's fastest-changing neighbourhood.

SHOPPING

Union Sq. has the most expensive marquees, from Disney and Nike to Saks Fifth Avenue and Tiffany. **Union St** (MUNI bus 45) caters to the stylishly trendy, pricey shops in stylish Victorian buildings offering jewellery, marbled paper, clothing, antiques, furnishings and bric-à-brac from around the world. **Haight St** (MUNI buses 6, 7, 71 or Metro N) is an ultra-trendy mix of fashion, food and body piercing. For bargain-basement shopping, **Yerba Buena Sq**. has six floors of factory outlet merchandise and **Six Sixty Center** (600 Third St; MUNI buses 15, 30, 45 or Caltrain MUNI Metro) has 20 factory outlet shops.

NIGHTLIFE

The Datebook Section in the *San Francisco Sunday Chronicle* is the most complete listing for traditional diversions; the *SF Bay Guardian* and *SF Weekly* concentrate on more avant-garde offerings.

The **American Conservatory Theatre** (ACT), 415 Geary S., Union Sq.; tel: (415) 749-2228 is San Francisco's leading repertory theatre company. **Theatre on the Square**, 450 Post St; tel: (415) 433-9500, is New York's off-Broadway theatre in San Francisco (open Tues–Sun). For a change, try **Audium** on Fri or Sat; 1616 Bush St; tel: (415) 771-1616, where sound sculptures from 136 speakers surrounds the audience, sitting in a darkened theatre. **Beach Blanket Babylon**, Club Fugazi, 678 Beach St; tel: (415) 421-4222, offers zany cabaret-style musical spoofs of popular culture. Performances Wed–Sun; adults only except Sun afternoon.

The world-class **San Francisco Opera** performs in the newly restored War Memorial Opera House (Van Ness Ave and McAllister St) Sept–Jan; tel: (415) 864-3330. Davies Symphony Hall is home to the **San Francisco Symphony**, tel: (415) 864-6000. Concerts are held regularly in **Grace Cathedral**, California's finest Gothic cathedral; tel: (415) 749-6350, and at **Old First Church**, Van Ness Ave and Sacramento St; tel: (415) 474-1608. A favourite for Sun picnics is the **Stern Grove Midsummer Music Festival**, 19th Ave and Sloat Blvd, a free outdoor summer festival with classical, opera, popular and jazz by top performers. The annual dance season of the **San Francisco Ballet**, 455 Franklin St; tel: (415) 865-2000, runs Jan–May.

DAY TRIPS

NAPA VALLEY

Napa is becoming a wine theme park, but only for people with serious money to spend. Prices are higher than in Sonoma County, crowds are bigger, and advance bookings a necessity. Crowds and prices increase to the south, or 'down valley', especially in summer. You can avoid some of the crowds by following the **Silverado Trail** along the eastern edge of the valley and taking one of the many cross-valley roads back to Hwy 29 as needed. Vineyards are thickest around St Helena, Rutherford, Oakville and Yountville; many wineries charge for tasting. The easiest way to see the greatest number of wineries – from the outside – is aboard the **Napa Valley Wine Train** $$$, which makes daily lunch and dinner runs up and down the valley; tel: (707) 226-2528. Amtrak Thruway buses connecting with the 'Capitol' and 'San Joaquin' trains (see p. 425) stop at the Wine Train Station (1275 McKinstry St). Buses from the Baylink Ferry Terminal run north to Napa, Yountville, Oakville, Rutherford, St Helena and Calistoga (a DayPass is good for unlimited travel on the ferry and buses.) By car, take I-80 then Hwy 29 north to Napa and all the towns up the valley.

PICNIC PROVISIONS

Napa Valley Olive Oil Manufacturer, 835 McCorkle Ave, St Helena, has a wonderful selection of breads, cheeses and sausages, along with fine olive oil. **Guigni's Grocery**, 1227 Main St, stocks many practical items and **Oakville Grocery Co.**, 7856 St Helena Hwy, Oakville is the ultimate up-market deli for picnic provisions.

Napa Valley Conference and Visitors Bureau, 1310 Napa Town Center; tel: (707) 226-7459, has general Napa Valley information. **Napa Chamber of Commerce**, 1556 1st St; tel: (707) 226-7455, is open 0900–1700. The **Tourist Information Office** at 4076 Byway East; tel: (707) 253-2929, is open 1000–1500.

Napa Valley Reservations Unlimited, 1819 Tanen; tel: (707) 252-1985 and **Bed and Breakfast Inns of Napa Valley**, tel: (707) 944-4444 can help with bookings. Try **Napa**

Town and Country Fairgrounds, 575 3rd St; tel: (707) 226-2164) for basic camping. **St Helena Chamber of Commerce**, 1508 Main St; tel: (707) 963-4456 is a good information source for B&Bs.

CALISTOGA At the northern end of the Napa Valley, Calistoga sits atop an active geothermal area. Sam Brannan created the town in 1859, hoping to emulate the highly profitable hot springs of Saratoga, New York (see p. 79). He ended up in San Francisco, but the **Sam Brannan Cottage** and the **Sharpsteen Museum** (1311 Washington St) keep his historic contributions alive. Spa packages start at about $50, depending on resort and options. **Old Faithful Geyser**, 1299 Tubbs Lane, erupts every 4 mins, recent earthquakes permitting, in a 60 ft blast of steam and water.

Robert Louis Stevenson State Park, 10 miles north along Hwy 29, offers the best view of wine country from Mt St Helena. Stevenson honeymooned in an abandoned miner's cabin on the mountain in 1880, which provided material for *Silverado Squatters*. He also penned the over-quoted 'bottled poetry' description of Napa wines. The 5-mile return walk to the 4344 ft peak is debilitating in summer, but pleasant in autumn or spring. The **Silverado Museum** in St Helena has one of the world's best Stevenson collections.

i **Calistoga Chamber of Commerce**, 1458 Lincoln 9, Calistoga, CA 94525; tel: (707) 942-6333.

Bed and Breakfast Exchange, 1458 Lincoln Ave; tel: (707) 942-2888. The only camping is at **Napa County Fairgrounds** $ 1435 Oak St; tel: (707) 942-5111.

SONOMA Sonoma was California's capital during a short bout of independence before the USA annexed California in 1847. Strict building controls have kept the downtown intact. Many are part of **Sonoma State Historic Park** (self-guided walking tours available). By car, take Hwy 29 north to Hwy 121. Golden Gate Transit buses run from San Francisco and link to local bus services from Petaluma and Santa Rosa. Sonoma Hwy (Hwy 12) runs north-west through the 'Valley of the Moon', Jack London's name for the Sonoma Valley. His beloved Beauty Ranch has become the **Jack London State Historic Park** (2400 London Ranch Rd, Glen Ellen). The park offers picnicking, a museum, the ruins of London's dream Wolf House, and miles of walking or riding trails. The 17-mile long valley now has about three dozen wineries, and is less commercialised (and cheaper) than the Napa Valley.

i **Sonoma Valley Visitors Bureau**, 453 First St E., Sonoma, CA 95476; tel: (707) 996-1090. Visitor centres are in Sonoma Plaza, and on Hwy 121, adjacent to Viansa Winery.

Sequoia and Kings Canyon National Parks

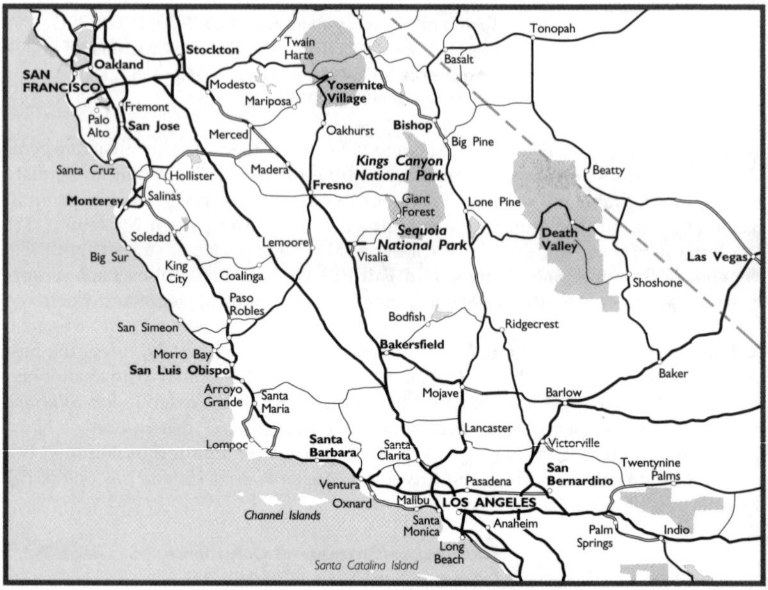

Notes

Yosemite Via runs buses from Fresno to Sequoia National Park – 5hrs 30mins.

Route Detail

Hwy 198 leads from Visalia to and through the parks (there is no public transport). Only one road penetrates Kings Canyon Park proper, the Kings Canyon Highway (Hwy 180), open only in summer. Other road access is limited and often closed in winter and barred to RVs: for driving information contact: (559) 565-3351.

These two contiguous parks contain some of California's most spectacular mountain scenery, some of the biggest living things on earth, and vast tracts of Sierra Nevada wilderness. Tortuous trails lead eastwards over the spine of the sierras to Mount Whitney – California's highest peak – and the Owens Valley, but innumerable easier paths wandering a few miles into the wilderness are an unforgettable introduction to the glories of outdoor California.

SEQUOIA NATIONAL PARK

Sequoia, the more southerly park, offers a variety of natural attractions, from caves and Mount Whitney to alpine meadows and crashing rivers – all of which pale beside the dense stands of giant sequoia redwood trees (*Sequoiadendron giganteum*), the largest living things on earth.

Access to the park is via Ash Grove, Ash Mountain and Big Stump Entrances; all off Highway 198.

Sequoia National Parks, Three Rivers CA 93271; tel: (559) 565-3341; www.nps/gov/seki.
Ash Mountain/Foothills Visitor Center; tel: (559) 565-3341; open daily 0800–1700.
Lodgepole Visitor Center; tel: (559) 565-3782; open daily 0800–1800 (May–Oct), Fri–Sun 1000–1600 (Nov–Apr).
Mineral King Visitor Center, open daily 0700–1500 May–Sept.

All park hotels are operated by **Sequoia National Park Reservations**, Three Rivers, CA 93271; tel: (559) 565-3134 or (888) 252-5757; fax: (559) 456-0542. Motels in Three Rivers (on Hwy 180, south of Ash Mountain Entrance) are open all year; some places in the park open summer only.
Mineral King Pack Station $$ Box 61, Three Rivers, CA 93271; tel: (559) 561-3404 (summer) or (559) 561-4142 (winter). Advance booking required.
Montecito-Sequoia Lodge $$ Generals Hwy (Hwy 180), between Sequoia and Kings Canyon; tel: (559) 565-3388 or (800) 843-8677; www.montecitosequoia.com. For advance reservations contact 2225 Grant Rd, Ste 1, Los Altos, CA 94024; tel: (650) 967-8612 or (800) 227-9900. Open all year.
Silver City High Sierra Rustic Family Resort $$ Box 56, Three Rivers, CA 93271; tel: (559) 561-3223 (late May–early Sept); or 2420 E. Hillcrest Ave, Visalia, CA 93292; tel: (209)

SEQUOIA AND KINGS CANYON NATIONAL PARKS

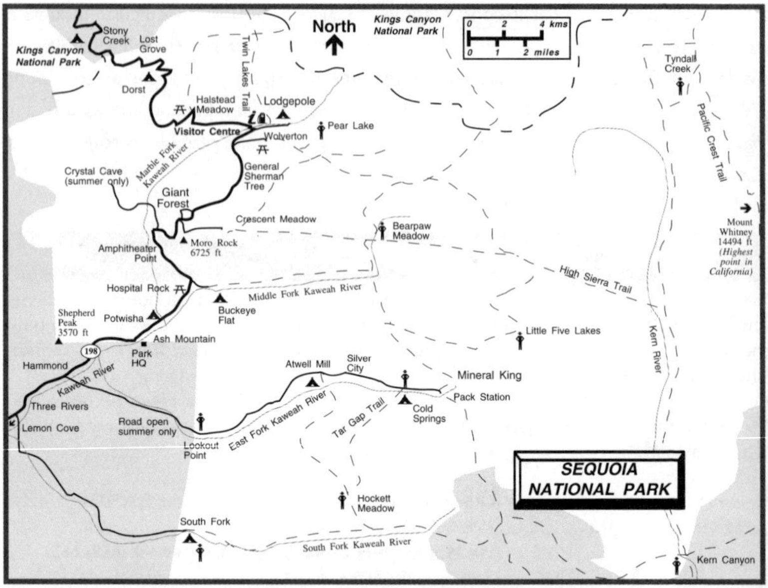

734-4109 (late Sept–early May). Lantern-lit cabins and chalets on the road to Mineral King in summer.
Wuksachi Village $$. Open all year.

Meals and picnic supplies are available in Wuksachi Village (a new facility near the Giant Forest) Lodgepole and Montecito-Sequoia all year.
Silver City Bakery and Restaurant $$ near Mineral King. Open in summer along with an adjoining general store.

HIGHLIGHTS **Mineral King** (turn-off 5 miles north of Three Rivers; no RVs or trailers) is a scalloped bowl at 7800 ft, the only bit of the park's high sierra country accessible by vehicle. Walt Disney tried to turn the scenic bowl into a ski resort in 1965 – thirteen litigious years later it was added to Sequoia National Park instead.

Hospital Rock, 5 miles beyond Ash Grove Entrance towards Giant Forest, marks an ancient native American village site. Look for pictographs on the surrounding boulders and 71 mortar holes, once used to grind acorns and seeds into flour.

Giant Forest, 30 miles from Big Stump Entrance and 16 miles from Ash Mountain Entrance, was named by John Muir, who first brought Yosemite to the world's attention in the 19th century (see p. 446). Four of the largest known sequoias grow in this grove. The biggest of them all is the **General Sherman tree**, 275 ft tall and 103 ft in circumference.

One of the best easy walks is the 2 mile paved **Congress Trail** (from the Sherman tree); pick up a self-guiding trail guide at the tree or at the Lodgepole Visitor Center nearby.

Crescent Meadow Road leaves the main road from the former Giant Forest Village in a scenic detour past several famous sites (not recommended for RVs). A set of nearly 400 concrete steps leads 300 ft up the side of **Moro Rock** (6725 ft) which gives a splendid 360° view stretching 150 miles from the spine of the sierras to the Central Valley. Save the staircase climb for clear days when vistas are not swathed in haze.

HIKING TRAILS

Hiking into the golden **Sawtooth Mountains** to the east is superb, as are wilderness horseback trips from **Mineral King Pack Station**, tel: (559) 561-3404. The ¼ mile **Cold Springs Nature Trail** is a less strenuous alternative.

Crescent Meadow itself, like most naturally grassy areas in the park, is actually a marsh, too wet to support sequoias and other trees. A flat 1½ mile trail circles the meadow to **Tharp's Log**, a sequoia hollowed into a cabin for Hale Tharp, who grazed sheep in the meadow in the 1850s.

KINGS CANYON NATIONAL PARK

The park got its name from the gaping canyon ripped into the salt-and-pepper granite of the high sierra by the raging torrent of the Kings River, gouged into a broad valley by ponderous glaciers. Just downstream from the confluence of the Middle and South Forks of the Kings River, the canyon plunges 8200 ft from the peak of Spanish Mountain, the deepest gorge in North America.

Access to the park is via Hyw 180 from Fresno, and Hwy 198 from Visalia. There are no petrol stations in the park, but Kings Canyon Lodge has a supply at premium prices.

Kings Canyon National Park, Three Rivers, CA 93271; tel: (559) 565-3341; www.nps/gov/seki.
Grant Grove Visitor Center, Grant Grove Village; tel: (559) 335-2856. Open daily 0800–1700.
Cedar Grove Visitor Center, just west of Cedar Grove Village; tel: (559) 565-3793. Open daily 0800–1800 (late June–Labor Day); Thur–Mon (May and Sept).

All accommodation in the park is booked through **Kings**

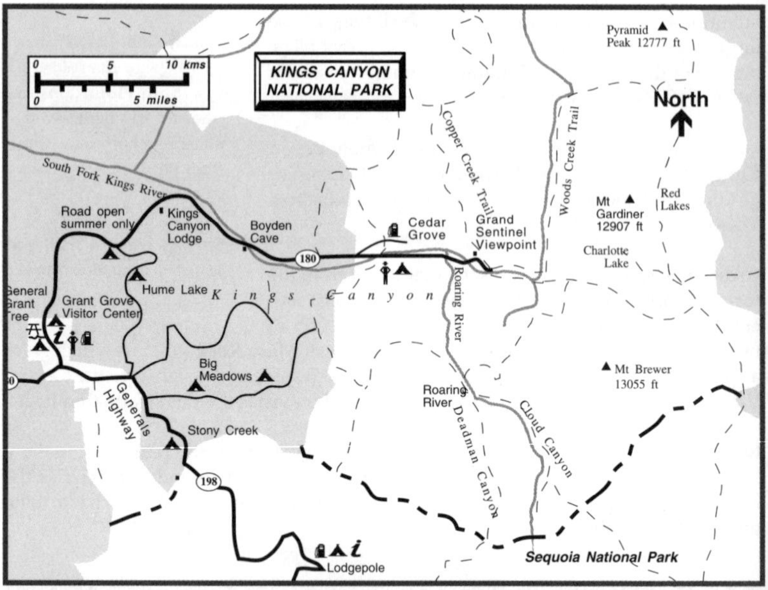

Canyon Park Services, Box 909, Kings Canyon NP, CA 93633; tel: (559) 335-5500.
Grant Grove Lodge $$. Open all year.
Cedar Grove Lodge $$. Open in summer.

In summer, picnic supplies and restaurant meals are available in **Grant Grove Village $$**, **Cedar Grove Village $$**, and **Kings Canyon Lodge $$–$$$**. Grant Grove remains open in winter.

HIGHLIGHTS Kings Canyon's most popular attractions are concentrated around **Grant Grove**, named after the **General Grant Tree**, officially the world's third largest tree at 267 ft tall and 107 ft in circumference. A paved path wanders for 0.3 mile through the grove, passing the **Fallen Monarch**, which has been a house and a stable, and the **Gamlin Cabin**, a rebuilt 1872 logger's cabin. Most of the major trees have been fenced off to protect their shallow root systems from trampling by adoring crowds.

A quieter alternative is the seldom-visited **North Grove Loop**, a 1½ mile trail that begins at the Grant Grove car park. The 2.2 mile **Dead Giant Loop** (from the lower end of the car park) passes a historic lumber mill pond on the way to a giant sequoia killed by girdling, or cutting through the living cambium layer just beneath the bark, which cut the flow of nutrients to the tree. The walk offers an instructive comparison between the ways National Park and National Forest lands are managed.

ON A CLEAR DAY ...
Panoramic Point is one of the most accessible vistas across the spine of the high sierra, with **Lake Hume** to the north below. The 4.7-mile return **Park Ridge Trail** offers views (on clear days) from the high peaks down the descending western ranges into the Central Valley.

From Grant Grove, **Kings Canyon Highway** runs east to Cedar Grove. Much of the road follows the canyon of the Kings River, here a sharp V shape. The sheer granite walls are laced with blue marble, pocked with yellow yucca plants and splattered with green and orange lichen, more easily visible beyond **Junction View**.

Cedar Grove is as close as Kings Canyon comes to civilisation. The seasonal village and visitor centre are named after the surrounding groves of incense cedars. The flat valley floor is ideal for leisurely cycle rides – from here it's 5 miles to Roads End.

The U shape of Kings Canyon, the unmistakable sign of past glacial activity, is most obvious from **Canyon Viewpoint** a mile to the east, while the V shape of the lower canyon, beyond the reach of glaciers, is typical of canyons carved by rivers.

Knapp's Cabin, a mile east of the viewpoint, was used to store equipment for opulent fishing expeditions staged by Santa Barbara businessman George Knapp during the 1920s. A mile further east is the car park for **Roaring River Falls**. An easy 5-min walk along a paved path leads to the falls.

The 1 mile loop trail through **Zumwalt Meadow** is one of the most scenic walks in either park. The trail crosses a suspension bridge to a view over the grassy meadow and **North Dome** (8717 ft), then descends through the meadow. Expect to see a variety of birds as well as a profusion of wildflowers – leopard lilies, shooting stars, violets, Indian paintbrush, lupins and others. Pick up a self-guiding map at the visitor centre. Just beyond is **Grand Sentinel Viewpoint**, with clear views of one of the most striking rock formations in the area, the Grand Sentinel (8504 ft).

Roads End, literally just that, is the start of a vast network of trails. Gruelling tracks cross the sierras through passes above 11,000 ft into the Owens Valley. The 8 mile return hike to **Mist Falls** is an easier way to see this area. The sandy trail starts relatively flat, but gains 600 ft in the final mile to the largest waterfall in the twin parks. Allow 4–6 hours for the hike. Return to Cedar Grove on the road, or, more interestingly, via the **Motor Nature Trail** on the north side of the river. This rough corrugated road is passable by passenger vehicles but *not* recommended for RVs.

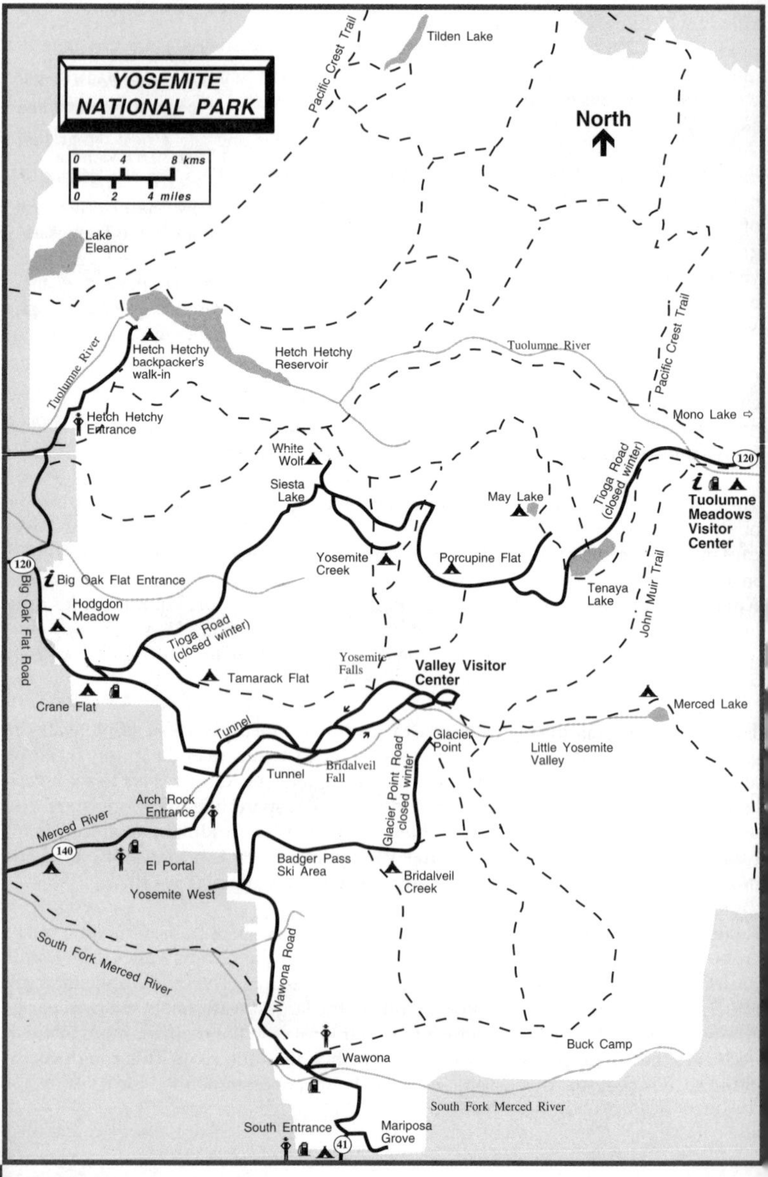
YOSEMITE
NATIONAL PARK
0 4 8 kms
0 2 4 miles
North
Tilden Lake
Pacific Crest Trail
Lake Eleanor
Hetch Hetchy backpacker's walk-in
Hetch Hetchy Reservoir
Tuolumne River
Hetch Hetchy Entrance
White Wolf
Siesta Lake
May Lake
Tioga Road (closed winter)
Mono Lake ⇨
120
Tuolumne Meadows Visitor Center
Yosemite Creek
Porcupine Flat
Tenaya Lake
John Muir Trail
Big Oak Flat Entrance
Big Oak Flat Road
Hodgdon Meadow
Tamarack Flat
Yosemite Falls
Valley Visitor Center
Crane Flat
Merced Lake
Tunnel
Glacier Point
Little Yosemite Valley
Bridalveil Fall
Glacier Point Road closed winter
Arch Rock Entrance
Merced River
140
El Portal
Badger Pass Ski Area
Bridalveil Creek
Yosemite West
Wawona Road
South Fork Merced River
Wawona
Buck Camp
South Entrance
Mariposa Grove
41

Waves of glaciers carved Yosemite into a colossal landscape that captivated a Scottish immigrant and itinerant mountain wanderer named John Muir more than a century ago. It's a wild wonder of soaring granite, deep gorges, mountain meadows and silent peaks that seem to touch the sky. Even Yosemite's trees are larger than life – giant sequoias in park groves are among the largest living organisms on the planet. Yosemite Falls, thundering 2425 ft to the valley floor, have a vertical drop greater than that of any other waterfall in North America and the fifth greatest in the world.

In retrospect, it's easy to blame Muir for the steadily growing popularity that has chipped away at Yosemite's beauty. His efforts were largely responsible for preserving the spectacular landscape inside a national park. But his success at protecting Yosemite was due primarily to his success at promoting the place as unique in all the world: and Muir was one of the best promoters California has ever seen. Once word got out, people from around the world came to test his tales of astounding beauty, including those on the very first Thomas Cook tour of America in the 1870s. Yosemite became a National Park in 1890. A century ago, it received a trickle of visitors. Today, park rangers warn of 'loving Yosemite to death'.

The problem is that the most famous sights – Half Dome, El Capitan, Yosemite Falls, Bridalveil Fall and others – are in Yosemite Valley, which attracts nearly all of the 4 million-plus people who come each year. The rest of the park is almost deserted, including hiking trails barely beyond shouting distance of the gridlocked valley floor.

If possible, *don't* visit the valley in the summer. If you absolutely must, park your car, hire a bicycle and laugh at the traffic jams. Free shuttles make an even easier alternative to driving.

GETTING THERE

From northern California, the park ($$) is reached via Arch Rock Entrance on Hwy 140 from Merced; the most direct route from southern California is Hwy 41 from Fresno, entering at South Entrance. There are also entrances on both east and west sides of the park from Hwy 120, which runs across the park (but is closed in winter).

VIA Adventures, tel: (209) 722-0366 or (800) 369-7275, operates Amtrak's Thruway bus service, connecting with the San Joaquin trains at Merced. VIA also offers one-day and overnight tour packages.

INFORMATION

Yosemite National Park, Box 557, CA 95389; tel: (209) 372-0200; www.nps.gov/yose.

The main visitor centre, as well as most accommodation, restaurants and other services, is in Yosemite Village. **Yosemite Valley Visitors Center**, at the west end of Yosemite Village Mall; tel: (209) 372-0299, is open 0900–1700 daily. Must-haves are the park brochure and the newsprint *Yosemite Guide*, both available at park entrances, and the *Yosemite Magazine*, from visitor centre bookshops.

Tuolumne Meadows Visitor Center, Tuolumne Meadows; tel: (209) 372-0263, is open early summer–Sept.

ANIMAL ALERT

It's wise to keep a distance from park animals; they can react unpredictably if approached too closely or surrounded. Black bears frequent the valley in search of the food visitors bring in – so follow park recommendations for storing food out of bears' way. If a bear is spotted, alert park rangers.

ACCOMMODATION

All accommodation in the park is run by **Yosemite Concession Services**. Advance bookings are essential Apr–Sept and at weekends and holidays all year – contact **Yosemite Reservations**, 5410 East Home, Fresno, CA 93727; tel: (209) 252-4848.

Yosemite Lodge $$ Yosemite Valley. Best value motel accommodation.

Ahwahnee Hotel $$$ Yosemite Valley. Grand hotel and dining room, worth a visit even if you aren't staying here.

Wawona Hotel $$$ in the south end of the park. Also has camping.

CAMPING Tents, cabins and campsites ($$) are scattered throughout Yosemite Valley. Campsite reservations are handled by DESTINET, 9450 Carroll Park Dr., San Diego, CA 92121; tel: (800) 436-7275 or (619) 452-8787. Advance reservations are essential in all seasons. During May–Sept, the **Camp Curry Campground Reservation Office** sometimes has last-minute cancellations, but demand is intense. Camping away from campsites is by permit only, obtainable from the park wilderness centre. Write as far in advance as possible to Wilderness Permits, PO Box 545, Yosemite, CA 95389, or tel: (209) 372-0740.. Half the permits allotted for most wilderness areas are assigned in advance, the other half on a first-come, first-served basis during the season.

FOOD

Village Grill $ Yosemite Village. Basic burgers and sandwiches.

Degnans Deli $ and **The Pasta Place** $. Yosemite Village. Variations on a similar theme.

Yosemite Lodge $$ Yosemite Valley. Has a budget-priced cafeteria and a moderate restaurant.

Wawona Hotel Dining Room $$ South Yosemite. Sunday brunch is particularly good.

Ahwahnee Hotel Dining Room $$$ Yosemite Valley. A better bet for breakfast and lunch than dinner – except for special events such as the Vintners' Holidays and the Chefs' Holidays, when dinners are outstanding.

Curry Village and Tuolumne Meadows both have grills open until the first snowfall; the Badger Pass Lodge offers simple meals in winter only. **Village Store** is a full grocery store, but picnic supplies are more expensive than outside the park.

HIGHLIGHTS

There are really three Yosemites within the park: **Yosemite Valley,** with the greatest concentration of attractions and visitors; **South Yosemite** and **Tioga Pass Rd**, which are almost as crowded. The more remote countryside remains relatively untouched.

YOSEMITE VALLEY Entering the park at the Arch Rock Entrance on Hwy 140, a one-way anticlockwise road loops through the valley. Most of the road is lined with parking spaces on one or both sides. A paved walking/cycling trail runs parallel to the road in the east end of the valley.

The route passes Bridalveil Fall, Sentinel Dome, the wedding chapel and Curry Village before reaching the east end of the valley, with Half Dome in the distance. The road then runs through campsites, passes the Ahwahnee Hotel beneath the valley wall, and comes to Yosemite Village.

Yosemite Falls cascade down the valley wall beyond the Village, almost across the highway from Yosemite Lodge. The road continues to a connector for the return loop, or beyond, past the sheer rock face of El Capitan, rising 7569 ft, to another return connector.

Glacier Point, perched some 321 ft above the valley

FREE SHUTTLES

Shuttle buses circle the eastern Yosemite Valley all year, running in non-stop loops from dawn to midnight. Seasonal shuttles serve other attractions such as the Badger Pass ski area, the Mariposa Grove of Giant Sequoias and trailheads between Yosemite Valley and Tuolumne Meadow.

Exploring Yosemite Valley on Foot

The most popular walks are the paved ½-mile trails to **Lower Yosemite Fall** and **Bridalveil Fall**, on opposite sides of the valley. The return walk to **Mirror Lake**, which reflects surrounding mountains, is 2 miles, most of it flat. With occasional help, all three trails can be navigated by wheelchairs.

One of the more popular longer valley walks is the 3-mile return hike up the **Vernal Fall Mist Trail** to Vernal Fall. Two miles beyond is **Nevada Fall**. Most visitors take all day over the 7-mile return trip because of the altitude. A special treat for the truly fit and determined is the 17-mile return hike up the granite hemisphere forming the 8842 ft back of **Half Dome**. Steel cables anchored in the rock help the final ascent.

floor, offers spectacular views of the valley, Yosemite Falls, Half Dome and much of the park. However, it's a circuitous 25-mile drive to get there, and access is easier from the south. Caravans and RVs are not permitted to use the road, but coach tours run there from the valley in the summer months.

South Yosemite

To reach **Mariposa Grove**, travelling from the south, turn right immediately beyond the South Entrance and follow the winding road 2 miles east to the paved parking area. This road is closed to all caravans and RVs more than 25 ft long because of restricted parking space. If parking at the grove is full, drive to Wawona and take the free shuttle back. The grove has toilets, drinking water, a museum and souvenir shop (fencing protects the shallow roots of the giant sequoias that dot the parking area). The **Mariposa Grove Museum** is on the site of a cabin built by Galen Clark, the first official guardian when the Yosemite Valley and Mariposa Grove were set aside as a state reserve in 1864. The museum focuses on the natural history of the sequoias.

The main grove is a 2-min stroll down a walking trail. During the summer an open-top tram tours the grove. Near the start of the trail is the **Fallen Monarch**, immortalised in an 1899 photograph of an entire US Cavalry troop, including horses, posing atop the tree. **Grizzly Giant**, an estimated 2700 years old, is one of the oldest living sequoias. The huge limb far up on the south side of the trunk is nearly 7 ft in diameter, larger than the trunk of any non-sequoia tree in the area.

About 150 ft beyond the Grizzly Giant is the **California Tunnel Tree**, cut in 1895 to allow stagecoaches to pass through. Millions of visitors passed through the Tunnel Tree between 1881, when it was cut open, and 1969, when it collapsed under the weight of a record snowpack. Weakened by the gigantic hole in its base, the tree may have died 1000 years prematurely.

From the park's southern entrance, Hwy 41 runs north, past the entrance to **Wawona Basin**. This valley, now largely taken over by a golf course, was a native American encampment and site of a roadside hostel built by Galen Clark in 1857 – Clark's Station was an overnight stop between Mariposa and the Yosemite Valley. The white Victorian gingerbread **Wawona Hotel**, built in 1879, is still a popular holiday destination.

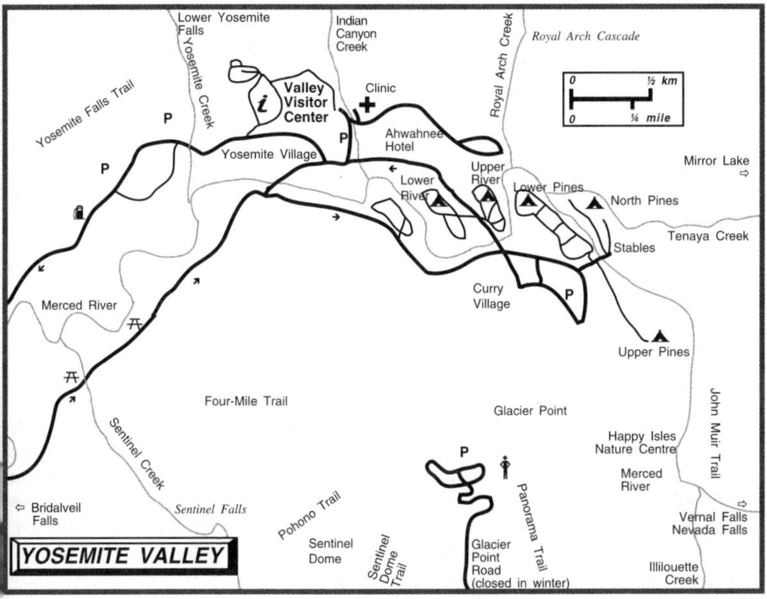

Just beyond the hotel is the **Yosemite Pioneer History Center**, which concentrates on the human history of Yosemite. The museum features a collection of historic cabins and other buildings moved to the site, plus several stagecoaches. There are stagecoach rides and living history demonstrations during the summer months.

Hwy 41 continues north towards Yosemite Valley, 27 miles ahead. It follows the western boundary of the park, winding from the crest of one ridge to the next. Fire scars are visible on both sides of the road in several places, the result of nearly a century of ruthless fire suppression in Yosemite (see box).

Yosemite Village

Village facilities include the Park Headquarters and Valley Visitor Center, stores, restaurants, a medical clinic, bicycle rental (around $20 a day) at Yosemite Lodge, a museum, the Indian Cultural Museum, an art activity centre and other services.

About 12 miles beyond Wawona is a left turn towards Yosemite West, a private development just outside the park boundaries. About ½ mile beyond is Glacier Point Rd, a turn-off to the right for Badger Pass and Glacier Point. The narrow, winding road (closed to caravans and RVs) twists through forests of pine and fir. It is open all year as far as the **Badger Pass Ski Area**. The remainder of the road is closed in winter, but cross-country skiers can continue all the way to Glacier Point.

The rest of the year it's a short, easy (and well-trodden) walk from the car park at the end of the road to **Glacier Point**, overlooking Yosemite Valley 3214 ft below. A 1 mile walk from the parking area leads to **Sentinel Dome** (8122 ft), 908 ft above Glacier Point. On full moon nights the valley below becomes a fairyland.

Beyond the Glacier Point Rd turn-off, Hwy 41 turns towards Yosemite Valley. **Inspiration Point**, 6 miles beyond the junction, has a fine view of the Gates of Yosemite. The Cathedral Rocks are on the right, El Capitan on the left, with Half Dome rising in the background. Continuing downhill leads through the tunnel to **Tunnel View**, the official viewpoint into Yosemite Valley. Bridalveil Fall is visible on the right. The view is on the left side of the road, but there is parking on both sides. Watch for pedestrians crossing the highway who are more intent on the view than on traffic. The parking area for Bridalveil Fall, and the beginning of the valley floor loop, is 1 mile further on.

TIOGA PASS The 60 miles across Yosemite National Park from **Crane Flat** over Tioga Pass in the Sierra Nevada and down to **Lee Vining**, just beyond the eastern boundary of the park, is one of California's best short drives, threading through lush alpine meadows along the spine of the Sierra Nevada. The road is usually closed by snow in Oct and seldom reopens before the end of May. The best guide to the sights, facilities and geography on the drive is the *Yosemite Road Guide*, published by the Yosemite Association and on sale throughout the park. Most lay-bys and vista points have picnic tables and explanatory signs keyed to local geography, plants or animals.

From Yosemite Village, follow the valley loop road 6 miles, passing El Capitan on the right. An excellent valley view across the Merced River is on the left side of the road just beyond El Capitan. At the junction with Hwy 140, bear to the right on Big

FIRE!

Until the 1960s, forest managers didn't realise that fire is an integral part of sierra forests. Many forest species, including redwoods, need fire to regenerate. The seeds need the bare soil created by natural fires in order to germinate, and open sunlight to grow. Historically, late summer fires swept through these forests every seven to twenty years, burning out undergrowth and fallen branches and leaving a layer of rich ash on the bare soil. Years of fire suppression allowed a build-up of debris and the proliferation of underbrush and shade-tolerant trees. When fires did start, they burned fiercely through the dense brush and fallen wood. Instead of rejuvenating the forest, fire destroyed everything in its path, leaving vast tracts of charred tree trunks.

The solution is controlled fire, called 'management fires', set by park personnel during damp autumn weather when winds are calm. Watch for signs which warn of management fires ahead. Any other fires should be reported to park personnel by dialling 911 from any telephone.

HETCH HETCHY VALLEY

For a look at what could have happened to Yosemite, continue on Big Oak Flat Rd to the Big Oak Flat Entrance. Exit the park, turn right onto Evergreen Rd towards Camp Mather and re-enter Yosemite at the Hetch Hetchy Entrance. Hetch Hetchy Valley was the visual equal of Yosemite Valley until it was dammed and drowned to provide electricity and drinking water for San Francisco in 1913. The National Park Service was created in 1916, charged to preserve and protect National Park lands from similar commercial attacks in the future. (The 52-mile detour to Hetch Hetchy and back takes about 2 hrs.)

Oak Flat Rd towards Tioga Pass. The road begins climbing almost immediately, affording broad views across the Merced River canyon; there is an observation point just beyond the first tunnel. Turn right onto Hwy 120, following signs for Yosemite Institute, Tuolumne Grove, Tuolumne Meadows and Tioga Pass.

The **Yosemite Institute** is an outdoor education institute on the left side of the highway above the **Tuolumne Grove** of sequoias. Walk down to the grove (summer or winter) along a 1-mile return trail. The grove contains 20 sequoias, including the **Dead Giant**, a tunnel tree that broke in two several years ago. Hwy 120 is closed just beyond the grove in winter.

The road continues climbing beyond the grove, following low ridges and shallow valleys between peaks topping more than 10,000 ft. **Siesta Lake**, 14 miles beyond the Tuolumne Grove, is a favourite photographic stop. The shallow lake, on the right-hand side of the road, mirrors the surrounding forests and mountain peaks. **White Wolf**, 1 mile beyond, has summer camping and eating facilities. **Tenaya Lake**, another 14 miles, is a favourite for fishing.

The highlight of the Tioga Pass Rd is **Tuolumne Meadows**, 6 miles from Tenaya Lake. The high country meadows, at an altitude of 8600 ft, are popular for camping, walking and fishing, and as a departure point for mountain climbing and exploration. Rangers at the visitor centre conduct daily walks and evening educational programmes in summer. Petrol, groceries, a restaurant, post office, guides, horses and other services are also available in summer.

The highway continues climbing towards **Tioga**

YOSEMITE OUT OF SEASON

Hwy 140 from Mariposa into Yosemite Valley seldom closes, but heavy snow closes some of the roads, such as Tioga Rd and Glacier Point Rd, usually mid Nov–late May. The park may be at its best in winter, when trees and waterfalls are rimmed with ice and the daily visitor count is in hundreds rather than tens of thousands. Badger Pass was the first commercial ski area in California (most runs are beginner and intermediate). Park rangers also lead snowshoe walks into the deep snows that blanket the surrounding forests. In autumn, winter and spring, carry tyre chains in case of unexpected snowstorms.

Pass (9945 ft) and the Tioga Pass Entrance just beyond. Food, petrol and accommodation, as overpriced as any inside Yosemite, begin about 2 miles below the park entrance. The last 12 miles of highway take long, sweeping turns down the eastern side of the Sierra Nevada, with magnificent vistas up and down the Lee Vining Canyon National Scenic Byway. Watch for a viewpoint on the right side of the road overlooking Tioga Lake, 5 miles below the park entrance. The panoramas across the Mono Basin and beyond are magical, especially in the warm sunlight of late afternoon.

The steep slope provides an exciting ride, swooping down the mountainside, but it can be extremely hard on the brakes, especially for RVs and caravans. The best driving tactic is to shift into low gear at Tioga Pass and use the brakes sparingly.

Notes
Merced is the stop for Yosemite. Reservations for San Joaquin trains can generally be made the same day of travel, except during busy holiday periods. Hwy 5 from Los Angeles leads to Hwy 99 which connects all the towns mentioned on this route.

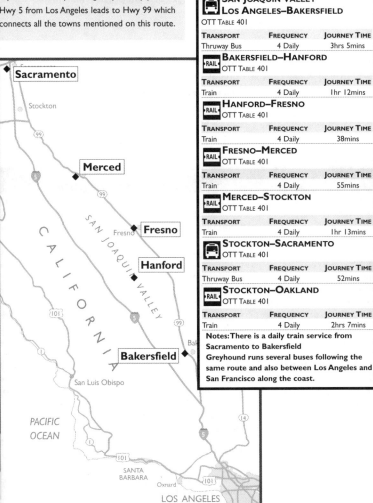

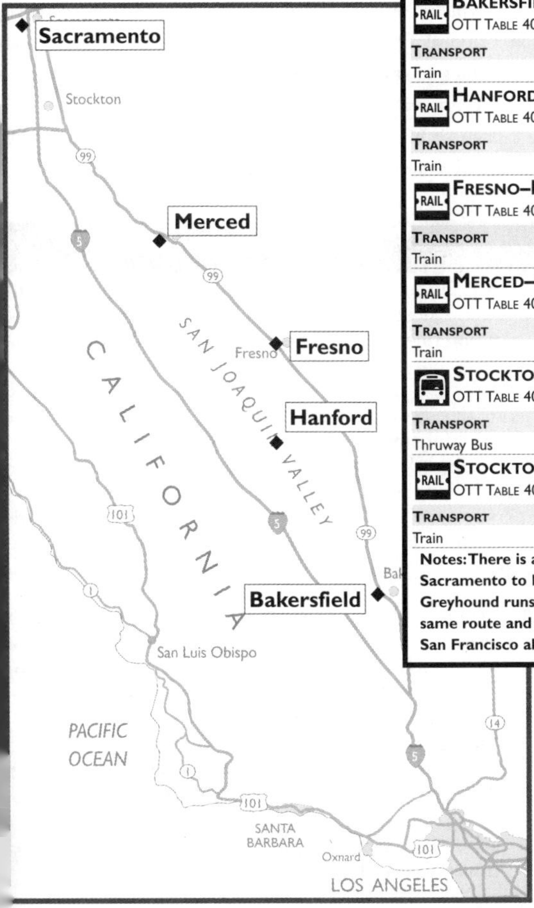

SAN JOAQUIN VALLEY
LOS ANGELES–BAKERSFIELD
OTT TABLE 401

TRANSPORT	FREQUENCY	JOURNEY TIME
Thruway Bus	4 Daily	3hrs 5mins

BAKERSFIELD–HANFORD
OTT TABLE 401

TRANSPORT	FREQUENCY	JOURNEY TIME
Train	4 Daily	1hr 12mins

HANFORD–FRESNO
OTT TABLE 401

TRANSPORT	FREQUENCY	JOURNEY TIME
Train	4 Daily	38mins

FRESNO–MERCED
OTT TABLE 401

TRANSPORT	FREQUENCY	JOURNEY TIME
Train	4 Daily	55mins

MERCED–STOCKTON
OTT TABLE 401

TRANSPORT	FREQUENCY	JOURNEY TIME
Train	4 Daily	1hr 13mins

STOCKTON–SACRAMENTO
OTT TABLE 401

TRANSPORT	FREQUENCY	JOURNEY TIME
Thruway Bus	4 Daily	52mins

STOCKTON–OAKLAND
OTT TABLE 401

TRANSPORT	FREQUENCY	JOURNEY TIME
Train	4 Daily	2hrs 7mins

Notes: There is a daily train service from Sacramento to Bakersfield
Greyhound runs several buses following the same route and also between Los Angeles and San Francisco along the coast.

San Joaquin Valley

On the 'San Joaquin'

California's Central Valley stretches from Redding to Bakersfield. It is called the Sacramento Valley in the north and the San Joaquin in the south, after corresponding rivers. The valley looks a lot like Kansas . . . except on clear days when the gently rising Sierra Nevada Mountain Range or Coastal Range are visible in the distance. Spring and Fall are the best time to visit.

Most of the larger towns and cities are located on the eastern side of the valley. Few are of much interest to visitors except for historic Hanford, the gateway towns of Visalia (Sequoia and Kings Canyon National Parks), Merced (Yosemite National Park) and Sacramento, California's Capitol and gateway to the Gold County and Lake Tahoe regions. Amtrak trains travel the length of the valley, from Stockton (with Thruway connection from Sacramento, the state capital) via Merced, Fresno and Hanford to Bakersfield (with Thruway coach links to Los Angeles and other parts of southern California).

SACRAMENTO

California's capital city began at **Sutter's Fort** (27th and L Sts; RT bus 30, 31), built by Swiss immigrant John Sutter, whose Coloma sawmill sparked the Gold Rush. Sutter's adobe administration building is largely original; the rest of the fort ($) is reconstructed.

Old Sacramento (I–L Sts along the Sacramento River), or 'Old Sac' has brick buildings dating back to the 1850s, skilfully mixed with modern buildings, wooden sidewalks and shade trees. The **California State Railroad Museum** ($) is America's largest railway museum, filled with splendidly restored locomotive engines, luxurious private carriages, sleepers and extensive displays on America's first transcontinental railway. A new **Waterfront Promenade** links Old Sacramento and the **Crocker Art Museum** $, 2nd and O Sts, the oldest art gallery west of the Mississippi.

Golden State Museum, 1020 O St is California's official museum, drawing upon the 120 million items in state archives. The domed **California State Capitol** (10th St between L and N Sts) is also an outstanding museum, thanks to extensive 1980s renovations that returned the government offices to turn-of-the-century splendour.

i **Sacramento Visitor Information Center**, 1104 Front St, Old Sacramento; tel: (916) 442-7644, has information, a post office and a 24-hr cash dispenser. Open daily 0900–1700.

Amtrak arrives downtown at 5th and I Sts. **Baylink** buses connect to the Vallejo–San Francisco ferry.

HI-Sacramento $ 900 H St; tel: (916) 443-1691. Former mansion, within walking distance of all major attractions.
***Delta King* Hotel** $$$ 1000 Front St; tel: (800) 825-5464. Restored steam paddlewheel boat on the Sacramento River.

River City Brewing Company $ 545 Downtown Plaza. Offers pub fare.
4th Street Grille $$ 400 L St. Uses pesticide-free produce in salads, pizzas and pastas.
Pilothouse Restaurant $$ *Delta King*; tel: (916) 441-4440. Known for its Sunday brunch.

MERCED

Merced is the transfer point for buses to **Yosemite National Park** (see p. 440). The 1875 **County Courthouse**, 21st and N Sts, houses the county museum. The exterior resembles the State Capitol in Sacramento, and is set in a lovely shady park.

Merced Conference and Visitors Bureau, 690 W. 16th St; tel: (800) 446-5353 or (209) 384-3333, open Mon–Fri 0830–1700, has accommodation information.

The Amtrak station is downtown at 324 W. 24th St.

Hostelling International $; tel: (209) 725-0407. Call for free pick-up.

The Branding Iron Restaurant $$ 640 W. 16th St. A steak house with a collection of cattle branding irons.

FRESNO

Fresno's **Metropolitan Museum of Art, History and Science** $, 1555 Van Ness Ave, and very own symphony – **William Saroyan Theatre**, 700 M St; tel: (559) 498-1524 – mark it as the valley's cultural hub. The art deco **Tower District** (Olive and Wishon Aves) features antique shops, bookshops, restaurants and several live theatres. **Forestiere Underground Gardens** is an underground labyrinth of 50-odd rooms created 1905–46 to protect fruit orchards and other crops from the blistering summer sun. $ 5021 W. Shaw Ave; tel: (559) 271-0734; open Wed–Sun 1000–1600 (June–Sept); Sat–Sun 1200–1500 (Oct–Nov).

Fresno Convention and Visitors Bureau, 808 M St; tel: (559) 233-0836 or (800) 788-0836; open Mon–Fri 0800–1700. It has an accommodation list.

Amtrak (2650 Tulare St) is located downtown.

George's Shish Kebab $$ 2405 Capitol St; across from Amtrak. A chance to try Armenian food.
Santa Fe $$ 935 Santa Fe Ave; across from Amtrak. Basque country cooking served family-style.

HANFORD

Historic Hanford's town square is surrounded by restored buildings including the 1896 **County Courthouse, La Bastille**, shops, restaurants and a carousel. **China Alley** features an 1893 Taoist temple, Temple Theater, herb shop, hand laundry and **Imperial Dynasty Restaurant**, operated by descendants of the once large Chinese community. **Hanford Fox Theater**, 326 N. Irwin St, is one of the few remaining Fox 'atmospheric' theatres, with a Wurlitzer pipe organ.

Hanford Visitor Agency, 432 W. 7th St; tel: (209) 582-0483, is located in the Amtrak station, three blocks from downtown. Open Mon–Fri 0900–1700.

Irwin Street Inn $$, 522 N. Irwin St, tel: (209) 584-9286. B&B near the town square.

BAKERSFIELD

The unbeatable combination of fertile soil and the smell of oil was an open invitation for settlers to Bakersfield. **Kern County Museum**, 3801 Chester Ave, has won national acclaim for its collection of historic structures dating from 1860 to 1930. **Buck Owens' Crystal Palace**, 2800 Buck Owens Blvd at Sillect Ave; tel: (661) 328-7560, features the music that put Bakersfield on the map as 'Nashville West'.

WHERE NEXT?

Bakersfield has Amtrak Thruway bus connections to Los Angeles (see p. 375), Santa Barbara (see p. 42), Orange County, Palm Springs and Las Vegas (see p. 401).

Visitor Center, 1325 P St; tel: (661) 325-5051, is open Mon–Fri 0830–1700.

Amtrak arrives downtown at 15th and F Sts.

Downtowner Inn $$ 1301 Chester Ave; tel: (661) 327-7122.

Cottage Sandwich Shop $ 1032 Truxton Ave.
Dewars $ 1120 Eye St. Has served ice cream since 1909.
Uricchio's Trattoria $$ 1400 17th St. Italian family cooking.

Redwood Empire Association, 280 Leavenworth St, San Francisco, CA 94133; tel: (415) 543-8334, has information in English and German on lodging, dining and attractions for California's coastal areas from San Francisco to southern Oregon.

ALTERNATIVE ROUTES

Keeping to Hwy 101 will take you on a slightly shorter inland route (372 miles) that runs roughly parallel to Hwy 1 before the two join at Leggett. On the way visit quintessentially Victorian American Old Pentaluma, Santa Rosa's Railroad Square Historic District (the station was one of the few buildings to survive the 1906 earthquake) and the northern California wineries between Hopland and Ukiah. Hwy 128, linking Cloverdale on Hwy 101 and Elk on Hwy 1, runs through the vineyards and orchards of Anderson Valley.

If you'd like to let someone else do the driving, the **Amtrak Thruway** bus operates daily from Emeryville (for San Francisco), north to Arcata, and the **Greyhound bus** from San Francisco to Portland travels the Redwood Highway daily – OTT Tables 377/549/883.

ROUTE DETAIL

Take Hwy 101 north from San Francisco to the Hwy 1 exit, 3 miles beyond the Golden Gate Bridge.

Follow Hwy 1 north to Leggett. 188 miles.

Rejoin Hwy 101 and continue north to Crescent City 415 miles.

For sleep and safety as well as the scenery, allow at least five days for the drive.

San Francisco – Oregon Border

Pacific Coast Highway North

Towering forests of coast redwoods, pastoral dairies, and a dramatic coastline of sea stacks and rocky bluffs isolate this north-westernmost section of California, while preserving its regional personality.

Timber and fishing were Redwood Empire's economic mainstays, and much of the region has not recovered financially or emotionally from the diminution of both. Local residents are polarised over preservation of forest, fishing and land resources, and animosities spill over into newspaper headlines as environmentalists and huge lumber companies become locked in literal and legal battles.

Despite Ronald Reagan's comment that, having seen one redwood, you've seen them all, the clumps and groves differ in character. Second growth allows much more light to penetrate the canopy, but the size and magnitude of one or more old-growth giants is simply astounding. The stretch of Hwy 101 between Phillipsville and Pepperwood is known as the Avenue of the Giants, while north of Arcata the Redwood National and State Parks collectively conserve some of the tallest, biggest and oldest natural objects on the planet.

MENDOCINO

San Francisco artists rescued Mendocino as the lumber industry died in the 1950s. They may have succeeded too well. The town looks like a film set (it has been one, many times), with picture-perfect New England-style buildings perched on the edge of the swirling Pacific Ocean. The whole community is a National Historic Preservation District, its original buildings intact, beautifully renovated, and almost invisible behind the crowds.

Mendocino Art Center, 45200 Little Lake St, remains the centre for arts and artists throughout the county. The Gallery and the Showcase exhibit local as well as outside artists. If the weather is reasonable, **Mendocino Headlands State Park** is a refreshing respite. Start at park headquarters, the Ford House on Main St, then continue along the sandstone cliffs sculpted by wind and wave. **Russian Gulch State Park**, just north of Mendocino, is another defunct lumber port. The park has 1200 acres of redwoods, rhododendrons, azaleas, ferns, berry bushes, trees, fishing and camping. **Jug Handle State Reserve**, just north of the Caspar Headlands, is a prime example of an ecological staircase. A succession of ancient marine terraces, each about 100 ft above the other, is home to a different set of plants, from salt-tolerant wildflowers near the water to redwoods high above.

Mendocino Coast Chamber of Commerce, 332 N. Main St, PO Box 1141, Fort Bragg, CA 95437; tel: (800) 726-2780 or (707) 961-6300.

Mendocino is filled with B&Bs and restaurants, mostly pricey. Advance bookings are essential all year.

FORT BRAGG

Fort Bragg is Mendocino without culture-vulture crowds and inflated prices. Main St is lined with Victorian buildings, renovated for local use as much as for the tourist trade – merchants decided it was faster, cheaper and more attractive to refurbish than to rebuild. A historic walking guide covers more than two dozen downtown buildings, including the **Fort Bragg Depot, Marketplace and Museum**, a renovated 1924 Ford motor dealership which has railway artefacts, engines, shops and food stalls. The **Skunk Train**, tel: (707) 964-6371, still runs through the mountains to Willits on Hwy 101. The **Guest House Museum**, 343 North Main St, displays the history of Fort Bragg and the timber industry in photographs and artefacts.

Fort Bragg-Mendocino Coast Chamber of Commerce, 332 N. Main St, Fort Bragg, CA 95437; tel: (707) 961-6300 or (800) 726-2780.

Although Mendocino gets most of the visitors, Fort Bragg is the largest town on the coast between San Francisco and Eureka and prices are considerably more reasonable.

The North Coast Brewing Co. $–$$ 444 N. Main St. Usually crowded for the beer and robust meals.

LEGGETT

This small, one-time lumber town is sometimes called the Gateway to the Redwoods. The first of a long string of redwoods parks is just north of town, and road signs begin calling Hwy 101 'The Redwood Highway'.

Smithe Redwoods State Reserve, 4 miles north of the town east of Hwy 101, is a preview of the coast redwood giants to come. It is favoured for fishing, picnicking, hiking to a 60 ft waterfall, and summer swimming in the Eel River's South Fork.

About 8 miles short of Garberville, **Richardson Grove State Park** $; tel: (707) 247-3318, provides services and an early glimpse of major stands of coast redwoods on the Hwy 101 route north. Families swim in the South Fork Eel River in summer; fishers enjoy steelhead later in the year. Camping is popular and cabins are for hire.

Leggett Valley Chamber of Commerce, 66502 Underwood Lane, Leggett, CA 95585; tel: (707) 925-6385.

Eel River Redwoods Hostel, 70400 Hwy 101; tel: (707) 925-6469. Open all year.

GARBERVILLE

Avenue of the Giants
Just north of Garberville, coast redwood groves extend for a narrow 31-mile strip along both sides of Hwy 101 from Phillipsville to Pepperwood, cutting left and right over the South Fork of the Eel River. Most are named in tribute to the group or individuals who in the early 20th century worked to save a small number of redwoods before they disappeared. Most groves have a lay-by to park and explore the forest.

Garberville serves as a hub for forestry, and for holidaymakers as a base for exploring the Avenue of the Giants and a convenient stopping point. Environmental protection v. lumbering friction is notable, while musicians and young counterculture types hang out for the atmosphere.

Garberville-Redway Chamber of Commerce, 773 Redwood Dr, Garberville, CA 95542; tel: (800) 923-2613 or (707) 923-2613; fax: (707) 923-4789, is open Mon–Fri 0900–1700, shorter hours in winter.

As a services hub, Garberville is well supplied with motels. **Benbow Inn** $$$ 445 Lake Benbow Dr. (1 mile south of Garberville); tel: (707) 923-2124 or (800) 355-3301; fax: (707) 923-2122; www.benbowinn.com. A stunning redwoods version of Tudor, with lovely flower gardens outside and a high-ceilinged lobby and dining room. Open Apr–New Year's Day.

Sicilitos $ 445 Conger St. Old advertising and sports team memorabilia decorate the walls; serves tasty Mexican food and traditional American fare.

HUMBOLDT REDWOODS STATE PARK

Most visitors' encounter with Humboldt Redwoods State Park, tel: (707) 946-2409, is restricted to the Avenue of the Giants, but its 52,000 acres extend to the awesome trees of **Rockefeller Forest**, estimated to represent 10% of remaining old-growth redwoods.

Stop at the convenient and informative visitor centre 2 miles north of Weott, which helps interpret the history of these resilient but endangered trees. A short path from here gives a rare opportunity to see all three species side by side: dawn redwood (*Metasequoia glyptostroboides*), coast redwood (*Sequoia sempervirens*) and giant redwood (*Sequoiadendron giganteum*). The visitor centre is open 0900–1700 (Mar–Oct), 1000–1600 (Nov–Feb).

FERNDALE

The town has trademarked its moniker, 'The Victorian Village', but for once the pretentions are justified. Settled in 1852, Ferndale's low-lying, lush pastures were perfect for dairy cattle. It prospered and, by the 1890s, dairymen in Cream City were building heavily embellished Victorian mansions called 'butterfat palaces'. Two subsequent earthquakes wrought havoc, but the homes, mansions, churches and Main St storefronts were repaired and repainted and once more ooze their charm through sun or frequent fogs.

Main St is the place for shops, galleries, restaurants, bakeries, a meat market, a pioneer museum and the **Kinetic Sculpture Museum** (see Arcata, p. 465). The **Ferndale Carriage Co.** (from Main and Washington Sts) offers horse-drawn carriage tours of Main St and the mansions. Ferndale is also a walker's paradise.

i **Ferndale Chamber of Commerce**, PO Box 325, Ferndale, CA 95536; tel/fax: (707) 786-4477.

Ferndale has five B&Bs, one hotel, three motels and a county fairground camping area, but book in advance, as the town is popular with tourists from San Francisco and Los Angeles.
Gingerbread Mansion Inn $$$ 400 Berding St; tel: (800) 952-4136 or (707) 786-4000; www.gingerbread-mansion.com. 1899 turreted and gabled Victoriana, with magnificent English formal garden landscaping and a perfect and perfectly incongruous palm tree.

EUREKA

No building in far northern California is more recognisable than the green Victorian **Carson Mansion**, built in 1885 by a lumber baron's employees to fill time. Now a private club, this centrepiece of Eureka's historic **Old Town** (B–I Sts, Waterfront–7th St), shows the 19th-century value of a good fishing harbour with access to lumber. Attractions include horse-drawn carriage rides, galleries, stores, restaurants and B&Bs. Salmon and Dungeness crab are still staples, though fishing is restricted.

i **Eureka! Humboldt County Convention and Visitors Bureau**, 1034 2nd St, Eureka, CA 95501; tel: (707) 443-5097 or (800) 346-3482; fax: (707) 443-5115; www.redwoodvisitor.org. Open Mon–Fri 0900–1200, 1300–1700.

Café Waterfront $$ 102 F St. Fine seafood and salads, a long wooden bar, a stained glass window with a heron and, most remarkable in this landmark Old Town Eureka building, wall paintings of flowers and natural scenes, even in the loo!
Samoa Cookhouse $ Samoa Bridge, Hwy 255. Large, family-style portions of lumberjack fare served here, in keeping with its status as the last surviving lumber camp cookhouse in the west. Prices are low, and the draw of a free museum to one side with artefacts and old-time pose-with-your-log lumber camp photographs is irresistible.

ARCATA

Youth, counterculture, environmentalism, organic produce and vegetarianism are bywords in this youthful enclave by Humboldt State University. Sand dunes and marshy wetlands are within a mile of an urban forest sheltering magnificent redwoods along trails. Bicycles are common, especially by the marshes and estuaries of the Mad River between Arcata Bay and McKinleyville.

The town square, **Arcata Plaza**, was set aside by original lumber company owners as a park and meeting place. Among well-restored buildings near the plaza are **Jacoby's Storehouse** (1857) , 8th and H Sts, its 2 ft thick stone walls sheltering two restaurants; the 1914 **Minor Theatre**, 10th and H Sts; tel: (707) 822-3456, the oldest operating cinema in the USA, enhanced by isinglass door panels; and the 1915 **Hotel Arcata**, 9th and G Sts.

THE KINETIC SCULPTURE RACE

On Memorial Day Weekend (late May) each year, this entertaining and curious spectacle begins at **Arcata Plaza**. Contestants take three days to navigate 38 miles to **Ferndale** on whimsical people-powered contraptions that are the essence of clever design, ornamentation and wackiness, in keeping with Arcata's nickname, Ecotopia. The idea emerged from race founder Hobart Brown's belief in a 'new Race, conceived in insanity, and dedicated to the proposition that all mechanical nightmares definitely are not created equal'. The mechanical sculptures that participate are displayed in Ferndale's **Kinetic Sculpture Museum** (p. 464).

One answer to timber clearing has been to preserve 575 acres on a slope east of Hwy 101 near the university, the **Arcata Community Forest/Redwood Park** (east on 14th St to Redwood Park Dr.). The area includes 10 miles of trails.

Birders are attracted to **Arcata Marsh and Wildlife Sanctuary** year round, but especially mid July–May. River otters and 200 species of birds are visible from trails and blinds on a flat track by grassy uplands, a freshwater marsh, a tidal slough, a brackish lake and mudflats, a system designed to purify wastewater naturally and return it to nature. The **Marsh Interpretive Center**, 600 S. G St; tel: (707) 826-2359, is open daily 0900–1700; call for tour information.

Arcata Chamber of Commerce/California Welcome Center, Arcata, CA 95521; tel: (707) 822-3619 or (800) 908-9464; fax: (707) 822-3515; www.arcata.com/chamber/. Ask for the excellent Victorian Building walking tour brochure.

Chain motels cluster around E. Guintoli Lane, downwind of fumes from the Louisiana Pacific processing plant. Closer to downtown, a smattering of B&Bs offer Victoriana. Book in advance for Kinetic Sculpture Race weekend in May.
Hotel Arcata $$ 708 9th St; tel: (800) 344-1221 or (707) 826-0217. Central and cheerful, a 1915 hunting lodge.

Abruzzi $$ 780 7th St (in Jacoby's Storehouse). Italian dinners nightly in historic building on Arcata Plaza.
Golden Harvest Café $$ 1062 G St. A wide range of dishes with a salad bar, two blocks north of Arcata Plaza.
North Coast Co-Op $ 811 I St. Forthright co-op selling groceries to all. Open 0700–2100.

TRINIDAD

Trinidad qualifies as no more than a hamlet, just south of Patrick's Point State Park, with more than its share of B&Bs and a fishing fleet. Its symbol is the red-roofed replica of the 1871 **Memorial Lighthouse**. A good spot to watch a dramatic sunset behind the Jew's-harp rocks rising from the sea is **Trinidad State Beach** (off Trinity St, north of Main St), with diving and swooping black oystercatchers. Trinidad Scenic Dr., south from Trinity St, parallels Hwy 101 and provides access to **Luffenholtz Beach County Park** and **Houda Point**.

Patrick's Point State Park, on the west side of Hwy 101 5 miles north of Trinidad, has superb views offshore to whale migrations, northwards to Agate Beach and Big Lagoon and south to Trinidad Head. There is a bluff-top Rim Trail and a Yurok (Native American) Village, with wooden houses, a sweat house and dance pit still reserved for use by tribal members.

Greater Trinidad Chamber of Commerce, PO Box 356; tel: (707) 677-1610.

REDWOOD NATIONAL AND STATE PARKS

The jointly managed state parks, Prairie Creek Redwoods, Del Norte Coast Redwoods and Jedediah Smith Redwoods (east of Crescent City) protect old-growth (over 250 years) coast redwoods. The parks are a World Heritage Site and an International Biosphere Reserve, accessible by car, RV or motorcycle, but much better enjoyed on foot, bicycle, or horseback. Trails are well-marked. Dress for frequent fog and rain. While coast redwoods and elk are the focus, the parks also conserve coastline, tidepools, waterfalls, oak woodlands and prairies. As tame as the stately trees look, it's a wild world out there of ticks, banana slugs, cougars (mountain lions) and bears (see p. 493)

Prairie Creek Redwoods State Park may be best known for the **Roosevelt elk** which roam around three areas (Davidson Rd, Elk Prairie, and remote Gold Bluffs) Aug–Oct. The huge animals cause traffic jams on Hwy 101, and many cars drive through the park without stopping. $ west of Hwy 101, 50–58 miles north of Eureka; tel: (707) 464-6101, ex. 5301.

Prairie Creek is rich in redwoods, with connecting trails circling through the major groves. Take either Newton B Drury Scenic Parkway exit from Hwy 101. The most dramatic redwoods are near the south exit, where the visitor centre offers previews of what's ahead. Stop and hike to **Big Tree**, a fenced specimen 304 ft high and 216 in in diameter, and to the twined multiple trunks of the **Corkscrew Tree**.

In **Del Norte Coast Redwoods State Park**, 7 miles south of Crescent City, old growth redwoods combine with a spectacular rocky coast and uncrowded trails.

Redwood National and State Parks, 1111 2nd St, Crescent City, CA 95531; tel: (707) 464-6101; www.nps.gov/redw.
Redwood Information Center, Hwy 101, 2 miles west of Orick. Open daily 0900–1700, with excellent whale-watching.
Prairie Creek/Elk Prairie Visitor Center, 8 miles north of Orick on Hwy 101. Open 0900–1700 in summer, 1000–1400 in winter.

HI Redwood National Park Hostel, 14480 Hwy 101 at Wilson Creek Rd; tel: (707) 482-8265 or (800) 909-4776, code 74. The Greyhound bus will stop here on request.

CRESCENT CITY

As elsewhere on the north coast, Crescent City, named after the shape of its bay, was long dependent upon fishing and timber. A tsunami tidal wave, caused by a major

Alaska earthquake in 1964, wiped out the harbour and downtown, and the rebuilt version gives the town a modern but bland character. Favourite local activities include fishing, bicycling, scuba diving and surfing in frigid waters.

Battery Point Lighthouse, at the west end of Front St, has perched on its well-eroded golden rock since 1856. It has lovely proportions from any angle, and at night its exterior is illuminated. Check in advance to walk the beach to a causeway at low tide. Open for guided tours Apr–Sept. **Pebble Beach Drive**, north from the lighthouse, looks west to sea stacks and **Castle Rock National Wildlife Refuge**, home to screeching birds and noisy sea lions. Go left on Washington Blvd to **Point St George**, with its namesake lighthouse 6 miles offshore.

Crescent City/Del Norte County Chamber of Commerce, 1001 Front St, Crescent City, CA 95531; tel: (707) 464-3174 or (800) 343-8300; www.delnorte.org. Open Memorial Day–Labor Day Mon–Fri 0900–1800, Sat–Sun 0900–1700.

Proximity to Oregon (where prices are lower and there's no state sales tax) keeps prices at Crescent City motels to bargain levels. Hwy 101 divides into north (M St) and south (L St) between Front and 9th Sts; most motels are found here. Others are near the harbour at Anchor Rd.

Jefferson State Brewery, 400 Front St, has a flavourful selection of beers in the 'state of mind' style of this region which, with south-western Oregon, periodically declares its independence from the USA.

WHERE NEXT?

Crescent City is the crossroads for more redwood parks eastwards and the Hwy 199 Smith River Wild and Scenic River drive to the Rogue River Region in Oregon. Up the increasingly wild coastline lies Seattle (see p. 467).

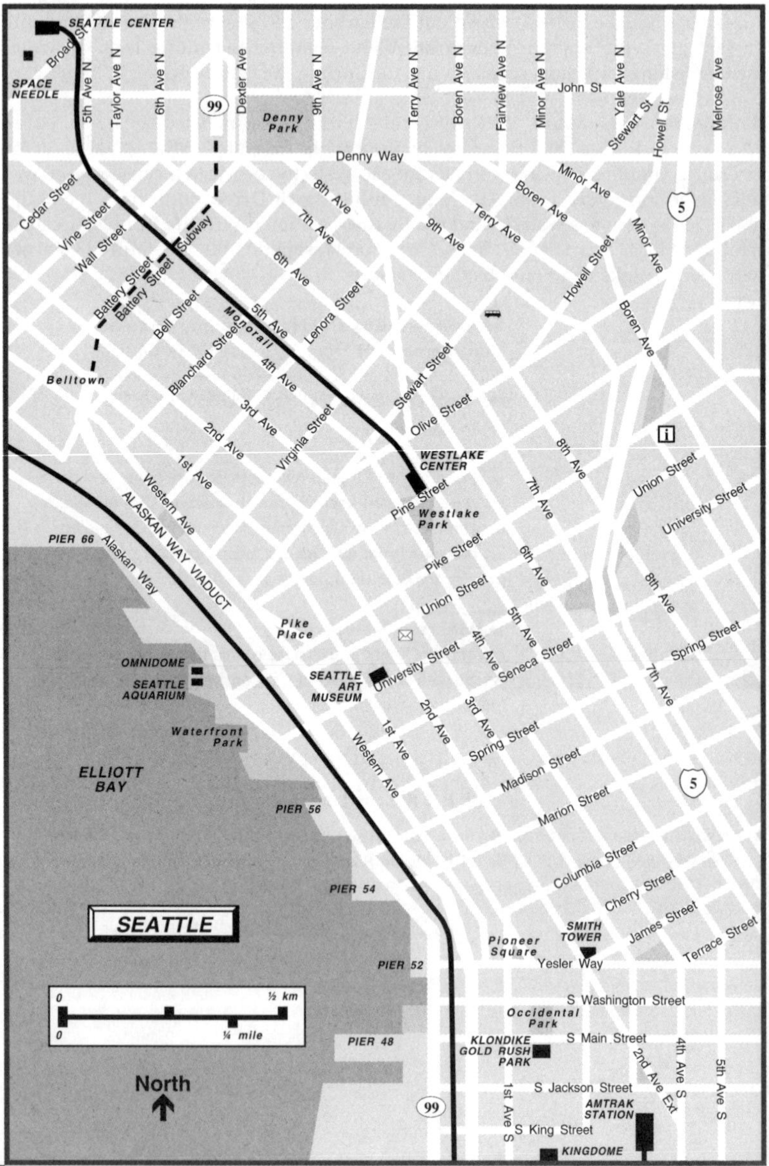
SEATTLE CENTER
Broad St
SPACE NEEDLE
5th Ave N
Taylor Ave N
6th Ave N
99
Dexter Ave
Denny Park
9th Ave N
Terry Ave N
Boren Ave N
Fairview Ave N
Minor Ave N
John St
Yale Ave N
Stewart St
Howell St
Melrose Ave
Denny Way
Minor Ave
Boren Ave
Terry Ave
9th Ave
8th Ave
7th Ave
6th Ave
5th Ave
4th Ave
3rd Ave
2nd Ave
1st Ave
Western Ave
Cedar Street
Vine Street
Wall Street
Battery Street
Battery Street
Subway
Bell Street
Blanchard Street
Monorail
Lenora Street
Virginia Street
Stewart Street
Olive Street
Howell Street
Minor Ave
Boren Ave
5
Belltown
WESTLAKE CENTER
Pine Street
Westlake Park
8th Ave
7th Ave
6th Ave
5th Ave
4th Ave
3rd Ave
2nd Ave
1st Ave
Western Ave
Union Street
University Street
PIER 66
Alaskan Way
ALASKAN WAY VIADUCT
Pike Street
Union Street
8th Ave
Pike Place
OMNIDOME
SEATTLE AQUARIUM
SEATTLE ART MUSEUM
University Street
Seneca Street
Spring Street
7th Ave
Waterfront Park
Spring Street
Madison Street
5
ELLIOTT BAY
PIER 56
Marion Street
Columbia Street
PIER 54
Cherry Street
SEATTLE
SMITH TOWER
James Street
Pioneer Square
Terrace Street
PIER 52
Yesler Way
0
½ km
0
¼ mile
S Washington Street
Occidental Park
PIER 48
KLONDIKE GOLD RUSH PARK
S Main Street
2nd Ave Ext
4th Ave S
5th Ave S
North
S Jackson Street
99
AMTRAK STATION
1st Ave S
S King Street
KINGDOME

Rainfall and mist-grown trees make Seattle the Emerald City. Puget Sound's deep blue waters combine with lead-grey skies and green-dappled parks in a lush, hilly city by the sea. A society built on commerce, timber and fishing is being transformed by the computer software industry and the aerospace giant, Boeing. Grunge bands put the city on the pop music map in the early 1990s, and gourmet coffee shops stoke the locals with caffeine. The result is a youthful population of forward-looking independent thinkers, rooted in pragmatic capitalism, living the good life at the north-western corner of the USA.

Seattle is known not so much for its wealth of sights as for its particular atmosphere and spectacular emergence as America's city of the 1990s. Pioneer Sq. downtown is a good place to get your bearings, as well as a grasp of Seattle's adventurous history, through a couple of beguiling museums. The new Seattle Arts Museum nearby is well worth a visit, while the crazy, now-notorious Space Needle commands your attention to the north. Most important, though, is to stroll the waterfront and the atmospheric Pike's Place Market, as well as various off-centre neighbourhoods, for a taste of the city's spunk and verve.

GETTING THERE AND GETTING AROUND

AIR Seattle-Tacoma International Airport (Sea-Tac) is about 10 miles from the centre. Gray Line Airport Express buses operate 0540–2335 every 20 mins between two Sea-Tac terminal stops and eight downtown hotels for $7.50. Metro Transit bus no. 194 runs every 30 mins from the lower level baggage claim.

RAIL/BUS Amtrak trains from Chicago, Vancouver and Los Angeles arrive at King St Station, 3rd Ave and S. Jackson St in southern downtown. Greyhound and regional buses use the terminal at 8th Ave and Stewart St.

BOAT Coming from Canada, one viable option is to travel by boat. **Victoria Clipper/Clipper Navigation**, tel: (206) 448-5000 or (1-800) 888-2535, runs passenger ferries between Victoria, British Columbia and Seattle's Pier 69. **Victoria Line**, tel: (206) 625-1881 or (1-800) 683-7977, operates a car and passenger ferry mid-May–Sept from Ogden Point, Victoria to Seattle's Pier 48.

For most trips, use **Metro Transit buses** (cheaper out of peak hours and for under-17s any time). You can buy a weekend and holiday All-Day Pass for the cost of two off-peak journeys. Travelling *towards* downtown, pay the driver as you enter; *from* downtown, pay as you exit. Buses are free 0600–1900 within the Downtown Seattle Ride Free Area (between 6th Ave, S. Jackson St, Alaskan Way and Battery St). A 1.3-mile tunnel speeds the passage of electric buses through downtown under 3rd Ave.

The **Waterfront Street Car** (same prices as buses) runs every 20 mins daily along Alaskan Way downtown; these historic green-and-cream trolleys are imported from Melbourne, Australia.

A legacy of the 1962 Seattle World's Fair, the **Monorail** is a fast way to travel from Westlake Center to Seattle Center, but it makes no stops.

INFORMATION

The Seattle-King County Convention and Visitors Bureau, 8th Ave and Pike St; tel: (206) 461-5800; fax: (206) 461-5855; www.seeseattle.org, is open Mon–Fri 0830–1700, Sat–Sun 1000–1600, and can give leads to the numerous walking, cycling and boat tours of the Seattle area.

SAFETY At night caution is advised outside the downtown and in the waterfront areas – take a taxi if you are dining away from downtown. Ask advise from the hotel concierge about which specific areas you should avoid.

MONEY Thomas Cook has a foreign exchange office downtown at Westlake Center (4th Ave and Pine St), open Mon–Sat 1000–1800, Sun 1200–1700, also offering sightseeing and transport information. There is another location at 906 3rd Ave, open Mon–Fri 0900–1700, Sat 1000–1400. Automatic cash dispensers abound throughout Seattle.

POST AND PHONES The main post office is at 301 Union St, open 0800–1730.

ACCOMMODATION

The visitors bureau has an extensive *Lodging Guide*, and the **Seattle Hotel Hotline**, tel: (206) 461-5882 or (1-800) 535-7071, books accommodation free of charge. Summer prices are high, but Nov–Mar the visitors bureau organises the Seattle Super Saver Package with discounts of up to 50%. **Seattle Bed & Breakfast Association**, tel: (206) 547-1020 or (1-800) 348-5630; www.seattlebandbs.com, has information on a dozen historic inns. A **Traveller's Reservation Service**, tel: (206) 364-5900; fax: (206) 367-0088; www.atravellersres.com books B&B accommodation throughout the region. At the bottom end, there is a good selection of hostels and a fair number of B&Bs, particularly in Capitol Hill. There are a few cheapish places in Belltown, north of Pike Place Market.

International AYH Hostel $ 85 Union St; tel: (206) 622-

5443; fax: (206) 682-2179. Within easy reach of the waterfront and Pike Place Market.

Vincent's Backpacker's Guest House $–$$ 527 Malden Ave E.; tel: (206) 323-7849. Pleasant setting in Capitol Hill and excellent rates.

Commodore Motor Hotel $$ 2013 2nd Ave; tel: (206) 448-8868 or (1-800) 714-8868; fax: (206) 269-0519. Easily the best hotel value downtown, just to the north-west of Pike Place Market. Dorm beds also available ($).

Kings Inn $$ 2106 5th Ave; tel: (206) 441-8833 or (1-800) 546-4760; fax: (206) 441-0730. In Belltown, basic but cheap.

Capitol Hill Guesthouse $$$ 1808 E. Denny Way; tel: (206) 650-4359 or (1-800) 281-6971; fax: (206) 325-7676. Tastefully decorated rooms in a restored 1908 home in Capitol Hill; guests have use of the kitchen.

Pensione Nichols $$$–$$$$ 1923 1st Ave; tel: (206) 441-7125. Great location near Pike Place Market, with views of Puget Sound.

Tugboat *Challenger* Bunk & Breakfast $$$–$$$$ 1001 Fairview Ave N.; tel: (206) 340-1201; fax: (206) 621-9208. At the south end of Lake Union near Capitol Hill.

Best Western Pioneer Square $$$$ 77 Yesler Way; tel: (206) 340-1234. Classy and an excellent location; reasonable for this price range.

FOOD AND DRINK

Dining can be a sublime art here. The pan-Asian dining trend is rooted in Seattle: the Pacific Rim includes both shores, and Seattle chefs invite adventurous dining. Seafood and Asian restaurants are easily found – for the best of these, head for the Waterfront and the International District respectively. For snacks and light meals, aim for the many food stalls in Pike Place Market.

Seattle is one of the few American cities that embraces European-style café culture, and trendy coffee spots all over town are well frequented day and night for a caffeine fix. Many also serve up beers and a variety of entertainment. Microbreweries are another north-west phenomenon, and speciality bars are rampant.

Le Panier Very French Bakery $ 1902 Pike Pl. Claims to have the best baguettes outside Paris.

Grand Central Baking Company $$ 214 1st Ave S. Eat delicious roast vegetable sandwiches by a fireplace, or outdoors overlooking totem poles in Occidental Park.

Sit and Spin $$ 2219 4th Ave. An urban launderette, where excellent budget vegetarian food meets counter-culture furniture and patrons.

Ivar's Acres of Clams **$$–$$$** Pier 54, Alaskan Way. Traditional clam house, bustling and basic.

Elliott's Oyster House and Seafood Restaurant **$$$** Pier 56, Alaskan Way. Fine for shellfish and relaxing on the pier.

Wild Ginger Asian Restaurant and Satay Bar **$$$–$$$$** 1400 Western Ave. Has perhaps the tastiest marriage of fresh ingredients in Pacific Rim recipes.

Space Needle **$$$–$$$$** Seattle Center, 219 4th Ave N. Two dining rooms revolving 500 ft above ground level: the casual Space Needle Restaurant and the slightly more expensive formal Emerald Suite.

Painted Table **$$$$** 92 Madison St. Named after its décor which resembles a bright, high-ceilinged art galley. Unique plates and fine food.

HIGHLIGHTS

DOWNTOWN

Hills, skyscrapers, espresso bars, sculptures and the presence of the sea define downtown Seattle. The central area's two foci are Pioneer Sq. and the area around Pike Place Market. In between, the city's skyline reaches upward, dominated by the 76-storey Columbia Tower. Back down on the ground, the Waterfront is a lively run of ferry docks, shops and restaurants. In fact, the city's greatest attractions are its streets and marketplaces, and much of Seattle is simply best explored outdoors – it is a joy to wander around, and all for free.

Pioneer Square is the place to head for a taste of Seattle's not-so-ancient roots in the timber trade and gold rush. During the city's initial rise to prominence, local businessman Henry Yesler built a lumber mill in the square, at the bottom of the so-called 'Skid Road', a long, narrow path down which logs were slid. The square is now an integral part of the **Pioneer Square Historic District**, with its 1909 pergola, a replica totem pole from a nearby Tlingit Indian village and a bust of Chief Sealth. The neighbourhood is characterised by graceful period red brick and stone buildings, very consciously restored to ply the tourist trade.

Seattle's precarious setting on the edge of Puget Sound has meant periodic flooding, and the incessant rain and steep hills lead to occasional landslides. Much of the original city is now well below the present street level. One of Seattle's real highlights is **Bill Speidel's Underground Tour**, a fascinating trip through the district's subterranean passages. What are now drainage and cabling channels were once street-level shops, lumber yards and brothels, and this 90-min tour, led by informed and amusing guides, reveals much of the history, squalor and colour. Tours ($$) leave regularly from Doc Maynard's pub at 601 1st Ave (on Pioneer Sq.).

The 42-storey Smith Tower nearby was built in 1914 as the tallest building outside New York City. The bright, crusty white structure is more appealing for its oddity than its beauty, and has an observation deck nominally open 1000–1900.

The **Klondike Gold Rush National Historic Park**, a few blocks south of Pioneer Sq. at 117 S. Main St, chronicles the general panic and the role of Seattle as the prospectors' jump-off point on their journey north. Open daily 0900–1700; free.

Just south of here the colossal **Kingdome**, Seattle's main sports complex, is scheduled for demolition. A new stadium being built next door should improve the otherwise overwhelming impersonality of this part of town. Abutting its eastern edge, the **International District**, formerly called Chinatown, is the city's focal point for recent Asian immigrants. Shabby and quiet, it's nevertheless a fun place to scout out Chinese groceries and Vietnamese restaurants – head for Jackson St between 5th and 8th Sts.

SEATTLE IN WOOD AND GOLD

From the original 1851 landing at Alki Bay, settlers moved to Elliott Bay and named their town Seattle after a friendly Duwamish chief, Sealth. The timber industry hit full stride almost immediately: millions of logs from the vast neighbouring forests were shimmied down the city's steep hills to sawmills near the water's edge. But it took Yukon gold to turn Seattle into a boom town. As the nearest sizable port city, it swelled overnight with fortune seekers and local merchants eager to make a buck. While most prospectors returned in financial ruin, Seattle reaped the spoils of the Klondike Gold Rush.

A huge black Hammering Man sculpture marks the **Seattle Art Museum** (SAM) at 100 University St, completed in 1991. This is one of the best places to see north-west native American art, which is complemented by African masks, east Asian scrolls, a swathe of European fine arts and contemporary American pop art. $ Open Tues–Sun 1000–1700 (Thur until 2100).

Harbor Steps Park connects the art museum to Alaskan Way in 104 wide steps with eight fountains. Alaskan Way runs along the **Waterfront**, the most interesting stretch of which is between about Pier 50 and Pier 70. A solid bunch of shops and restaurants along the piers is happy to part you from your tourist dollars as you drink up the atmosphere. Stop at the **Seattle Aquarium** at Pier 59 for large window views of Puget Sound fish. Highlights include adorable sea otters and the fascinating Pacific salmon, which swim – leaping over falls where necessary – hundreds of miles upstream to inland spawning waters. $$ Open 1000–1700 (until 1900 in summer). Waterfront Park has nice spots for picnicking and summer concerts, and the **Pike Place Hill Climb** stairs ascend to Pike Place Market.

Seattle's bounty overflows at **Pike Place Market**, 7 acres of food stalls, restaurants,

Gray Line, tel: (206) 626-5208, offers narrated bus tours of the city's main sights.

crafts, produce and flower sellers, gift shops and fishmongers. Open year-round, the market draws thousands of residents at weekends; arrive early on Sat morning to see the finest produce and fish. A stroll along Pike St towards the water brings you to the famous yell-and-fish-throw performed by fishmongers at Pike Place Fish when a customer places an order.

BELLTOWN A skid row for decades between the waterfront, Seattle Center and downtown, Belltown is now filled with small restaurants, clubs, galleries and consignment clothing shops patronised by the grunge set and techno-heads.

The 1962 Seattle World's Fair forced the little-known city to polish its attractions and add the **Space Needle** as its icon. Now horribly anachronistic, the needle none the less offers spectacular 360° views from its 520 ft high observation deck – when the weather is good. $$ Open 0800–midnight.

Fantastic views of the striking Seattle skyline are best had from ferries serving Puget Sound islands such as Bainbridge and Vashon. Washington State Ferries, tel: (206) 464-6400 or (1-800) 843-3779, has regular commuter ferries from Pier 52.

Other sights of interest here include the **Pacific Science Center**, **Children's Museum** and **Fun Forest Amusement Park** (collectively the Seattle Center). Along with the Space Needle, the futuristic **Monorail** has dated badly over the past 40 years, but is still the best way to get here from the centre.

CAPITOL HILL AND THE UNIVERSITY DISTRICT Further east, elegant Capitol Hill holds some lovely mansions, and is Seattle's center of gay life, with good restaurants, coffeehouses and shops. **Volunteer Park** is a lazy green space with a conservatory and 75 ft moss-covered water tower. It contains the **Seattle Asian Art Museum**, with excellent Pacific Rim collections; $ open Tues–Sun 1000–1700, Thur 1000–2100. The Kado Tea Garden within the museum is open at weekends for teas and pastries.

Seattle is home to 35,000 students of the University of Washington, whose campus is north of Capitol Hill. While short on sights, the University District is a great place for chic boutiques and cafés.

FREMONT Across the Lake Washington Ship Canal, Fremont is a self-appointed Seattle Left Bank, where a salvaged 53 ft rocket steams up at what residents consider the centre of the universe. 'Republic of Fremont' mottos like *delibertas quirkas* and 'Freedom to be Peculiar' flaunt the humour of this ultra-trendy district. Lenin's statue watches over the **Sunday Flea Market** on Fremont Ave N., and nearby a sculpture, the **Fremont Troll,** munches a Volkswagen bug under the

BOEING BOEING

In 1916, the Boeing Company began making military planes; today it is by far the world's largest passenger aircraft manufacturer. Its century of achievement is showcased at the **Museum of Flight** some 30 mins south of central Seattle at 9404 E. Marginal Way S. More than 50 aircraft are on display, including the Boeing 707 Airforce One used by Presidents Eisenhower and Johnson. $$ Open daily 1000–1700 (Thur until 2100). To see where Boeing puts its planes together, make for the **Boeing Tour Center** near Everitt, about 30 miles north of Seattle. Tours take you through nearly 100 acres of assembly plant, and are popular, so call ahead: tel: (1-800) 464-1476.

Aurora Bridge. **Redhook Ale Brewery**, a few streets west on N. Canal St, is an institution over 'a huge natural reservoir holding the largest proven beer reserve in the world'.

SHOPPING

Local crafts such as Pacific North-west art and replica totem poles can be obtained in several shops. Pike Place Market and the streets north are good for these; try Made in Washington, 2221 2nd Ave, and Stonington Gallery, 2030 1st Ave. Also in this area is the Westlake Center, the indoor heart of downtown shopping. The Waterfront is handy for souvenir shopping, particularly around Pier 54. Pioneer Sq. is another good browsing zone and Pioneer Sq. Mall has antiques. Elliott Bay Book Company, 101 S. Main St, is Seattle's rainy day magnet, famed for author readings.

NIGHTLIFE

The Seattle music scene has produced such names as Jimi Hendrix in the 1960s, and Nirvana and Pearl Jam in the 1990s; the 'Seattle Sound' has much to do with the city's current identity, though grunge bars are already out. Theatre and classical music are also well represented. The **Seattle Symphony**, tel: (206) 215-4747, has a new home, Benaroya Hall downtown at 2nd Ave and University St; while the **Seattle Opera**, tel: (206) 389-7699, puts on grand spectacles at its Seattle Center home. Several local free papers list cultural and nightlife events, including *Seattle Weekly*'s Wed 'Going On' section, *Eastside Week* and the bi-weekly *The Rocket.*

Central Saloon, 207 1st Ave S. Popular century-old bar near Pioneer S.q, with occasional live bands.

Bohemian Café, 111 Yesler Way. A variety of jazz, blues and rock acts most nights.

Speakeasy Café, 2304 2nd Ave. Belltown café/bar with light food and events including concerts, poetry readings and films.

Dimitriou's Jazz Alley, 2033 6th Ave. Seattle's leading jazz club, featuring national acts.

Vogue, 2018 1st Ave. Established part of the city's club scene, amid the galleries and bars of Belltown.

Virginia Inn, 1937 1st Ave. Lively beer place near Pike Place Market.

MOE's Mo'Roc'n Café, 325 E. Pike St. Fairly good rock-'n'-roll bar/café near Pike Place Market.

Redhook Ale Fremont Brewery and **Trolleyman Pub**, 3400 Phinney Ave N. Good budget food and brews in this nationally known microbrewery.

DAY TRIPS

Puget Sound and the Olympic Peninsula cry out for exploration. Islands in the sound are easily reached by ferry, and the stunning peaks and rainforests of Olympic National Park possess a mystical beauty. While you *could* try any of the following on a day trip, their appeal makes it not really worth the effort for less than a weekend jaunt.

SAN JUAN ISLANDS

It takes a high tolerance for tranquillity to enjoy the San Juan Islands between Sept and May, and an equally high tolerance for queues in summer. Some 700 islands dot the sparkling blue waters of Puget Sound. Only San Juan Island has an incorporated town, named Friday Harbor. This is also the most accessible and varied of the islands: wildflowers carpet forest meadows in spring, while orchards gone wild produce apples, pears and cherries. The waters are busy with seals and the largest population of orcas (killer whales) in the world; America's largest concentration of bald eagles keeps company overhead.

San Juan's claim to historical fame is its role in the so-called Pig War, a British–American skirmish over possession in which the only casualty was a pig. Reconstructed fortresses at the southern and western edges of the island tell the tale. Friday Harbor has a **Whale Museum**, and the easiest way to see the real thing is to cross the island west to **Lime Kiln Point State Park**; prime time for whale-watching is May–Aug. Bicycles can be rented from Island Bicycles, 380 Argyle; tel: (360) 378-4941.

GETTING THERE

Victoria Clipper has a daily passenger ferry from Seattle's Pier 69 to Friday Harbor May–Sept (weekends only Oct–Apr). Advance booking is required in summer and recommended all year. If you're bringing a car, take the Washington State Ferries service from Anacortes, a 2 hr drive north of Seattle. San Juan Central Reservations, tel: (360) 378-6675, handles accommodation bookings for the entire island, which include everything from campsites to motels to a luxurious isolated resort. Be sure to call before arriving.

OLYMPIC PENINSULA Seattleites look west towards the Olympic Peninsula with awe. Jagged mountaintops are riddled with glaciers – 10 miles of them on Mount Olympus – and the rain here is a part of the scenery, creating an unusual northern rainforest.

> **GETTING THERE**
> Greyhound buses run twice daily between Seattle and Port Angeles, a 3 hr trip, but transport around the park is scarce. A number of motels line the main streets in Port Angeles, and a private hostel, at 511 E. 1st St; tel: (360) 452-7494, has cheap dorm beds. Clallam Transit, tel: (360) 452-4511, runs buses Mon–Sat from Port Angeles to Neah Bay and Hurricane Ridge (ski season only).

Much of the peninsula is contained within the **Olympic National Park**, the main point of entry to which is Port Angeles. The main visitor centre, which dispenses good driving and hiking maps, is in Race St; open daily 0800–1600 (until 2000 in summer); tel: (360) 452-4501. This is the start of a dramatic upward drive along **Hurricane Ridge**, with breathtaking views of the Strait of Juan de Fuca. In the north-west corner of the park, **Sol Duc hot springs** is a resort at which you can soak in mineral baths (daily May–Sept, otherwise weekends only). The astonishing **Hoh Rain Forest** lies on the western slopes of the mountains, which are lashed by massive Pacific storms. Over 200 in of precipitation per year feed a virgin temperate rainforest, perpetually blanketed in a greenish twilight.

At the north-western tip of the peninsula, beyond park boundaries, Neah Bay is the only town on the **Makah Reservation**, a salmon fishing port and home of the Makah Indians. For 500 years, the tribe kept the secret of Ozette Village, which was buried beneath a landslide. Artefacts uncovered in the 1970s now contribute to exhibits at the **Makah Museum**; $ open Wed–Sun 1000–1700 (daily in summer).

PORT TOWNSEND First settled in 1792, Port Townsend's large, calm harbour rests in the rainshadow of the Olympic Peninsula. In the mid-19th century, bars, brothels and gambling were a social mainstay. Red-brick buildings from the time are now preserved as hotels, restaurants and shops, while high society Victorian homes, on a bluff above, offer magnificent vistas of the still-busy docks.

> **GETTING THERE**
> Olympic Bus Lines, tel: (360) 452-3858 or (1-800) 550-3858, serves Seattle's Greyhound station twice a day.

Port Townsend bursts with accommodation, but the city is very popular with weekenders. Port Townsend Visitors Center, 2437 E. Sims Way, tel: (360) 385-2722 or (1-800) 499-0047, can help. There's a hostel at nearby Fort Worden, tel: (360) 385-0655.

WHERE NEXT?

Tucked in under the Canadian border, Seattle is only a short stop from Vancouver.

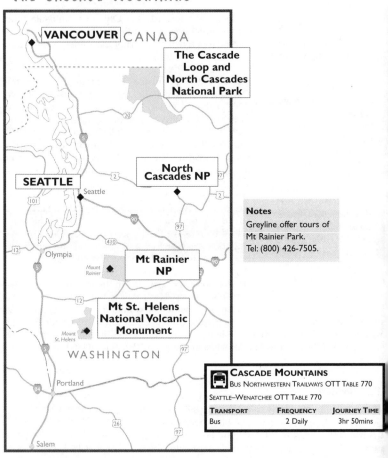

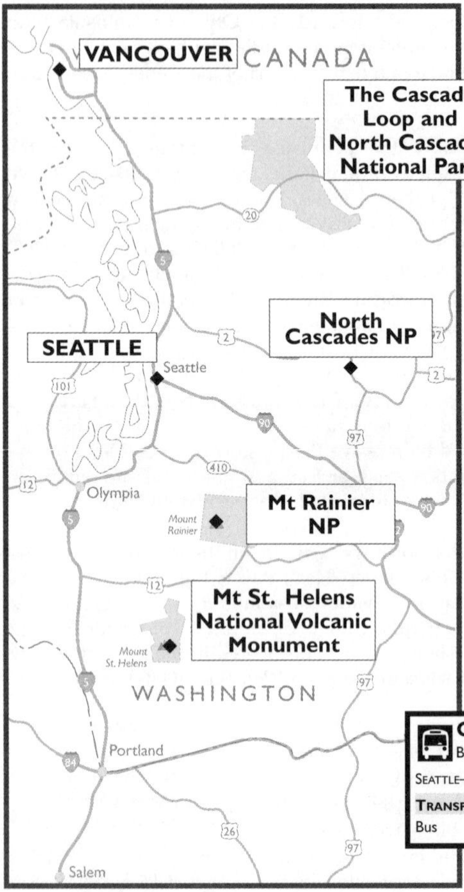

Notes
Greyline offer tours of Mt Rainier Park.
Tel: (800) 426-7505.

CASCADE MOUNTAINS
BUS NORTHWESTERN TRAILWAYS OTT TABLE 770

SEATTLE–WENATCHEE OTT TABLE 770

TRANSPORT	FREQUENCY	JOURNEY TIME
Bus	2 Daily	3hr 50mins

Within an hour's drive east of Seattle, the dramatic, brooding Cascade Mountains offer a surprising swathe of snow-covered peaks on a par with the Rockies. On clear days (rare as they are) you can see Mount Rainier from Seattle, and townies make a beeline for this part of the mountains. Further south, Mount St Helens' notorious 1980 volcanic eruption lends a certain volatility to the range.

Exploring on Public Transport

It is possible, though difficult and time-consuming, to get to the area by public transport. Greyhound buses run from Seattle along Hwy 2 through Leavenworth and on to Wenatchee. There is no public transport to the national park, but towns and villages to the south get you close, and offer equally wonderful scenery: local bus companies serve Chelan and points along Lake Chelan, across which a boat takes you to Stehekin.

The northern Cascades are far less visited, and the Cascade Loop, a circular highway route, slips through the upper reaches and the beautiful North Cascades National Park. Towns in the area hold little interest, although they are useful bases for accommodation, information and picking up supplies for hikes – such as fresh apples, for which Washington state is famous.

THE CASCADE LOOP AND NORTH CASCADES NATIONAL PARK

The linking of three highways to the north-east of Seattle creates the 400 miles of the Cascade Loop. The loop consists of two parallel roads leading off I-5 north of Seattle – a southern stretch, Hwy 2, and a northern stretch, Hwy 20 – both of which connect to Hwy 97 towards the north central part of the state.

The German-influenced town of **Leavenworth**, on Hwy 2, is a small commercial hub in the region, with a visitor centre, bicycle rental shops and cheap accommodation.

On around the loop, **Chelan**, on Hwy 97, is a pretty place from which you can catch a morning ferry across beautiful Lake Chelan, surrounded by stunning purple-green mountains. On the northern tip of the lake, the village of **Stehekin** makes a launch pad for the northern Cascades, with a ranger's station, bicycle rental and shuttle buses to take you further into the hills.

En Route

Just 25 miles east of Seattle off I-90, Snoqualmie Falls is a fantastically misty waterfall, familiar to many from David Lynch's TV series *Twin Peaks*. Short hikes lead in many directions from the falls, including one up Mount Si, which affords great views of the Cascades.

Pushing right up to the Canadian border, the **North Cascades National Park** is far less frequented than Mount Rainier or many others in the Pacific Northwest, partly because of its sheer isolation and lack of tourist facilities. This renders its high glaciers and nearly impenetrable forest all the more enticing.

i Leavenworth Chamber of Commerce, P O Box 327, Leavenworth, WA 98826; tel: (509) 548-5807.
North Cascades National Park Visitor Center, Sedro-Woolley; tel: (360) 856-5700, isn't even in the park, but way

back west on Hwy 20. It's open Mon–Fri 0800–1630 (plus weekends in summer). A small ranger's station on Hwy 20 in the park provides maps and wild camping permits.

Evergreen Motor Inn $$–$$$ 1117 Front St, Leavenworth; tel: (509) 548-5515. There's no shortage of cheap places to stay in Leavenworth, but this is a useful base if you want security.
Brickhouse Inn $$–$$$ 304 Wapato Ave, Chelan; tel: (509) 682-2233. Reasonably priced rooms in a Victorian-style home.
Silver Bay Inn $$$–$$$$ 10 Silver Bay Rd, Stehekin; tel: (509) 682-2212. A finely situated B&B.

MOUNT RAINIER NATIONAL PARK

Think of Mount Rainier, and think of 100 inches of snow, frequent rain, fog, mist, and even occasional brilliant sunshine or starshine glinting from the summit. Of two million annual visitors, 10,000 hikers attempt the snowy 14,411 ft summit – the highest in the Cascades and a world-class climb. For the less vertically inclined, subalpine wildflowers are profuse throughout the summer months, and the lower slopes of the mountain are cloaked in Douglas fir.

The main point of access to the park in which Mount Rainier sits so haughtily is Hwy 706 (off Hwy 7 from Tacoma) through Nisqually entrance. Roads through the park are deliberately narrow, slowing traffic and preserving scenic vistas in a timeless setting. A few miles into the park, **Longmire** is a collection of buildings including a museum, general store, lodge and restaurant. Further up the slopes of Mount Rainier, the few buildings in **Paradise** include a year-round visitor centre, lodge, restaurant and facilities for hikers, climbers and snowshoers. The Guide House, tel: (360) 569-2227, can help with equipment, passes and guides. Nearby **Narada Falls** is a sheer 168 ft drop of clear water into a pool below, and beyond, the winding **Nisqually Glacier** is known to move 3 ft per day.

In summer you can drive on around the base of Mount Rainier and link up with Hwy 410, which leads through the park's north-eastern White River entrance; the route is usually closed during the winter months. This is a staging area for short hikes to **Emmons Glacier**, and from here a narrow, switchback highway ascends to **Sunrise**, a summer-only visitor centre at 6100 ft.

Mount Rainier National Park Headquarters, Ashford; 9 miles west of the Nisqually entrance; tel: (360) 569-2211 for information.
Jackson Visitor Center, Paradise, is open daily mid Apr–Oct, Sat–Sun the rest of the year.

There are cheapish motels in Ashford, and **Mount Rainier Guest Services**, tel: (360) 569-2275; fax: (360) 569-2770, books rooms at lodges in Longmire and Paradise (both $$$–$$$$). There are campsites, all with RV hookups, near each park entrance, all first-come, first-served. Each of the park's developed areas mentioned above has dining facilities, though only Longmire remains open year-round.

MOUNT ST HELENS NATIONAL VOLCANIC MONUMENT

If there was ever any doubt that the white-capped Cascade Range was formed by shattering volcanic upheaval, Mount St Helens dispelled it with a terrifying explosion on 18 May 1980. The blast was the latest in a series of Mount St Helens eruptions, many of which had been viewed by Klickitat native Americans. The mountain has been a justifiably popular destination since its grand statement, and scientists have been surprised by the speed of nature's regeneration. Insects, small animals, birds and seeds survived under the pyroclastic flow or in caves; this and the mountain's gaping wound, plus the sight of acres of stunted trees, make it an extraordinary sight. The visitor centre in Amboy issues permits for volcano climbing. A long trail encircles the mountain, and there are many shorter hikes to take in the unusual scenery.

THE MOUNT ST HELENS ERUPTION

A lateral blast lopped the peak's height from 9677 ft to 8383 ft in minutes, spewing a hazy, smoking grey vertical plume 11 miles high, and sending half a cubic mile of pumice, ash and glacial ice down the north face. The Toutle River to the west clogged and the 40 ft deep Columbia River Channel was mired in rock and debris. Trees 150 ft tall toppled like straws up to 17 miles from the explosion, and ash rained down for hundreds of miles. Dust and gases from the eruption affected weather around the globe.

Visitor Center, Amboy (south of the volcano, off Hwy 503 and I-5, closer to Portland); tel: (360) 750-3900. There are several visitor centres along Hwy 504 (which heads east off I-5) leading to the mountain.

There are several motels in the town of Kelso (off I-5 west of the mountain), such as the **Aladdin Motor Inn** $$ 310 Long Ave; tel: (360) 425-9660. A number of campsites surround the mountain.

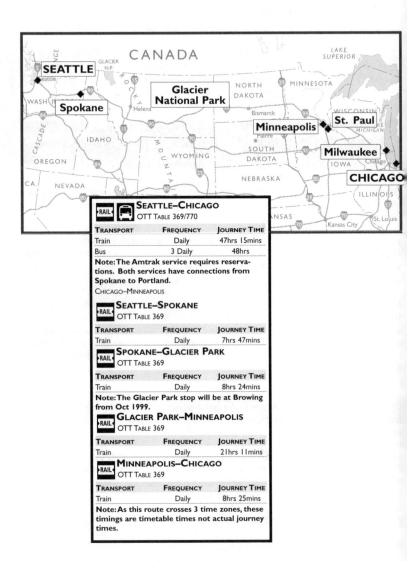

SEATTLE–CHICAGO

OTT TABLE 369/770

TRANSPORT	FREQUENCY	JOURNEY TIME
Train	Daily	47hrs 15mins
Bus	3 Daily	48hrs

Note: The Amtrak service requires reservations. Both services have connections from Spokane to Portland.

CHICAGO–MINNEAPOLIS

SEATTLE–SPOKANE

OTT TABLE 369

TRANSPORT	FREQUENCY	JOURNEY TIME
Train	Daily	7hrs 47mins

SPOKANE–GLACIER PARK

OTT TABLE 369

TRANSPORT	FREQUENCY	JOURNEY TIME
Train	Daily	8hrs 24mins

Note: The Glacier Park stop will be at Browing from Oct 1999.

GLACIER PARK–MINNEAPOLIS

OTT TABLE 369

TRANSPORT	FREQUENCY	JOURNEY TIME
Train	Daily	21hrs 11mins

MINNEAPOLIS–CHICAGO

OTT TABLE 369

TRANSPORT	FREQUENCY	JOURNEY TIME
Train	Daily	8hrs 25mins

Note: As this route crosses 3 time zones, these timings are timetable times not actual journey times.

On 'The Empire Builder'

Traversing a vast northern stretch of the USA, Amtrak's 'Empire Builder' makes a two-day journey across some of the country's most dramatic mountain scenery, most desolate prairies and richest farmland. From Seattle, the train flies through the snowy Cascade Mountains and across central Washington. After Spokane, the route takes in a piece of northern Idaho and more mountain scenery follows in western Montana. The train slips along the southern boundary of Glacier National Park, one of the very finest in the land.

En Route

Before it turns on its long journey eastward, look out the left-hand side of the train to see the jagged mountain tops of Olympic National Park, across Puget Sound.

On the Portland route, keep your eyes open (right-hand side of the train) for the plunging cascades of Bridal Veil and Multnomah Falls and the graceful contours of Mount Hood as the train runs through the Columbia River Gorge.

Montana's northern Rocky Mountains are as haunting as any, but between eastern Montana and Minnesota, as the train sprawls across the empty North Dakota plain, the trip can drag a bit if you're not simply dazzled by the vastness of it all. Wisconsin and Minnesota form part of America's heartland, and the tracks cross rolling fields of corn and beans, skirting thousands of lakes. There are two cities of note. Milwaukee, a blue-collar town on the shores of Lake Michigan, is one of the country's beer-brewing capitals, while Minneapolis and St Paul (known as the Twin Cities) share some excellent museums, fine architecture and a balanced flavour.

SPOKANE

Home to the first non-native settlement in the Pacific North-west, Spokane has become the only genuine city in Washington east of the Cascades. Built at the largest falls on the Spokane River, it's the commercial and cultural capital of the Inland Empire, a vast area stretching north into British Columbia, east to the Rocky Mountains, south to the Columbia River and west to the Cascades. Lumbermen, fur traders, farmers, barkeepers, prostitutes and missionaries followed the railway to Spokane, and the economy was fuelled by rich mining strikes in nearby Idaho and British Columbia. It remains one of the most pleasant cities in the region.

Riverfront Park is Spokane's defining feature, and was the site of the 1974 World's Fair. **Spokane Falls**, in the centre of the park, were an important native American fishery and settlement, and later became the base from which a sawmill developed into today's city. Best viewing spots are from the gondola cable cars ($; running daily 1100–2100 except in winter) or the footbridge directly over the falls – though the spray can be drenching.

Many fine brick and stone buildings from the ebullient industrial years survive in the city centre. **Cheney Cowles Museum and Historic Campbell House**, 2316 W. First Ave, is an 1898 mansion with displays on the history of the Inland Empire.

The **Convention and Visitors Bureau**, 926 W. Sprague St; tel: (1-800) 248-3230; or the **Visitor Information Center**, 201 W. Main Ave; tel: (509) 747-3230.

Amtrak pulls in at 221 W. First St.

Advance booking is strongly recommended. The closest campsite is at Riverside State Park, 6 miles north.
Suntree Inn $$ 211 S. Division St; tel: (509) 838-6630. Simple budget rooms near centre.
Fotheringham House $$$–$$$$ 2121 W. 2nd Ave; tel: (509) 838-1891; fax: (509) 838-1807. An 1891 house, easily the city's most comfortable B&B with the tastiest breakfast.

Northwest cuisine (especially salmon) features prominently.
Birkenbeiner Brewery $$ 35 W. Main Ave. The best brewery in town, with a lively international menu that mixes Thai, Mexican, German, Italian and Louisiana Cajun.
Two Moon Café $$–$$$ in the Mars Hotel, 300 W. Sprague Ave. Trendy place with one of the best wine lists in town.

GLACIER NATIONAL PARK

One of the National Park Service's jewels, Glacier National Park ($) is a wilderness of rocky peaks, cold glacial lakes, thousands of waterfalls and dense pine forest. By far the heaviest tourist season is summer, when the park's one through road is open.

Amtrak stops at East Glacier Park (summer only), and at Essex and West Glacier Park (year round). The park service runs shuttle buses along this route between East Glacier and West Glacier, but there is no other transport into or within the park. Coming by train, West Glacier is your most viable option, as it's only 2 miles from here to the Apgar Visitor Center on beautiful **Lake McDonald**.

The area around Lake McDonald is as good a place as any to spend time if you're without a vehicle; it has camping, lodging and dining facilities. You can take sunset cruises on the lake or rent your own rowing boat, and the lower slopes of the park can be explored on foot from here. Unless you want to embark on a several-day hike, though, **Going to the Sun Road** is the only way to reach the park's upper reaches. Despite the heavy traffic, the ribbon of highway elicits oohs and aahs at every turn, as it weaves a path along mountain slopes. The views are simply awesome, and the ecology of the park – purple wildflowers, mountain goats – and Montana's famous big sky, can leave you breathless. With the right equipment, it's easy to slip off travelled routes and escape. The road emerges at St Mary Entrance, where another visitor centre and basic facilities are available.

i Glacier National Park, PO Box 128, West Glacier, Montana 59936; tel: (406) 888-7800.

It is essential to book a room before arriving. All reservations are handled by **Glacier Park Inc.**, tel: (602) 207-6000, and these include lodges and cabins at the main entrances and in more remote sections. There is an **HI hostel** in East Glacier on Hwy 49; tel: (406) 226-4426; handy for the train station, but not so accessible to the park without your own car. There are more than a dozen campsites near the entrances and main road, and these fill up fast in summer.

MINNEAPOLIS AND ST PAUL

The twin cities of Minneapolis and St Paul, on opposite sides of the Mississippi River, exemplify the sense of cleanliness, order and general wholesomeness of the American Midwest. Both are attractive and have plenty to offer culturally, as well as pretty lakes nearby for a swim in summer.

Minneapolis is affectionately referred to as the 'Minneapple' by its residents, and has a nice stretch of parkland along the Mississippi to complement several good museums. Downstream a few miles and on the opposite bank, central St Paul is presided over by the stern state capitol and its grand cathedral. The two city centres are linked by express bus 94BCD.

A good place to start is the **Riverfront** in Minneapolis, a scenic stretch known alternatively as the Mississippi Mile. The city was founded by a fur trader in the 1840s, and the cobbled streets and restored buildings give a feel of the time. A modern glass-and-steel skyline now overshadows the 1929 **Foshay Tower** (821 Marquette Ave), which has an observation deck. Several blocks south-west of centre, Vineland Pl. and Lyndale Ave S., the **Walker Art Center** is a great contemporary arts gallery with a huge sculpture garden. $ Open Tues–Sat 1000–1700 (Thur until 2000), Sun 1100–1700. An equal distance south of downtown, the excellent **Minneapolis Institute of Arts**, 2400 3rd Ave S., has art from virtually all corners of the globe covering five millennia. In addition to the Rembrandts, Van Goghs, Cézannes and

Winters in the Midwest are severe. You will need to come equipped with padded waterproof layers for sightseeing out of doors, but the trappings of modern comfort in the Twin Cities have bestowed both cities with a skyway system of glass passages linking downtown office buildings.

Mirós, the gallery has fine collections of African, East Asian and Peruvian artefacts. Open Tues–Sat 1000–1700 (Thur until 2100), Sun 1200–1700; free.

St Paul preserves its feeling of grandeur with stately monuments and fine Victorian mansions. The art deco **City Hall and Courthouse** near the Wabasha St Bridge are complemented by a three-storey white onyx statue, the 'Vision of Peace'. The **Minnesota History Center**, 345 Kellogg Blvd, presents the lakes, dairies and heavily Scandinavian-influenced culture of the state. Open Tues–Sat 1000–1700 (Thur until 2100), Sun 1200–1700; free. Uphill to the north is the **State Capitol**, while to the west the **Cathedral of St Paul**, built in 1915, is modelled after St Peter's in Rome. Summitt Ave winds down and around the cathedral's base past beautiful old homes of some of the wealthier early 20th-century citizens.

South of town near the airport, at the intersection of Hwys 5 and 55, **Fort Snelling** was built in 1819 as a wilderness outpost; today it does a good job of presenting early Minnesota history. $ Open May–Oct, Mon–Sat 1000–1700, Sun 1200–1700. Take bus no. 7 from Minneapolis or no. 9 from St Paul.

People come from around the world to visit the outrageous **Mall of America**, easily the world's largest shopping mall. Serious shoppers won't want to miss the 500-plus stores and amusement park rides. Express bus no. 80 from Minneapolis, and bus no. 54 from St Paul, make the run regularly.

The **Minneapolis Visitor Information Center** is at 40 S. 7th Street; tel: (612) 335-5827; www.minneapolis.org. The **St Paul Convention and Visitors Bureau** is at 175 W. Kellogg Blvd; tel: (612) 265-4900 or (1-800) 627-6101; www.stpaulcvb.org.

The Amtrak station, 730 Transfer Rd, near University Ave, is about midway between the city centres on the St Paul side.

The Twin Cities' welcoming Midwest style carries over into its gracious B&Bs. Always ask about weekend rates at hotels.

MINNEAPOLIS

City of Lakes International House/Hostel $ 2400 Stevens Ave S.; tel: (612) 871-3210. Budget dorm beds and private rooms in historic mansion. Bus nos. 10, 17 or 18 southbound to 24th Street and Nicollet Ave.

Hotel Amsterdam $$ 828 Hennepin Ave; tel: (612) 288-0459. Reasonable downtown establishment.

Evelo's B&B $$–$$$ 2301 Bryant Ave S; tel: (612) 374-9656. Victorian B&B within walking distance of Walker Art Center.

ST PAUL **Chatsworth B&B** $$$ 984 Ashland Ave; tel: (612) 227-4288. Victorian home near the governor's mansion.

Although standard Midwest fare is readily available, the Twin Cities have a cosmopolitan array of cuisines from which to choose. The best places to look are the Warehouse District (around 3rd St S. and Hennepin Ave) and Nicollet Mall in Minneapolis, and along St Peter's St in St Paul.

MINNEAPOLIS **8th St Grill** $$ 800 Marquette Ave. Popular downtown Minneapolis bar and grill.

Ben Coleman's Caribbean Splash $$–$$$ 106 N. 3rd St. A surprise in these parts: Jamaican jerk chicken and ginger beer.

Café Brenda $$–$$$ 300 1st Ave N. Warehouse District café specialising in vegetarian and seafood dishes.

ST PAUL **Babanis Kurdish Restaurant** $$–$$$ 544 St Peter St. America's first Kurdish café, a pleasant downtown St Paul affair.

Taste of Scandinavia $$$–$$$$ Landmark Center, 75 W. 5th St. Appropriately for the cities' rich Scandinavian heritage, an ever-changing array of salmon, venison and meatballs.

MILWAUKEE

To most Americans, Milwaukee means one thing: beer. Although the industry has gone through some big shakeups in the past few years, with corporate buyouts siphoning off business, the city's identity depends in large part on this legacy, and the nation's second largest brewery, Miller, still holds the fort. Milwaukee's character derives from its largely German immigrant, working-class population, and this influence is evident today in the city's neighbourhoods and many bars. A good art museum and various brewery tours complete the attractions.

Although Milwaukee is not a prime tourist destination, a few sites do merit your attention. The **Riverwalk** development improves the city's otherwise drab downtown, a stretch of the Milwaukee River devoted to shops, restaurants and strolling space. On the lakefront, the **Milwaukee Art Museum** features European and American paintings and sculpture, decorative arts and a good collection of American and Haitian folk art. $ 750 N. Lincoln Memorial Dr.; open Tues–Wed and Fri–Sat 1000–1700, Thur 1200–2100, Sun 1200–1700.

To understand the importance of beer in Milwaukee's economy and social life, visit the **Captain Frederick Pabst Mansion**. The founder of the Pabst brewery (no longer in Milwaukee) built his home in the Flemish Renaissance style; the opulent interior attests to his wealth. $$ 2000 W. Wisconsin Ave, west of centre; open Mon–Sat 1000–1500, Sun 1200–1530. More enticing are the free samples given out after the **Miller Brewing Company** tour. The huge brewery, at 4251 W. State St, is open Mon–Sat 1200–1530; free. Take bus no. 71 west from the centre.

SUMMERFEST

A defining characteristic of the city is its location on Lake Michigan. In June, all Milwaukee turns out for the food and music of Summerfest on its shores.

Wisconsin's capital, Madison, is a lively, pretty college town an hour west of Milwaukee. Frequent buses make the trip daily.

Milwaukee's friendly **Visitor Information Center** is located at 510 W. Kilbourn Ave; tel: (1-800) 231-0903; www.milwaukee.org. Open Mon–Fri 0800–1700.

The Amtrak station is about a mile west of centre at 433 W. St Paul Ave.

Business travellers are the city's main hotel draw, but there are also plenty of B&Bs. The only hostel is way out of town.

Red Barn Hostel $ 6750 W. Loomis Rd, Greendale; tel: (414) 529-3299. Open May–Oct only. Accessible by bus no. 10 from W. Wisconsin Ave; change to bus no. 35 at Southway and Loomis Rd. Bicycles and canoe rental available.

Ambassador Hotel $$–$$$ 2308 W. Wisconsin Ave; tel: (414) 342-8400; fax: (414) 931-0279. Art deco central hotel.

County Clare $$$–$$$$ 1234 N. Astor St; tel: (414) 272-5273; fax: (414) 290-6300. Irish-style B&B near the lake.

German cuisine meets the Midwest on happy plates of meat and potatoes. Fish from a multitude of nearby lakes is another speciality. Wash it all down with beer, of course.

Milwaukee Ale House $$–$$$ 233 N. Water St. Pushing the local tradition, this small brewery serves German and Cajun food to go with its ales, riverfront views and live music.

Karl Ratzsch's Restaurant $$$ 320 E. Mason St. Central European schnitzels and sausages are highlights of the menu.

Third Street Pier $$$ 1110 N. Old World 3rd St. Seafood and steaks downtown on the Milwaukee River.

WHERE NEXT?

See p. 246 for the city guide to Chicago. If doing this journey in reverse, see pp. 468 and 478 for Seattle and the Cascade Mountains.

ENTRY FORMALITIES

For travellers from British Commonwealth countries, entry into either the United States or Canada is generally routine. Customs and immigration officials are paid to take their jobs very seriously, and those at entry points into the United States are known for being particularly thorough. Both Canada and the United States have had problems with illegal immigration: quite often visitors overstay tourist and student visas. Don't view this as inhospitable, just as standard precautions.

If it's any consolation, the trip through customs and immigration lines is just as annoying to US citizens returning home as it is for holidaymakers from abroad. Officials have *carte blanche* to ask any question, search anyone or anything, and do it in any manner they see fit. In reality, most inspectors are polite to a fault, but the only defence against an inspector who got out of the wrong side of the bed is to have passport, visa, proof of support and return ticket in order.

PASSPORTS AND VISAS

All non-US citizens must have a valid full passport and, except for Canadians, a visa, in order to enter the United States.

Visitors requiring a visa must obtain one from the US embassy in their country of residence in advance of arrival. Citizens of Britain, New Zealand and Ireland may complete a visa waiver form, which they generally receive with their air tickets if the airline is a 'participating carrier'. Provided nothing untoward is declared, such as a previous entry refusal or a criminal conviction, which would make application for a full visa mandatory, the waiver exempts visitors from the need for a visa for stays of up to 90 days. It also allows a side trip overland into Mexico or Canada and return. In the UK, your local Thomas Cook branch can advise on obtaining a US visas (which last for the life of your passport).

Documentation regulations change frequently and are complex for some nationalities; confirm your requirements with the nearest US embassy or consulate at least 90 days before you plan to depart for the USA.

Take a few passport photos with you and photocopy the important pages and any visa stamps in your passport. Store these safely, together with a note of the numbers of your travellers' cheques, credit cards and insurance documents, separate from the documents themselves. If you lose your wallet or are unfortunate enough to be robbed, you will at least have some identification, and replacing the documents will be much easier. Apply to your nearest consulate (see Embassies and Consulates, p. 499 for addresses and phone numbers) to replace your passport.

A valid passport is required for entry into Canada, but no visa is required for citizens of Australia, New Zealand, Republic of Ireland, South Africa, the UK or the US. Citizens of countries other than Canada and the US who plan to return to the USA after visiting Canada should check with US immigration officials that their visa, if one is required, permits a return.

Although brief crossings into and return from neighbouring Canada are generally permitted, they can be time consuming if an official targets you for a car search. If you're not carrying illegal drugs, alcohol, firearms or agricultural products, and if your documents are in order, you should have no difficulty entering the USA or Canada.

There are generally no restrictions on taking hire cars across the border in either direction, but check when making your initial booking and again when picking up the vehicle. It is also wise to ensure that vehicle insurance purchased in one country is valid in the other.

Both the USA and Canada prohibit the importation of weapons, narcotics or certain non-approved pharmaceutical products. Carry doctors' prescriptions with documentation (such as a doctor's letter) to prove that medications are legitimate.

Customs Allowances

Personal duty-free allowances which can be taken into the USA by visitors are: 1 litre of spirits or wine, 120 cigarettes and 100 (non-Cuban) cigars, and up to $100 worth of gifts.

Personal duty-free allowances which can be taken into Canada by visitors are: 1.14 litres (40 fl oz) of spirits or wine or 8.5 litres (300 fl oz, 24 bottles/cans) of beer or ale, 50 cigars, 200 cigarettes and 400 g (14 oz) loose tobacco.

On your return home you will be allowed to take the following:

Australia: goods to the value of A$400 (half for those under 18) plus 250 cigarettes or 250 g tobacco and 1 litre alcohol.

Canada: goods to the value of C$300, provided you have been away for over a week and have not already used up part of your allowance that year. You are also allowed 50 cigars plus 200 cigarettes and 1 kg tobacco (if over 16), and 1.14 litres (40 oz) alcohol.

New Zealand: goods to the value of NZ$700. Anyone over 17 may also take 200 cigarettes or 250 g tobacco or 50 cigars or a combination of tobacco products not exceeding 250 g in all; plus 4.5 litres beer or wine and 1.125 litres spirits.

South Africa: Goods to the value of 500 Rand. Anyone over 18 may also take 400 cigarettes, 50 cigars and 250 g tobacco, plus 2 litres wine and 1 litre spirits, plus 50 ml perfume and 250 ml toilet water.

UK: The allowances for goods bought outside the EU and/or in EU duty-free shops are: 200 cigarettes or 50 cigars or 100 cigarillos or 250 g tobacco; plus 2 litres still table wine and 1 litre spirits or 2 litres sparkling wine; plus 60 cc/ml perfume and 250 cc/ml toilet water.

Street prices for alcohol, tobacco, perfume and other typical duty-free items beat most duty-free shops at airports.

A–Z

EARTHQUAKES

Earthquakes are a fact of life in California and not unknown further north in Washington State and Oregon. Archaeological evidence, Native American accounts and settlers' diaries all record major quakes in Oregon, Washington and British Columbia, although not in recent years.

If you feel a mild earthquake, treat it like an amusement park ride. If items start falling from shelves, lamps sway or it becomes difficult to walk because of a quake, take cover. Crawl under the nearest solid table for protection against falling objects. If there's no table handy, brace arms and legs in an interior doorway. Stay away from windows, bookcases, stairs or anything else that could fall or break. Don't run outside – glass, masonry and live power lines could be falling.

If you are driving, pull off the road and stop – it's almost impossible to control a vehicle when the road won't hold still. Once the quake is over, treat it like any other civil emergency. Make sure everyone is safe and provide all help possible to the wounded. And get ready for the next shake: there are always aftershocks.

ELECTRICITY

The USA uses 110 volt 60 Hz current. Two- or three-pin electrical plugs are standard. Electrical gadgets from outside North America require plug and power converters. Both are difficult to obtain in the USA. Beware of buying electrical appliances in the USA: few gadgets on the US market can run on 220 volt 50 Hz power. Exceptions are battery-operated equipment such as radios, cameras and portable computers – or a few dual-voltage models of electric shavers and hair dryers.

North American video equipment, which uses the NTSC format, is not compatible with the PAL and SECAM equipment used in most of the rest of the world – prerecorded video tapes sold in the USA and Canada will therefore not work with other equipment unless specifically marked as compatible with PAL or SECAM. Blank videotapes purchased in North America, however, can be used with video recorders elsewhere in the world.

EMERGENCIES

To telephone **police** in an emergency, ring 911. The USA has no national police force, and there are many different police jurisdictions within any area, each with its own force. Even locals don't know whether state, county or town police have jurisdiction in any given situation, but 911 emergency personnel will see that the proper help is sent at once.

The Royal Canadian Mounted Police – the RCMP or Mounties of film and television fame – are a national force which seldom deals with local problems. Mounties only wear their famous red dress uniform for formal functions and occasional public appearances. Yes, you may ask a Mountie for help.

In case of **medical emergency**, also ring 911. Ambulance, paramedic, police, fire brigade or other public safety personnel will be dispatched immediately.

Hospital emergency rooms are the places to go in the event of life-threatening medical problems. If a life is at risk, treatment will be swift and top-notch, with payment problems sorted out later. For more mundane problems, doctors' offices, 24 hr walk-in health clinics and urgent care units are available in urban areas and many rural communities.

In Canada, government-run programmes provide health care for all, including visitors. Non-Canadians must pay for treatment, but prices are a bargain compared to most other industrialised countries. This is not so in the USA.

HEALTH AND HEALTH HAZARDS

The USA is basically a healthy place to visit. No inoculations are required and commonsense is enough to avoid most health problems. Eat and drink normally (or at least sensibly) and avoid drinking water that didn't come from the tap or a bottle. Most ground water, even in the high mountains, is contaminated with giardia and other intestinal parasites. Be sure to drink plenty of non-alcoholic liquids, especially in hot weather. Too little water is a particular problem when travelling from the coast to the dry interior.

The following advice covers some of the hazards you might encounter and precautions you should take.

WILDLIFE

Especially in parks and wilderness areas of the west, wildlife can be a problem. **Cougars** (also called bobcats, mountain lions and pumas) would rather run than fight, but can be vicious if defending a den or accidentally cornered. Avoid hiking alone and never let small children run ahead or fall far behind. If you meet a cougar, never try to run or hide – you won't escape and either behaviour signals that you're prey. Instead, be aggressive. Stand your ground. Try to appear larger by raising your arms or opening up a jacket. Should the cougar approach, shout and throw sticks or stones. Show that you're ready to fight. And if attacked, fight with all you've got. Pummel, kick, hit with anything hard, and try to scratch the cougar's eyes. Prove that you're not an easy target, and it will probably look for something easier – like a hare.

Bears are a more serious threat. They're large, strong, fast-moving, always hungry, and smart enough to connect humans with the food they carry. Parks and campsites have detailed warnings on how to store food safely to avoid attack. When possible, hang anything edible (including toothpaste) in bags well above the ground or store it in metal lockers. Never feed bears, as they won't know when the meal is over. Shouting, banging pots and throwing stones usually persuade curious bears to look somewhere else for a meal.

Coyotes are common, if somewhat shy, inhabitants throughout the west and east. About the size of a small German shepherd dog, coyotes prey on mice and small rodents. You're most likely to see them hunting in open fields or meadows early and late in the day, or near cleared roads in winter. They rarely pose any threat to humans.

Few people in the northern USA ever see **snakes** outside a zoo. The only poisonous snake native to the region is the rattlesnake, found only in drier areas east of the Pacific Northwest. They, along with other poisonous snakes, grow more common in the woodlands and wet areas further south. Only a handful of people each year across North America die from rattlesnake bites, usually while trying to catch them. Rattlers are harmless if left alone (as all snakes should be). The markings vary with the species, but all have diamond-shaped heads and rattles in their tails. Most, but not all, rattle a warning.

In the wild, look where you're walking; don't put hands or feet on ledges which you can't see; and before sitting down, make sure something hasn't already claimed the spot.

The **squirrels** and **chipmunks** that haunt many parks may look cute, but it is not uncommon for those trying to hand-feed them to end up being bitten instead. Rabies is endemic in the USA, so if bitten by an animal, try to capture it for observation of possible rabies, then go to the nearest emergency medical centre. You must seek immediate treatment – if left too late the disease is untreatable and fatal. Squirrels and chipmunks also carry fleas that transmit serious diseases.

TICK-BORNE DISEASES Don't wear shorts for hikes through the inviting grasslands, forests and mountains. Instead, cover up with long trousers, long-sleeved shirts, and insect repellent The risk of contracting **Lyme disease** from ticks which thrive in moist climates is rising by the year, as the deer ticks that carry it spread northwards. Lyme disease is frequently misdiagnosed and usually mistaken for rheumatoid arthritis. Typical symptoms include temporary paralysis, arthritic pains in the hand, arm or leg joints, swollen hands, fever, fatigue, headaches, swollen glands, heart palpitations and a circular red rash around the bite up to 30 days later. Early treatment with tetracycline and other drugs is nearly 100% effective; late treatment often fails. Symptoms may not appear for three months or longer after the first infected tick bite, but the disease can be detected by a simple blood test.

In the west, ticks also carry **Rocky Mountain spotted fever**, **Colorado tick fever** and **tularemia**. All are treatable, but it's easier to avoid the diseases in the first place. Cover up while hiking and check skin for ticks at midday and again in the evening. Look for tiny dark dots. Ticks especially like to hide in hair on the head and at the back of the neck.

POISONOUS PLANTS The most common hiking problem in the west is **poison oak**, found primarily in southern Oregon and north along the coast into Washington. This oak-like plant is usually a shrub, sometimes a creeper, and always a trailside hazard. Variable leaf shapes make the plant difficult to identify, although the leaves always occur in clusters of three and usually look like rounded oak leaves. Leaves are bright, glossy green in spring and summer, bright red in autumn, and dead in winter – but not forgotten.

In the east, watch for **poison ivy**, also with three shiny leaves that turn reddish in the autumn. It is a low-growing plant, often creeping across the ground.

The two plants have similar affects on those who brush against them. All parts of the plant – leaves, stems and flowers – exude a sticky sap that causes an intense allergic reaction in most people. The most common symptoms are red rash, itching, burning, and weeping sores. The best way to avoid the problem is to avoid the plant. Second best is to wash skin or clothing that has come into contact with the plant immediately in hot, soapy water. If you are afflicted, drying lotions such as calamine or products containing cortisone provide temporary relief, but time is the only cure.

SEXUALLY TRANSMITTED DISEASES The best way to avoid Aids or other sexually transmitted diseases (or STDs, as they're usually called) is to avoid promiscuous sex. In anything other than long-term, strictly monogamous relationships, the key phrase is 'safe sex'. Use condoms in any kind of sexual intercourse – they're very strongly encouraged by prostitutes plying the sex trade. Condoms can be bought in drug stores, pharmacies and supermarkets, and from vending machines in some public toilets.

MAPS

The best one-stop sources of maps are the American Automobile Association (AAA) and Canadian Automobile Association (CAA), which distribute their maps through local affiliates. State, regional, county and city maps are available free at all association offices, but only to members. Fortunately, most motoring clubs around the world have reciprocal agreements with the AAA and CAA to provide maps and other member services. Be prepared to show a membership card to obtain service.

The most detailed road maps are produced by Arrow Map Inc., 50 Scotland Blvd, Bridgewater MA 02324; tel: (508) 279-1177. Wire-bound and folding Arrow maps are sold at booksellers, news-stands, souvenir shops and airports. Detailed inland maps are available from DeLorme Map Co., Rte 1, Freeport ME 04032; tel: (207) 865-4171.

Rand McNally road maps and atlases are probably the best known of the ranges available outside the USA, in the travel section of bookshops and more specialist outlets. Each state produces a road map of its own, good for travelling within the state, but chauvinistically ending with its own borders, often without indicating so much as the route number of a road continuing on the other side. Like other information you will be sent, these vary greatly in quality and detail. The most detailed, not surprisingly, is tiny Rhode Island's, which usually has local road sign names as well as route numbers.

For wilderness travel, US Geological Survey topographic maps show terrain reliably; they can be purchased in sporting goods stores in each area. For hiking along the Appalachian Trail, which runs the length of eastern USA, get maps and guidebooks from the **Appalachian Mountain Club**, 5 Joy St, Boston MA 02108; tel: (617) 523-0636 – indispensable. In remote areas of the west, logging companies sometimes provide the most accurate and up-to-date off-road maps, available through travel information centres and timber industry information centres. But getting lost in the wilderness is a genuine possibility even with the best of maps in hand, so if you are thinking of driving off the beaten track, always carry a topographic map and compass in addition to any other maps and guides. Sierra Club and Wilderness Press publish the most up-to-date and reliable maps and guides to more remote areas. Outdoor supply shops and good booksellers stock maps of this kind as well

Before leaving civilisation behind, compare every available map for discrepancies, then check with forest or park personnel. Most are experienced wilderness enthusiasts themselves, and since they're responsible for rescuing lost hikers, they have a vested interest in dispensing the best possible information and advice.

OPENING TIMES

Office hours are generally Mon–Fri 0900–1700, although tourist offices also keep short Saturday hours all year, and weekend hours in summer. Many banks open from 0900 or 1000 to 1500 or 1600; a few stay open Thur to 1900 and Sat 0900–1300. Cash dispenser machines are ubiquitous and open 24 hrs. Petrol stations generally open from early morning until late at night; a few stay open 24 hrs on major travel routes.

In major cities, big stores, supermarkets and shopping centres open at 0900 or 1000 Mon–Sat and close at 2000 or 2100, with shorter hours Sun. Small shops keep standard business hours. Sunday opening hours for many stores and businesses are slightly shorter.

Many restaurants, museums and legitimate theatres close Mon, but most tourist attractions are open seven days a week in summer. Many tourist attractions are closed Sept–May, corresponding with the normal school year, but some are open during school vacations, which vary from state to state.

POSTAL SERVICES

Every town of any size has at least one post office. Hours vary, although all are open Mon–Fri, morning and afternoon. Major US Postal Service branches are open Sat, and only a select few Sun. Stamps may be purchased from machines in some pharmacies and convenience stores. Some hotels sell stamps through the concierge; large department stores may have a post office; and some supermarkets sell stamps at the checkout counter. Stamp machines are installed in some stores, but a surcharge may be included in the cost.

Poste restante is available at any post office, without charge. Mail should be addressed in block lettering to your name, Poste Restante/General Delivery, city, state, postal code, and United States of America or Canada (do not abbreviate). Mail is held for 30 days at the post office branch that handles General Delivery for each town or city, usually the main office. Identification is required for mail pick-up.

Postal rates are lower in the USA than in Canada. Letters and cards with correct postage may be dropped in blue boxes outside postal branches or on street corners; parcels weighing more than 1 lb must be handed to a postal clerk for security reasons.

Post everything going overseas as air mail (surface mail takes weeks or even months). If posting letters near an urban area, overseas mail should take about one week. Add a day or two if posting from remote areas.

All US mail must include the five-digit zip code (also use the four-digit suffix if you know it).

PUBLIC HOLIDAYS

North America's love affair with the road extends to jumping in the car for holiday weekends. Local celebrations, festivals, parades or neighbourhood parties can disrupt some or all activities in town. This works both ways, either keeping shops and businesses open longer hours or closing them earlier. Local museums which are normally open only on certain days will often open during local festivals.

The Fourth of July (Independence Day) is celebrated in every city and town with cookouts, concerts and fireworks. Memorial Day (30 May) and St Patrick's Day (17 March) are occasions for parades, which may tie up traffic for a few minutes or a few hours, even on numbered routes which become the main street of small towns they pass through.

The following holidays are celebrated nationally:

New Year's Day	(1 Jan)
Martin Luther King Jr Day	(third Mon in Jan)
Presidents' Day	(third Mon in Feb)
Memorial Day	(last Mon in May)
Independence Day	(4 July)
Labor Day	(first Mon in Sept, unless Mon falls on 1 Sept)
Columbus Day	(second Mon in Oct)
Veterans' Day	(11 Nov)
Thanksgiving Day	(fourth Thur in Nov)
Christmas Day	(25 Dec).

On these days post offices and government offices close, as do many businesses and shops. Large department stores stay open and hold huge sales. Convenience stores, supermarkets, liquor stores and petrol stations generally remain open (sometimes with curtailed hours). Nearly everything closes on New Year's Day, Thanksgiving Day and Christmas Day, including many restaurants. If you find yourself without a place to eat on Christmas Day, look for the nearest Chinese restaurant, which will very likely be open.

Some states have special holidays. Massachusetts celebrates Patriot's Day on 19 April and Boston celebrates Evacuation Day on 17 March, the day the British troops left Boston. (In practice, however, it is celebrated by Irish-heavy Boston as St Patrick's Day.)

Canadian National holidays include New Year's Day (1 Jan); Good Fri and Easter Mon (Mar or Apr); Victoria Day (late May); Canada Day (1 July); Labour Day (early Sept); Thanksgiving (mid-Oct); Remembrance Day (11 Nov); Christmas Day (25 Dec) and Boxing Day (26 Dec).

Call in advance before visiting an attraction on a public holiday as frequently there are special hours. National and state park campsites and accommodation must be reserved in advance for all holidays. Easter, Thanksgiving and Christmas are family holidays, so accommodation is usually available and may even be discounted (to fill hotels and motels). On other holidays Americans are 'mobile', so book early.

TELEPHONES

Public telephones are everywhere, and are located on street corners or inside restaurants, hotels and other public buildings, indicated by a sign with a white telephone receiver depicted on a blue field. Enclosed booths, wall-mounted or free-standing machines are all used. If possible, use public phones in well-lit, busy public areas.

Dialling instructions are in the local white pages telephone directory. Phone numbers are always seven digits, preceded by a three-digit area code when calling outside the local area. In some places (Maryland is one), you must dial the area code even if it is a local call. For all long-distance calls, precede the area code with a 1, or with 0 if calling collect (i.e. reversing the charges).

Like all long-distance numbers, the 800/888 area code must be preceded by a 1, e.g. 1 (888) 123-4567. Some telephone numbers are given in letters, i.e. 1 (800) VAN-RIDE – telephone keys have both numbers and letters. A few numbers have more than seven letters to finish a business name. Don't worry: US phone numbers never require more than seven numerals, plus three for the area code.

The North American telephone system is divided into local and long-distance carriers. Depending on the time of day and day of the week, it may be cheaper to call across the country than to call 30 miles away. After 1700, Mon–Fri, and all weekend, rates are lower. A local call usually costs $0.35; a computer voice will come on-line to ask for additional coins when needed. Pre-paid phone cards are gaining popularity and may be purchased at pharmacies, news-stands and convenience stores.

INFORMATION

For local number information, dial 411. For long-distance phone information, dial 1, the area code, then 555-1212. 0 reaches an operator, but remember that operator-assisted calls will be more expensive. There will be a charge for information calls. Most phone numbers with the 800 or 888 area code are toll-free. Those with a 900 area code charge the caller for information or other services, often at high per-minute rates.

Many hotels and motels add a stiff surcharge to the cost of a call from a room; nearly all charge a service fee of $0.50–$1.50 per call for local calls and those using a credit card, even to toll-free 800 or 888 numbers. Nearly every hotel, however small, will have pay telephones in the lobby, where you can go to make calls.

Before you travel, ask your local phone company if your phone card will work in North America. Most do, and come with a list of contact numbers. However, remember that the USA has the cheapest overseas phone rates in the world, which makes it cheaper to fill pay

INTERNATIONAL DIALLING

Dial 011-country code-city code (omitting the first 0 if there is one)-local number. Some country codes are:

Australia	61
New Zealand	64
Republic of Ireland	353
South Africa	27
UK	44

So to call central London, for example, dial: 011-44-171-local number.

Dial an international operator on 00 for enquiries or assistance.

phones with quarters than to reverse charges. A credit card may be convenient, but only economical if you pay the bill immediately.

TOILETS

'Restroom' or 'bathroom' are the common terms in the USA, and 'washroom' in Canada; 'toilet' is acceptable. Americans do not usually recognise 'WC'. Whatever the term, most are marked with a figure for a male or a female; 'Men' and 'Women' are the most common terms. Occasionally, a restroom may be used by both sexes. Restaurants sometimes use supposedly cute terms or pictures to replace the standard 'Men' and 'Women' signs, often to fit in with the theme of the establishment, and these can be confusing. Common in seafood and waterfront eateries are 'Buoys' and 'Gulls'; 'Colts' and 'Fillies' are popular in places with a western theme. Travellers in a hurry find these tedious, especially when pseudo-Scottish theme places use 'Laddies'. Fortunately, it's a trend that's dying out.

Most businesses, including bars and restaurants, reserve restrooms for clients. Petrol stations provide keys for customers to access restrooms. Public toilets are sporadically placed, but well marked. Public toilets are not common along city streets, but roadside rest stops often have them. Hotels, museums and other tourist attractions have them too, of course, as do department stores and shopping malls. Small shops usually do not.

USEFUL ADDRESSES AND CONTACT NUMBERS

EMBASSIES AND CONSULATES

AUSTRALIA	**Embassy:** 1601 Massachusetts Ave N.W., Washington DC 20096; tel: (202) 797-3000.
	150 E. 42nd St, 34 Floor, New York, NY 10017; tel: (212) 351 6500
	1 Bush St, 7th Floor, San Francisco CA 94104; tel: (415) 362-6160.
CANADA	**Embassy:** 501 Pennsylvania Ave N.W., Washington DC 20003; tel: (202) 481-1740.
	Plaza 600, Suite 412, Seattle WA 98101; tel: (206) 443-1372.
NEW ZEALAND	**Embassy:** 37 Observatory Circle N.W., Washington DC 20008; tel: (202) 328-4800.
	2461 Warrenton Dr., Houston, TX 77024; tel: (847) 384-5497.
	1 Maritime Plaza, Suite 700, San Francisco, CA 94111; tel: (415) 399-1255.
	Box 51059, Seattle WA 98115; tel: (206) 525-0271.
REPUBLIC OF IRELAND	**Embassy:** 2234 Massachusetts Ave N.W., Washington DC 20008; tel: (202) 462-3939.

	655 Montgomery St, San Francisco CA 94104; tel: (415) 392-4214.
	Chase Building, 535 Boylston St, Boston, MA 02116; tel: (627) 267-9330.
	400 N. Michigan Ave, Chicago, IL 60611; tel: (312) 337-1868.
SOUTH AFRICA	**Embassy:** 3051 Massachusetts Ave N.W., Washington DC 20008; tel: (202) 232-4400.
	50 N. La Cienega Blvd, Suite 300, Beverly Hills CA 90211; tel: (310) 657-9200.
	200 S. Michigan Ave, 6th Floor, Chicago, IL 60604; tel: (310) 939-7929.
UK	**Embassy:** 3100 Massachusetts Ave N.W., Washington DC 20008; tel: (202) 462-1340.
	820 First Interstate Center, Seattle WA 98101; tel: (206) 622-9255.
	Suite 850, 1 Sansome St, San Francisco, CA 94104; tel: (415) 981-3030.
	Suite 2110, Sun Trust Center, 200 S. Orange Ave, Orlando, FL 32801; tel: (407) 426-7855.

TOURIST INFORMATION

In the USA, each state is responsible for its own tourism promotion. Ask for information you need to be sent to you well in advance to allow time for overseas shipping of large packets. While travelling in the USA, you can call tourist information offices to ask questions or seek advice, although many state offices are not able to recommend accommodation. They can, however, steer you to the local chambers of commerce or information offices in the city or town where you are going.

Local tourist information centres (TICs) are not government-run bureaux, but are often staffed by volunteers. While some have regular hours, others vary with the day of the week, season or schedule of the individual who works there. Often those run by local chambers of commerce are, oddly, open 0900–1700 on weekdays, but not at weekends when travellers are the most abundant.

If you have access to the Internet, search for websites; most states and several regions and cities are developing these and some are filled with practical information, even pictures of B&Bs and hotels. Many have links that allow you to enquire about rates and availability, as well as to make reservations. At the least they will give you an idea of what is available at your destination.

Alabama Bureau of Tourism and Travel, 410 Adams Ave, Montgomery AL 36117; tel: (205) 242-4670 or (800) 252-2262.

Arizona Tourism, 1100 West Washington, Phoenix AZ 85007; tel: (602) 542-8687 or (800) 842-8257.

Arkansas Dept of Parks and Tourism, 1 Capitol Mall, Little Rock AR 72201; tel: (501) 682-7777 or (800) 643-8383.

California Division of Tourism, 801 K St, Ste 1600, Sacramento CA 95814; tel: (916) 322-2881 or (800) TO-CALIF; fax: (916) 322-3402; www.gocalif.ca.gov/.

Colorado currently has no tourism office; contact the regional Grand Circle Association, PO Box 987, Page AZ 86040; tel: (520) 645-3232. This agency provides information on the entire south-west mountain country.

Connecticut Office of Tourism Department of Economic and Community Development, 505 Hudson St, Hartford CT 06106; tel: (800) CT-BOUND; www.state.ct.us/tourism.

Delaware Council for International Visitors, PO Box 831, Wilmington DE 19899; tel: (302) 656-9928; www.state.de.us/tourism/intro.htm.

Florida Tourism, PO Box 1100, 661 E. Jefferson St, Tallahassee FL 32302; tel: (904) 487-1462; fax (904) 224-2938. In the UK: ABC FLORIDA, Box 35 Abingdon, Oxon OX14 4TB; tel: (0891) 600555.

Georgia Department of Industry, Trade and Tourism, PO Box 1776 Atlanta GA 30301; tel: (404) 656-3590 or (800) 847-4842.

Idaho Parks and Recreation Dept, 5657 Warm Springs Ave, Boise ID 83720; tel: (208) 334-4199.

Illinois Office Of Tourism, 620 E. Adams St, Springfield IL 62701; tel: (217) 782-7500.

Indiana Division of Tourism, 1 North Capitol 77, Indianapolis IN 46204; tel: (317) 232-8860.

Iowa Department of Economic Development, 200 E. Grand Ave, Des Moines IA 50309; tel (515) 281-3100 or (800) 345-4692.

Kansas Department of Commerce, 700 South West Harrison, 1300, Topeka KS 66603; tel: (913) 296-3481 or (800) 252-6727.

Kentucky Department of Travel Development, 500 Metro St, Frankfurt KY 40601; tel: (502) 564-4930 or (800) 225-8747.

Louisiana Travel Office, PO Box 94291, Capitol Station, Baton Rouge LA 70804; tel: (504) 925-3800 or (800) 633-6970.

Maine Publicity Bureau PO Box 2300, Hallowell ME 04347-2300; tel: (207) 623-0363; Maine Office of Tourism: www.visit-maine.com.

Maryland Office of Tourism Development, Department of Business and Economic Development, 217 E. Redwood St, Baltimore MD 21201; tel: (410) 767-6270; www.mdisfun.orf/mdisfun.

Massachusetts Office of Travel and Tourism, 100 Cambridge St,

13th Floor, Boston MA 02202; tel: (800) 447-MASS, ext 300; www.mass-vacation.com.

Michigan Travel Bureau, 333 South Capitol, Suite F, Lansing MI 48909; tel: (517) 335-1876 or (800) 543-2937.

Minnesota Office of Tourism, 100 Metro Sq., St Paul MN 55101-2112; tel: (612) 296-5029 or (800) 657-3700.

Mississippi Division of Tourism, 1301 Walter Siller Bldg, 55 High St, Jackson MS 39209; tel: (601) 359-3414 or (800) 647-2290.

Missouri Division of Tourism, PO Box 1055, Jefferson City MO 65102; tel: (314) 751-4133.

Montana Travel, PO Box 200533, Helena MT 59620; tel: (406) 444-2654 or (800) 541-1447.

Nebraska Department of Economic Development, PO Box 94666, Lincoln NE 68509; tel: (402) 471-3796 or (800) 228-4307.

Nevada Commission on Tourism, PO Box 30032, Reno NV 89520; tel: (702) 687-4332 or (800) 638-2328; fax: (702) 687-6779; www.travelnevada.com.

New Hampshire Office of Vacation Travel, PO Box 586, Concord NH 03301; tel: (603) 271-2666; www.visitnh.gov.

New Jersey Division of Travel and Tourism, 1 W. State St, Trenton NJ 08625; tel: (609) 292-2470.

New Mexico Department of Tourism, 491 Old Santa Fe Trail, Santa Fe NM 87501; tel (505) 827-0291 or (800) 545-2040.

Nevada Commission of Tourism, Capitol Complex, Carson City NV 89710; tel: (702) 687-4322.

New York State Division of Tourism, 1 Commerce Plaza, Albany NY 12245; tel: (518) 474-4116.

New York City Convention and Visitors Bureau, 42nd at Times Square, New York NY 10036; tel: (212) 397-8222.

North Carolina Travel and Tourism Division, 301 N. Wilmington St, Raleigh NC 27601; tel: (919) 733-4171 or (800) 847-4862.

North Dakota Promotion Division, Liberty Memorial Bldg, Capitol Grounds, Bismark 58505; tel: (701) 224-2525 or (800) 437-2077.

Ohio Office of Travel and Tourism, 77 S. High St, PO Box 1001, Columbus OH 43215; tel: (614) 466-8844.

Oklahoma Tourism and Recreation Dept, 500 Will Rogers Bldg, Oklahoma City OK 73105; tel: (405) 521-2409 or (800) 652-6552.

Oregon Tourism Commission, 775 Summer St N.E., Salem OR 97310; tel: (800) 547-7842 or (503) 986-0000; fax: (503) 986-0001.

Pennsylvania Office of Tourism, 453 Forum Bldg, Harrisburg PA

17120; tel: (717) 787-5453. In the UK: 11–15 Betterton St, London WC2H 9BP; tel: (0171) 470 8801; www.libertynet.org/phila-visitor.

Rhode Island Tourism Division, 1 W. Exchange St, Providence RI 02903; tel: (800) 556-2484 or (401) 222-2601; www.visitrhodeisland.com.

South Carolina Department of Parks Recreation and Tourism, 1205 Pendleton St, Columbia SC 29201; tel: (803) 724-0122.

South Dakota Division of Tourism, 221 South Central, PO Box 1000, Pierre SD 57051; tel: (605) 773-3301 or (800) 843-1930.

Tennessee Department of Tourist Development, PO Box 23170, Nashville TN 37202; tel (615) 471-2158.

Texas Division of Tourism, PO Box 12728, Austin TX 78711; tel (512) 463-8586 or (800) 888-8839.

Utah Travel Council, 300 N. State St, Salt Lake City UT 84114; tel: (801) 538-1030.

Vermont Department of Tourism and Marketing, 134 State St, PO Box 1471, Montpelier VT 0560-1471; tel: (802) 828-3236; www.travel-vermont.com.

Virginia Division of Tourism, 901 E. Byrd St, Richmond VA 23219; tel: (804) 786-2051. In the UK: 1st floor, 182–4 Addington Rd, Selsdon, Surrey CR2 8LB; tel: (0181) 651 4743; www.virginia.org.

Washington DC Convention and Visitors Association, 1212 New York Ave N.W., Washington DC 20005; tel (202) 789-7000. In the UK: see Regional Information, below.

Washington State Division of Tourism, Box 42500, Olympia WA 98504; tel: 800-544-1800 or (360) 753-5630.

West Virginia Division of Tourism and Parks, State Capitol, Charleston WV 25305; tel: (800) CALL-WVA.

Wisconsin Division of Tourism, 123 W. Washington St, PO Box 7606, Madison WI 53707; tel: (608) 266-2161 or (800) 432-8748.

Wyoming Travel Commission, College Drive, Cheyenne WY 82002; tel: (307) 777-7777.

REGIONAL AND OTHER INFORMATION Information, brochures, maps and itinerary planning are also available from **Discover New England**, 34 Francis Grove, Wimbledon, London SW19 4DT; tel: (0181) 544 1000; fax: (0181) 542 6556. In the USA, the address is 1250 Waterbury Rd, Box 3809, Stowe VT 05672 02536; tel: (802) 253-2500; fax: (802) 253-9064; www.discovernewengland.com.

Destinnations New England, tel: (UK) (01707) 644 450; (USA) (508) 790-0577, fax (508) 790-0565; email: destinn@capecod.net; www.newenglandinns.co.uk; a travel

HOTEL AND MOTEL CHAINS

In the following list, the first number is for use in the USA and Canada. Subsequent numbers are for making reservations from other countries. Telephone numbers with area codes 800 or 888 are free calls from pay telephones (although not from in-room phones in most hotels).

Budgetel Inn
(800) 428 3438
Best Western
(800) 528 1234
Australia (1 800) 222 422
Ireland (800) 709 101
NZ (09) 520 5418
South Africa (011) 339 4865
UK (0800) 393130
Comfort Inn
(800) 228 5150
Australia (008) 090 600
Canada (800) 888 4747
Ireland (800) 500 600
NZ (800) 8686 888
UK (0800) 444 444
Clarion
(800) CLARION
(800) 268 1133
Days Inn
(800) 325 2525
UK (01483) 440470
DoubleTree Inn
(800) 222 8733
Econo Lodge
(800) 424 6423
worldwide (800) 221 2222
Embassy Suites
(800) 362 2779
Australia 02 959 3922
Canada 416 626 3974
NZ 09 623 4294
SA 11 789 6706
UK (01992) 441517
Fiesta Americana (800) Fiesta-1; (800) 343 7821
Friendship Inns
(800) 424 6423
Hampton Inns
(800) 426 7866
Holiday Inn
(800) 465 4329
Australia (800) 221 066
Ireland (800) 553 155
NZ (0800) 442 222
South Africa (011) 482 3500
UK (0800) 897121
Hostelling International
(800) 444 6111
UK (0171) 248 6547
Howard Johnson
(800) 654 2000
Australia 02 262 4918
UK (0181) 688 1418
Hilton
(800) 445 8667
Australia (800) 222 255
NZ (800) 448 002
South Africa (011) 880 3108
UK (0345) 581595
Inter-Continental
(800) 327 0200
UK (0345) 581 237
Marriott (800) 228 9290
Australia (800) 251 259
NZ (800) 441 035
UK (800) 221222
Motel 6 (not toll-free) (505) 891 6161
Novotel
(800) NOVOTEL
Quality Inn (800) 228 5151
Quality Suites
(800) 228 5151
Radisson (800) 333 3333
Ireland (800) 557 474
NZ (800) 443 333
UK (800) 191991
Residence Inn
(800) 331 3131
Australia (800) 251 259
Ireland (800) 409929
NZ (800) 441035
Ramada (800) 854 7854
UK (800) 181 737
Red Carpet Inns
(800) 251 1962
Red Lion Hotels and Inns
(800) 547 8010
Red Roof Inns
800) 843 7663
Rodeway Inn
(800) 228 2000
Sheraton
(800) 325 3535; (800) 325 1717 (hearing impaired)
Australia (008) 073 535
Ireland (800) 535 353
NZ (0800) 443 535
UK (0800) 353535
Sonesta (800) SONESTA; (800) 766 3782
Suisse Chalet
(800) 524 2538
Super 8 (800) 800 8000
Travelodge (800) 578 7878
Australia (800) 622 240
Ireland (800) 409 040
NZ (800) 801 111
South Africa (011) 442 9201
UK (0345) 404040
Venture Inn (888) 483 6887
Westin (800) 228 3000

planning and reservation service, which can secure accommodation at selected New England inns.

Capital Region USA, 375 Upper Richmond Rd West, East Sheen, London SW14 7JG; tel: (0181) 392 9187; www.washington.org; has information about the Washington DC, Virginia and Maryland area.

Washington State Bed & Breakfast Directory, 2442 N.W. Market St, 355, Seattle WA 98107; tel: (800) 647-2918, lists B&Bs around Washington.

For national park, monument and seashore information, contact **National Parks of the West**, Western Region Information Center, Fort Mason, Bldg 201, San Francisco CA 94125; tel: (415) 556-0560; www.nps.gov.

Canada also has active federal tourism promotion offices, usually located in Canadian consulates around the world. In the UK, **Tourism British Columbia** is located at British Columbia House, 3rd Floor, 1 Regent St, London SW1Y 4NS; tel: (0171) 930 6857.

WEIGHTS AND MEASURES

Officially, the USA is converting to the metric system. In truth, few people have changed and metric measures are rarely seen. (A few road signs show both miles and km.) The non-metric US measures are the same as imperial measures except for fluids, where US gallons and quarts are five-sixths of their imperial equivalents. See conversion tables, overleaf. Canada has long since joined the metric world.

Clothing sizes are the same as or very close to imperial sizes for menswear, tights and children's clothing. Women's sizes are quite different. Shoe and hat sizes are close enough to be confusing, but not close enough to fit.

DISTANCES (approx. conversions)

1 kilometre (km) = 1000 metres (m) 1 metre = 100 centimetres (cm)

Metric	Imperial/US	Metric	Imperial/US	Metric	Imperial/US
1 cm	3/8 in.	10 m	33 ft (11 yd)	3 km	2 miles
50 cm	20 in.	20 m	66 ft (22 yd)	4 km	2½ miles
1 m	3 ft 3 in.	50 m	164 ft (54 yd)	5 km	3 miles
2 m	6 ft 6 in.	100 m	330 ft (110 yd)	10 km	6 miles
3 m	10 ft	200 m	660 ft (220 yd)	20 km	12½ miles
4 m	13 ft	250 m	820 ft (275 yd)	25 km	15½ miles
5 m	16 ft 6 in.	300 m	984 ft (330 yd)	30 km	18½ miles
6 m	19 ft 6 in.	500 m	1640 ft (550 yd)	40 km	25 miles
7 m	23 ft	750 m	½ mile	50 km	31 miles
8 m	26 ft	1 km	5/8 mile	75 km	46 miles
9 m	29 ft (10 yd)	2 km	1½ miles	100 km	62 miles

24-HOUR CLOCK

(examples)

0000 = Midnight	1200 = Noon	1800 = 6 pm
0600 = 6 am	1300 = 1 pm	2000 = 8 pm
0715 = 7.15 am	1415 = 2.15 pm	2110 = 9.10 pm
0930 = 9.30 am	1645 = 4.45 pm	2345 = 11.45 pm

TEMPERATURE

Conversion Formula: °C × 9 ÷ 5 + 32 = °F

°C	°F	°C	°F	°C	°F	°C	°F
-20	-4	-5	23	10	50	25	77
-15	5	0	32	15	59	30	86
-10	14	5	41	20	68	35	95

WEIGHT

1kg = 1000g 100 g = 3½ oz

Kg	Lbs	Kg	Lbs	Kg	Lbs
1	2¼	5	11	25	55
2	4½	10	22	50	110
3	6½	15	33	75	165
4	9	20	45	100	220

FLUID MEASURES

1 ltr.(l) = 0.88 Imp. quarts = 1.06 US quarts

Ltrs.	Imp. gal.	US gal.	Ltrs.	Imp. gal.	US gal.
5	1.1	1.3	30	6.6	7.8
10	2.2	2.6	35	7.7	9.1
15	3.3	3.9	40	8.8	10.4
20	4.4	5.2	45	9.9	11.7
25	5.5	6.5	50	11.0	13.0

MEN'S SHIRTS

UK	Europe	US
14	36	14
15	38	15
15½	39	15½
16	41	16
16½	42	16½
17	43	17

MEN'S SHOES

UK	Europe	US
6	40	7
7	41	8
8	42	9
9	43	10
10	44	11
11	45	12

MEN'S CLOTHES

UK	Europe	US
36	46	36
38	48	38
40	50	40
42	52	42
44	54	44
46	56	46

LADIES' SHOES

UK	Europe	US
3	36	4½
4	37	5½
5	38	6½
6	39	7½
7	40	8½
8	41	9½

LADIES' CLOTHES

UK	France	Italy	Rest of Europe	US
10	36	38	34	8
12	38	40	36	10
14	40	42	38	12
16	42	44	40	14
18	44	46	42	16
20	46	48	44	18

AREAS

1 hectare = 2.471 acres

1 hectare = 10,000 sq meters

1 acre = 0.4 hectares

This index lists places and topics in alphabetical sequence. All references are to page numbers. **Bold** numbers refer to map pages. To find routes between cities, see pp. 8–9.

If you enjoyed using this book, or even if you didn't, please help us improve future editions by taking part in our reader survey. Every returned form will be acknowledged, and to show our appreciation we will give you £1 off your next purchase of a Thomas Cook guidebook. Just take a few minutes to complete and return this form to us.

When did you buy this book? ______________________

Where did you buy it? (Please give town/city and if possible name of retailer)

____

____

When did you/do you intend to travel in USA? ______________________

For how long (approx.)? ______________________

How many people in your party? ______________________

Which cities and other locations did you/do you intend mainly to visit?

____

____

____

How will you travel around the USA? By Rail ☐ By Car ☐ By Bus ☐ By Air ☐

____

Did you/will you:

☐ Make all your travel arrangements independently?

☐ Travel on an Amtrak pass? ☐ Travel on a Greyhound Pass?

☐ If you purchased a rail or bus pass, where did you buy it? ______________________

☐ Use other passes or tickets, please give brief details: ______________________

____

Did you/do you intend to use this book:

☐ For planning your trip?

☐ During the trip itself?

☐ Both?

Did you/do you intend also to purchase any of the following travel publications for your trip?

☐ *Thomas Cook Overseas Timetable*

☐ *Thomas Cook World Timetable Independent Traveller's Edition*

☐ Other guidebooks or maps, please specify

____

____

Have you used any other Thomas Cook guidebooks in the past? If so, which?

____

____

Reader Survey

Please rate the following features within this guide for their value to you
(Circle vu for 'very useful', u for 'useful', nu for 'little or no use'):

The 'Travelling around the USA' section on pages 14–28	vu	u	nu
The 'Cross-country route' section on pages 29–30	vu	u	nu
The 'Travel Basics' section on pages 31–50	vu	u	nu
The 'Travel Directory' section on pages 540–569	vu	u	nu
The recommended routes throughout the book	vu	u	nu
Information on towns and cities	vu	u	nu
The maps of towns and cities	vu	u	nu

This book will be updated annually, which allows us to amend and enhance the information we include within it, but we need our readers to tell us what they would like to see changed and improved. Please use this space to make any comments you have concerning this book.

Your age category: under 21 21–30 31–40 41–50 over 50

Your name: Mr/Mrs/Miss/Ms
(First name or initials)
(Last name)

Your full address: (Please include postal or zip code)

Your daytime telephone number:

Please detach this page and send it to: **The Editor, Independent Traveller's USA, Thomas Cook Publishing, PO Box 227, Peterborough PE3 6PU, United Kingdom.**

We will be pleased to send you details of how to claim your discount upon receipt of this questionnaire.

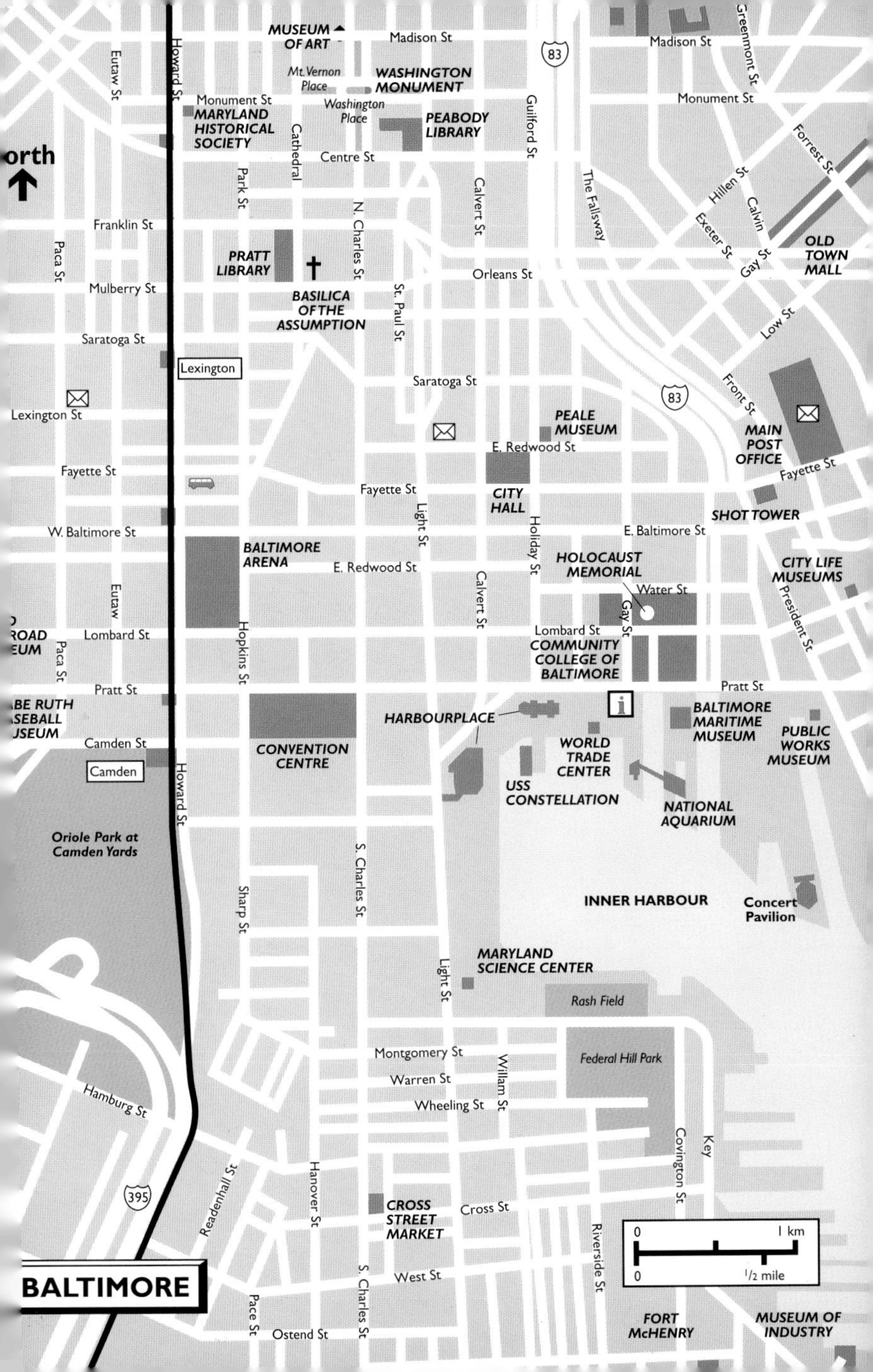
BALTIMORE
North
MUSEUM OF ART
WASHINGTON MONUMENT
Mt. Vernon Place
Washington Place
PEABODY LIBRARY
MARYLAND HISTORICAL SOCIETY
PRATT LIBRARY
BASILICA OF THE ASSUMPTION
Lexington
PEALE MUSEUM
CITY HALL
MAIN POST OFFICE
OLD TOWN MALL
SHOT TOWER
CITY LIFE MUSEUMS
HOLOCAUST MEMORIAL
BALTIMORE ARENA
COMMUNITY COLLEGE OF BALTIMORE
BABE RUTH BASEBALL MUSEUM
HARBOURPLACE
BALTIMORE MARITIME MUSEUM
PUBLIC WORKS MUSEUM
CONVENTION CENTRE
WORLD TRADE CENTER
USS CONSTELLATION
NATIONAL AQUARIUM
Camden
Oriole Park at Camden Yards
INNER HARBOUR
Concert Pavilion
MARYLAND SCIENCE CENTER
Rash Field
Federal Hill Park
CROSS STREET MARKET
FORT McHENRY
MUSEUM OF INDUSTRY
Madison St
Monument St
Centre St
Franklin St
Mulberry St
Orleans St
Saratoga St
Lexington St
Fayette St
W. Baltimore St
E. Baltimore St
E. Redwood St
Water St
Lombard St
Pratt St
Camden St
Montgomery St
Warren St
Wheeling St
Cross St
West St
Ostend St
Hamburg St
Eutaw St
Howard St
Paca St
Park St
Cathedral
N. Charles St
St. Paul St
Calvert St
Guilford St
The Fallsway
Light St
Holiday St
Gay St
Hopkins St
Sharp St
S. Charles St
Hanover St
Readenhall St
Pace St
William St
Riverside St
Covington St
Key
Greenmount St
Forrest St
Hillen St
Calvin
Exeter St
Low St
Front St
President St
83
395
0
1 km
1/2 mile

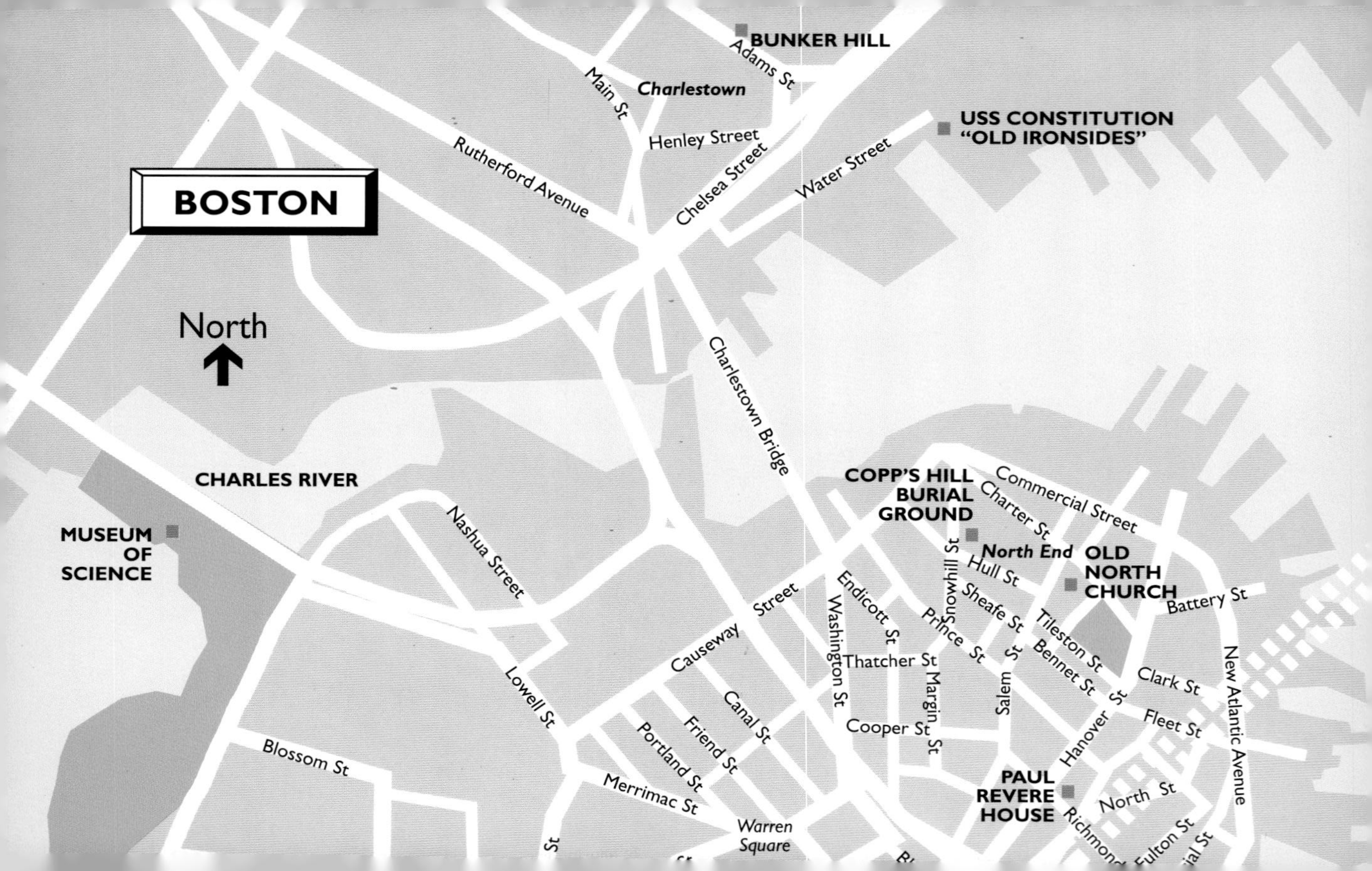
BOSTON
North
BUNKER HILL
Charlestown
Adams St
Main St
Henley Street
Chelsea Street
Water Street
Rutherford Avenue
USS CONSTITUTION
"OLD IRONSIDES"
Charlestown Bridge
CHARLES RIVER
MUSEUM
OF
SCIENCE
Nashua Street
Lowell St
Blossom St
Merrimac St
Portland St
Friend St
Canal St
Causeway Street
Warren
Square
Washington St
Endicott St
Thatcher St
Cooper St
Margin St
Prince St
Snowhill St
Salem St
COPP'S HILL
BURIAL
GROUND
North End
Charter St
Commercial Street
Hull St
Sheafe St
Tileston St
Bennet St
OLD
NORTH
CHURCH
Battery St
Clark St
Fleet St
Hanover St
New Atlantic Avenue
PAUL
REVERE
HOUSE
North St
Richmond
Fulton St

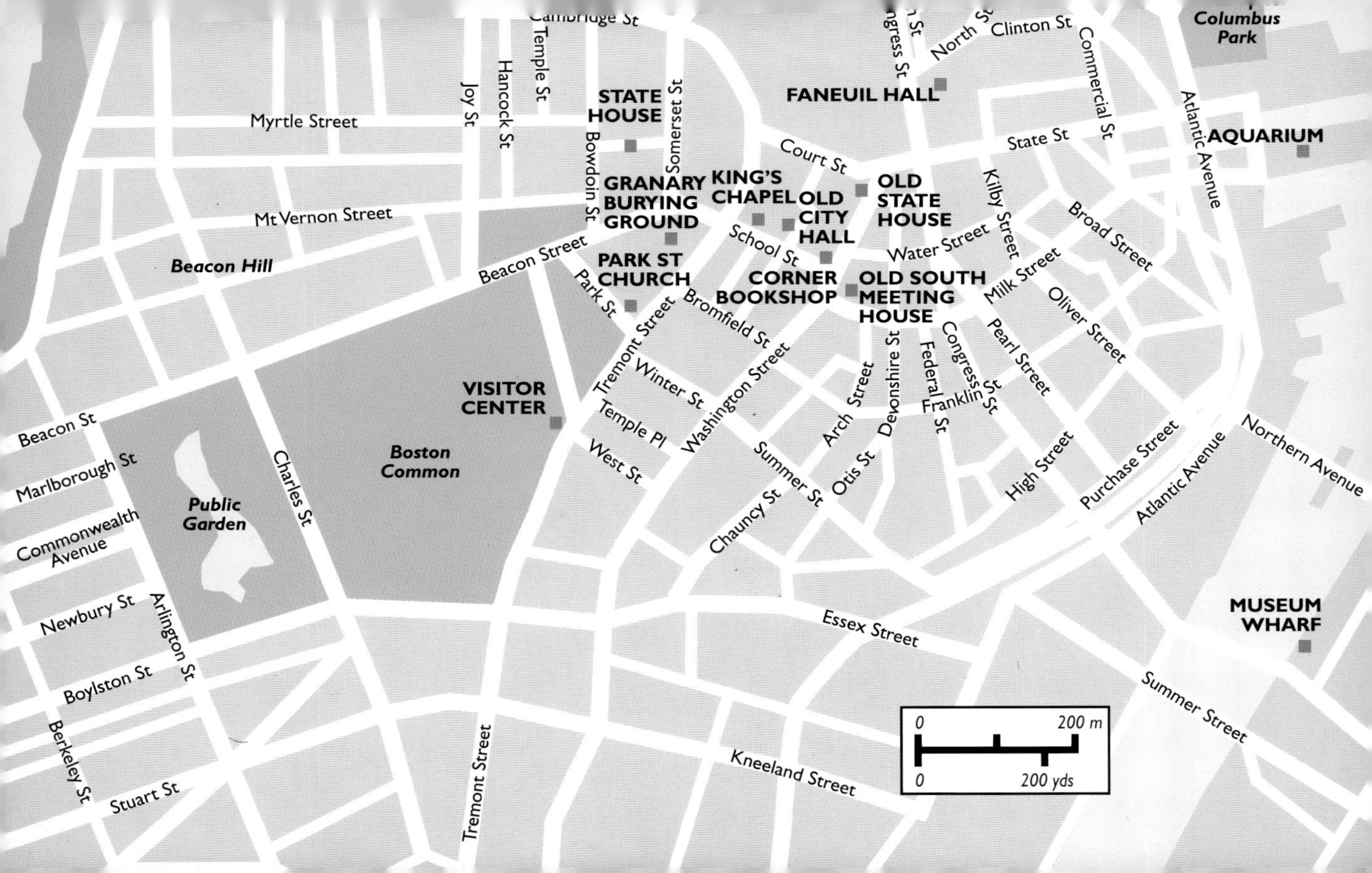
FANEUIL HALL
STATE HOUSE
GRANARY BURYING GROUND
KING'S CHAPEL
OLD CITY HALL
OLD STATE HOUSE
PARK ST CHURCH
CORNER BOOKSHOP
OLD SOUTH MEETING HOUSE
AQUARIUM
MUSEUM WHARF
VISITOR CENTER
Columbus Park
Beacon Hill
Boston Common
Public Garden
Myrtle Street
Mt Vernon Street
Joy St
Hancock St
Temple St
Bowdoin St
Somerset St
Court St
State St
Commercial St
Clinton St
North St
Atlantic Avenue
Beacon Street
School St
Water Street
Kilby Street
Broad Street
Milk Street
Oliver Street
Park St
Tremont Street
Bromfield St
Washington Street
Winter St
Temple Pl
West St
Summer St
Chauncy St
Arch Street
Otis St
Devonshire St
Federal St
Franklin St
Congress St
Pearl Street
High Street
Purchase Street
Northern Avenue
Essex Street
Summer Street
Kneeland Street
Charles St
Beacon St
Marlborough St
Commonwealth Avenue
Newbury St
Arlington St
Boylston St
Berkeley St
Stuart St
0
200 m
0
200 yds

BOSTON SUBWAY

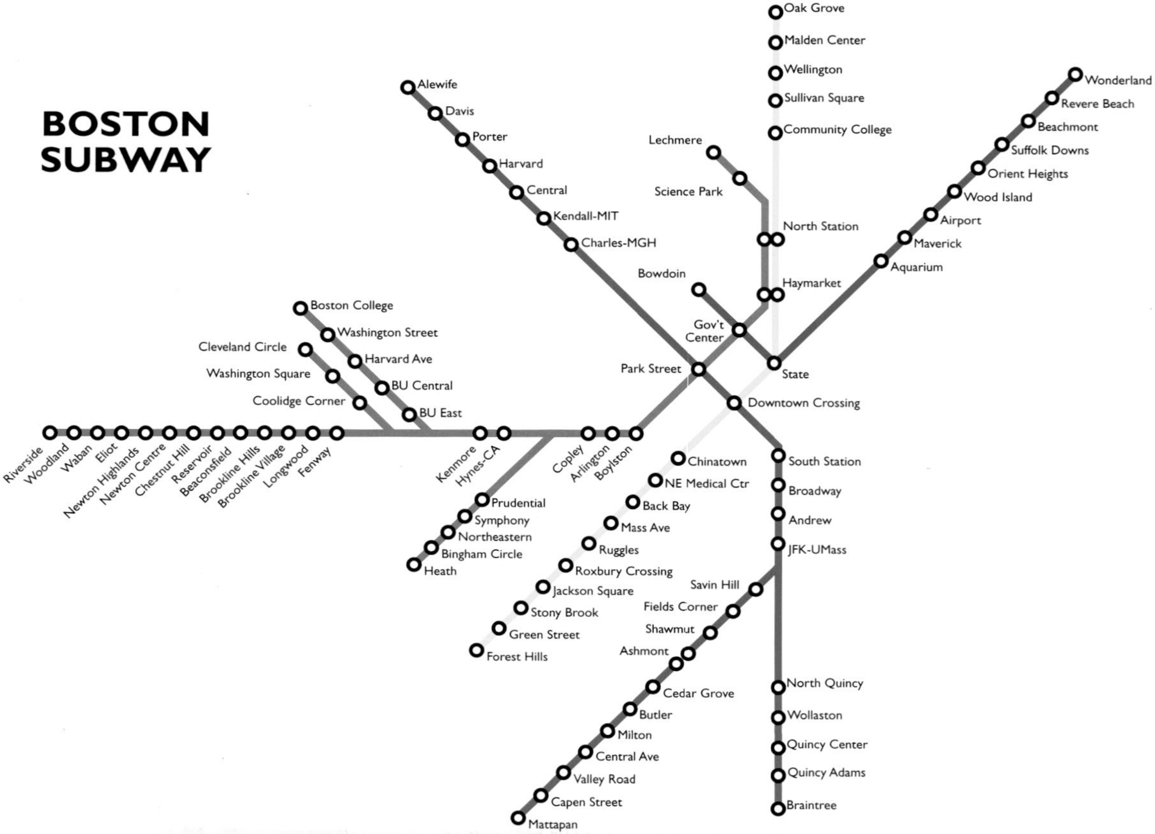

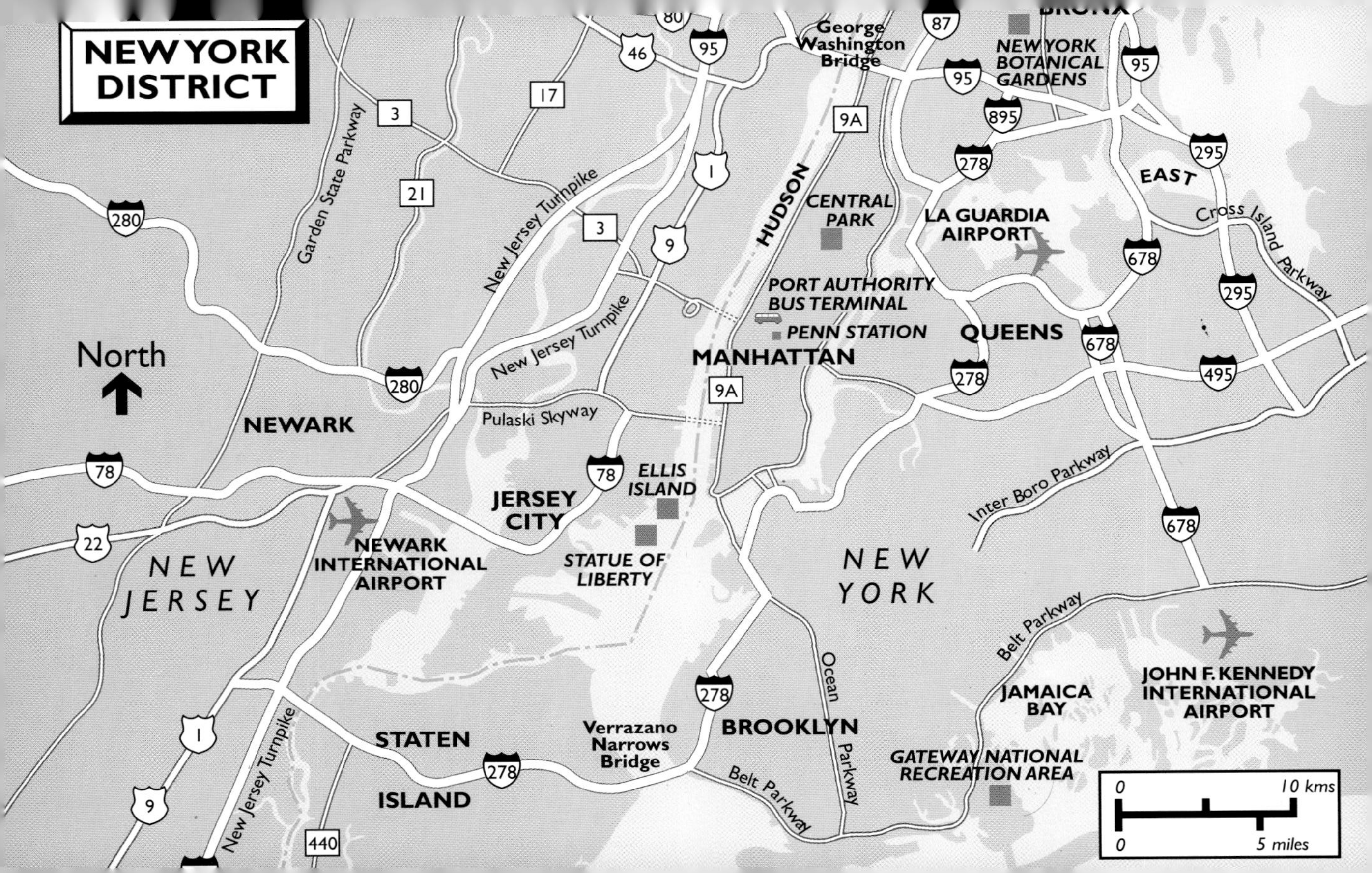
NEW YORK DISTRICT
North
NEWARK
NEW JERSEY
NEWARK INTERNATIONAL AIRPORT
JERSEY CITY
ELLIS ISLAND
STATUE OF LIBERTY
STATEN ISLAND
Verrazano Narrows Bridge
BROOKLYN
NEW YORK
MANHATTAN
PORT AUTHORITY BUS TERMINAL
PENN STATION
CENTRAL PARK
HUDSON
George Washington Bridge
NEW YORK BOTANICAL GARDENS
LA GUARDIA AIRPORT
QUEENS
EAST
Cross Island Parkway
Inter Boro Parkway
Belt Parkway
Ocean Parkway
JAMAICA BAY
JOHN F. KENNEDY INTERNATIONAL AIRPORT
GATEWAY NATIONAL RECREATION AREA
Garden State Parkway
New Jersey Turnpike
Pulaski Skyway
0 10 kms
0 5 miles
80
46
95
87
895
295
678
495
278
9A
3
17
21
1
9
280
78
22
440

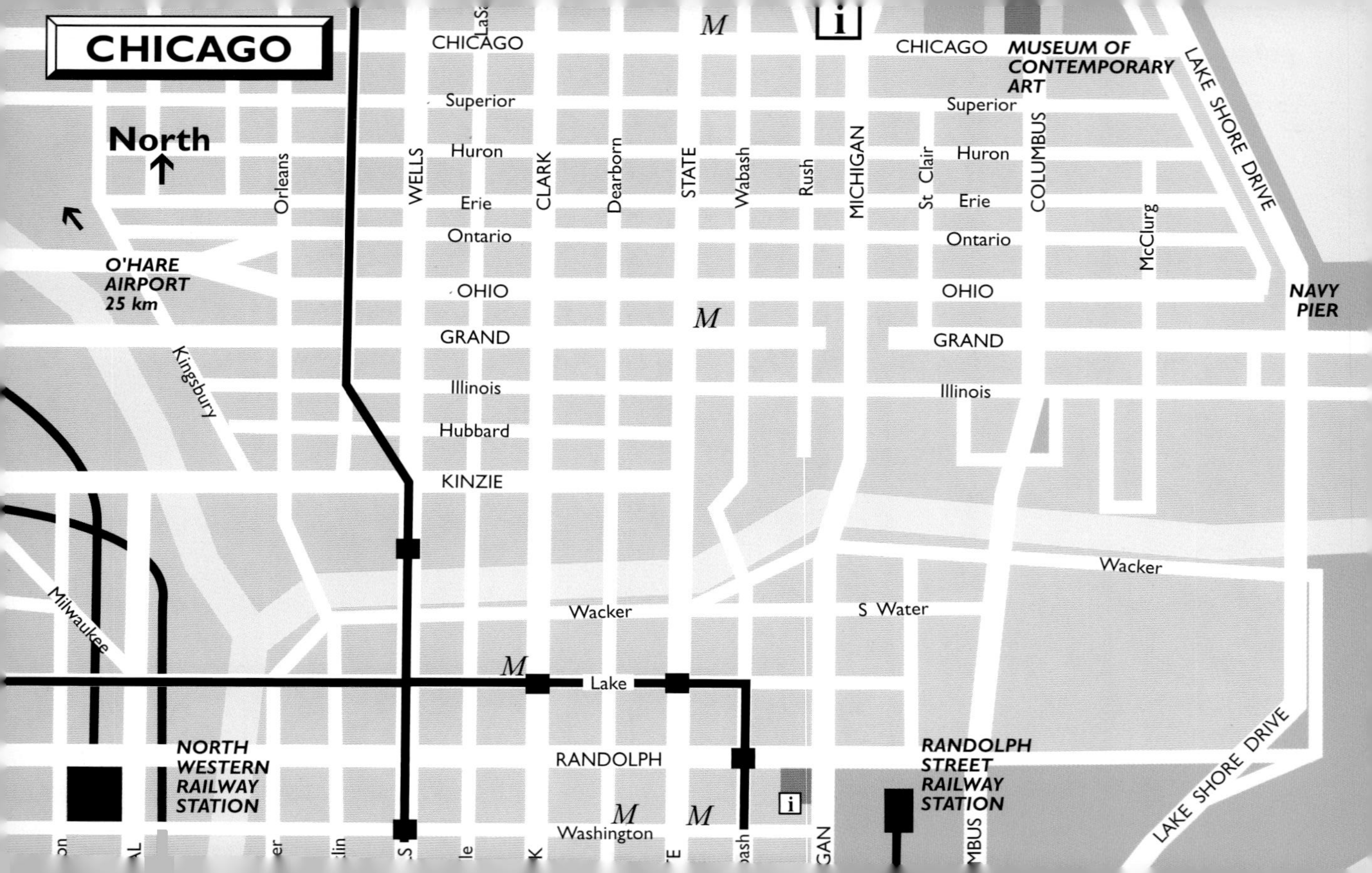
CHICAGO
North
O'HARE AIRPORT 25 km
Kingsbury
Milwaukee
Orleans
WELLS
CLARK
Dearborn
STATE
Wabash
Rush
MICHIGAN
COLUMBUS
McClurg
LAKE SHORE DRIVE
NAVY PIER
MUSEUM OF CONTEMPORARY ART
CHICAGO
Superior
Huron
Erie
Ontario
OHIO
GRAND
Illinois
Hubbard
KINZIE
St Clair
Wacker
S Water
Lake
RANDOLPH
Washington
RANDOLPH STREET RAILWAY STATION
NORTH WESTERN RAILWAY STATION
LAKE SHORE DRIVE

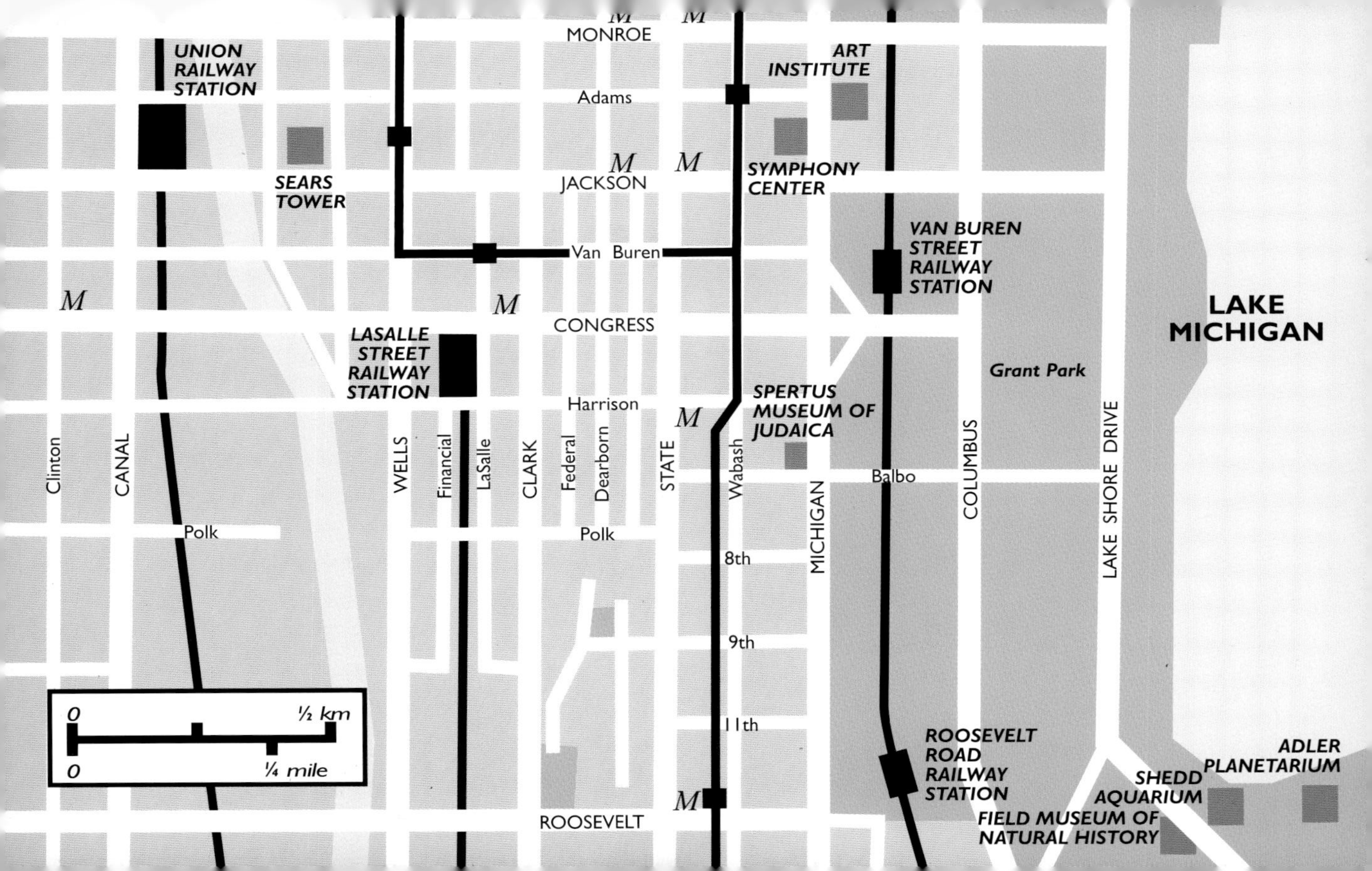

LAKE MICHIGAN
UNION RAILWAY STATION
SEARS TOWER
LASALLE STREET RAILWAY STATION
VAN BUREN STREET RAILWAY STATION
ROOSEVELT ROAD RAILWAY STATION
ART INSTITUTE
SYMPHONY CENTER
SPERTUS MUSEUM OF JUDAICA
Grant Park
ADLER PLANETARIUM
SHEDD AQUARIUM
FIELD MUSEUM OF NATURAL HISTORY
MONROE
Adams
JACKSON
Van Buren
CONGRESS
Harrison
Polk
Balbo
8th
9th
11th
ROOSEVELT
Clinton
CANAL
WELLS
Financial
LaSalle
CLARK
Federal
Dearborn
STATE
Wabash
MICHIGAN
COLUMBUS
LAKE SHORE DRIVE
M
0
½ km
0
¼ mile

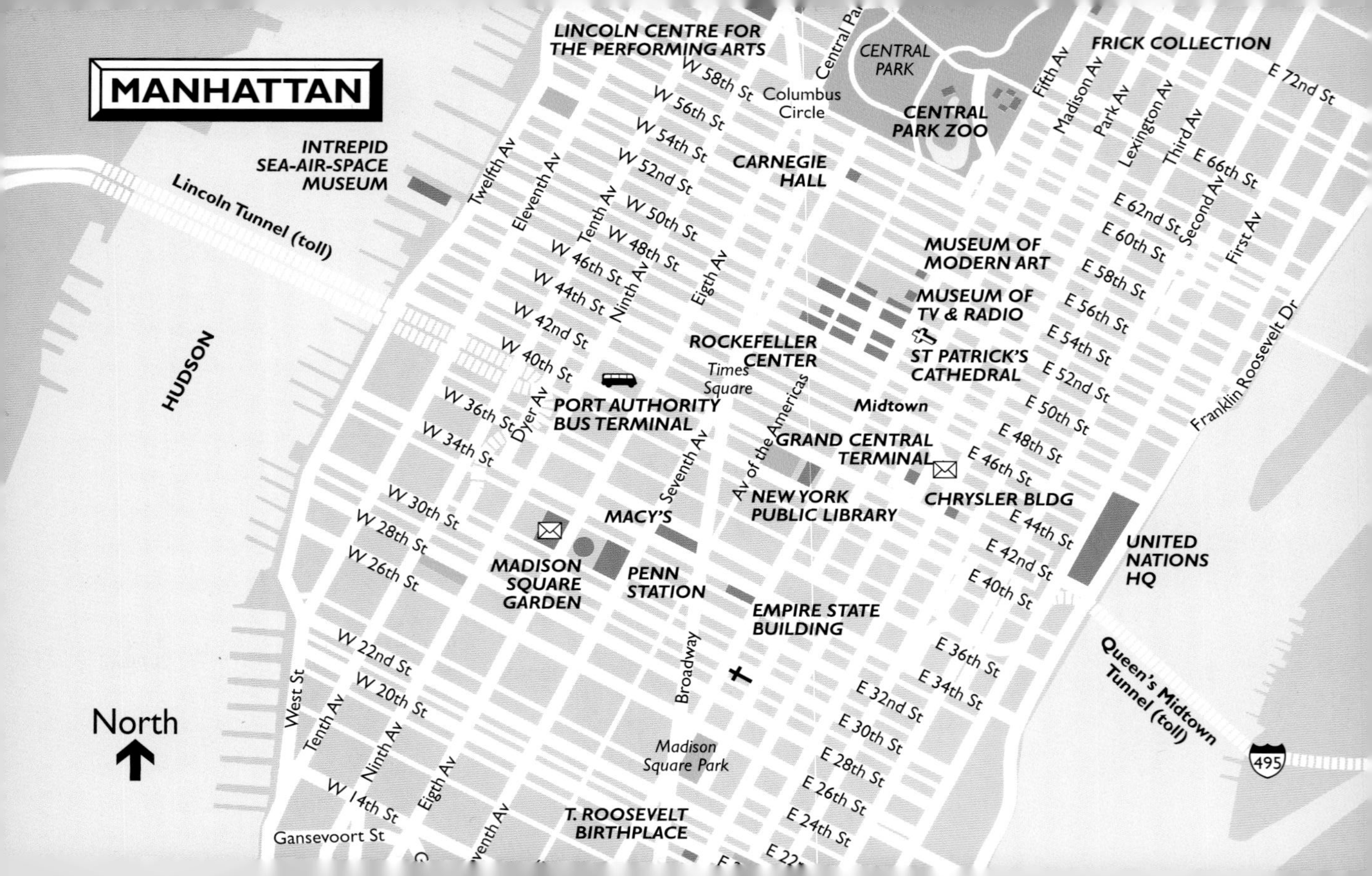
MANHATTAN
LINCOLN CENTRE FOR THE PERFORMING ARTS
FRICK COLLECTION
CENTRAL PARK
CENTRAL PARK ZOO
Columbus Circle
Central Park
INTREPID SEA-AIR-SPACE MUSEUM
Lincoln Tunnel (toll)
HUDSON
CARNEGIE HALL
MUSEUM OF MODERN ART
MUSEUM OF TV & RADIO
ST PATRICK'S CATHEDRAL
ROCKEFELLER CENTER
Times Square
Midtown
PORT AUTHORITY BUS TERMINAL
GRAND CENTRAL TERMINAL
CHRYSLER BLDG
NEW YORK PUBLIC LIBRARY
UNITED NATIONS HQ
MACY'S
MADISON SQUARE GARDEN
PENN STATION
EMPIRE STATE BUILDING
Queen's Midtown Tunnel (toll)
495
Madison Square Park
T. ROOSEVELT BIRTHPLACE
North
Twelfth Av
Eleventh Av
Tenth Av
Ninth Av
Eigth Av
Seventh Av
Av of the Americas
Fifth Av
Madison Av
Park Av
Lexington Av
Third Av
Second Av
First Av
Franklin Roosevelt Dr
Dyer Av
Broadway
West St
Gansevoort St
W 58th St
W 56th St
W 54th St
W 52nd St
W 50th St
W 48th St
W 46th St
W 44th St
W 42nd St
W 40th St
W 36th St
W 34th St
W 30th St
W 28th St
W 26th St
W 22nd St
W 20th St
W 14th St
E 72nd St
E 66th St
E 62nd St
E 60th St
E 58th St
E 56th St
E 54th St
E 52nd St
E 50th St
E 48th St
E 46th St
E 44th St
E 42nd St
E 40th St
E 36th St
E 34th St
E 32nd St
E 30th St
E 28th St
E 26th St
E 24th St

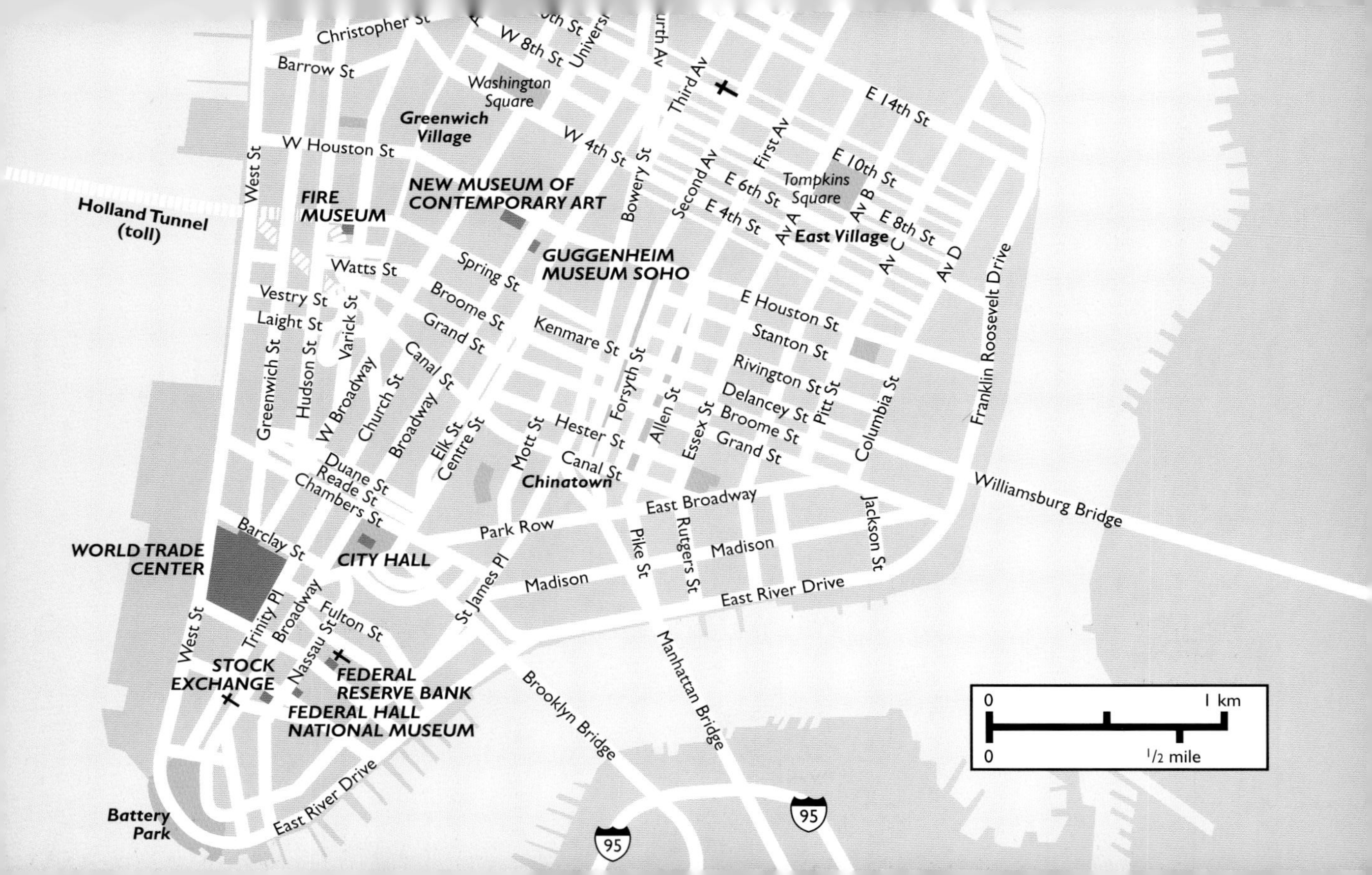

Christopher St
W 8th St
Barrow St
Washington Square
Greenwich Village
Third Av
E 14th St
W Houston St
W 4th St
First Av
E 10th St
West St
Holland Tunnel (toll)
FIRE MUSEUM
NEW MUSEUM OF CONTEMPORARY ART
Bowery St
Second Av
E 6th St
Tompkins Square
Av B
E 8th St
E 4th St
Av A
East Village
Av C
Av D
Franklin Roosevelt Drive
GUGGENHEIM MUSEUM SOHO
Watts St
Spring St
Broome St
Vestry St
Laight St
Varick St
Grand St
Kenmare St
E Houston St
Stanton St
Rivington St
Pitt St
Delancey St
Broome St
Grand St
Columbia St
Greenwich St
Hudson St
W Broadway
Church St
Canal St
Broadway
Elk St
Centre St
Mott St
Hester St
Forsyth St
Allen St
Essex St
Canal St
Chinatown
Duane St
Reade St
Chambers St
East Broadway
Jackson St
Williamsburg Bridge
Park Row
Barclay St
WORLD TRADE CENTER
CITY HALL
Pike St
Rutgers St
Madison
Madison
St James Pl
East River Drive
West St
Trinity Pl
Broadway
Fulton St
Nassau St
STOCK EXCHANGE
FEDERAL RESERVE BANK
FEDERAL HALL NATIONAL MUSEUM
Brooklyn Bridge
Manhattan Bridge
Battery Park
East River Drive
95
95
0
1 km
0
1/2 mile

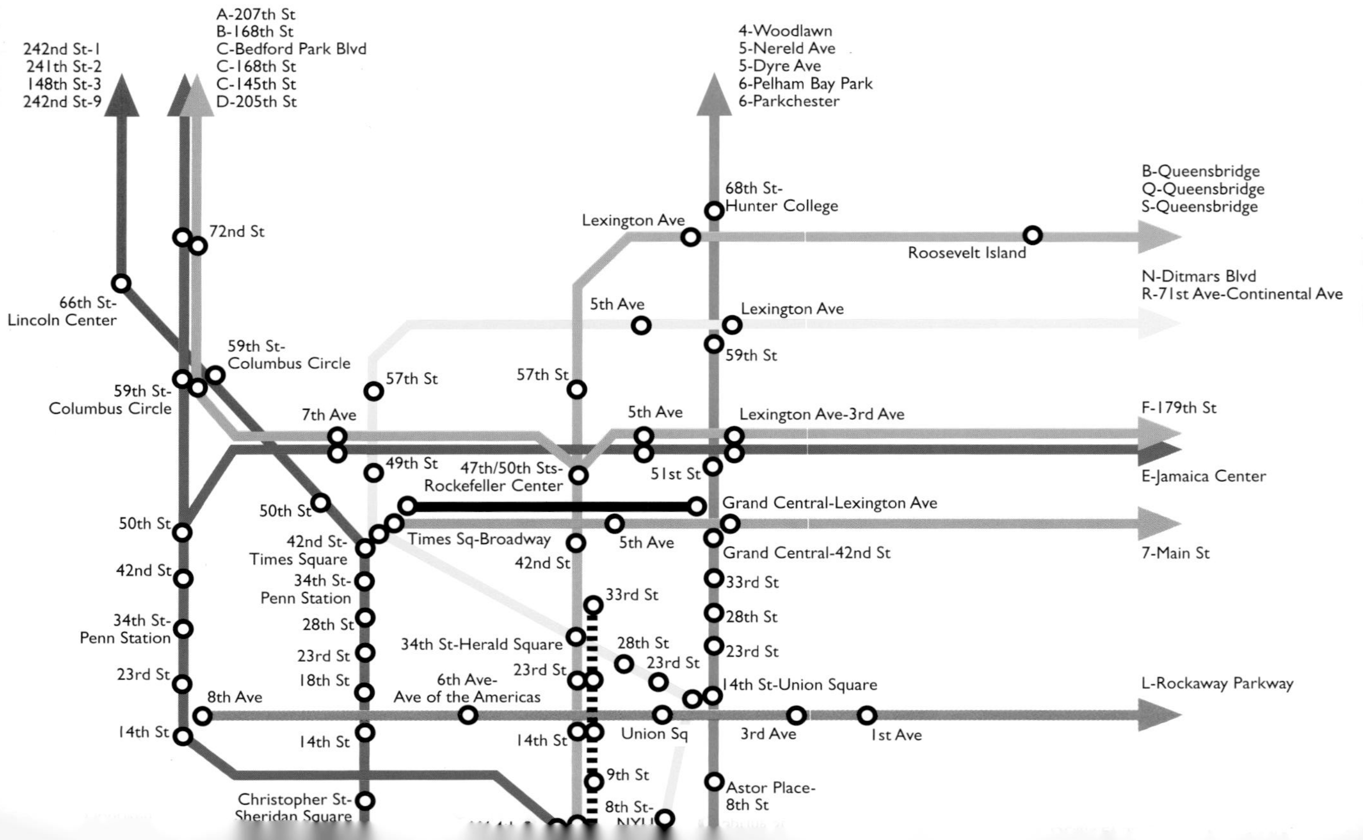
242nd St-1
241th St-2
148th St-3
242nd St-9
A-207th St
B-168th St
C-Bedford Park Blvd
C-168th St
C-145th St
D-205th St
4-Woodlawn
5-Nereld Ave
5-Dyre Ave
6-Pelham Bay Park
6-Parkchester
B-Queensbridge
Q-Queensbridge
S-Queensbridge
68th St-
Hunter College
Lexington Ave
Roosevelt Island
N-Ditmars Blvd
R-71st Ave-Continental Ave
72nd St
66th St-
Lincoln Center
5th Ave
Lexington Ave
59th St
59th St-
Columbus Circle
59th St-
Columbus Circle
57th St
57th St
7th Ave
5th Ave
Lexington Ave-3rd Ave
F-179th St
49th St
47th/50th Sts-
Rockefeller Center
51st St
E-Jamaica Center
50th St
50th St
Grand Central-Lexington Ave
42nd St-
Times Square
Times Sq-Broadway
5th Ave
42nd St
Grand Central-42nd St
7-Main St
42nd St
34th St-
Penn Station
33rd St
33rd St
28th St
34th St-
Penn Station
34th St-Herald Square
28th St
28th St
23rd St
23rd St
23rd St
23rd St
23rd St
18th St
6th Ave-
Ave of the Americas
14th St-Union Square
8th Ave
L-Rockaway Parkway
14th St
14th St
14th St
Union Sq
3rd Ave
1st Ave
9th St
Astor Place-
8th St
Christopher St-
Sheridan Square
8th St-
NYU

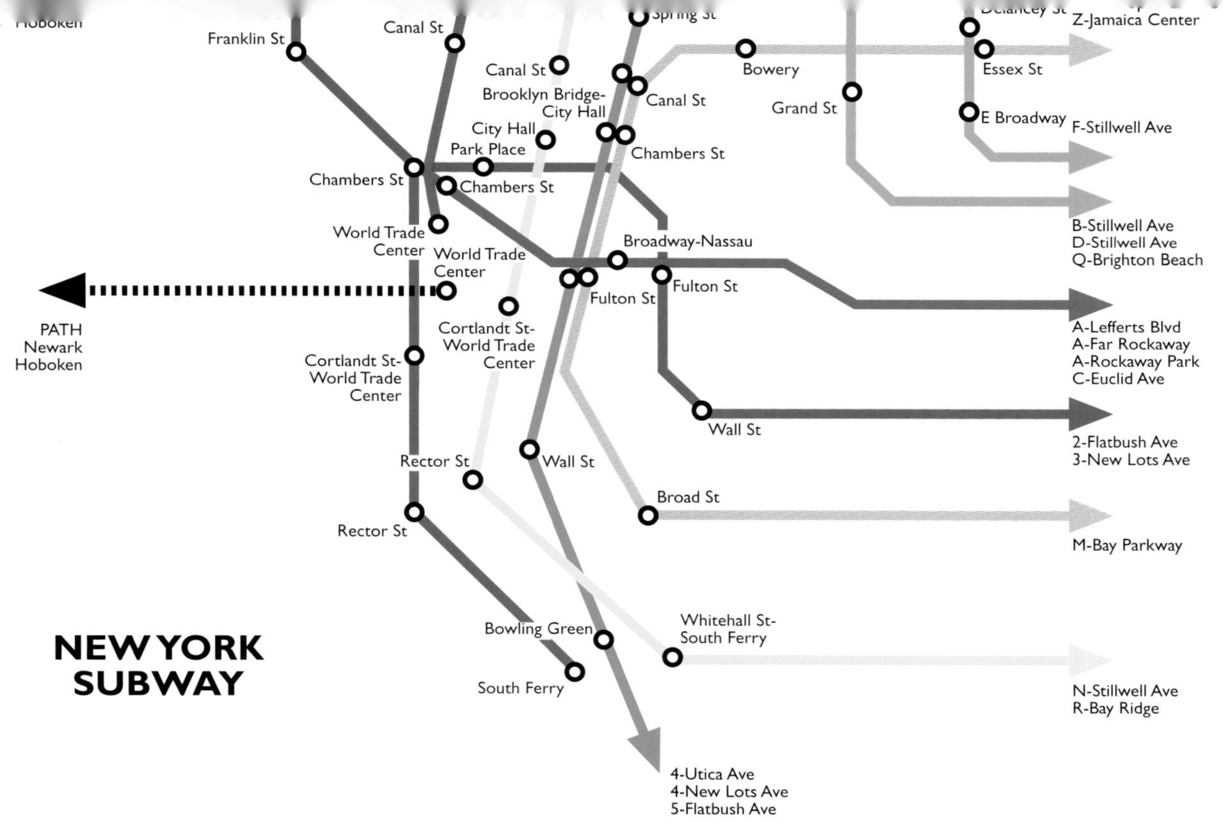
NEW YORK
SUBWAY
Franklin St
Canal St
Canal St
Brooklyn Bridge-
City Hall
City Hall
Park Place
Chambers St
Chambers St
Chambers St
World Trade
Center
World Trade
Center
Broadway-Nassau
Fulton St
Fulton St
Cortlandt St-
World Trade
Center
Cortlandt St-
World Trade
Center
Rector St
Rector St
Wall St
Wall St
Broad St
Bowling Green
South Ferry
Whitehall St-
South Ferry
Canal St
Bowery
Grand St
Essex St
E Broadway
PATH
Newark
Hoboken
Z-Jamaica Center
F-Stillwell Ave
B-Stillwell Ave
D-Stillwell Ave
Q-Brighton Beach
A-Lefferts Blvd
A-Far Rockaway
A-Rockaway Park
C-Euclid Ave
2-Flatbush Ave
3-New Lots Ave
M-Bay Parkway
N-Stillwell Ave
R-Bay Ridge
4-Utica Ave
4-New Lots Ave
5-Flatbush Ave

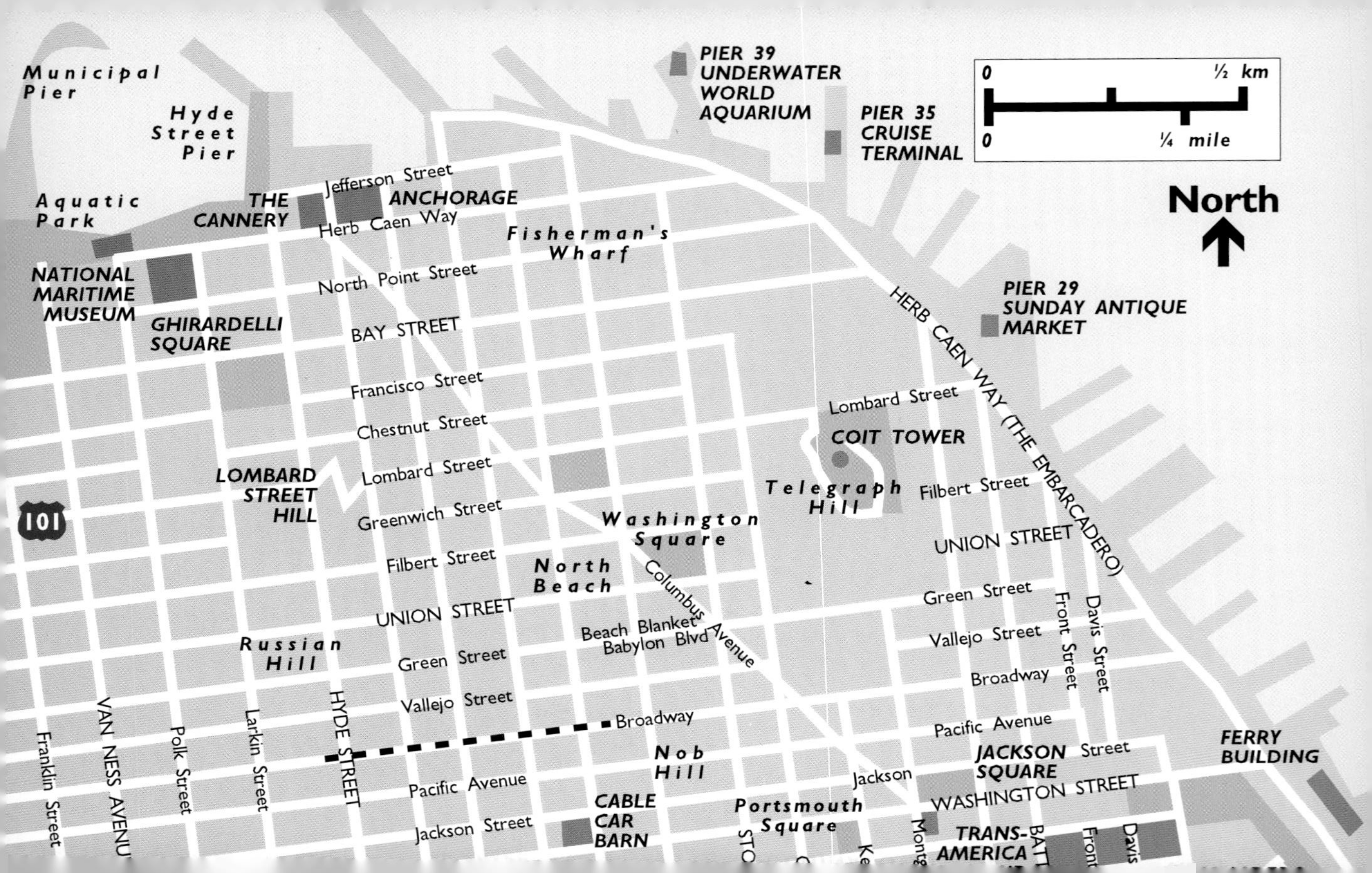

Municipal Pier
Hyde Street Pier
Aquatic Park
THE CANNERY
Jefferson Street
ANCHORAGE
Herb Caen Way
Fisherman's Wharf
PIER 39 UNDERWATER WORLD AQUARIUM
PIER 35 CRUISE TERMINAL
0 ½ km
0 ¼ mile
North
NATIONAL MARITIME MUSEUM
GHIRARDELLI SQUARE
North Point Street
BAY STREET
Francisco Street
Chestnut Street
Lombard Street
Greenwich Street
Filbert Street
UNION STREET
Green Street
Vallejo Street
Broadway
Pacific Avenue
Jackson Street
LOMBARD STREET HILL
101
HERB CAEN WAY (THE EMBARCADERO)
PIER 29 SUNDAY ANTIQUE MARKET
Lombard Street
COIT TOWER
Telegraph Hill
Filbert Street
Washington Square
North Beach
Columbus Avenue
Beach Blanket Babylon Blvd
UNION STREET
Green Street
Vallejo Street
Broadway
Front Street
Davis Street
Russian Hill
Franklin Street
VAN NESS AVENU
Polk Street
Larkin Street
HYDE STREET
Nob Hill
CABLE CAR BARN
Portsmouth Square
Jackson
Pacific Avenue
JACKSON SQUARE
Street
WASHINGTON STREET
FERRY BUILDING
TRANS-AMERICA

SAN FRANCISCO
CALIFORNIA STREET
Pine Street
Bush Street
Sutter Street
Post Street
GEARY STREET
O'Farrell Street
Ellis Street
Eddy Street
Turk Street
Golden Gate Avenue
McAllister Street
GROVE STREET
Hayes Street
Fell Street
Oak Street
Page Street
Gough Street
101
GRACE CATHEDRAL
CHINATOWN
Financial District
CROCKER GALLERIA
M
MONTGOMERY ST BART/Muni Metro
Union Square
POWELL STREET BART/Muni Metro
YERBA BUENA GARDENS
MUSEUM OF MODERN ART
ST MARY'S CATHEDRAL
HALLIDIE PLAZA
SAN FRANCISCO SHOPPING CENTER
OLD MINT
MARKET STREET
MISSION STREET
Howard Street
Folsom Street
Harrison Street
Bryant Street
Brannan Street
Townsend Street
Main Street
BEALE STREET
Fremont Street
First Street
SECOND STREET
Third Street
FOURTH STREET
Fifth Street
SIXTH STREET
Seventh Street
EIGHTH STREET
Ninth Street
TENTH STREET
Civic Center
CITY HALL
EMERGENCY HOSPITAL
M CIVIC CENTER BART/Muni Metro
M Muni Metro
18 km
South Park
80
280
CALTRANS RAILROAD STATION

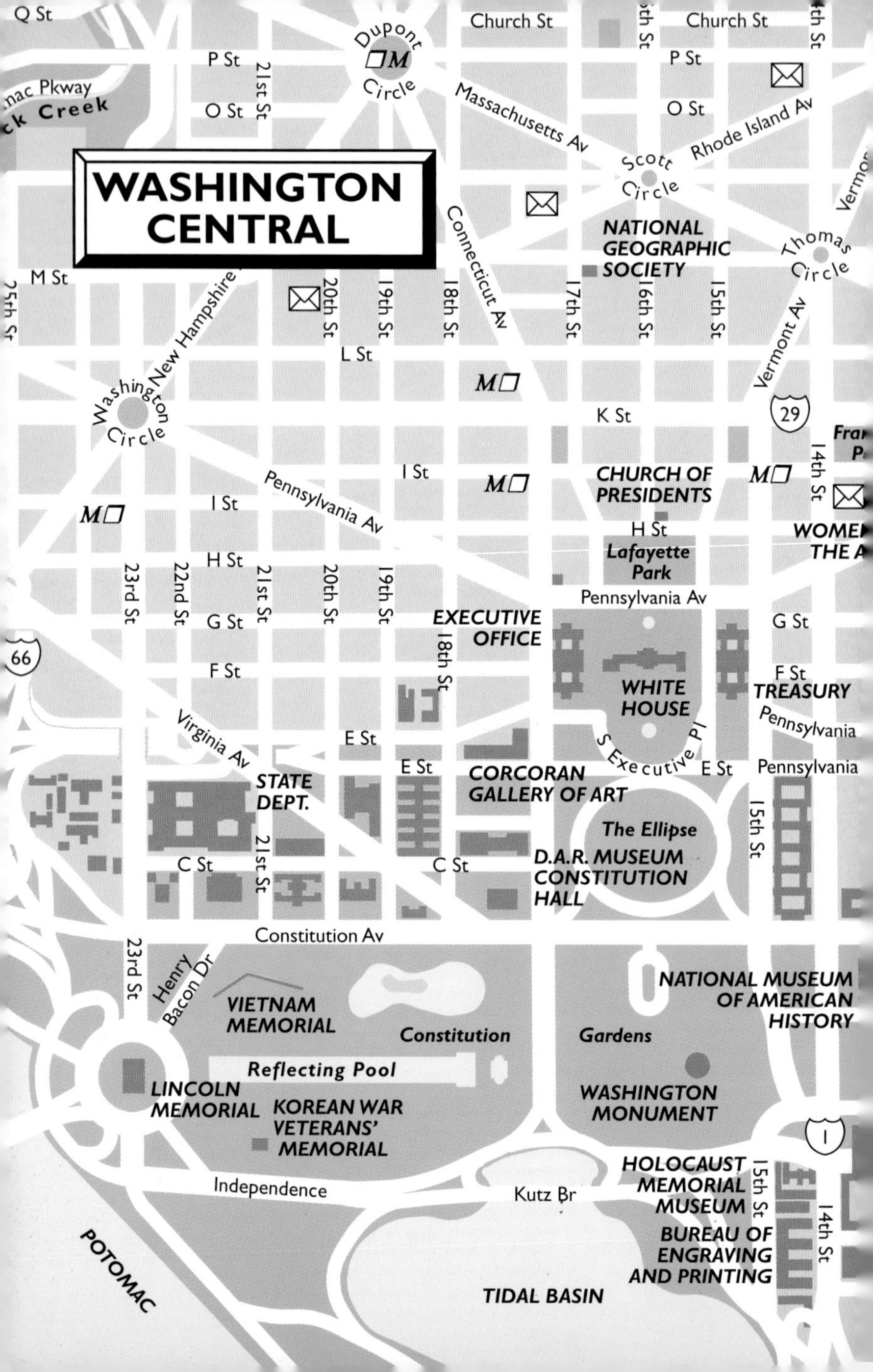
WASHINGTON CENTRAL
Q St
Church St
Church St
Dupont Circle
P St
P St
21st St
O St
O St
Rock Creek
Massachusetts Av
Rhode Island Av
Scott Circle
Connecticut Av
NATIONAL GEOGRAPHIC SOCIETY
Thomas Circle
M St
25th St
New Hampshire
20th St
19th St
18th St
17th St
16th St
15th St
Vermont Av
L St
Washington Circle
K St
29
I St
I St
Pennsylvania Av
CHURCH OF PRESIDENTS
14th St
H St
H St
Lafayette Park
23rd St
22nd St
21st St
20th St
19th St
Pennsylvania Av
G St
G St
EXECUTIVE OFFICE
66
18th St
F St
F St
WHITE HOUSE
TREASURY
Pennsylvania
Virginia Av
E St
E St
S Executive Pl
E St
Pennsylvania
STATE DEPT.
CORCORAN GALLERY OF ART
The Ellipse
15th St
21st St
C St
C St
D.A.R. MUSEUM CONSTITUTION HALL
Constitution Av
23rd St
Henry Bacon Dr
NATIONAL MUSEUM OF AMERICAN HISTORY
VIETNAM MEMORIAL
Constitution
Gardens
Reflecting Pool
LINCOLN MEMORIAL
KOREAN WAR VETERANS' MEMORIAL
WASHINGTON MONUMENT
1
HOLOCAUST MEMORIAL MUSEUM
15th St
Independence
Kutz Br
14th St
BUREAU OF ENGRAVING AND PRINTING
POTOMAC
TIDAL BASIN

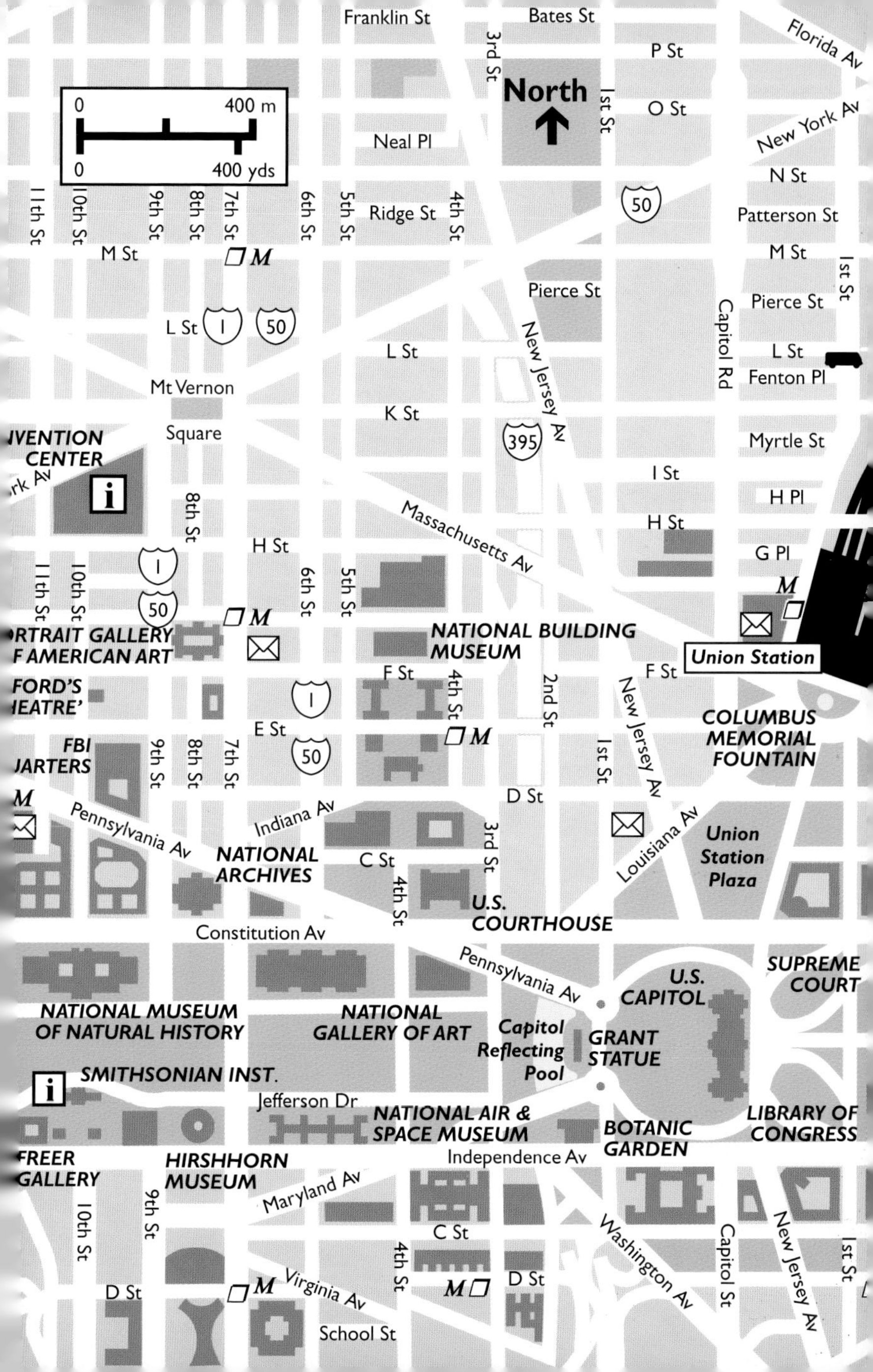

Franklin St
Bates St
P St
Florida Av
3rd St
North
1st St
O St
New York Av
0
400 m
0
400 yds
Neal Pl
N St
50
11th St
10th St
9th St
8th St
7th St
6th St
5th St
Ridge St
4th St
Patterson St
M St
M
M St
1st St
Pierce St
Pierce St
Capitol Rd
L St
1
50
L St
L St
Fenton Pl
Mt Vernon
Square
New Jersey Av
K St
395
Myrtle St
NVENTION
CENTER
rk Av
i
I St
H Pl
8th St
Massachusetts Av
H St
H St
G Pl
1
11th St
10th St
6th St
5th St
M
50
M
RTRAIT GALLERY
F AMERICAN ART
NATIONAL BUILDING
MUSEUM
Union Station
F St
F St
FORD'S
HEATRE'
4th St
2nd St
New Jersey Av
1
E St
COLUMBUS
MEMORIAL
FOUNTAIN
M
FBI
JARTERS
9th St
8th St
7th St
50
1st St
D St
M
Pennsylvania Av
Indiana Av
3rd St
Louisiana Av
Union
Station
Plaza
NATIONAL
ARCHIVES
C St
4th St
U.S.
COURTHOUSE
Constitution Av
Pennsylvania Av
SUPREME
COURT
U.S.
CAPITOL
NATIONAL MUSEUM
OF NATURAL HISTORY
NATIONAL
GALLERY OF ART
Capitol
Reflecting
Pool
GRANT
STATUE
i
SMITHSONIAN INST.
Jefferson Dr
NATIONAL AIR &
SPACE MUSEUM
BOTANIC
GARDEN
LIBRARY OF
CONGRESS
FREER
GALLERY
HIRSHHORN
MUSEUM
Independence Av
Maryland Av
10th St
9th St
C St
4th St
Washington Av
Capitol St
New Jersey Av
1st St
D St
M
Virginia Av
M
D St
School St

WASHINGTON DC METRO

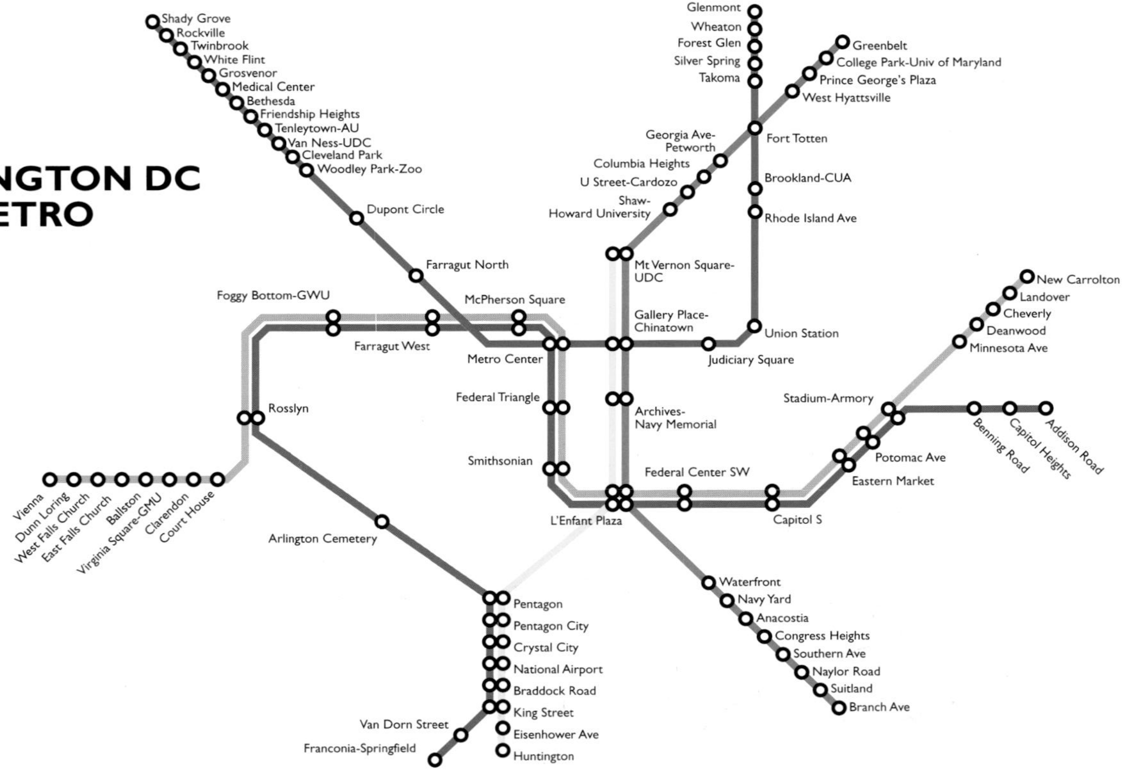

Shady Grove
Rockville
Twinbrook
White Flint
Grosvenor
Medical Center
Bethesda
Friendship Heights
Tenleytown-AU
Van Ness-UDC
Cleveland Park
Woodley Park-Zoo
Dupont Circle
Farragut North
Metro Center
Gallery Place-Chinatown
Judiciary Square
Union Station
Rhode Island Ave
Brookland-CUA
Fort Totten
Takoma
Silver Spring
Forest Glen
Wheaton
Glenmont
Greenbelt
College Park-Univ of Maryland
Prince George's Plaza
West Hyattsville
Georgia Ave-Petworth
Columbia Heights
U Street-Cardozo
Shaw-Howard University
Mt Vernon Square-UDC
Archives-Navy Memorial
L'Enfant Plaza
Waterfront
Navy Yard
Anacostia
Congress Heights
Southern Ave
Naylor Road
Suitland
Branch Ave
Vienna
Dunn Loring
West Falls Church
East Falls Church
Ballston
Virginia Square-GMU
Clarendon
Court House
Rosslyn
Foggy Bottom-GWU
Farragut West
McPherson Square
Federal Triangle
Smithsonian
Federal Center SW
Capitol S
Eastern Market
Potomac Ave
Stadium-Armory
Minnesota Ave
Deanwood
Cheverly
Landover
New Carrolton
Benning Road
Capitol Heights
Addison Road
Arlington Cemetery
Pentagon
Pentagon City
Crystal City
National Airport
Braddock Road
King Street
Eisenhower Ave
Huntington
Van Dorn Street
Franconia-Springfield